Fodor's

THE COMPLETE AFRICAN SAFARI PLANNER

2nd Edition

Fodor's Travel Publications   New York, Toronto, London, Sydney, Auckland
www.fodors.com

Eugene Fodor:
The Spy Who Loved Travel

As Fodor's celebrates our 75th anniversary, we are honoring the colorful and adventurous life of Eugene Fodor, who revolutionized guidebook publishing in 1936 with his first book, *On the Continent, The Entertaining Travel Annual.*

Eugene Fodor's life seemed to leap off the pages of a great spy novel. Born in Hungary, he spoke six languages and graduated from the Sorbonne and the London School of Economics. During World War II he joined the Office of Strategic Services, the budding spy agency for the United States. He commanded the team that went behind enemy lines to liberate Prague, and recommended to Generals Eisenhower, Bradley, and Patton that Allied troops move to the capital city. After the war, Fodor worked as a spy in Austria, posing as a U.S. diplomat.

In 1949 Eugene Fodor—with the help of the CIA—established Fodor's Modern Guides. He was passionate about travel and wanted to bring his insider's knowledge of Europe to a new generation of sophisticated Americans who wanted to explore and seek out experiences beyond their borders. Among his innovations were annual updates, consulting local experts, and including cultural and historical perspectives and an emphasis on people—not just sites. As Fodor described it, "The main interest and enjoyment of foreign travel lies not only in 'the sites,' . . . but in contact with people whose customs, habits, and general outlook are different from your own."

Eugene Fodor died in 1991, but his legacy, Fodor's Travel, continues. It is now one of the world's largest and most trusted brands in travel information, covering more than 600 destinations worldwide in guidebooks, on Fodors.com, and in ebooks and iPhone apps. Technology and the accessibility of travel may be changing, but Eugene Fodor's unique storytelling skills and reporting style are behind every word of today's Fodor's guides.

Our editors and writers continue to embrace Eugene Fodor's vision of building personal relationships through travel. We invite you to join the Fodor's community at fodors.com/community and share your experiences with like-minded travelers. Tell us when we're right. Tell us when we're wrong. And share fantastic travel secrets that aren't yet in Fodor's. Together, we will continue to deepen our understanding of our world.

Happy 75th Anniversary, Fodor's! Here's to many more.

Tim Jarrell, Publisher

FODOR'S THE COMPLETE AFRICAN SAFARI PLANNER

Editors: Alexis Crisman Kelly, Douglas Stallings

Writers: Claire Baranowski, Sanja Cloete-Jones, Lee Middleton, Sean Pattrick, Kate Turkington

Production Editor: Jennifer DePrima

Maps & Illustrations: David Lindroth and Mark Stroud, *cartographers;* Bob Blake, Rebecca Baer, *map editors;* William Wu, *information graphics*

Design: Fabrizio La Rocca, *creative director*; Guido Caroti, Siobhan O'Hare, *art directors*; Tina Malaney, Nora Rosansky, Chie Ushio, Jessica Walsh, Ann McBride, *designers*; Melanie Marin, *senior picture editor*

Cover Photo: (Cheetah on termite mound, Masai) Paul Goldstein/age fotostock

Production Manager: Angela L. McLean

2nd Edition

ISBN 978-0-679-00924-5

ISSN 1941-0336

SPECIAL SALES

This book is available at special discounts for bulk purchases for sales promotions or premiums. Special editions, including personalized covers, excerpts of existing books, and corporate imprints, can be created in large quantities for special needs. For more information, write to Special Markets/Premium Sales, 1745 Broadway, MD 6-2, New York, NY 10019, or e-mail specialmarkets@randomhouse.com.

AN IMPORTANT TIP & AN INVITATION

Although all prices, opening times, and other details in this book are based on information supplied to us at press time, changes occur all the time in the travel world, and Fodor's cannot accept responsibility for facts that become outdated or for inadvertent errors or omissions. So **always confirm information when it matters,** especially if you're making a detour to visit a specific place. Your experiences—positive and negative—matter to us. If we have missed or misstated something, **please write to us.** Share your opinion instantly through our online feedback center at fodors.com/contact-us.

PRINTED IN SINGAPORE

10 9 8 7 6 5 4 3 2

CONTENTS

Fodor's Features

MAPS

ABOUT THIS BOOK

Our Ratings

Sometimes you find terrific travel experiences and sometimes they just find you. But usually the burden is on you to select the right combination of experiences. That's where our ratings come in.

As travelers we've all discovered a place so wonderful that its worthiness is obvious. And sometimes that place is so experiential that superlatives don't do it justice: you just have to be there to know. These sights, properties, and experiences get our highest rating, **Fodor's Choice**, indicated by orange stars throughout this book.

Black stars highlight sights and properties we deem **Highly Recommended,** places that our writers, editors, and readers praise again and again for consistency and excellence.

By default, there's another category: any place we include in this book is by definition worth your time, unless we say otherwise. And we will.

Disagree with any of our choices? Care to nominate a place or suggest that we rate one more highly? Visit our feedback center at www.fodors.com/feedback.

Budget Well

Hotel and restaurant price categories from ¢ to $$$$ are defined in the opening pages of each chapter. For attractions, we always give standard adult admission fees; reductions are usually available for children, students, and senior citizens. Want to pay with plastic? **AE, DC, MC,** and **V** after restaurant and hotel listings indicate whether American Express, Diners Club, MasterCard, and Visa are accepted.

Restaurants

Unless we state otherwise, restaurants are open for lunch and dinner daily. We mention dress only when there's a specific requirement and reservations only when they're essential or not accepted—it's always best to book ahead.

Hotels

Hotels have private bath, phone, TV, and air-conditioning and operate on the European Plan (aka EP, meaning without meals), unless we specify that they use the Continental Plan (CP, with a continental breakfast), Breakfast Plan (BP, with a full breakfast), or Modified American Plan (MAP, with breakfast and dinner) or are all-inclusive (including all meals and most activities). We always list facilities but not whether you'll be charged an extra fee to use them, so when pricing accommodations, find out what's included.

Listings	
★	Fodor's Choice
★	Highly recommended
⊠	Physical address
✛	Directions or Map coordinates
⌂	Mailing address
☎	Telephone
🖷	Fax
⊕	On the Web
✍	E-mail
✍	Admission fee
☉	Open/closed times
Ⓜ	Metro stations
▭	Credit cards
Hotels & Restaurants	
🏨	Hotel
⌕	Number of rooms
⚲	Facilities
⦿|	Meal plans
✕	Restaurant
⟲	Reservations
🏛	Dress code
⟍	Smoking
⚇⚇	BYOB
Outdoors	
⚐	Golf
⛺	Camping
Other	
☾	Family-friendly
⇨	See also
⊠	Branch address
☞	Take note

Your Safari

WHAT'S WHERE

The following numbers refer to chapters.

3 Kenya. Part of East Africa, you can expect golden lions, red-robed warriors, snow-capped mountains, pristine white beaches, orange sunsets, and coral-pink dawns. You'll also experience some of the world's most famous safari destinations—Masai Mara, Mt. Kilimanjaro, the Rift Valley—and world-class beach destinations like Diani Beach and the tiny town of Lamu.

4 Tanzania. Also part of East Africa, Tanzania attracts far fewer tourists than Kenya and South Africa, even though it boasts some of Africa's greatest tourist attractions—the Serengeti, the Great Migration, Olduvai Gorge, Ngorongoro Crater, Selous Game Reserve, and Lake Victoria.

5 South Africa. Africa's most developed country, at the very tip of the continent, is many worlds in one: modern bustling cities, ancient rock art, gorgeous beaches, fabulous game lodges, well-run national parks, mountain ranges, desert, and wine lands. It's home to Kruger National Park and the Kwa-Zulu Natal reserves.

6 Botswana. The country itself is a natural wonder with terrains that vary from vast salt pans to the pristine waterways of the Okavango Delta. Expect lots of game, few tourists, and stars brighter than you'll ever see—the Kala-hari Bushmen say that you can hear them sing.

7 Namibia. From the Namib Desert—the earth's oldest—to the fog-enshrouded Skeleton Coast, from the great game park of Etosha to Damara-land's stark beauty and desert elephants, to bustling small cities with a fascinating mix of colonial and modern, you've never been anywhere like Namibia.

8 Victoria Falls. Shared by Zambia and Zimbabwe, Vic Falls is one of the natural wonders of the world, unsurpassed by anything. The adventure center of Africa, adrenaline junkies can try everything from bungee jumping and white-water rafting, to canoeing, rappelling, and Jet Skiing.

9 Seychelles. Located in the Indian Ocean 932 mi off Africa's eastern coast, this archipelago of 115 islands lies just northeast of Madagascar and has some of the world's best-preserved natural habitats and pristine beaches. The main island, Mahé, is home to the international airport and the capital city, Victoria.

SKELETON

NAMIB

Swakopmund
Walvis Bay

COAST

Luder

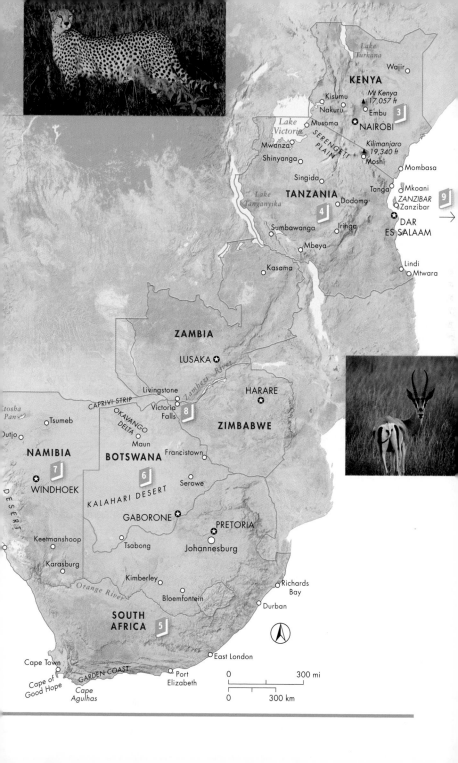

WHEN TO GO

You can visit the parks covered in this book most of the time. However, in the dry season (read: winter) vegetation is low and surface water is scarce, making it easier to spot game. But it's much cheaper to travel in the low and shoulder seasons, when the bush looks much more beautiful—although you will encounter rain sometimes and it will be harder to spot game—and there are lots of baby animals. It also gets *very* hot everywhere from December to the end of February.

To find out exactly what the weather will be for your destination, **African Weather Forecasts** (⊕ *www.africanweather.net*) lists weather information for the entire continent.

The Seasons

The seasons in sub-Saharan Africa are opposite of those in North America. Summer is December through March, autumn is April and May, winter is June through September, and spring is October and November. The Seychelles follows a similar pattern, with the notable addition that stormier seas make winter unsuitable for keen divers.

Winter is usually high season throughout safari areas because it's the driest time of the year and game is easiest to spot. The exception is South Africa and Seychelles, where high season is linked with the summer vacation schedules of South Africans (December through mid-January), and both the European summer vacations (July–August) and Christmas holidays (December–January) in the Seychelles.

When we say "Low season," we're saying that this is the rainy season. Although the rains are intermittent—often occurring in late afternoon—the bush and vegetation are high and it's more difficult to spot game. It can also get very hot and humid during this time. However, the upside is that there are far fewer tourists, lodge rates are much cheaper (often half price), and the bush is beautifully lush and green. Plus there are lots of baby animals, and if you're a birder all the migrant species are back from their winter habitats. Seychelles' low season occurs during the cusp times of February–April and October–November, which can be the nicest times to visit in terms of both weather (especially April and November) and better prices.

High season, also called dry season, refers to the winter months in East and Southern Africa when there is little to no rain at all. Days are sunny and bright, but the nights are cool. In the desert, temperatures can plummet to below freezing, but you will be snug and warm in your tent wherever you stay. The landscape will be barren and dry (read: not very attractive), but that lack of surface water means that game must use permanent water holes where it can be easily seen. This is the busiest tourist time.

The shoulder season occurs between summer and winter; it's our fall in the States. The rains are just beginning, tourist numbers are decreasing, and the vegetation is starting to die off. Lodges will offer cheaper rates.

Seasonal Access to Parks

		Summer				Fall		Winter				Spring	
		Dec	Jan	Feb	Mar	Apr	May	Jun	Jul	Aug	Sep	Oct	Nov
BOTSWANA	The Okavango Delta	●	●	●	●	●	●	●	●	●	●	●	●
	Moremi Wildlife Reserve	●	●	●	●	●	●	●	●	●	●	●	●
	Chobe Nat'l Park	●	●	●	●	●	●	●	●	●	●	●	●
	Kwando Game Reserve	●	●	●	●	●	●	●	●	●	●	●	●
KENYA	Masai Mara	●	●	●	●	●	●	●	●	●	●	●	●
	Amboseli Nat'l Park	●	●	●	●	●	●	●	●	●	●	●	●
	Tsavo Nat'l Park	●	●	●	●	●	●	●	●	●	●	●	●
	Laikipia Plateau	●	●	●	●	●	●	●	●	●	●	●	●
NAMIBIA	Namib Naukluft Park	●	●	●	●	●	●	●	●	●	●	●	●
	Damaraland	●	●	●	●	●	●	●	●	●	●	●	●
	Etosha Nat'l Park	●	●	●	●	●	●	●	●	●	●	●	●
SOUTH AFRICA	Kruger Nat'l Park	●	●	●	●	●	●	●	●	●	●	●	●
	Sabi Sands Game Reserve	●	●	●	●	●	●	●	●	●	●	●	●
	KwaZulu-Natal Parks	●	●	●	●	●	●	●	●	●	●	●	●
	Kgalagadi Transfrontier Park	●	●	●	●	●	●	●	●	●	●	●	●
TANZANIA	Serengeti Nat'l Park	●	●	●	●	●	●	●	●	●	●	●	●
	Ngorongoro Crater	●	●	●	●	○	○	●	●	●	●	●	●
	Lake Manyara Nat'l Park	●	●	●	●	●	●	●	●	●	●	●	●
	Selous Game Reserve	●	●	●	○	○	○	●	●	●	●	●	●
	Gombe Stream and Mahale Mountains Nat'l Parks	●	●	●	●	●	●	●	●	●	●	●	●

KEY: ● = Low Season, Park Open ● = Shoulder Season Park Open ● = High Season Park Open
○ = Low Season, Park Closed ○ = Shoulder Season Park Closed ○ = High Season Park Closed

IF YOU LIKE

The Out of Africa Experience

Turn back the clock to the great, glorious days of the early safaris, when Ernest Hemingway and Teddy Roosevelt stalked the golden grasses of the plains with the Big Five in their rifle sights. Forget the rifles, but shoot as much as you like—with cameras. We have the perfect spots.

Cottars 1920s Safari Camp, Kenya. For an original safari replay it doesn't get much better than this—claw-foot tubs, antique rugs, wrought-iron candlesticks, old gramophones, polished butlers' trays—all under white safari tents.

Finch Hatton's, Kenya. Live your every African dream at this classy camp where you'll dine at a table sparkling with silver and crystal as strains of Mozart softly fill the African night.

Il Moran, Kenya. Situated where Kenya's first colonial governors used to twirl their handlebar moustaches and sip their G&Ts while on safari, you will enjoy the exclusive location, teeming game, and bygone elegance.

King's Pool, Botswana. From the ancient tree dominating the main deck to the lush accommodations, everything is on a regal scale—a tribute to the European royalty who used to hunt in this area.

Selati Lodge, South Africa. Formerly a private hunting lodge, the early-1900s ambience stems from genuine train memorabilia. Old leather suitcases, antique wooden chairs, and signals recall the days of an 1870s train line.

Serena Kirawira Camp, Tanzania. Any well-heeled Victorian traveler would feel at home in this elegant pioneer setting—polished wooden floors, antique furniture, copper urns, and shining brass lamps.

To See the Great Migration

No matter where you stay during the Great Migration, you'll be assured of unforgettable sights. But we've highlighted a few camps where sightings may be even more spectacular. Remember that world weather cycles are changing—there's no guarantee that at that particular place and time your game-viewing will always live up to the National Geographic TV Channel.

Grumeti River Camp, Tanzania. Watch out for galloping wildebeest at this exclusive camp on the banks of the famed Grumeti River, where you'll be perfectly positioned to witness one of the greatest shows on earth.

Little Governors' Camp, Kenya. A ferry ride across the Mara River and a short walk escorted by armed guides takes you to this lovely camp sited directly in the path of the wildebeest migration.

Mara Serena Safari Lodge, Kenya. If you get tired of looking at the endless grasslands where the migration takes place in front of your eyes, then spot game at the lodge's own busy water hole.

Naibor Camp, Kenya. Situated in a particularly game-rich area 20 minutes away from one of the legendary migration river crossings, this is the perfect base for watching the migration.

Sayari Camp, Tanzania. This camp is perfectly poised for watching the Mara River crossing, when hundreds of thousands of wildebeest plunge into the crocodile-infested water on their journey north.

Serengeti Under Canvas, Tanzania. This luxury mobile camp follows the migration, staying put for a couple of months and then moving north with the herds. Not cheap but worth every penny.

Drop-Dead Luxury

So you want the whole game experience but don't want to rough it? No problem. Our favorites will tempt you to defect from the real world and live like kings and queens.

The Banyan Tree, Seychelles. One of Seychelles' most romantic resorts, the Banyan Tree's white Victorian style buildings and truly impeccable service lend this gem a colonial feel.

Mala Mala, Mpumalanga, South Africa. One of the oldest and most distinguished of all Southern African bush lodges, this is the haunt of royalty, celebs, and the jet set.

Mombo Camp, Botswana. The spacious, graciously decorated en suite rooms of this legendary camp may have a tented feel, but they are ultraluxurious with great game-watching views.

Ngorongoro Crater Lodge, Tanzania. The theme here is Great Zimbabwe ruins meets SS *Titanic* baroque, and your abode will be palatial and the game-viewing equally fabulous.

North Island, Seychelles. This private island of granite cliffs and powder-white beaches hosts 11 villas that are each as large as most peoples' homes, kitted out in a Robinson Crusoe–envisioned-by-Galliano dream.

Ntwala Island Lodge, Namibia. This lodge, 80 km (50 mi) upstream from the Victoria Falls, comprises four spectacular art deco–meets-Africa chalets built on a cluster of islands linked by walkways.

Shompole Lodge, Kenya. You'll feel like you're a part of an Arabian Nights fantasy when you enter your multipeaked thatch-roof tent and see your personal pool and the views of the Rift Valley's distant plains and mountains.

Singita, Sabi Sands, South Africa. Hide yourself away at this gorgeous bush getaway, with superb game and service to match.

Thanda Main Lodge, Kwa-Zulu Natal, South Africa. This exquisite lodge has beehive-shape dwellings that blend elements of royal Zulu with an eclectic pan-African feel. Shaka never had it this good.

To Get Out of the Vehicle

Game drives are thrilling but sometimes, particularly if you are a second-time visitor to Africa and have ticked off your Big Five, you'd like to get up close and personal with the African bush and its inhabitants. Here are some of the best ways to really get down to nature.

Footsteps Across the Delta, Botswana. Learn the secrets of the Okavango—on foot and by mokoro—with outstanding guides. Enjoy game drives, night drives, boat trips, and fishing as well.

Lewa Wilderness, Kenya. Game drives here are action packed, but try game spotting from a different angle—on top of a camel or from the back of a horse—or on your own two feet.

Offbeat Safaris, Kenya. Riding alongside thousands of plains game is a once-in-a-lifetime experience, but only if you're an experienced rider and fit enough to ride four or six hours a day.

Olduvai Tented Camp, Tanzania. Go walking in the Ngorongoro highlands with genuine Masai warriors at this no-frills camp that's just south of the Serengeti border.

Rhino Walking Safaris, South Africa. You'll leave for morning guided walks from one of three tiny camps situated in central Kruger's pristine bushveld.

IF YOU LIKE

To Get Away from the Crowds

We can't whisk you away from all civilization and people, but we know that if you choose any of the following camps and lodges you'll be assured of privacy and exclusivity.

Duba Plains, Botswana. Based deep in the Okavango Delta, this tiny camp on an isolated island has superb game-viewing. Only two 4x4 open game vehicles operate in the whole reserve so you're assured of exclusivity.

Jack's Camp, Botswana. If you're bold spirited, reasonably fit, and enjoy a rugged pioneer experience, then Jack's is for you. Try quad-biking, sleeping out under the stars, or walking with the bushmen.

Loliondo Mobile Camp, Tanzania. Get away from the big lodges and busy safari routes and put yourself in the expert hands of your guide, cooks, waiters, and camp attendants, and experience a true old-style private safari.

Mnemba Island, Tanzania. For the ultimate beach escape where time stands still, where sand, sea, and horizon melt into each other, this exclusive lodge with only 20 guests is hard to beat.

Sand Rivers Selous, Tanzania. Above a wide bend of the Rufiji River—hundreds of miles away from touristy Africa—this lodge is just about as isolated and exclusive as you can get.

Sarara Tented Camp, Kenya. At this small remote tented camp below the Mathews Mountains in the 75,000 acre Namunyuk Wildlife Conservation Trust, the only strangers in the night you'll see are the wildlife residents.

!Xaus Lodge, South Africa. Located in one of South Africa's most remote parks, !Xaus (pronounced Kaus) provides great hospitality, game drives, desert walks, and introductions to the local bushmen.

To Interact with the Locals

Of course you want to see lots of game, but may want to meet the local people, too. Although many of the cultural and village visits are not entirely authentic given the need for tourist dollars, we've tried to find you the genuine article. Go with an open mind, a nonjudgmental approach, and a friendly smile.

Deception Valley Lodge, Botswana. At Central Kalahari's only lodge you'll meet the desert-dwelling Naru people, who built it entirely by hand. Expect pure magic during a three-hour walk with the bushmen themselves.

Il'Ngwesi Lodge, Kenya. Learn about hunting, gathering honey, animal trapping with indigenous poisons, and fashioning beadwork at the nearby Masai village.

Kichwa Tembo Tented Safari Camp, Kenya. A visit to a nearby Masai village is a must at this sought-after camp. The tribe's young men will explain their culture in English learned at the local school.

Lake Manyara Serena Lodge, Tanzania. Take a guided walk to Mto wa Mbu, a small town that's home to more than 100 different tribes. Here you'll visit homes, a school, a church, the market, and a banana-leaf bar.

Ol Seki Mara Camp, Kenya. At this eco-friendly camp you'll visit authentic, nontouristy Masai villages, where you might be lucky enough to witness a genuine betrothal or post-initiation ceremony.

Serra Cafema, Namibia. Only the nomadic Himba people share this awesome remote area, and a visit to a local village will be a life-changing experience.

To Bring the Kids

More and more families want their kids to share in their safari experience, and more lodges are catering to kids with programs designed especially for them. Always find out in advance which camps welcome kids, as many still don't allow kids under 12. Remember: good behavior is essential. You don't want to spoil someone's safari of a lifetime.

Berg-en-Dal, Kruger Park, South Africa. Kids can explore in safety at this attractive, fenced camp, which has a great pool and curio shop. Get them to walk around the camp's perimeter and spot game.

Kwando, Botswana. Kids learn to track, make plaster casts of spoor, spot game, cook over the boma fire, tell stories, catch and release butterflies, make bush jewelry, and learn about ecology.

Ngorongoro Serena Lodge, Tanzania. Apart from game drives, there are picnic lunches, balloon trips, and guided walks to the crater's rim or along the nature trail around the lodge.

Okaukuejo Camp, Etosha, Namibia. The 24-hour floodlighted water hole—regarded as one of the finest in Africa—will keep kids entranced for hours. They can sit, stand, or run (quietly) around.

Pafuri Camp, South Africa. This lovely camp in Kruger's far north has a superb children's program and special family accommodations that give everybody privacy. Kids will love Crooks Corner, where baddies on the run used to hide.

Voi Wildlife Lodge, Kenya. This is a popular family destination (kids under 2 stay free, 2–12 at half price), so don't expect peace and tranquility. There's a kids' play area, pool, DVDs, and wildlife games.

An Animal Encounter

If you've set your heart on one particular animal, read on because these camps will provide incredible, once-in-a-lifetime experiences.

Addo Elephant Back Safaris, South Africa. Be introduced to a small group of trained African elephants. Take a short elephant ride, go for a scenic walk through the bush with them, touch them, feed them, and watch them bathe.

Crocodile Camp, Kenya. Get your cameras clicking at the nightly crocodile feeding at the Galana River, when staff members call individual crocs by name and throw food to them.

Greystoke Mahale, Tanzania. About 60 of the area's 1,000 or so wild chimpanzees live in the forest near this gorgeous lodge on a deserted beach, so you have an excellent chance of spotting them.

Londolozi, South Africa. This is the place to see leopards. The most beautiful and successful of all feline predators, watching a leopard move through the bush is a truly awesome sight.

Ol Kanyau Camp, Kenya. The focus is on elephants, which have been studied here for nearly 40 years. You'll never forget the thrill of your first nose-to-trunk introduction to one of the 52 great matriarchal herds.

Palmwag Rhino Camp, Namibia. If it's rhinos you're after, especially the rare black rhino, then this remote tented camp in the heart of the 400,000-hectare (1-million-acre) private Palmwag Reserve is a must.

Cousine Island, Seychelles. Tiny Cousine's rehabilitation has resulted in the return of thousands of nesting seabirds. A stay in one of the four luxurious villas is a birder's delight.

IF YOU LIKE

To Stay in Eco-Lodges

Want to do a little good while you experience the trip of a lifetime? Never sacrificing luxury, these spots look after the environment, the local communities, and the wildlife so you can feel good while you're having fun.

Amboseli Porini Camp, Kenya. A silver eco-award winner, this camp is co-owned with the local Masai community. You'll see very few visitors (numbers are limited to 12 per day), but lots of game, including predators and elephants.

Campi ya Kanzi, Kenya. This was the first camp in Kenya to be gold rated by Ecotourism Kenya for its efforts in sustainable tourism and is one of the most environmentally friendly camps in East Africa.

Delta Camp, Botswana. A major conservation plus for this enchanting camp set deep in the Okavango is that motorboats are not used; the emphasis is on preserving the purity of the environment.

Saruni Camp, Kenya. This exclusive eco-friendly lodge just outside the Masai Mara boasts the Masai Wellbeing Space, which uses local plants for its treatments and is considered one of the best spas in Kenya.

Vuyatela, Djuma, Sabi Sands, South Africa. This vibey camp mixes contemporary African township culture with modern Shangaan culture. The owners are passionate about community involvement and have established a day-care center for the local children.

Wilderness Damaraland Camp, Namibia. A joint community venture with the local *riemvasmakers* (thong makers), this eco-friendly isolated camp has won numerous awards for its successful integration of local communities, the environment, and wildlife.

To Go to the Beach

Going on Safari isn't only about seeing game these days; it's also about where you're going to go before or after your safari to unwind. Luckily, there are plenty of beach resort options to pick from in this part of the world.

Alfajiri Beach Villa, Kenya. Near Diani Beach, these double-story villas are some of the most luxurious in the world; each has its own pool that borders the Indian Ocean. You can go on safari or hang out at the beach and play in the water—there are all sorts of water activities on offer.

The Four Seasons Resort, Seychelles. Located on one of Mahé Island's most beautiful bays, this gorgeous resort helps visitors enjoy its perfect slice of white sand with fantastic beach service (loungers, towels, and bar service), plenty of ship-shape equipment from snorkeling gear to kayaks, and one of the island's best snorkeling areas.

Kiwayu Safari Village, Kenya. Located northeast of Lamu, this village is one of the most romantic spots in all of Kenya. The area is known for its deep-sea fishing, and the hotel is close to the Kiunga Marine National Reserve—a great place for snorkeling. Make sure you book far in advance.

Mnemba Island, Tanzania. For the ultimate beach escape head to this tiny island off the tip of Zanzibar. There are diving and snorkeling off a pristine coral reef, and you might just rub elbows with the rich and famous.

Ras Nungwi, Tanzania. You'll find this resort on the northern tip of Zanzibar overlooking the Indian Ocean's turquoise waters. The balmy breezes and numerous lounge areas beg you to just sit down and relax, but if you can't, there are water sports, a

spa, and local tours to Stone Town, spice plantations, and Jozani Forest.

Rocktail Beach Lodge, South Africa. If you're in the mood for pristine beaches, surf fishing, amazing scuba diving, and snorkeling, then coming to this lodge nestled in the Maputaland Coastal Reserve will be the perfect beach getaway after your safari.

Zimbali Lodge, South Africa. With direct access to the beach, this lodge near Durban is set in one of the last remaining coastal forests in the Kwa-Zulu Natal province. Play golf, go horseback riding, or swim in the pool on the beach.

Natural Wonders

Sub-Saharan Africa is home to amazing game, welcoming people, and awe-inspiring natural wonders.

The Great Migration. This annual journey of more than 2 million animals through Kenya and Tanzania is a safari seeker's Holy Grail; some consider it to be one of the world's greatest natural wonders.

Mt. Kilimanjaro. Kili, as it's fondly called, is one of the continent's highest peaks and the tallest free-standing mountain in the world. It's one of the easier mountains to climb; about 12,000 people each year set out for the summit.

The Namibia Dunes. Located in Namib Naukluft Park, the largest game park in Africa, lie the mythical Namibia sand dunes. Said to be the highest dunes in the world, this is an adventure seeker's dream.

The Ngorongoro Crater. Nearly 3 million years old, this World Heritage site in northern Tanzania is a haven for wild game. Though it does get busy during high season, your experiences far outweigh the annoyances.

Okavango Delta. At its peak, the world's largest inland delta covers some 16,000 square km (6,177 square mi) of northwest Botswana.

Skeleton Coast. Littered with the skeletons of old boats, this part of the Namibian coast is beautiful, but bleak. The bushmen call it "The Land God Made in Anger."

Victoria Falls. More than 91 meters (300 feet) high and visible from 50 km (31 mi) away, the Falls are one of the world's seven natural wonders.

Vallée de Mai. Located on Praslin Island, in the Seychelles, this World Heritage Site protects some of the last ancient virgin Mascarene forest in the world, and is the only place on earth where the unique double coconut or Coco de Mer palms grow wild and abundantly.

WHAT'S YOUR BUDGET?

When setting a budget, consider how much you want to spend and keep in mind three things: your flight, the actual safari costs, and extras. You can have a low-budget self-catering trip in one of South Africa's national parks or spend a great deal of money in one of the small, pampering, exclusive camps in Botswana. Almost every market has high-priced options as well as some economical ones.

Luxury Safaris

The most popular option is to book with a tour operator and stay in private lodges, which are owned and run by an individual or company rather than a government or country. Prices at these lodges include all meals and, in many cases, alcoholic beverages, as well as two three- to five-hour-long game-viewing expeditions a day. Occasionally high-end lodges offer extra services such as spa treatments, boat trips, or special-occasion meals served alfresco in the bush. Prices range approximately from US$350 to US$1,600 per person per night sharing a double room. If you travel alone, expect to pay a single supplement because all safari-lodge rooms are doubles.

Safaris on a Shoestring

Don't let a tight budget deter you. There are many opportunities for great big-game experiences without going over the top. And, you won't have to completely abandon the idea of comfort and style either. Below are some money-saving tips that every budget can appreciate.

1. Drive yourself and/or self cater. The least expensive option is to choose a public game park—Kruger National Park in South Africa, for example—where you drive yourself and self-cater (shop for and prepare all meals yourself). Most South Africans travel this way. The price of this type of trip is approximately a tenth of that for private, fully inclusive lodges.

Rates for national-park camps, called rest camps, start at about $34 a day for a two-bed *rondavel* (a round hut modeled after traditional African dwellings) and go up to $85 for a four-bed bungalow. Budget about $6 for breakfast, $8 for lunch, and $12 for dinner per person for each day on the trip. You will need to factor in park entry fees, however, and these can add quite considerably to the cost of your trip.

Driving yourself can be enjoyable, but keep in mind that you will have to identify all the animals yourself, and you can't go off-road. Hire a guide from the main office of the park; it's inexpensive and will add a great deal to your experience. South Africa, Botswana, and Namibia are the best places to self-drive, as road conditions are good. Elsewhere, you may need a 4x4 vehicle. Cars are difficult to rent in Zimbabwe, and the roads are very poor in Kenya. Keep in mind that car rentals can be expensive.

2. Stay in an accommodation outside the park or in a nearby town. This cuts down on the "mark-ups" that you may experience for the convenience of staying inside a park and you can come into the park on day-trips, so you won't miss anything.

3. Stick to one park, or visit a lesser-known one, and keep your trip short. The high-end safari-goer may visit up to four different parks in different terrains and areas of the country, but the budget traveler would do well to stick to just one. Lesser-known parks can be just as good as famous ones, and sometimes being far from the madding crowds is a luxury in itself. Many travelers tack a two- or three-day safari onto the end of a beach holiday; this is enough time to see the Big Five and get a

good understanding of the animals you'll encounter.

4. Mobile camping safaris are another option. Travel is by 4x4 (often something that looks like a bus), and you sleep in tents at public or private campsites. There are different levels of comfort and service, and the price varies accordingly; at the lower end, you will pitch your own tent and help with cooking, but with a full service mobile camping safari, your driver/guide and a cook will do all the setup. The cost will also vary according to the number of people on the tour. You'll really feel at one with nature and the wildlife if you take this option, but you will need to be able to put up with a certain level of roughing it. A full-service safari costs in the region of $100–$200 a day—a quarter of what you'd spend at a private lodge.

5. Book a private lodge in the off-season. Many lodges—South Africa's Sabi Sands area, for example—cost about US$800 per person per night during the high season but can drop to about US$500 a night during the slower months of July and August; on average savings can be 30%–40%. In the rainy season, however, roads may be impassable in some areas and the wildlife hard to spot, so do your research beforehand. Sometimes, the high season merely correlates with the European long vacation. In South Africa, the low season is from May to September, mostly because Cape Town is cold and wet during this time. Regions north of the country, such as Kruger, are excellent for game-viewing during this time, as the winter is the dry season and grasses are short. Early mornings and nighttime can get cold, but the daytime is usually dry and sunny. You'll also have the benefit of fewer crowds, although if you're very social, you may find the off-season too quiet. If you're a honeymooner, it's perfect.

6. Cheap flights are out there, but you'll have to work for them. Aggregators such as Skyscanner.net and ebookers.com can help you search for the best fares that meet your requirements. American travelers will save money by flying through Europe. Book a flight to a regional hub like Nairobi or Johannesburg, and then catch a connecting flight to your destination. Many of Kenya's budget airlines fly from Nairobi to destinations in Tanzania, and South Africa's budget airline Kulula.com flies from South Africa to Namibia and Zimbabwe. For flights to South Africa, look into flying via Dubai or Doha. You'll add extra time to your flight, but you could save big. Always book at least two months in advance, especially during the high season.

7. Budget for all aspects of your trip and watch out for hidden extras. Most safaris are all-inclusive so you don't think about the cost of your sundowner drink, snacks on your game drive, or cocktail at mealtime. However, some lodges, such as the Fairmont Mara Safari Club in Kenya, charge extra for drinks and excursions (e.g., a visit to a Masai village). You can keep your costs down by going to a place where things are à la carte and pay only for the things you deem important. Be aware that local beer is usually cheap, but wines are often imported (outside of South Africa) and are quite expensive.

When you book your trip, be clear as to whether extras such as airport transfers, use of equipment (including sleeping bags on some mobile-camping safaris) and entry fees are included in the fee.

Besides airfare and safari costs, make sure you budget for tips, medications, film, and

other sundries such as souvenirs. Plan to stay at a city hotel on your first and last nights in Africa—it'll help you adjust to jet lag and makes things altogether easier. Expect to pay from US$50 for basic accommodations to US$750 a night in the most luxurious hotels. If you do splash out on your safari, but want to keep costs down elsewhere, look out for special offers—sometimes South African lodges will throw in a free night's accommodation in Cape Town, for example, and this can turn out to be a great bargain.

Plan to spend US$15–$25 a day (per traveler) on gratuities. In South Africa tips are on the higher end of this range and usually are paid in rand (the local currency); you may also use U.S. dollars for tips, however. Elsewhere in Southern Africa, U.S. currency is preferred.

Stock up on film before you head out into the bush; a roll costs about US$20 in a safari camp.

8. Book your trip locally, or at the last minute. Last-minute deals can offer massive discounts, as long as you are prepared to be flexible about everything to do with your trip. Alternatively, book a trip locally once you are at your destination. This is popular in Kenya and Tanzania but is really an option only if you have plenty of time. You can also gather a group of people at your lodgings and do a group booking. This way you'll have the benefit of a guide, too, with the cost shared among a number of people.

QUESTIONS TO ASK A SAFARI SPECIALIST

Don't forward a deposit to a safari specialist (a general term for a safari operator or African-tour operator) until you have considered his or her answers to these questions. Once you have paid a deposit, you're liable for a penalty if you decide to cancel the arrangements for any reason.

■ Do you handle Africa exclusively?

■ How many years have you been selling tours in Africa?

■ Are you or any of the staff native to the continent?

■ To which professional organizations do you belong? For example, the American Society of Travel Agents (ASTA) or the United States Tour Operators Association (USTOA)?

■ Has your company received any accolades or awards relating to Africa?

■ Can you provide a reference list of past clients?

■ How often do you and your staff visit Africa?

■ Have you ever visited Africa yourself?

■ What sort of support do you have in Africa?

■ Do you charge a fee? (Agents and operators usually make their money through commissions.)

■ What is your cancellation policy?

■ Can you handle arrangements from start to finish, including flights?

■ What is your contingency plan in case of war or terrorism?

SAFARI PLANNING TIMELINE

Six Months Ahead

■ Research destinations and options and make a list of sights you want to see.

■ Start a safari file to keep track of information.

■ Set a budget.

■ Search the Internet. Post questions on bulletin boards and narrow your choices.

■ Contact a travel agent to start firming up details.

■ Choose your destination and make your reservations.

■ Buy travel insurance.

Three to Six Months Ahead

■ Find out which travel documents you need.

■ Apply for a passport, or renew yours if it's due to expire within six months of travel time. Many countries now require at least two empty pages in your passport.

■ Confirm whether your destination requires visas and certified health documents.

■ Arrange vaccinations or medical clearances.

■ Research malaria precautions.

■ Book excursions, tours, and side trips.

One to Three Months Ahead

■ Create a packing checklist. ⇨ *See our list in Chapter 9.*

■ Fill prescriptions for antimalarial and regular medications. Buy mosquito repellant.

■ Shop for safari clothing and equipment.

■ Arrange for a house and pet sitter.

One Month Ahead

■ Get copies of any prescriptions and make sure you have enough of any needed medicine to last you a few days longer than your trip.

■ Confirm international flights, transfers, and lodging reservations directly with your travel agent.

Three Weeks Ahead

■ Using your packing list, start buying articles you don't have. Update the list as you go.

Two Weeks Ahead

■ Collect small denominations of U.S. currency ($1 and $5) for tips.

■ Prepare to pack; remember bag size and weight restrictions.

One Week Ahead

■ Suspend newspaper and mail delivery.

■ List contact numbers and other details for your house sitter.

■ Check antimalarial prescriptions to see whether you need to start taking medication now.

■ Arrange transportation to the airport.

■ Make two copies of your passport's data page. Leave one copy, and a copy of your itinerary, with someone at home; pack the other separately from your passport. Make a PDF of these pages that can be accessed via e-mail.

A Few Days Ahead

■ Get pets situated.

■ Pack.

■ Reconfirm flights.

One Day Ahead

■ Check destination weather reports.

■ Make a last check of your house and go through your travel checklist one final time.

WHO'S WHO

There's no substitute for a knowledgeable tour operator or travel agent who specializes in Africa. These specialists look out for your best interests, are aware of trends and developments, and function as indispensable backups in the rare instance when something goes wrong.

African safari operator. Also referred to as a ground operator, this type of outfitter is a company in Africa that provides logistical support to a U.S.–based tour operator by seeing to the details of your safari. An operator might charter flights, pick you up at the airport, and take you on game-viewing trips, for example. Some operators own or manage safari lodges. In addition, an operator communicates changing trends and developments in the region to tour operators and serves as your on-site contact in cases of illness, injury, or other unexpected situations.

African tour operator. Based in the United States, this type of company specializes in tours and safaris to Africa and works with a safari outfitter that provides support on the ground. Start dates and itineraries are set for some trips offered by the operator, but customized vacations can be arranged. Travelers usually find out about these trips through retail travel agents.

Air consolidator. A consolidator aggressively promotes and sells plane tickets to Africa, usually concentrating on only one or a few airlines to ensure a large volume of sales with those particular carriers. The airlines provide greatly reduced airfares to the consolidator, who in turn adds a markup and resells them directly to you.

Retail travel agent. In general, a travel agent sells trip packages directly to consumers. In most cases an agent doesn't have a geographical specialty. When called on to arrange a trip to Africa, the travel agent turns to an African-tour operator for details.

Before you entrust your trip to an agent, do your best to determine the extent of his or her knowledge as well as the level of enthusiasm he or she has for the destination. There are as many travel companies claiming to specialize in Africa as there are hippos in the Zambezi, so it's especially important to determine which operators and agents are up to the challenge.

After choosing a tour operator or travel agent, it's a good idea to discuss with him or her the logistics and details of the itinerary so you know what to expect each day. Ask questions about lodging, even if you're traveling on a group tour. A lodge that is completely open to the elements may be a highlight for some travelers and terrifying for others, particularly at night when a lion roars nearby. Also ask about the amount of time you'll spend with other travelers. If you're planning a safari honeymoon, find out if you can dine alone when you want to, and ask about honeymoon packages.

TOUR OPERATORS

Our list of tour operators hardly exhausts the number of reputable companies, but those listed were chosen because they are established firms that offer a good selection of itineraries ranging from overland safaris, walking and fly-in safaris, under-canvas safaris, or safari lodges. Although various price options are offered, we suggest that where possible you go for all-inclusive packages, which will cover every aspect of your safari, from flights and road transfers to game drives, guided game walks, food, drinks, and accommodations.

Abercrombie & Kent (✉ *USA* ☎ *800/554–7016* ⊕ *www.abercrombiekent.com*). In business since 1962, this company is considered one of the best in the safari business and is consistently given high marks by former clients. From your first decision to go on safari to its successful conclusion, A&K offers seamless service. It has a professional network of local A&K offices in all its destination countries, staffed by full-time A&K experts. It is also renowned for its top tour directors and guides. The head office in the States is located in Illinois.

Africa Adventure Company (✉ *USA* ☎ *954/491–8877* ⊕ *www.africa-adventure.com*). For more than 20 years this Florida-based company has planned safaris of all kinds. It also specializes in all sorts of tours that you can add on to your safari, from exploring cities, gorilla trekking, and fishing, to diving, beaching, and lots more.

Africa Serendipity (✉ *USA* ☎ *212/288–1714* ⊕ *www.africaserendipity.com*). This New York–based company has excellent Africa-based operators with more than 50 years' experience, specializing in Kenya and Tanzania exclusively. They offer top accommodations, top guides, and excellent service, and always help you plan your safari, beach escape, city stay, or tour down to the last detail.

Africa Travel Resource (✉ *UK* ☎ *44/1306–880–770; 888/487–5418 in the U.S. and Canada* ⊕ *www.africatravelresource.com*). This is a Web-based resource site that provides you with numerous trip possibilities. After you've browsed to your heart's content and made all the relevant decisions, the operator will do the easy part and book the trip for you. So, if you're looking to plan a trip to Mt. Kilimanjaro, you can search through the huge resource base and choose your perfect trip.

&Beyond (✉ *South Africa* ☎ *27/11809–4300 in South Africa; 888/882–3742 in U.S.* ⊕ *www.andbeyond.com*). Formerly CC Africa, this highly experienced tour operator has 16 years of service to the safari-going public. It offers ready-made trips and tours to all parts of Southern or East Africa or can tailor one to your needs, from the budget variety to the lavish. It offers some of the best destinations and accommodations in Africa (read: it owns and manages all its properties), from the Okavango to remote Indian Ocean islands. It specializes in honeymoon packages.

Big Five (✉ *USA* ☎ *800/244–3483* ⊕ *www.bigfive.com*). Offering more than 100 tours to Africa, this Florida-based operator promises its clients a trip of a lifetime—if you're not happy with the tour choices, Big Five will custom create one for you. You can be assured that whatever trip you do choose, your knowledgeable agent will be able to draw on personal experience to assist you. Founded in 1973, Big Five focuses on low-impact, sustainable tourism and patronizes environmentally responsible lodgings.

Cheli & Peacock (✉ *Kenya* ☎ *254/20/60–4053* ⊕ *www.chelipeacock.com*). Based in Nairobi, Cheli & Peacock features small luxury camps and lodges in Kenya's top national parks and reserves. The variety of locations covers a broad selection of ecosystems, game, and conservation. Each agent creates a safari itinerary that best suits the likes and dislikes of each client producing once-in-a-lifetime experiences.

Gamewatchers Safaris (✉ *Kenya* ☎ *254/20/712–3129* ⊕ *www.porini.com*). This Nairobi-based company specializes in delivering tailored safaris to small camps and lodges in East Africa. They can also include beach getaways in your package. Every guest is guaranteed a personal, authentic travel experience and the opportunity to experience the magic of the African bush while helping protect Africa's wildlife, ecosystems, and cultures.

Journey Beyond (✉ *South Africa* ☎ *27/11/781–9210* ⊕ *www.journey-beyond.com*). Definitive sub-Saharan independent travel specialist offering comprehensive safari services to select travel operators and agents. Known for its responsible and caring service to individuals and groups.

Ker & Downey (✉ *Kenya* ☎ *800/423–4236* ⊕ *www.kerdowney.com*). One of the oldest and most respected safari companies in Africa, Ker & Downey also has an office in Texas. The company utilizes its exclusive camps to provide traditional safari experiences. Accommodation options range from rustic to deluxe.

Micato Safaris (✉ *USA* ☎ *212/545–7111* ⊕ *www.micatosafaris.com*). Family-owned and -operated, this award-winning New York–based operator offers deliberately luxurious trips driven by a sustainable ethos. Safari lodges enchant with such unadulterated luxuries as private

plunge pools and personal butlers. Cultured safari guides educate, instruct, and amuse, while itineraries offer an irresistible array of experiences from the sophisticated pleasures of Cape Town to the celebrated savannas of the Serengeti and the near-spiritual beauty of the Kalahari.

Moremi Safaris and Tours (✉ *South Africa* ☎ *27/11/706–0861* ⊕ *www.moremi-safaris.com*). This South African–based company has provided opportunities and given expert advice for individuals or special-interest groups on Botswana, Zimbabwe, Zambia, Namibia, Seychelles, and South Africa for nearly 30 years.

NatureFriend Safaris (✉ *Namibia* ☎ *264/61/23–4793* ⊕ *www.naturefriendsafaris.com*). This small, dynamic Namibian company, which also operates Dune Hopper Air Taxis, has flexible fly-in packages from Windhoek or Swakopmund to the Sossusvlei area. It also offers a wide range of exclusive fly-in safaris (called wing-in by the operator) to other tourist destinations in Namibia, including Skeleton Coast, Damaraland, and Etosha.

Orient-Express Safaris (✉ *South Africa* ☎ *27/21/483–1600* ⊕ *www.orient-express-safaris.co.za*). A member of the Small Luxury Hotels of the World organization, this operator owns three strategically located camps in some of Botswana's most diverse ecosystems and most desirable destinations: Chobe National Park, Moremi Wildlife Reserve, and the Okavango Delta. All the camps have identical thatch-tented lodging and furnishings, plus plenty of bells and whistles.

Premier Tours (✉ *USA* ☎ *800/545–1910* ⊕ *www.premiertours.com*). Based in Philadelphia but owned and operated by people from Africa, Premier specializes in

Outfitter	Location	Tel. no.	Website	Countries it covers
Abercrombie & Kent	USA	800/554-7016	www.abercrombiekent.com	Kenya, Tanzania, South Africa, Botswana, Namibia, Zambia, Zimbabwe
African Adventure Company	USA	800/882-9453	www.africa-adventure.com	Kenya, Tanzania, South Africa, Botswana, Namibia, Zambia, Zimbabwe
African Extravaganza	Namibia	26/61/37-2100	www.african-extravaganza.com	Namibia
Africa Serendipity	USA	212/288-1714	www.africaserendipity.com	Kenya, Tanzania
African Travel Resource	UK	0845/450-1520	www.africantravelresource.com	Kenya, Tanzania, South Africa, Botswana, Namibia, Zimbabwe
Big Five	USA	800/244-3483	www.bigfive.com	Kenya, Tanzania, South Africa, Botswana, Namibia, Zambia
CC Africa Safaris & Tours	South Africa USA	27/11/809-4300 888/882-3742	www.ccafrica.com	Kenya, Tanzania, South Africa, Botswana, Namibia, Zimbabwe
Cheli & Peacock	Kenya	254/20/60-4053	www.chelipeacock.com	Kenya
Damaraland Trails & Tours	Namibia	061/23-4610	no web	Namibia
Desert & Delta Safaris	South Africa	27/11/706-0861	www.desertdelta.co.za	Botswana, Zambia, Zimbabwe
Fazendin Portfolio	USA	303/895-9583	www.fazendinportfolio.com	Kenya, Tanzania, South Africa, Zambia
Gamewatchers Safaris	Kenya	254/20/712-3129	www.porini.com	Kenya, Tanzania
Islands in Africa	South Africa	27/11/706-7207	www.islandsinafrica.com	Botswana, Namibia
Ker & Downey	USA	800/423-4236	www.kerdowney.com	Kenya, Tanzania, South Africa, Botswana, Namibia, Zambia
Micato Safaris	USA Kenya	800/642-2861	www.micatosafaris.com	Kenya, Tanzania, South Africa, Botswana, Namibia, Zambia
NatureFriend Safaris	Namibia	264/61/23-4793	www.naturefriendsafaris.com	Botswana, Namibia, Zambia
Orient Express	South Africa	27/11/481-6052 800/237-1236	www.orient-express-safaris.com	South Africa, Botswana, Namibia, Zambia
Premier Tours	USA	800/545-1910	www.premiertours.com	Kenya, Tanzania, South Africa, Botswana, Namibia, Zimbabwe
Sardius Tours	Kenya	254/20/201—5094	www.sardiustours.com	Kenya, Tanzania
Skeleton Coast Safaris	Namibia	264/61/22-4248	www.skeletoncoastsafaris.com	Namibia
Skyview of Africa	Kenya	254/20/375-1672	www.skyviewofafrica.com	Kenya, Tanzania
Tanzania Odyssey	UK	866/356-4691	www.tanzaniaodyssey.com	Tanzania
Thompsons Africa	South Africa	27/31/275-3500	www.thompsonssa.com	Kenya, Tanzania, South Africa, Botswana, Namibia, Zambia, Zimbabwe
Wilderness Safaris	South Africa	27/11/807-1800	www.wilderness-safaris.com	South Africa, Botswana, Namibia, Zambia, Zimbabwe

adventure tours for anyone from 18 to 55. It is a founding member of the United Nations Environment Program's initiative on sustainable tourism development and offers consolidated airfares to Africa.

Roar Africa (✉ *USA* ☎ *877/762–7237* ⊕ *www.roarafrica.com*). New York– and South Africa–based ROAR Africa offers a one-of-a-kind travel service for personalized, custom tours of southern Africa. The founders' family dates back to 1688, ensuring that trips are designed by specialists whose wealth of information and well-established network can only come from years of actually living there.

Skeleton Coast Fly-In Safaris (✉ *Namibia* ☎ *264/61/22–4248* ⊕ *www. skeletoncoastsafaris.com*). This fly-in safari company runs superb four- and six-day trips to the Skeleton Coast that include visits with the Himba people, who, with their red-ocher body coverings, elaborate plaited hair, and intricate bead necklaces and leather aprons, live much as they have for centuries.

Skyview of Africa (✉ *Kenya* ☎ *254/20/252– 8721* ⊕ *www.skyviewofafrica.com*). This Kenyan-owned and -operated company offers a wide range of memorable safaris in Kenya and Tanzania to international clients. Destinations include the Ngorongoro Crater, the Serengeti, Masai Mara, Amboseli, and even a Mt. Kenya climb.

Tanzania Odyssey (✉ *UK* ☎ *866/356–4691 in the U.S.* ⊕ *www.tanzaniaodyssey.com*). Based in London with offices in Arusha and Dar-es-Salaam, this knowledgeable company has spent more than 12 years creating tailor-made itineraries to suit every individual requirement, from safaris and beach holidays to honeymoons. They are the only company to have taken extensive video footage of each and every lodge in Tanzania and Zanzibar.

Thompsons Africa (✉ *South Africa* ☎ *27/ 11/770–7700* ⊕ *www.thompsonssa.com*). Thompsons, which has been given awards for excellence by the South Africa Travel Industry and South African Airways, works with every budget to plan all types of tours, including day trips and safaris. Agents are available 24 hours a day to answer your questions.

Wilderness Safaris (✉ *South Africa* ☎ *27/ 11/257–5000* ⊕ *www.wilderness-safaris. com*). One of Africa's most respected and innovative tour operators, Wilderness assures you impeccable service, gorgeous destinations and accommodations, and game galore. It operates a seven-day fly-in safari from Windhoek, which covers most of the main tourist destinations in Namibia. It also owns the majority of lodges in Botswana and offers all kinds of packages and a choice of "premier," "classic," "vintage," or "camping wild" camps in a great variety of locations and ecosystems, from the delta to the Kalahari Desert. It has mobile safaris and custom tours for all Botswana destinations and specializes in honeymoon packages.

WHAT TO EXPECT
WHILE ON SAFARI

Your safari will be one of the most memorable trips you'll ever take, and it's essential that your African experience matches the one you've always imagined. Nothing should be left to chance, and that includes where you'll stay and how you'll get around.

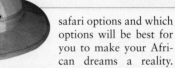

If you already know what the term *bush* means, then you've read all the books and brochures and watched all the movies and TV shows about Africa and African safaris and are ready to book the real thing.

But what happens if the chalet you get is not what you expected it to be, or your game-viewing vehicle does not quite look like those you've seen in the movies?

Read on to figure out what you really can expect when booking lodging and safari options and which options will be best for you to make your African dreams a reality. After all, you should get the very best from your experience. This is a once-in-a-lifetime trip.

By the way, *bush* is a term used to describe the natural setting of your safari—be it in forests, plains, or on riverbanks. The expression "going to the bush" means going away from urban areas and into the wilderness.

Above: Making friends with giraffes in South Africa

LODGING

The days are long gone when legendary 19th-century explorer Dr. David Livingstone pitched his travel-stained tent under a tree and ate his sparse rations. But whether you go simple in a basic safari tent with an adjacent bucket shower and long-drop toilet, choose ultra-comfort in a mega-tent or canvas-and-thatch chalet, or go totally over-the-top in a glass-walled aerie-cum-penthouse with a state-of-the-art designer interior, you'll still feel very much part of the bush.

LUXURY LODGES

Kings Pool

Some would say that using the word *luxury* with *safari lodge* is redundant, as *all* such lodges fall into this category. But there's *luxurious*, and then there's *luxurious*. Options in the latter category range from *Out of Africa* accommodations with antique furniture, crystal, and wrought-iron chandeliers, to thatch-roofed stone chalets, Tuscan villas, and suites that wouldn't seem out of place in midtown Manhattan. In all, you can expect to find a/c; in many there will be a small library, a spa, a gift shop, and Internet service. You may even have your own plunge pool.

PERMANENT TENTED CAMPS

Think luxurious, oh-so-comfortable, and spacious...in a tent. This no ordinary tent, though. Each has its own bathroom, usually with an outdoor shower; a wooden deck with table and chairs that overlooks the bush; and carpet or wooden floors, big "windows," and an inviting four-poster (usually) bed with puffy pillows and fluffy blankets (for those cold winter months). The public space will comprise a bar, lounge, dining areas, viewing decks, usually a pool, and a curio shop. Some will have internet, a/c, and private plunge pools.

Severin Safari Camp

POTTY TALK

Using the bathroom in the bush will be an eye-opening experience for you. If you're camping, very often bathing will be via bucket shower, which is a hot water–filled canvas bucket dangling from a tree. And your toilet? Well that might be a long hole in the ground below a toilet seat—it's called a long-drop toilet. Picture a very rustic outhouse with canvas walls.

MOBILE TENTED CAMPS

CC Africa

This option varies enormously. You could have the original, roomy walk-in dome tent (complete with canvas bedrolls, crisp cotton bedding on GI stretchers, open-air flush toilets, and bucket showers) that's ready and waiting for you at day's end. Or you could have luxury tents (with crystal chandeliers, antique rugs, and shining silver) that stay in one place for a few months during peak seasons. They are all fully serviced (the staff travels with the tents), and you'll dine under the stars or sip coffee as the sun rises.

NATIONAL PARK ACCOMMODATIONS

What you'll get in this category depends on which park you're in and what type of lodgings you're looking for. Accommodations can vary from camp sites to simple one-room rondavels (round huts) with en-suite bathroom; safari tents to two- to four-bed cottages; or possibly a top-of-the-range guest house that sleeps eight people. With the exception of some camping sites, all national-park accommodations are fully serviced with staff to look after you.

Rondavels at Taita Hill Lodge, Kenya

TRANSPORTATION

Your safari transportation is determined by your destination and could range from custom-made game-viewing vehicles (full-service safari) to a combi or minivan (basic safari or self-drive). There shouldn't be more than six people per vehicle. To make sure you experience every view, suggest to your ranger that visitors rotate seats for each drive. Be warned if you're going it alone: roads in Africa range from superb to bone-crunching. Plan your route carefully, arm yourself with reliable maps, and get up-to-date road conditions before you go.

OPEN-SIDED LAND ROVERS

This is the most common game-viewing vehicle, usually a Land Rover or a Land Cruiser. Each vehicle seats six to eight people. Sit beside the ranger/driver if you're a bit unsteady, because you won't have to climb up into the rear. The back seats tend to be bumpy, but you get great views, and you'll hear every word the driver says if you choose the seats behind him. The more expensive the camp, the fewer people in the vehicle.

POP TOPS

Used mainly in East Africa, because of dirt, dust, and rain, these hard-topped minivans pop up so you can stand up, get a better view, and take photos in every direction. If you're claustrophobic or very tall, this might not be the vehicle for you, but there are outfitters that have larger vehicles that can "stretch." If it gets really hot outside, you'll be happy to close up and turn on the a/c. Make sure water and sodas are available.

SMALL PLANES

As many camps and lodges are inaccessible by land, or are in very remote places, you'll often fly in 6- to 10-seat plane. This is particularly true in Botswana's Okavango Delta. Always take a bottle of water with you (small planes can get very hot), and make sure you have medication ready if you're prone to motion sickness. Keep in mind the strictly enforced luggage restriction: 12 kg (26 lbs) of luggage in a soft bag that can squeeze into the plane's small hold. Flights can be bumpy, and landing strips are often just baked earth.

MINIVANS

It's unlikely that you'll use one of these unless you are on a very cheap safari or a self-drive—they are, however, perfect for the Namib Desert. The advantage is that they sit high off the ground and provide much better views; some outfitters offer vehicles that can expand. If you're self-driving, make sure you get a van with a/c and power steering. The farther north you go, check out your prospective vehicle's year and make sure it's as recent as possible.

WATERCRAFT

If your lodge is on or near a river, expect to go out in a boat. Options range from the big sunset safari boats with bar and bathroom on the Zambezi and Chobe rivers to a six- or eight-seater along the Okavango and smaller rivers, where your amenities include a cool box of drinks and snacks but no toilet. One of the highlights of your stay in the Okavango Delta will be gliding in a *mokoro* (a canoe) poled by an expert local waterman through papyrus-fringed channels where hippos and crocs lurk.

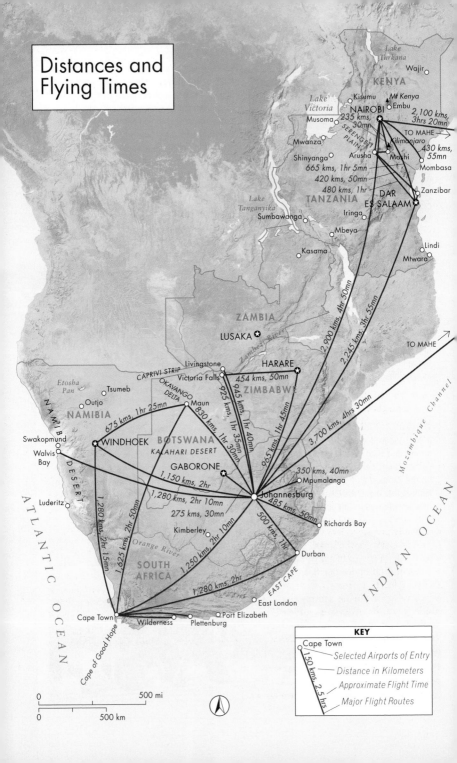

SPECIAL CONSIDERATIONS

Children on Safari

Most safari operators and private game reserves don't accept children under a certain age, usually under 8, but sometimes the age limit is as high as 12. This age limit is largely for safety reasons. Animals often respond, not in a positive manner, to something that is younger, slower, or smaller than they are. And even though you might think your six- or seven-year-old adores all sorts of animals and bugs, you'd be surprised how overwhelmed kids can become, out of the comfort of their home and backyard, by the size and multitude of African insects and wildlife.

Take into account, also, that when you're following a strange schedule and getting in and out of small planes, safari vehicles, boats, and the like with other people whom you probably won't know, there often is no time to deal with recalcitrant children—and fussing will, you can be guaranteed, annoy the other people in your plane or lodge, who have spent a great deal of money for what may be a once-in-a-lifetime safari trip.

One option, if you can afford it, is to book a private safari where no other people are involved and you dictate the schedule. Many private lodges will rent you the entire property for the length of your stay; this is often the only way these camps allow children under age 8 on safari. At the very least, a camp will require that you pay for a private safari vehicle and guide if you have children under 12. Be advised that, even if you're renting the whole camp, babies and toddlers still aren't allowed out on game-viewing trips.

One great family option is to stay with &Beyond, formerly CC Africa, a safari operator with children's programs at several of its upscale camps throughout Southern and East Africa. While you follow your own program, your kids pursue their own wilderness activities; you all meet up later for meals and other activities.

A much cheaper alternative is also one of the most enjoyable for a safari as a family: a self-driving trip where you stay at national parks. No destination is better in this regard than Kruger National Park in South Africa, where there are comfortable accommodations and lots of other families around. You'll be able to set your own schedule, rent a cottage large enough for the entire family, and buy and prepare food you know your children will eat.

It's best not to visit malarial areas with children under age 10. Young kidneys are especially vulnerable to both the effects of malaria and the side effects of malaria prophylactics. You might opt to practice stringent nonchemical preventive measures, but know the risks: malaria's effects on young children are much worse than they are on older people.

Going on safari with babies also isn't recommended. Some lodges, such as those at Mala Mala, provide babysitting service for infants, but babies aren't allowed out in safari vehicles. The sound of an infant crying puts most predators on alert—dangerous to other passengers as well as the child. Keep in mind also that the bush is often a hot and dusty place with little in the way of baby-friendly amenities. You'd have to bring all your own supplies, and if something were to go wrong there would be no way to get immediate help until a flight could be arranged.

People with Disabilities

Having a disability doesn't mean you cannot go on safari. It's important, however, to plan carefully to ensure that your needs can be adequately met. South African lodges, especially the high-end private ones, are the easiest to navigate and have the fewest steps. Keep in mind that all-terrain 4x4 vehicles don't have seat belts, so you need enough muscle control to keep yourself upright while the vehicle bumps along the unpaved roads. Getting in and out of these elevated vehicles can also be challenging. Mala Mala Game Reserve in South Africa is completely accessible and even has specially equipped four-wheel-drive safari vehicles with harness seat belts. Many of Kruger's camps have special accommodations.

Older Travelers

Safaris everywhere welcome older travelers. However, before you book a safari, find out as many details as possible about how taxing a trip might be both physically and mentally. Consider the types of accommodations (for example, find out whether a lodge is built on an incline or has many stairs, and whether bathrooms have grab bars) as well as how much time will be spent in the elements, such as in the hot sun where it's easy to dehydrate, and whether there are daily activities such as canoeing that are physically challenging.

SHOULD YOU TAKE THE KIDS?

Consider the following if you're thinking about bringing children to a private safari lodge:

■ **Are they afraid of the dark?** A safari camp that runs on generator-powered batteries will have minimal lights at night.

■ **Are they startled easily?** Large animals may come quite close to rooms or tents or near safari vehicles.

■ **Are they comfortable with strangers?** Most meals at safari lodges are at communal tables, and shared six-seat planes are the basic form of transportation between remote safari camps.

■ **Are they troubled by bugs?** The African bush can be filled with moths as big as small birds as well as a host of other flying and crawling insects.

■ **Are they picky eaters?** Meals are usually buffet style and food for camps is often ordered at least a month in advance, so your child's favorite food may not be available.

TYPES OF SAFARIS

Luxury Lodge–Based Safaris

The majority of safari-goers base their trips at luxury lodges, which pack the double punch of outstanding game-viewing and stylish, atmospheric accommodations. A lodge may be made up of stone chalets, thatch-roof huts, rondavels, or large suitelike tents. Mosquito nets, leather furnishings, and mounted trophies add to the ambience. Dinners are served inside or in an open-air *boma* (traditional thatch dining enclosure). All have hot-and-cold running water, flush toilets, toiletries, laundry service, electricity, and, in most cases, swimming pools. Some lodges also have air-conditioning, telephones, hair dryers, and minibars. The most lavish places also have private plunge pools.

Make no mistake—you pay for all this pampering. Expect to spend anywhere from US$400 to US$1,300 per person per night, depending on the season. All meals, beverages, house wines, game drives, and walks are included. A three-night stay is ideal, but two nights are usually sufficient to see the big game.

The time you spend at a private lodge is tightly structured. With some exceptions, the lodges offer almost identical programs of events. There are usually two three- to four-hour game drives a day, one in the early morning and another in the evening. You spend a lot of time sitting and eating, and in the afternoon you can nap and relax. However, you can always opt for an after-breakfast bush walk, and many lodges now have spas and gyms. If you're tired after your night drive, ask for something to be sent to your room, but don't miss the bush *braai* (barbecue) and at least one night in the boma.

On game drives at bigger camps, rangers stay in contact with one another via radio.

If one finds a rhino, for example, he relays its location to the others so they can bring their guests. It's a double-edged sword. The more vehicles you have in the field, the more wildlife everyone is likely to see. But don't worry, most lodges are very well disciplined with their vehicles, and there are rarely more than three or four at a sighting. As your vehicle arrives, one already there will drive away. In choosing a game lodge, remember to check how much land a lodge can traverse and how many vehicles it uses. Try to go on a bush walk with an armed ranger—an unforgettable experience, as the ranger can point out fascinating details along the way.

All lodges arrange transfers from nearby airports, train stations, or drop-off points. In more remote areas most have their own private airstrips carved out of the bush and fly guests in on chartered aircraft at extra cost. If you're driving yourself, the lodge will send you detailed instructions because many of the roads don't appear on maps and lack names.

Fly-in Safaris

The mode of transportation for fly-in safaris is as central to the experience as the accommodations. In places such as northern Botswana, where few roads are paved, or northern Namibia, where distances make road transfers impractical, small bush planes take you from lodge to lodge. These planes are usually six-seat Cessna 206 craft flown by bush pilots. The planes have no air-conditioning and in summer can be very hot, especially in the afternoon. Bring a bottle of water with you. But most flights are short—approximately 30 minutes or so—so bite the bullet or you'll miss out on some of the really fabulous destinations.

Flying from destination to destination is a special experience. The planes stay at low altitudes, allowing you to spot game along the way: you might see elephant and buffalo herds lined up drinking along the edges of remote water holes, or large numbers of zebras walking across the plains. Fly-in safaris also allow you to cover more territory than other types of safaris. In Botswana, for example, the trip between the diverse game destinations of the Moremi Wildlife Reserve in the Okavango Delta and northern Chobe National Park is 40 minutes by plane; it would take six hours by vehicle, if a road between these locations existed.

Hopping from place to place by plane is so easy and fast that many travelers make the mistake of cramming their itineraries with too many lodges. Plan your trip this way and you'll spend more time at airstrips, in planes, and shuttling to and from the airfields than tracking animals or enjoying the bush. You will glimpse animals as you travel back and forth—sometimes you'll even see them on the airstrips—but you won't have time to stop and really take in the sights. Try to spend at least two nights at any one lodge; three nights is better.

The best way to set up a fly-in safari is to book an all-inclusive package that includes airfare. (It's impractical to try to do it yourself.) A tour operator makes all the arrangements, and many offer standard trips that visit several of its lodges. For example, in Botswana, Orient-Express Safaris has a package that includes three camps in three very different locations.

Be sure to pack light. In Southern Africa the maximum weight allowed for luggage is 26 kilos (57 pounds) (South Africa is the exception to this rule). Your bag should be a soft-sided duffel with a lock

or something similar, so the pilot can easily fit it into the small cargo area. At most private lodges, laundry is included.

■ **TIP→ If your bag is over the weight limit, or if you weigh more than 220 pounds, you will be required to purchase an additional plane seat (usually about US$100).**

Walking Safaris

Many lodges offer walks as an optional way to view game. On a walking safari, however, you spend most, if not all, of your time in the bush on foot, accompanied by an armed guide. Because you're trekking through big-game country, there's an element of danger. But it's the proximity to wilderness that makes this type of trip so enchanting—and exciting. Of course, you can't stop every step of the way or you'd never get very far, but you will stop frequently to be shown something—from a native flower to spoor to animals—or to discuss some aspect of animal behavior or of tracking.

Walking treks take place on what are known as wilderness trails, which are natural tracks made by animals and are traversed only on foot, never by vehicle, to maintain their pristine condition. These trails usually lead into remote areas that you would never see on a typical safari. In some cases porters carry the supplies and bags. Accommodation is usually in remote camps or occasionally in tents.

■ **TIP→ If you consider a walking safari, you must factor in your physical condition.** You should be in good health and be able to walk between 6.4 and 16 km (4 and 10 mi) a day, depending on the scope of the trip. Some trips don't allow hikers under age 12 or over age 60 (but Kruger Park makes exceptions for those over 60 if you produce a doctor's certificate). Also, you shouldn't scare easily. No guide has time

for people who freeze up at the sight of a beetle, spider, or something more menacing; guides need to keep their attention on the wilds around them and on the group as a whole. Guides are armed, and they take great caution to keep you away from trouble. To stay safe, always listen to your guide and follow instructions.

Mobile and Overland Safaris

Most mobile-safari operations are expertly run but are aimed at budget-conscious travelers. They are mostly self-sufficient camping affairs with overnights at either public or private campgrounds, depending on the safari's itinerary and price. Sometimes you stay at basic lodges along the way. Travel is often by something that looks like a 4x4 bus.

For young, hardy people, or the young at heart, mobile safaris are a great way to see the land from ground level. You taste the dust, smell the bacon cooking, stop where and when you want (within reason), and get to see some of the best places in the region. Trips usually run 14 to 21 days, although you can find shorter ones that cover fewer destinations. Prices start at US$750 and climb to US$2,500 for all-inclusive trips. Not sure whether all-inclusive is right for you? Consider combining a mobile safari with a lodge-based one, which gives you the best of both worlds. A minimum of 10 nights is recommended for such an itinerary.

Self-Drive Safaris

A self-drive safari, where you drive yourself in your own rental vehicle, is a great option for budget travelers and for those who feel comfortable seeing the bush without a ranger at hand to search out game or explain what you're seeing. Some popular and easiest-to-navigate options are South Africa's Kruger National Park,

Pilanesburg National Park, Hluhluwe-Imfolozi Game Reserve, and Kgalagadi Transfrontier Park, and Namibia's Etosha National Park. These parks have paved, well-marked roads and a wide range of accommodations that include family-size chalets, small huts, tents, and camping sites. You may buy your own groceries and cook for yourself at all of these areas; some options, especially in Kruger, have restaurants and stores on-site.

If possible, rent a van or a 4x4, since the higher off the ground you are the better your chances of spotting game (although a two-wheel-drive car is fine); remember that you have to stick to marked roads. In addition to patience, you'll need drinks, snacks, and a ready camera. Keep your eyes and ears open and you may come across game at any time, in any place.

■TIP→ Purchase a good park map that shows roads, watering holes, different eco-zones, and the types of animals you can expect to find in each. You can buy these maps when you enter a park or at rest-camp shops, and it would be foolish to pass them up.

Plan you game drive routes around as many water holes and rivers as possible. Except during the height of the summer rains, most game come to permanent water sources to drink. In winter, when the land is parched, a tour of water holes is bound to reap great rewards. Even better, take a picnic lunch and park at the same watering hole for an hour or two, especially in winter, when the car interior doesn't become too hot. Not only will you see plenty of animals, but you'll find yourself slipping into the drama of the bush.

THE CHANGING CONTINENT

This age-old proverb illustrates the intricate dance performed daily by countless species in the African bush. The continent is home to the greatest population of wildlife on the planet, but by 1986, Central Africa had lost about half of its wildlife habitats while the number of extinct plants in Southern Africa increased from 39 to 58 between 1980 and 1995 alone. More than 700 vertebrate species and about 1,000 species of trees are threatened with extinction in Africa. The balance between African wildlife and its environment—not to mention indigenous peoples—is delicate; it shifts unpredictably as Mother Nature plays her hand.

Poaching

Fueled by a growing demand in Asia as well as online sales in the United States, the killing of elephants for their tusks has reached levels not seen since 1989. Elephant populations are actually increasing across Southern Africa, but herds in Central and Western Africa continue to struggle.

The Convention on International Trade in Endangered Species of Wild Fauna and Flora (CITES), attended by 172 countries every two to three years, offers a chance for members to review conservation progress as well as make amendments to the list of endangered species. Today, CITES offers protection, in varying degrees, to more than 30,000 species of plants and animals worldwide. In 2007, there was good news for conservationists when the convention approved a decade-long suspension of trade in elephant ivory. Almost simultaneously, scientists announced a breakthrough procedure that matches the genetic profile of poached ivory to the region in Africa where the elephant came

from. This promises to be an invaluable tool for anti-poaching enforcement.

The victory for the elephants at CITES did not come without a price, however. The approval of a one-off sale of stockpiled ivory by a handful of African nations was a compromise. Naturally, this raises concerns that any ivory sales will stimulate illicit markets. Other animals in high demand by poachers include crocodiles for their skins, rhinoceroses for their tusks, hippos for their teeth, monkeys for their pelts, and chimps for medical research.

The Many Consequences of War

Ironically, one of the most far-reaching causes of wildlife extinction on the African continent is one of the least obvious: the erosion of the environment caused by war and government instability. In the words of Kenyan environmentalist and Nobel Peace Prize–winner Wangari Mathai, we can only hope that "in a few decades, the relationship between the environment, resources, and conflict may seem almost as obvious as the connection we see today between human rights, democracy, and peace."

In previously war-torn Angola many elephants migrating into the country have had their trunks and legs blown off by land mines, condemning them to

excruciating deaths because without its trunk, an elephant can't eat. The situation is getting better, and elephants are learning to navigate away from the land mines, though no one knows how or why they have the sense to do this. And in Southern Africa, during the 1970s, '80s, and '90s, the South African Defense Force played a major role in the decimation of Africa's elephant and rhinoceros populations. Initially, this was undertaken as a way of helping to fund the wars in Angola and Mozambique with illicit ivory sales, but it gradually became an organized ring for profiteering at very high levels of the Apartheid government.

There is hope. Bodies such as the African Union are fostering an open dialogue on conflicts, which may have once been viewed as regional, and the African Ministerial Conference on the Environment has tried to foster discussions on land degradation and water resource management. By taking small steps, Africa has made considerable progress toward creating a healthier ecosystem for both humans and wildlife.

Global Climate Change

In 2006, an international coalition of "green groups" released a report that predicted climate change will hit Africa hardest. The report indicated that although climates across Africa have always been erratic, there will be new extremes in its near future if the effects of global warming are not reversed. Temperatures in the Nile basin are rising and are expected to continue to rise, while the famous icecap on Mt. Kilimanjaro is fast disappearing. This will have serious implications for the rivers that depend on the ice melt for their flow, which in turn affects access to water by both human and animal populations.

In addition, while the semi-arid regions of Southern Africa become drier, parts of equatorial Africa are getting wetter.

Although a lack of environmental regulations in Africa may be in some small way to blame, the greatest threat is caused by economic activity in the wealthier, industrial countries of the Western world. It is believed that global greenhouse-gas emissions will need to be cut by up to 90% in order to mitigate the detrimental effects of global warming in Africa. It is vital for every traveler to remember that when you return to your everyday life, what you do on a daily basis will affect the future of the creatures you just experienced. Though the situation may seem overwhelming, if each individual does his part in reducing his carbon footprint, progress can be made.

Flora and Fauna

FLORA AND FAUNA PLANNER

Do's and Don'ts

Never attempt to attract an animal's attention. Don't imitate sounds, clap hands, pound the vehicle, or throw objects.

Respect your driver and guide's judgment. They have more knowledge and experience than you. If they say no, there's a good reason.

Doing a self-drive? Stay in the vehicle, drive slowly, and keep ample distance between you and the wildlife.

Walking safaris. Stay downwind from the animals, stay quiet, and obey your guide's instructions.

Never litter. Any tossed item can choke or poison animals.

Never attempt to feed or approach animals. This is especially important at lodges and campgrounds where animals are accustomed to humans.

No smoking. The bush ignites easily.

Dress in neutral tones. If everyone is wearing earth tones, the animal sees one large vegetation-colored mass.

Avoid body fragrances. It's for the animals and your fellow travelers.

Wildlife Safety and Respect

Nature is neither kind nor sentimental. Do not be tempted to interfere with the natural processes. The animals are going about the business of survival in a harsh environment, and you can unwittingly make this business more difficult. Don't get too close to the animals and don't try to help them cross some perceived obstacle; you have no idea what it's really trying to do or where it wants to go. If you're intrusive, you could drive animals away from feeding and, even worse, from drinking at water holes, where they are very skittish and vulnerable to predators. That time at the water hole may be their only opportunity to drink that day.

Never feed any wild creature. Not a cute monkey, not an inquisitive baboon, not a baby tree squirrel, or a young bird out of its nest. In some camps and lodges, however, animals have gotten used to being fed or steal food. The most common animals in this category are baboons and monkeys; in some places they sneak into huts, tents, and even occupied vehicles to snatch food. If you see primates around, keep all food out of sight, and keep your windows rolled up. (If a baboon manages to get into your vehicle, he will trash the interior as he searches for food and use the vehicle as a toilet.)

Never try to get an animal to pose with you. This is probably the biggest cause of death and injury on safaris, when visitors don't listen to or believe the warnings from their rangers or posted notices in the public parks. Regardless of how cute or harmless they may look, these animals are not tame. An herbivore hippo, giraffe, or ostrich can kill you just as easily as a lion, elephant, or buffalo can.

Immersion in the African safari lands is a privilege. In order to preserve this privilege for later generations, it's important that you view wildlife with minimal disturbance and avoid upsetting the delicate balance of nature at all costs. You are the visitor, so act like you would in someone else's home: respect their space. Caution is your most trusted safety measure. Keep your distance, keep quiet, and keep your hands to yourself, and you should be fine.

Nighttime Safety

Never sleep out in the open in any area with wildlife. If you're sleeping in a tent, make sure it's fully closed as in zipped or snapped shut; if it's a small tent, place something between you and the side of the wall to prevent an opportunistic bite from the outside. Also, if you are menstruating, be sure to dispose of your toiletries somewhere other than in or near your tent. All in all, if you're in your tent and not exposed, you should be quite safe. Few people lose their lives to lions or hyenas. Malaria is a much more potent danger, so keep your tent zipped up tight at night to keep out mosquitoes.

Never walk alone. Most camps and lodges insist that an armed ranger accompany you to and from your accommodation at night, and rightly so.

Best Viewing Times

The best time to find game is in the early morning and early evening, when the animals are most active, although old Africa hands will tell you that you can come across good game at any time of day. Stick to the philosophy "you never know what's around the next corner," and keep your eyes and ears wide open all the time. If your rest camp offers guided night drives on open vehicles with spotlights—go for it. You'll rarely be disappointed, seeing not only big game, but also a lot of fascinating little critters that surface only at night. Book your night drive in advance or as soon as you get to camp.

Driving Directions

Approach animals cautiously and quietly and "feel" their response. As soon as an effect is noted, slow down or stop, depending on the circumstances. Human presence among wild animals never goes unnoticed. In the Serengeti and Masai Mara, cheetah survival is being jeopardized by guides who try to drive too close to them, thereby giving up the cheetah's location to its prey or sometimes just chasing away the skittish cat, thus impacting the animal's ability to hunt, eat, and ultimately survive. Not all game guides and rangers are sensitive to this, their focus being on giving you the best sighting. But if you feel uncomfortable, say so.

Choosing a Field Guide

Arm yourself with specialized books on mammals and birds rather than a more general one that tries to cover too much. Airports, lodges, and camp shops stock a good range, but try to bring one with you and do a bit of boning up in advance. Any bird guide by Ken Newman (Struik Publishers) and the *Sasol Guide to Birds* are recommended.

Making a List, Checking It Twice

Many national parks have reception areas with charts that show the most recent sightings of wildlife in the area. To be sure you see everything you want to, stop at the nearest reception and ask about a spotting chart, or just chat with the other drivers, rangers, and tourists you may encounter there, who can tell you what they've seen and where.

FINDING THE BIG FIVE

The fauna that can be found on an African safari is as varied and vast as the continent's landscape. Africa has more large animals than anywhere else in the world and is the only place on earth where vast herds still roam the planes.

		African Buffalo	Elephant	Leopard	Lion	Rhino
BOTSWANA	The Okavango Delta	●	●	●	●	●
	Moremi Wildlife Reserve	●	●	●	●	●
	Chobe Nat'l Park	●	●	●	●	●
	Kwando Game Reserve	●	●	●	●	○
KENYA	Masai Mara	●	●	●	●	●
	Amboseli Nat'l Park	●	●	●	●	●
	Tsavo Nat'l Park	●	●	●	●	●
	Laikipia Plateau	●	●	●	●	●
NAMIBIA	Namib Naukluft Park*	○	○	◑	◑	○
	Damaraland	○	●	○	○	●
	Etosha Nat'l Park	●	●	●	●	●
SOUTH AFRICA	Kruger Nat'l Park	●	●	●	●	●
	Sabi Sands Game Reserve	●	●	●	●	●
	KwaZulu-Natal Parks	●	●	●	●	●
	Kgalagadi Transfrontier Park	○	○	●	●	○
TANZANIA	Serengeti Nat'l Park	●	●	●	●	●
	Ngorongoro Crater	●	●	●	●	●
	Lake Manyara Nat'l Park	●	●	●	●	○
	Selous Game Reserve	●	●	●	●	●
	Gombe Stream and Mahale Mountains Nat'l Parks**	○	○	○	○	○

*This park is noted for its stunning scenic beauty - not game
**These parks are primarily for primate viewing - chimpanzees and monkeys
KEY: ● = yes   ◑ = Rarely   ○ = No

There's nothing quite like the feeling of first setting eyes on one of the Big Five—buffalo, elephant, leopard, lion, and rhino—in the African bush. Being just a few feet from these majestic creatures is both terrifying and exhilarating, even for the most seasoned safari-goer.

THE BIG 5

updated by
Kate Turkington

The Big Five was originally a hunting term referring to those animals that posed the greatest risk to hunters on foot—buffalo, elephant, leopard, lion, and rhino. Today it has become one of the most important criteria used in evaluating a lodge or reserve, though it should never be your only criterion.

THE AFRICAN BUFFALO

Often referred to as the Cape buffalo, this is considered by many to be the most dangerous of the Big Five because of its unpredictability and speed. Do not confuse it with the docile Asian water buffalo as the Cape buffalo is a more powerful and untameable beast with a massive build and short strong legs. They have few predators other than human hunters and lions. It generally takes an entire lion pride to bring down an adult buffalo, although calves, weak and sick adults can be taken by wild dog and spotted hyena. Lions risk being mobbed by the herd when they do attack, and are sometimes trampled and gored.

Cape buffalo can reach up to 1,800 pounds and in the wild can live up to 15 or so years, much longer if they are in captivity. Never found very far from water, they are grazers and widespread throughout sub-Saharan Africa, especially in Kenya, Tanzania, Botswana, Zambia, Zimbabwe and South Africa. Large, mixed herds can number up to a few hundred, and in the Serengeti, during the rains, in their thousands. You shouldn't fear a herd, but beware lone old males which have mostly been thrown out of the herd and are now bad-tempered and volatile. Known as "Dagha Boys"—dagha is the clay mixture used for building traditional huts—they spend much of their days in mud wallows and are usually thickly coated in the stuff. While seemingly lethargic these old boys can turn on a dime and charge like lightning. If you are charged, run for cover or climb the nearest tree.

THE ELEPHANT

The largest of the land animal, it once roamed the continent by the millions. Today, according to the World Wildlife Fund (WWF), the population, mainly found in Southern and Eastern Africa, is between 470,000 and 600,000. The continent's forest elephants (of central and West Africa) are still under severe threat.

African elephants are divided into two species. Savannah elephants are the largest, at 13 feet and 7 tons, and can be found by lakes, marshes, or grasslands. Forest elephants have an average height of 10 feet and weight of 10,000 pounds. They're usually found in central and West African rainforests.

An elephant's gestation period is 22 months—the longest of any land animal. The aver-

age calf is 265 pounds. When calves are born, they are raised and protected by the entire herd—a group of about 10 females led by the oldest and largest. Males leave the herd after 15 years, often living with other males or alone.

When an elephant trumpets in a showy manner, head up and ears spread, it's a mock charge—frightening but not physically dangerous. If an elephant stomps the ground, holds its ears back and head forward, and issues a loud, high-pitched screech, this means real trouble. A charging elephant is extremely fast and surprisingly agile. If you're on foot make for the nearest big tree or embankment; elephants seldom negotiate these obstacles. If you're in a vehicle, hit the gas.

THE RHINO

There are two species of these massive primeval-looking animals in Africa: the black, or hook-lipped rhino, and the white, or square-lipped rhino. Both species have poor eyesight but excellent hearing, and because of their erratic tempers, they may sometimes charge without apparent reason. These animals are surprisingly agile for their size. The white rhino is slighter taller (up to 60 inches at the shoulder) and heavier at over two tons, the black rhino is shorter and stockier by a few inches and can weigh up to one and a half tons. Although they share habitats, the white rhino is a grazer eating only grasses, the black, a browser, eating leaves and shrubs. The black rhino which is more aggressive than the white, prefers thick thornveld and dense vegetation, while the white sticks more to open grassland and the plains. Both love to wallow in mud. They mark their territory by means of defecating in individual middens, or dung heaps, which they make along rhino paths and territorial boundaries, regularly patrolling these 'signposts' on the look out for intruders.

The black rhino tends to be more solitary unless it is a very small mother/father/calf group; the white rhino stays together in small groups called crashes. Calves of both species stay with their mothers until they are four or five, when they leave to find a new territory.

Sadly, the survival of this incredible mammal is under serious threat from poaching. Today, many are protected in sanctuaries or reserves, but poaching is a constant threat – in South Africa in 2010 alone, 126 rhino had been slaughtered for their horns by mid-year. These are traded on the black market as aphrodisiacs (an empty claim) and as potential dagger handles in the Middle East to symbolize wealth and power. However, major efforts by conservationists are in hand to try to stem the problem.

■TIP➔ When a rhino is about to charge, it lowers it head, snorts, and launches into a swift gallop of up to 30 miles an hour. If you're on foot, best bet is to climb the nearest tree.

THE LION

Known as the king of beasts—the Swahili word for lion, "simba," also means "king," "strong," and "aggressive"—this proud animal was once found throughout the world. Today, the majority of the estimated 23,000 lions are found in sub-Saharan Africa—a small population are also found in India—in grasslands, savannah, and dense bush.

Watching a lion stalk its prey can be one of the most exciting safari encounters. Females do most of the hunting, typically setting up a plan of attack, which is then carried out by the pride. Lionesses take turns hunting and this collective labor allows them to conserve their energy and survive longer in the bush. They are most active from dusk to dawn. A pride consists of between four and six adults but occasionally may go up to 20 or even 30. Botswana's Savuti region is known for its large prides. The males, identified by their gorgeous golden-red manes, are often brothers who behave territorially; their main task is to protect the females and the cubs. Typically, the females in the pride will give birth at approximately the same time, and the cubs will be raised together. Litters usually consist of two to three cubs that weigh about three pounds each. Sometimes, males that take over a pride will kill existing cubs so that they can sire their own with the lioness.

Lions can sleep for up to 18 hours a day. Lounging about in the grass, lions will often lick each other, rub heads, and purr contentedly. But don't be fooled by their charms. When a lion moves, it can do so with awesome speed and power—a charging lion can cover 330 feet in four seconds. If you come face to face with a lion, never, ever turn your back and try to run—that is your death warrant. Your best bet is to stand as still as possible and try to outface the lion.

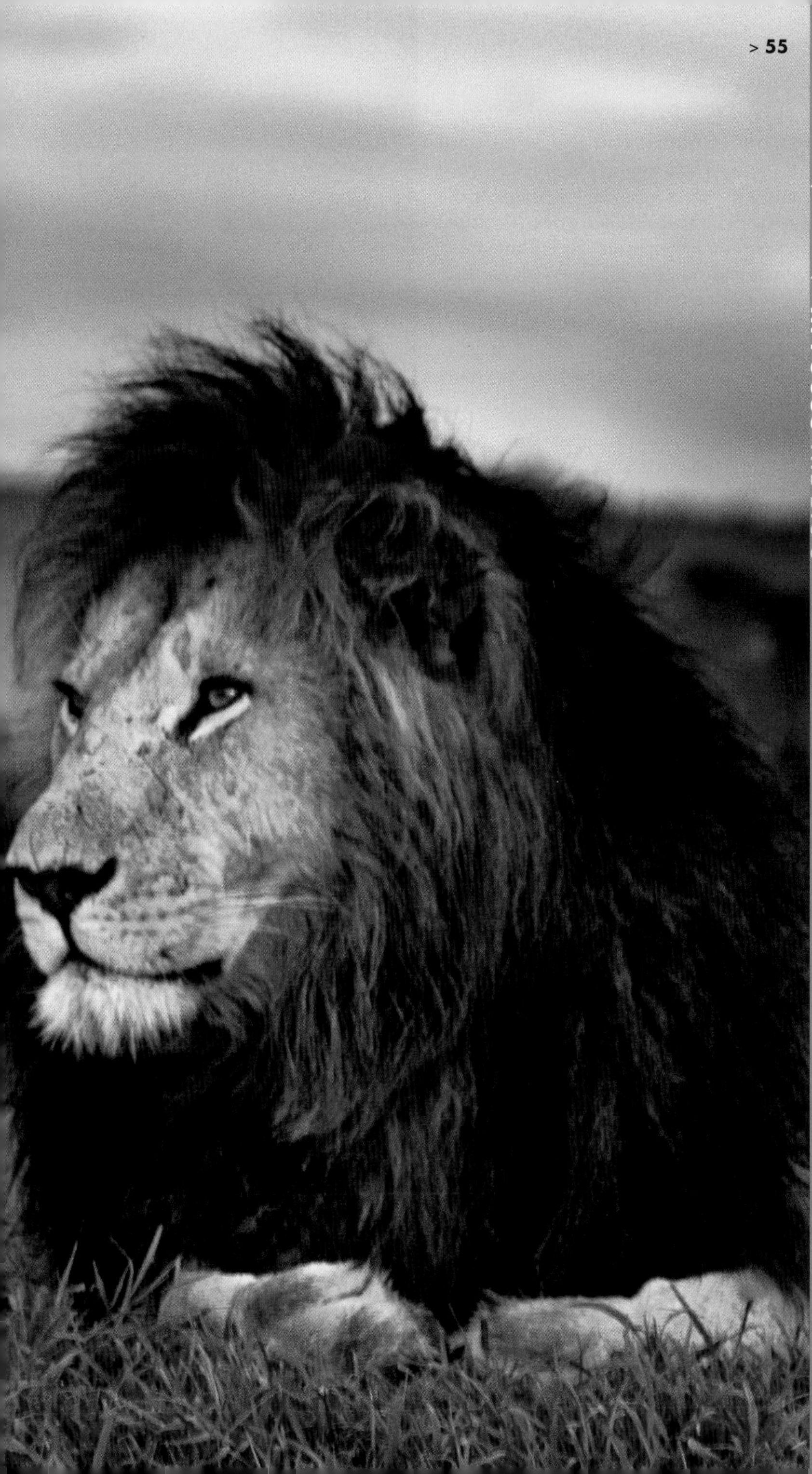

THE LEOPARD

Secretive, stealthy and shrewd, the leopard is the most successful predator of all Africa's big cats. They are often difficult to spot on safari, primarily because they are nocturnal, but if you go on a night game drive your chances will increase tremendously. South Africa's Sabi Sands area has the highest density of leopards in the world and you would be very unlucky not to see one there.

Leopard can vary in appearance, their coat ranging from a light tawny hue in dry areas to darker shades in the forest. Their spots, called rosettes, are round in East Africa, but square in Southern Africa. Leopard can also be found in India, China, Siberia, and Korea. The female leopard, whose litter usually ranges from about one to three cubs, will keep her young hidden for about two months after birth, then feed and nurse them for an additional three months or so until her cubs are strong enough to roam with her. What about dad? Male leopards play no part in rearing the cubs. In fact, the male is usually long gone by the time the female gives birth. He leaves her after they mate, although he has been known to return to kill the cubs, hence the reasoning behind keeping them hidden for the first few months of their lives.

Leopard use a combination of teeth and razor-sharp claws to kill their prey; it's not uncommon for a leopard's lunch to be taken away by lion or hyena. In order to avoid this, the leopard will often drag their larger kills into a tree where they can dine amongst the leaves in relative peace and quiet.

THE LITTLE 5

We've all heard of the Big Five, but keep a look out for the Little Five, a term given to the animals with names that include the Big Five: antlion, buffalo weaver, elephant shrew, leopard tortoise, and rhinoceros beetle.

RHINOCEROS BEETLE

The rhinoceros beetle grows up to two inches long. It has large spikes—similar in appearance to a rhino's tusks—that are used in battle with other rhino beetles, or for digging, climbing, and mating.

LEOPARD TORTOISE

The largest tortoise in Africa, the leopard tortoise can grow up to two feet long and weigh up to 100 pounds. It lives in the grasslands of East and Southern Africa and doesn't mate until it's at least 12 years old. Its name stems from its black and yellow-spotted shell, which resembles a leopard's coat.

ELEPHANT SHREW

These ground-dwelling mammals range in size from that of a mouse to a large rabbit. They live in lowland forests, woodlands, rocky outcrops, and deserts and eat small fruits and plants. They get their name from their long nose, which resembles a miniature elephant's trunk.

ANTLION

Also known as a "doodlebug" because of the winding patterns it leaves in the sand when building traps, the antlion makes its home on dry, sandy slopes sheltered from the wind. Essentially larva, it eventually grows into an insect akin to a dragonfly.

RED-BILLED BUFFALO WEAVERS

These black birds with red bills and legs make big sturdy communal nests out of sticks which are defended by the dominant male and nearly always face westward. Inside, the nests are separate chambers with individual tunnels leading to the outside. Their mating is unique amongst birds as it lasts up to two minutes instead of seconds as in most birds.

FAUNA

OTHER ANIMALS

You'll be amazed by how many visitors ignore a gorgeous animal that doesn't "rank" in the Big Five or lose interest in a species once they've checked it off their list. After you've spent a few days in the bush, you will hopefully understand the idiocy of racing about in search of five animals when there are 150 equally fascinating species all around you. Here are a few to look out for.

Baboons

(A) These are the most adaptable of the ground-dwelling primates and can live in all manner of habitats as long as they have water and a safe place to sleep. Baboons travel in groups of up to 40 animals, sleeping, eating, and socializing together. Although they are hugely entertaining to watch, always keep your vehicle windows rolled up. Like other animals, they can be vicious when they feel threatened, and they have huge canine teeth. They eat mainly plants, but will also consume small quantities of meat.

Cheetah

(B) Reaching speeds of 70 mph, Cheetahs are the world's fastest land animal—they have slender, muscular legs and special pads on their feet for traction. With its characteristic dark spots, the cheetah also has a distinctive black "tear" line running from the inside corner of its eye to the mouth. A solitary, timid creature, cheetahs are found mainly in open savanna. Males and females can sometimes be seen together after mating, but usually one or two males—often brothers—are alone and females are with the cubs. Cheetahs generally prey on gazelle and impala. Sadly, this stunning cat is one of the most endangered animals, due to shrinking habitat, loss of prey, and disease.

Giraffe

(C) The biggest ruminant and tallest living animal, giraffes are social creatures that live in loose herds that can spread out over half a mile. Although there are no leaders, the males fight over females using a "necking" technique, winding their necks around each other, pushing and shoving. Giraffes either walk or gallop and are ubiquitous in most national parks. It's easy to tell the difference between males and females. The tops of the male's horns are bare and shiny from fighting; the females have bushy tips like paintbrushes.

Hippo

(D) Though they may be comical looking, these are actually one of Africa's most dangerous animals. The most common threat display is the yawn, which is telling you to back off. Most guides will give them a wide berth. Never get between a hippo and its water, as this will appear to them that you're trying to corner them and may result in an attack. The comical nighttime sounds of hippos snorting and chortling will be one of your safari's most memorable experiences.

Impala

(E) One of the most populous animals in the African bush, impalas can be found in grasslands and wooded areas, usually near water. Similar in appearance to a deer, these one-of-a-kind antelopes are reddish-brown with white and black markings. A typical herd has one dominant male ruling over his harem, although bachelor herds are usually in the vicinity, with hopeful individuals awaiting their turn to oust the ruling male. It's a hugely successful animal because it is both a grazer and a browser.

FAUNA

Springbok

(F) This cinnamon-color antelope has a dark brown stripe on its flanks, a white underside, and short, slender horns. It often engages in a mysterious activity known as "pronking," a seemingly sudden spurt of high jumps into the air with its back bowed. Breeding takes place twice a year, and the young will stay with their mothers for about four months. These herbivores travel in herds that usually include a few territorial males.

African Wild Dogs

(G) Also called the "painted dog" or "painted wolf" because of each uniquely spotted coat, the wild dog is headed toward extinction with numbers about 3,000 and shrinking. This highly social animal with batlike ears and a furry tail lives in small packs of about 15; only the alpha male and female are allowed to breed. Intelligent and quick, wild dogs hunt as a coordinated pack running down

their prey, which varies from antelopes to zebras, until exhausted. They have an amazingly successful catch rate of 85%.

Wildebeest

(H) Living on the savanna plains of Kenya and Tanzania, this herbivore is an odd-looking creature: large head and front end, curved horns, and slender body and rear. Often called "the clowns of the veld" they toss their heads as they run and kick up their back legs. Mothers give birth to their young in the middle of the herd, and calves are up and running within days.

Zebra

(I) Africa has three species: the Burchell's or common zebra, East Africa's Grevy's zebra (named after former French president Jules Grevy), and the mountain zebra of South and Southwestern Africa. All have striped coats and strong teeth for chewing grass and often travel in large herds. A mother keeps its foal close for

2

the first few hours after birth so it can remember her stripes and not get lost. Bold and courageous, a male zebra can break an attacking lion's jaw with one powerful kick.

Hyena

(J) Hyenas live in groups called clans and make their homes in dens. They mark their territory with gland secretions or droppings. Cubs are nursed for about 18 months, at which point they head out on hunting and scavenging sprees with their mothers. Both strategic hunters and opportunists, hyenas will feed on their own kill as well as that of others. Aggressive and dangerous, African folklore links the hyena with witchcraft and legends, a fact that has been exacerbated in popular culture such as *The Lion King*.

Nile Crocodile

(K) Averaging about 16 feet and 700 pounds, this croc can be found in sub-Saharan Africa, the Nile River, and in Madagascar. They eat mainly fish but will eat almost anything, including a baby hippo or a human. Although fearsome looking and lightning quick in their attack, they are unusually sensitive with their young, carefully guarding their nests until their babies hatch. Their numbers have been slashed by poachers, who seek their skins for shoemakers.

Bush Baby

(L) These small nocturnal primates, which make cries similar to that of a human baby, range in size from 2 ounces to 3 pounds. During the day, they stay in tree hollows and nests, but at night you'll see them leaping and bouncing from tree to tree in pursuit of night-flying insects. Their main predators are some of the larger carnivores, genets, and snakes.

FAUNA

BIRDS

Many people come to Africa solely for the birds. There are thousands of winged beauties to ooh and aah over; we mention a few to look out for.

Bateleur Eagle

(A) This spectacular bird found through-out sub-Saharan Africa is probably one of the best known birds in Africa. Mainly black with a red back, legs, and beak and white underneath its wings, the Bateleur eagle can fly up to 322 km (200 mi) at a time in search of prey, which includes antelope, mice, other birds, snakes, and carrion. They mate for life, often using the same nest for several years.

Lappet-Faced Vulture

(B) The largest and most dominant of the vultures, this scavenger feeds mainly on carrion and carcasses that have been killed by other animals. The most aggressive of

the African vultures, it will also, on occasion, kill other weaker birds or attack the nests of young birds as prey. The Lappet-faced vulture has a bald head and is pink in color with a wingspan of up to 8½ feet.

Lilacbreasted Roller

(C) This stunning-looking bird with a blue and lilac-colored breast is found in the open woodland and savanna plains throughout sub-Saharan Africa. It's usually solo or in pairs sitting in bushes or trees. Both parents nurture the nest and are extremely territorial and aggressive when it comes to defending it. During mating, the male flies up high and then rolls over and over as it descends, making screeching cries.

Kori Bustard

(D) One of the world's heaviest flying birds is found all over Southern and Eastern Africa. Reaching almost 30 pounds and about 3½ feet in length, the male is much

larger than the female but both are gray in color, have crests, and gray and white necks. Although it does fly, the majority of its time is spent on land where it can find insects, lizards, snakes, and seeds. One male mates with several females, which then raise the young on their own.

Pel's Fishing Owl

(E) A large, monogamous, ginger-brown owl with no ears, bare legs, and dark eyes, it lives along the banks of rivers in Kruger Park, South Africa's Kwa-Zulu Natal province, Botswana's Okavango Delta, and Zimbabwe. One of only three fishing owls in the world, it hunts at night with its sharp talons and dozes in tall trees during the day. The owls communicate with each other through synchronized hooting at night as they guard their stretch of riverbank.

Wattled Crane

(F) The rarest African crane is found in Ethiopia, Zambia, Botswana, Mozambique, and South Africa. A gray-and-white bird, it can reach up to 5 feet tall and, while mating, will nest in pairs along the shallow wetlands of large rivers. They are omnivorous and sometimes wander onto farmlands where they are vulnerable to poisoning by farmers. They occur in pairs or sometimes in large flocks especially in the Okavango Delta. Recently, the crane has been added to the "endangered" list and is on South Africa's "critically endangered" list.

FLORA

Although the mammals and birds of Africa are spectacular, we'd be remiss if we didn't mention the amazing plant life of this varied landscape. The floral wealth of the African continent is astounding, with unique, endemic species growing in all parts—the South African Cape has one of the richest of the world's six floral kingdoms. There are also several species of non-native plants and trees in Africa that have become the subject of lively environmental debates due to their effect on the environment.

TREES

African Mahogany

(A) Originally from West Africa, you'll find this majestic tree in warm humid climates like riverine forests; you'll also find them in the Florida everglades. A member of the Khaya genus, the mahogany requires significant rainfall in order to thrive and can reach up to 140 feet with a 6-foot trunk diameter. Its much-prized, strong, richly colored wood is sought after for furniture making and boat building.

Baobab

(B) A huge, deciduous quirky-looking tree that grows throughout mainland Africa, the baobab has a round, hollow trunk with spiny-looking branches growing out at the top in all directions—it almost looks like it's upside down with the roots sprouting out at the top. Known for storing water in its trunk, the baobab lives in dry regions and can live up to 400 years; some have lived for more than 1,000 years. The hollow trunks have been home to a prison and a post office.

Fever

(C) The fabled fever tree, which thrives in damp, swampy habitats throughout sub-Saharan Africa, has a luminous, yellow-green bark that's smooth and flaky, and its branches have white thorns and clusters of yellow flowers. It is so-named because

before mosquitoes were known to carry malaria, travelers often contracted the disease where fever trees grew and thus they were wrongly thought to transmit malaria. Bees are attracted by the sweet smell of the flowers, and birds often nest in its branches as the thorns offer extra protection against predators.

Fig

(D) There are as many as 50 species of fig trees in Southern and East Africa, where they may reach almost gigantic proportions, growing wherever water is nearby. Although figs provide nourishment for a variety of birds, bats, and other animals, they are most noted for their symbiotic relationship with wasps, which pollinate the fig flowers while reproducing. The fig seed is dispersed throughout the bush in the droppings of animals who feed on the rich, juicy fruit.

Jackalberry

(E) The large, graceful jackalberry, also known as the African ebony, is a riverine tree found all over sub-Saharan Africa. It can grow up to 80 feet tall and 16 feet wide. It bears fragrant white flowers and a fleshy yellow fruit that jackals, monkeys, baboons, and fruit-eating birds love. Its bark and leaves are used in traditional medicine with proven pharmacological benefits.

Sausage

(F) This unique tree, found in Southern Africa, bears sausagelike fruits that hang from ropelike stalks. The tree grows to be about 40 feet with fragrant red flowers that bloom at night and are pollinated by bats, insects, and the occasional bird. The fresh fruit, which can grow up to 2 feet long and weigh as much as 15 pounds, is poisonous but can be made into various medicines and an alcohol similar to beer.

FLORA

PLANTS

Magic Guarri

This round shrub grows along floodplains and rivers. It has dark green leaves and white or cream-color flowers, and its fruit is fleshy and purple with a seed in its center. The fruit can be fermented to produce an alcoholic beverage, and the bark is used as a dye in basket making. The twigs have been used as toothbrushes, while the root can be used as mouthwash. The wood, sometimes used to make furniture, is said to have magical or supernatural powers and is never burned as firewood.

Strelitzia Flower

(G) Also known as Bird of Paradise or the crane flower, the strelitzia is indigenous to South Africa. It grows up to 6½ feet tall with a beautiful fan-shaped crown with bright orange and bluish-purple petals that grow perpendicular to the stem, giving it the appearance of a graceful bird.

Welwitschia mirabilis

(H) With its long, wide leathery leaves creeping over the ground, this somewhat surreal-looking plant is also one of the world's oldest plants; it's estimated that welwitschia live to about 1,500 years, though botanists believe some can live to be 2,000 years old. It's found in the Namib Desert and consists solely of two leaves, a stem base, and roots. The plant's two permanent leaves lie on the ground getting tattered and torn, but grow longer and longer each summer.

Wild Thyme

(I) Also called creeping thyme, wild thyme grows mainly in rocky soil and outcrops. Its fragrant flowers are purple or white, and its leaves are used to make herbal tea. Honeybees use the plant as an important source of nectar. There is also a species of butterfly whose diet consists solely of wild thyme.

Cape Fynbos

(J) There are six plant kingdoms—an area with a relatively uniform plant population—in the world. The smallest, known as the Cape Floral Kingdom or Capensis, is found in South Africa's southwestern and southern Cape; it's roughly the size of Portugal or Indiana and is made up of eight different protected areas. In 2004 it became the sixth South African site to be named to the UNESCO World Heritage list.

Fynbos, a term given to the collection of plants found in the Cape, accounts for four-fifths of the Cape Floral Kingdom; the term has been around since the Dutch first settled here in the 1600s. It includes no less than 8,600 plant species including shrubs, proteas, bulbous plants like gladiolus and lachenalias (in the hydrangea family), aloes, and grasslike flowering plants. Table Mountain alone hosts approximately 1,500 species of plants and 69 protea species—there 112 protea species worldwide.

From a distance, fynbos may just look like random clusters of sharp growth that cover the mountainous regions of the Cape, but up close you'll see the beauty and diversity of this colorful growth. Many of the bright blooms in gardens in the U.S. and Europe, such as daisies, gladioli, lilies, and irises, come from indigenous Cape plants.

Kenya

WELCOME TO KENYA

TOP REASONS TO GO

★ **The Great Migration.** Millions of plains game move in an endless cycle of birth and death from Tanzania's Serengeti to Kenya's Masai Mara.

★ **Eyeball Big Game.** Visiting Kenya's legendary national parks and game reserves guarantees that you'll see the Big Five as well as huge herds of plains animals and hundreds of colorful birds.

★ **Africa's Fabled Tribe.** The tall and dignified red-robed Masai have held explorers, adventurers, and writers in thrall for centuries.

★ **Beach Escapes.** Miles of white sandy beaches lined by an azure ocean and water sports galore. From diving and snorkeling to windsurfing, there's something for everyone.

★ **Turn back the Past.** Check out ancient history along the coast where Arab traders and Vasco da Gama once sailed. In the World Heritage tiny town of Lamu you'll find an Arabic way of life unchanged for centuries.

1 Masai Mara. Located in Southern Kenya, in the area known as the Great Rift Valley, the park covers 1,510 km (938 mi) at altitudes of 1,500 meters to 2,100 meters above sea level. It's considered by many to be the world's greatest game park because of the abundance of animals located here. During July and August when the Great Migration reaches here, you can see hundreds of thousands of wildebeest, zebra, and gazelles feeding on the new grass, followed by dozens of predators.

2 Amboseli National Park. The snow-capped peak of Kilimanjaro, huge herds of elephants, and quintessential Kenyan landscape (open plains, acacia woodland, grasslands, bush, and marshland) greet you along the Tanzania border.

3 Tsavo National Park. Once known for its legendary man-eating lions, Tsavo, which is made up of Tsavo East and West, is now home to peaceful prides and loads of other game. The park's close proximity to the coast makes it a great choice for those who want to combine beach and beasts.

4 Laikipia Plateau. Fast becoming Kenya's hottest game destination, the area is home to the Samburu National Reserve, which boasts more game per square mile than anywhere else in the country, and some of its classiest camps and lodges.

GETTING ORIENTED

3

Kenya lies on Africa's east coast. It's bordered by Uganda to the west, Tanzania to the south, Ethiopia to the north, Somalia to the northeast, and the Indian Ocean to the southeast. It's a land of amazing diversity with extraordinary tourist attractions: great game reserves including Masai Mara and Samburu, the Great Rift Valley, fertile highlands, parched deserts, long pristine beaches and coral reefs, marine parks, mountains such as Mt. Kenya and Mt. Meru, and rivers and lakes, including Lake Turkana—its largest lake. Its two major cities couldn't be more different. Nairobi, the capital, is a bustling city where colonial buildings rub shoulders with modern skyscrapers. Steamy Mombasa on the coast retains its strong Arabic influence and history as it continues to be Kenya's largest and busiest port. Kenya is also home to the Masai, who've roamed the plains for centuries.

ETHIOPIA

CHALBI DESERT

GEILO HILLS

LAIKIPIA PLATEAU

BOJI PLAIN

○ Wajir

4

Samburu National Reserve

SOMALIA

Mt. Kenya 5,199 m

Meru National Park

Meru

EQUATOR

Nyeri ○   Mt. Meru 4,566 m

○ Garissa

Embu ○

YATTA PLATEAU

NAIROBI ✪

Nairobi National Park

Tsavo National Park

Amboseli National Park

2

3

KENYA BEACH

○ Lamu

Kipini

Tsavo

INDIAN OCEAN

Mt. Kilimanjaro 5,895 m

○ Malindi

Mombasa ○

| 0 | | 50 mi |
| 0 | | 50 km |

GREEN LODGINGS IN KENYA

Kenya is home to two cultural (Lamu Old Town and Sacred Mijikenda Kaya Forests) and two natural (Lake Turkana National Parks and Mt. Kenya National Park/Natural Forest) UNESCO World Heritage sites. It's also home to 49 national parks and countless private reserves.

(above) Cottars 1920s Safari Camp; (opposite upper right) Porini Rhino Camp; (opposite bottom left) Il Ngwesi Camp

Ensuring that these natural and cultural wonders last for generations to come is paramount. It's especially important when you realize that African Lion, Grevy's Zebra, Black Rhinoceros, African Elephant, and Cheetah are all on the endangered species list. But how can you be sure you're traveling green? By being a responsible ecotourist and staying in accommodations that put high value on preserving these things as well. To help you in this quest, we've listed a few places you can stay on safari that are eco-conscious. Of course our list is not exhaustive, but it's a starting place.

BRINGING UP THE CHIMPS

Established in 1993, Sweetwaters Chimpanzee Sanctuary (🌐 www.olpejetaconservancy.org) provides lifelong refuge to chimpanzees. Today, the sanctuary, located in the Ol Pejeta Conservancy, has more than 40 chimps in its protection. Visitors to the conservancy have free access to the sanctuary, which is open daily, but anyone can make a donation.

KENYA'S GREEN LODGES

Though the folks at **Cottars 1920s Safari Camp** (☎ *888/870–0903* ⊕ *www.cottars.com*) tread lightly on the environment, this remains one of Africa's most exclusive and luxurious camps. The owners pay the local Masai community for land use and have helped finance the local school and nearby clinics so that the camp and its activities are seen as a part of the surrounding land and its people. ⇨ *See Permanent Tented Camps, in Masai Mara for more information about the camp.*

Il Ngwesi Camp (☎ *020/203–3122* ⊕ *www.ilngwesi.com*) is a shining example of how a safari lodge can reduce poverty and strengthen partnerships between the tourist trade and local communities in Africa. Built only with local materials, the camp is completely solar powered, and its water comes from a nearby spring and is gravity fed to the lodge. The local Masai community helped build and continues to run the camp through a communal group. ⇨ *See Luxury Lodges, in Laikipia Plateau for more information about the camp.*

Porini Rhino Camp (☎ *020/712–2504* ⊕ *www.porini.com*) is the largest black rhino sanctuary in East Africa. The camp has no permanent structures and is strategically constructed around trees and shrubs to minimize the human footprint on the natural landscape. The camp uses solar power for electricity, and water is heated with eco-friendly, sustainable charcoal briquettes; there is no generator. The conservancy is owned by the local Masai, and the camp is run with the aim of creating income for the tribe. ⇨ *See Permanent Tented Camps, in Laikipia Plateau for more information about the camp.*

Campi ya Kanzi (☎ *720/461–300* ⊕ *www.maasai.com*) was the first camp in Kenya to be gold rated by Ecotourism Kenya for its efforts in sustainable tourism. It's also co-owned by the local Masai. There is an additional US$100 per-person, per-day conservation fee, which entirely benefits the local Masai community. ⇨ *See Permanent Tented Camps, in Amboseli National Reserve for more information about the camp.*

IS YOUR OPERATOR GREEN?

Before booking your trip, question several operators about their relationship to the communities where their safaris take place. Ask about the company's philosophies on recycling, energy efficiency, water conservation, and waste management. Also find out whether the company, or the lodges it uses, provides economic opportunities for local communities. Many reputable outfitters have established foundations that make donations to local peoples or wildlife, and some will even arrange trips to nearby schools, orphanages, or neighborhoods.

GREEN IS YOUR LODGE GREEN?

Before booking a hotel, lodge, or camp in Kenya, check to see if the property has been rated by Ecotourism Kenya (⊕ www.ecotourismkenya.org). Ratings are given based upon the properties efforts to promote environmental, social, and economic values. Participation is voluntary on the part of the hotel, lodge, or camp, but ratings are determined by a pre-set list of criteria.

Updated
by Claire
Baranowski

Kenya is where "going on safari" started. A hundred years
or so ago, visitors from all over the world, including Teddy
Roosevelt, started traveling to Africa, lured by stories of mul-
titudes of wild animals; there were more than 3 million large
mammals roving East Africa's plains at the time. Today millions of visitors continue to flock to this East African nation
each year. Although humans have made their mark, Kenya
still holds onto its pristine wilderness.

But Kenya's tourism industry, the main source of foreign revenue, is very
susceptible to perceptions of tourist safety. Tourism declined in the late
1990s following a series of attacks on tourists and the terrorist bombing
of the U.S. Embassies in Nairobi and Dar es Salaam in 1998, but visitor
numbers were on the rise again before the crisis in 2007–2008. Widely
televised at the time, the ethnic violence that arose after disputed election results still tarnishes Kenya's reputation, even though no tourists
were in any danger. The crisis was, however, a large contributing factor
to a new constitution being signed into law in August 2010. Thought to
be the most significant political event to have taken place in the country
since independence, this new constitution introduces a U.S.-style system
of checks and balances, aimed at limiting presidential powers and keeping corruption in check. It will take years to implement, but there is a
new optimism among Kenyans and, more than ever, there seems to be
no reason to consider Kenya unsafe as a tourist destination.

Kenya's human history dates back at least 6 million years. In 2001 the
controversial Millennium Man was discovered near Lake Baringo in
the northwest. This find and Richard and Mary Leakey's discovery of
Homo habilis in the '60s fuel ongoing excavations.

Today there are more than 70 ethnic groups in Kenya that range from
the Masai, Samburu, Kikuyu, and Turkana tribes to the Arabs and
Indians that settled on the coast and the descendants of the first white
settlers in and around Nairobi and the Kenya highlands. In Nairobi,
about 40% of the population is Kikuyu—a Bantu people numbering

more than 6 million. Islam arrived along the coast in the 8th century, followed in the 15th century by Portuguese explorers and sailors who came looking for the sea route to India. During the rule of Seyyid Said of Oman in the 1830s, German, British, and American merchants established themselves on the coast, and the notorious slave routes were created.

The British created what was then known as British East Africa in the late 1800s. After a much publicized and often sensationalized struggle by native Kenyans against British rule in the 1950s, known as the Mau Mau era, Kenya finally won independence in 1963.

If there were animal karma, some of Kenya's great parks, like the Masai Mara, would be an animal's nirvana, because this is food paradise. It's an abundantly stocked raptor restaurant that offers something for every predator's palate: a hyena hamburger place, a jackal fast-food joint, cheetah takeaways, banquets for bat-eared foxes, breakfast, lunch, and dinner for leopards, feasts for lions, and lush grazing for vegetarians.

Don't be put off by people who say that there are far too many tourists, which sometimes makes you feel like you're in a big zoo. Although the Masai Mara is much more crowded with visitors than neighboring Tanzania's Serengeti, you'll still get a superb year-round game experience, and your safari could be cheaper, too. Kenya has a compact and easily accessible tourist circuit, and the authorities are now limiting visitor numbers in national parks, as they do in South Africa's Kruger Park.

Kenya is not just about big game. It has a gorgeous tropical coastline with white sandy beaches, coral gardens, superb fishing, and snorkeling, diving, and vibey beach resorts. Traditional triangular-sailed dhows still ply their trade providing unforgettable seafood to the surrounding restaurants. You'll discover unique islands with ancient stone Arab buildings, where a donkey is the main means of transport, and where time really does seem to have stood still.

PLANNING

WHEN TO GO

Generally speaking, Kenya, which straddles the equator, has one of the best climates in the world with sunny, dry days; daytime temperatures average between 20°C (68°F) and 25°C (77°F). The coast can get hot and humid, though sea breezes cool things down, and the mountainous regions can get very cold—remember there's snow all year round on the highest peaks. Try to avoid the long rains of March and April or the short rains of October, November, and December because park roads can become impassable and mosquitoes are at their busiest and deadliest. Game-viewing is at its best during the driest seasons (May–September, January, and February) because the lack of surface water forces

FAST FACTS

Size 582,645 square km (224,960 square mi)

Capital Nairobi

Number of National Parks 49, including the Masai Mara National Reserve, Amboseli National Park, and Tsavo National Park.

Number of Private Reserves Too many to count, but includes Laikipia Plateau and Lewa Wildlife Conservancy.

Population Approximately 38 million.

Big Five You'll find them all here.

Language Kiswahili is the official language, but most people speak English.

Time Kenya is on EAT (East Africa Time), which is three hours ahead of Greenwich Mean Time and eight hours ahead of North America's Eastern Standard Time.

game to congregate at water holes. Safari high season is July–November when the annual wildebeest migration is in full swing, but it's much cheaper to go in the low season (April and May) when rates drop dramatically. High season at the coast is September through January (the hottest time is December and January), but avoid Christmas and New Year periods as holiday resorts are packed. If you're a birder, aim to visit between October and April when the migrant species have arrived.

GETTING HERE AND AROUND

AIR TRAVEL

When booking flights, check the routing carefully as some involve stopovers or require you to change airlines. Several flight options from America require long layovers in Europe before connecting to Nairobi or Mombasa. This is especially true for the cheaper flight options.

Airports Jomo Kenyatta International Airport (JKIA) (NBO ✉ Nairobi ☎ 020/661–1000 or 020/822–111). **Moi International Airport** (MBA ✉ Mombasa ☎ 041/343–3211 or 041/343–4021). **Wilson Airport** (WIL ✉ Nairobi ☎ 020/501–941).

Air Travel Resources in Kenya Kenya Airports Authority (⊕ www. kenyaairports.co.ke).

FLIGHTS

Most major European and African airlines fly into Jomo Kenyatta International Airport (JKIA), Kenya's major airport. There are no direct flights from the U.S. to Kenya; indirect flights leave from most major cities, i.e., New York, Chicago, Atlanta. Flying via London, Amsterdam, or Dubai is a popular option. There are plenty of cheap and efficient domestic flights available, including daily flights on Air Kenya between Nairobi and Mombasa, Malindi and Lamu. Air Kenya also flies daily to Amboseli, Diani Beach, Kiwayu, the Masai Mara, and Samburu. Two other local airlines, Safarilink and Fly540, cover similar destinations. There are also numerous charter flights available from Nairobi to the major tourist destinations and individual lodges and camps. When you book your safari, it's a good idea to ask your accommodation destination to book your internal flights for you as part of your package.

Kenya Airways offers flights directly to Mombasa's Moi International from a variety of European and African destinations. Kenya Airways and Thomsonfly fly from London to Mombasa, and Condor flies to Frankfurt from Mombasa.

Emirates offers flights to Jomo via Dubai, and Qatar Airways via Doha. British Airways offers direct flights to Nairobi. KLM flies to Nairobi via Amsterdam. Virgin Atlantic Airways flies directly from London Heathrow to Nairobi. Connections to Mombasa from Nairobi can be made several times a day using AirKenya, Kenya Airways, or Fly540.

Airport departure tax is included in your scheduled flight tickets, but check before you leave home. If not, US$40 is payable upon departure from Kenyan airports. Departure tax for internal flights is Ksh100.

International Airlines British Airways (☎ 0844/493–0787 in U.K. ⊕ www. britishairways.com). **Condor** (☎ 180/570–7202 in Germany ⊕ www.condor.com). **Emirates** (☎ 0844/800–2777 in U.K.; 800/777–3999 in U.S. ⊕ www.emirates. com). **KLM** (☎ 0871/222–7740 in U.K. ⊕ www.klm.com). **Thomsonfly** (Corsair ☎ 0871/231–4787 in U.K. ⊕ www.thomsonfly.com). **Virgin Atlantic Airlines** (☎ 800/821–5438 in U.S., 0844/874–7747 in U.K., 020/278–9100 in Kenya ⊕ www.virgin-atlantic.com).

Domestic Airlines Air Kenya (☎ 020/391–6000 ⊕ www.airkenya.com). **Fly540** (☎ 0722/540–540/0733/540–540 ⊕ www.fly540.com). **Kenya Airways** (☎ 020/327–4747 ⊕ www.kenya-airways.com). **Safarilink** (☎ 020/6000–777 ⊕ www.flysafarilink.com).

CHARTER FLIGHTS

The major charter companies—African Sky Charters, East African Air Charter, Phoenix Aviation, and Safarilink—run daily shuttles from Jomo Kenyatta International Airport and Wilson Airport to numerous destinations in East Africa including safari spots, Mombasa, and Nairobi. Safarilink also flies to Mt. Kilimanjaro. All flights should be booked directly thorough the charter service.

Charter Companies African Sky Charters (☎ 020/601–467). **East African Air Charter** (☎ 020/603–858 ⊕ www.eaaircharters.co.ke). **Phoenix Aviation** (☎ 020/604–048 or 0733/632–769 ⊕ www.phoenixaviation.co.ke). **Safarilink** (☎ 020/6000–777 ⊕ www.flysafarilink.com).

CUSTOMS AND DUTIES

Each person may bring 200 cigarettes (or 50 cigars or 250g of tobacco), one bottle of spirits or wine and up to 568ml of perfume. The tobacco and alcohol allowance applies only to people 18 and over.

Contact Kenya Customs Service Department (⊕ www.kra.go.ke).

HEALTH AND SAFETY

Kenya is a relatively poor country, and crime is a reality for residents and tourists alike, although by following a few basic precautions you will be fine.

Mugging, purse snatching, and pickpocketing are rife in big towns. Leave good jewelry and watches at home, and unless you're on safari, keep cameras, camcorders, and binoculars out of sight. Always lock valuables in the hotel or lodge safe. If you must carry valuables, use a money belt under your clothes; keep some cash handy so you don't reveal your money belt in public. Bring copies of all your important documents and stash them away from the originals. Carry extra passport photos in case you need new documents fast. Don't venture out on foot at night. Never take food or drink from strangers—it could be drugged.

Be on the lookout for street scams like hard-luck stories or appeals to finance a scholarship. Don't be fooled if a taxi driver says upon arrival that the fee you negotiated was per person or that he doesn't have change for large bills. Be polite but firm if you are stopped by police officers charging you with an "instant fine" for a minor infraction. If you ask to go to the police station, the charges are often dismissed.

You'll need full medical travel insurance, and if you're planning to dive, trek, or climb, make sure your insurance covers active pursuits. Check with your health care provider to see what vaccinations might be necessary for your destination(s); you may need a yellow-fever certificate if you arrive via another African country. Always use sunscreen and bug repellent with DEET. HIV/Aids is rampant, and malaria is rife in certain areas (not in Nairobi but definitely on the coast and game reserves).

The Flying Doctors Service offered by AMREF provides air evacuation services for medical emergencies in Kenya, Tanzania, and Uganda, or anywhere within a 1,000 km (621 mi) radius of Nairobi. The planes fly out of Nairobi's Wilson Airport 24 hours a day, 365 days a year. They also provide transportation between medical facilities, fly you back to Europe, Asia, or North America, or provide you with an escort if you're flying on a commercial carrier.

Embassies U.S. Embassy (✉ *United Nations Ave., Gigiri, Nairobi* ☎ *020/363–6000*).

Emergencies Kenya Police (☎ *999* ⊕ *www.kenyapolice.go.ke*).

Medical-Assistance Companies The Flying Doctors Service (☎ *020/315–454 landline; 073/363–9088 mobile* ⊕ *www.amref.org*).

HOLIDAYS

If a public holiday falls on a Sunday, it will be observed the next day, Monday. Muslim festivals are timed according to local sightings of phases of the moon; dates vary accordingly. During the lunar month of Ramadan that precedes Eid al-Fitr, Muslims fast during the day and feast at night, and normal business patterns may be interrupted. Many restaurants are closed during the day, and there may be restrictions on smoking and drinking.

"These pups were playing when suddenly something in the distance got their attention.... [I]t took Mom with breakfast to get their attention!" —Stephanie Menke, Fodors.com member

MONEY MATTERS

The official currency is the Kenya shilling. Available notes are 50, 100, 200, 500, and 1,000 shillings. Available coins are 1, 5, 10, 20, and 40 shillings.

At this writing, the schilling was trading at about Ksh80 to US$1. It is still relatively inexpensive given the quality of lodgings, which cost probably two-thirds the price of comparable facilities in the United States, although some hotels in the cities have been known to charge expensive rates for tourists.

To avoid administrative hassles, keep all foreign-exchange receipts until you leave the region, as you may need them as proof when changing any unspent local currency back into your own currency.

As the shilling is a relatively weak currency, hotels tend to quote in U.S. dollars. However, for small amounts, such as restaurants, shopping, and tips, it's easiest to withdraw shillings from an ATM once you're in the country. If you pay with dollars, you may find the exchange rate used is lower than the official one.

ATMS AND BANKS

Banks open at 9 on weekdays and close at 3; on Saturday they open at 9 and close at 11. Banks are closed on Sunday. Many banks can perform foreign-exchange services or international electronic transfers. Try to avoid banks at their busiest times—at 9 and from noon to 2 on Friday, and at month's end—unless you're willing to arrive early and line up with the locals. Major banks in Kenya are Barclays, Kenya Commercial, and Standard Chartered.

Major credit cards such as Visa and MasterCard are accepted at Kenyan banks and by ATMs. Most ATMs accept Cirrus, Plus, Maestro, Visa Electron, and Visa and MasterCard; the best place to withdraw cash is at an indoor ATM, preferably one guarded by a security officer. If you're unsure where to find a safe ATM, ask a merchant.

Contacts Central Bank of Kenya (✉ *Haile Selassie Ave., Nairobi* ☎ *020/286–1000* ⊕ *www.centralbank.go.ke*).

COMMUNICATIONS

PHONES

CALLING WITHIN KENYA

Local landline calls are quite cheap, but hotels add hefty surcharges to phone calls. Prepaid cards for public telephones can be purchased at cafés, newsstands, convenience stores, and telephone company offices. City codes are (020) for Nairobi, (041) for Mombasa, (042) for Malindi, (040) for Diani Beach, and (012) for Lamu; include the first 0 when you dial within the country. When making a phone call in Kenya, always use the full 10-digit number, including the area code, even if you're in the same area. Telkom Kenya now offers VoIP calling-card services, for cheap international calls at Ksh15 per minute.

Directory inquiry numbers are different for each cell-phone network. Safaricom is 191 and Zain is 111. These calls are charged at normal rates, but the call is timed only from when it is actually answered. You can, for an extra fee, get the call connected by the operator.

Contacts Directory Assistance (☎ *020/323–2000*). **Telkom Kenya** (⊕ *www.telkom.co.ke*).

CALLING OUTSIDE KENYA

When dialing out from Kenya, dial 000 before the international code. So, for example, you would dial 000 (0001) for the United States. Other country codes are 00044 for the United Kingdom, 00027 for South Africa, and 00033 for France.

Access Codes MCI WorldPhone (☎ *0800/220–111 from Kenya*).

MOBILE PHONES

The biggest mobile-phone service providers in Kenya are Zain (formerly Celtel Kenya) and Safaricom.

If you have brought your cell phone to Kenya, you can activate inbound roaming on Zain's network by selecting "settings" in your phone menu, then "phone Settings," followed by "network selection," then "manual selection," and then "Zain" or 63903 or "yes." Safaricom also has part-nerships with service providers in a number of countries that can set up international roaming on your phone. A cheaper alternative is to buy a Kenyan pay-as-you-go SIM card and top up the airtime as you need it.

Contacts Zain (☎ *111 from phone or 0733/100–111* ⊕ *www.ke.zain.com*). **Safaricom** (☎ *100 from phone or 020/427–2100 24-hour helpline* ⊕ *www.safaricom.co.ke*).

RESTAURANTS

Kenya prides itself on game meat, and the seafood, organically grown vegetables, and tropical fruits (such as passion fruit, papaya, and mangoes) are excellent. Sample traditional Indian and Arab food when you're near the coast, and look for Kenyan-grown tea and coffee and Tusker beer, a local brew. "Swahili tea" is very similar to chai in India. You'll find most cuisines, from Chinese to French to Ethiopian, in restaurants in Nairobi.

⇨ *For information on what you can expect at the restaurants and hotels on the Kenyan coast, see the Beach Escapes section below.*

HOTELS AND LODGES

There are more than 2,000 licensed hotels, camps, and lodges in Kenya. There are modern hotels in Nairobi, but some older establishments offer comparable service and comfort plus colonial ambience. Price categories in this chapter treat all-inclusive lodges differently from other lodgings (see chart below). Lodging, meals, and activities are included at private lodges; find out in advance if park fees (US$60 to US$100 per day) are included. There are no elevators in lodging facilities outside hotels in big cities, but most everything is at ground level. Children are not always welcome at lodges. Some camps, lodges, and coastal hotels are closed during rainy months; ask in advance.

Hotel prices usually include dinner and a full English breakfast. Many lodges and hotels offer special midweek or winter low-season rates. Campsites have few or no facilities and are not really an option for a visitor with time restrictions or for first-timers. There are all kinds of luxurious beach accommodations available, but these resorts get crowded during holiday season, so it's essential to book in advance.

⇨ *For information on plugging in while on Safari, see Electricity, in the On Safari chapter.*

	WHAT IT COSTS IN U.S. DOLLARS				
	¢	$	$$	$$$	$$$$
Safari Camps and Lodges	under $200	$200–$450	$451–$750	$751–$1,000	over $1,000
Hotels	under $100	$100–$150	$151–$200	$201–$250	over $250
Dining	under $5	$5–$10	$11–$20	$21–$30	over $30

All prices refer to an all-inclusive per-person, per-night rate, including 12.5% tax, assuming double occupancy. Hotel prices are for a standard double room in high season. Restaurant prices are per person for a main course at dinner, a main course equivalent, or a prix-fixe meal.

PASSPORTS AND VISAS

Your passport must be valid up to six months after you leave Kenya. Single-entry visas (US$25), valid for three months, are available at Nairobi's Jomo Kenyatta International Airport (you can use US$, euros, or UK pounds sterling) and can be used to move freely between Kenya and Tanzania.

TAXES

In Kenya the value-added tax (V.A.T.), currently 16%, is included in the price of most goods and services, including accommodations and food. To get a V.A.T. refund, foreign visitors must present receipts at the airport and carry purchased items with them or in their luggage. Fill out Form V.A.T. 4, available at the airport V.A.T. refund office. Make sure that your receipts are original tax invoices, containing the vendor's name and address, V.A.T. registration number, and the words "tax invoice." Refunds are paid by check, which can be cashed immediately at an airport bank or refunded to your credit card with a small transaction fee. Visit the V.A.T. refund desk in the departures hall before you go through check-in, and organize receipts as you travel. Officials will go through your receipts and randomly ask to view purchases.

Airport taxes and fees are included in the price of your ticket.

Contacts Kenya Revenue Authority (☎ 020/281–7700 ⊕ www.kra.go.ke).

TIPPING

Tipping isn't mandatory, but porters do expect something, and 10% is customary in restaurants. Some hotels have a gratuity box for you to put a tip for all of the staff at the end of your stay. Tip your safari driver and guide approximately US$10–US$15 per person, per day.

VISITOR INFORMATION

There's no official tourist office in Nairobi and the one in Mombasa isn't very good. Your best option is to consult the Kenya Tourist Board Web site before you leave home. Kenya Tourism Federation, which represents the private sector of the tourism industry, has a good tourist help line, and the Web site for Kenya Wildlife Services is a good source if you're going to a national park.

Visitor Information Kenya Tourist Board (☎ 020/274–9000 ⊕ www. magicalkenya.com). **Kenya Tourism Federation** (☎ 020/600–4767 ⊕ www. kenyatourism.or.ke). **Kenya Wildlife Services** (⊕ www.kws.org).

MUST-SEE PARKS

Unfortunately, you probably won't be able to see all of Kenya in one trip. So we've broken down the chapter by **Must-See Parks** (Masai Mara National Reserve, Amboseli National Park, Tsavo National Park, Laikipia Plateau, and Samburu National Reserve) and **If You Have Time Parks** (Nairobi National Park, Meru National Park, Lakes Nakuru, and Naivasha) to help you better organize your time. We suggest though, that you research *all* of them before you make your decision.

MASAI MARA

Game
★★★★★

Park Accessibility
★★★★★

Getting Around
★★★★★

Accommodations
★★★★★

Scenic Beauty
☆★★★★

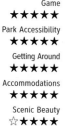

The legendary Masai Mara Game Reserve ranks right up there with Tanzania's Serengeti National Park and South Africa's Kruger National Park in terms of the world's finest wildlife sanctuaries.

Established in 1961, some 275 km (171 mi) southwest of Nairobi, it covers an area of 1,800 square km (702 square mi) and is demarcated by the Serengeti in the south, the Loita Hills in the east, the Esoit Oloololo escarpment in the west, and the Itong Hills in the north. It's also part of the Serengeti ecosystem that extends from northern Tanzania into southern Kenya. This ecosystem of well-watered plains supports one of the largest populations of numerous animal groups on earth. There are more than 2 million wildebeest; 250,000 Thomson's gazelle (arguably the prettiest of all antelope); 200,000 zebra; 70,000 impala; 30,000 Grant's gazelle; and a huge number of predators including lion (the largest population in Kenya), leopard, cheetah, jackal, hyena, and numerous smaller ones. There are also more than 450 species of birds, including 57 species of raptors. Every January, one of the greatest natural shows on earth begins, when the wildebeest start to move in a time-honored clockwise movement around the Serengeti toward the new fresh grazing in the Masai Mara. It's an unforgettable experience.

Local communities, not Kenya Wildlife Services, manage this reserve giving the Masai—who are pastoralists—the rights to graze their stock on the perimeters of the reserve. Although stock is lost to wild animals, the Masai manage to coexist peacefully with the game, and rely only on their own cattle for subsistence; in Masai communities wealth is measured by the number of cattle owned. You'll see the Masai's *man-yattas*—beehive huts made of mud and cow dung—at the entrance to the reserve. The striking appearance of the Masai, with their red robes and ochre-dyed and braided hair, is one of the abiding images of Kenya. Many lodges offer visits to traditional Masai villages and homes, and although inevitably, these visits have become touristy, they are still well worth doing. Witnessing the dramatic *ipid*, a dance in

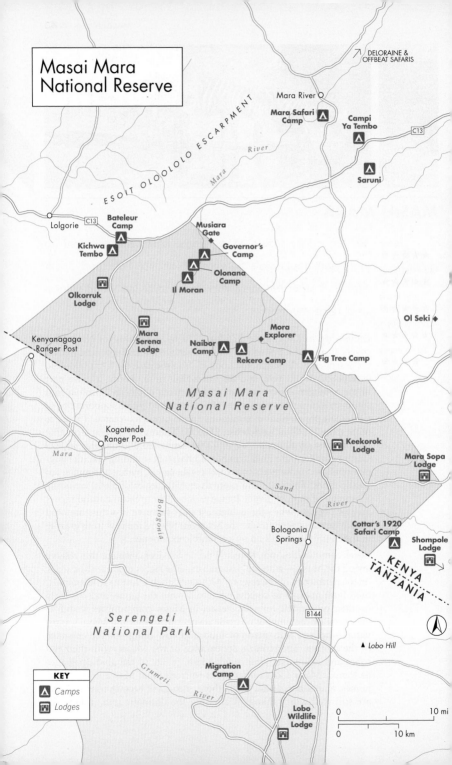

Masai Mara National Reserve

DELORAINE & OFFBEAT SAFARIS

Mara River

Mara Safari Camp

Campi Ya Tembo

C13

ESOIT OLOOLOLO ESCARPMENT

Mara River

Saruni

Lolgorie

C13

Bateleur Camp

Musiara Gate

Governor's Camp

Kichwa Tembo

Olonana Camp

Il Moran

Ol Seki

Olkorruk Lodge

Kenyanagaga Ranger Post

Mara Serena Lodge

Mora Explorer

Naibor Camp

Rekero Camp

Fig Tree Camp

Masai Mara National Reserve

Kogatende Ranger Post

Mara River

Keekorok Lodge

Mara Sopa Lodge

Sand River

Cottar's 1920 Safari Camp

Bologonia

Bologonia Springs

Shompole Lodge

KENYA
TANZANIA

Serengeti National Park

B144

▲ Lobo Hill

Grumeti River

Migration Camp

Lobo Wildlife Lodge

KEY
- ▲ Camps
- ▣ Lodges

0   10 mi

0   10 km

which the *moran* (warriors) take turns in leaping high into the air, will keep your camera clicking nonstop. However, the future fate of the instantly recognizable Masai is inextricably bound up with the growth of tourism—it seems certain that their unique nomadic way of life in which they seasonally followed the new grazing with their flocks will be forced to change.

3

The Masai people named the reserve *mara,* which means spotted, but whether mara applies to the landscape, which is spotted with vegetation, or the hundreds of thousands of wildebeest and other game that spot the landscape, is anybody's guess.

GETTING HERE AND AROUND

Most people fly to the Mara from Nairobi Wilson or JKIA airport, and scheduled daily air services (half an hour flight) land at eight airstrips in the area. The cost is approximately $120 each way. If you're a nervous flyer, note that you will usually travel in small turbo prop aircraft; many tour operators offer a driving option. The Mara is 168 mi from Nairobi and takes approximately six hours to drive. You will need a four-wheel-drive vehicle. Do not attempt to drive in the rainy season. Once in the park, there are well established, signposted roads, but make sure you know exactly where you are going before you depart. Park entry fees are $80 per person, but this is always included in package tours.

WHEN TO GO

There's no real best time to visit the Mara, but most people come in the July–October dry season, when the Great Migration is taking place and there are plenty of wildebeest and zebras for the lions, leopards, and cheetahs to prey upon. There's no guarantee of seeing any epic river crossings, however. The rainy season is April and May and November, and many roads become inaccessible.

WHERE TO STAY

All prices have been quoted in high-season rates, as most people will want to come during the migration. However, at low and mid-season, rates can be considerably cheaper. Check for special offers before you book.

LUXURY LODGES

$ ☐ **Mara Serena Safari Lodge.** Perched high on a hill deep inside the reserve, attractive mud-color, domed huts echo the style and shape of the traditional Masai *manyattas.* Each hut has rooms that echo the ethnic theme of the exteriors with soft, honey-color furnishings and a personal balcony that overlooks the plains and the distant Esoit Oloololo escarpment—the views are spectacular. Though it's highly unlikely, if you do get tired of gazing out at the endless rolling grasslands where the migration takes place each year, then keep watch at the busy water hole below the restaurant for a continuous wildlife show. Activities include ballooning (expensive but the trip of a lifetime), guided walks, bush barbecues, and game drives. After bouncing around in an open-sided game vehicle, it's great to enjoy a relaxing massage at the Maisha Spa. The Masai dancing is also spectacular. **Pros:** amazing views from the bedrooms; the break-

fasts at the hippo pool. **Cons:** the decor is a bit dated; rooms lack tea- and coffee-making facilities. ☎ 050/22059 or 020/284–2000 ⊕ www. serenahotels.com ➭ 74 rooms ⚲ In-room: no a/c, safe, no TV. In-hotel: restaurant, bar, pool, spa ➡ AE, DC, MC, V ⍾ FAP.

$–$$
ⵂ **Saruni.** This exclusive eco-friendly lodge lies just outside the Masai
ⵜ Mara National Reserve, inside Mara North Conservancy in a remote
Fodor'sChoice valley of olive and cedar trees. Each of the six cottages has polished
★ wooden floors and is furnished with hand-carved cedarwood beds, Persian rugs, African art, colonial antiques, and comfortable chairs. You'll
dine at a long table at Kuro House, the main lodge, which combines an
eclectic mix of old-style Africa and modern design. The Italian cuisine
here is superb, but there's also a wide international menu available that
uses fresh, locally grown, organic produce. You can also participate
in a bush barbecue or dine alone by candlelight on your veranda. The
library has a superb collection of Africana—it's definitely worth a visit.
Children of all ages are welcome. The tucked-away Masai Wellbeing
Space, which uses local plants for its treatments, is run by one of Italy's
most famous spas, Centro Benessere Stresa, and is considered one of
the best spas in Kenya. All the guides are members of the Kenya Professional Safari Guides Association, and Saruni supports the innovative
Koyiaki Guiding School, which trains young Kenyans. Make sure you
factor in the $80 per-person, per-day park fees into your expenses as
this is not included in the lodge's fees. **Pros:** this is the only small lodge
in the Masai Mara, with a maximum of 12 guests at a time; specialized guiding, such as bird-watching, is available; there's a forest view.
Cons: a high altitude of 2,000 meters (6,000 feet) means cold nights
and sometimes cold days; the access road is rough. ☎ 254/734–764616
or 050/224–24 ⊕ www.sarunicamp.com ➭ 6 cottages ⚲ In room: no
a/c, safe, no TV. In-hotel: bar, spa ➡ MC, V ⍾ FAP.

$–$$
ⵂ **Saruni Wild.** You certainly won't come across another vehicle at this
exclusively sited camp in the northern section of the Masai Mara ecosystem. It has three comfortable Bedouin-looking tents with en-suite
bathrooms with hot and cold running water and flush toilets. One of
the tents is suitable for families, with two bedrooms and bathrooms.
You can track elephants on foot or take action-packed night drives
when you have more than a good chance of spotting a leopard, as well
as other nocturnal animals such as bush babies and genets. **Pros:** one
of the few camps offering exclusive use with only one booking at a
time; there's a high chance of seeing rare nocturnal species. **Cons:** it's
far from the more popular migration routes during migration time; no

pool. ☎ *254/734–764616 or 050/224–24* ⊕ *www.saruniwild.com* ⤵ *3 tents* ⬥ *In-room: no a/c, safe, no TV. In-hotel: bar* ▣ *MC, V* ⦿ *FAP.*

PERMANENT TENTED CAMPS

\$\$\$ ⊡ **Bateleur Camp.** Who can forget the final scene in *Out of Africa* when two lions, symbolic of the Karen Blixen/Denys Finch-Hatton love affair, are silhouetted lying on a hill amid the African bush? If you're among the many who saw that movie and began fantasizing about your own African experience, then you'll be happy to know that this totally private and very romantic world-class camp is just below that famous hill. The spacious tents are pitched under an A-frame wood structure with polished wooden floors and a wooden deck with steps leading down to the bush and encircling trees below. A massive four-poster bed dominates the tent's interior—a handy, long, padded stool, great for sitting on while putting on and taking off your boots after a game drive or bush walk, sits at the foot of the bed. The public areas—also made of wood and canvas—are decorated with old leather armchairs, antique Persian rugs, and a well-stocked but small library. The game-viewing will keep you busy by day and night, but do try to include a picnic on the edge of the Great Rift Valley—it will induce dreams of those who once hunted and gathered here millennia ago. **Pros:** the service is excellent; there are unexpected surprise touches along the way. **Cons:** there's no telephone or Internet access at the camp; no bath (showers only). ☎ *27/11/809–4300* ⊕ *www.andbeyond.com* ⤵ *18 tents* ⬥ *In-room: no a/c, safe, no TV. In-hotel: bar, pool* ▣ *MC, V* ⦿ *FAP.*

\$\$\$ ⊡ **Cottars 1920s Safari Camp.** If you want to turn back the clock and immerse yourself in the kind of original safari ambience that Ernest Hemingway enjoyed, then it doesn't get much better than this. From the superb and gracious service to the casual touches of antique luxury—claw-foot tubs, faded antique rugs, wrought-iron candlesticks, old gramophones, polished butlers' trays—all under authentic white safari tents, the Cottar family's 80 years of experience certainly shows. Sit outside your own spacious tent on a wooden rocking chair and watch the hills and valleys below, or relax in the deep red armchairs of the main tented lounge and admire the old photos and prints. At night as you sip a brandy snifter under the soft glow of oil lamps by a log fire, you'll forget all about the 21st century. The tents, with separate lounge and bedroom areas and floor-level canvas decks, are in a huge, 250,000-acre exclusive concession between the Masai Mara, Serengeti, and Loliondo reserves. Because it's a private concession, you won't see the masses of other tourists that you can hardly help bumping into elsewhere in the Masai Mara itself. Because they operate just outside the reserve, Cottars' game vehicles are also allowed off-road, which means more freedom to follow game. The legendary fourth-generation Kenyan Calvin Cottar could be your guide (at extra cost), but his experienced colleagues won't let you down either. Enjoy a quiet moment in the tented reading room, or rest in a hammock by the natural rock pool. **Pros:** complimentary massages are included in the rate; you will seldom see another game vehicle. **Cons:** hair dryers can be used only in the office; rate does not include air transfers. ☎ *020/603–090; 888/870–0903 toll-*

free in U.S. ⊕ *www.cottars.com* ⇨ *6 tents* � *In-room: no a/c, safe, no TV In-hotel: bar, pool* ▭ *AE, DC, MC, V* ⦿ *FAP.*

$ ⌂ **Fairmont Mara Safari Club.** Although the camp area has manicured lawns and flowers, it is surrounded on three sides by the croc- and hippo-filled Mara River, so you are always close to the wildlife. Spacious tents are set on stilts with private balconies that overlook the river. The bedspread of the four-poster mosquito-netted beds are made of the iconic red cloth used for Masai warrior robes, while brightly colored handwoven rugs, comfortable chairs, and big windows ensure *aprés-safari* comfort. The main lodge is themed old-style safari with deep padded-leather-and-fabric armchairs, beaded lamps, an open fireplace, and an inviting wood-paneled bar. Keep family and friends informed of your big-game adventures with Internet access in the library, or write in your journal on the spacious outside deck that leads to a pool, complete with bar and private massage tents. Forgo one morning game drive in favor of a hot-air-balloon safari over the Mara plains followed by a bush champagne breakfast—you'll thank us—or stroll in the footprints of the hippo-trodden path, escorted by a Masai warrior (four people minimum). **Pros:** rooms have hair dryers; the views of the river from the rooms are excellent. **Cons:** it's not in the park itself or near any migration routes; sundowners and bush walks cost extra. ☎ *020/226–5555* ⊕ *www.fairmont.com* ⇨ *50 tents* ⚭ *In-room: no a/c, safe, no TV. In-hotel: restaurant, bar, pool, spa* ▭ *AE, MC, V* ⦿ *FAP.*

$ ⌂ **Fig Tree Camp.** This budget option on the banks of the Talek River overlooks the plains and its location in the north end of the reserve gives it easy access to all the game areas. You'll stay in a safari tent or stone-and-thatch chalet, both furnished in African ethnic themes, but you should try for a tent with a river view; be sure to have taken your malaria *muti* (muti is the generic African word for medicine). Both tents and chalets are en suite and have small verandas or balconies. There are two bars, an indoor and outdoor eating area, and a treehouse coffee deck where you can watch the passing animal show. Don't expect the ultimate in luxury, but you'll get good value for your money and also get to meet lots of international visitors. There's electricity only from 4 to 9 AM, noon to 3 PM, and 6 PM to midnight. If you want more luxury and exclusivity, go for one of the Ngaboli tents, where you'll sleep in a four-poster bed and have lots more room. Bonuses for camp guests include lectures, a resident nurse, and an in-house medical clinic. Activities are extra: night safaris, bush walks, champagne breakfasts, and bush dinners range in price from US$55 to US$100. **Pros:** three game drives a day are included; there's evening entertainment with Masai dancers or music. **Cons:** hot showers are available only at certain times; tents are located close to each other so can be noisy. ☎ *020/605–328* ⊕ *www.madahotels.com* ⇨ *38 tents, 27 chalets* ⚭ *In room: no a/c, safe, no TV. In-hotel: restaurant, bar, pool* ▭ *AE, DC, MC, V* ⦿ *FAP.*

$$ ⌂ **Il Moran.** One of the famous Governors' Camps, Il Moran is where Kenya's first colonial governors used to twirl their handlebar moustaches and sip their gin and tonics while on safari—as you can imagine, it boasts an exclusive location that's teeming with game. *Il Moran*, which means warrior in Masai, sits on the edge of the plains, nestled

"Early in the morning in the Masai, Mara, we came across these . . . cubs, walking along a dirt road in the midst of a sea of long golden grass. . . ." —Nick Gordan, Fodors.com member

in a private forest on the banks of the Mara river. Once upon a time there were 20 tents here, but the owner decided to reduce the number of visitors so as to give you an even more exclusive experience. Today there are just 10 tents, imaginatively furnished with stunningly original furniture hand-carved from ancient olive trees, the antique Persian rugs that seem obligatory in so many safari accommodations, battered old leather suitcases, and glowing oil lamps. There are once-in-a-lifetime game drives and guided bush walks, but treat yourself to the hot-air-balloon ride (an extra cost) with a champagne breakfast in the bush to follow. **Pros:** the beds are very comfortable; there's a maximum of four guests per game vehicle. **Cons:** they no longer offer fishing or night drives. ☎ 020/273–4000 or 020/273–4001 ⊕ www.governorscamp.com ➯ 10 tents ⚐ In-room: no a/c, safe, no TV. In-hotel: bar, pool, spa ⊟ AE, MC, V ⫣⎮ FAP.

$

Fodor's Choice

★

Kichwa Tembo Tented Safari Camp. Kichwa Tembo, which means head of the elephant in Kiswahili, is one of Kenya's most sought-after camps. Perched on the edge of a riverine forest below the Oloololo Escarpment, the camp lies directly in the path of the migration. The en-suite tents are spacious and have seemingly never-ending views of the plains from the verandas. You'll be surrounded by the unforgettable sounds of the African night as you drift off to sleep. During the day you can take a dip in the shady pool between activities or just relax on your veranda while you fill out your bird and mammal lists. Don't forget to keep an eye out for passing animals: there'll be predators galore, as well as blue- and red-tailed monkeys, the mischievous banded mongoose, and, if you're really lucky, the endangered black rhino. The candlelit dinner on the banks of the Sabaringo River is a must-do for anyone.

The staff here is attentive and charming. **Pros:** there's an excellent curio shop; Internet access. **Cons:** no bathtubs; hair dryers in luxury tents only. ☎ 27/11/809–4300 ⊕ *www.andbeyond.com.com* ⤳ *40 tents* ⚲ *In-room: no a/c, safe, no TV. In-hotel: bar, pool* ▤ *MC, V* ⌑ *FAP.*

$ ⛺ **Little Governors' Camp.** Getting to this camp is an adventure in itself. First you take a ferry across the Mara River followed by a short, escorted—by armed guides—walk (you don't want to be lion's snack before your safari even starts) before arriving at this gorgeous little camp that was described by BBCTV as "the prime wild life real estate in the world." It was also rated the top safari camp in Kenya by the prestigious World Travel Awards for 2007. The accolades are not surprising, as you can be assured of superb service and comfortable accommodations. Each tent is built on a wooden platform and has an en-suite bathroom with constant hot and cold running water and flush toilet—this may seem normal, but most places can provide hot water only at the end of the day (after solar power has heated it) or in the morning (after the donkey boiler has been lighted). Lighting, as at many of the traditional Masai Mara camps, is by gas, kerosene lantern, and candlelight. If you're lucky enough to be here during a full moon, you can watch the game come and go at the large water hole in front of the camp. You'll eat superb home-cooked meals under a blue sky or at night in a candlelit dining tent. If you need to stretch your legs after a muscle-clenching, nerve-wracking game drive, go on a guided walking safari or visit a nearby Masai village and join in the ipid jumping dance with the warriors. **Pros:** the camp sits directly in the path of the wildebeest migration; the tents are enormous. **Cons:** you have to cross a river before departing on any game drives; there's no electricity at night. ☎ *020/273–4000 or 020/273–4001* ⊕ *www.governorscamp.com* ⤳ *17 tents* ⚲ *In-room: no a/c, safe, no TV. In-hotel: bar, pool* ▤ *AE, MC, V* ⌑ *FAP.*

$$ ⛺ **Mara Explorer.** At this intimate little camp tucked in a riverine forest on a bend on the Talek River, you'll be able to watch elephants wading, hippos snorting, and all other sorts of game from your outdoor claw-foot bathtub that overlooks the river. Of course, a cocktail of choice from your personal butler makes the scene so much more appealing. A handcrafted wooden bed dominates the en-suite tent, but there's still room for the bedside tables fashioned from logs, old chests, and weather-beaten tin trunks that serve as tables, and an old-fashioned rocking chair where you can sit and tick off your mammal and bird lists. Move a little farther outside and you can laze on your wooden deck, savoring every tranquil moment. You'll be awed by the number of predators you see—lion, leopard, cheetah, hyena—preying on the plains herbivores. All the Masai Mara activities are available, and you'll particularly enjoy the breakfast picnics where the lions can watch *you* feeding. You'll eat delicious meals in an open-air dining area, which looks out over the river, and there are a cozy lounge and small library for those moments when you want to sit still. **Pros:** the camp is a short drive from the airstrip; meals are taken overlooking the river. **Cons:** hot water is available only at fixed times; there's no pool. ☎ *020/444–6651*

⊕ *www.heritage-eastafrica.com* ⤳ *10 tents* ⟁ *In-room: no a/c, safe, no TV. In-hotel: bar* ⊟ *AE, DC, MC, V* ⊙*FAP.*

$$ 🔆 **Naibor Camp.** Only 20 minutes away from one of the legendary migration river crossings, this stylish camp doesn't exclusively follow the old traditional safari camp feel, but it aims for a fusion of old and new with pale khaki and white mesh tents, minimalist hand-carved wooden furniture, roof-to-ceiling earth-color drapes, and plain couches and chairs highlighted with ethnic-patterned cushions. The whole camp lives up to its name—*naibor* means simplicity and space in Kiswahili—but you'll never lose that essential sense of being on an African safari. The spacious tents on the banks of the Talek River are furnished with handwoven straw mats, a hand-carved figwood bed, and simple bedside tables. There's a big private veranda from where you can catch the elephants going down to drink, or listen to and watch the myriad birds. The game here is exceptionally good, but give yourself a break from that plethora of plenty and go for an all-day walk, try mountain biking, go honey-hunting, visit Lake Victoria for a day, or do what everybody *must* in the Mara and take a balloon ride. **Pros:** it's sociable, with drinks around the fire; excellent bird walks; there's room service for drinks and snacks. **Cons:** there's no pool, bucket showers only (although they are hot). ☏ *020/251–3147* ⊕ *www.naibor.com* ⤳ *9 tents* ⟁ *In-room: no a/c, safe, no TV. In-hotel: bar* ⊟ *MC, V* ⊗ *Closed Apr., May, and Nov.* ⊙*FAP.*

$$$ 🔆 **Olonana Camp.** Named after an honored Masai chief, this attractive eco-friendly camp in game-rich country rests on the northwestern border of the reserve overlooking the Mara River and the Oolololo escarpment. Feeling really lazy? Hibernate in your huge wooden-floor tent—it's more like a mini-pavilion—prop yourself up on pillows in your queen-size bed and watch the river below. There are floor-to-ceiling mosquito-proofed "windows" and stone-walled en-suite bathrooms with his and her basins and stools, and a roomy shower. Feeling energetic? Take a guided bush walk or hike up the escarpment. Don't let the lodge's manyatta-styled entrance fool you. Once inside the main lodge you'll find the understated luxury of hand-carved wooden furniture; cream, russet, and brown linens; handwoven African rugs; and indigenous art and artifacts. The reed-roofed main viewing deck overlooks a hippo pool with daylong entertainment from these overgrown clowns. The food is superb, and you have the option to dine with your fellow guests or on your own veranda. There is an inviting pool, a small but good library, and excellent opportunities to observe the everyday lives of the Masai in the adjacent village. **Pros:** the honeymoon tents are beautiful; you can watch hippos from your tent. **Cons:** no Internet in rooms; water pressure in showers can be weak. ☏ *020/695–0002 or 020/695–0244* ⊕ *www.sanctuaryretreats.com* ⤳ *14 tents* ⟁ *In-room: no a/c, safe, no TV. In-hotel: bar, pool* ⊟ *AE, MC, V* ⊙*FAP.*

$$ 🔆 **Ol Seki Mara Camp.** This eco-friendly camp is in the pristine northern regions of the reserve. It was built by the Allan family but is now managed by the Giovando family, who have more than 38 years of safari experience. It's named after the *olseki* or sandpaper tree, which is a Masai symbol of peace, harmony, and wealth. Set on round wooden platforms on a rocky outcrop surrounded by bird-filled trees, the

Ol Seki

Mara Explorer

Bateleur

12-sided tents look as if they are sailing through the bush. Inside, it's all space and light, with simple, stylish furnishings. The lean, clean effect is carried through to the attractive dining tent and library, which has a fireplace. The tents have been refurbished, and two new suites (with two bedrooms each) have private living and dining areas, as well as their own kitchens, ensuring the ultimate in privacy. There's a full range of activities, including morning and night game drives with lots of game—you might get one of Kenya's few woman guides—bush picnics, star-gazer walks, botanical walks, and visits to authentic, nontouristy Masai villages, where you might be lucky enough to witness a genuine betrothal or postinitiation ceremony. **Pros:** hot and cold running water; there's power supply 24 hours a day and Internet and telephone on request. **Cons:** it's located outside the reserve; game might not be as dense (but you won't encounter other vehicles). ☏ *020/242–5060* ⊕ *www.olseki.com* ⇨ *8 tents* ⚲ *In-room: no a/c, safe, no TV. In-hotel: bar, pool* ⊟ *MC, V* ☺ *Closed Apr.* ⫫*FAP.*

$$ ⌂ **Rekero Camp.** The Beaton family, owners of this seasonal tented camp, settled in Kenya more than a century ago and helped pioneer the country's conservation movement. The camp, tucked away in a grove of trees more than 40 km (25 mi) from the main tourist throng farther east, is beautifully situated on a river bank near the confluence of the Talek and Mara rivers. You'll sleep in one of only eight tents (which include two family tents), each hidden from the other and all with great views of the plains and the river. There's an ancient wildebeest crossing practically on your doorstep, so you won't have to bounce around for hours in an open-sided game vehicle to find the game. But when you do find game, there won't be hordes of other visitors to spoil the sight. Tents are bright and comfortably furnished with double beds, handwoven rugs, and en-suite bathrooms with flush toilets and canvas bucket showers. As the camp is unfenced, expect all kinds of game to wander past your tent, but you'll be safe within your canvas walls, and a Masai warrior will escort you to and from the main areas. **Pros:** the unfenced camp means you can hear animals up close; great location next to a river crossing point. **Cons:** there's no running water, TVs, or phones (although they do have solar power to recharge camera batteries). ☏ *No phone* ⊕ *www. rekerocamp.com* ⇨ *8 tents* ⚲ *In-room: no phone, no a/c, safe, no TV. In-hotel: bar* ⊟ *AE, DC, MC, V* ☺ *Closed Apr.* ⫫*FAP.*

BUDGET LODGING

$ ⌂ **Keekorok Lodge.** This unpretentious lodge has rather basic accommodations, but it was the first lodge built in the Masai Mara. Though it's a bit gray at the temples, its superb location—directly in the path of the wildebeest migration—means you won't have to leave camp to see animals galore. You'll stay in a Sand River stone chalet or A-frame wood-and-stone bungalow, both simply furnished with comfortable beds, mosquito nets, and an en-suite old-fashioned white-tiled bathroom with bath and overhead shower. Outside there's a small stone veranda with a rustic table and camping chairs. There's a 300-meter (984 feet) raised wooden walkway that leads to a viewing deck with great views of the plains and a hippo pool. The camp is unfenced, so you'll often see elephants and buffalos round its perimeter. Activities

"We watched in awe as the cheetah chose his prey and set out on the chase." —The Swain Family, Fodors.com members

include lectures on the Masai culture, wildlife video viewings, hot-air-balloon rides, or tanning by the small pool. **Pros:** seeing animals outside your room; beds are comfortable. **Cons:** food is buffet style; Internet access is expensive. ☎ *050–22680 or 020/650–392* ⊕ *www.africanmeccasafaris.com* ⬐ *12 chalets* ☖ *In-room: no a/c, safe, no TV. In-hotel: bar, pool* ⊟ *AE, DC, MC, V* ⦿❙ *FAP.*

$ 🏨 **Mara Sopa Lodge.** Located on a hillside near the Ooloolaimutia Gate, ☾   this budget lodge (*sopa* means welcome in the Masai language) is one of the most popular in the reserve. Even though they're always busy, the delightfully friendly and experienced staff will make you feel special. You'll sleep in a *rondavel* (small, round, thatch-roof hut) that has a tiny veranda and is simply but pleasantly furnished in traditional African style with lots of earth-color soft furnishings. The brightly decorated public areas are nestled among flowering plants and trees; notices telling you about mealtimes, balloon booking times, how to book a picnic, and other information are pasted throughout the main area. Don't expect all the bells and whistles of the luxury lodges—hot water is available only mornings and evenings—but the setting and the feeling of Africa on your doorstep more than compensate. Plus, there's a great pool to cool off in after a hot dusty game drive, where events such as Masai dancing or African food are held. There's also a quaintly named "Wild Animals Viewing Deck" in camp. Because you're more than 6,000 feet above sea level, you'll be cool in summer and will definitely need a jacket or sweater in winter. **Pros:** it's very near the entrance to the reserve; you can see hyenas and bush babies feeding. **Cons:** hot water is available only at limited times; rondavels are located close to each other. ☎ *020/375–0183 or 020/375–0235* ⊕ *www.sopalodges.*

com ↝ *77 rondavels, 12 suites, 1 presidential suite* ⚶ *In-room: no a/c, safe, no TV. In-hotel: restaurant, bar, pool* ⊟ *AE, DC, MC, V* ⭐ *FAP.*

$ ⚠**Offbeat Safaris.** A truly wonderful and unique way to see game and experience Kenya close up is to go on a horse safari; you should do this only if you're an experienced rider—you want to be able to gallop if you meet a hungry predator—and if you're fit enough to ride four to six hours a day. Your safari begins at Deloraine, the beautiful old colonial mansion owned by Tristan and Lucinda Voorspuy, who keep more than 80 horses on the estate—Tristan served in the British Household Cavalry, so he really knows his oats. The estate, which has welcomed British royalty, is on the western edge of the Great Rift Valley on the lower slopes of Mt. Londiani. When you choose the Mara safari, you'll stay at small rustic but comfortable tented camps along the way, sometimes spending two or three nights at the same camp, depending on which route you choose. But even if you get a bit saddle-sore, riding alongside hundreds of thousands of plains game is a once-in-a-lifetime experience. **Pros:** an adventurous and original way of viewing game; a bit of a hidden secret. **Cons:** must be an experienced horseback rider; it's tricky getting photos when you are on horseback. ☎ *054/62–31081* ⊕ *www.offbeatsafaris.com* ⊟ *AE, DC, MC, V* ⭐ *FAP.*

BETWEEN MASAI MARA AND AMBOSELI NATIONAL PARK

LUXURY LODGE

$$ ⬚ **Shompole Lodge.** Midway between Masai Mara and Amboseli, not far from the Kenya/Tanzania border, is the exquisite Shompole Lodge, which looks out onto the Rift Valley's distant plains and mountains. The Shompole Conservancy, a group venture with the Masai, consists of 56,000 hectares (138,379 acres) teeming with game. Built on huge stilted wooden platforms, each tent rests under a multipeaked thatch roof, which also shelters a spacious open living area built of local stone and wood. As you lie on your deck beside your personal pool, look out to the horizon. You'll feel as if you're taking part in an Arabian Nights fantasy. The main building continues the theme of light, space, water, and air. It'll be hard to drag yourself away, even for the amazing game drives, breakfast in the fig-tree forest, or a walk at Lake Natron to see the million-plus flamingos. **Pros:** each room has a private plunge pool; you can dine in your room or communally. **Cons:** rooms have showers only; conservation fees ($45 per day) are not included. ✉ *Shompole Conservancy* ☎ *020/884–135* ⊕ *www.shompole.com* ↝ *6 rooms, 2 suites* ⚶ *In-room: no a/c, no TV. In-hotel: restaurant, bar, pool* ⊟ *MC, V* ⭐ *FAP.*

AMBOSELI NATIONAL RESERVE

Game
☆☆★★★
Park Accessibility
★★★★★
Getting Around
★★★★★
Accommodations
★★★★★
Scenic Beauty
★★★★★

Amboseli National Reserve, immediately northwest of Mt. Kilimanjaro and 240 km (150 mi) southeast of Nairobi on the Tanzanian border, is certainly one of the most picturesque places in the whole of Africa to watch game. Where else could you watch a great herd of elephants trudging slowly across a wide empty plain dominated by Africa's highest mountain, Kilimanjaro?

At dawn, as the cloud cover breaks and the first rays of sun illuminate the snow-capped 5,895-meter (19,340-foot) peak, you'll be awed by the colors—rosy pinks and soft reds—of the sky that provide the perfect backdrop for the plains below. It gets even better at dusk, when the whole area is backlighted, and the mountain stands out in stark relief against the swiftly setting fiery sun. That's the pretty picture. The reality, though slowly improving, is that one of Kenya's most visited parks has become a dustbowl of overused tourist trails, traffic jams, and irresponsible off-road driving.

Amboseli has a checkered history. First established as a natural reserve in 1948, it was returned to Masai ownership and management in 1961 but soon became environmentally degraded with too many cattle and too many tourists. Some 10 years later, 392 square km (151 square mi) were designated a national park, and cattle-grazing was forbidden. This angered the mainly pastoral Masai, who took their revenge by killing a majority of the rhino population. Eventually peace was restored with some expedient land swapping, and today there's a responsible environmental program that controls the well-being of the game, puts limits on tourist numbers, and enforces a strict policy on off-road driving.

There are five different habitats in Amboseli: open plains, acacia woodland, thornscrub, swamps, and marshlands. To the west is the Ol Doinyo Orok massif and Lake Amboseli, which is usually dry. But when the heavy rains return, so do the flamingos, and the whole surrounding area becomes green and lush again. Expect some impassable roads at these times, as well as when the lake is completely dry because the fine alkaline dust that blows up from the lake's surface is hell for tires.

Amboseli is filled with great game: zebra, warthog, giraffe, buffalo, impala, wildebeest, the long-necked minigiraffe-like gerenuks, and baboons galore. But your chances of seeing predators are much less than in the Masai Mara. Lions were hunted to almost the point of extinction by the Masai because they killed their herds of cattle. Those that survived are still skittish and often not comfortable with vehicles. If a predator is spotted, it is often surrounded by far too many vehicles and put under great stress. Interestingly, the hunting methods of cheetah within the park have changed dramatically because of tourist pressure. Accustomed to hunting at dawn and dusk, they've now resorted to hunting at midday—tourist siesta time—with poorer success rates, thus their numbers are decreasing. But if it's elephants you're after, then Amboseli is the place. Perhaps the oldest and most studied elephant population in sub-Saharan Africa lives here. There are more than 1,000 of these great pachyderms today, and because they are accustomed to visitors and vehicles you'll experience eyeball-to-knee-high close encounters.

Game-viewing is best around the main swamps of Enkongo Narok, which means black and benevolent, and the Amboseli landmark, Observation Hill. Enkongo Narok, in the middle of the park, is where you can see water seeping up from the lava rocks. Observation Hill provides a surefire opportunity to spot game, especially elephants, as it looks out over the plains.

Birdlife is also prolific, with more than 420 recorded species. There are dozens of birds of prey including more than 10 different kinds of eagles. In the swamp areas, which are fed by the melting snow of Kilimanjaro, seasonal flamingo and more than 12 species of heron are among the profusion of water birds.

GETTING HERE AND AROUND
Amboseli is 260 km (160 mi) from Nairobi. Scheduled flights from Nairobi's Wilson Airport and Mombasa land at three airstrips. Note that you'll be flying in a small aircraft. The journey by road takes about four hours. The last 10 mi are full of pot-holes, so you'll need a 4x4. There's no public transport within the park. Park fees are $40 per person. This fee is included in package tours and most lodges.

WHEN TO GO
January and February, and June to September are the best times to come here. Avoid April and May, the rainy season, as roads become impassable. There might also be rain in November and December.

WHERE TO STAY

LUXURY LODGES
$ **Amboseli Serena Safari Lodge.** Situated plumb in the middle of the park, beside a natural flowing spring, this lodge enjoys spectacular views of Mt. Kilimanjaro. Pink guest cottages line narrow paved walkways, and although trees and shrubs give you some privacy, they also take away

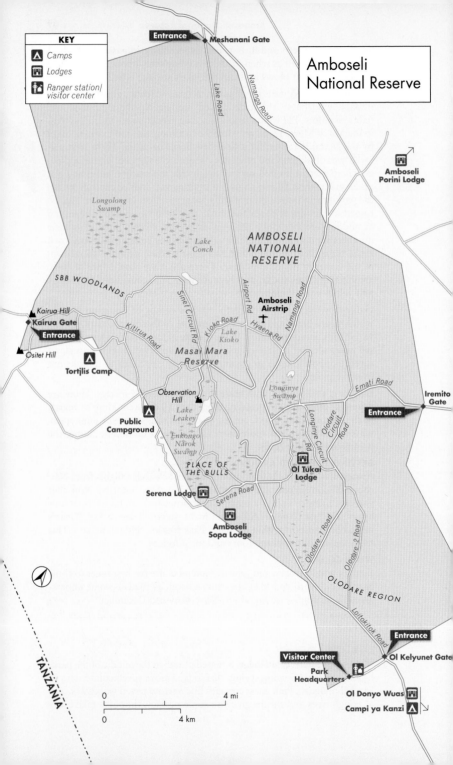

your view. The food, cooked with homegrown herbs and vegetables, is excellent, particularly the homemade pasta. Because the lodge is near the Enkongo Narok Swamp, there's always plenty of game around. Take a game drive, go walking with a Masai guide, enjoy a bush breakfast, and always remember to keep your doors and windows closed to keep out marauding vervet monkeys, which look cute but can make off with your belongings. The rooms are small, and fairly basic, with a couple of twin beds with eye-catching pink and purple bedspreads, a small dressing table, and en-suite bathroom. What the lodge lacks in luxury is more than made up by the friendly and helpful staff. **Pros:** good value for money; the lodge balcony has views out onto the plains. **Cons:** the pool is heavily shaded by trees; not all the rooms have views. ☎ *050/22059 or 020/284–2000* ⊕ *www.serenahotels.com* ⤳ *96 rooms* ♨ *In-room: no a/c, safe, no TV. In-hotel: restaurant, bar, pool* ☐ *AE, DC, MC, V* ¶⊙¶ *FAP.*

$ ⊡ **Amboseli Sopa Lodge.** Although this attractive lodge wasn't around when Ernest Hemingway wrote *The Snows of Kilimanjaro*, he would have enjoyed much the same spectacular views and wildlife as you, because he stayed nearby while writing it. The lodge is in lush established gardens in the foothills of Mt. Kilimanjaro near the Tanzanian border. You'll stay in roomy mud-and-thatch en-suite hut, gaily decorated with wood, animal motifs, and brightly colored soft furnishings. Enjoy a hearty breakfast and lunch buffet inside in the big African-theme dining room, or eat out beside the pool, where there's also a pleasant poolside bar. In the evening sit down to a four-course meal where you can choose between European, African, or Asian dishes. There is a stunning lounge area and great viewing deck. It's also a great place for kids—there's plenty of room for them to run around, a lovely pool, and babysitters are always available if you want to be child-free for an evening. The lodge offers lots of activities, which are an additional cost, including game drives, guided walks, and trips to Masai villages. If you want to have a go at climbing Mt. Kilimanjaro, the lodge can arrange that, too. **Pros:** the backdrop of Mt. Kilimanjaro; the hotel arranges night feeding of the animals. **Cons:** the lodge is half an hour's drive from Amboseli itself; hot water can be erratic. ☎ *020/375–0183 or 020/375–0235* ⊕ *www.sopalodges.com* ⤳ *83 rooms* ♨ *In-room: no a/c, safe, no TV. In-hotel: restaurant, bar, pool* ☐ *MC, V* ¶⊙¶ *FAP.*

PERMANENT TENTED CAMPS

$ ⊡ **Amboseli Porini Camp.** This exclusive, back-to-nature tented camp is located in the remote and game-abundant Selenkay Conservancy, a few miles north of Amboseli National Park. A silver eco-award winner, the camp is co-owned with the local Masai community. Because the area is relatively new to tourism, you'll see few visitors (numbers are limited to 18 per day), but lots of game including lion, leopard, cheetah, and the ubiquitous Amboseli elephants. Birdlife is prolific, with lots of raptors. Big, comfortably furnished tents are solar-powered and have en-suite bathrooms with a basin, shower, and flush toilet. You'll eat hearty, home-cooked meals outside the mess tent while being serenaded by birdcalls by day and nocturnal animals by night. Game drives are taken in an open-sided safari vehicle—yours will be the only one for miles. You'll visit a Masai village, take an informative walk in a dry riverbed, enjoy a picnic lunch in Amboseli itself, and at night you'll return to your own little private spot in the African wilderness. The all-inclusive price covers round-trip road transfers, Amboseli park fees, conservancy fees, all game drives, sundowners, walks with Masai warriors, Masai village visits, full board, and free house wines, beer, and soft drinks. **Pros:** the camp benefits the local community and is eco-friendly; there are few visitors but lots of game. **Cons:** solar power rather than electricity; no pool. ☎ *020/712–2504 or 020/712–3129* ⊕ *www.porini.com* ⇝ *9 tents* ⚴ *In-room: no a/c, safe, no TV. In-hotel: restaurant* ☰ *MC, V* ¶⨀¶ *FAP.*

$ ⛺ **Tortillis Camp.** This multi-award-winning rustic bush camp is named after the flat-topped *Acacia tortilis* trees that surround the camp. The main thatch-roof open bar, lounge, and dining room overlook a water hole and have superb views of Mt. Kilimanjaro and Mt. Meru in neighboring Tanzania. Your large tent sits under a huge thatch canopy and is raised up on a small platform with wooden floors, a king-size bed, and an en-suite bathroom with hot showers and flush toilets. If you want to catch up on your journal or bird and mammal lists, then relax on the comfortable furniture on your personal sitting area, or laze by the pool in between activities (such as game drives or guided bush walks, which the lodge provides at an extra cost). There's also a family house with one double and one twin-bed room if you don't fancy splitting up between two tents. The mainly northern-Italian food is delicious and is whipped up from the owner's original family recipes. The food is made even tastier by homegrown herbs and vegetables. There's a minimum two-night-stay requirement. **Pros:** stunning views of Mt. Kilimanjaro; excellent library; lots of elephants and great birdlife. **Cons:** the tents are on the small side; many of them are down steep steps. ☎ *020/6003–053/4 or 020/6003–090/1* ⊕ *www.tortilis.com* ⇝ *17 tents, 1 family house* ⚴ *In-room: no a/c, safe, no phone. In-hotel: restaurant, bar, pool* ☰ *MC, V* ¶⨀¶ *FAP.*

BUDGET LODGING

¢ ⛺ **Ol Tukai Lodge.** Just 3 km (2 mi) east of Amboseli National Park, this
☺ is an ideal location to spot game such as the famously studied Amboseli elephants. In fact, Ol Tukai claims that this is the best place in the world to watch elephants. Apart from the plains game and its attendant predators, there are more than 400 species of birds to be identified, and Ol Tukai offers specially designed bird walks through its grounds for

Amboseli Serena Safari Lodge Bedroom interior

Camp ya Kanzi

Ol Donyo Wuas

"Amboseli Park was dry, and the plain was hazy at dusk. The cheetahs were stalking under the watchful eyes of the wildebeest." —Liz1940, Fodors.com member

beginners and experts alike; it's a wonderful opportunity to introduce yourself or the kids to the world of birds. This resort manages to be both modern and traditional—its facilities are world class, but its feel and ambience are unmistakably African. The resort is set amid acres of well-kept lawns dotted with the familiar symbol of the plains—*Acacia tortilis* trees—and has a superb view of Mt. Kilimanjaro. En-suite chalets, built of local stone and slate, are furnished with handcrafted wooden furniture and decorated with faux animal-skin fabrics, rugs, and throws; each has a personal veranda. Public areas are open and spacious; everywhere you go you'll have a different view. For that special group celebration, choose the three-bedroom stone and wood Kibo Villa, tucked away in its own private 5 acres where you can self-cater or eat at the main lodge. Babysitters are available. **Pros:** rooms are very spacious; the views of Kilimanjaro are fantastic. **Cons:** game drives and other activities are not included in the price; no a/c. ☎ *020/444–5514* ⊕ *www.oltukailodge.com* ↰ *80 chalets, 1 villa* ☆ *In-room: no a/c, safe, no TV. In-hotel: restaurant, bar, pool* ▭ *AE, DC, MC, V* ⫶⦿⫶ *FAP.*

NEAR AMBOSELI AND TSAVO EAST AND WEST

LUXURY LODGES

$$–$$$ ⛺ **Ol Donyo Wuas.** This camp is perched on a hillside, so every suite has great views of the plains, Mt. Kilimanjaro, and the watering holes. No two of the ten large suites in six stand-alone villas are the same. They all have rooftop "star beds," which are accessed from the veranda by a winding stone staircase. They allow you the option of sleeping under the stars but with all the comforts of your suite just below. All but two

of the suites have private pools, too. Some villas have four beds each and private sitting rooms and are ideal for families or small groups of friends. Excellent food and friendly, attentive service are the norm. Meals are taken in the centrally positioned dining room with a big open fireplace for those chilly nights. You have the option of camping out for two or three days, with support crew and a mobile tented camp, by foot or horseback. **Pros:** the horizon pool has stunning views of Mt. Kilimanjaro; suites have indoor and outdoor showers as well as bathtubs; the "star beds" are an indescribable experience. **Cons:** there's less concentrated game than in the main areas, but no other people; no a/c. ☎ *020/600–457 or 020/605–108* 🌐 *www.bush-and-beyond.com* *10 suites* *In-room: no a/c, safe, no TV. In-hotel: restaurant, bar, pool* *MC, V* *Closed Apr.* *FAP.*

3

PERMANENT TENTED CAMPS

$$ Fodor's Choice ★ **Campi ya Kanzi.** One of the most environmentally friendly camps in East Africa, this lovely camp, whose name means "Camp of the Hidden Treasure" in Kiswahili, is in the Kuku Group Ranch, the natural corridor between Amboseli and Tsavo National Parks. It was the first camp in Kenya to be gold rated by Ecotourism Kenya for its efforts in sustainable tourism, and has won other prestigious international ecotourism awards. It's also co-owned by the Masai from the ranch area and Luca Belpietro and his wife, Antonella Bonomi. The ranch itself stretches 1,115 square km (400 square mi) from the foothills of Mt. Kilimanjaro to the Chyulu Hills in the north, and because of the different altitudes you'll find all sorts of habitats, from wide plains and riverine bush to high mountain forests. You'll also find plenty of game—more than 50 mammals and 400 bird species—but few tourists. To see all this, choose between game drives (where the game is really wild and not used to vehicles), guided game walks, botanical walks, birdwatching, and cultural visits. Take your kids to the Masai school and open their eyes to a completely different way of life. The main lounge and dining areas are in Tembo (Elephant) House, which has superb views of Mt. Kilimanjaro, the Taita Hills, and Chyulu Hills. All the tents have great views, as well as wooden floors, a veranda, and an en-suite bathroom with bidet, flush toilet, and hot and cold running water. The Hemingway and Simba tented suites boast king-size beds, a dressing room, en-suite bathroom with his-and-her washbasins, and verandas overlooking Mt. Kilimanjaro. Note that there is an additional US$100 per-person, per-day conservation fee, which entirely benefits the local Masai community. **Pros:** the cottages are very private; staff are from the local Masai community. **Cons:** no bathtubs; no pool. ☎ *720/461–300* 🌐 *www.maasai.com* *6 tents, 2 suites* *In-room: no a/c, safe, no TV. In-hotel: restaurant, bar* *AE, MC, V* *FAP.*

TSAVO NATIONAL PARK

Game
☆☆★★★
Park Accessibility
☆★★★★
Getting Around
☆★★★★
Accommodations
☆★★★★
Scenic Beauty
☆★★★★

At almost 21,000 square km (8,108 square mi), Tsavo National Park is Kenya's largest park. It includes the areas of Tsavo West and Tsavo East. Both stretch for about 130 km (80 mi) along either side of Nairobi/Mombasa Highway, the main road from Nairobi to Mombasa. It's amazing that just a few miles away from the constant thunder of motor traffic on Kenya's busiest road is some of Kenya's best wildlife viewing.

TSAVO WEST

Tsavo West covers 7,065 square km (2,728 square mi), which is a little less than a third of the total area comprising all of Kenya's national parks. It lies to the west of the Chyulu Hills—said to be the world's youngest mountains at only a few hundred years old—and with its diverse habitats of riverine forest, palm thickets, rocky outcrops and ridges, mountains and plains, is more attractive and certainly more accessible than Tsavo East. It's also a lot more crowded. In the north, heavily wooded hills dominate; in the south there are wonderful views over the Serengeti Plains. Take a boat ride or go birding on Lake Jipe, one of the most important wetlands in Kenya. If you like birds, you'll be keen to get a glimpse of the whitebacked night heron, African skimmers, and palm-nut vultures. The lake, which lies in the park's southwest corner on the Kenya/Tanzania border, is fed from the snows of Kilimanjaro and the North Pare mountains. There's evidence of volcanic activity everywhere in the park, especially where recent lava flows absorb the rainfall. In one spectacular spot, this rainfall, having traveled underground for 40 km (25 mi) or so, gushes up in a pair of pools at Mzima Springs, in the north of the park. There's a submerged hippo blind here, but the hippos have gotten wise to tourists and often move to the far side of the pools. Because of the fertile volcanic soil and abundance of water, the park is brimming with animal, bird, and plant life. You'll see lion and cheetah—especially in the dry season when the grass is low—spotted hyena, buffalo, the beautiful Masai giraffe, and all kinds of antelope, including Thompson's and Grant's gazelle—the prettiest of the antelope.

GETTING HERE AND AROUND

Tsavo West is approximately 100 km (62 mi) from Mombasa, making it a good option if you're staying by the coast or plan to visit the coast after your safari. There's no public transport to the park, so you'll have to self-drive or fly from Mombasa or Wilson Nairobi airport. If you drive yourself, be aware that signage in the park is unclear and you'll need a GPS. Park fees are $50 per person.

WHEN TO GO

You will have a good experience whenever you go, but bear in mind that the long rains are from March to May, and the short rains are October to December. January to March can be very hot.

WHERE TO STAY

LUXURY LODGES

$ ⛺ **Kilaguni Lodge.** This lovely old lodge was Kenya's first lodge in a national park. Timber, stone, and thatch buildings complement the natural wilderness surroundings and when it's not wreathed in clouds, there's a good view of Mt. Kilimanjaro. You can watch game and birds from any one of several viewing decks, or enjoy a drink in the bar carved out of rocks. En-suite rooms are decorated in the ubiquitous African-theme fabrics, but are comfortable and spacious. Buffet meals with plenty of variety are way above the average. You can book all sorts of activities at the lodge, including morning and afternoon game drives, bush breakfasts and dinners, and guided walks. **Pros:** there's an on-site medic; there's a busy watering hole that can be viewed from the hotel. **Cons:** not all rooms have great views; room decor is a bit dated. ☎ *050/22059 or 020/284–2000* ⊕ *www.serenahotels.com* ⬚ *56 rooms* ⚘ *In-room: no a/c, safe, TV (some). In-hotel: restaurant, bar, pool* ⊟ *AE, DC, MC, V* ⦿ *FAP.*

$ ⛺ **Sarova Salt Lick Game Lodge.** Set in the Taita Hills just outside the park is this uniquely designed lodge. Honey-color rondavels with dark brown thatch roofs sit high above the ground on stilts and overlook a chain of small floodlighted water holes. You may feel you're in the middle of a fantasy, but this is real Africa—there is a lot of big game just outside your door. The entire lodge is on raised stilts, offering 24-hour game-viewing opportunity. The en-suite round rooms are comfortably if basically furnished, but it's the experience you're here for, not the room decor, although the public areas are sumptuously decorated with rugs, batiks, and a number of authentic African artifacts. Request a top room or one over a water hole for a close-up encounter with elephants, buffalos, and lots of other game. Be sure to visit the underground viewing room at night, because you've a better chance of spotting nocturnal animals like civets, porcupine, and maybe even a leopard. The food is excellent with lots of fresh homegrown vegetables. **Pros:** the underground viewing room; watching animals from your bed. **Cons:** no pool;

not all rooms have good views. ☏ *043/203–0540 or 043/203–0625* ⊕ *www.sarovahotels.com* ⇥ *96 rooms* ⌂ *In-room: no a/c, safe, no TV. In-hotel: restaurant, bar, pool* ▤ *AE, DC, MC, V* ⦿ *FAP.*

PERMANENT TENTED CAMPS

$ ⊡ **Finch Hattons.** If you saw the movie *Out of Africa*, then you'll have some idea, even if it's rather over-romanticized, of who Denys Finch Hatton was. At the turn of the 20th century he left his native England and fell in love not only with Karen Blixen but also with Kenya. A big-game hunter and host extraordinaire, he soon cultivated a reputation for leading classy, exclusive safaris for American tycoons and British royalty, among others. His legend lives on in this superb camp—frequently voted "Best Tented Camp in Africa" by top writers and travelers—where your every whim is catered to, your every dream of Africa comes true, and where you'll dine at a table sparkling with silver and crystal as strains of Mozart (Denys's favorite composer) softly fill the African night. The camp is in groves of old acacia trees around a natural spring that is home to numerous hippos, crocodiles, and different species of birds near the Kenya/Tanzania border. The tents are luxuriously furnished with antique furniture, wooden chests, and even a daybed on your personal veranda. It's expensive, but this lodge is worth it. **Pros:** you'll see an extraordinary array of wildlife right in the camp; food and service are outstanding. **Cons:** game drives and park fees are extra; the generator is switched off at 11:30 PM. ☏ *20/553–237 or 20/351–8391* ⊕ *www.finchhattons.com* ⇥ *50 tents* ⌂ *In-room: no a/c, safe, no TV. In-hotel: restaurant, bar, pool, Wi-Fi* ▤ *AE, DC, MC, V* ⦿ *FAP.*

BUDGET LODGING

¢ ⊡ **Ngulia Safari Lodge.** High on the edge of the Ndawe escarpment with
⟳ panoramic views of the plains below, this unassuming, basic lodge offers all the generic game park activities (not included) plus spacious en-suite rooms all overlooking the wide savanna. Thatch and wood *bandas* (thatch and canvas bungalows) raised just above ground level, each with its own veranda, blend in aesthetically with the bush environment. Inside they have tiled floors and brightly colored soft furnishings. There's a pool surrounded by flowering shrubs and trees, two bars, and a restaurant with good home-cooked food. Because the lodge is in the park, you don't have to travel far to see lots of big game: lions, cheetahs, a leopard if you're lucky, elephants, buffalos, and hundreds of pretty little gazelles. **Pros:** lodge overlooks a watering hole; you have a good chance of seeing a leopard. **Cons:** bathrooms are dated; pool area is not shady. ☏ *866/527–4281 U.S. toll-free reservations* ⊕ *www. africanmeccasafaris.com* ⇥ *52 rooms* ⌂ *In-room: no phone, no a/c, safe. In-hotel: restaurant, bar, pool* ▤ *AE, DC, MC, V* ⦿ *FAP.*

NATIONAL PARKS ACCOMMODATIONS

Public campsites are run by the local Masai communities, but because there are no facilities this is really not an option, unless you're a hard-core camper.

¢ ⊡ **Kamboyo Guest House.** This reasonably priced, self-catering government guesthouse is 8 km (5 mi) from the Mtito Andei Gate, an easy 240-km (149-mi) drive from Nairobi. Built of red brick and red tiles,

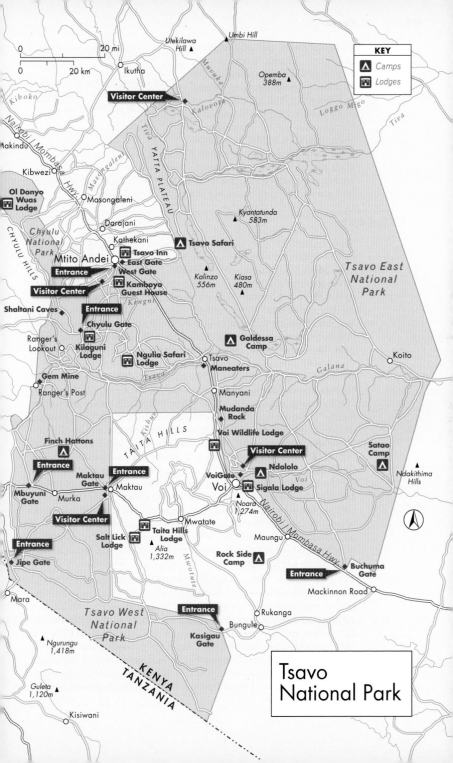

KEY

⛺ Camps
🏠 Lodges

0 ——— 20 mi
0 ——— 20 km

Kiboko

Ikutha

Visitor Center

Utekilawa Hill ▲

Umbi Hill

Opemba 388m ▲

Muvuka

Kalovoto

Loggo Migo

Tiva

Makindu

Nairobi | Mombasa Hwy

Kibwezi

Ol Donyo Wuas Lodge 🏠

Masongaleni

Tiva

YATTA PLATEAU

Masongaleni

Kyantatunda 583m ▲

Tsavo East National Park

Darajani

Chyulu National Park

Kathekani

🏠 **Tsavo Inn**

Mtito Andei

East Gate
Entrance
West Gate

▲ **Tsavo Safari**

Kalinzo 556m ▲

Kiasa 480m ▲

Koito

CHYULU HILLS

Visitor Center

Kamboyo Guest House 🏠

Entrance

Shaltani Caves ◆

Kengni

Chyulu Gate

Ranger's Lookout ○

Kilaguni Lodge 🏠

Ngulia Safari Lodge 🏠

⛺ **Galdessa Camp**

Tsavo
Maneaters ◆

Galana

Gem Mine ◆

Ranger's Post

Tsavo

Manyani ◆

Mudanda Rock ◆

Finch Hattons ⛺

TAITA HILLS

Kishus

Voi Wildlife Lodge 🏠

Visitor Center

Ndololo ⛺

Satao Camp ⛺

Ndakithima Hills ▲

Entrance

Maktau Gate

Entrance

Maktau

Voi Gate ◆
Voi
🏠 **Sigala Lodge**

Voi

Mbuyuni Gate

Murka

Visitor Center

Noara 1,274m

Mwatate

Salt Lick Lodge 🏠

Taita Hills Lodge 🏠

Alia 1,332m ▲

Maungu

Rock Side Camp ⛺

Entrance

Jipe Gate ◆

Entrance

Buchuma Gate ◆

Mara

Tsavo West National Park

Entrance

Rukanga

Mackinnon Road

Ngurungu 1,418m ▲

Kasigau Gate ◆

Bungule

KENYA

TANZANIA

Guleta 1,120m ▲

Kisiwani

Tsavo National Park

it has four clean, sparsely furnished bedrooms. Linens, soap, towels, and basic kitchen implements are provided; bring drinking water and firewood. You are allowed up to 10 guests; it's a bit of a squash, but worth it for the proximity to attractions such as Mzima Springs.

> **PARK ESSENTIALS**
>
> If you are only visiting for the day, you can buy a permit (US$40 per adult, US$20 per child).

Book early at the lodge or Kenya Wildlife Service. **Pros:** there's a fireplace and outside shower. **Cons:** electricity from 6 to 10 PM only; there are only two bathrooms, one en suite. ☎ *0456/22483* ⊕ *www.kws.org* ↝ *1 guesthouse* ♿ *In-room: kitchen* ⊟ *AE, DC, MC, V.*

TSAVO EAST

More inaccessible than its sister park, Tsavo East—11,747 square km (4,535 square mi)—is also one of Kenya's least visited parks. It's a fairly harsh landscape of scrubland dotted with huge baobab trees, but photographers will revel in the great natural light and the vast plains stretching to the horizon. There's lots of greenery along the banks of the Voi and Galana rivers, and the big Aruba Dam, built across the Voi, attracts game and birdlife galore. You'll see herds of elephant and buffalo, waterbuck, and all kinds of animals coming to drink at the dam. The Lugard Falls, on the Galana River, is more a series of rapids than actual waterfalls; walk along the riverbank to catch a glimpse of the water-sculpted rocks. Legend has it that the falls were named after the first British Pro-Consul, who volunteered for Kenya's Colonial Service to escape an unrequited love affair at home. Another fascinating feature in the park is the 290-km-long (180-mi-long) Yatta Plateau, one of the world's longest lava flows. It runs parallel to the Nairobi/Mombasa Highway and is 5 to 10 km (3 to 6 mi) wide and 305 meters (1,000 feet) high. Mudanda Rock, a 1.5-km (2-mi) outcropping, is a water catchment area. You'll see plenty of wildlife coming to drink at the dam below. There's a lot of game in this park, including zebras, kongoni antelope, impala, lion, cheetah and giraffe, and rarer animals such as the oryx, lesser kudu, and the small klipspringer antelopes, which can jump nimbly from rock to rock because of the sticky suction pads under their feet. And yes, it's true: those fat and hairy marmotlike creatures you see sunning themselves on the rocks—the hyraxes—are first cousins to elephants.

The park became infamous in the late 1890s when the Man Eaters of Tsavo, a pride of lions that specialized in human flesh, preyed on the Indian migrant laborers who were building the railway. More than 130 workers were killed; the incident was retold in the 1996 thriller, *The Ghost and the Darkness,* starring Val Kilmer. In the 1970s and '80s Tsavo became notorious once again for the widespread poaching that decimated the elephant population and nearly wiped out rhinos altogether. Today, thanks to responsible management, enlightened environmental vision, and proper funding, both elephant and rhino populations are on the rise.

GETTING HERE AND AROUND

Tsavo East is 233 km (148 mi) south of Nairobi and 250 km (155 mi) north of Mombasa. There are nine airstrips. There's no public transport within the park. Park entry fees are $50 per person, although this is always included in a package tour.

WHEN TO GO

Tsavo East is accessible all year round, so the peak season is actually based on demand months such as migration time in Kenya (July–October) and also vacationers getting away during the winter months—especially Europeans. That being said, March to May is the rainy season, and there are short rains in October and December. Humidity is high from December to April.

THE LEGEND OF THE BAOBAB

Legend has it that when the gods were planting the earth, the baobab refused many locations. In anger, the gods threw them out of heaven and they landed upside down. Take a good look. When not in leaf, they look exactly as if their roots are sticking up into the air.

3

WHERE TO STAY

LUXURY LODGES

$–$$ Fodor's Choice ★ **Galdessa Camp.** The ultimate in luxury, this stunningly beautiful camp is on the south bank of the Galana River, and many consider it to be one of Kenya's best camps; we agree. Overlooking the Yatta Plateau upstream from the Lugard Falls, it's actually two camps; the main lodge has 12 spacious bandas, including one honeymoon banda; the other, private camp (exclusive use only) has three bandas, also including a honeymoon one. Each lodge has its own lounge, dining area, and bar overlooking the river. The elegant and imaginatively decorated bandas are built on wooden platforms with an A-frame thatch roof and a private veranda that has breathtaking river views. There's an en-suite bathroom with flush toilet and bucket shower. If you want total privacy, then opt for the honeymoon bandas, which have separate verandas on stilts—perfect for canoodling to your heart's content under the stars. Don't be surprised if you see a pride of lions strolling along the riverbank or crocodiles and hippos right in front of your banda, as during the dry season many animals come to the river to drink. **Pros:** bush walks are excellent; the quality and standard of the food is superb. **Cons:** there's no pool; dinners are off a set menu. ☎ *040/320–2431 or 040/320–2218* 🌐 *www.galdessa.com* ⇨ *15 bandas* 🛎 *In room: no a/c, safe, no TV. In-hotel: restaurant, bar* 💳 *MC, V* 🍽 *FAP.*

PERMANENT TENTED CAMPS

$ **Satao Camp.** This small and friendly camp lies on a traditional migration route, so it's not short of game. It's not short on comfort either. You'll stay in one of 20 tents placed in a semicircle looking out onto a water hole, each with its own veranda. All are built under individual thatch canopies and shaded by ancient tamarind trees. There's a handmade bed inside your green canvas tent, with lots of attractive African-patterned soft furnishings. The bathrooms are en suite with flush toilet and a bucket shower, which the attentive staff makes sure is hot and ready when you are. The food is wholesome and fresh, and it's great to sit under the 200-year-old tamarind tree and watch the elephants at

Galdessa

Salt Lick Safari Lodge

Galdessa

the water hole. There's a thatch viewing deck on stilts where you can sit and read, or just watch, wait, and see what walks up. There's an attractive dining area under thatch, but lunch is usually taken alfresco under the trees. Kids under 2 stay free, and those 2 to 12 pay 50% of the adult rate. **Pros:** you'll probably see elephants at the watering hole; it's fully equipped for people with disabilities. **Cons:** there's no pool; tents do not have mosquito nets. ☎ *020/243–4600 or 011/47–5075* ⊕ *www.sataocamp.com* ⤹ *16 tents, 4 suites* ⚐ *In-hotel: restaurant, bar* ▭ *AE, MC, V* ⦿ *FAP.*

BUDGET LODGINGS

¢ 🏨 **Rock Side Camp.** Between Tsavo East and West, this former hunting camp *(formerly Westermann's Safari Camp)* is a great base to explore both parks. The Tozers, who live here permanently, have transformed this delightful getaway into a luxury destination that's simply but tastefully decorated with en-suite facilities. Accommodations are at the foot of a rocky *kopje* (small hill) that look out toward plains in the foreground and mountains in the background. It's all about personal service and individual attention here. Food is homemade, often homegrown, and delicious. The camp doesn't offer game drives, but you can go for a walk in the bush, climb up the kopje, or just sit with the tipple of your choice and watch the spectacular sunsets. **Pros:** Rock Side is inexpensive because it's not in the park; it's been upgraded. **Cons:** activities are not offered; they don't take credit cards. ☎ *043/30–028 or 043/30–233* ⊕ *www.westermannssafaricamp.com* ⤹ *12 bandas, 11 cottages* ⚐ *In-hotel: restaurant, bar, pool* ▭ *No credit cards* ⦿ *FAP.*

¢ 🏨 **Voi Wildlife Lodge.** Set in 25 acres on the boundary of Tsavo East
Ⓢ National Park, this resort lodge—only 5 km (3 mi) off Nairobi/Mombasa Highway, a four-hour drive from Nairobi, and a two-hour drive from Mombasa—is a good place to combine with a beach holiday. Don't expect perfect peace and tranquility though, as it's a popular family destination (kids under 2 stay free, 2–12 at half price). Apart from the obligatory game drives, which are extra but always action packed and fruitful, there's plenty to do at the lodge. The viewing deck is a great place to spot game any time of day and night. If you're feeling active, there is pool, badminton, and table tennis, a pool with a poolside Jacuzzi, and aerobics classes at the inviting spa. Bringing the kids? Ask about the babysitting services. There's also a children's play area outside and a discovery room inside with wildlife DVDs and games. Accommodations include comfortable en-suite rooms or an en-suite tent that'll give you the feeling of camping. There are specially designed rooms for physically handicapped people near the lobby. **Pros:** lovely swimming pool; all rooms overlook the watering hole. **Cons:** no a/c; drinks are expensive. ☎ *020/712–5741* ⊕ *www.voiwildlifelodge.com* ⤹ *88 rooms* ⚐ *In-room: no a/c, safe, no TV. In-hotel: restaurant, bar, pool, spa* ▭ *MC, V* ⦿ *BP, MAP, FAP.*

LAIKIPIA PLATEAU

Game
☆★★★★

Park Accessibility
☆★★★★

Getting Around
☆☆★★★

Accommodations
☆☆★★★

Scenic Beauty
☆★★★★

Stretching all the way to Ethiopia and the Sudan, Laikipia Plateau, gateway to Kenya's little-visited northern territory, is not in itself a national park or reserve, but it has become one of Kenya's most recent conservation successes. It's primeval Eden without hordes of game vehicles and flashing cameras.

Amid spectacular scenery, traditional ways of pastoral life continue side by side with an abundance of free-roaming game. Comprising a series of privately owned farms and ranches in an area roughly half the size of Wales, it's rapidly becoming a major tourist destination. In 1992 the Laikipia Wildlife Forum (⊕ *www.laikipia.com*) was formed to combine the interests and efforts of both the privately owned ranches and the communal landowning local communities. Local communities banded together to form their own big ranches and have managed to keep up a traditional way of life as well as embracing tourism. A rewarding by-product of this development has been to foster both cultural identity and community solidarity. This is high country, with altitudes from 1,700 meters (5,577 feet) to 2,600 meters (8,530 feet), so bring those sweaters and jackets. Habitats range from arid semi-desert, scrubland, and sprawling open plains in the north and south, to the thick forests of cedar and olive trees in the east. Two rivers, the Ewaso Ng'iro and Ewasa Narok, dominate the area, which also includes the Laikipia National Reserve and the Lewa Wildlife Conservancy. The area around the Laikipia National Reserve has one of the biggest and most diverse mammal populations in Kenya—only the Masai Mara can boast more game. The Big Five, including black and white rhino, are all present, plus the wide-ranging wild dogs; there's even a chance of seeing the rare aquatic sitatunga antelope. Keep an eye out for Grevy's zebra, which is more narrowly striped than its southern cousin. It was once hunted almost to extinction for its fine desirable skin, but is reestablishing itself well in the area. A visit to one of Kenya's last great true wilderness areas

is a must before it becomes as crowded as some of the better-known reserves and parks farther south.

SAMBURU NATIONAL RESERVE

In the far north of the plateau, north of Mt. Kenya, is the remote Samburu National Reserve. It's highly regarded by experienced travelers and old Africa hands alike as perhaps the best reserve in Kenya. The drive from the foothills of Mt. Kenya into the semi-desert is awesome, and where the road follows the river, you'll be treated to the unusual spectacle of riverine bush and forest on the one side and desert on the other. Again, there's game galore, if you don't spot at least one lion, cheetah, or leopard, or even all three—in addition to giraffe, hippo, antelope, elephant, baboons, vervet monkeys, oryx, and zebra—you might want to get your eyes tested because this whole area hasn't yet become as commercialized as those along the Kenya/Tanzanian border. You'll be privy to a genuine traditional way of life as you watch the red-robed Samburu tribesmen, former kin to the Masai, bringing their cattle down to the river to drink. The lives of the Samburu, like their kinsmen, are centered round their livestock, their traditional source of wealth. After initiation, boys become morans (warriors) whose role it is to protect both humans and livestock from drought, famine, and predators. In Samburu don't be surprised to come across the native camels padding along through the arid savanna.

GETTING HERE AND AROUND

The reserve is about six hours' drive from Nairobi. Unless you've lots and lots of time, however, it's not a good idea to attempt these far northern areas on your own. Choose one of the many superb private lodges instead, which will look after your transport arrangements from Nairobi. There are two airstrips.

WHEN TO GO

Samburu is good all year around, but late May to early October is a good time to visit as there will be lots of game around due to a great deal of vegetation along the Ewaso Nyiro River, the main source of water to the reserve. November and April are peak rainy-season times.

WHERE TO STAY

LUXURY LODGES

$$ 🔅 **Laragai House.** For a once-in-a-lifetime experience of doing things like the Old Colonials once did, consider booking this opulent thatch-and-stone family home that's furnished with antiques, imported furniture, fine china and crystal, and beautiful paintings and is surrounded by gorgeous manicured gardens. The staff is hard to better in terms of service and friendliness. Alas, you can stay here only when the owners are not in residence, but it's worth waiting for. It sleeps 12 people in ultimate luxury, and there's extra room if necessary for kids and guides. **Pros:** heated pool; great for a family getaway. **Cons:** there's an additional $90 per-person conservation fee; there's no à la carte menu. ☎ 020/600–6759 or 020/712–579999 ⊕ *www.borana.co.ke* 🖙 *8 rooms* 🖒 *In-room: DVD, Wi-Fi. In-hotel: pool* ▤ *MC, V* ❑❘ *FAP.*

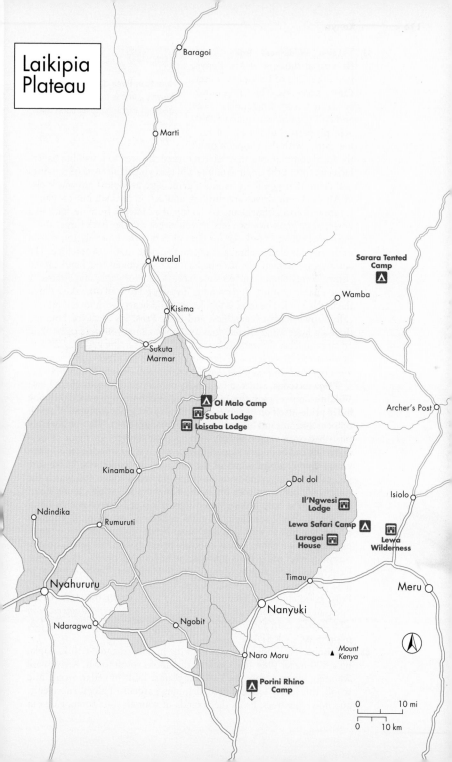

$$ ⟦⟧ **Lewa Wilderness Trails.** Lewa Downs, at the foot of Mt. Kenya, is another one of Laikipia's conservation successes. The Craig family emigrated from England in 1924 and still lives on the same 65,000-acre property, but instead of raising cattle, with the cooperation of

> **DID YOU KNOW?**
>
> More than three-quarters of all Kenya's game is found on private land, not in the national parks and reserves.

the local communities they have returned the area to a wildlife haven. Descendants of the original family will lead you on all sorts of activities and claim that you'll see as much game here as almost anywhere else in Africa. Game drives are thrilling and action packed, but try game-spotting from a different angle—on top of a camel or from the back of a horse, or on your own two feet. (If you've got a dodgy back forget about the camel riding.) Look out for Grevy's zebra, the more elegant cousin of the regular plains zebra, and the rare aquatic sitatunga antelope. The cottages are attractively furnished with a big wooden bed, hand-carved chests, comfy chairs, and en-suite bathroom. Hot water and electricity are available morning and evening; if you need to cool off, take a dip in the lovely pool. The food is wholesome and hearty with lots of organically grown herbs, vegetables, and fruit. **Pros:** it's ideal for families; there's a huge range of activities available. **Cons:** you need to book in advance; bucket showers. ⊠ *Lewa Wildlife Conservancy* ☎ *64/31405 or 20/607–197* ⊕ *www.lewawilderness.com* ⤳ *8 cottages* ⚴ *In-room: no a/c, no phone. In-hotel: bar, tennis court, pool, shop* ⊟ *MC, V* ⦿ *FAP.*

$ ⟦⟧ **Il'Ngwesi Lodge.** Situated on a rocky outcrop in the north of the Lewa Wildlife Conservancy, this intimate and environmental award-winning lodge prides itself on its successful efforts to integrate community development and sustainable environmental management. The comfortably furnished open-walled bandas with open-air showers are made of local materials and built on a slope—their fronts rest on wooden stilts—thus giving uninterrupted views of the surrounding wilderness. Make sure you take the opportunity to sit out at the main lodge and watch the water hole below or cool off on the horizon pool, which gently flows down into the bush below; water is gravity-piped from a nearby natural spring. You'll see plenty of game including lion, leopard, cheetah, hyena, the elusive wild dog, and large herds of elephant and buffalo, plus the plains game. Learn about hunting, gathering honey, animal trapping with indigenous poisons, or fashioning beadwork with the local Masai at the nearby Masai Cultural Manyatta. You won't want to miss the dancing of the warriors and maidens—it's the genuine article. **Pros:** good children's facilities; you can sleep under the stars. **Cons:** open-air showers only; no a/c. ☎ *020/203–3122* ⊕ *www.ilngwesi.com* ⤳ *6 bandas* ⚴ *In-room: no a/c, safe, no TV. In-hotel: restaurant, bar, pool* ⊟ *MC, V* ⦿ *FAP.*

$$ ⟦⟧ **Loisaba.** This lodge sits plumb in the middle of game-rich Laikipia, on a 300-meter (984-foot) plateau that looks south to Mt. Kenya with stunning views across the Laikipia plains. Built of cedar, stone, and wood, this lovely lodge is nestled among gardens of aloes, succulents, and flowering trees. From the veranda of your en-suite room, gaze out

Sabuk

Sabuk

Il'Ngwesi Lodge

at the dizzying views or just watch the water hole below with its passing show of animals. If you fancy something even more special, opt for one of the star beds (closed in November), which have been created with the local community. Don't expect a meager stretcher under the stars. You'll stay in an en-suite "platform" with half-covered thatch roof, hand-crafted furniture, and wooden floors set among big rocks. The Kiboko star beds overlook a water hole, whereas the Koija star beds overlook the Ewaso Nyiro river. Every evening your friendly and attentive Laikipia Masai attendants will wheel out your double bed under the star-studded clear night sky, where, carefully shrouded under a mosquito net, you can watch the world turn. If you're looking for something even more different, go for a quad bike ride. It's not only a thrilling experience but also contributes directly to sponsoring a classroom for the local kids. **Pros:** other activities include game drives, tennis, horseback riding, and camel trekking; laundry service is included. **Cons:** no a/c; Internet connection is slow. ☎ *020/6003–054 or 6003–090* ⊕ *www.loisaba.com* ⤳ *7 rooms, 6 star beds* ♿ *In-room: no a/c, safe, no TV, Wi-Fi. In-hotel: restaurant, bar, tennis court, pool, spa* ▭ *MC, V* ⎟⦿⎟ *FAP.*

$$ ▦ **Ol Malo.** Choose a luxurious tent or a thatch cottage perched on ☾ a cliff edge at this lovely camp to the west of Samburu overlooking Mt. Kenya. You'll find yourself under the personal supervision of the owners, Rocky and Colin Francombe. Spacious and elegant tents with elephant-theme interiors have en-suite bathrooms made out of natural rock, while the stone-and-thatch cottages, some built on two levels, have king-size beds and baths that you can lie in and look out at the passing wildlife. The main lodge, also built of natural rock and olive wood, is cozy and comfortable. There's a huge pool, which clings to the rock edge, spilling its waters to the rocks below. Drives are extremely rewarding with game galore, but for something a little different try a camel ride (not for bad backs), a nature walk, an overnight stay in the Look Out Hut—a little wooden hut in the bush—or go camping under the stars. Horseback riding is a fascinating way to spot game: there are also safe and friendly ponies for kids, and children's gift packs on arrival, plus other kids' activities. There's also the opportunity to meet and mix with the local Samburu people and to take part in some of their activities. **Pros:** it's very child-friendly; the afternoon tea is excellent. **Cons:** no a/c, no TV in rooms. ☎ *20/600–457* ⊕ *www.olmalo.com* ⤳ *4 cottages, 2 tents* ♿ *In-room: no a/c, safe, no TV. In-hotel: restaurant, bar, pool* ▭ *AE, DC, MC, V* ⎟⦿⎟ *FAP.*

$$ ▦ **Sabuk Lodge.** This lodge organically created out of local thatch, stone, and wood clings to a hillside on the northwest of the Laikipia Plateau. Overlooking the ever-flowing Ewaso N'giro River, the lodge offers spectacular views and great hospitality. In between activities, lie on your uniquely designed handcrafted big bed in your charming open-fronted room and gaze out at the river below. If you can't tear yourself away from the view, then just move into the bathroom, slip in the deep stone bath, flip water over the edge to the rocks below and keep gazing. The comfortable main open-sided lodge ensures you're never far away from those memorable views. On chilly nights a roaring log fire keeps you cozy and warm. Food is plentiful, fresh, and delicious with superb

breakfasts on the viewing deck. Spend a night out under the stars at a fly camp after a day's camel safari, go walking, birding, or fishing, or try tubing down the river. Game is plentiful, and you should see elephants, lions, leopards, giraffe, Grevy's and plains zebras, and much, much more. Because there are no fences, the game can wander at will. **Pros:** the food is excellent; camel safaris highly recommended. **Cons:** rooms don't have safes; no à la carte menus. ☎ *071/813–9359 or 020/359–8871* ⊕ *www.sabuklodge. com* ⌁ *5 cottages* ⌂ *In-room: no a/c, no TV. In-hotel: bar, pool* ⊟ *AE, DC, MC, V* ⦶ *FAP.*

PERMANENT TENTED CAMPS

$$ ⛺ **Lewa Safari Camp.** If it's rhinos you're after, then this delightful but small tented camp in the 65,000-acre Lewa Conservancy, right where the old Rhino Sanctuary headquarters used to stand, is for you. There's a comfortable main building for eating and relaxing, and wide verandas outside each tent for soaking up the beautiful environs. But if it's game-viewing you're after, then one of the camp's expert team of professional guides will take you on an exhilarating drive. Spacious tents protected by a sturdy thatch roof have comfortable beds, a desk for keeping up on those precious journal notes, and spacious en-suite bathrooms. The food is homegrown and tasty. Bird-watching is spectacular in this area, but it's likely that while you're watching out for feathered friends, you're likely to spot big game as well, including lions. Burn up some calories and have a unique experience at the same time by going on a guided game walk. **Pros:** tents are private; very few other vehicles. **Cons:** bucket showers; no a/c. ⊠ *Lewa Wildlife Conservancy* ☎ *64/31405 or 20/607–197* ⊕ *www.lewasafaricamp.com* ⌁ *12 cottages* ⌂ *In-room: no a/c, safe, no TV. In-hotel: restaurant, bar, pool* ⊟ *MC, V* ⦶ *FAP.*

$$ ⛺ **Porini Rhino Camp.** Opened in summer 2007, this delightful eco-
★ friendly tented camp is nestled among Kenya's ubiquitous *Acacia tortilis* trees in a secluded valley in the Ol Pejeta Conservancy. This 90,000-acre stretch of game-rich wilderness lies between the snow-capped Mt. Kenya and the foothills of the Aberdares. This location treats guests to a double whammy—abundant game including the Big Five and the endangered black rhino and superb views across the open plains. Each beautifully placed tent has stunning views from its personal veranda, and inside there's an en-suite bathroom with flush toilet and bucket shower with hot water heated by solar power. Sip sundowners from a carefully chosen vantage point, and then take a spectacular night drive. By day stretch your legs on a guided bush walk with a Masai guide or have your heartstrings tugged at the nearby Sweetwaters Chimpanzee Sanctuary. If you're feeling extra energetic and really want to walk on

the wild side, then the camp also offers walking safaris. ■TIP→ **The all-inclusive price includes round-trip transfers by air from Nairobi, Ol Pejeta conservancy fees, all game drives, sundowners, walks with Masai warriors, full board, and free house wines, beer, and soft drinks.** **Pros:** the camp benefits the local community and is eco-friendly; single supplements are reasonable. **Cons:** it can be cooler than reserves south of the country; there is only solar power, no electricity; no pool. ⊠ *Ol Pejeta Conservancy* ☎ *020/712–2504 or 020/712–3129* ⊕ *www.porini.com* ⤴ *6 tents* ☰ *MC, V* ⍩○⍠ *AI.*

$$ ⛺ **Sarara Tented Camp.** This small, tented camp lies below the peaks of the Mathews Mountains in the 850,000-acre Namunyak Wildlife Conservation Trust, a community project between landowners and the local Samburu people. Accommodation is in six spacious tents, sited under pole-supported thatch roofs with flush toilets and open-air showers. There is also a two-bedroom house with a shared sitting/dining area. The main sitting room and dining area sits on stilts in front of the water hole and natural rock pool—yes, you swim here overlooking the water hole and you are quite safe—with stunning views of the Mathews Mountains. Game is plentiful with resident lion and leopard, and there's an excellent chance of seeing wild dog as there are two packs in the area. Look out for the attractive colobus monkeys when you go for a guided hike in the forest. Go donkey trekking in the mountains, or take a camel safari with an overnight stop at a fly camp. **Pros:** there's a wide range of activities available; staff are from the local community. **Cons:** it's off the beaten track; no power points in tents; Wi-Fi is available only during the day. ☎ *020/6000–457* ⊕ *www.sararacamp.com* ⤴ *6 tents* ⛱ *In-room: no a/c, safe, no TV. In-hotel: restaurant, bar, pool, Internet terminal, Wi-Fi hotspot* ☰ *AE, DC, MC, V* ⊗ *Closed Apr. 15–end of May and Nov.* ⍩○⍠ *FAP.*

IF YOU HAVE TIME

Although we've gone into great detail about the must-see parks in Kenya, there are many others to explore if you have time. Here, we mention a few good ones.

NAIROBI NATIONAL PARK

The most striking thing about Nairobi National Park, Kenya's oldest national park, is not a mountain or a lake, but the very fact that it exists at all. This sliver of unspoiled Africa survives on the edge of a city of almost 3 million people. Where else can you get a photo of animals in their natural habitat with skyscrapers in the background? As you travel into the city from Jomo Kenyatta International Airport, you're likely to see gazelles grazing near the highway.

The park is tiny compared with Kenya's other game parks and reserves; it covers only 117 square km (44 square mi). It's characterized by open plains that slope gently from west to east and rocky ridges that are covered with rich vegetation. Seasonal streams run southeast into the Mbagathi Athi River, which is lined with yellow fever and acacia trees.

Continued on page 126

Blue wildebeest in Tanzania's Serengeti National Park

THE GREAT MIGRATION

by Kate Turkington

Nothing will prepare you for the spectacle that is the Great Migration. This annual journey of more than 2 million animals is a safari-seeker's Holy Grail, the ultimate in wildlife experiences. Some say it's one of the world's greatest natural wonders.

The greater Serengeti ecosystem, which includes Kenya's Masai Mara (north) and Tanzania's Serengeti (south), is the main arena for this awesome sight. At the end of each year during the short rains—November to early December—the herds disperse into the southeast plains of Tanzania's Seronera. After calving early in the new year (wildebeests drop up to 8,000 babies a day), huge numbers of animals start the 800-km (497-mi) trek from these now bare southeast plains to lush northern pastures. On the way they will face terrible, unavoidable danger. In June and July braying columns—40-km (25 miles) long—have to cross the crocodile-infested Grumeti River. Half of the great herds which successfully survive the crossing will stay in northern Tanzania, the other half will cross over into Kenya's Masai Mara. In early October the animals begin their return journey back to Seronera and come full circle, only to begin their relentless trek once again early the following year.

WHO'S MIGRATING

What will you see during the migration?

More than **2 million** wildebeest
250,000 Thompson's gazelle
200,000 zebra
70,000 impala
30,000 Grant's gazelle

In addition, huge numbers of predators follow the herds. You're likely to see lion, leopard, cheetah, jackal, hyena, and numerous smaller predators.

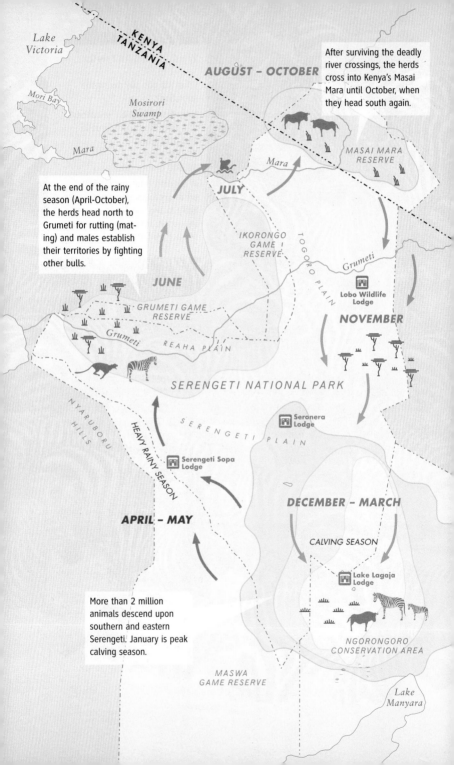

Lake Victoria

Mori Bay

Mara

Mosirori Swamp

KENYA
TANZANIA

AUGUST – OCTOBER

After surviving the deadly river crossings, the herds cross into Kenya's Masai Mara until October, when they head south again.

Mara

MASAI MARA RESERVE

JULY

At the end of the rainy season (April-October), the herds head north to Grumeti for rutting (mating) and males establish their territories by fighting other bulls.

IKORONGO GAME RESERVE

TOGORO PLAIN

Grumeti

Lobo Wildlife Lodge

JUNE

GRUMETI GAME RESERVE

Grumeti

REAHA PLAIN

NOVEMBER

SERENGETI NATIONAL PARK

NYARUBORU HILLS

HEAVY RAINY SEASON

SERENGETI PLAIN

Seronera Lodge

Serengeti Sopa Lodge

APRIL – MAY

DECEMBER – MARCH

CALVING SEASON

Lake Lagaja Lodge

More than 2 million animals descend upon southern and eastern Serengeti. January is peak calving season.

NGORONGORO CONSERVATION AREA

MASWA GAME RESERVE

Lake Manyara

DRIVEN BY DINNER

STAGGERING NUMBERS

The Great Migration, as we know it, is a fairly young phenomenon, having only started in the 1960s when wildebeest numbers exploded. However, an estimated 250,000 wildebeests don't survive the annual migration.

WHERE THE MAGIC HAPPENS

The Serengeti more then lives up to its awesome reputation as an amazing spot to see wildlife and it's here that the Great Migration begins and ends. The park's ecosystem supports some of the most abundant mammal populations left anywhere on earth and it covers almost 15,000 square km (9,320 square mi) of seemingly endless plains, riverine bush, forest and scrubland roughly the size of Northern Ireland or Connecticut. It stretches between the Ngorongoro highlands, Lake Victoria, and Tanzania's northern border with Kenya. It was named a UNESCO World Heritage Site in 1978 and an International Biosphere Reserve (a UNESCO international conservation area) in 1981.

WHEN TO GO

Because rainfall patterns are unpredictable, it's difficult to anticipate timings for the migration. But usually, by the beginning of each year, the grazing on the southeast plains of Serengeti's Seronera is exhausted and the herds start to move northwest into Tanzania's Western Corridor. The actual crossing of the Grumeti River, usually between June and July, when an unrivalled bloody spectacle of terrified frantic wildebeest and huge lashing crocodiles unfolds, is a gruesome, unforgettable spectacle. You'll see hundreds of thousands of animals between March and November, including predators. Seronera in March, April and May is an ideal time for a safari because there are huge concentrations of predators preying on all the baby animals. Safaris are much cheaper between April and June, and although you may not witness the actual river crossings, you'll still be privy to prime game-viewing experiences. Plus there will be far fewer vehicles.

In the west the river runs through a deep gorge where rocky outcrops are the favored habitat of leopards.

Fences separate the park from the nearby communities of Langata and Karen, but they do not always prevent the occasional leopard or lion from snacking on a dog or horse. This is because of an open corridor to the south that allows wildebeest and other animals to move to other areas in search of food; researchers believe the annual migration in this area was once as spectacular as that in the Serengeti.

Despite the urban pressures, the park contains a good variety of wildlife, especially during the dry season. Animals migrate here from other areas knowing that there's always a source of permanent water. You can see the Big Five, minus elephants as the area is not big enough to support them. ■TIP→ If you want to see baby elephants, visit the David Sheldrick Elephant Orphanage close to the main entrance of the park. Zebras, elands, impalas, and Grant's and Thomson's gazelles are well represented. Warthogs and ostriches are common on the open plains. Larger game includes Masai giraffes, which browse in the woodland, and a herd of 50 black rhinos, sometimes found in the light bush around the forest area; black rhinos have been particularly successful here because it has been easier to keep track of and control poachers. Hippos can be spied in the larger pools of the Mbagathi Athi River as well as from a nature trail in the eastern section of the park. In the extreme western border of the park, a low ridge covered by a stand of hardwood trees is home to herds of bushbucks and impalas as well as some of the park's olive baboons. Impala Point, at the edge of the ridge, makes a good vantage point to scan the plains with binoculars for concentrations of game.

Predators include about 30 resident lions—you've an excellent chance of seeing a lion kill—and cheetahs. Rangers keep a careful note of the movements of the larger animals, so it is worth asking at the gate where to look for lions or rhinos.

More than 500 species of permanent and migratory birds have been spotted in the park. Around the dams used to create marshes you will find Egyptian geese, crowned cranes, yellow and saddle-billed storks, herons, African spoonbills, sacred ibis, hammerkops, Kittlitz's sand plovers, and marabou storks. In the plains look for secretary birds, vultures, helmeted guinea fowls, bustards, yellow-throated sand grouse, larks, pipits, and Jackson's widow birds, which display their long tails and attractive plumage during the long rains in May and June. The forests hold cuckoo shrikes, sunbirds, waxbills, flycatchers, and warblers.

GETTING HERE AND AROUND

A 20-minute drive from downtown Nairobi (7 km [4 mi]), the park's network of paved and all-weather dirt roads can be negotiated by cars and vans, and junctions are generally signposted and clearly marked on the official park map, which you can pick up at the gate or any bookstore or tourist office. Open-roof hatches are not permitted in the park. Do not leave your vehicle except where permitted, as unsuspecting tourists have been mauled by lions and attacked by rhinos.

BOOKING AND VISITOR INFO

Most safari operators will arrange a trip, usually four to five hours long, to the park. Otherwise, you can take a taxi. For $65, you can arrange to visit the Animal Orphanage and take a safari walk, arranged by the park. The park is very busy on weekends, when locals visit.

Contact **Kenya Wildlife Service** (☎ 020/6000–800 reservations ⊕ www.kws. org ✉ $40 ☉ Daily 6 AM–7 PM).

WHERE TO STAY

There are no accommodations inside the park.

MERU NATIONAL PARK

Situated 370 km (230 mi) northeast of Nairobi and west of Mt. Kenya, this little-visited park (1,810 square km [699 square mi]) offers some of Kenya's wildest country, but was taken off the mainstream safari circuit and deleted from safari operators' destination lists because of the lawless poachers who wiped out the white-rhino population in the 1980s. Although the Kenyan government has gotten a grip on the security situation, the park still finds it difficult to shake off its negative image. But rest assured that all is now well and the park is a safe and fulfilling destination—after all, this is the place where wildlife champions Joy and George Adamson hand-reared Elsa the lioness made famous by the 1966 film *Born Free.*

A successful rehabilitation program reintroduced elephants and rhinos to the park in 2001; both populations are doing well. There is a lot of other game here, including buffalo, lion, leopard, cheetah, hippo, lesser kudu, hartebeest (grassland antelope), Grevy's and Burchell's zebra, the gerenuk (a mini-giraffe), the reticulated or Somali giraffe, waterbuck, oryx, and Grant's gazelle. The park is part of an ecosystem that includes Kora National Park and Mwingi, Rahole, and Bisanadi reserves. It straddles the equator and is home to a great variety of habitats, including scrubland dotted with baobab trees, lush green grasslands, and riverine forests. Tana, Kenya's longest river, is fed by 13 rivers that create a superb habitat for bird life as well. Check out the Somali ostrich, raptors such as the red-necked falcon and the palm-nut vulture, and that mega-score on serious birder's life list, the Pel's fishing owl, which hides in the huge ancient trees along the rivers.

GETTING HERE AND AROUND

There is a daily flight to Meru National Park from Nairobi Wilson Airport with Airkenya, which takes 1¾ hours. You can drive from Nairobi; the road is not particularly bad but it takes five to six hours. If you are already at a property in the area, it can make sense to drive. Visitors would need a 4x4 vehicle for driving within the park.

Contact **Kenya Wildlife Service** (☎ 050/50407 ⊕ www.kws.org ✉ $50 per day ☉ Daily 6–6).

WHERE TO STAY
LUXURY LODGES

$$ ⊞ **Elsa's Kopje.** This lodge is set above George Adamson's original camp-site, where he and his wife, author Joy Adamson, released their lioness Elsa (after which the lodge is named) back into the wild. It's a strikingly attractive lodge both for its elevated position and for its imaginatively designed thatch cottages. Each cottage is unique, with boulders for walls, trees growing through the roof, and spacious interiors furnished with handcrafted furniture, hand-woven rugs, and earth-toned cushions, throws, and bedspreads. All the cottages have complete privacy, but if you would like your family to stay together and have your own private infinity swimming pool, go for Elsa's Private House, which sleeps 4 (extra beds can be added for kids) and has a small garden. Watch the plains game ambling through the grasslands from your veranda or view predators or rhinos in open-sided game vehicles before sundowners at the palm-fringed hippo pools. The home-cooked, homegrown food is principally northern Italian, but if you're not a pasta person, there's plenty more to choose from. **Pros:** delicious homegrown vegetables; free laundry service. **Cons:** not all rooms have tubs; no a/c. ☎ 20/600–4053 ⊕ *www.elsaskopje.com* ↪ *9 cottages, 1 private house* ⅄ *In-room: no a/c, safe, no TV. In-hotel: restaurant, bar, pool* ⊟ *MC, V* ⅋ *FAP.*

$ ⊞ **Leopard Rock Lodge.** Antique furniture, Persian rugs, and understated elegance characterize this exclusive lodge, which sprawls out along the banks of the Murera River. You'll stay in one of the thatch and wood bandas, with his-and-her en-suite bathrooms; or a family cottage or suite, all with stunning views. The food is superb even by high Kenyan standards, and there's a great wine list and open-air kitchen. The lodge offers a pottery workshop and an unforgettable pool that allows you to come safely nose to nose—there's a glass panel between the river and the pool—with crocs in the river. **Pros:** other activities on offer include fishing and bird-watching; there's a pool bar and Jacuzzi. **Cons:** dinner requires formal dress; no a/c. ☎ 20/600–0031 ⊕ *www.leopardmico.com* ↪ *15 cottages, 5 family cottages, 10 suites* ⅄ *In-room: no phone, no a/c, safe. In-hotel: pool* ⊟ *AE, DC, MC, V* ⅋ *FAP.*

THE LAKES OF KENYA

In addition to its great game parks, Kenya is home to huge beautiful lakes that are often covered with uncountable flocks of flamingos. Here's just a snapshot of four of them.

LAKE NAIVASHA

One of the Rift Valley's few freshwater lakes, Lake Naivasha is a popular spot for day-trips and weekends away from Nairobi. The pleasant forested surroundings, which are a far cry from the congestion and noise of Nairobi, are another big draw. Keep an eye out for the yellow fever trees, and the abundant populations of birds, monkeys, and hippos. Such an attractive location lured a group of settlers to build their homes on its shores. Known collectively as "White Mischief," these settlers were internationally infamous for their decadent, hedonistic lifestyle.

A 1987 movie of the same name, starring Greta Scacchi, was based on a notorious society murder set during this time.

GETTING HERE AND AROUND

Lake Naivasha is a one to two hour drive from Nairobi. There are two routes—a shorter but badly pot holed route along the escarpment, or a longer but better maintained road, the A104 Uplands, which leads to Naivasha town. Hotels and lodges in the area will arrange pickups from Nairobi, and taxis can transport you around the area. Safarilink has a flight from Nairobi Wilson airport.

EXPLORING

Cross over by boat to **Crescent Island Wildlife Sanctuary** (☎ 0733/579–935 🕮 $20), where you can see giraffes, zebras, and other plains herbivores, but absolutely no predators.

WHERE TO STAY

Need a pick-me-up or a place to stay while you're here? **La Belle Inn** (☎ *050/202–1007* ✉ *labelleinn@kenyaweb.co*) is a great place for breakfast or a terrace sundowner. It also has a business center with Internet access. **Crater Lake Tented Camp** (⊕ *www.africanmeccasafaris. com*) is a classy place to stay with great views of the lake. **Lake Naivasha Simba Lodge** (⊕ *www.marasimba.com*), though primarily a conference center, has lovely grounds, big rooms, and loads of facilities.

LAKE TURKANA

The tip of Lake Turkana, in Kenya's northwest, runs into the Ethiopian highlands, but the rest of Kenya's biggest lake stretches for 250 km (155 mi) south. Sometimes called the Jade Lake because of its vivid green color, it's a shallow alkaline lake in the Great Rift Valley that has been drying up alarmingly over the past decade. Surprisingly, it's still home to the legendary giant Nile perch, huge herds of hippos and more Nile crocodiles than anywhere else in the world—more than 20,000 reside here. There's abundant birdlife with many European migrants wintering around its shores.

GETTING HERE AND AROUND

The roads to Lake Turkana are in bad condition, so it's better to fly. Fly540 flies daily from Nairobi JKIA to Lodwar, via Kitale.

Contact **Kenya Wildlife Service** (☎ *020/600–800* ⊕ *www.kws.org*).

WHERE TO STAY

Lobolo Camp (⊕ *www.bush-and-beyond.com*) makes a good base and boats can be hired for US$250 per day.

LAKE VICTORIA

Kenya shares Africa's biggest freshwater lake with its neighbors, Uganda and Tanzania. Tanzania has the lion's share: 49%; Uganda has 45%; Kenya only 6%. The lake is so huge (68,000 square km [26,000 square mi]) that it has its own weather system with unpredictable storms, squalls, and high waters just like the ocean. The dhow was first introduced to Lake Victoria by Arab slave traders, and the local Luo shipbuilders quickly adopted the shape and lateen sail. You'll see fishing fleets of white-sailed dhows all over the lake, fishing mainly for the delicious Nile perch. These fish, which can reach the size of a fully

Kenya's Tribes

KIKUYU

The Kikuyu account for almost 25% of the country's total population. Most Kikuyu live around Mt. Kenya, and because of the fertility of the land there, they have become largely a pastoralist people, farming the rich fields around the mountain and up in the Kenyan highlands. The Mau Mau Rebellion (1952–58) was a sad time in Kikuyu—and Kenyan—history, with frustrations among Kenyan tribes toward the colonizing British resulting in guerilla warfare. During this time, many Kikuyu were killed and detained in British camps. This difficult era spurred the move toward independence, and in 1964 Jomo Kenyatta, a Kikuyu, became Kenya's first president. Kenya's third president, Mwai Kibaki, is also Kikuyu, as is Nobel Peace Prize–winner and Greenbelt Movement founder Wangari Maathai.

LUO

Mainly in Western Kenya, the Luo tribe is one of the country's largest, accounting for about 15% of the population. Most members make their living through fishing and farming. The culture is rich in musical traditions, and the sounds and melodies common in their music are said to be the basis for Kenya's modern pop music. Raila Odinga, the top opposition-party leader who ran against Mwai Kibaki in the much disputed 2007 presidential election, is Luo. Odinga and Kibaki entered into a power-sharing government in early 2008. Barack Obama's father was from the Luo tribe.

MASAI

Known to be great warriors, the Masai are also largely associated with Kenya. This red-clad tribe is mainly found in southern Kenya and Tanzania. *To find out more about this ethnic group, see Tanzania's Tribes box in Chapter 4.*

grown shark, now account for about 80% of the fish in the lake. Their presence still arouses controversy. On the one hand, they are the basis for a multimillion-dollar processing and export industry; on the other, scientists say they are destroying the lake's ecosystem.

GETTING HERE AND AROUND

Kenya Airways and Fly540 fly from Nairobi to Kisumu. The flight takes approximately 45 minutes. The airport is 4 km (2.5 mi) out of the center of town (a 10-minute drive). Renovation and expansion of the airport should be completed at the end of 2010 and is expected to boost tourism as well as local business. Driving from Nairobi will take about 5½ hours. When you are in Kisumu, bicycle taxis are a quick and cheap way of getting around.

EXPLORING

Kisumu, on Lake Victoria's shore, is the main town of western Kenya, and Kenya's third largest, although it lacks the post-independence prosperity and development of Mombasa and Nairobi. It's got a bit of a run-down feel reminiscent of some of the small towns on the Indian Ocean coast.

If you're a birder, head for **Ndere Island National Park** (⊠ *$5* ⊗ *Daily 6–6*) or the **Kisumu Bird Sanctuary** (⊠ *No fee* ⊗ *Dawn–dusk*), both breeding grounds for hundreds of water birds. April to May is the best season.

WHERE TO STAY

Rusinga Island Lodge (⊕ *www.rusinga.com*) and **Mfangano Island Camp** (⊕ *www.governorscamp.com*) are top-of-the-range luxury lodges.

GATEWAY CITY

As Nairobi is Kenya's capital city and the main hub for visitors, it's very likely that you'll be spending an overnight here between flights. The following information will help you plan those hours productively and safely.

NAIROBI

The starting point for safaris since the days of Teddy Roosevelt and Ernest Hemingway, Nairobi is still the first stop for many travelers headed to the wildlife parks of East Africa. Just over a century ago Nairobi was little more than a water depot for the notorious "Lunatic Express." Every railhead presented a new nightmare for its British builders. Work was halted by hungry lions (a saga portrayed in the film *The Ghost and the Darkness*) as well as by masses of caterpillars that crawled on the tracks, spoiling traction and spinning wheels. Nearsighted rhinos charged the noisy engines. Africans fashioned jewelry from the copper telegraph wires, leading to a head-on collision between two engines after the communication wires were cut. The budget ballooned to 59,500 ($19,685) a mile, an enormous amount of money in 1900.

Nairobi, which means "cool water" in the language of the Masai, wouldn't remain a backwater for long. In her 1942 memoir, *West with the Night*, aviatrix Beryl Markham wrote that less than three decades after it was founded, the city "had sprung from a collection of corrugated iron shacks serving the spindly Uganda Railway to a sprawling welter of British, Boers, Indians, Somalis, Abyssinians, natives from all over Africa and a dozen other places." Its grand hotels and imposing public buildings, she wrote, were "imposing evidence that modern times and methods have at last caught up with East Africa."

Today Nairobi's skyline surprises first-time visitors, whose visions of the country are often shaped by wildlife documentaries on the Discovery Channel or news reports about poverty on CNN. Since it was founded little more than a century ago, Nairobi has grown into one of the continent's largest capitals. Some early architecture survives here and there, but this city of almost 3 million people is dominated by modern office towers.

This is not to say the city has lost all its charm—the venerable Norfolk and Stanley hotels recall the elegance of an age long since past, and the big black taxis from London lend a sense of style. Sometimes you can even describe the city as beautiful. After a good rain the city seems to have more green than New York or London. Brilliant bougainvillea line the highway from the airport, flame trees shout with color, and, in October, the horizon turns lavender with the blossoms of jacaranda.

But Nairobi has more than its share of problems. This city that grew too fast has paralyzing traffic jams, with many unsafe or overloaded vehicles on the road, and no hint of emissions control. Crime is on the rise, and stories about muggings and carjackings have led to the capital's moniker "Nairobbery." In addition, there is a growing disparity between rich and poor. Private estates on the edge of Nairobi resemble those of Beverly Hills or Boca Raton, with elaborate wrought-iron fences surrounding opulent mansions with stables, tennis courts, and swimming pools. The upper crust is known as the *wabenzi,* with *wa* a generic prefix for a people or tribe and *benzi* referring to the ubiquitous Mercedes-Benz cars lining the driveways. Not far away you can glimpse vast mazes of tin shacks, many with no electricity or running water.

These problems have pushed many travelers to the sanctuary of the suburbs. The Ngong Hills, consisting of "four noble peaks rising like immovable darker blue waves against the sky," mark the southwestern boundaries of Nairobi, embracing the townships of Langata and Karen. The latter is named after Baroness Karen Blixen, who wrote under the pen name Isak Dinesen about her life on a coffee farm here. Purple at dusk, the Ngong Hills are a restful symbol of *salaam,* Swahili for "peace." Here people take a deep breath, toast the setting sun, and discuss the remains of the day.

Exclusive guest homes, such as the Giraffe Manor, Ngong House, and the House of Waine, provide a sense of peace in the suburban bush. Some of the better boutiques selling everything from antiques to art are found in Karen and Langata. The suburb of Langata lies on the edge of the Nairobi National Park, a great introduction to the magnificent wildlife of Kenya. No wonder many visitors return here year after year. They discover how Blixen felt when she wrote in one of her letters: "Wherever I may be in future, I will always wonder whether there is rain on the Ngongs."

GETTING HERE AND AROUND

Nairobi National Park is to the south of the city, with Jomo Kenyatta International Airport and Wilson Airport on the park periphery. Karen and Langata, suburbs of Nairobi, are southwest of the city center, and the Ngong Hills, on the edge the Great Rift Valley, are beyond them. Muthaiga, Gigiri, and Limuru are to the north.

Most major European airlines fly into Jomo Kenyatta International Airport (JKIA), Kenya's major airport, which is 15 km (9 mi) from the city. The airport has several ATM-equipped banks and Bureaux de Change where you can change money. Barclays Bank, National Bank of Kenya, and Transnational Bank have branches and 24-hour money changing daily. You can also use the ATMs, although some accept only Visa. It usually takes about 40 minutes to drive from the airport to the city center by taxi (about US$20; always negotiate first) or regular shuttle bus, although protracted road works mean that it can take 90 minutes in rush hour. Many hotels have shuttle service; be sure to organize this when you book your room.

Wilson Airport 6 km (4 mi) south of the city on the Langata Road is Nairobi's second airport. It's used for domestic, charter, and some international flights. A taxi into the center of town is about $12.

There are plenty of cheap and efficient domestic flights available, including daily flights on Air Kenya between Nairobi and Mombasa Malindi, and Lamu. Air Kenya also flies daily to Amboseli, Kiwayu Lamu, Malindi, the Masai Mara, and Meru. Fly540 flies from Nairobi JKIA to Lamu, Malindi, the Masai Mara and Mombasa, and Safarilink flies from Nairobi Wilson to Diani Beach, Lamu, Amboseli, Samburu, Tsavo, and the Masai Mara. When you book a local flight, make sure to note which airport it departs from.

You're probably only in Nairobi overnight or for a few hours, so you definitely won't need a car. Take a taxi. There's an 80 km (50 mi) per hour speed limit, and it's compulsory to buckle up. Always negotiate the price before setting out. Locals travel around on matatus (passenger minivans carrying up to 15 passengers), but the drivers are notoriously reckless and the vehicles not always road worthy.

EMERGENCIES
Police in general are friendly and helpful to tourists. There are two private hospitals (avoid the government hospitals) with excellent staff and facilities, which have 24-hour pharmacies. There are plenty of pharmacies all over downtown Nairobi. Consult your concierge or host.

ESSENTIALS
Airports Jomo Kenyatta International Airport (NBO ☎ 020/822–111 ⊕ www.kenyaairports.co.ke). **Wilson Airport** (WIL ☎ 020/501–941 ⊕ www. kenyaairports.co.ke).

Emergency Contacts Central Police Station (✉ University Way ☎ 020/221–6183; 999 for all emergencies). **Aga Khan Hospital** (✉ Parklands Ave., Parklands ☎ 020/366–2025). **Nairobi Hospital** (✉ Argwings Kodhek Rd. ☎ 020/284–5000).

EXPLORING
TOP ATTRACTIONS
☼ **David Sheldrick Orphanage for Rhinos and Elephants.** Take a morning excursion, which you can book through your tour guide or hotel concierge, to this amazing rescue center that was set up by Daphne Sheldrick after the death of her husband, David, who was famous for his anti-poaching activities in Tsavo National Park. You'll be able to watch baby elephants at play or having a bath, knowing that one day when they're old enough they will be successfully reintroduced into the wild. It's an absolutely unmissable and heartwarming experience. Make a donation, however small, or go for gold and adopt your own baby elephant. ■ TIP→ **Avoid visiting on Saturdays and Sundays in July and August as it gets very busy.** ✉ Entrance is at Maintenance Gate on Magadi Rd. ☎ 020/230–1396

or 0733/891–996 ⊕ *www.sheldrickwildlifetrust.org* ✉ *Ksh500* ⊙ *Daily 11* AM*–noon.*

★ **Nairobi National Museum.** On Museum Hill off Chiromo Road, this interesting museum has good reproduction rock art displays and excellent prehistory exhibits of the archaeological discoveries of Richard and Mary Leakey. When working near Lake Turkana in the 1960s, the Leakeys discovered the skull and bones of *Homo habilis,* believed to be the ancestor of early humankind. Their findings established the Rift Valley as the possible Cradle of Humankind, although both South Africa's Sterkfontein Caves and Ethiopia's Hadar region claim the same distinction. There are also excellent paintings by Joy Adamson, better known as the author of *Born Free,* and a good collection of Kenya's birds and butterflies. The Kenya Museum Society takes guided bird walks every Wednesday morning at 8:45. There are some good craft shops and a museum shop, and it's worthwhile popping in to the Kuona Trust, the part of the museum that showcases young Kenyan artists. ⊠ *Museum Hill, off Chiromo St., Nairobi* ☎ *020/374–2161 or 020/374–2131* ⊕ *www.museums.or.ke* ✉ *Ksh 800* ⊙ *Daily 8:30–5:30.*

Nairobi National Park. ⇨ *See If You Have Time, above, for more information about this park.*

Karen Blixen Museum. *Out of Africa* author Karen Blixen lived in this estate from 1913 to 1931. This is where she threw a grand dinner party for the Prince of Wales and where she carried on a torrid relationship with aviator Denys Finch Hatton. The museum contains a few of her belongings and some of the farm machinery she used to cultivate the land for coffee and tea. There's also some of her furniture, but most of it is found in the McMillan Library in Nairobi. There is a magnificent view of the surrounding hills from her lawn, which is dominated by euphorbia, the many-armed plant widely known as the candelabra cactus. On the way to the museum you may notice a signpost reading NDEGE. On this road, whose Swahili name means "bird," Finch Hatton once landed his plane for his visits with Blixen. After his plane crashed in Voi, he was buried nearby in the Ngong Hills. Guides will take you on a tour of the garden and the house, but there is little reference to the literary works by Blixen, who wrote under the pen name Isak Dinesen. ⊠ *Karen Rd., Karen* ☎ *02/800–2139* ⊕ *www.museums.or.ke* ✉ *Ksh 800* ⊙ *Daily 9–6.*

WORTH NOTING

City Market. Designed in 1930 as an aircraft hangar, this vast space is a jumble of color, noise, and activity. Head to the balcony to view the flower, fruit, and vegetable stands on the main level. Outside the market entrance is Biashara Street, where you'll find all sorts of tailors, haberdashers, and seamstresses. Look for *kikois* and *kangas,* traditional fabrics worn by Kenyan women. They make for colorful sarongs that are good for wearing over a bathing suit or throwing over a picnic table. They're half the price here than in the hotel shops. ⊠ *Muindi Mbingu St.* ☎ *No phone* ✉ *Free* ⊙ *Mon.–Sat. 8–4.*

⟳ **Railway Museum.** Established to preserve relics and records of East African railways and harbors, this museum is enormous fun for rail enthusiasts and children of all ages. You can see the rhino catcher that Teddy Roosevelt rode during his 1908 safari and climb into the carriage where Charles Ryall, a British railroad builder, was dragged out a window by a hungry lion. There are great photos and posters, plus silver service from the more elegant days of the overnight train to Mombasa. Rides on steam trains take place on the second Saturday of each month. ⊠ *Station Rd. near Uhuru Hwy.* ☎ *020/222–1211* ⌗ *Ksh 400* ⊙ *Daily 8:15–5.*

OFF THE BEATEN PATH

Olorgesailie. Set in the eastern branch of the Great Rift Valley, Olorgesailie is one of Kenya's best-known archaeological sites. Discovered in 1919 by geologist J. W. Gregory, the area was excavated by Louis and Mary Leakey in the 1940s. They discovered tools thought to have been made by residents of the region more than a half million years ago. A small museum shows some of the axes and other tools found nearby. The journey here is unforgettable. As you drive south on Magadi Road, you'll find that past the town of Kiserian the route climbs over the southern end of the Ngong Hills, affording fine views of the entire valley. Volcanic hills rise out of the plains as the road drops into dry country where the Masai people graze their herds. ⊠ *65 km (40 mi) south of Nairobi* ☎ *02/742–131* ⊕ *www.museums.or.ke* ⌗ *Ksh 500* ⊙ *Daily 9–6.*

WHERE TO EAT

$$
STEAKHOUSE

✕ **Carnivore.** A firm fixture on the tourist trail, Carnivore became famous for serving wild game. Although this is no longer the case, you can still get crocodile, camel, and ostrich as well as beef and lamb. The emphasis, as ever, is firmly on meat, and lots of it. Waiters carry the sizzling meat to your table on long skewers and carve whatever you wish onto the cast-iron platters that serve as plates. Only when you offer a little white flag of surrender do they stop carving. As strange as it may seem, there are also many excellent choices for vegetarians. There's an à la carte option if you feel your appetite may not be equal to the set menu. ⊠ *Langata Rd., between Nairobi and Langata* ☎ *02/600–5933* ⊕ *www. tamarind.co.ke* ⌂ *Reservations essential* ▭ *AE, DC, MC, V.*

$$
MEDITERRANEAN

✕ **Moonflower.** Although the road leading here is steep and bumpy, once you're inside the property (Moonflower is part of the Palacina Hotel), you will find the restaurant a tranquil oasis. Tables are on an open-air patio, looking out onto trees and next to a soothing fountain. The menu is mainly Mediterranean with Swahili touches and is wonderfully varied, ranging from salads (Niçoise, grilled chicken, couscous) to burgers, steaks, pasta, and chicken. Fish dishes include red snapper with lime hollandaise, and there are some good vegetarian options. Lunchtime is popular with local businessmen, and a jazz band plays on Wednesday, Friday, and Saturday nights. The Palacina Hotel ($$) is has tastefully decorated rooms and all modern amenities. ⊠ *Palacina Hotel, Kitale Ln., off Denis Pritt Rd., Kilimani* ☎ *20/251–7717* ⊕ *www.palacina. com/moonflower* ▭ *AE, MC, V.*

$$$
SEAFOOD

✕ **Tamarind.** Hands down the finest seafood restaurant in town, Tamarind is famous for its deep-fried crab claws, ginger crab, and *piri piri* (spicy, buttery prawns grilled over charcoal). Everything is flown up

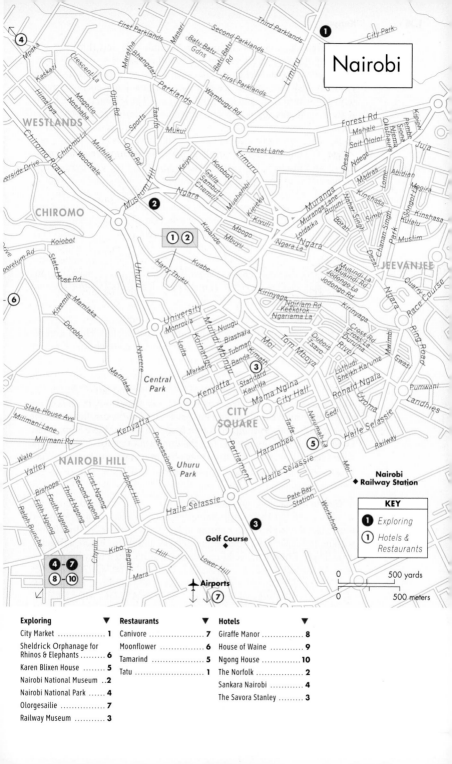

Nairobi

daily from the coast, including the Malindi sole and the Kilifi oysters, tiny but very flavorful and served either raw or as classic oysters Rockefeller. Try the delicious *kokonda,* based on a famous dish from Fiji—raw fish and shrimp are marinated in lime juice, coconut cream, fennel, mustard seed, and local chili peppers. The setting is quite lovely, with stained glass by renowned Kenya artist Nani Croze. ⊠ *National Bank of Kenya, Harambee Ave.* ☎ *20/225–1811* ⊕ *www.tamarind. co.ke* ⌲ *Reservations essential* ⊟ *AE, DC, MC, V.*

$$
STEAKHOUSE

✕ **Tatu.** The interior of the Norfolk Hotel's fine-dining restaurant is minimalist and modern, with large black-and-white prints of tribespeople on the walls, an open-plan kitchen, leather tablecloths, and soft lighting in muted shades of orange, yellow, and green. The menu specializes in steaks, with some interesting sides, such as truffled Parmesan fries and mac and cheese. There's a fantastic selection of seafood, too, including Mombasa spiny lobster, giant tiger prawns, Nile perch, and classic comfort dishes such as chicken potpie. The wine list features New World labels with a good selection by the glass. Waitresses in beautiful kanga-print dresses round off what is altogether a very elegant dining experience. ⊠ *Norfolk Hotel, Harry Thuku Rd.* ☎ *20/250–900* ⊕ *www. fairmont.com* ⊟ *AE, DC, MC, V.*

WHERE TO STAY

The two landmark lodgings in the capital, the Norfolk Hotel and the Sarova Stanley Hotel, have thrown their doors open to visitors for more than a century. Both have been renovated in recent years and now have everything from health clubs to business centers. Newer luxury hotels, such as Sankara Nairobi, are giving them a run for their money.

Although corporate travelers may need to stay in Nairobi, those wishing to get away from the hustle and bustle can head to the distilled air of the Ngong Hills, which prompted Karen Blixen to write, "Here I am, where I ought to be." Many visitors feel the same affinity with this landscape where several country establishments offer more peaceful surroundings.

Lodging reviews have been abbreviated in this book. For expanded reviews, please go to Fodors.com.

$$$$

Giraffe Manor. Yes, giraffes really do pop their heads through the windows and bat their improbable eyelashes at you at this stately old look-alike gabled Scottish hunting lodge. **Pros:** the rate is all-inclusive, with no hidden extras; nonguests can book a table for lunch, subject to availability. **Cons:** you need to book ahead as it's often fully booked; no pool. ⊠ *Koitobos Rd., Karen, Nairobi* ☎ *020/89–1078, 020/89–0949, or 073/281–2896* ⊕ *www.giraffemanor.com* ⤳ *6 rooms* ⌂ *In-room: no a/c, safe, no TV. In-hotel: restaurant, Wi-Fi* ⊟ *AE, DC, MC, V* ⊺◯⫶*AI.*

$$$

House of Waine. You'll find nostalgia, history, and romantic surroundings at this family-owned boutique hotel. **Pros:** there's a full-board or bed-and-breakfast option; rooms are very large; the swimming pool is heated. **Cons:** the dining room needs updating; the wooden floors can be noisy. ⊠ *Near junction of Masai La. and Bogani Rd. 20/260–1455 or 20/89–1553* ⊕ *www.houseofwaine.com* ⤳ *11 suites* ⌂ *In-room: safe, Wi-Fi. In-hotel: restaurant, bar, pool* ⊟ *AE, MC, V* ⊺◯⫶*FAP.*

$$$$ Ngong House. A contrast to the
rather grand, colonial-era hotels
such as the Norfolk and Stanley,
Ngong House is a fabulous boutique hotel located in the quiet suburb of Karen. **Pros:** the design of the
treehouses is wonderfully quirky;
guests are invited to gather by
the bonfire for pre-dinner drinks.
Cons: the pool is small; no a/c.
⊠ *Ngong Road, Karen 020/891–
856 or 0722/434–965* ⊕ *www.
ngonghouse.com* ⤸ *9 rooms* ⅁ *In-
room: no a/c, safe, no TV, Wi-Fi.
In-hotel: restaurant, bar, pool*
▤ *AE, DC, MC, V* ⅣⓄⅠ *BP, MAP,
FAP.*

$$$$ The Norfolk Hotel. This grand old colonial lady will take you back to
the heady early days when settlers, adventurers, colonial officers, and
their ladies arrived in the capital to make their names and their fortunes. **Pros:** the breakfast buffet is the best in town; the terrace is a great
place to watch the world go by. **Cons:** Internet use is not free; some of
the older rooms need updating. ⊠ *Harry Thuku Rd. 020/221–6940;
866/840–8208 toll-free in U.S.* ⊕ *www.fairmont.com* ⤸ *129 rooms, 18
suites, 6 luxury cottages* ⅁ *In-room: safe, Wi-Fi. In-hotel: restaurant,
bar, pool* ▤ *AE, DC, MC, V* ⅣⓄⅠ*FAP.*

$ Sankara Nairobi. This stylish city hotel is conveniently located in West-
lands, close to a number of restaurants and shopping centers, although
you will find all you need for a relaxing stay in the hotel itself. **Pros:**
varied dining options; the hotel has been beautifully designed. **Cons:** the
pool is small; spa treatments are expensive. ⊠ *Woodvale Grove, West-
lands* ☎ *020/420–8000 or 020/249–0210* ⊕ *www.sankara.com* ⤸ *156
rooms* ⅁ *In-room: safe, Wi-Fi, DVD. In-hotel: restaurant, bar, pool,
gym, spa* ▤ *AE, DC, MC, V* ⅣⓄⅠ*BP.*

$ The Sarova Stanley. Also one of Nairobi's oldest hotels, the Stanley
was named after the journalist Henry Morton Stanley who immortal-
ized himself by discovering a long-lost Scots explorer with one of the
best sound bites in history: "Dr. Livingstone, I presume?" **Pros:** security is good; the pool is heated. **Cons:** it's right in the hustle and bustle
of downtown Nairobi; standard rooms are small. ⊠ *Corner Kenyatta
Ave. and Kimati St. 020/316–377* ⊕ *www.sarova.co.ke* ⤸ *217 rooms*
⅁ *In-room: safe, Wi-Fi. In-hotel: restaurant, bar, pool, gym* ▤ *AE, DC,
MC, V* ⅣⓄⅠ*BP.*

BEACH ESCAPES

Intricately carved doorways studded with brass and white walls draped with bougainvillea distinguish the towns that dot Kenya's coastline. Arab traders who landed on these shores in the 9th century brought their own culture, so the streets are dominated by a different style of dress and architecture from what you see in other parts of Kenya. Men stroll the streets wearing traditional caps called *kofias* and billowing caftans known as *khanzus,* while women cover their faces with black veils called *bui-buis* that reveal only their sparkling eyes.

The creation of Swahili, a combination of Arabic and African Bantu, came about when Arab traders married African women. Swahili comes from the Arabic words *sahil,* meaning "coast," and *i,* meaning "of the." As seductive as the rhythm of the sea, Swahili is one of the most melodic tongues on earth. The coastal communities of Lamu, Malindi, and Mombasa are strongholds of the language that once dominated communities from Somalia to Mozambique.

Mombasa, the country's second-largest city, was once the gateway to East Africa. Karen Blixen described people arriving and departing by ship in the book *Out of Africa.* Mombasa's harbor still attracts a few large cruise ships, but nothing like the hundreds that sailed here before World War I. In Lamu, a Swahili proverb prevails: *Haraka haraka haina baraka* (Haste, haste, brings no blessing). The best-preserved Swahili town in Kenya, Lamu has streets hardly wide enough for a donkey cart. Narrow, winding alleyways are lined with houses set tight against one another. It is said that the beautifully carved doors found here are built first, then the house constructed around them. By the same token, a mosque is built first, and the town follows. Due north—the direction of Mecca—is easy to discern because of the town's orientation.

Azure waters from Lamu to Wasini are protected by the 240-km (150-mi) coral reef that runs parallel to the coast. Broken only where rivers cut through it, the reef is home to hundreds of species of tropical fish. The beaches themselves have calm and clear waters that hover around 27°C (80°F). As Ernest Hemingway put it, "The endless sand, the reefs, the lot, are completely unmatched in the world."

Be sure to get your feet in this ivory white sand. A few days at the coast is an ideal way to round off a safari trip.

PLANNING

GETTING HERE AND AROUND

Getting to the towns along the Kenya Coast is easier than ever. Mombasa has an international airport, but you can fly directly to Malindi, Diani Beach, or Lamu. Travel by car around Mombasa is fairly safe, but the road to Lamu has been plagued by armed robberies. Avoid this route if at all possible.

RESTAURANTS

The excellent cuisine reflects the region's rich history. Thanks to Italians, basil is everywhere, along with olive oil, garlic, and fresh lettuce. The Portuguese introduced tomatoes, corn, and cashews. Everything is combined with pungent spices such as coriander and ginger and the rich coconut milk often used as a cooking broth.

The Indian Ocean delivers some of the world's best fishing, so marlin, sailfish, swordfish, kingfish, and many other types of fish are on every menu. Not surprisingly, sashimi made from yellowtail tuna is favored by connoisseurs (and was listed on menus here as "fish tartare" before the rest of the world discovered Japanese cuisine). Prawns can be gargantuan, and wild oysters are small and sweet. Diving for your own lobster is an adventure, but you will easily find young boys happy to deliver fresh seafood to your door. You can even place your order for the next day.

HOTELS

Accommodations along the Kenya Coast range from sprawling resorts with several restaurants to small beach houses with kitchens where you can prepare your own meals. To really get a sense of the region, consider staying in a private home. Most accommodations along the coast can arrange snorkeling, windsurfing, waterskiing, and deep-sea fishing.

MOMBASA

You may well find yourself in Mombasa for a few hours or an overnight stop. The city (which is actually an island linked to the mainland by a ferry) is a strange mixture of culture, religion, and history—it's the second oldest trade center with Arabia and the Far East. Today it still plays an important role as the main port for Kenya. Although it lacks the beautiful beaches of the north and south, it has a rich, fascinating history. Visit the Old Town with its Arab influence, narrow streets lined with tiny shops and souks (markets), where you can watch an appealing array of traditions and maybe see a belly dancer performing her rhythmic enticing talents in one of the numerous cafés. The Old Harbour, frequented by numerous dhows, is an ideal place to arrange a short cruise on one of these local boats that have plied the oceans for centuries. Fort Jesus, designed by an Italian and built by the Portuguese in the late 16th century, is a major visitor draw and well worth a visit. In summer there's an impressive sound and light show.

GETTING HERE AND AROUND

Kenya Airways and Fly540 have daily flights between Nairobi and Mombasa, and from Mombasa you can fly to Malindi and Lamu. Safaris to Tsavo East or Tsavo West can also depart from here. The airport is located 10 km (6 mi) from the city center, on the mainland. Several taxi companies operate from the airport and have fixed rates to either the center of town or the beach resorts. You can also arrange for your hotel to pick you up.

Taxis in Mombasa are inexpensive. The drivers are friendly and helpful and will wait or return to collect you if you ask.

MONEY MATTERS

Barclay's Bank has several ATMs in Mombasa. There's one on Malindi Road, on Kenyatta Avenue near Digo Road, on Nkrumah Road near Fort Jesus, and on the main road out of Mombasa to Nairobi. If you want to change money, Forex Bureau has exchange shops on Digo Road near the Municipal Market and near the entrance of Fort Jesus.

SAFETY

The best way to see Mombasa is on foot, but you should not walk around at night. If you take a taxi at night, make sure it delivers you all the way to the door of your destination. Purse snatchers are all too common. Beware of people who might approach you on Mombasa's Moi Avenue offering to become your guide. Tell them "*Hapana, asante sana*" ("No, thank you") and move on.

VISITOR INFORMATION

Mombasa Coast Tourist Information (MCTA), near the Tusks, sells books on city sights such as Fort Jesus. It's open weekdays 8–4:30 and Saturday 8–12:30. The best map is *The Streets of Mombasa Island*, which sells for Ksh 500 ($7.50).

ESSENTIALS

Emergencies Emergency Hotline (☎ 999 from a Kenyan landline; 112 from a mobile phone). **Mombasa Central Police Station** (☎ 041/225–501). **Tourist 24-hour Helpline** (☎ 020/604–767 or 020/605–485).

Hospitals Aga Khan Hospital (✉ Vanga Rd., Kizingo, Mombasa ☎ 041/222–7710). **Pandya Memorial Hospital** (✉ Dedan Kimathi Rd. ☎ 041/231–3577).

Taxis Kenatco Taxis Ltd (✉ Ambalal House, Mombasa Trade Centre, Nkrumah Rd. ☎ 041/222–7503).

Visitor Info Mombasa Coast Tourism Association (✉ Moi Ave. Mombasa ☎ 041/222–5428 ✍ mcta@africaonline.co.ke).

THE BEACH BOYS

The hawkers and hustlers known as "beach boys" are the scourge of Kenya's coastline, although their numbers have reportedly dwindled. They sell everything from boat rides and souvenirs to drugs and sex, and their incessant pestering can ruin a beach walk (hotels employ guards to keep them off their premises, so you're okay when you're in your hotel grounds). A strategy may be to go on a boat trip or purchase something from one of them, and in theory, the rest should leave you alone. Otherwise, be firm and don't engage if you're not interested. The problem is far less pronounced in Lamu.

EXPLORING

Anglican Cathedral. Built in the early part of the last century, the cathedral is a memorial to Archbishop James Hannington, a missionary who was executed in 1885. The influence of Middle Eastern Islamic architecture is clear in the frieze, the dome, and the tall, narrow windows. The paneling behind the high altar is reminiscent of the cathedral in Stone Town. ⊠ *Nkrumah Rd. and Cathedral Rd.*

Basheikh Mosque. Like other Swahili towns, Mombasa probably had a Muslim community from the time it was founded. This mosque, painted cream and white, is said to be built on a foundation dating from the 11th century. Its purposeful square facade reflects the best in Islamic architecture. ⊠ *Old Kilindini Rd. at Kibokoni Rd.*

Fort Jesus. This massive edifice was built in the late 16th century by the Portuguese, who were keen to control trade in the region. When the Omanis captured the fort at the end of the 17th century, they made some adjustments. The walls were raised to account for the improved trajectory of cannons mounted aboard attacking ships. By the end of the 18th century, turrets were erected. For water, the garrison relied on wells. There is a large pit cistern in the center of the compound, which some guides say was the bath of the harem—an intriguing notion. The captain's house retains some traces of the Portuguese—note the outline of the old colonnade. The exhibits at the museum include an important display on ceramics of the coast, beautiful carved doors studded with brass, and the remains of a Portuguese gunner, *San Antonio de Tanna*, which sank outside the fort at the end of the 17th century. Objects from the ship—shoes, glass bottles, a powder shovel, and cannon with its muzzle blown away—bring the period to life. There are also exhibits of finds from archaeological excavations at Gedi, Manda, Ungwana, and other sites. ⊠ *End of Nkrumah Rd.* 🖃 *Ksh 800* ⊗ *Daily 8–6.*

Moi Avenue. Like to shop? The city's most popular shopping strip is also the city's main thoroughfare Moi Avenue, famous for the two pairs of giant tusks that dominate the road. The section of road between the tusks and Digo Road (bullets 5 and 6 on the map) has a number of curio booths and souvenir stands. Harria's Gift Shop, just before the Tusks, is a good place to get an idea of what's on offer and prices. Good items to buy are woven baskets, carvings, and beadwork. You'll have to bargain hard, but it's more relaxed here than in Nairobi. ⊠ *Moi Ave.*

New Burhani Bohra Mosque. The elaborate facade and soaring minaret of this mosque overlook the Old Harbor. Built in 1902, it's the third mosque to occupy this site. ⊠ *Buchuma Rd..*

Tusks. Dominating Moi Avenue are the famous elephant tusks that cross above the roadway. They were erected to commemorate the 1952 visit of Britain's Princess Elizabeth, now Queen Elizabeth II. Up close, they can be somewhat disappointing, as they are made of aluminum. ⊠ *Moi Ave. at Uhuru Gardens.*

WHERE TO EAT AND STAY

Lodging reviews have been abbreviated in this book. For expanded reviews, please go to Fodors.com.

$ ✕ **Blue Room.** Famous for its *bhajias* (deep-fried pastries filled with veg-
INDIAN etables), this family-owned Indian restaurant has been in business for
more than 50 years. It seats 140 people, making it one of the largest
restaurants in the city. The menu features more than 65 items of both
Western and Indian origin, and its bright clean interior with tiled floors
and plenty of chairs and tables keeps people coming. The curries and
Indian vegetarian dishes are especially good, as are the tasty snacks. Try
the samosas, kebabs, or even fish-and-chips. There's also an ice-cream
parlor and DVD-rental shop. You'll find a cybercafé inside, where you
can send an e-mail back home. ⊠ *Intersection of Haile Selassie Rd. and
Digo Rd.* ☎ *011/2224–021* ⊕ *www.blueroomonline.com* ⊟ *No credit
cards* ⊗ *Daily 9* AM*–10* PM.

$$ ✕ **Hunter's Bar.** This small, intimate international restaurant is one of
STEAKHOUSE Mombasa's best, very popular with foreign visitors and Mombasa's
expatriates. With trophy animals mounted on the walls, the place
resembles a hunting lodge. Although it serves a wide range of dishes
including excellent seafood and venison, Hunter's is best known for
its mouthwatering steaks and homemade desserts like apple pie. It's
also a good place to stop for a cold beer. ⊠ *M. Mkomani Rd., Nyali*
☎ *011/471–771* ⊟ *DC, V* ⊗ *Closed Sun.*

$$$ ✕ **Tamarind.** What the Carnivore restaurant does for meat in Nairobi,
SEAFOOD this fine restaurant does for seafood in Mombasa. A 15-minute drive
from downtown and a welcome house cocktail—a *dawa* made of lime,
vodka, honey, and crushed ice—will introduce you to a memorable
meal and unforgettable experience. Overlooking a creek flowing into
the sea, the restaurant is designed like an old Moorish palace with
fountains, high arches, and tiled floors. If you love seafood, you'll be
in heaven. You can also take a lunch- or dinner-dhow cruise ($75 for
a set menu) around Tudor Creek and soak up some sun and sea air by
day, or watch the moon rise over Mombasa Old Town by night, as soft
Swahili music makes the food and wine go down even better. ⊠ *Silo
Rd., Nyali* ☎ *041/471–747 or 0733/623–583* ⊕ *tamarind.co.ke* ⊟ *AE,
DC, MC, V* ⊗ *12:30–2:30* PM*, 7–10:30* PM.

¢ ⌂ **Castle Royal Hotel.** Originally built in 1919, this gleaming white old
colonial building is in Mombasa's town center only a short distance
away from the old town and Fort Jesus. **Pros:** the central location is
unbeatable; rooms have fridges. **Cons:** some of the rooms are very noisy;
there's hot water in the mornings and evenings only. ⊠ *Moi St., Central
Mombasa* ☎ *041/222–8780* ⊕ *www.sentrim-hotels.com* ⇱ *48 rooms*
⌂ *In-room: safe. In-hotel: restaurant, bar* ⊟ *AE, DC, MC, V* ⊙| *BP.*

$$$$ ⌂ **The Serena Beach Hotel and Spa.** This gorgeous resort at Shanzu Beach
was built to resemble a 13th-century Arab town. **Pros:** there's a free
daily shuttle to Mombasa town; the spa is good. **Cons:** the pool is
small; Internet is not free. ☎ *050/22059 or 020/284–2000* ⊕ *www.
serenahotels.com* ⇱ *166 rooms* ⌂ *In-room: safe. In-hotel: restaurant,
bar, tennis court, pool, spa* ⊟ *AE, DC, MC, V* ⊙| *MAP.*

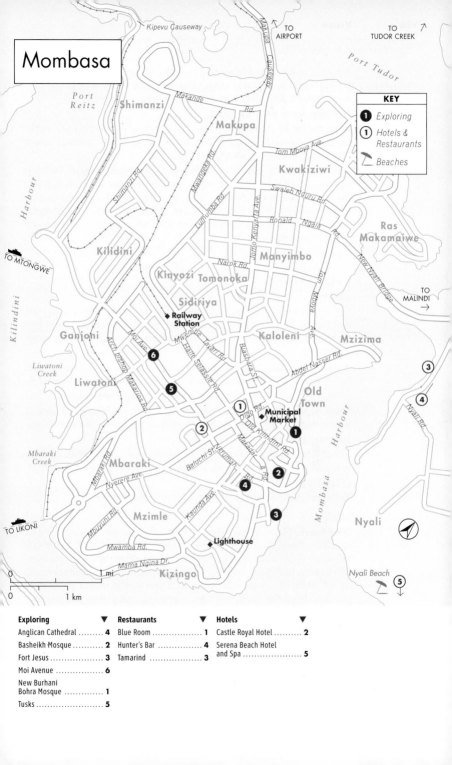

Mombasa

SOUTHERN BEACHES

Kenya's coast south of Mombasa has some of the country's most beautiful beaches. The highway from Mombasa runs all the way to the Tanzania border, providing easy access to a string of resorts.

GETTING HERE AND AROUND

Most people fly into Mombasa's Moi International Airport and make their way down the coast by taxi, rental car, or hotel shuttle. There is an airstrip at Ukunda for charter flights.

You must take the Likoni Ferry to travel south of Mombasa. Two ferries run simultaneously, departing about 20 minutes apart, with fewer departures late in the day and in the evening. Vehicles are charged by length, usually about Ksh 90 per car. Pedestrians ride free. Matatus leave the city center (in front of the post office) on a regular basis down to the ferry terminal.

MONEY MATTERS

Barclay's Bank has an ATM in Ukunda, north of the junction headed for Diani Beach.

SAFETY

If you take a taxi at night, make sure it delivers you all the way to your destination. Tourist Police officers patrol beaches, but don't tempt fate by bringing jewelry, cameras, or cash. Women should not walk alone on the beach.

If you are walking from Tiwi to Diani, consult the tidal chart beforehand. A creek that you must swim across at high tide is known as "Panga Point," after the machete used as a weapon by muggers.

Drink plenty of bottled water and wear sunscreen. It's a good idea to wear a thick T-shirt to protect your back from sunburn when snorkeling.

TELEPHONES

The city code for Diani Beach and the surrounding communities is 040. If you are calling from outside Kenya, drop the "0" in the city code.

ESSENTIALS

Visitor Info Ukuna Tourism (✉ *Private Safaris Bldg., Ukunda Rd.*).

BEACHES

Diani Beach. Once a true tropical Eden with gorgeous weather and equally gorgeous scenery this 20-km (12-mi) stretch of sand, 30 km (19 mi) south of Mombasa, is the most developed along the southern coast. One reason that it's so popular is that the reef filters out the seaweed, so the sandy shores are truly pristine. If you stay in one of the private cottages, local fishermen will take your order and deliver lobsters and other delicacies of the deep to your door.

Shimon. Just 60 km (37 mi) south of Diani, on the tip of a peninsula known for its excellent deep-sea fishing you'll find the village of Shimoni, which means "place of the holes." Ocean currents dug out a maze of coral caves, one of them 11 km (7 mi) long. This catacomb was used as an underground tunnel for loading slaves onto dhows. You can see iron shackles that still remain on the cave walls.

EXPLORING

Mwana Mosque. This well-preserved 16th-century mosque, also known as Kongo Mosque or Diani Persian Mosque, stands at the mouth of the Mwachema River. The high-ceilinged prayer room is still used regularly by worshippers. The mosque is surrounded by baobab trees, which grow to great size here since there are no elephants to root them out. ■TIP→ It's respectful for lady visitors to cover their heads, shoulders, and knees in whatever mosque they visit. A good tip is to carry a scarf and a kikoi to wrap around the body if necessary. A small donation is required. ⊠ *In baobab grove between Diani and Tiwi, accessed through the grounds of the Indian Ocean Beach Resort.*

Jadini Forest. You'll find the remains of the Jadini Forest, which once covered the whole of the coastal area, at the southern end of Diani. It's home to vervet monkeys, troops of baboons, and endangered Angolan black-and-white colobus monkeys, as well as butterflies and birds. It's a great place for a picnic with lots of nature trails, but watch out for thieving monkeys! The Colobus Trust offers one-hour guided primate walks (US$5) as well as 1½-hour night walks (US$7) where you can see bush babies as well as monkeys. ⊠ *Close to Papillon Beach* ☎ *0711/479–453* 🖃 *US$5* ☉ *Mon.–Sat. 8–5.*

Kisite-Mpunguti Marine National Park. A few miles off the coast, this 28-square-km (11-square-mi) national park is known for its beautiful coral gardens. Staghorn, brain, mushroom, and pencil are just a few of the ore than 40 varieties of coral that have been identified. And more than 250 species of fish have been spotted feeding around the reef, including butterfly fish, parrot fish, and angelfish. Humpback dolphins are a common sight, as are big schools of bonitos and frigate mackerels. The entire protected area, just past Wasini Island, is in shallow water and can be easily reached by motor boat or dhow. You can arrange a day-trip from boat captains at the dock in Shimoni. ⊠ *4–8 km (2–5 mi) from Shimoni* ⊕ *www.kws.org* 🖃 *$20.*

Wasini Island. Take a walk to the ancient Arab settlement near the modern village of Wasini Island. Here you'll find the ruins of 18th- and 19th-century houses and a Muslim pillar tomb inset with Chinese porcelain. If you're into snorkeling or diving, make this a definite stop. You can book an excursion or hire a motorboat from Ksh 1,500 to Ksh 3,000 one-way. Remember to dress respectfully when walking around the village. ⊠ *1 km (½ mi) from Shimoni* ☎ *040/52410* ⊕ *www.wasini-island.com.*

WHERE TO EAT

$ ✕ **African Pot.** This relaxed beach-
AFRICAN front restaurant, made of thatch
and wood, is in front of the Coral
Beach cottages, 300 meters (984
feet) north of Ukunda junction,
Diani Beach. It serves excellent
Swahili food, including the traditional *ugali*—some say it's the
inspiration for grits—greens, and
gumbo. Live African music is occa-
sionally featured here. ⊠ *Near entrance to Coral Beach Cottages, Diani*
☎ *040/320–3890* ▤ *No credit cards.*

WORD OF MOUTH

"There are some beautiful beach resorts on the Kenyan coast, including Alfajiri on the Diani Coast south of Mombasa. There's also Lamu and Manda Islands north of Mombasa and very remote and romantic." —sandi

$$ ✕ **Ali Barbour's Cave.** You can dine in a naturally formed cave deep
FRENCH underground or on an outdoor terrace at this popular seafood restau-
rant. You can't go wrong with the crab salad marinated with lemon and
chilies. You can also choose excellent French food. There is a shuttle
bus that will pick up people staying in the Diani Beach area. ⊠ *Be-*
tween Diani Sea Lodge and Trade Winds ☎ *040/320–2033* ⊕ *www.*
dianibeachkenya.com ⌁ *Reservations essential* ▤ *AE, DC, MC, V.*

$ ✕ **Sundowner.** This cheap but cheerful thatch bar and eatery is a five-
AFRICAN minute walk from the Diani Beach Chalets. It serves good seafood,
including grilled and fried fish, tasty local food and curries, and an
excellent English breakfast. Local beer and drinks are also cheap here.
⊠ *Southern end of Diani Beach* ☎ *No phone* ▤ *No credit cards.*

WHERE TO STAY

It may seem odd that there are no addresses listed for the hotels in this
section, but this is the norm. Most of the hotels and resorts are located
on one or two roads running parallel to the beach. The properties are
not usually numbered, so landmarks are used to guide people instead.
Everyone knows where all the places are, so you don't need to instruct
a taxi driver with specific details.

Lodging reviews have been abbreviated in this book. For expanded
reviews, please go to Fodors.com.

$$$$ ▥ **Alfajiri Beach Villa.** Built of stone and thatch, these double-story villas
are some of the most luxurious villas in the world, and are elegantly
furnished with the wit and style you would expect of owner and host
Marika Molinaro, one of Kenya's top interior designers. **Pros:** daily
menus are tailored to your preferences; villas have private pools. **Cons:**
the beach next to the hotel is not suitable for swimming; you may find
you don't use all the included activities, such as golf, gym, and yoga.
☎ *0733/630–491 or 0722/727–876* ⊕ *www.alfajirivillas.com* ⤳ *3 villas*
⌂ *In-hotel: restaurant, bar, pool* ▤ *AE, DC, MC, V* ⦿ *FAP.*

$$$ ▥ **Diani Reef Beach Resort and Spa.** This luxurious resort will make sure you
get the best out of your beach break. **Pros:** the staff are extremely friendly;
organized activities are good. **Cons:** wine and Internet use is expensive;
resident monkeys can be annoying. ☎ *040/320–2723 or 040/320–3308*
⊕ *www.dianireef.com* ⤳ *300 rooms* ⌂ *In-room: safe, Wi-Fi. In-hotel: res-*
taurant, bar, tennis court, pool ▤ *AE, DC, MC, V* ⦿ *MAP.*

$$$$ ⊤ **Indian Ocean Beach Resort.** This beachfront resort stretches for 500 meters (1,640 feet) along the Indian Ocean amid 10 hectares (25 acres) of indigenous gardens. **Pros:** security staff keep the beach vendors away; the staff set up dining areas in different parts of the resort. **Cons:** use of the safe is extra; alcohol is expensive. ☎ *040/320–3730* ⊕ *www. jacarandahotels.com* ↬ *100 rooms* ♿ *In-room: safe. In-hotel: 3 restaurants, bars, tennis court, pool* ▭ *AE, DC, MC, V* ❙❂❙ *MAP.*

MALINDI

3

Malindi, the country's second largest coastal town, is 120 km (75 mi) north of Mombasa and has been an important port for hundreds of years. In ancient Chinese documents, "Ma Lin De" is referred to as a stop on the trade route. The town battled with Mombasa for control of the coast, which explains why Portuguese explorer Vasco da Gama received such a warm welcome when he landed here in 1498 but was given the cold shoulder in Mombasa. The Vasco da Gama Cross, made from Portuguese stone, sits on a promontory on the southern tip of the bay. Malindi has become very much an Italian holiday destination, and although it is laid-back, it has a somewhat seedy atmosphere, and sex tourism is rife. That being said, the beaches are picture-postcard-perfect, with white sand and coconut palms, there are some good restaurants in the town and some excellent resort hotels. Old Town is a great place to hunt for colorful fabrics, antiques, and sandals, and the beach is clean and attractive, although it does get a bit seaweedy in spring. Malindi has two nearby parks, Malindi and Watamu. These are marine parks, where you can watch fish and corals from a glass-bottom boat or snorkel, but the collection or destruction of shells is strictly forbidden. It also offers deep-sea fishing and other water sports. It's an easy place to get around because there are lots of *tuk tuks* (auto rickshaw) and *boda bodas* (bicycle taxis), which are everywhere day and night.

GETTING HERE AND AROUND

Kenya Airways and Fly540 fly to Malindi frequently.

Taxis are inexpensive. The drivers are friendly and helpful and will wait or return to collect you if you ask. There are lots of tuk tuks, and although the journey can be bumpy, they're an easy and inexpensive way to get around town.

MONEY MATTERS

In Malindi, there are several ATMS dotted around the town, including at the Barclay's Bank.

SAFETY

The best way to see Malindi is on foot, but you should not walk around at night. If you take a taxi at night, make sure it delivers you all the way to the door of your destination. Purse snatchers are all too common.

ESSENTIALS

Visitor Info Malindi Tourist Office (✉ *Malindi Complex, Lamu Rd., Malindi* ☎ *No phone* ⊕ *www.malindikenya.com*).

EXPLORING

Jamaa Mosque. The 14th-century tombs beside this mosque are among the oldest in Malindi. It was here in the 1800s that slaves were auctioned weekly until 1873. ⊠ *Near Uhuru Park.*

Malindi Marine Park. Home to an impressive variety of colorful coral, you'll find two main reefs here that are separated by a deep sandy-bottom channel. There's very little commercial fishing in the area, which means the kingfish found here are trophy size. The water ranges from 25°C (77°F) to 29°C (84 °F), making this a particularly pleasant place to snorkel or scuba dive. If you want to stay dry, try one of the glass-bottom boats, although visibility is not generally very good. ⊠ *Offshore from Malindi* ⊕ *www.kws.org* ⊡ *US$15 entry fee* ☉ *Dawn–dusk.*

Malindi Museum. Delve into some of Malindi's fascinating history at this museum, which was once the home of a 19th-century trader. You'll find it on the seafront near the Malindi jetty and the fish market. It has temporary exhibitions and also serves as a visitor information center. ⊕ *www.museums.or.ke* ⊡ *Ksh 500* ☉ *Daily 9–6.*

WHERE TO EAT

$
ITALIAN
✕ **Baby Marrow.** Malindi's fine-dining option is, naturally, Italian owned, so you'll be able to sample prosciutto *e melone,* pizzas, and a variety of pastas (including baby marrow [zucchini] ravioli) alongside such seafood dishes as ginger and black-pepper crab, jumbo prawns, and lobster. Seating is under an attractive thatched roof, and it's rather romantic at night. ⊠ *Vasco da Gama Rd.* ☎ *0733/542–584* ⊟ *No credit cards.*

¢
CAFÉ
✕ **Baobab café.** Eat breakfast, lunch, or dinner or just have a beer or juice at this friendly, cheerful restaurant. There's a choice of soup, burgers, pasta, grills, steak, and seafood. The fish curry is particularly good. ⊠ *On sea front, close to Portuguese church* ☎ *042/31699* ⊟ *No credit cards.*

¢
PIZZA
✕ **I Love Pizza.** Overlooking the bay, this place is famous for its, you guessed it, pizza, although there are also some sophisticated seafood dishes, such as kingfish carpaccio with horseradish, and risotto with clams, prawns, and squid. The calamari salad is excellent. ⊠ *Vasco da Gama Rd.* ☎ *042/20672* ⊟ *No credit cards.*

¢
AFRICAN
✕ **The Old Man and the Sea.** Near the fishing jetty, this stylish former Arab house has been lovingly restored and is known as one of the best places in town for its fresh seafood. Try the marinated prawns wrapped in smoked sailfish, a Malindi specialty, or the red snapper with a champagne sauce. ⊠ *Vasco da Gama Rd.* ☎ *042/213–1106* ⊰ *Reservations essential in high season* ⊟ *MC, V.*

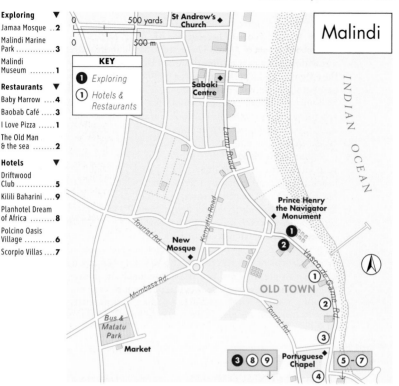

WHERE TO STAY

Rates are very high in season—June through October—but prices drop dramatically off-season. It's best to stick to lodging near the beach as downtown gets noisy, is not always safe, and accommodations can be squalid.

Lodging reviews have been abbreviated in this book. For expanded reviews, please go to Fodors.com.

$ 🏨 **Driftwood Club.** In an attractive garden, these Swahili-style individual bandas, each with a thatch roof and small veranda, are seconds away from the pool and beach. ■ TIP→ **Ask for a banda directly facing the sea. Pros:** there are excellent rates for children; rooms have good a/c. **Cons:** use of the in-room safe is extra; some bandas look out onto the walkway so are not very private. ✛ *3 km (2 mi) south of Malindi* ☎ *042/212–0155 or 0721/724–489* ⊕ *www.driftwoodclub.com* ⤴ *37 rooms* ♿ *In-room: safe, no TV. In-hotel: restaurant, bar, pool* ⊟ *AE, V* ⍾⊙⍾ *BP.*

$$ 🏨 **Kilili Baharini.** This elegant resort, much favored by Italians, is in large grounds amid a profusion of tropical flowering plants 4 km (2½ mi) from Malindi. **Pros:** rooms have a/c; there are five pools. **Cons:** lunch is buffet only; airport transfers not included. ⊠ *Casuarina Rd., Malindi* 🖂 *Box 93, Malindi, Kenya* ☎ *042/212–1264* ⊕ *www.kililibaharini.com*

↝ *29 rooms, 6 suites* ⚘ *In-room: safe. In-hotel: restaurant, bar, pool, spa* ⊟ *AE, V* ⊙ *Closed May–July* ¦⊙¦ *BP, MAP, FAP.*

$$$$ 🏨 **Planhotel Dream of Africa.** There are four Planhotels stretched out in a row down this part of the coast, but Dream of Africa is the jewel in the crown, and the perfect place for a honeymoon or some après-safari pampering. **Pros:** with only 35 rooms, it's one of the smallest hotels in Malindi; all alcohol except premium brands included. **Cons:** the beds are a little hard; rooms do not look out onto the ocean. ⊠ *Casuarina Rd.* ☎ *042/20444* ⊕ *www.planhotel.com* ↝ *35 rooms* ⚘ *In-room: safe, Wi-Fi. In-hotel: restaurant, bar, pool, spa* ⊟ *AE, MC, V* ¦⊙¦ *FAP.*

¢ 🏨 **Polcino Oasis Village.** These white thatch-roof en-suite apartments with kitchenette, sleeping one to three people, are right on Silver Sands beach, 3 km (2 mi) from town. **Pros:** rates include breakfast; the pool is big. **Cons:** it's noisy; apartments are in a four-story block. ⊠ *Tourist Rd.* ☎ *042/31995* ⊕ *www.holidays-kenya.com* ↝ *130 cottages* ⚘ *In-room: safe, no a/c. In-hotel: restaurant, bar, pool* ⊟ *AE, V* ¦⊙¦ *BP.*

¢ 🏨 **Scorpio Villas.** Thatch-roof cottages filled with handcrafted furniture such as huge Zanzibar beds and day couches are scattered around the exotic gardens of this resort near the Vasco da Gama Cross. **Pros:** the half-board option allows you to choose lunch or dinner; rooms have fridges. **Cons:** use of the safe is extra; payment by cash only. ⊠ *Harambee Rd., Malindi* ☎ *042/212–0194* ⊕ *www.scorpiovillas.co.ke* ↝ *25 villas* ⚘ *In-room: no phone, a/c, safe. In-hotel: restaurant, bar, pools* ⊟ *No credit cards* ¦⊙¦ *FAP.*

LAMU

Designated a UNESCO World Heritage Site in December 2001, Lamu Old Town is the oldest and best-preserved Swahili settlement in East Africa. Some 260 km (162 mi) north of Mombasa—and just two degrees below the Equator—Lamu is separated from the mainland by a narrow channel that's fringed with thick mangroves protected from the sea by coral reefs and huge sand dunes. Visit this tiny town and you'll feel like you've gone back in time. Winding narrow alleyways lead past the ornate carved doorways and coral rag walls of magnificent merchant houses to the bustling waterfront. Life goes on much as it did when Lamu was a thriving port town in the 8th century; there are no cars (all transport and heavy lifting is by donkey) and more than 1,000 years of East African, Omani, Yemeni, Indian and Portuguese influence has resulted in a unique mix of cultures, reflected in the faces of its inhabitants as well as the architecture and cuisine. A stronghold of Islam for many centuries, you'll see men in *kofias* (traditional caps that Muslims wear) and *khanzus* (white caftanlike robes Muslim men wear) and women in *bui-buis* (black veils that Muslim women wear). Some merchant houses have been converted into gorgeous boutique hotels, and rooftop restaurants offer abundant, fresh seafood for very little, but be warned, the breeze can bring with it the smell of donkey pats and open drains, along with the haunting sounds of the Muslim call to prayer.

The island is roughly divided into two parts: Lamu Town, in the south, and Shela, a smaller, quieter village in the north and next to the beach. Some visitors split their holiday between staying on both sides of the island, or opt to stay on Manda Island or in further flung hotels on the far northern or southern edges. You can walk between Lamu Town or Shela in about 45 minutes; a popular option is to walk one way and take a boat back. The beach offers 13 km (8 mi) of unspoiled coastline, although it's not the white-sand perfection of Malindi or the Mombasa beaches. Be sure not to stray out of sight if you're on your own. Lamu is generally very safe, but it's best to be careful.

It's very easy to relax into the pole-pole ("slowly" in Swahili) pace of life in Lamu, spending hours on the beach or on your hotel terrace reading a book and sipping on a delicious fresh fruit juice. There is plenty for the energetic to do here, however: you can go windsurfing, kayaking, fishing, snorkeling and, if you're lucky, see pods of wild dolphins or turtles laying their eggs (or hatching) in the sand. You can also take a dhow cruise to visit ancient, mysterious ruins on Pate and Manda Toto islands.

Tourism hasn't made much of an impact on Lamu, and that's what makes it so special, although this sadly won't last forever. Lamu has become a hot destination for global glitterati: Princess Caroline of Monaco has a house here along with any number of other notables. Foreigners are also restoring many of the large coral rag houses, something locals cannot afford to do. In time locals will be priced out of town, and a proposed port, if it does come to be built, will destroy the ambience of the place forever.

GETTING HERE AND AROUND
Flights land on Manda Island, and a speedboat takes about 10 minutes to get to Lamu (your hotel will pick you up). Lamu is a very easy town to get around because it is so small. The cobbled streets are laid out in a grid fashion with the main street, Harambee Avenue, running parallel to the harbor.

Kenya Airways has daily flights from Nairobi. AirKenya has frequent flights to Lamu and Kiwayu from Nairobi, Mombasa, and Malindi. It also offers hops from Lamu to Kiwayu. Fly540 flies here from Nairobi and Malindi.

Most hotels can arrange for a trip by dhow from Lamu to Shela or Matondoni (where you can watch dhows being built). Find out the going price from your accommodation and confirm with the captain before setting out. You can also head to neighboring islands such as Manta, Manda Moto, and Pate. More distant destinations, such as Kiwayu and Kipungani, are more expensive.

FESTIVALS AND SEASONAL EVENTS
The Maulidi festival, marking the birth of Muhammad, has been celebrated on Lamu for more than a century. Dhow races, poetry readings, and other events take place around the town's main mosques. Maulidi, which takes place in the spring, attracts pilgrims from all over Kenya.

SAFETY

The best way to see Lamu town is on foot, but you should not walk alone at night. Crime is rare in this part of Kenya, but it's better to be on the safe side.

TELEPHONES

The area code for Lamu is 040. If you are calling Lamu from outside Kenya, dial the country code, 254, the area code, 040, and the local number.

EXPLORING

Donkey Sanctuary. Donkeys are the main transport in Lamu, and the sanctuary was started in 1987 by Elisabeth Svendsen, a British doctor, to protect and look after the working donkeys. It's now managed and run in conjunction with the KSPCA (Kenya Society for the Protection and Care of Animals). There's a treatment clinic where locals can get their donkeys wormed, a training center, and a resting place for a few of the old animals that can no longer work. If you don't want to go inside, you can eyeball a few donkeys over the low wall in front of the yard. An annual prize is given to the Lamu donkey in the best physical condition. ⊠ *Kenyatta Rd.* ⊕ *www.thedonkeysanctuary.org.uk* ⊠ *Donations accepted* ⊙ *Weekdays 9* AM–1 PM.

Jumaa Mosque. Located in the north of the town, just off Harambee Avenue, Jumaa is the second oldest mosque in Lamu. It dates from 1511, and was used up until the late 1800s for trading slaves. ⊠ *Off Harambee Ave.*

Kiwayu Island. This strip of sand is 50 km (31 mi) northeast of Lamu. The main attraction of Kiwayu Island is its proximity to Kiunga Marine National Reserve, a marine park encompassing Kiwayu Bay. The confluence of two major ocean currents creates unique ecological conditions that nurture three marine habitats—mangroves, sea-grass beds, and coral reefs. Here you have a chance of catching a glimpse of the most endangered mammal in Kenya, the manatee. Because of its tasty flesh, this gentle giant has been hunted to near extinction all along Africa's eastern coast. The best way to get here is to charter a dhow from Lamu. If you can muster a group of six people, it should cost you about US$15–US$20 per person including food, water, and snorkeling equipment. Otherwise, your lodge or hotel will arrange the trip for you; it's 90 minutes by speedboat.

Lamu Fort. This imposing edifice, which was completed in 1821, marks the southern corner of the town. It was used as a prison from 1910 to 1984, when it became part of the country's museum system. Today, it is a central part of the town as it hosts conferences, exhibits, and theater productions. If you have a few moments, climb up to the battlements for some great views of Lamu. ⊠ *Kenyatta Rd.* ⊕ *www.museums.or.ke* ⊠ *Free* ⊙ *Daily 8–6.*

Lamu Museum. You enter the museum through a brass-studded door that was imported from Zanzibar. Inside there are archaeological displays showing the Takwa Ruins excavations, some wonderful photos of Lamu taken by a French photographer from 1846 to 1849 (you'll be amazed at how little has changed in Lamu), some intricately carved Lamu

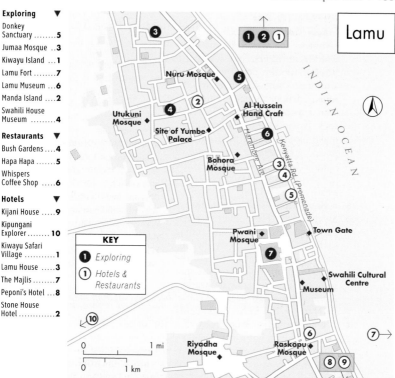

headboards and throne chairs, and a library. In the Balcony Room upstairs is a fascinating display of musical instruments including the famed Siwa Horn, which is made of brass and resembles elephant tusks; the Pate Siwa horn, made of ivory, is now in Nairobi Museum. Dating from the 17th-century, they're reputed to be the oldest surviving musical instruments in sub-Saharan Africa. ⊠ *Kenyatta Rd.* ⊕ *www.museums. or.ke* ⊠ *Ksh 500* ⊗ *Daily 8–6.*

Manda Island. Just across the channel from Shela, the mostly uninhabited Manda Island once held one of the area's largest cities. The once-thriving community of Takwa was abandoned in the 17th century, and archaeologists have yet to discover why. Reached by taking a dhow up a baobab tree-lined creek, the ruins are a popular day-trip from Lamu and Shela. ⊠ *10 min by boat from Lamu.*

Swahili House Museum. This beautifully restored Swahili merchant's house has original period furniture. Notice the traditional beds with woven bases of rope, and the finely carved Kalinda screen in the main room. There's a garden full of flowering tropical shrubs and trees and the original well. ⊠ *A few blocks south of Juma Mosque, Old Town* ⊕ *www.museums.or.ke* ⊠ *Ksh 500* ⊗ *Daily 7:30–5:45.*

WHERE TO EAT

$ ✕ **Bush Gardens.** Service isn't the
SEAFOOD fastest in the world at this lively waterfront eatery, but it's worth waiting for the delicious seafood and fresh fish—definitely try the tuna, shark, or snapper. Entrées are served with coconut rice or french fries. If you stop by for breakfast, make sure to sample the fresh fruit juices. ⊠ *Harambee Ave., south of main jetty, Lamu* ☎ *071/493–4804* ☾ *Daily 7 AM–10 PM* ▭ *No credit cards.*

$ ✕ **Hapa Hapa.** With a name that is
SEAFOOD Swahili for "Here, Here," Hapa Hapa is known for its outstanding seafood. Make sure to try the barracuda. This restaurant is on the waterfront, making it a great spot to watch the fishing boats heading out into the Indian Ocean. ⊠ *Harambee Ave., south of main jetty, Lamu* ☎ *042/633–145* ▭ *No credit cards.*

¢ ✕ **Whispers Coffee Shop.** Located in the same building as the Baraka
CAFÉ Gallery (which has a wonderful collection of African art, jewelry, and souvenirs for sale), this upscale café has a pretty, quiet courtyard where you can relax over a cappuccino. There's also a lunch and dinner menu, focusing on salads, pastas, and deli items, or you can order a packed lunch to take away. The homemade ice creams are good. ⊠ *Harambee Ave., Lamu* ☎ *042/463–2024* ▭ *No credit cards* ☾ *Closed May–July.*

WHERE TO STAY

Most of the restaurants and hotels in Lamu town are along the seafront or the road parallel to it, called Harambee Avenue. The locals are very helpful, and if you take a guided tour of the town, which we highly recommend, you will soon have oriented yourself.

Lodging reviews have been abbreviated in this book. For expanded reviews, please go to Fodors.com.

$ ⊞ **Kijani House.** While hotels such as Lamu House and Peponi boast decor straight out of the pages of a glossy style magazine, Kijani House, located in right on the waterfront in Shela, represents a more low-key, old-fashioned style of Swahili living. **Pros:** rooms look out onto the waterfront; the hotel is five minutes' walk from the beach. **Cons:** can get hot at night; no Internet. ⊠ *Shela Sea Front* ☎ *020/243–5700 or 0725/545–264* ⊕ *www.kijani-lamu.com* ⟿ *11 rooms* ⌂ *In-room: no a/c, safe, no TV. In-hotel: restaurant, bar, pool* ▭ *MC, V* ☾ *Closed May–June* ⦿| *BP.*

$$$$ ⊞ **Kipungani Explorer.** On the southern tip of Lamu Island, this lodge is for anyone who's looking for a truly secluded getaway. **Pros:** the hotel's engagement with the local community; the sunsets from the

swimming pool. **Cons:** electricity is on only 8 AM to noon and 6 PM to midnight; full-board option only. ⊠ *Kipungani* ☎ *020/444–2115* ↗ *15 cottages* ⊕ *kipungani. heritage-eastafrica.com* 👌 *In-room: no a/c, safe, no TV. In-hotel: restaurant, bar, pool* ¶◎¶ *BP.*

$$$$ 🏨 **Kiwayu Safari Village.** Fifty kilometers (31 mi) northeast of Lamu you'll find one of the most romantic destinations in Kenya. **Pros:** the bandas are beautifully furnished; there are great water-sport activities on offer. **Cons:** no swimming pool; trips to Lamu are extra. ⊠ *Kiwayu Island* ☎ *020/600–9414 or 020/600–891* ⊕ *www.kiwayu.com* ↗ *18 cottages* 👌 *In-room: no a/c, safe, no TV. In-hotel: restaurant, bar, Wi-Fi* ☰ *AE, DC, MC, V* ⊙ *Closed end Apr.–mid-July.*

$$ 🏨 **Lamu House.** The rooms in this boutique hotel, located next to the Donkey Sanctuary on Lamu's waterfront, are all different, but each one is superbly decorated in traditional Swahili style and has a separate dressing room and a terrace looking out either onto the water or the town. **Pros:** each room has a fridge; there's a daily boat shuttle to Shela Beach; breakfast is available all day. **Cons:** it can be noisy as it's in the center of town; no a/c. ⊠ *Lamu Sea Front* ☎ *042/633–491* ⊕ *www. lamuhouse.com* ↗ *10 rooms* 👌 *In-room: safe, no a/c, no TV. In-hotel: restaurant, bar, pool, spa, Wi-Fi* ☰ *MC, V* ¶◎¶ *BP.*

$$$ 🏨 **The Majlis.** The rooms in this spectacular hotel on Manda Island are in three villas, and as each has a sitting room with white couches, antique Swahili furniture, and African paintings and sculptures, you'll feel as though you are staying in an ultrastylish private beach house. **Pros:** unforgettable dhow sunset cruises; an excellent beach; rooms have a/c. **Cons:** trips to Lamu are not included; alcohol is not included in the full-board option. ⊠ *Manda Island* ☎ *020/261–7496 or 0718/195–499* ⊕ *www.themajlisresorts.com* ↗ *25 rooms* 👌 *In-room: safe, no TV, Wi-Fi. In-hotel: restaurant, bar, pool* ☰ *AE, MC, V* ¶◎¶ *FAP.*

$ 🏨 **Peponi's Hotel.** Peponi's is well known for its beachfront location in Shela, lovely accommodations, and superb food. **Pros:** only hotel guests get seating on the outside balcony at dinner; morning tea is served in your room; it's very close to the beach. **Cons:** pool area is small; the staff are very keen to arrange all your activities for you; dinner must be ordered by 5 PM. ☎ *020/802–3655 or 0722/203–082* ⊕ *www.peponi-lamu.com* ↗ *24 rooms* 👌 *In-room: no a/c, safe, no TV. In-hotel: restaurant, bar, pool* ☰ *AE, DC, MC, V* ⊙ *Closed May and June* ¶◎¶ *BP, MAP, FAP.*

¢ 🏨 **Stone House Hotel.** This lovely 18th-century house is in the heart of Old Lamu. **Pros:** good value; in the heart of Lamu Town. **Cons:** no safes in the rooms; can be noisy. ☎ *042/633–544* ↗ *10 rooms, 4 share bath* 👌 *In-room: no a/c, no TV. In-hotel: restaurant, bar* ☰ *No credit cards* ¶◎¶ *BP, MAP, FAP.*

Tanzania

WELCOME TO TANZANIA

TOP REASONS TO GO

★ **The Great Migration.** This annual movement is one of the great natural wonders of the world.

★ **Big Game Adventures.** You'll be amazed at how close up and familiar you get not only with the Big Five, but with thousands of other animals as well.

★ **Sea, Sand, and Sun.** Tanzania's sun-spoiled but deserted beaches are lapped by the turquoise blue waters of the Indian Ocean. Swim, snorkel, scuba dive, sail, fish, or just chill on soft white sands under waving palm trees.

★ **Ancient Cultures.** From the traditional red-robed, bead-bedecked nomadic Masai in the north to the exotic heady mix of Arab and Africa influences in Zanzibar, you'll encounter unique peoples and cultures just about everywhere you go.

★ **Bird-Watching.** Stay glued to your binoculars in one of the finest bird-watching destinations in the world. You'll be able to watch hundreds of species in a variety of habitats.

1 Serengeti National Park. It'll be just how you imagine it and more: endless plains of golden grasses, teeming herds of game, stalking predators, wheeling vultures. You won't be disappointed.

2 Ngorongoro Crater. Bump down the steep descent road through primeval forest to the crater floor where you'll find the biggest concentration of predators on earth.

3 **Lake Manyara National Park.** Tree-climbing lions, huge troops of baboons, elegant giraffes, harrumphing hippos, myriads of birds, ancient forest, lakeside plains, and towering cliffs characterize this enchanting, little-visited park.

4 **Selous Game Reserve.** Escape the tourist crowds in the world's second largest conservation area where you can view game on foot, by boat, or from your vehicle.

5 **Gombe Stream and Mahale Mountains National Parks.** Follow in the footsteps of world-famous primatologist Jane Goodall and come face-to-face with wild chimpanzees. It's an unforgettable wildlife encounter.

GETTING ORIENTED

Covering an area of 886,037 square km (342,100 square mi), which includes the islands of Mafia, Pemba, and Zanzibar, Tanzania is about twice the size of the state of California. It's bordered by the Indian Ocean in the east, Kenya to the north, and Mozambique to the south. The country is home to some of the most coveted tourist destinations in the world: Serengeti, Ngorongoro Crater, Zanzibar, Lakes Victoria, Tanganyika, and Malawi, and Mt. Kilimanjaro, Africa's highest freestanding mountain. Tourism doesn't come cheap, but you'll be rewarded with spectacular views, legions of game, and unique marine experiences. It also boasts more than 1,130 bird species. Traveling distances are vast, so be prepared for lots of trips in different-size planes, or bite the bullet and face the notoriously bad potholes and seriously bumpy surfaces of dirt roads.

KENYA

Ngorongoro Crater Mt. Meru 4,566 m Mt. Kilimanjaro 5,895 m
Arusha
Lake Manyara Arusha National Park
Moshi

3

Lake Manyara National Park Tarangire National Park

M A S A I   S T E P P E

P A R E   M T S

Dodoma

Tanga
Wete
PEMBA
Mkoani
Mkokotoni
Koani
Stone Town **ZANZIBAR**

Morogoro Kibaha
DAR ES SALAAM

Iringa

Selous Game Reserve

4

Mohoro

MAFIA

I N D I A N   O C E A N

Lindi
Mtwara

Songea

MOZAMBIQUE

GREEN LODGINGS IN TANZANIA

Home to half of the annual Great Migration, Tanzania plays host to thousands and thousands of animals every year. Being eco-conscious in every way possible ensures that this amazing natural wonder continues for years to come.

(above) Serengeti Under Canvas; (opposite upper right and bottom left) Chumbe Island

A controversial two-lane highway has been proposed across the Serengeti National Park. If built, the road, some 40 mi long, would connect Arusha with Musoma, on the eastern shore of Lake Victoria. The road, meant to facilitate commercial transportation in the region, would allow truck traffic to bisect the Great Migration route and could disrupt one of nature's greatest spectacles and the largest mass-migration of large mammals. Activists are trying to stop the construction, or at least change the route of the highway. But on other fronts, Tanzania is quite green.

There are numerous eco-conscious lodgings in Tanzania; our list is a mere drop in the bucket. However, it's a starting place that we hope inspires you to travel green. And, remember that no matter where you travel, always minimize the negative impact on your surroundings while nurturing the cultural integrity of indigenous peoples.

OPERATOR'S INTEGRITY

To make sure that your operator's practices are green, inquire with a watchdog agency such as Tourism Concern (⊕ *www.tourismconcern.org.uk*) or Green Globe (⊕ *www.greenglobe.org*). Conservation organizations such as World Wildlife Fund (⊕ *www.worldwildlife.org*) or the African Wildlife Foundation (⊕ *www.awf.org*) also promote green tourism standards.

GREEN LODGES IN TANZANIA

Chumbe Island (☎ *024/223–1040* ⊕ *www.chumbeisland. com*), between the Tanzanian coast and the islands of Zanzibar, is the country's first marine national park. It's home to 400 species of coral, 200 species of fish, and a boutique luxury hotel. The island's ecotourism concept was the brainstorm of a German conservationist who, since the early 1990s, has succeeded in developing it as one of the world's foremost marine sanctuaries. Seven thatch bungalows with specially built roofs catch rainwater that is funneled into bathrooms through a tank in the floor. Electricity is solar powered, and toilets are doused in sweet-smelling compost and later cleaned. Scuba diving, snorkeling, island hikes guided by expert rangers, and outrigger boat rides leave you with plenty to do while you absorb the lesson of sustainability at Chumbe.

Set within 31,000 mi of Tanzania wilderness in the Selous Game Reserve, **Sand Rivers Selous** (☎ *022/286–5156* ⊕ *www.nomad-tanzania.com*) might be the closest you'll get to nature in all of Africa. Seven cottages made of stone and thatch are raised on stakes above the Rufiji River; the cottages have open fronts that look out over the surrounding woodlands and river. Perhaps most important for green travelers, though, is Sand Rivers Selous's involvement in the Selous Rhino Trust. In partnership with the Tanzania Division of Wildlife, the owners and a few dedicated partners have identified 16 black rhino in the region—a triumph for a part of the world that once supported at least 3,000 of these great beasts. Today, the black rhino numbers at no more than a handful in Tanzania and the rest of Africa, but the trust is steadily working to change this with constant monitoring and conservation support at Sand Rivers Selous. ⇨ *See Luxury Lodges, in Selous Game Reserve for more information about the camp.*

Think no electricity, no running water, and vast plains. Now think hot-bucket showers, romantic canvas tents, Indian rugs, and fine cuisine. Top it off with the knowledge that you're contributing to the welfare of the local Masai communities and you've got a stay at **Serengeti Under Canvas** (☎ *011/809–4300* ⊕ *www.andbeyond.com*), a camp within the Klein's Camp Private Concession in northern Tanzania. Tanzania Under Canvas is part of the &Beyond group of camps that works to implement education and AIDS awareness programs in local communities through the Africa Foundation, a nonprofit rural development organization focused on sustainable development. Tanzania Under Canvas also offers guests night drives, visits to local Masai settlements, and interpretive bush walks, which also contribute to the immersing international travelers in indigenous cultures for the mutual benefit of both. ⇨ *See Mobile Tented Camps, in Serengeti National Park for more information about the camp.*

Updated by
Sean Pattrick

Tanzania is the quintessential, definitive Africa of your dreams. And who wouldn't want to visit a place where the names of its legendary travel destinations roll off the tongue like an incantation: Zanzibar, Serengeti, Olduvai Gorge, Mt. Kilimanjaro, Lake Tanganyika, Lake Victoria, the Rift Valley, the Ngorongoro Crater, Olduvai Gorge, the Cradle of Humankind.

Great plains abound with legions of game, snow-capped mountains soar above dusty valleys, rain forests teem with monkeys and birds, beaches are covered in sand as soft and white as talcum powder, and coral reefs host myriads of jewel-like tropical fish. Although Tanzania is one of the poorest countries in the world—its economy depends heavily on agriculture, which accounts for almost half of its GDP—it has more land (more than 25%) devoted to national parks and game reserves than any other wildlife destination in the world. Everything from pristine coral reefs to the crater highlands, remote game reserves, and the famous national parks are protected by government law and placed in trust for future generations.

The East African coast appears to have first been explored by the Phoenicians in approximately 600 BC. Bantu peoples arrived about 2,000 years ago and a few 4th-century Roman coins have turned up at the coast. We can tell from ancient writings that the Romans certainly knew about Mt. Kilimanjaro and the great inland lakes, but nobody is quite sure how they came by this knowledge. By AD 100, trade with India and the Middle East was well established, and many city-states ruled by local sultans sprang up along the coast. The Portuguese first arrived at the end of the 15th century looking for a trade route to India, but their hold on the country was shattered when the sultan of Oman captured Mombasa in 1698; 150 years later the capital was transferred here from Oman. The slave trade dominated the coast and the interior from the early 1800s. It was only after the passionate first-hand accounts given by Dr. Livingstone in the 1850s and his proposing its abolition that the slave trade was finally eradicated in 1918, when the British took control

FAST FACTS

Size 945,203 square km (364,898 square mi).

Capital Dar es Salaam, though legislative offices have been transferred to Dodoma, which is planned as the new national capital.

Number of National Parks 15, including the Serengeti, Tarangire, Lake Manyara, Gombe Stream, Ruaha, Selous, Katavi, and Mt. Kilimanjaro.

Number of Private Reserves Too many to count, but includes the Singita Grumeti Reserves.

Population Approximately 42 million.

Big Five All the Big Five, including black and white rhinos.

Language Official languages are Kiswahili and English.

Time Tanzania is on EAT (East Africa Time), which is three hours ahead of Greenwich Mean Time and eight hours ahead of Eastern Standard Time.

4

of Tanzania. This was followed in the Scramble for Africa by German rule. Germany was determined to make the colony self-sufficient by planting coffee and cotton, efforts which failed. Tanzania returned to British hands after World War I and finally won its independence in 1964. It's now a stable multiparty democracy. Dar es Salaam is still the country's capital, but the legislative offices have been transferred to the central city of Dodoma, which was chosen to be the new national capital in 1973; the transfer is slow moving because of the great expense. The National Assembly already meets there on a regular basis.

Tanzania has always been the poor relation of Kenya in terms of tourist numbers, but in recent years numbers of visitors are increasing along with a better infrastructure and tourist facilities.

There are two circuits you can follow in Tanzania: the conventional northern tourist circuit, which includes the Serengeti and Ngorongoro Crater, or the lesser traveled southern tourist circuit of Selous Game Reserve and Ruaha, Mahale, and Gombe national parks among others. You'll be amply rewarded for the often lengthy traveling to these southern locations by having the places much more to yourself and usually at cheaper rates.

Serengeti *is* all it's cracked up to be with endless plains of golden grasses (Serengeti means "endless plain" in the Masai language), teeming game, abundant bird life, and an awe-inspiring sense of space and timelessness. Ngorongoro Crater justly deserves its reputation as one of the natural wonders of the world. The ride down onto the crater floor is memorable enough as you pass through misty primeval forest with wild orchids, swinging vines, and chattering monkeys, but once on the floor you could well be in the middle of a National Geographic TV program. You can follow in the footsteps of legendary hunters and explorers when you visit Selous Game Reserve in the south. Although it's the second largest conservation area in the world after Greenland National Park, only 5% of the northern part is open to tourists; but don't worry, you'll see all the game and birds you could wish for with the advantage of seeing it by boat and on foot. If it's chimpanzees you're after, then Gombe Stream and Mahale Mountains national parks are the places to head for. A lot of traveling (much of it by boat)

> **DID YOU KNOW?**
>
> Tanzania is one of the world's largest producers of cashews, exporting more than 100,000 tons of raw nuts each year.

is required, but the experience is well worth the effort and you'll join only a small community of other privileged visitors who have had the unique experience of coming face-to-face with wild chimpanzees.

The animals aren't the only wonders Tanzania has to offer. There are the islands of Zanizibar, Pemba, and Mafia, as well as Mt. Kilimanjaro, Mt. Meru, and the three great lakes of Victoria, Tanganyika, and Malawi. Wherever you go, you are guaranteed travel experiences that you'll remember for the rest of your life.

PLANNING

WHEN TO GO

There are two rainy seasons: the short rains (*mvuli*) October through December and the long rains (*masika*) from late February to early May. Given the influence of global warming, these rains are not as regular or intense as they once were. It's best to avoid the two rainy seasons because many roads become impassable. Ngorongoro Crater is open all year, but the roads become extremely muddy and difficult to navigate during the wet seasons. High season is January to the end of September, but prices are much higher during this time. Make sure you find out in advance when the lodge or destination of your choice is closed as many are open only during the dry season. The coast is always pretty hot and humid, particularly during the rains, but is cooler and more pleasant the rest of the year. The hottest time is December just before the long rains. In high-altitude areas such as Ngorongoro highlands and Mt. Kilimanjaro, temperatures can fall below freezing.

GETTING HERE AND AROUND

AIR TRAVEL

Most travelers arrive in Tanzania through Dar es Salaam airport. Many airlines fly directly to Dar es Salaam from Europe, but there are no direct flights from the United States.

KLM offers the only daily flights to Dar es Salaam from Amsterdam's Schipol airport. Other airlines that fly here frequently are Air India, Air Zimbabwe, Air Tanzania, British Airways, Egypt Air, Emirates, Ethiopian Airlines, Kenya Airways, South African Airways, and Swissair. British Airways has one flight daily from Dar es Salaam to London. Air Tanzania has daily flights to Dar es Salaam from destinations within East Africa. Air Tanzania has several daily flights to Zanzibar.

Airlines Air India (☎ 022/215–2642 ⊕ www.airindia.com). **Air Tanzania** (☎ 022/211–8411 ⊕ www.airtanzania.com). **Air Zimbabwe** (☎ 022/212–3526 ⊕ www.airzimbabwe.com). **British Airways** (☎ 022/211–3820 ⊕ www. britishairways.com). **Emirates** (☎ 022/211–6100 ⊕ www.emirates.com). **Ethiopian Airlines** (☎ 022/211–7063 ⊕ www.ethiopianairlines.com). **Kenyan Airways** (☎ 022/211–9377 ⊕ www.kenya-airways.com). **KLM** (☎ 022/213–9790 ⊕ www.klm.com). **South Africa Airways** (☎ 022/211–7044 ⊕ www.flysaa.com). **Swiss Air** (☎ 022/211–8870 ⊕ www.swiss.com).

AIRPORTS AND TRANSFERS

Julius Nyerere International Airport, formerly Dar es Salaam International Airport, is about 13 km (8 mi) from the city center. Plenty of white-color taxis are available at the airport and will cost you about Tsh 15,000 to the city center. This can usually be negotiated. Most hotels will send drivers to meet your plane, if arranged in advance.

Airports Arusha Airport (☎ 027/741–530 or 027/744–317). **Julius Nyerere International Airport** (☎ 022/284–4324). **Kilimanjaro International Airport** (☎ 027/255–4252 ⊕ www.kilimanjaroairport.co.tz). **Zanzibar Airport** (☎ 024/223–3979 ⊕ www.zanzibar-airport.com).

CHARTER FLIGHTS

The major charter companies run daily shuttles from Dar es Salaam to popular tourism destinations, such as Serengeti. Keep in mind that you probably won't get to choose the charter company you fly with. The aircraft you get depends on the number of passengers flying and can vary from very small (you will sit in the co-pilot's seat) to a much more comfortable commuter plane. ■TIP→ **Those with a severe fear of small planes might consider road travel instead.**

Due to the limited space and size of the aircraft, charter carriers observe strict luggage regulations: luggage must be soft sided and weigh no more than 44 lbs (20 kg).

Contacts Coastal Air (✉ Stone Town ☎ 222/842–700). **Flightlink** (✉ Dar es Salaam ☎ 022/284–3073). **Precision Air** (☎ 022/212–1718 ⊕ www. precisionairtz.com). **Tanzanair** (✉ Dar es Salaam ☎ 022/284–3131 or 022/211–3151 ⊕ www.tanzanair.com). **Sky Aviation** (✉ Dar es Salaam ☎ 022/284–4410).

CUSTOMS AND DUTIES

You can bring in a liter of spirits or wine and 200 cigarettes duty fee. The import of zebra skin or other tourist products requires a CITES (Convention of International Trade in Endangered Species of Wild Fauna and Flora) permit. Although you can buy curios made from animal products in Tanzania, your home country may confiscate them on arrival. Don't buy shells or items made from sea turtles.

⇨ *For information on CITES and what you can and cannot bring into the U.S., see Customs and Duties, in the On Safari chapter.*

HEALTH AND SAFETY

Malaria is the biggest health threat in Tanzania, so be vigilant about taking antimalarials and applying bug spray. Consult with your doctor or travel clinic before leaving home for up-to-date antimalarial medication. At time of writing HIV/AIDS is less a risk than in some other African countries, but the golden rule is *never* to have sex with a stranger. It's imperative to use strong sunscreen: remember you are just below the equator, where the sun is at its hottest. Stick to bottled water and ensure that the bottle seal is unbroken. Put your personal medications in your carry-on and bring copies of prescriptions.

The Flying Doctors Service offered by AMREF provides air evacuation services for medical emergencies in Kenya, Tanzania, and Uganda or anywhere within a 1,000 km (621 mi) radius of Nairobi. The planes fly out of Nairobi's Wilson Airport 24 hours a day, 365 days a year. They also provide transportation between medical facilities, fly you back to Europe, Asia, or North America, or provide you with an escort if you're flying on a commercial carrier.

SHOTS AND MEDICATIONS

Be up to date on yellow fever, polio, tetanus, typhoid, meningococcus, rabies, and hepatitis A. It's not necessary to have a cholera jab, but if you are visiting Zanzibar it's sensible to get a cholera exception form from your GP or travel clinic. Visit a travel clinic eight to 10 weeks before you travel to find out your requirements. If you are coming to Tanzania for a safari, chances are you are heading to a malarial game reserve. Millions of travelers take oral prophylactic drugs before, during, and after their safaris. It is up to you to weigh the risks and benefits of the type of antimalarial drug you choose to take. If you are pregnant or traveling with small children, consider a nonmalarial region for your safari.

Embassies U.S. Embassy (✉ 686 Old Bagamoyo Rd., Dar es Salaam 022/266–8001).

Emergencies Police Hotline (📞 999 or 111).

Medical-Assistance Companies The Flying Doctors Service (📞 022/211–6610 in Dar es Saalam, 022/212–7187 in Arusha ⊕ www.amref.org).

MONEY MATTERS

The regulated currency is the Tanzanian shilling (Tsh). Notes are 500, 1,000, 2,000, 5,000, and 10,000. At this writing, the exchange rate was about Tsh 1,163 to US$1.

To avoid administrative hassles, keep all foreign-exchange receipts until you leave the region, as you may need them as proof when changing any unspent local currency back into your own currency at the airport when you leave. Better still, don't leave yourself with any Tsh—you won't be able to change them outside of Tanzania.

Bargaining, especially at market places, is part of the shopping experience. But always be aware of the exchange rate and pay appropriately—

you don't want to underpay, but you also don't want to be charged exorbitant "tourist" prices.

Most large hotels accept only U.S. dollars; some budget hotels will also accept Tanzanian shillings.

ATMS AND BANKS

There are banks in all major cities and ATMs; you can draw cash directly from an ATM in Dar es Salaam, Arusha, and Mwanza. Most ATMs accept Cirrus, Plus, Maestro, Visa Electron, Visa, and MasterCard. The best place to withdraw cash is at an indoor ATM, preferably one guarded by a security officer. If you're unsure where to find a safe ATM, ask a merchant. Most machines will not let you withdraw more than the equivalent of about $150 at a time.

4

COMMUNICATIONS

MAIL

If you make a purchase, try your best to take it home on the plane with you, even if it means packing your travel clothes and items into a box and shipping those to your home, or buying a cheap piece of luggage and paying the excess weight fees. If you buy something from a store accustomed to foreign visitors, they will likely already have a system for getting your items to you, often in a surprising few weeks' time.

PHONES

If you run across a number with only five digits, it's a remnant of the old system that was changed in 1999. Because telephone communications are difficult, many people in the travel business have mobile phones.

CALLING WITHIN TANZANIA

The "0" in the regional code is used only for calls placed from other areas within the country.

CALLING OUTSIDE TANZANIA

To call from abroad, dial the international access number 00, then the country code 255, then the area code 24, and then the telephone number, which should have six or seven digits.

MOBILE PHONES

Vodacom and Zain are the main service providers in Tanzania. The best option is to bring your own phone (if it's not locked to a particular network) or rent a phone and buy a SIM card on arrival. The starter packs for pay-as-you-go cell phones are very reasonable. You will have to buy credit for your phone, but this is easily done at shops or roadside vendors.

Contacts Vodacom (⊕ www.vodacomco.tz). **Zain** (⊕ www.tz.zain.com). **Zantel** (⊕ www.zantel.co.tz).

HOTELS AND LODGES

You'll find the ultimate in luxury at many of the safari camps, lodges, and coastal resorts and hotels. We highly recommend that you opt for a private camp or lodge if possible, because everything is usually included—lodging, transport to and from the lodge, meals, beverages including excellent house wines, game drives, and other activities. Check in advance whether park fees are included in your rate, as these can get very expensive if you have to pay them daily. The southern safari circuit is cheaper in general, but you will need to factor in the cost of transport. Many lodges and hotels offer low-season rates. If you're opting for a private game lodge, find out whether they accept children (many specify only kids over 12), and stay a minimum of

two nights, three if you can. If you're traveling to the more remote parks, allow for more time. National park accommodations are few and very basic. Unless you are a hardcore camper, we advise that you stick with another type of accommodation. It's essential to note that more often than not, there will not be an elevator in your lodge—which are usually one story—and because of the rustic locations, accommodations are not wheelchair-friendly. You'll encounter lots of steps, rocky paths, dim lighting, and uneven ground. The price categories used for lodging in this chapter treat all-inclusive lodges differently from other lodgings; see the price chart below for details.

⇨ *For information on plugging in while on Safari, see Electricity, in the On Safari chapter.*

RESTAURANTS AND FOOD

Food in the lodges is plentiful and tasty, and if you head to the coast, you'll dine on superb seafood and fish with lots of fresh fruit and vegetables. All places now have at least one vegetarian course on the menu.

There is a very cosmopolitan flavor about a city like Dar es Saalam with it's large expat community. There are restaurants to suit all tastes and budgets.

WHAT IT COSTS IN U.S. DOLLARS				
¢	**$**	**$$**	**$$$**	**$$$$**
Safari Camps and Lodges	under $200	$200–$450	$451–$750	$751–$1,000	over $1,000
Hotels	under $100	$100–$150	$151–$200	$201–$250	over $250
Dining	under $5	$5–$10	$11–$20	$21–$30	over $30

All prices refer to an all-inclusive per-person, per-night rate including 12.5% tax, assuming double occupancy. Hotel prices are for a standard double room in high season. Restaurant prices are per person for a main course at dinner, a main course equivalent, or a prix-fixe meal.

PASSPORTS AND VISAS

Most visitors require a visa to enter Tanzania. You can buy one upon arrival—make sure you have at least $100 cash as the visa price has recently increased, and does so all the time, and two passport pictures—but get one ahead of time if possible. Visas are valid for three months and allow multiple entries. Passports must be valid for 6 months after your planned departure date from Tanzania.

TIPPING

If you've been given good service, tip accordingly. For a two- or three-night stay at a lodge or hotel tip a couple of dollars for small services, US$2–US$5 per day for room steward and waiter. Your guide will expect a tip of US$15–US$20 per day per person; if he's gone out of his way for you, then you may wish to give him more. It's a good idea to carry a number of small-denomination bills. U.S. dollars are acceptable almost everywhere, but if you're planning to go to more remote places, then shillings are preferred.

VISITOR INFORMATION

The Tanzanian Tourist Board (TTB) has offices in Dar es Salaam and Arusha. The tourist board's Web site is a great online source for pre-trip planning.

Contacts Tanzania National Parks (✉ *Opposite Cultural Heritage Centre, Serengeti Rd.* ☎ *027/250–1930* ⊕ *www.tanzaniaparks.com*). **Tanzanian Tourist Board** (☎ *022/211–1244* ⊕ *www.tanzaniatouristboard.com*).

MUST-SEE PARKS

Unfortunately, you probably won't be able to see all of Tanzania in one trip. So we've broken down the chapter by **Must-See Parks** (Serengeti National Park, Ngorongoro Conservation Area, Lake Manyara National Park, Selous Game Reserve, and Gombe Stream and Mahale Mountains national parks) and **If You Have Time Parks** (Arusha National Park, Tarangire National Park, and Ruaha National Park) to help you better organize your time. We suggest though, that you read about all of them and then choose for yourself.

SERENGETI NATIONAL PARK

Game
★★★★★
Park Accessibility
★★★★★
Getting Around
★★★★★
Accommodations
★★★★★
Scenic Beauty
☆★★★★

The very name Serengeti is guaranteed to bring a glint to even the most jaded traveler's eye. It's up there in that wish list of legendary destinations alongside Machu Picchu, Angkor Wat, Kakadu, Killarney, and the Great Pyramid of Giza. But what distinguishes Serengeti from all its competitors is its sheer naturalness.

It's 15,000 square km (5,791 square mi) of pristine wilderness and that's it. Its Masai name *Serenget*, means Endless Plain. A primeval Eden par excellence, named a World Heritage Site in 1978 and an International Biosphere Reserve in 1981, Serengeti is all it's cracked up to be. You won't be disappointed.

This ecosystem supports some of the most plentiful mammal populations left anywhere on earth, and the animals here seem bigger, stockier, stronger, and sturdier than elsewhere in Africa. Even the scrub hares are bigger than their southern neighbors, loping rather than scampering over the tussocks and grassy mounds. Hyenas are everywhere and raptors are in perpetual motion—tawny eagles, kestrels, harriers, kites, buzzards, and vultures. Expect to see at least one baby wildebeest that has fallen by the wayside lying alone encircled by patient, voracious vultures or prowling hyenas.

But let's put you right in the picture. You'll probably land at a busy landing strip, maybe near Ntuti, where a dozen open-sided vehicles wait to pick up the new arrivals. Don't worry about lots of vehicles. In your few days driving around the Serengeti you'll certainly see others, but not too many. As you leave the airstrip, your vehicle will weave its way through herds of zebra and gazelle. Rufous-tailed weavers, endemic to northern Tanzania, flutter up from the sandy road. The plains stretch endlessly with misty mountains faint in the distance. At first the plains are ringed by trees, but then only an occasional and solitary tree punctuates the golden grasses. Wherever you stay, you'll be looked after royally, with comfortable accommodation, good food, a dawn chorus of bubbling birdsong, and an evening serenade of whooping hyenas with a backing group of softly calling lions.

What will you remember about the Serengeti? The unending horizons and limitless plains. The sheer space. The wildebeest. The oh-so-beautiful Thomson's and Grant's gazelles. The bat-eared foxes playing in the early morning sun. Lions galore, and in particular, the one that may wander past your tent one night and roar under the blazing stars. The hosts of water birds by the streams, lakes, and rivers. The flat-topped acacia trees, ancient guardians of this windswept wilderness. The quiet. The Big Country. Knowing how small is your place in the interconnectedness of all things. And how privileged you are to be able to experience the wonder of it all.

GETTING HERE AND AROUND

The drive from Arusha to Serengeti is about eight hours or 325 km (202 mi). While there are places to refuel, breakdown facilities are virtually nonexistent. The roads outside of the cities are mostly dirt, and you'll have a lot of potholes to contend with on many of them; a 4x4 vehicle would be best if you are renting a car. While you can drive to the Serengeti from Arusha, Lake Manyara, Tarangire, or Ngorongoro Crater, we suggest flying in, as it's quick, less of a headache, and gives one the sense of the scale of the landscape. There are scheduled and charter flights to the Serengeti from Arusha, Lake Manyara, and Mwanza. The flights are daily. A flight from Arusha to Serengeti South is an hour long, the flight from Dar es Salaam to Arusha is two hours. Most tour operators will arrange the flights for you, and lodges will be sure to have someone pick you up at the airstrip.

WHEN TO GO

If you want to see the wildebeest migration, visit December through July; if you want to see predators, June through October.

TIMING

The route and timing of the wildebeest migration is unpredictable. With that said, you should allow at least three days to be assured of seeing the migration on your visit, longer if you would like to see more interactions with predators.

WHERE TO STAY

LUXURY LODGES

$$$ ☒ **Klein's Camp.** This lovely little camp, named after the 1920s American big-game hunter Al Klein, is built on the crest of the Kuka Hills with 360-degree panoramic views. Because it lies just outside the national park on a 24,710-acre private conservancy leased from the local Ololosokwan community, you can go on unrestricted game drives and three-hour bush walks—night drives are particularly thrilling. A visit with your Masai guide to his village will be another highlight. Stone and thatch cottages have en-suite bathrooms and a private veranda with great views over the Grumeti River valley. The separate dining and lounge area and very comfortable large bar have stunning views. Game is very good, especially along the river. **Pros:** great service and attention to detail; off-road game driving is allowed at this camp—not

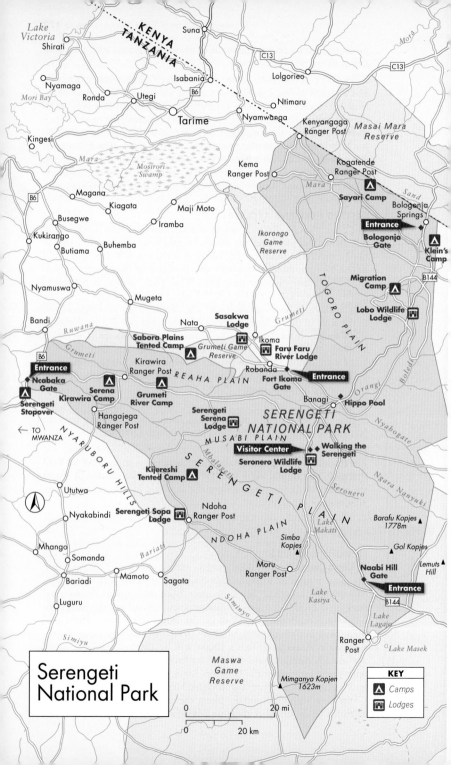

great for the environment but good to get up close to the animals. **Cons:** hot water available twice a day or on request; there's no electricity from about 11 PM to 4 AM, but battery-powered lamps are provided. ☎ *27/11/809–4300* ⊕ *www.andbeyond.com* ➦ *10 cottages* ⚒ *In-room: no phone, no a/c, safe, no TV. In-hotel: bar, pool, shop* ⊟ *AE, DC, MC, V* ◎| *FAP.*

$$$$ 🏠 **Sasakwa Lodge.** This is one of three camps in the Grumeti Reserve, a 350,000-acre concession in Serengeti's Western Corridor. If you're at all familiar with the Singita name, you'll know it is associated with some of the most luxurious and elegant lodges in the Sabi Sands Private Reserve in South Africa. This superlative lodge, built in the style of a 1920s East African ranch house, adds more luster to the Singita name. You'll stay in one of the honey-color stone cottages, each elegantly furnished with hand-carved furniture, cream and white throws, cushions, and lamps, and copies of antique animal prints lining the high walls. Need some downtime? Sit out on your deck and watch for game, luxuriate in your own heated pool, or laze in your lounge and listen to the state-of-the-art sound system. There are game drives here—the game is as good as it gets—but there is also horseback riding and mountain biking, all with an armed guard in attendance. Enjoy a massage before a fine dinner served with crystal and silver. **Pros:** wonderful views of the vast Serengeti plains; it's part of the migration route; there is a wide range of exciting activities offered. **Cons:** the lodge is quite formal, but many may think that is a pro. ☎ *021/683–3424* ⊕ *www.singita.com* ➦ *9 cottages, 1 villa* ⚒ *In-room: a/c, safe, Wi-Fi. In-hotel: restaurant, bar, tennis courts, pool, spa, no kids under 10* ⊟ *AE, MC, V* ⊘ *Closed Apr. and May* ◎| *FAP.*

$$ 🏠 **Serengeti Serena Lodge.** Situated high on a hill with superb views over the central Serengeti, the two-story thatch cottages are shaped like Masai huts and are among indigenous trees. Each is individually decorated with handcrafted African furniture and colorful Africa-theme soft furnishings. If you need to unwind, head to your wooden balcony and gaze far out over the plains. You'll get lost in your thoughts and the view. If you're in a sociable mood, head to the huge bar and dining area, also rondavel-shaped, which is supported by tall carved figures of Masai maidens and warriors. The food here is tasty and plentiful, and there's a gorgeous horizon pool with another great view. All the Serengeti activities are on offer and are included, but it's worth spending those extra pennies on an exclusive balloon safari and champagne breakfast. **Pros:** there are great views of the Serengeti from the lodge; the expanse of open plains make it ideal for hot air ballooning. **Cons:** with 66 rooms, it's larger than most safari lodges, giving it an impersonal feel; when the hotel is full you may have to wait in line for the buffet meal. ☎ *028/262–1507* ⊕ *www.serenahotels.com* ➦ *66 rooms* ⚒ *In-room: no a/c, safe, no TV. In-hotel: restaurant, bar, pool* ⊟ *AE, DC, MC, V* ◎| *FAP.*

PERMANENT TENTED CAMPS

$$$$ 🏠 **Faru Faru River Lodge.** The third camp in the Grumeti concession in Serengeti's Western Corridor—it joins Sabora Plains Tented Camp and Sasakwa Lodge—is sprawling but intimate and is built in the style of

"It's a battle of wills and for this lucky lion. . . . The lion's jaw and claws clench the wildebeest's face until it reaches a point of suffocation." —normalind, Fodors.com member.

a classic East African safari camp under sycamore trees on a hill that overlooks a gorgeous pool and the bush beyond. Local rock, wood, and thatch dominate the main buildings, but you'll sleep in a classic East African tented suite from where you can watch the game at the water hole below from your Victorian-style claw-foot tub or from your veranda. Buffalo, elephant, topi (an East African antelope), and giraffe all come to drink, as do predators, while black-and-white colobus monkeys scream and swing in the trees along the river. The Great Migration moves through the reserve between June and August, although there's plenty of game all year round. Bird life is prolific with more than 400 species including lots of raptors. Viewing decks and public areas jut out over the rock pool and overlook the Grumeti River, making imaginative use of local stone and wooden poles; although the effect is rustic, there is nothing rustic about the elegantly furnished tents and superb service. Dine alone with your personal waiter in attendance, or mingle with the other guests and swap fireside stories after a day's game-viewing. ■TIP→ No children under 10 are allowed unless the lodge is booked on an exclusive use basis. **Pros:** the service and personal attention are outstanding. **Cons:** sleeping under a tent, albeit a luxury tent, might not suit all tastes. ☎ *021/683–3424* ⊕ *www.singita.com* ⤳ *6 tented suites* ⌂ *In-room: a/c, safe, Internet. In-hotel: restaurant, bar, tennis courts, pool, spa, no kids under 10* ▤ *AE, MC, V* ☻ *Closed Apr. and May* ⎢◯⎢*FAP.*

$$$ ⛺ **Grumeti River Camp.** Situated on the banks of a Grumeti River tributary, this is one of the most exclusive tented camps in the Serengeti. En-suite tents are furnished much like you would see on the set of a Hollywood movie trying to do Africa chic. There are handmade wooden beds decorated with metal posts and bedheads, deep blue chairs with

Ghanaian Kente (handwoven fabric from Ghana) cloth cushions, hand-blown Kenyan glass, colorful rugs, and woven tables. The service is flawless, and there's an abundance of birdlife and game with resident hippos munching outside the tents at night. This is &Beyond at its best. **Pros:** great for hippo-viewing as the lodge overlooks the banks of the river. **Cons:** outdoor showers can be a bit chilly in the early mornings. ☏ 27/11/809–4300 ⊕ www.andbeyond.com ⤳ 10 tents ♿ In-room: no a/c, safe, no TV. In-hotel: bar, pool, shop ▭ AE, DC, MC, V ⫲ FAP.

$$$ ⛺ **Migration Camp.** Because this lovely camp is sited in northeast Serengeti among the rocky Ndasiata Hills, you won't see as many vehicles as you would nearer Seronera in the center of the park, but the game is all here. It's hard to believe that the accommodation is actually tented because it looks so luxurious. Spacious tents with hand-carved wooden furniture, big windowlike screens, en-suite bathroom, and a veranda facing the Grumeti River give you a ringside seat of the migration. The main areas with their deep leather chairs, sofas, handsome rugs, and elegant fittings seem more like a gentlemen's club you'd find in London or Washington, D.C., than a tent. Game is good all year round, but when the migration passes through it is awesome. Take a guided game walk from the camp, laze at the pool, or catch up on your reading in the small library. Too fast paced for you? May we suggest sitting on your veranda to watch what's happening game-wise in the surrounding wilderness. Food and service match the surroundings and accommodation in quality and style. Elewana recommends that you book through a safari specialist rather than directly. **Pros:** 360-degree views from the deck; complimentary laundry service. **Cons:** camp is about a three-hour trip from Central Serengeti; lots of steps may be a problem for people with mobility issues. ⇨ See the Tour Operators chart in Chapter 1, Your Safari for operator suggestions. ☏ 027/254–0630 ⊕ www.elewana.com ⤳ 20 tents ♿ In-room: no phone, no a/c, safe, no TV. In-hotel: restaurant, bar, pool, Wi-Fi ▭ AE, MC, V ⫲ FAP.

$$$$ ⛺ **Sabora Plains Tented Camp.** It's not often that you'll stay in a marquee-shaped tent elegantly furnished with silk curtains, antique furniture, stylish African artifacts, and a/c, but that's what you'll get at this ultra-luxurious camp set among green lawns adjacent to the Great Migration route. The game-abundant terrain ranges from open plains and rocky outcrops to riverine forest and woodlands in this 350,000-acre Grumeti concession in Serengeti's western corridor. At night, glowing gas lamps transform the tents raised on polished wooden platforms into a bush fairyland, although the only winged creatures you see will be the night birds and the fluttering moths. If you're an experienced rider, galloping across the plains with zebra and wildebeest is an unforgettable experience. For a more soothing experience, have a spa treatment on your veranda as you gaze out at the never-ending plains. At night, enjoy the brilliance of the night sky before or after a superlative meal. **Pros:** wide, open spaces; archery, stargazing safaris, mountain biking, and tennis are all available. **Cons:** children under 10 years old can be accommodated if the lodge is booked on an exclusive-use basis. ☏ 021/683–3424 ⊕ www.singita.com ⤳ 6 tents ♿ In-room: safe, Internet, Wi-Fi. In-hotel: restaurant, bar, tennis courts, pool, spa, no kids under 10 ▭ AE, MC, V ⊘ Closed Apr. and May ⫲ FAP.

$$ ⬚ Sayari Camp. Overlooking the Mara River in Serengeti's northwest, where the park borders Kenya's Masai Mara National Park, this small tented camp is perfectly poised for watching the river crossing—hundreds of thousands of wildebeest plunge into the crocodile-infested water on their relentless journey north. The unforgettable sightings of this natural wonder of the world (between July and November) often exceed those of next-door Masai Mara. The spacious en-suite tents, with hot water safari showers and flush toilets, colorfully decorated with handwoven rugs and wall hangings, are only a few hundred meters away from the river, so you can sit and relax in comfort while the herds build up on the bank. Then, at the appropriate moment, you can make your move and start clicking away. The Wedge, a nearby plain, is home to permanent spring-fed water and attracts thousands of antelope and other plains animals. Because this area of Serengeti is less visited than the west and south but still has an abundance of game and birdlife, you may not see another vehicle—always a huge bonus. Get there before the word gets out—you'll feel at the end of the world. **Pros:** the camp's isolated location means you'll have the game all to yourself; off-road driving is allowed on game drives. **Cons:** as there are few trees on the plains you can see the other tents from your own. ☎ 027/250–2799 ⊕ *www.asilialodges.com* 📷 *8 tents ⌂ In-room: no phone, no a/c, safe, no TV. In-hotel: restaurant, bar* ▭ *AE, MC, V* ⧆ *FAP.*

$$$ ⬚ Serena Kirawira Camp. Turn back the clock and stay at a camp that any well-heeled Victorian traveler would have felt completely at home in. Colonial comfort meets Africa in this gorgeous tented camp overlooking the western corridor just west of Seronara. Kirawira is a member of the Small Luxury Hotels of the World group, but that won't surprise you as the elegant pioneer ambience—polished wooden floors, gleaming antique furniture, handmade patchwork bedspreads, copper urns, and shining brass lamps—wraps itself around you. Your spacious double en-suite tent faces the endless plains where you can go for exhilarating game-packed drives and guided walks. Venture farther afield to go fishing or sailing on Lake Victoria. A crocodile safari—brave souls go out at night to track and watch crocs—by the Grumeti River will be a highlight, as will your meals; the food here is some of the Serengeti's finest. **Pros:** friendly staff; great food; beautiful Victorian-theme camp. **Cons:** camp is a five-hour journey from the Ngorogoro Crater; tsetse flies can be a problem in this area. ☎ 028/262–1518 ⊕ *www.kirawiracamp.com* 📷 *25 tents ⌂ In-room: no a/c, safe, no TV. In-hotel: restaurant, bar, pool, no kids under 7* ▭ *AE, DC, MC, V* ⧆ *FAP.*

MOBILE TENTED CAMPS

$$$ ⬚ Nduara Loliondo. If you want to do your own thing away from the big lodges and busy safari routes, then this small, intimate mobile camp, formerly Loliondo Mobile Camp, is for you. Taking up to eight travelers at a time, the "pack up and go" camp is run by Nomad Tanzania, a fitting name for a company that specializes in moving you to the game at the right place at the right time. Put yourself in the expert hands of your guide, cooks, waiters, and camp attendants to experience a true old-style safari. Accommodation is in one of four comfortable tents with hot bucket showers, bush toilet, and a big mess tent where you'll

Grumeti River Camp, Serengeti National Park

Grumeti River Camp

Klein's Camp,

Klein's Camp, Serengeti National Park

get together at the end of a hot dusty day. Your own vehicle and knowledgeable driver-guide stays with you for the length of your safari, and you can choose to do what you want, where you want. After a day's activities you'll enjoy sipping a glass of chilled white wine by the roaring campfire as you relive your experiences. Nomad operates several mobile camps in Tanzania, but they do not take direct bookings or publish their rates, so you'll need to contact your own safari operator for more information. **Pros:** as this camp is not located in the Serengeti park but on the outskirts, there is the freedom for game drives at night and bush walks. **Cons:** the migration will sometimes pass through but is not guaranteed in the Loliondo area; there are no credit-card facilities so bring cash if you want to tip the staff. ⊕ *www.nomad-tanzania. com* ⤳ *4 tents* ♿ *In-room: no phone, no a/c, safe, no TV* ▭ *AE, DC, MC, V* ⦿ *FAP.*

$$$

Fodor's Choice

★

🏨 Serengeti Under Canvas. This &Beyond mobile camp follows the migration beginning (usually in March) in Serengeti's northeast near Lake Ntutu on a small bluff with splendid acacia trees overlooking a small river. The camp stays put for a couple of months at a time and then moves northward with the herds. Comfortable walk-in tents (Tanzania's largest) with chandeliers that tinkle in the breeze (yes, there's even electricity) have en-suite bucket showers, copper washbasins, a flush toilet, deep, comfortable beds with crisp linen and fluffy mohair blankets, Indian rugs, a dawn chorus of joyous birdsong, and an evening serenade of whooping hyenas with back vocals by softly calling lions. If you want to rough it in the bush, this is not your place, because you'll be pampered at every turn. But you're never cocooned away from the surrounding natural wonders. This is the most marvelous way to experience the migrations, the wonders of Serengeti and Africa. It's certainly not cheap, but it is definitely worth every penny. **Pros:** an authentic safari experience; you won't lift a finger; largest walk-in tents in Tanzania. **Cons:** all this luxury and pampering will cost you. ☎ *27/11/809–4300* ⊕ *www.andbeyond.com* ⤳ *6 tents* ♿ *In-room: no phone, no a/c, safe, no TV* ▭ *AE, DC, MC, V* ⦿ *FAP.*

BUDGET ACCOMMODATIONS

¢ **🏨 Serengeti Stop Over.** If you're coming by road from Mwanza, this is a convenient stopover just outside the national park. Accommodation is in clean basic en-suite *bandas* (bungalow), and there's a small restaurant and bar. Friendly knowledgeable staff can arrange safaris into the park, fishing and boating trips to Lake Victoria, and cultural visits to nearby villages. Lake Victoria is within walking distance. If available, you can hire a safari vehicle for US$150 per day. **Pros:** an affordable camp run as a community initiative with the local Sukuma people. **Cons:** located outside the park. ☎ *028/262–2273 or 0748/422–359* ⊕ *www.serengetistopover.com* ⤳ *10 rooms* ♿ *In-room: no phone, no a/c, safe. In-hotel: restaurant, bar* ▭ *AE, MC, V* ⦿ *BP.*

¢ **🏨 Seronera Wildlife Lodge.** Although this big popular lodge is attractively located around huge rocks and boulders that are next to a number of water holes, it's also plumb in the middle of Serengeti—an ideal place for superb wildlife-viewing. But don't expect the levels of service and

"It was January, and all of the babies were being born. I loved watching the interactions of the moms with their babies, and of course watching out for the predators." —Nicki Geigert, Fodors.com member

luxury you would get from some of the smaller, more exclusive camps. However, it's cheap and cheerful, with small, rather drab en-suite rooms with king-size beds and big windows, and a cafeteria-style restaurant and bars that come alive in the evenings when the day's game-viewing or ballooning experiences are shared. (You're only five minutes from balloon lift-off here.) The food is hearty and wholesome with a tasty evening buffet, often accompanied by the snorts and harrumphing of the nearby hippos. You'll certainly see lots of game at close quarters, but lots of other visitors and vehicles, too. **Pros:** good location in the middle of the Serengeti. **Cons:** the walls between the rooms are thin; the 75 rooms are old-fashioned accommodation blocks built in the 1970s. ☎ *027/254–4595* ⊕ *www.hotelsandlodges-tanzania.com* ⤶ *75 rooms* ⚒ *In-room: no a/c, safe, no TV. In-hotel: restaurant, bar, pool, shop* ▭ *AE, MC, V* ⦿ *FAP.*

NGORONGORO CRATER

Game
★★★★★
Park Accessibility
★★★★★
Getting Around
☆★★★★
Accommodations
★★★★★
Scenic Beauty
★★★★★

Ngorongoro Crater ranks right up there among Africa's must-visit wildlife destinations: Serengeti, Masai Mara, Etosha, Kruger Park, and the Okavango Delta. Almost every would-be safari-goer wants to come here, and rightly so. One of only three UNESCO World Heritage sites in Tanzania (together with the Serengeti and the Selous Game Reserve), the crater is often called the Eighth Wonder of the World.

It lies in the Biosphere Reserve of the Ngorongoro Conservation Area, which covers 8,300 square km (3,204 square mi) in northern Tanzania. This reserve was specifically planned to accommodate both the traditional Masai communities and tourists. You'll see Masai villagers grazing their sheep and cattle all over.

The Ngorongoro Crater lies in a cluster of other volcanoes (sometimes seen rather ominously smoking) that borders the Serengeti National Park to the north and west. It's actually a collapsed volcano or *caldera*. The original volcano, which may have been higher than Kilimanjaro, collapsed in on itself over time and now forms a perfect basin. Once inside you'll feel like you're at the bottom of a deep soup bowl with very steep sides. The basin, measuring 18 km (11 mi) in diameter, lies 500 meters (1,640 feet) below the rim, which towers above it at about 2,200 meters (7,217 feet) above sea level.

Believed to have formed some 2 million years ago, the crater harbors an astonishing variety of landscapes—forests, peaks, craters, valleys, rivers, lakes, and plains—including the world-famous Olduvai Gorge, where some of our earliest human ancestors once hunted and gathered. ⇨ *See the Olduvai Gorge box, below.*

PARK ESSENTIALS

Entrance fees increase all the time, but in 2010 it cost US$50 per person to enter the Ngorongoro Conservation area.

The very steep and bumpy drive into the crater—don't be surprised if you encounter at least one vehicle with a puncture—begins high up in the forest. At dawn, thick mist drifts through the trees and visibility is next to nothing. Although this lush highland forest looks exactly like a rain forest, it's not. It's a *mist* forest, which depends on a regular and abundant amount of mist and drizzle. If you look closely enough, you'll see the particles of mist swirling like raindrops among the ancient trees. The aptly named pillarwood trees stand sentinel over the strangler figs, the croton trees, the highland *bersama* (a local plant), and purple wild tobacco flowers. The tree trunks and branches are home to thousands of epiphytes—specialized plants such as arboreal orchids and ferns—which cling to their hosts and absorb moisture with their own aerial roots. Look for the orchids among the curtains of Old Man's Beard, or hanging tree moss.

4

Monkeys, bushbuck, bush pigs, and elephants frequent the forest, although it's unlikely you'll see them. What you will see if you are staying in one of the crater lodges are well-mown lawns, which are not the result of hardworking gardeners but that of zebras and buffaloes, which after dark seek sanctuary from predators here. It's not dogs you hear barking after sundown but the warning calls of vigilant zebras and baboons. The crater floor, dominated by a huge flamingo-filled alkaline lake, holds the highest concentration of predators in the world—lions, hyenas, jackals, leopards. Cheetahs can occasionally be seen but fall prey to lions and hyena, which the nervous and fragile cheetah is no match for. Big herds of plains game such as Thomson's and Grant's gazelle, impala, giraffe, zebra, and wildebeest are easy meat for the thoroughly spoiled predators that need to expend very little energy to score a megameal. You'll probably see at least one pride of bloated lions lying on their backs, paws in air, stuffed and totally damaging their noble image as the King of Beasts. Make sure you ask your guide to point out a black or white rhino if he spots one. This is also a great place to take a boat safari down one of the hippo-dense rivers.

Birdlife is also spectacular with some endemic species: the Rufous-tailed weaver, Schalow's wheatear, and large flocks of the incredibly beautiful crowned cranes. Because this is a continuous killing ground, you'll quickly become a vulture expert. If you're a birder, ask for a guide who knows his birds well because not all the guides do.

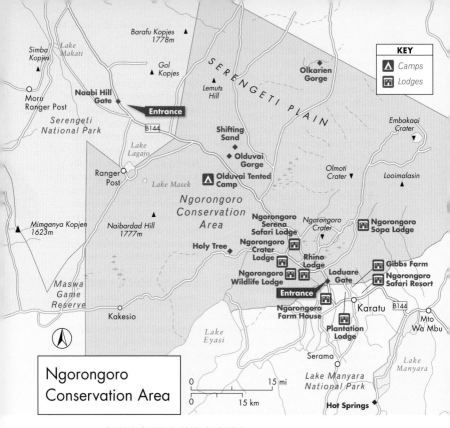

KEY

▲ Camps

▥ Lodges

Ngorongoro
Conservation Area

0   15 mi

0   15 km

GETTING HERE AND AROUND

Ngorongoro is about 180 km (112 mi) from Arusha by road. You can also fly into the crater rim airstrip or Ndutu Lodge airstrip. Tour operators can arrange your transfer in advance.

WHEN TO GO

Avoid April and May as these months are particularly wet in the crater.

SAFETY AND PRECAUTIONS

Be prepared for thick early morning mist all year round, which makes it quite chilly. Be sure to pack warm clothes.

TIMING

Because there is no restriction on the number of vehicles, there can be well over a hundred at one sighting in the high season. It's amazing to have a close-up encounter with some of Africa's finest game, but not if you're surrounded by other vehicles and often very noisy, boisterous tourists. It's best to go down as early as possible (the gates open at 6:30) to avoid the later traffic jams. But the crater is a once-in-a-lifetime experience so grit your teeth, ignore all the other tourists, and enjoy one of the world's most spectacular destinations.

WHERE TO STAY ON THE CRATER RIM

LUXURY LODGES

$$$$ 🔲 **Ngorongoro Crater Lodge.** Imagine walking into a Hollywood film set where the spectacular setting is literally "Great Zimbabwe ruins meets SS *Titanic* baroque." Clusters of stilted rooms with woven conical banana-leaf domes and fancifully carved stone chimneys cling to the crater's rim and somehow blend in with the natural surroundings. Your palatial abode has polished wooden floors, leather armchairs, and a dramatic mix of furniture and styles, including crystal chandeliers and hand-wrought local lamps. Ceiling-high swaths of silk taffeta drapes frame a small veranda with some of the world's most awesome views. Hand-carved doors lead to a massive bathroom with fresh-cut roses, a freestanding tub, and a tessellated tile shower straight out of a Roman villa. The main dining room has a 1920s ocean liner stateroom feel, but the adjacent lounge comes straight from an old English country house. It's a daring, glamorous mix of competing styles and themes that somehow works. However, the standards of food and service don't quite match the boldness of the architecture and opulence of the interiors. **Pros:** beautiful views over the Crater; iPod docks, a fireplace, and a hairdryer in the rooms. **Cons:** crater can be crowded with vehicles in peak season. ☎ 27/11/809–4300 ⊕ *www.andbeyond. com* ⬅ *30 rooms* ♿ *In-room: Internet. In-hotel: bar, pool, spa, shop* ▭ *AE, DC, MC, V* ⃝ *FAP.*

$$ 🔲 **Ngorongoro Serena Safari Lodge.** Imagine a medieval keep set deep into a hillside on the rim of an ancient volcano, surrounded by tropical rain forest. Imagine hand-built walls of russet-colored river stones, winding corridors, heavy wooden doors, and bushman paintings on cream interior walls. Imagine a tiled balcony overlooking one of the most famous and awesome views in the world. This is Serena Ngorogoro Safari Lodge. Built so unobtrusively to fit in with the natural surroundings, it's hard to spot the lodge even from the nature trail that winds around it. All the rooms have superb views overlooking the crater, and when you come back exhausted and exhilarated from your fill of one of the most amazing animal spectacles on earth, you'll still want to sit and gaze out at the mountain-ringed caldera, the vast herds roaming the plains, and the pink masses of flamingos on the water's edge. Your room has lots of hanging and storage space, polished wooden floors, earth-toned soft furnishings, comfortable beds and a big bathroom with his and her basins, a shower that a family of Thomson's gazelles could take refuge

CLOSE UP

The Cradle of Mankind

If you're interested in evolution and human origins, Olduvai Gorge, a World Heritage Site, is a definite must. It's about a 90-minute drive from the Ngorongoro Crater and is accessible only via a badly maintained road. The gorge, about 48 km (30 mi) long, is part of the Great Rift Valley, which stretches along East Africa. It has played a key role in palaeoanthropologists' understanding of the history of humanity providing clues dating from about 2.5 million years ago. There is a small museum at the gorge, but it doesn't really do justice to the magnitude of fossil discoveries made here.

Locals actually call Olduvai "Oldupai," which is the Masai name for a sisal plant, *Sansevieria ehrenbergii,* which grows all over in the area. The view overlooking the gorge is spectacular, and for a few extra shillings or dollars, your guide will be easily persuaded to take you down into the gorge where important fossils were found.

It's all a rather makeshift affair, and the guides aren't all fluent in English, so you may struggle to understand explanations inevitably filled with the Latin names of fossils.

Archaeological rock stars like the Leaky family have made some of these important discoveries:

■ *Paranthropus boisei* dating back 2.5 million years. These hominids had massive jaws and large, thickly enameled molars suitable for crushing tough vegetation. Their bite was several times more powerful than that of modern humans.

■ The first specimens of *Homo habilis,* which lived about 2 million to 1.6 million years ago. This is the earliest known named species of the Homo genus. Scientists believe that *Homo habilis* was one of the first hominid species that could make and use stone tools, enhancing our ancestors' adaptability and chances of long-term survival.

■ The world's oldest stone tools dated about 2 million years old, which are very primitive—basically just crude tools fashioned from pebbles.

By Tara Turkington

in, a wooden desk and chair, and old-fashioned lamps that look straight out of a colonial governor's residence. After the early morning mist has cleared, enjoy further spectacular views from the split-level bar and dining room where the food is wholesome and hearty. The whole place speaks of comfort with a classy, authentic bush ambience. **Pros:** location, location, location; close to crater entrance; nightly Masai dancing. **Cons:** most often cold and misty in morning; no safe in room; lots and lots of stairs that might challenge the less than nimble; a long, tiring ride on bad roads into and out of the crater (but that's true of all the crater lodges). ☎ *027/254–5555 or 027/253–7053* ⊕ *www.serenahotels.com* ➵ *75 rooms* ⌂ *In-room: a/c, Wi-Fi. In-hotel: restaurant, bar, pool, spa, shop* ═ *AE, DC, MC, V* ⏀ *FAP.*

$ ▥ **Ngorongoro Sopa Lodge.** The best thing about this acceptable but rather shabby lodge on the eastern edge of the crater is the spectacular sunset views from the bar lounge, the dining room, the gardens, swimming pool, and some of the guest rooms. Not all the rooms have great

views, however, so try for a room on the top floor in the higher numbers. Some rooms in the lower level have no view at all. Rooms are big with simple but outdated furnishings and dim lighting—regard it as 1970s retro and then it becomes fun. Hot water is only available at certain hours, so check with the desk when you arrive. The public areas where you meet up with your safari guides each morning are big and noisy until the safaris leave. If you're looking for peace and quiet, stay behind and just enjoy the views. Food is plentiful and varied, and the hotel has a relaxed, welcoming atmosphere and friendly staff. If you're a birder, you will particularly enjoy the lodge's forested grounds full of many different species. A bonus is the lodge's private ascent and descent road, which takes hours off traveling into the crater. **Pros:** wonderful views down into the Crater; heaters and hot-water bottles can be provided if you get cold. **Cons:** large lodge, and the number of guests makes it impersonal; rooms lacking in charm. ☎ *027/250–0630 or 027/250–0639* ⊕ *www.sopalodges.com* ⤳ *96 rooms* ⚘ *In-room: no phone, no a/c, safe, no TV. In-hotel: restaurant, bar, pool, shop* ☰ *MC, V* ⑂ *FAP.*

WHERE TO STAY IN THE NGORONGORO CONSERVATION AREA

LUXURY LODGING

$ ⛏ **Gibbs Farm.** If it weren't for the profusion of flowering plants and trees and sunny weather, you could believe yourself in an English country house at this working organic coffee farm midway between Lake Manyara and the Ngorongoro Crater. The 1929 farmhouse has managed to retain its old-fashioned charm with a wide veranda, intimate lounges, inviting reading nooks, and a bar and dining room that look much as they must have done almost 100 years ago. Small but luxurious guest cottages with en-suite bathrooms are scattered throughout the gardens and provide a perfect base to explore the crater and Lake Manyara National Park, as well as a perfect respite from exhilarating game drives. Expect delicious home-cooked food served with organic veggies and fruit from the farm's own gardens. The coffee is superb. Take advantage of the Masai health and beauty treatments developed by a third-generation Masai healer at the farm's Living Spa in the Oseru Forest Clinic. **Pros:** farm atmosphere; home-grown, organic vegetables and coffee; management dedicated to sustaining the land and supporting the nearby communities. **Cons:** the very bumpy road to the crater will take roughly an hour to get to the park gate. ☎ *027/253–4397* ⊕ *www.gibbsfarm.net* ⤳ *20 rooms* ⚘ *In-room: no phone, no a/c, safe, no TV. In-hotel: restaurant, bar, pool, shop* ☰ *AE, MC, V* ⑂ *MAP.*

$ ⛏ **Ngorongoro Farm House.** Once the home and coffee plantation of a 19th-century German settler, this beautifully renovated property facing the Oldeani volcano now consists of three camps of 40 spacious cottages built and decorated in old colonial style. Cottages and the thatch-roof main farmhouse are set in lovely gardens only 5 km (3.1 mi)

> **DID YOU KNOW?**
>
> A white rhino baby follows its mother, but a black rhino baby walks in front of its mother.

"Flying in unison over the Ngorongoro Crater, the large wingspan and bold colors of the crowned cranes provide a stark contrast to the natural browns and greens of the crater floor." —jechaft, Fodors.com member

from the Ngorongoro Lolduare gate. You'll sleep under a thatch roof in a large, airy bedroom with an en-suite bathroom and veranda. The main farmhouse has a bar, library, restaurant, and lounge. The food is delicious and uses lots of organic vegetables and herbs from the farm's own gardens. If you're looking for some downtime, spend some time by the pool or just wander round the gardens and spot birds. Excursions include trips to the crater and conservation area as well as face-to-face encounters with local communities (not included in the quoted price). **Pros:** home cooking using fresh, farm-produced dairy and vegetables yearround; cell reception; fireplace in the rooms. **Cons:** rooms look a little lackluster from the outside; some are far from main lodge, making it less appealing to mobility-impaired people. ☎ *7027/250–4093* ⊕ *www.tanganyikawildernesscamps.com* ➘ *50 rooms* ♿ *In-room: no phone, no a/c, safe, no TV. In-hotel: restaurant, bar, pool, shop* ▭ *AE, MC, V* ⑩ *MAP.*

$ 🏨 **Plantation Lodge.** Traditional Africa meets contemporary classic in the stylish interiors of this exquisite lodge set in established gardens amid coffee plantations only 4 km (2½ mi) from the Ngorongoro Crater. Cottages are furnished in a clean, uncluttered style that employs African motifs, prints, and artifacts complemented by the creams, browns, and whites of the soft furnishings, the wooden furniture, and terra-cotta tiled floors. Beautiful en-suite tiled bathrooms continue the theme of space and light, as do the public areas where you can dine in style at a massive long wooden table with your fellow guests, or have a romantic candlelit dinner à deux in the garden or on your private veranda. Food is homegrown and tastily prepared, and there's a list of good South African wines. ⇨ *See the South African Wine primer, in Chapter 5, South*

Gibb's Farm

Gibb's Farm

Ngorongoro Serena Safari Lodge

Africa, for more information about these great wines. The lodge can arrange your entire safari for you, or just your daily activities; neither is included in the quoted price. The lodge has many repeat guests and the guestbook echoes the word *Paradise* written over and over again. **Pros:** this is a small lodge so you will have a bit of peace and quiet; fireplace in each room. **Cons:** an hour's drive from the crater. ☎ 027/253–4405 ⊕ *www.plantation-lodge.com* 🛏 *16 rooms* ♿ *In-room: no phone, no a/c, safe, no TV. In-hotel: restaurant, bar, pool, shop* ▤ *AE, MC, V* ⦿*I MAP.*

PERMANENT TENTED CAMPS

$ 🚹 **Olduvai Tented Camp.** You'll have the opportunity to go walking in the Ngorongoro highlands with genuine Masai warriors at this no-frills, but untouristy camp. Built within a circle of *kopjes* (rocky outcrops) just south of the Serengeti border in the Ngorongoro Conservation Area, the camp operates in complete harmony with the Masai. It's the closest camp to the Olduvai Gorge, which is only a 40-minute drive from the Ngorongoro Crater. The food is not the greatest, but the location and feeling of being in genuine contact with the wild more than compensate for the basic cuisine. The game is particularly abundant December through May, and guests have been kept awake all night during the migration by the snuffling and snorting of thousands of wildebeest. Tents have wooden floors and thatch roofs with basic chemical toilets and bucket showers. There are two thatch rondavels for eating and sitting, and an open fire pit where you'll reminisce after the day's activities, which can include a variety of superb walking safaris, game drives, or a trip to the Olduvai museum. All activities are included. **Pros:** closest camp to the Olduvai Gorge; comfortable and unassuming lodgings; benefits the local community. **Cons:** food could be improved upon. ☎ 866/6–*SAFARI from U.S.* ⊕ *www.africatravelresource.com* 🛏 *16 tents* ♿ *In-room: no phone, no a/c, no TV. In-hotel: restaurant, bar, shop* ▤ *MC, V* ⦿*I FAP.*

BUDGET LODGING

¢ 🚹 **Ngorongoro Safari Resort.** If you're looking for something cheap and cheerful and don't mind being on the main road next to a garage and a very popular campsite, then this well-run property will hit the spot. Set in pleasant gardens in the middle of the lively little town of Karatu, the resort's rooms are retro 1970s with flounced satin bed frills, print curtains, and big windows, but they are also clean and comfortable with en-suite hot showers and complementary bottled drinking water. The resort is ideally situated along the main road to the Ngorongoro Crater, Olduvai Gorge, Lake Eyasi, and Serengeti. There are a couple of very interesting daily excursions, including a visit the Iraqw people of the Ngorongoro highlands and a guided walk that meanders through forest highlands to a nearby waterfall. **Pros:** short 15- to 20-minutes' drive to Ngorongoro Gate. **Cons:** located on the main road; no wild animals can be seen in the camp. ☎ 027/253–4287 ⊕ *www. ngorongorocampandlodge.com* 🛏 *32 rooms* ♿ *In-room: no a/c. In-hotel: restaurant, bar, pool, shop* ▤ *AE, MC, V* ⦿*I BP.*

LAKE MANYARA NATIONAL PARK

Game
☆☆★★★

Park Accessibility
★★★★★

Getting Around
☆☆★★★

Accommodations
☆☆★★★

Scenic Beauty
☆★★★★

In the Great Rift Valley south of Serengeti and the Ngorong-oro Crater lies the Cinderella of Tanzania's parks—the often overlooked and underrated Lake Manyara National Park. When Ernest Hemingway faced the rusty-red rocks of the almost 2,000-foot-high rift valley escarpment that dominates the park, he called it "the loveliest place I have seen in Africa."

Lake Manyara National Park is small, stretching only some 330 square km (127 square mi) along the base of the escarpment with two-thirds of its surface taken up by shallow alkaline Lake Manyara. This serene flat lake is one of the so-called Rift Lakes, which stretch like jewels along the floor of the Rift Valley.

The park may be small, but what it lacks in size it makes up for in diversity. Its range of ecosystems at different elevations makes for dramatic differences in scenery. At one moment you are traveling through a fairy-tale forest (called groundwater forest) of tumbling, crystal-clear streams, waterfalls, rivers, and ancient trees, the next you're bumping over flat, grassy plains that edge the usually unruffled lake, pink with hundreds of flamingos.

In the deep forest where old tuskers still roam, blue monkeys swing among huge fig and tamarind trees, giant baobabs, and mahoganies, using their long tail as an extra limbs. They've got orange eyes, roman noses, and wistful expressions. In the evenings as motes of dusty sunlight dance in the setting sun, there's an excellent chance of spotting troops of more than 300 olive baboons (better looking and furrier than their chacma cousins) sitting in the road, grooming each other, chatting, and dozing, while dozens of naughty babies play around them and old granddaddies look on with knowing eyes.

The thick, tangled evergreen forest eventually gives way to acacia woodlands with tall, flat-topped acacias and fever trees and finally to open

"All of a sudden . . . a downpour [began]. The wildebeests pulled in tighter to one another and just huddled together to stay protected. I thought that it created . . . an ethereal look." —Nicki Geigert, Fodors.com member

plains where hundreds of elephants, buffalo, and antelope roam, accompanied by Masai giraffes so dark they look as if they have been dipped in chocolate. This is a great place to see hippos at close hand as they lie on the banks of the lake, or as they begin to forage as dusk approaches. The park is known for its tree-climbing lions, not common to see, but you can be sure if one vehicle glimpses them then the bush telegraph will quickly reach your truck, too. No one really knows why they climb and roost in trees, but it's been suggested by one former warden of the park that this unusual behavior probably started during a fly epidemic when the cats climbed high to escape the swarms of biting flies on the ground. He suggests that the present ongoing behavior is now part of their collective memory.

If you're a birder then put this park on your must-visit list. Because of the great variety of habitats, there is a great variety of birds; more than 400 species have been recorded. As you drive through the forest you'll hear the Silvery-cheeked hornbills long before you see them flapping noisily in small groups among the massive trees, braying loudly as they fly. The edges of the lake as well as its placid surface attract all manner of water birds large and small. Along the reed-fringed lakeshore you'll see huge pink clouds drifting to and fro. These "clouds" are flocks of flamingos, not so prolific as they once were before the El

PARK ESSENTIALS

If you are only passing through Lake Manyara National Park, you can buy a permit (US$25) at the gate. You can get a good map and a bird checklist at the park's headquarters at the gate as you drive in from Mto Wa Mbu.

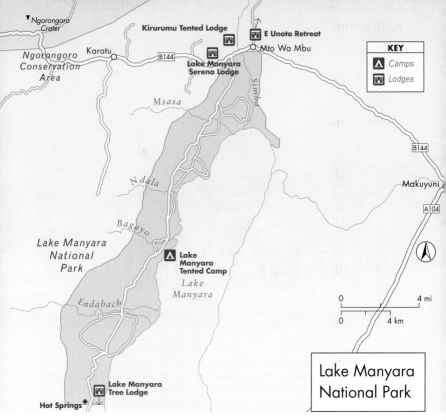

Niño floods of the late '90s, but now building up steadily again year by year. White-backed pelicans paddle through the water as the ubiquitous African fish eagle soars overhead. Other water birds of all kinds congregate—waders, ducks, geese, storks, spoonbills, egrets, and herons. In the thickets at the base of the red escarpment overlooking the lake, which angles up dramatically at 90 degrees, watch out for Nubian woodpeckers, the very pretty and aptly named Silver birds (flycatchers), Superb, Ashy, and Hildebrand's starlings, Yellow wagtails, trilling cistocolas, Red-cheeked cordon bleus, Peter's twinspots, Bluenecked mousebirds, and every cuckoo imaginable. The Red-and-yellow barbet is known as the "bed-and-breakfast bird" for its habit of living where it eats—in termite mounds. The park is also a raptor's paradise, where you can spot up to 51 daytime species, including dozens of Augur Buzzards, small hawks, and harriers. Deep in the forest you might be lucky enough to see Africa's most powerful eagle, the crowned eagle, which is strong enough to carry off young antelope, unwary baboons, and monkeys. At night listen for up to six different kinds of owl, including the Giant Eagle owl and the diminutive but very vocal African Scops owl.

"Remember, keep hydrated while on safari!" —alfredlind, Fodors.com member

GETTING HERE AND AROUND

You can get here by road or charter or scheduled flight from Arusha or en route to Serengeti and Ngorongoro Crater. The entrance gate to Lake Manyara National Park lies 1½ hours or 126 km (80 mi) west of Arusha along a newly surfaced road. There are daily flights that are 20 minutes from Arusha. Your safari operator or lodge can help you organize your transfers.

WHEN TO GO

During the dry season (May–October), it's easier to see the larger mammals and track their movements because there's less foliage. The wet season (November–April) is a great time for bird-watching, glimpsing amazing waterfalls, and canoeing.

WHERE TO STAY

LUXURY LODGES

$ **E Unoto Retreat.** Overseen by its American vice president who lives on the property, this stylish "Tanzania Masai luxury lodge," which lies at the foot of the Rift Valley escarpment, has attractive Masai-theme bungalows. Interiors boast hand-carved, funky, king-size wooden beds with colorful local beadwork complemented by handwoven rugs and woven lampshades. Outside, your personal balcony has bird's-eye views over Lake Miwaleni and the lofty escarpment. There are four honeymoon suites and, rare for safari lodges, another four are wheelchair-friendly. There's a lively outdoor bar, and the excellent international cuisine, complete with a great kids' menu, is served in the open-air restaurant. The very friendly and knowledgeable staff will arrange your excursions such as game drives in the park, mountain biking, or walking with a Masai guide to the nearby village to find out more about the local Masai people. **Pros:** The lodge provides employment, health care, and education to the local community, who also have shares in the lodge; wheelchair-friendly. **Cons:** electricity available only at certain times of the day. ☎ *0744/360–908* ⊕ *www.maasaivillage.com* ⇨ *25 cottages* △ *In-room: no phone, no a/c, safe, no TV. In-hotel: restaurant, bar, pool* ⊟ *AE, DC, MC, V* ⦿ *FAP.*

$$ ⛺ **Lake Manyara Serena Lodge.** Although not situated in the actual park, this lodge scores major points for its breathtaking views. On the edge of the escarpment overlooking the lake, the cluster of comfortably furnished en-suite double-story rondavels celebrates the area's legendary birdlife with its avian theme of sweeping cone-shaped thatch roofs and interior brightly colored "winged" frescoes. A stream that attracts all kinds of birdlife runs through the property. Another big bonus for this attractive but not very private lodge is the program of varied activities. You can choose from a microlite plane ride to look at the Great Rift Valley from 1,500 feet up; take an hour-long gentle nature walk; or if you're more energetic, hike in the forest and clamber over rivers, navigate thickly forested hillsides, and get spectacular views over the lake. Exhilarating mountain-bike rides take you down the Rift Valley escarpment and to the lakeshore. A very special outing is a village walk to the nearby town of Mto wa Mbu, which is home to more than 100 different tribes, although estimates vary according to whom you're talking with. However many there are, it's certain that there are dozens of different languages being spoken—this is apparently one of the richest linguistic mixes in Africa. You'll visit individual homes, a school, a church, and the market and end up at a banana-leaf bar with a fruit tasting. **Pros:** lovely infinity pool and rooms with views over the lake; two rooms are wheelchair-friendly. **Cons:** rooms could do with a revamp. ☎ *027/253–9162 or 027/254–5555* ⊕ *www.serenahotels.com* ⇨ *54 rooms* △ *In-room: no a/c, safe, no TV, Wi-Fi. In-hotel: restaurant, bar, pool* ⊟ *AE, DC, MC, V* ⦿ *FAP.*

$$$ ⛺ **Lake Manyara Tree Lodge.** The 10 tree houses of the camp—the only one in Lake Manyara National Park—are cradled in the boughs of giant mahogany trees. It's a Swiss Family Robinson setting without the DIY aspect. You'll be greeted at forest-floor-level entrance by an array of upturned wooden canoes before climbing up to the main areas built under ancient branches heavy with foliage, fruit, and flowers. Your huge wooden thatch bedroom decorated with looped ropes of palm fronds

Lake Manyara Tree Lodge

Lake Manyara Tree Lodge

has its own lounge area and en-suite bathroom where you can relax in a bubble bath as birds flit past the big window. Take time to sit on your wooden deck suspended above the forest floor as old elephants browse beneath you and tumultuous birdsong fills the air. There's fine dining by soft gas lamps as owls call. Bush picnics, game drives, and bird-watching trips are all part of the memorable experience at this enchanting camp. **Pros:** stay in a treehouse; there's a chance of seeing the famous Manyara tree-climbing lions when out on a game drive (not into your treehouse, though!); the long ride to the lodge from the air strip is treated as a game drive so you could see some amazing animals on the way. **Cons:** lodge is a three-hour drive from the Manyara airstrip on a bumpy road. ☎ 27/11/809–4300 ⊕ *www.andbeyond.com* ⤴ *10 rooms* ♿ *In-room: no phone, no a/c, safe, no TV. In-hotel: bar, pool, shop* ⊟ *AE, DC, MC, V* ⦶ *FAP.*

PERMANENT TENTED CAMPS

$ ⊞ **Kirurumu Tented Lodge.** The 20 secluded double tents of this highly regarded, intimate camp set among indigenous bush high on the escarpment will make you feel much closer to Africa than some of the bigger lodges. Spacious thatch-roof tents, each with its own veranda, are built on wooden platforms with great views overlooking Lake Manyara. Gaily decorated with animal-motif furnishings, woven straw mats, and carved bedside lamps, all tents have an en-suite bathroom with flush toilet and ceramic hand basins. Larger family tents are also available. Known for its excellent food and friendly service, the camp is an ideal base for game drives in the park, mountain biking, horseback riding, hiking, and bird-watching. For something very special go fly-camping in the forest, but fix this with the lodge in advance. After an action-packed day, sip your sundowner in the attractive open-sided bar before enjoying a memorable meal in the restaurant with stunning views over the Rift Valley floor. **Pros:** plenty of room for families; lovely view over the Rift Valley and Lake Manyara; coffee-making facilities in the rooms. **Cons:** bumpy 6-km (3.7-mi) drive to the camp; no mosquito nets. ☎ 027/250–7011 or 027/250–7541 ⊕ *www.kirurumu.com* ⤴ *22 tents* ♿ *In-room: no phone, no a/c. In-hotel: restaurant, bar* ⊟ *AE, DC, MC, V* ⦶ *FAP.*

BUDGET ACCOMMODATIONS

¢ ⊞ **Lake Manyara Tented Camp (aka Migunga Forest Camp).** The main attraction of this secluded bush camp, apart from its reasonable price, is its location in an indigenous forest just 2 km (1.2 mi) from the town of Mto wa Mbu. En-suite tents with hot-water showers are basic and comfortable, and meals are included in the price. There's a pleasant bar and restaurant, and the staff will arrange game drives and other activities for you. **Pros:** located in a beautiful fever-tree forest; camp has a laid-back atmosphere; only about a 15-minute drive to the park entrance. **Cons:** camp is outside Lake Manyara Park. ☎ 0754/300806 or 0754/611818 ⊕ *www.swalasafaris.com* ⤴ *9 tents* ♿ *In-room: no phone, no a/c, no TV. In-hotel: restaurant, bar* ⊟ *AE, DC, MC, V* ⦶ *FAP.*

SELOUS GAME RESERVE

4

Game
☆☆★★★
Park Accessibility
☆★★★★
Getting Around
☆★★★★
Accommodations
☆☆★★★
Scenic Beauty
☆★★★★

Most visitors come away from Selous (sel-oo) Game Reserve acknowledging that this is Africa as it is—not as tourism has made it. The reserve is one of only three World Heritage sites in Tanzania. A true untamed wilderness, the reserve covers 50,000 square km (19,305 square mi) and comprises 5% of Tanzania. Selous Game Reserve is the largest national park in Africa and the second largest in the world.

Only Greenland National Park at 972,000 square km (375,398 square mi), which is larger than England and France combined, beats Selous. But before you get too excited over the statistics, although Selous is still arguably the biggest area of protected pristine wilderness left in Africa, most of it is off-limits to tourists. The reserve is bisected from west to east by Tanzania's biggest river, the Rufiji, and only the area north of the river is open to visitors. So although it's teeming with game, it forms only about 5% of the total park.

The other 95% is mainly leased to hunting concessions. Hunting is still a very contentious issue, and although both sides passionately argue a plausible case, it's hard for many people to accept that shooting some of Africa's most beautiful and precious animals just for fun is ethically acceptable. However, hunting is under strict government control, and half of each substantial hunting fee is put back into the management and conservation of the reserve. It's possible that without this money the Selous would not exist, and rampant poaching would take over.

The visitor area of Selous north of the Rufiji River stretches for about 1,000 square km (386 square mi) and has great game-viewing and bird-watching opportunities. The fact that there are very few lodges adds to the area's exclusivity. These are along and beside the Rufiji River, which rises in Tanzania's highlands, then flows 250 km (155 mi) to the Indian Ocean. The Rufiji boasts the highest water-catchment area in East Africa. A string of five small lakes—Lake Tagalala, Lake Manze,

Lake Nzerekea, Lake Siwando, and Lake Mzizimia—interlinked by meandering waterways gives something of an Okavango Delta feel to the area and the birdlife—more than 400 recorded species—is prolific as are the huge crocodiles and lumbering hippos.

There are major advantages to visiting this park. First, although tourist numbers are now creeping up, there's no chance whatsoever that you'll be game-viewing in the middle of a noisy bunch of vehicles. Our advice is to get here quickly before the jungle telegraph spreads the news of its many attractions.

Another major draw is that much of your game-viewing and bird-watching will be done from the water. Because Selous is a game

SELOUS'S NAMESAKE

Captain Frederick Courtenay Selous (sel-oo) was a famous English explorer and Great White Hunter who roamed the area in the late 1800s. Considered by many to be the greatest hunter of all time, he recounted his adventures in best-selling books of the day, and his safari clients included none other than Teddy Roosevelt. He was killed by a German sniper at Beho Beho in 1917 while scouting for the British against the German *Schutztruppe* (a mixed force of German troops and local Africans) during World War I. His grave lies where he fell.

reserve, not a national park, a larger range of activities is permitted, so you can walk, camp, and go on a boat safari. There's nothing quite like watching a herd of elephants showering, playing, and generally having fun as you sit in a boat in the middle of a lake or river. As you watch, lots of other game including buffalo and giraffe will also amble down to the banks to quench their thirst. If giraffes are your favorite animals, Selous will delight you because it is one of the few places in Africa where you can see big herds of up to 50.

Another Selous bonus, especially if you've been bouncing about in a game vehicle for days in other parks, is that you can walk in the Selous, not alone but with an armed ranger. Although the game can be skittish as it is not as habituated as in Serengeti or Ngorongoro, walking through the bush or beside a river is a rare opportunity to get up close with nature, and you never know what's around the next corner. Your lodge will organize a short three-hour walk, or if you want to camp out in the bush, an overnight safari.

Selous still has a major problem with poaching, which decimated the elephant population and all but made the biggest herd of black rhino in the world extinct. In the 1980s the number of black rhino, previously estimated at 3,000, fell alarmingly to almost none. Today, thanks to the efforts of international and local conservation organizations, the black rhino has been pulled back from almost certain extinction to approximately 150 individuals, and, together with other game numbers, is increasing all the time. There are now approximately 65,000 elephants, 8,000 sable antelope, and an estimated 50,000 puku antelope, but you'll be lucky to see either sable or puku as they tend to stick to the thick bush or inaccessible areas of the park. What you almost certainly will see is the endangered African wild dog. Selous has up to

1,300 individuals in several wide-ranging packs: double that of any other African reserve. Three packs range north of the Rufiji, so there's a good chance of spotting these "painted wolves," especially from June to August when they are denning and stay put for a few months.

Selous is a birder's mecca with more than 400 species. Along the river with its attendant baobab trees and borassus palms, expect to see different species of herons from the aptly named Greenback heron to the Malagasy squacco heron, which winters here. Storks, skimmers, and little waders of all kinds dig in the mud and shallow water, while at dusk you may get a glimpse of the rare ginger-color Pel's Fishing Owl, which screeches like a soul in torment. In summer, flocks of hundreds of brightly colored Carmine bee-eaters flash crimson along the banks where they nest in holes, and kingfishers of all kinds dart to and fro.

PARK ESSENTIALS

If you are brave enough to go it alone in the park, you will need a 4x4 and very good driving skills. Don't even attempt to visit during the rainy season (March–May), as roads are impassable. Permits cost US$30 per person per day plus US$30 per vehicle. If you are camping, you will be required to hire an armed guard at US$15–US$20 per day. You can also hire a guide for about US$15–US$20 per day.

GETTING HERE AND AROUND

The best way to get to Selous is by charter or scheduled flight from Dar es Salaam or Arusha. Arusha to Selous is a three-hour flight, Dar es Salaam to Arusha is a two-hour flight. There is also the option of getting there by road from Dar, which will take eight hours. However, we recommend that you fly, especially between February and April, when the road conditions can become very bad because of the rainy season. Your operator or lodge should be able to help you arrange your transportation.

WHEN TO GO

May to October is the best time to visit, as it is the driest. During the long rains from February to May most of the camps are not accessible.

WHERE TO STAY

LUXURY LODGES

$$ **Beho Beho.** Regarded by many safari aficionados as being one of the best in East Africa for its accommodation, superb views over the floodplains, fine dining, and impeccable service, this ultraluxurious camp was the first in the Selous to be built in the cool highlands northwest of Lake Tagalala. Lake Tagalala is reputed to have more crocodiles than almost anywhere else in Africa. You'll see why as you chug along on a boat safari. Eight stone-and-thatch chalets with private en-suite bathrooms, a dressing room, and two verandas overlooking the wide floodplains are beautifully decorated with travel-worn leather trunks and suitcases, African artifacts, old maps and prints, writing desks, hand-carved wooden furniture, and comfortable Zanzibari day beds. Although not on the river, a pool in front of the camp plays host to

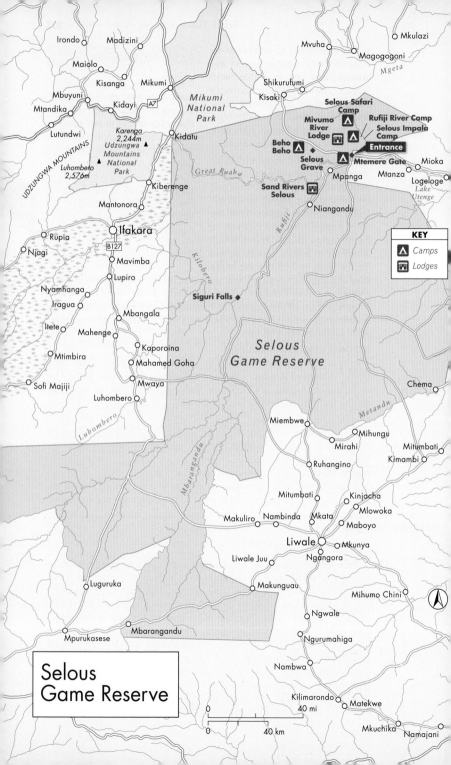

Selous
Game Reserve

buffalo, hippo, and whatever game happens to be in the area, including lion, elephant, and wild dog. You'll visit the hot sulfur springs of Maji Moto, where you can swim in the deep natural pools. If you stay more than four nights, seize the opportunity to camp out on the banks of the dry Beho Beho River. After first

> **DID YOU KNOW?**
>
> There are more elephants in Selous than anywhere else in Africa. An estimated 65,000 live in the reserve, comprising almost 10% of Africa's total.

walking through a remote part of the Selous with an armed guide for an hour or two, you'll think that you have strayed into an Arabian Nights fantasy as you catch sight on the sumptuously furnished tents at Bush Camp. Bookings are made through the U.K.'s Africa Reps. **Pros:** you don't have to leave the camp to see lots of wildlife; communal eating means that you can share safari stories and meet new people; private dining can be arranged on request. **Cons:** no night drives are allowed in the park; vehicles have to be back in the camp at dusk. ☎ *44/193226–0618 in U.K.* ⊕ *www.behobeho.com* ⮑ *8 chalets* ♿ *In-room: no a/c, safe, no TV. In-hotel: restaurant, bar, pool, no kids under 12* ▭ *AE, DC, MC, V* ☉ *Closed mid-March–early June* ⊙ *FAP.*

$$$$ 🛏 **Sand Rivers Selous.** Deep in the southwest corner of Selous, this lodge is just about as isolated and exclusive as you can get. Sited in the Sand River area above a wide bend of the Rufiji River, the stone and thatch lodge and chalets are literally and metaphorically hundreds of miles away from tourist Africa with its ubiquitous curio shops and gawking tourists. Your open-fronted en-suite chalet has a king-size bed, elegant wooden furniture, elegant cream and white soft furnishings, carefully chosen African artifacts, and great river views. In front of the main lodge, which is shaded by a 1,500-year-old baobab tree, there's a stone walkway that curves along the riverbank, where you can sit and watch cavorting hippos and dozing crocs. Apart from its game drives, the lodge prides itself on its walking safaris; you don't have to be super fit, but a ramble through the surrounding wilderness with some of Tanzania's best guides is something you'll never forget. Watch birds and game from a gently chugging boat, or spend a night fly-camping beside Lake Tagalala to a soundtrack of roaring lions, chortling hippos, and splashing crocs. The boat trip through Stiegler's Gorge (named after a Swiss explorer who got taken out here by an elephant in 1907) is your best chance of seeing a leopard. The lodge does not take direct bookings. **Pros:** beautiful location; river cruises available. **Cons:** mischievous monkeys have been known to raid the rooms, so put your belongings safely away; no mobile phone reception. ☎ *022/286–5156* ⊕ *www. nomad-tanzania.com* ⮑ *8 chalets* ♿ *In-room: no a/c, safe, no TV. In-hotel: restaurant, bar, pool* ▭ *AE, DC, MC, V* ⊙ *FAP.*

PERMANENT TENTED CAMPS

$ 🛏 **Rufiji River Camp.** This unpretentious great-value-for-the-money camp Fodor's Choice is the oldest in the reserve and it shows; the friendly owner and his · ★ experienced staff have got things absolutely right. On a wide bend on the Rufiji at the end of the eastern sector of the reserve, you'll stay in one of 20 spacious no-frills but comfortable en-suite tents spread out

4

Sand Rivers Selous

Beho Beho Safari Lodge

Selous Safari Camp

along the river. The home-cooked Italian cuisine is excellent, but if you're not a pasta fan, there are plenty of other options. Depending on the length of your stay you can choose any or all of the activities on offer including game drives, boat safaris, and overnight fly-camping. This camp also stays open throughout the rainy season (March–May), but you will need to book well in advance if you intend to visit then. Game is prolific, you won't have to leave camp to see elephants, buffalo, and all sorts of other game, including a good chance of seeing wild dogs. Sit out on the sunset deck and wait for Africa's wildlife to come to you. **Pros:** game-viewing can be done on foot, by boat, or vehicle; variety of game-viewing options gives you a different perspective of the wildlife and allows you to see a wide variety of animals, large and small. **Cons:** monkeys can be a problem in camp as they try to steal food from tables— don't feed them. ☎ *078/423–7422* ⊕ *www.rufijirivercamp.com* ⇨ *20 tents* ⚙ *In-room: no phone, no a/c, no TV. In-hotel: restaurant, bar, pool* ▣ *AE, DC, MC, V* ⊙ *FAP.*

WORD OF MOUTH

"We stayed at the Selous Safari Camp - luxurious tents right by the lake, great food amazing guides. All in all a very well run place. One of the main attractions for us was the option of not only jeep based safaris but boats on the lake/river which were amazing. We also opted for fly camping one night which involved long hike (option to go by jeep) which was still ranks as one of the most memorable experiences of my travelling life—fine food and wines in the middle of nowhere—fantastic." —crellston

$$
Fodor's Choice
★

🕱 **Selous Impala Camp.** This attractive small camp on Lake Mzizimia's shores nestles among borassus palms and riverine bush with great views over the Rufiji. Tents on wooden platforms raised on stilts, each with its own en-suite bathroom and private veranda, have comfortable African-theme soft furnishings and rustic handmade wooden furniture. Join other guests in the main thatch lounge or on the viewing deck overlooking the river for meals and sundowners. If you're here in the dry season between June and October, you'll see plains game galore as the animals come to drink at the perennial river. As well as elephant, buffalo, hippo, antelope of all kinds, and the always lying-in-wait crocodiles, there's a good chance of spotting lion and wild dog. Selous boasts more than 400 species of birds, so keep that bird-spotting list nearby at all times. Go for a guided game walk with an armed ranger, a game drive, or a boat safari; visit Stiegler's Gorge or the Maja Moto hot springs; or just chill out at this comfortable and unpretentious camp. ▪**TIP**➔ There are some very good deals available if you fly in with Coastal Aviation, which operates the camp. **Pros:** you rarely see any other vehicles on game drives; the staff are very knowledgeable; overall a fantastic camp. **Cons:** as there are fewer game vehicles in the area, animal sightings are not as prolific as in the north. ☎ *022/211–7959 or 022/211–7960* ⊕ *www.tanzaniaodyssey.com* ⇨ *7 tents* ⚙ *In-room: no phone, no a/c, safe, no TV. In-hotel: restaurant, bar, pool* ▣ *AE, DC, MC, V* ⊙ *FAP.*

$$$ 🕱 **Selous Safari Camp.** In the middle of the riverine bush on the banks of Lake Nzerakera, this luxuriously appointed camp comprises nine tents built on wooden platforms, which blend in graciously with the surrounding wilderness. The open-sided spacious tents, each with two verandas, are tastefully decorated in creams, browns, and whites with a big bed, antique wooden chests, hand-carved settles, and colorful rugs. An en-suite bathroom with his-and-her brass hand basins and an open-air hot-water shower overlooks the bush. Public palm-thatch areas of polished wood platforms ringed with rope and wood rails have comfortable cane furniture, African artifacts, camp chairs, and elegant pieces of furniture from a bygone age. The camp is unfenced, so be prepared for all sorts of game to wander past your tent or the main viewing deck. At night the camp takes on a fairy-tale atmosphere when it is lit by dozens of softly glowing gas lanterns. Activities include game drives and guided walks, boating, bird-watching, or just relaxing on the veranda. **Pros:** you rarely see any other vehicles on game drives; great food; lovely view over the lake. **Cons:** the boat trip up the Rufiji river is not available all year round. ☎ *022/213–4802* ⊕ *www.selous. com* ↝ *9 tents* ⚐ *In-room: no a/c, safe, no TV. In-hotel: restaurant, bar, pool* ☰ *MC, V* ⦿ *FAP.*

BUDGET ACCOMMODATION

$$ 🏨 **Mivumo River Lodge.** It's hard to believe that this gorgeous new lodge set high on a bluff above Tanazania's biggest river, the mighty Rufiji, could exist in such an utterly remote and wild area. There are 12 large thatch-roof suites with wall-to-ceiling windows, a big en-suite bathroom with chandelier, his-and-her marble basins, a claw-foot bath, and a handcarved wooden screen and mirrors. A big outdoor deck overlooks the river with loungers from where you can watch hippos snooze or crocodiles sunbathe, an umbrella to shade you from the noonday sun, and a table and chairs to have your morning tea. If you feel like cooling off, there's a personal cold-water Jacuzzi. Sumptuous golden taffeta curtains, 1950s retro furniture, carved wooden lamps, polished wooden floors, handmade rugs, and a desk with a zebra-skin surface all mix and match to give a unique African feel. The public areas are on three levels with superb river views, a pool deck, a viewing deck, and big sheltered thatch sitting and dining area where you'll have your sundowner, followed by a beautifully served tasty meal. Daylong drives into the middle of the reserve where giraffe and lion abound are spectacular. If you're a birder, the water birds at Tagalala Lake will keep you ticking furiously. You'll enjoy a picnic under palms by one of the lakes before more game-spotting in the huge area known as Little Serengeti. A boat trip up the Stiegler Gorge (named after a famous early 1900s elephant hunter) is a must. **Pros:** real, wild Africa; abundant game; boat trips down Rufiji River. **Cons:** lots of steps in lodge; very rough bumpy roads. ☎ *027/254–5555* ⊕ *www.serenahotels.com* ↝ *12 rooms* ⚐ *In-room: a/c, safe, TV. In-hotel: restaurant, bar, pool, spa, laundry service, no kids under 7* ☰ *AE, DC, MC, V* ⦿ *FAP.*

4

GOMBE STREAM AND MAHALE MOUNTAINS NATIONAL PARKS

Game
☆☆☆☆★

Park Accessibility
☆☆☆★★

Getting Around
☆☆☆☆★

Accommodations
☆☆☆★★

Scenic Beauty
★★★★★

If your heart is set on tracking our nearest animal relatives—the intriguing, beguiling, and oh-so-human chimpanzees—then take the time and effort to get to one or both of these rarely visited but dramatically beautiful parks. You'll meet very few other visitors, and very few other people on earth will share your experience.

The best time to see chimps is toward the end of the dry season, July–October, when they come out of the forest and move lower down the slopes—sometimes even to the beach.

Don't go trekking if you have a cold, flu, or any other infectious diseases. Chimps are highly susceptible to human diseases, and you certainly wouldn't wish to reduce the chimp population even further.

GOMBE STREAM NATIONAL PARK

Bordering Burundi to the west, Tanzania's smallest national park—only 52 square km (20 square mi)—is easily one of the country's loveliest. It's tucked away on the shores of Africa's longest and deepest lake, Lake Tanganyika, 420 mi long and 30 mi wide. The lake is a veritable inland sea, the second deepest lake in the world after Russia's Lake Baikal. This small gem of a park 3.5 km (2.2 mi) wide and only 15 km (9.3 mi) long stretches from the white sandy beaches of the blue lake up into the thick forest and the mountains of the Rift escarpment behind.

Though the area is famous for its primates, don't expect Tarzanlike rain forest because the area is mainly covered with thick Brachystegia woodland. There are also strips of riverine bush alongside the many streams that gouge out steep valleys as they make their way from the highlands to flow down into the lake.

You've got to be determined to get here because Gombe is accessible only by boat. But you'll be amply rewarded with one of the most exciting animal encounters of a close kind that is still possible on our planet. You'll hear the chimps long before you see them. A series of hoots and shrieks rising to a crescendo of piercing whoops sounds like a major primate battle is about to begin. But it's only the members of the clan identifying one another, recognizing one another, and finally greeting one another.

PARK ESSENTIALS

Entry fees for Gombe are US$120 per 24 hours, the highest of any park in Tanzania. The Mahale entry fee is US$100. Your guide will cost US$25. No kids under 7. Because of the traveling time you will need to spend at least two nights in either or both of the parks.

Gombe became famous when Brit Jane Goodall came to the area in 1960 to study the chimpanzee population. At the time she wasn't known or recognized as the world-renowned primatologist she would later become. Sponsored by the legendary paleontologist Louis Leakey of Olduvai Gorge, Goodall came to Gombe as an eager but unqualified student of chimpanzees. At first many of her amazing unique studies of chimp behavior were discounted because she was young, unknown, and not a respected scientist. How could a chimpanzee be a hunter and meat-eater? How could a chimpanzee possibly use grass stalks and sticks as tools? Whoever had heard of inter-troop warfare? Today her groundbreaking work is universally acknowledged. Read more about her and her experiences at Gombe in her best-selling book *In the Shadow of Man*. You'll also be able to meet descendants of those chimpanzees she studied and made famous. Fifi, who was only three when Goodall arrived at Gombe in 1960, survived to the millennium.

But be warned—to follow in Jane or Fifi's footsteps you need to be fairly fit. Keeping up with a group of feeding and moving chimpanzees as they climb hills and forage in deep valleys can be very strenuous work. But the effort will be worth it—there's nothing on earth quite like coming face-to-face with a chimpanzee or accompanying a group as they make their way through the forest.

GETTING HERE AND AROUND

Kigoma is connected to Dar es Salaam and Arusha by scheduled flights, and to Mwanza, Dar es Salaam and Mbeya by rough dirt roads. Kigoma to Dar es Salaam is a three-hour flight; from Kigoma to Arusha is roughly a two-hour flight. The drive from Kigoma to Mwanza is roughly 575 km (357 mi), and the roads are bad. If you go by bus it will take two days. The lodge can arrange your travel to and from your destination, talk to your safari operator about getting to and from the camps.

WHEN TO GO

The chimps don't roam very far during the wet season: February–May and November–mid--December. It'll be easier to find them, and you'll have better opportunities to photograph them, during the dry months of June–October and late December.

TIMING

Strict rules are in place to safeguard you and the chimps. Allow at least two days to see them—they are in a wild state, so there are no guarantees where they'll be each day.

WHERE TO STAY

LUXURY LODGES

¢ **Kigoma Hilltop Hotel.** On a hill overlooking the lake about 2 km (1.2 mi) from Kigoma's town center, this hotel makes an ideal base for your chimpanzee trekking. You'll stay in a comfortable no-frills cottage with a/c, a mini-refrigerator, satellite TV, and an en-suite bathroom. What puts the hotel above any other in the area is that it not only arranges your excursions for you, but also has all kinds of water-sports equipment for hire. Go snorkeling, fishing, swimming, or just chill out on the private beach. There is also a gym, business services, and a large pool. Try delicious Indian food at the restaurant, or stay conventional and stick with Western food. No alcohol is sold, but you can bring your own. **Pros:** lovely view of Lake Tanganyika from your balcony **Cons:** limited menu. ☎ *028/280–4435 or 028/280–4436 ⊕ www. chimpanzeesafaris.com ⤴ 8 tents ⚘ In-room: a/c, refrigerator. In-hotel: restaurant, pool ⊟ AE, DC, MC, V ⊚ BP.*

MAHALE MOUNTAINS NATIONAL PARK

Just south of Gombe on the shores of Lake Tanganyika lies Tanzania's most remote national park. Thirty times bigger than Gombe, Mahale is a stunningly beautiful park with crystal-clear streams, soaring forested mountains, and deserted, white sandy beaches. Mt. Nkungwe at 2,460 meters (8,070 feet) dominates the landscape. More than 700 chimpanzees live in the area and are more accessible and more regularly seen than at Gombe.

In 1965 the University of Kyoto in Japan established a permanent chimpanzee research station in Mahale at Kisoge, about a kilometer from the beach. It's still going strong and remains highly respected.

There are no roads in Gombe or Mahale: all your game-viewing and chimpanzee tracking is done on foot. If you're a couch potato, stick with the National Geographic TV channel. What will you see other than chimpanzees? You'll almost certainly see olive baboons, vervet monkeys, red-, blue-, and red-tailed colobus monkeys, and some exciting birds. More than 230 bird species have been recorded here, so look out for crowned eagles, the noisy trumpeter hornbills, and the "rasta" birds (the crested guinea fowls with their black punk hairdos). Don't expect to see big game; although there are roan antelope, elephant, giraffe, buffalo, lion, and wild dog in the eastern savanna and woodland, these areas are largely inaccessible. But you're not here for big game. You're here to meet your match.

GETTING HERE AND AROUND

Arrange a charter flight from Arusha, Dar es Salaam, or Kigoma. The flight to Greystoke Mahale is around three to four hours from Arusha. The flight from Dar to Arusha is two hours. There is also the National Park motorboat from Kigoma, which will take three to four hours.

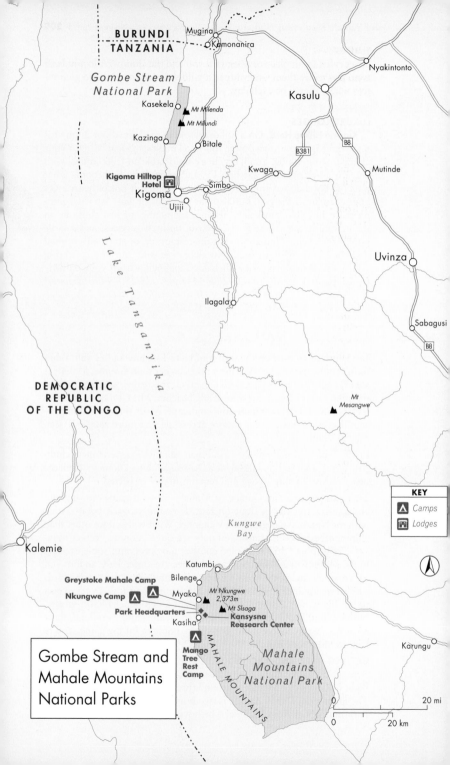

WHEN TO GO

The dry season, May–October, is best for forest walks, although there is no problem in the light rains of October and November.

WHERE TO STAY

LUXURY LODGES

$$$

Fodor's Choice

★

🛏 **Greystoke Mahale.** If you were a castaway, this would be heaven. It's difficult to imagine almost anywhere on earth that's as wildly beautiful and remote as this exotic camp on the eastern shore of Lake Tanganyika. Six wood and thatch bandas nestle on the forest rim. Behind them thickly wooded mountains rise almost 2,500 meters (8,200 feet); in front of them white sands stretch to the peaceful azure waters of the lake. Tarzan, of course, was really Lord Greystoke, so this aristocrat of camps is well-named. Your banda has furniture of bleached dhow wood, a rustic toilet and shower, and a lower and upper wooden deck with views over the lake. The main building is loosely based in the style of a Tongwe chief's hut, although many of your meals will be taken on the beach, at night by glowing lanterns. It's not easy to get here: a four-hour flight from Arusha followed by a two-hour boat ride. But once here you won't ever want to leave. About 60 of Mahale's 1,000 or so wild chimpanzees live in the forest near Greystoke, so you have an excellent chance of spotting them. Go snorkeling, birding, or just chill. Bookings are made only through reputable tour operators. ■TIP→ There are no roads within 100 km (62 mi) of camp, and access is only by light aircraft using the shared charter flights that operate on Mondays and Thursdays from Arusha only. Flights leave early in the morning and return to Arusha early evening that same day. The flight to Greystoke Mahale is around 3–4 hours, and upon arrival at the airstrip there is an approximately 90-minute dhow trip down the lake to reach the camp. ⇨ *See the Tour Operators chart in Chapter 1, Your Safari, for operator suggestions.* **Pros:** very secluded in the Mahale mountains; the camp gives you the opportunity to watch wild chimpanzees up close and personal. **Cons:** trekking up after the chimps is hard work; long flight to get there. ⊕ *www.greystoke-mahale.com* ⊸ *6 bandas* ⚹ *In-room: no phone, no a/c, no TV. In-hotel: restaurant, bar* ⊟ *AE, DC, MC, V* ⦿ *FAP.*

NATIONAL PARKS ACCOMMODATIONS

¢

🛏 **Mango Tree Rest Camp.** If you are on a tight budget and prepared to rough it, this national-park rest camp on the beach near the middle of Mahale hits the spot. All the rooms have mosquito nets and are clean. Some have en-suite bucket showers, others make use of the communal bucket showers, although you can always swim in the crystal-clear lake. There's no running water or electricity—kerosene lamps provide light—but a small shop at Park HQ sells bottled water (but bring your own just in case of shortages), beer, and a few basics. Bring all your

DID YOU KNOW?

Illegal trafficking is the greatest threat to Tanzania's endangered chimpanzee population. Highly coveted for medical research, zoos, and as pets, baby chimps are taken by force resulting in the death of many protective adults.

provisions from Kigoma. Hire a local cook to rustle up grilled fish or local food such as rice, beans, and *chapattis* (a type of Indian bread) for you. Pay park fees at the park's headquarters at the northern end of the park where you disembark before coming to the camp. Bookings can be made through any of the Kigoma travel agencies or directly through the senior park warden if he answers his phone. **Pros:** an inexpensive option if you're on a budget but really want to see the chimps. **Cons:** this is as rough as it gets, especially if you're used to nice accommodations. ☎ *8821/6217–7242* ♻ *In-room: no a/c, safe, no TV. In-hotel: shop* ▭ *No credit cards.*

IF YOU HAVE TIME

If you still have time after you've explored our picks for Must-See Parks, put the following parks on your list, too: Arusha National Park, Tarangire National Park, and Ruaha National Park.

ARUSHA NATIONAL PARK

Don't overlook the tiny Arusha National Park. Though it covers only 137 square km (58 square mi), it has more to see than many much larger reserves. You'll find three distinct areas within the park: the forests that surround the Ngurdoto Crater, the brightly colored pools of the Momella Lakes, and the soaring peaks of Mt. Meru. And with the city of Arusha only a 32 km (20 mi) drive to the northeast, it's easy to see the park in a day.

Established in 1960, the park was originally called Ngurdoto Crater National Park, but after the mountain was annexed in 1967 it became known as Mt. Meru National Park. Today it is named for the Warusha people who once lived in this area. The Masai also lived here, which is why many of the names for sights within the park are Swahili.

🏛 *Tanzania National Parks, Box 3134, Arusha, Tanzania* ☎ *027/255–3995* ⊕ *www.tanzaniaparks.com* ✉ *$35* ☉ *Daily 6:30–6:30.*

GETTING HERE AND AROUND

A 40-minute drive from Arusha and approximately 60 km (37 mi) from Kilimanjaro International Airport. The lakes, forest, and Ngurdoto Crater can all be visited in the course of a half-day visit.

WHEN TO GO

To climb Mt. Meru, the best time is between June and February, although it may rain in November. The best views of Kilimanjaro are December through February.

EXPLORING

Ngurdoto Forest and Crater. After entering the park through the Ngurdoto Gate, you'll pass through the fig, olive, and wild mango trees of the Ngurdoto Forest. Farther along is the Ngurdoto Crater, which is actually a caldera, or collapsed crater. Unlike the nearby Ngorongoro Crater, this caldera appears to have had two cones. There are no roads into the crater itself, so the buffalo and other animals that make their homes in the swampy habitat remain protected. You can drive around the rim,

Continued on page 220

MOUNT KILIMANJARO by Debra Bouwer

Kilimanjaro, a dormant volcano on the roof of Africa, is one of the closest points in the world to the sun (Chimborazo in the Andes is the closest). It's also the highest peak on the continent and the tallest free-standing mountain in the world. So great is her global attraction that approximately 12,000 people from around the world attempt to reach her mighty summit each year.

Rising to an incredible height of 5,895 meters (19,336 feet) above sea level, Mt. Kilimanjaro is a continental icon. She towers over the surrounding Amboselli plains and covers an area of about 750 sq km (290 sq mi). On a clear day, she can be seen from 150 km (93 mi) away. Thousands attempt to reach Kilimanjaro's highest peak, but only about 64% will officially make the summit, known as Uhuru Peak. Many reach the lower Stella Point at 5,745 meters (18,848 feet) or Gilmans' Point, at 5,681 meters (18,638 feet), which earns them a certificate from the Kilimanjaro Parks Authority.

The origin of the name Kilimanjaro has varying interpretations. Some say it means "Mountain of Greatness," others believe it to mean "Mountain of Caravans." There is a word in Swahili, "kilima" which means top of the hill and an additional claim is that it comes from the word "kile-makyaro" which, in the Chagga language, means "impossible journey." Whatever the meaning, the visual image of Kilimanjaro is of a majestic peak.

Top: Southern Giraffe with Mt. Kilimanjaro in the background, as seen from Amboseli National Park in Kenya

IS KILIMANJARO EASY TO CLIMB?

Kilimanjaro is one of the few high peaks in the world that can be climbed without any technical gear. Most climbers head up her flanks with the aid of trekking poles, while others abandon their poles for a camera and a zoom lens. Don't let the ease fool you though, the lack of oxygen near the summit radically slows down one's ascent. Here, oxygen levels in the air decrease to about 60% of levels at the coast. A simple act of rolling up a sleeping bag can wear you out. Walking and ascending slowly will help your body adapt to these diminished oxygen levels.

About 12,000 thrill seekers arrive on the mountain each year, each accompanied by an entourage of 4 to 6 people that include porters, guides, and a cook.

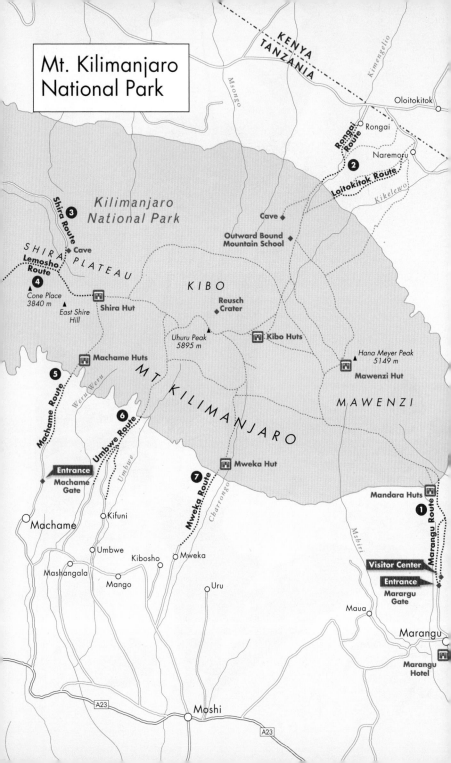

TREKKING KILI

Up, up, and away. Hikers ascend Kilimanjaro.

WHERE TO START

Most treks head out from Moshi, a bustling town at the mountain's base whose streets are lined with tourist stalls, tailors, banks and restaurants. Here you'll find registered guides and accredited trekking companies that will arrange your climb. We like Nomadic Adventure (⊕ *www.nomadicadventures.co.za)* because they offer great personal service, have climbed the mountain many times themselves, and get involved in the big Kilimanjaro Cleanup, a project that hauls thousands of pounds of waste off the mountain each year.

WHEN TO GO

The warmest, clearest trekking days are mid-December to February or September and October. June, July, and August are superb trekking months too, but evening temperatures tend to be colder. The wettest months are November, early December, April, and the start of May, which brings some snow.

Daytime temperatures range from 28°C (85°F) to 38°C (100°F) in the forest, but plummet to a frigid -2°C (28°F) to -16°C (3°F) at the summit. A general rule of thumb: with every 200 meters gained, the temperature drops by one degree.

THE ROUTES

There are seven routes to the summit: Marangu, Rongai, Shira, Lemosho, Machame, and Umbwe—all have long drop toilets. ❶ **Marangu** is the shortest (it takes a minimum of 5 days) and thus most popular route with accommodations in huts equipped with bunk beds, public dining areas, and flush toilets. Some even have solar heated showers. The other routes, which take at least six days to trek, require camping. ❷ **Rongai** (or **Loitokitok**) is the quietest as it heads out close to the Kenyan border, a far distance from Moshi. Along with Marangu, Rongai is classified as an easier route. ❸ **Shira**, ❹ **Lemosho** and ❺ **Machame** are steep and difficult, but also more scenic as they head through the distinct geographical zones: forest, shrub land, alpine desert, and snow fields. ❻ **Umbwe** is the steepest, but also the most direct ascent to the summit. ❼ **Mweka** can only be used as a descending route from the western side.

GEOLOGY & TERRAIN

Mount Kilimanjaro has five different types of terrain that you'll encounter while trying to reach the summit.

Forests

Cultivated Farmlands: Around the outskirts of Moshi near the base of the mountain are endless subsistence plantations of maize and banana. Small villages line the routes up to the various starting points on Kilimanjaro, and small children play in the fields.

Forests: The forest zone spreads around the base of the mountain; it is hot, humid, and generally wet. Starting at about 5,900 feet—there's cultivated farmland below this—the forest reaches up to 2,800 meters (9,186 feet) and is home to a myriad of small creatures and primates, including the black-and-white colobus monkey. Tall trees reach for the sunlight, their feet firmly anchored into a maze of roots on which cling mosses and brightly colored flowers including the rare and exotic impatiens Kilimanjari flower, unique to this mountain. Lichens hang in sheets and small birds dart to and fro.

Shrubland/Heath Zone

Shrubland or Heath Zone: At the edge of the forest zone, the vegetation suddenly changes to shrubland that's full of flowers, shrubs like the 6 meters (20 feet) high erica arborea, and daisy bushes that grow as big as pompoms. This zone extends up to about 12,467 feet where the landscape turns into alpine desert.

Alpine Desert

Alpine Desert: As the shrubs of the heath zone diminish in size, one enters the alpine desert, full of gnarled volcanic lava rock. Small burrows shelter the hyrax and field mice that eke out a living in this desert moonscape. Large white-naped ravens scavenge among the sand and stone.

Glaciers

Glaciers and Summit: As the desert rises to 16,404 feet, the summit of the mountain looms above, her flanks covered in ashen scree. Massive age old glaciers, hanging as though suspended in time, are slowly receding as the planet warms. Here among these towing blocks of ice at 19,340 feet, is Uhuru Peak, the summit of Kilimanjaro.

Summit

While other mountains are taller, Kilimanjaro is at the equator making it one of the closest to the sun.

KILIMANJARO VERSUS EVEREST

	Kilimanjaro	Everest
How tall from sea level?	19,340 feet	29,035 feet
Temperatures at the summit?	Below 0°C (32°F) to as much as -20°C (-4°F) with wind chill factor	From -15°C (5°F) to -100°C (-148°F) in extreme conditions
How many deaths occur each year from people trying to climb to the top?	Guides estimate about 12 a year, though there are no official figures	6 in 2005; 10 in 2006
How long does it take to climb to the top?	A minimum of 5 days	Between two and three months depending on which route you take
What is the most treacherous stretch?	There really isn't a treacherous stretch, but rather the Barranco Wall, which is a steep rock section climbed when doing the Machame, Shira, Lemosho and Umbwe Routes, is the trickiest	Any section above 24,606 feet is classified as the Death Zone

TIPS

1) Check out the internet or trekking magazines for tour operator suggestions

2) Choose an operator that is registered, has registered guides, has porters' interests at heart, an environmental policy, etc.

3) Communicate any health problems to your tour operator when you book

4) Choose your route according to what you want: scenery, challenge, type of accommodation, size of group

5) For a quiet climb on a well travelled route, avoid the full moon, as this is when the summit night is the busiest

6) Train about 2 months before you leave—this also helps to "train your brain" that you are heading off for a challenge. Squats, lunges and lots of hill walking with a pack are essential

7) Fly with your boots on—that way you won't lose them if your luggage gets lost

8) Read up on altitude sickness and symptoms and take the necessary medication with you

9) Drink 3-5 liters of water a day. The rule is 1 liter per 1,000 meters (3,280 feet) ascent

10) Add in acclimatisation days if possible or consider climbing Mt. Meru first

11) Take only photos; leave only footprints

where you'll find a misty landscape covered with date palms, orchids, and lichens. The grasslands to the west are known as Serengeti Ndogo ("Little Serengeti") and boast a herd of Burchell's zebras, thriving because there are no lions nearby.

Many baboons and other monkeys are found in the Ngurdoto Forest. Elegant black-and-white colobus monkeys spend most of the morning basking in the sun in the highest parts of the forest canopy, then later move lower in the branches to feed on the tender vegetation. Colobus monkeys do not drink water but get all their moisture from their food. They are endangered because their lovely fur was prized by humans.

Momella Lakes. From Ngurdoto Crater drive northeast to the Momella Lakes. Reedbuck and waterbuck are common sights near the dirt road. There are numerous observation points along the way for getting a closer look at the more than 400 species of birds that have been spotted in the area. The lakes were created by lava flow from nearby Mt. Meru; each is a distinct color because of the varying mineral content in the water. Each lake, therefore, attracts different types of birds. Keep an eye out for the flamingos that feed on the algae.

Mt. Meru. From the Momella Lakes the road toward Mt. Meru leads into a forest with a profusion of wildflowers. Here you'll encounter dik-diks and red forest duikers. Rangers can accompany you on walks to the rim of Meru Crater, where you'll have a breathtaking view of the sheer cliffs rising to the summit. Keep an eye out for a diminutive antelope called the klipspringer.

Because it is not as well known, the slopes of Mt. Meru are blissfully uncrowded. Although Meru looks diminutive alongside Kilimanjaro, do not underestimate what it takes to climb to the top. You must be in good shape, and you need to allow time to acclimatize. Climbing Mt. Meru itself takes at least three days. The route begins at the Momella Gate, on the eastern side of the mountain. Huts along the way sleep 24–48 people, but inquire beforehand whether beds are available; if not, you should bring a tent. You can arrange for no-frills journeys up the mountain through the park service, or book a luxury package through a travel company that includes porters to carry all your supplies. Either way you'll be accompanied by an armed guard to protect you from unfriendly encounters with elephant or buffalo.

TARANGIRE NATIONAL PARK

Although this lovely 2,600-square-km (1,004-square-mi) park is an easy drive from Arusha—just 118 km (71 mi) southwest—and adjacent to Lake Manyara, it has continued to be something of a well-kept secret. This relative secrecy is odd because during the dry season it's part of the migratory movement and is second only to Ngorongoro Crater in concentration of wildlife. The best time to visit is July through September, when thousands of parched animals flock to the watering holes and thousands more make their long way to the permanent water of the Tarangire River.

GAME-VIEWING

During the dry season, huge herds of elephant, eland, oryx, zebra, buffalo, wildebeest, giraffe, and impala roam the park. Hippos are plentiful and pythons can sometimes be seen in trees near the swamps. If you want to spot waterbuck or the mini-giraffe, the gerenuk, head for the Mkungero Pools. Tarangire is much more densely wooded than Serengeti with acacia, mixed woodland, and the ubiquitous baobab trees, although you'll find grasslands on the southern plains where cheetahs hunt.

There are more than 500 species of birds in Tarangire National Park, including martial and bateleur eagles. Especially good bird-watching can be done along the wetlands of the Silale Swamp and around the Tarangire River. Yellow-collared lovebirds, hammerkops, helmeted guinea fowl, long-toed lapwings, brown parrots, white-bellied go-away birds, and a variety of kingfishers, weavers, owls, plovers, and sandpipers make their homes here. A shallow alkaline lake attracts flamingos and pelicans in the rainy season. Raptors are plentiful, including the palm-nut vulture and lots of eagles. You may hear a cry that sounds quite similar to the American bald eagle but is in fact its look-alike cousin the African fish eagle.

ANCIENT ART

Kolo, just south of Tarangire, is where you'll find some of the most accessible Kondoa rock paintings. From the last stage of the Stone Age, these illustrations on cave walls depict hunting scenes using stylized human and animal figures. These fragile documents of an era long past were studied by Mary Leakey, who wrote a book about them called *Africa's Vanishing Art*. At a nearby site Leakey discovered "pencils" in which ocher and other pigments had been ground and mixed with grease. Later excavations revealed that some were 29,000 years old. ⌂ *Tanzania National Parks, Box 3134, Arusha, Tanzania* ☎ *027/250–1930* ⊕ *www.tanzaniaparks.com* ✉ *$35* ◷ *Mon.–Fri. 9–5, Sat. 9–noon.*

GETTING HERE AND AROUND

An easy drive from Arusha or Lake Manyara following a surfaced road to within 7 km (4 mi) of the main entrance gate. Charter flights from Arusha and the Serengeti are also possible. The flight from Arusha to southern Serengeti is roughly 1½ hours; the drive is 335 km (208 mi), which will take around eight hours.

WHEN TO GO

You can visit year round, but the dry season (May–September) is the best for sheer numbers of animals.

RUAHA NATIONAL PARK

Remote and rarely visited, Ruaha is Tanzania's second largest park—10,300 square km (3,980 square mi). Oddly enough, it attracts only a fraction of the visitors that go to Serengeti, which could be because it is less well-known and is difficult to access. But East Africa Safari aficionados claim it to be the country's best-kept secret. There are huge concentrations of buffalos, elephants, antelope, and more than 400 bird species.

Classified as a national park in 1964, it was once part of the Sabia River Game Reserve, which the German colonial government established in 1911. Ruaha is derived from the word "great" in the Hehe language and refers to the mighty Ruaha River, which flows around the park's borders, and it's only around the river that the park is developed for tourism with a 400-km (249-mi) road circuit. The main portion of the park sits on top of an 1,800-meter (5,900-foot) plateau with spectacular views of valleys, hills, and plains—a wonderful backdrop for game-viewing. Habitats include riverine forest, savanna, swamps, and acacia woodland.

GETTING HERE AND AROUND

Most visitors arrive by charter flight from Dar es Salaam, Selous, the Serengeti, or Arusha. The flight is 2½ hours to Ruaha from Arusha or Dar es Salaam, and one hour from Selous. It's possible to drive to Ruaha but just takes longer. Visitors often drive from Dar es Salaam, but not many drive from Arusha. The drive to Ruaha from Dar es Salaam is roughly 10 hours through Iringa. The roads do get a bit bumpy as you near the park. Safari companies will arrange road transfers if you so wish. If time is of the essence, fly; if it is interaction and experience (atmosphere) of the various places you would like on route to Ruaha, drive.

The best time to visit is May through December because, although even in the wet season the all-weather roads are passable, it's incredibly difficult to spot game at that time because of the lush, tall vegetation. If you're into bird watching, lush scenery, and wildflowers, you'll like the wet season (January–April).

TIMING

Four nights will give you the chance to fully experience the varied areas of the park.

GAME-VIEWING

There are elephant, buffalo, lion, spotted hyena, gazelle, zebra, greater and lesser kudu, and giraffe roaming this park. If you're lucky, you might even see roan and sable antelope or witness a cheetah hunt on the open plains in the Lundu area. Lion are well habituated to vehicles, so you would be very unlucky not to spot at least one

RUAHA ESSENTIALS

There's an entrance fee of US$25 per person, per 24-hour visit, and it must be paid in cash. Ask at your lodge for a copy of the Ruaha booklet, which has maps, checklists, and hints on where to look for particular species.

pride, and if you've set your heart on seeing wild dogs, then try to come in June or July when they are denning; this makes them easier to spot than at other times because they stay in one place for a couple of months. There are also lots of crocs and hippos in the river areas. Bird "specials" include the lovely little Eleonaora's falcon (December through January is the best time to spot one), Pel's fishing owl, and the pale-billed hornbill.

ANIMAL THREATS

Poaching has been a serious problem in this park as the rhino was at one point hunted to near extinction. But in 1988, the Tanzanian government joined with the WWF (the World Wildlife Fund) to initiate the Selous Conservation Programme, which has eased the problem considerably. The international ban on ivory in the 1990s has also contributed to increasing elephant numbers.

WHERE TO STAY
LUXURY LODGES

$$ **Jongomero Tented Camp.** This is the only camp in the southwest corner of Ruaha National Park. If you've come to see animals, but no other trucks or people, then this is your place. The tents, which have furniture that was made from the wood of old dhows, are perched along the banks of the (sometimes dry) Jongomero River—when you're at the lodge's bar, check out the bowl filled with handmade nails that were collected as the boats were disassembled. Take your morning or afternoon tea out on your veranda—you might catch a glimpse of a few passing animals. The food is excellent, and there is always something packed away for you when you're out on your drives. The pool is a great place to relax and ponder all that you've seen during your day, and the view of the setting sun is incredible. If you're interested, game walks with your own personal armed national parks guard, can be arranged. **Pros:** enthusiastic staff; spacious tents; great food; there's a sense of luxury everywhere. **Cons:** tsetse flies are in the area and around the camp. ☎ 022/213–4802 ⊕ www.ruaha.com ⇥ 8 tents ⚘ In-room: no phone, no a/c, safe, no TV. In-hotel: restaurant, bar, pool ⊟ MC, V ⃞ FAP.

$$ **Kigelia Camp.** Set in a forest of baobabs and sausage trees along the Ifaguru sand river, Kigelia has a prime location in Ruaha. This camp has a peaceful, relaxed atmosphere. The tents, are spacious, cool, and inviting. Every tent is furnished with unique, locally crafted furniture made from old dhows. This is a perfect place to sit in the tranquility and shade of a sausage tree and relax, quietly watching the passing wildlife. A very friendly staff and good service are the mark of this welcoming camp. The game in this area during the dry months is exceptional. **Pros:** classic tented safari camp feel with a few modern twists; there is a living room with reading material, gift shop, and fire pit. **Cons:** the camp is an hour's drive from the airstrip; children under 10 are excluded unless

the camp is booked exclusively. ☎ *754/927–694* ⊕ *www.kigeliacamp. com* ⇆ *6 tents* ♿ *In-room: no a/c, no safe, no TV. In-hotel: laundry service* ▭ *DC, MC, V.*

\$\$ 🛏 **Mwagusi Safari Camp.** This well-established camp is situated on the shady banks of the Mwagusi River, giving it a prime position in Ruaha for game-viewing. The large, cool, comfortable bandas, crafted from local and organic materials, are tucked into the sandy banks, giving each a secluded view. Wake up to fresh brewed coffee delivered by friendly staff and take in stunning views along the river on your private veranda. It's not unusual to encounter wildlife on your door step. Elephants are regular visitors to the camp, as well as large prides of lion. Mwagusi is an owner-run camp, and that is evident in all aspects. **Pros:** delicious food; excellent guides; friendly service. **Cons:** bandas are rustic looking from the outside. ☎ *44/182261–5721 in U.K.* ⊕ *www.mwagusicamp. com* ⇆ *10 tents* ♿ *In-room: no a/c, no safe, no TV. In-hotel: laundry service, shop* ▭ *DC, MC, V* 🍴 *FAP.*

\$ 🛏 **Tandala Camp.** Because Tandala is in a private conservancy 13 km (8 mi) outside the entrance gate, guests can take guided night drives, early morning game walks, or go fly camping—none of which you can do within the park. There are no frills here, but it's very comfortable, and you stay in an en-suite tent that's built on a wooden platform that overlooks a seasonal river. There's an attractive restaurant and bar area beside the small swimming pool. A nearby water hole attracts game at all times, particularly during the dry season, although elephants are hanging around most of the time. **Pros:** great views from your tent's raised deck over a water hole that is frequented by game. **Cons:** very bumpy road to the Ruaha park entrance (15 minutes). ☎ *026/270–3425* ⊕ *www.tandalatentedcamp.com* ⇆ *10 tents* ♿ *In-room: no phone, no a/c, no TV. In-hotel: restaurant, bar, pool* ▭ *DC, MC, V* 🍴 *FAP.*

GATEWAY CITY

4

Many visitors to Tanzania will find themselves with a layover in Dar es Salaam or Arusha before or after their safari. For some ideas and suggestions to help determine where you should stay, eat, and, if you have time, some sights to visit, read on.

DAR ES SALAAM

Dar es Salaam means "haven of peace" in Arabic, and paradoxically that's just what you'll find in this bustling port city on the Indian Ocean. Although it has grown to become Tanzania's most important commercial center, Dar es Salaam still recalls its origins as a fishing village. The reason is the city's inhabitants, who go out of their way to make newcomers feel at home. When someone says *"Karibu!"* when you meet, they are saying "Welcome!" Although Dar has transformed itself in the last decades into a modern bustling city, its mix of Arabic, German, English, Asian, and Swahili cultures gives it great charm, albeit a scruffy charm. Situated almost midway between Kenya in the north and Mozambique in the south at the edge of the sparkling blue Indian Ocean, Dar es Salaam's harbor is crowded with the hand-hewn canoes and triangular-sailed dhows that have distinguished the region for centuries. The palm-lined shore is lively with men selling freshly caught fish, mending giant nets, and scrubbing down their boats, while women nearby are roasting crayfish over open fires or stirring pots of soup. As with Zanzibar, one of your most abiding memories will be of the pungent scents and heady aromas of spices, food, and tropical flowers.

Now the graceful triangular-sailed dhows share the harbor with mammoth tankers, as the sleepy village has been transformed into one of East Africa's busiest ports, second only to Kenya's Mombasa. The country's major commercial center, Dar es Salaam has also become its largest city, home to more than 3.5 million inhabitants. Dar es Salaam also serves as the seat of government during the very slow move to Dodoma, which was named the official capital in 1973. The legislature resides in Dodoma, but most government offices are still found in Dar es Salaam.

In the early 1860s, Sultan Seyyid Majid of Zanzibar visited what was then the isolated fishing village of Mzizima, on the Tanzanian coast. Eager to have a protected port on the mainland, Majid began constructing a palace here in 1865. The city, poised to compete with neighboring ports such as Bagamoyo and Kilwa, suffered a setback after the sultan died in 1870. His successor, his half-brother Seyyid Barghash, had little interest in the city, and its royal buildings fell into ruins. Only the Old Boma, which once housed royal guests, still survives.

The city remained a small port until Germany moved its colonial capital here in 1891 and began constructing roads, offices, and many of the public buildings still in use today. The Treaty of Versailles granted Great Britain control of the region in 1916, but that country added comparatively little to the city's infrastructure during its 45-year rule.

IF YOU HAVE TIME

Travel 70 km (43 mi) north to the historically fascinating town of Bagamoyo, where old buildings such as the Catholic Museum, on the grounds of the Holy Ghost Mission, and the Old Fort are well worth visiting. At the Old Fort, once an Arab trader's slave prison, you can see the underground tunnel along which slaves were herded to waiting dhows. The damp walls bore witness to the most terrible human suffering. It was in Bagamoyo that Henry Morton Stanley arrived after his three-year journey across Africa.

Tanzania gained its independence in 1961. During the years that followed, President Julius Nyerere, who focused on issues such as education and health care, allowed the capital city to fall into a decline that lasted into the 1980s. When Benjamin William Mkapa took office in 1985, his market-oriented reforms helped to revitalize the city. The city continues to evolve—those who visited only a few years ago will be startled by the changes.

Dar es Salaam itself continues to grow and prosper with new hotels and restaurants mushrooming almost overnight and is now luring visitors that once might have scurried past on their way to the Serengeti. It doesn't hurt that the city has a bustling waterfront, interesting neighborhoods, and sights like the National Museum, which contains the famous fossil discoveries by Richard and Mary Leakey, including the 1.7 million-year-old hominid skull discovered by Mary Leakey in the Olduvai Gorge in 1959.

GETTING HERE AND AROUND

To find your way around central Dar es Salaam, use the Askari Monument, at the intersection of Samora Avenue and Azikiwe Street as a compass. Most sights are within walking distance. Four blocks northeast on Samora Avenue you'll find the National Museum and Botanical Gardens; about seven blocks southwest stands the Clock Tower, another good landmark. One block southeast is Sokoine Drive, which empties into Kivukoni Front as it follows the harbor. Farther along, Kivukoni Front becomes Ocean Road.

Along Samora Avenue and Sokoine Drive you'll find banks, pharmacies, grocery stores, and shops selling everything from clothing to curios. Northwest of Samora Avenue, around India, Jamhuri, and Libya streets, is the busy Swahili neighborhood where merchants sell all kinds of

Dar es Salaam

INDIAN OCEAN

UPANGA

KISUTU

Golf Course

Botanical Gardens

MCHAFUKOGE

Kariako Market

KARIAKOO

Clock Tower

Harbour

Malindi Wharf

KIGAMBONI

Kurusini Creek

Main Quay

0		500 yards
0		500 m

KEY

- ① Exploring
- ① Hotels & Restaurants

Exploring ▼	**Restaurants** ▼	**Hotels** ▼
Askari Monument 1	Bandari Grill 5	Mövenpick Royal Palm Hotel 3
Tanzania National Museum 2	Sawasdee 6	Sea Cliff Hotel 2
	Serengeti 4	The Souk 1

items, including Tanzania's best *kangas* (sarong or wrap). Farther west you'll find the large Kariakoo Market.

Do not buy tickets for transport, especially on ferries, trains, or buses, from anyone other than an accredited ticket seller.

Julius Nyerere International Airport, formerly Dar es Salaam International Airport, is about 13 km (8 mi) from the city center. Plenty of white-color taxis are available at the airport and will cost you about Tsh 15,000 to the city center. This can usually be negotiated. Most hotels will send drivers to meet your plane if arranged in advance.

Ferries operated by Sea Ferries Express to Zanzibar depart daily at 7:15, 10:30, 1, and 4:15 from the Zanzibar Ferry Terminal. The two-hour journey costs about Tsh 45,500 ($40). The Kigamboni ferry to the southern beaches runs continuously throughout the day and departs from the southern tip of the city center, where Kivukoni Front meets Ocean Road. The five-minute ride costs about Tsh 200 ($2) one-way.

Taxis are the most efficient way to get around town. During the day they are easy to find outside hotels and at major intersections, but at night they are often scarce. Ask someone to call one for you. Taxis don't have meters, so agree on fare before getting in. Fares run about Tsh 2,000 within the city.

SAFETY

Dar es Salaam is among the safest cities in East Africa. It's fine to wander around by yourself during the day, but after dark it's best to stick with your companions. Because taxis are cheap, it's a good idea to use them at night. The area with the most street crime is along the harbor, especially Kivukoni Front and Ocean Road.

Foreign women tend to feel safe in Dar es Salaam. But remember, women in Dar es Salaam never wear clothing that exposes their shoulders or legs. You should do the same. You'll feel more comfortable in modest dress.

VISITOR INFORMATION

The Tanzania Tourist Board's head office is in Dar es Salaam. It has maps and information on travel to dozens of points of interest around Tanzania and is very helpful. The staff will discuss hotel options with you and assist you in making reservations.

ESSENTIALS

Embassies American Embassy (⊠ 686 Old Bagamoyo Rd., Msasani ☎ 022/266–8001 ⊕ www.tanzania.usembassy.gov).

Ferries Kigamboni Ferry (⊹ The mainland port is located at Magogoni near the main fish market past the Kilimanjaro Kempinski Hotel ☎ 022/286–2796). **Sea Ferries Express** (⊠ Sokoine Dr., Dar es Salaam ☎ 022/213–7049). **Zanzibar Ferry Terminal** (⊠ Sokoine Dr., Dar es Salaam).

Visitor Info Tanzania Tourist Board (⊠ 3rd fl., IPS Building, corner of Azikiwe St. and Samora Ave., Dar es Salaam ☎ 022/213–1555 information; 022/211–1244 head office ⊕ www.tanzaniatouristboard.com ⊙ Weekdays 9–5, Sat. 9–noon).

BEACHES

The beaches north and south of Dar es Salaam are irresistible for those seeking the calm, cool waters of the Indian Ocean. Kunduchi Beach and Oyster Bay, just north of Dar es Salaam, offer a range of lodgings from thatch-roof bungalows to luxury high-rises. Open-air bars, cafés, and restaurants sit so close to shore you can feel the sea breeze. When you tire of swimming, you can snorkel around the coral reefs or sail in dhows to small islands such as Bongoyo and Mbudya.

EXPLORING

Askari Monument. This bronze statue was erected by the British in 1927 in memory of African troops who died during World War I. (The word *askari* means "soldier" in Swahili.) It stands on the site of a monument erected by Germany to celebrate its victory here in 1888. That monument stood only five years before being demolished in 1916. ⊠ *Samora Ave. and Azikiwe St.*

A REAL GEM

Looking for that one-of-a-kind gift or keepsake? How about jewelry with tanzanite in it? Given by Masai fathers to mothers upon the birth of their child, this deep-blue stone, discovered in 1967, is unique to Tanzania. And though you can purchase the gems just about anywhere these days, you can't beat the prices or the bargaining you'll find in the shops of Arusha and Dar es Salaam—you'll be able to purchase loose stones, existing pieces, or customize your own design. ⚠ Do not buy any tanzanite from street vendors. Nine times out of 10 it will be a fake stone.

Tanzania National Museum. Apart from the Leakey fossil discoveries, which are some of the most important in the world, there are also good displays of colonial exploration and German occupation. ⚠ If you take pictures or have a camera at the museum, you will be charged—$3 for a camera and $20 for a video camera. ⊠ *Near Botanical Gardens, between Samora Ave. and Sokoine Dr.* ☎ *212–2030 or 211–7508* ▨ *US$3* ☉ *Daily 9:30–6.*

WHERE TO EAT

You can spend days sampling Dar es Salaam's varied cuisine. There's no need to spend a lot, as *hotelis* (cafés) offer heaping plates of African or Indian fare for less than Tsh 5,000 ($5). Typical *chakula* (food) for an East African meal includes *wali* (rice) or *ugali* (a damp mound of breadlike ground corn) served with a meat, fish, or vegetable stew. A common side dish is *kachumbari,* a mixture of chopped tomatoes, onions, and cucumbers. Even less expensive are roadside stalls, such as those that line the harbor, offering snacks such as chicken and beef kebabs, roast corn on the cob, and *samosas* (triangular pastries stuffed with meat or vegetables). If you're in the mood for something sweet, try a doughnutlike *mandazi.* Wash it all down with a Tusker or Safari, local beers, or with *chai* (a hot tea served with milk, sugar, and spices).

Should you be in the mood for something fancier, upscale hotels offer cosmopolitan meals and elaborate buffets for as much as $30. Even at the toniest of restaurants, reservations are rarely required. Restaurants

Tanzania's Tribes

The Masai are a seminomadic people from Kenya and northern Tanzania whose distinct customs and dress have given them relative notoriety in the Western world. The Masai women wear colorful beaded jewelry, and men and women often wear bright red blankets over their shoulders. The tribe is patriarchal in structure and Masai elders make important decisions for each tribe. A famous rite of passage for Masai boys involves the circumcision of the penis without anesthetic: this process is a painful one, but in order to become warriors the boys are meant to endure it without any display of discomfort. Masai culture also dictates that boys must kill a lion before being circumcised.

Although this practice is less common these days, Masai who hunt lion rarely face any legal consequence. Wealth is measured in terms of cattle in the Masai community, and thus, cattle are considered sacred; they believe that cows are a gift from God. Since the Masai move about so much, their homes—called *inkajijik*, or *boma*—are made from materials they find in their surroundings. They are generally constructed of mud, sticks, grass, and cow dung and are circular in shape. A typical Serengeti scene (and a beautiful one, if you are lucky enough to come across it) is a wide savanna peppered with baobab trees and earthen Masai boma.

in hotels generally are open until at least 10:30 PM, even on Sunday, although the hours of local restaurants vary.

$ ╳ **Bandari Grill.** Long one of Dar es Salaam's best values, this place
ECLECTIC attracts the city's movers and shakers. The seemingly endless buffet features traditional Tanzanian cuisine as well as selections from other countries. The beef tenderloin tips with king prawns is always a favorite. There's also a sports bar where executives kick back after a long day. Enjoy live music most evenings, or stop by for breakfast or lunch. ✉ *Azikiwe St. and Sokoine Dr.* ☎ *022/211–7050* ▭ *AE, MC, V* ⊘ *Daily 7 AM–11:30 PM.*

$$ THAI Fodor's Choice ★ **Sawasdee.** With a name that means "welcome" in Thai, Sawasdee has a peaceful atmosphere and attentive service that make it one of the best eateries in the city. Tanzania's first Thai restaurant, Sawasdee serves authentic dishes—duck in brown sauce, fish in ginger, chicken in green curry—prepared by a highly esteemed chef from Bangkok. The restaurant on the 9th floor of the New Africa Hotel overlooks the sparkling lights of the harbor. ✉ *New Africa Hotel, Azikiwi St. and Sokoine Dr.* ☎ *022/211–7050* ▭ *AE, MC, V* ⏲ *No lunch weekdays.*

$$ ECLECTIC Fodor's Choice ★ **Serengeti.** Sumptuous buffets have made this restaurant on the ground floor of the Royal Palm Hotel a favorite among tourists as well as business executives. The cuisine changes nightly—Monday, Thursday, and Sunday are reserved for Asian fare; Tuesday, Wednesday, and Friday are the nights to go for European-style meals. Saturday the chef turns his attention to East African foods. The restaurant is also open for lunch and dinner, including the champagne breakfast, which is a Sunday morning ritual among the regulars. ✉ *Mövenpick Royal Palm Hotel, 20 Ohio St.* ☎ *022/211–2416* ▭ *AE, MC, V* ⏲ *Daily 6:30–10:30* PM.

WHERE TO STAY

Lodging reviews have been abbreviated in this book. For expanded reviews, please go to Fodors.com.

$ **Hotel Sea Cliff.** Only 15 minutes from downtown on the edge of the Msasani Peninsula, this classy hotel has good size, comfortable rooms (but insist on one with a sea view), three restaurants, a casino, a pool, and a gym. **Pros:** close to shopping centers and other activities in the city; great view. **Cons:** large, business-orientated hotel. ✉ *20 Ohio St., Msasani Peninsula* ☎ *752/555–500* 🌐 *www.hotelseacliff.com* *85 rooms* *In-room: safe. In-hotel: restaurant, room service, bar, pool, gym* ▭ *AE, DC, MC, V* *BP.*

$$$ **Mövenpick Royal Palm Hotel.** Dar's classiest hotel (formerly the Sheraton) is surrounded by pleasant gardens and is next to Gymkhana Golf Course, which is open to the public. **Pros:** all that you would expect from a five-star hotel. **Cons:** it is not convenient to the airport and does not have great views. ✉ *20 Ohio St.* ☎ *211–2416* 🌐 *www.moevenpick-hotels.com* *230 rooms* *In-room: a/c, safe, Internet. In-hotel: restaurant, room service, bar, pool, gym* ▭ *AE, DC, MC, V* *BP.*

¢ **The Souk.** Located in the Slipway, a shopping and leisure complex in a converted boatyard, the Souk is a great place for an overnight or base for exploration from Dar. **Pros:** convenient for restaurants and shopping; hotel arranges island trips. **Cons:** located in a large, busy shopping center; night noise from restaurants may be disturbing. ✉ *The Slipway, Chole Rd., Msasani Peninsula* ☎ *022/260–0893* 🌐 *www.slipway.net* *20 rooms* *In-room: a/c, safe, Internet. In-hotel: restaurant, room service, bar, pool, gym* ▭ *AE, MC, V* *BP.*

ARUSHA

Arusha could be any small town in sub-Saharan Africa—dusty, crowded, and forgettable. A couple of pleasant features do distinguish it, however: potted plants line the potholed streets (put there by the plant nurseries just behind the sidewalks), and on a clear day, you can see Mt. Meru, Africa's fifth highest mountain at 4,556 meters (14,947 feet), looming in the distance.

The town is bisected by the Nauru River. The more modern part is to the east of the river where most of the hotels, safari companies, and banks are located; west of the river is where the bus station and main market are. Most people spend an overnight here either coming or going. There's not really much to see and do in Arusha.

GETTING HERE AND AROUND

There are no direct flights from the United States. Generally you need to connect through a city on the mainland, the easiest being Dar es Saalam.

You will be approached immediately after you land by taxi drivers. Be sure to agree on a price before getting in, as taxis do not have meters. The fare to downtown Arusha is approximately US$25.

SAFETY

It's unlikely that you would want to explore Arusha at night, but if you do, take a taxi. As in any East African city, muggings and purse snatching are common.

VISITOR INFORMATION

The Tanzanian Tourist Board (TTB) has an Arusha office where you can pick up maps and brochures for the area. Tanzania National Parks also has an office here that can help you book accommodations or answer any of your safari questions.

ESSENTIALS

Airports Arusha Airport (*ARK* ☎ *027/741–530 or 027/744–317* ⊕ *www. tanzaniairports.com*).

Hospitals AICC Hospital (✉ *Old Moshi Rd., Arusha* ☎ *027/254–4392*).

Visitor Info Arusha Tourist Information Center (✉ *Boma Rd.* ☎ *057/503–843* ⊕ *www.tanzaniatouristboard.com*).

WHERE TO EAT AND STAY

Hotel reviews have been abbreviated in this book. For expanded reviews, please go to Fodors.com.

$$
ASIAN **Stiggy's.** Long one of Arusha's most popular dining spots, this authentic Thai restaurant is run by a husband-and-wife team from Australia and Thailand. But take a taxi if you plan to go here—it's not safe to walk in the area. The bar has a pool table and is a great place to hang out. ✉ *Old Moshi Rd.* ☎ *0754/37–5535* ⊟ *AE, MC, V* ⊘ *Tues.–Sun. noon–midnight.*

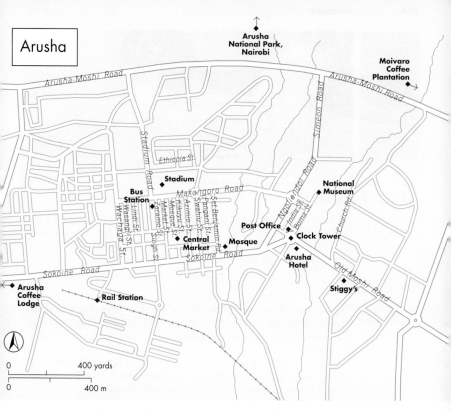

$$$ **Arusha Coffee Lodge.** Being 5 km (3 mi) from town and five minutes from Arusha Airport makes this a great option for pre- or post-safari layovers. **Pros:** beautiful setting; easy access to the airport. **Cons:** near the highway so you can hear traffic. ☒ *Serengeti Rd., Airport vicinity* ☎ *027/254–0630* ⊕ *www.elewana.com* ⤳ *18 rooms* ♿ *In-room: safe. In-hotel: restaurant, bar, pool* ▭ *MC, V* ⦿ *BP.*

$$$–$$$$ **The Arusha Hotel.** Bang in the middle of town, opposite the clock tower, this recently refurbished hotel built in 1894 retains a colonial feel, with elegantly decorated rooms and lovely gardens running down to the Themi River. **Pros:** walking distance from banks, shops, and the International Conference Centre. **Cons:** not all the rooms have a/c. ☒ *Main Rd.* ☎ *027/250–7777* ⊕ *www.thearushahotel.com* ⤳ *86 rooms* ♿ *In-room: safe, Internet. In-hotel: restaurant, bar, pool, spa* ▭ *MC, V* ⦿ *BP.*

¢   **Moivaro Coffee Plantation Lodge.** There are stunning views of the changing colors of Mt. Kilimanjaro from the grounds of this coffee plantation. **Pros:** only 7 km (4 mi) from Arusha: set among 40 acres of coffee plantations and gardens; rooms have ceiling fans and mosquito netting. **Cons:** the standard of the food could be improved. ☒ *6 km (4 mi) east of Arusha* ☎ *027/250–6315* ⊕ *www.moivaro.com* ⤳ *40 rooms* ♿ *In-room: no phone, no a/c, no TV, Internet. In-hotel: restaurant, room service, bar, tennis court, pool, spa, Internet* ▭ *MC, V.*

BEACH ESCAPES

Looking for a little R&R after your safari? Tanzania has 1,424 km (883 mi) of beautiful, pristine coastline just waiting for you to explore. Looking for an island getaway? Tanzania has those, too. Zanzibar and Mnemba Island are perfect spots to kick back and relax.

ZANZIBAR

Updated by
Kate Turkington

This ancient isle once ruled by sultans and slave traders served as the stepping stone into the African continent for missionaries and explorers. Today this jewel in the Indian Ocean attracts visitors intent on discovering its sandy beaches, pristine rain forests, or boldly colored coral reefs. Once known as the Spice Island for its export of cloves, Zanzibar has become one of the most exotic flavors in travel, better than Bali or Mali when it comes to beauty that will make your jaw drop.

Separated from the mainland by a channel only 35 km (22 mi) wide, and only six degrees south of the equator, this tiny archipelago—the name Zanzibar also includes the islands of Unguja (the main island), Pemba, and Mnemba—in the Indian Ocean was the launching base for a romantic era of expeditions into Africa. Sir Richard Burton and John Hanning Speke used it as their base when searching for the source of the Nile. It was in Zanzibar where journalist Henry Morton Stanley, perched in an upstairs room overlooking the Stone Town harbor, began his search for David Livingstone.

The first ships to enter the archipelago's harbors may have belonged to the Phoenicians, who are believed to have sailed in around 600 BC, and since then every other great navy in the Eastern Hemisphere has dropped anchor here at one time or another. But it was Arab traders who left an indelible mark. Minarets punctuate the skyline of Stone Town, where more than 90% of the residents are Muslim. In the harbor you will see dhows, the Arabian boats with triangular sails. Islamic women with their faces covered by black boubou veils scurry down alleyways so narrow their outstretched arms could touch buildings on both sides. Stone Town received its odd name because most of its buildings were made of limestone and coral, which means exposure to salty air has eroded many foundations. Flat rooftops, perfectly suited for the deserts where many of the oldest inhabitants originated, merely collected rain. After more than a few roofs collapsed from the standing pools, residents started changing their construction methods. As you gaze out upon the rooftops in the evening, you may now notice vaulted A-frames, the better to drain the water during monsoons.

The first Europeans who arrived here were the Portuguese in the 15th century, and thus began a reign of exploitation. As far inland as Lake Tanganyika, slave traders captured the residents or bartered for them from their own chiefs, then forced the newly enslaved to march toward the Indian Ocean carrying loads of ivory tusks. Once at the shore they were shackled together while waiting for dhows to collect them at Bagamoyo, a place whose name means "here I leave my heart." Although it's estimated that 50,000 slaves passed through the Zanzibar slave market each year during the 19th century, many more died en route.

Tanganyika and Zanzibar merged in 1964 to create Tanzania, but the honeymoon was brief. Zanzibar's relationship with the mainland remains uncertain as calls for independence continue. "Bismillah, will you let him go," a lyric from Queen's "Bohemian Rhapsody," has become a rebel chant for Zanzibar to break from Tanzania. The archipelago also has tensions of its own. Accusations of voting irregularities during the elections in 2000 and 2005 led to violence that sent scores of refugees fleeing to the mainland. Calm was quickly restored. As the old proverb goes, the dogs bark and the caravan moves on.

Zanzibar's appeal is apparent to developers, who are intent on opening restaurants, hotels, and even water-sapping golf courses. But so far the archipelago has kept much of its charm. It retains the allure it had when explorer David Livingstone set up his expedition office here in 1866.

Zanzibar Island, locally known as Unguja, has amazing beaches and resorts, incredible dive spots, acres and acres of spice plantations, the Jozani Forest Reserve, and Stone Town. Plus, it takes little more than an hour to fly there. It's a great spot to head for a post-safari unwind.

Stone Town, the archipelago's major metropolis, is a maze of narrow streets lined with houses featuring magnificently carved doors studded with brass. There are 51 mosques, six Hindu temples, and two Christian churches. And though it can rightly be called a city, much of the western part of the larger island is a slumbering paradise where cloves, as well as rice and coconuts, still grow.

Jozani Forest Reserve is home to the rare Kirk's red colobus monkey, which is named after Sir John Kirk, the British consul in Zanzibar from 1866 to 1887. The species is known for its white whiskers and rusty coat. Many of the other animals that call this reserve home are endangered because 95% of the original forests of the archipelago have been destroyed. Reserves have been established to harbor such species as the blue duiker, a diminutive antelope whose coat is a dusty bluish-gray.

Although the main island of Unguja feels untouched by the rest of the world, the nearby islands of Pemba and Mnemba offer retreats that are

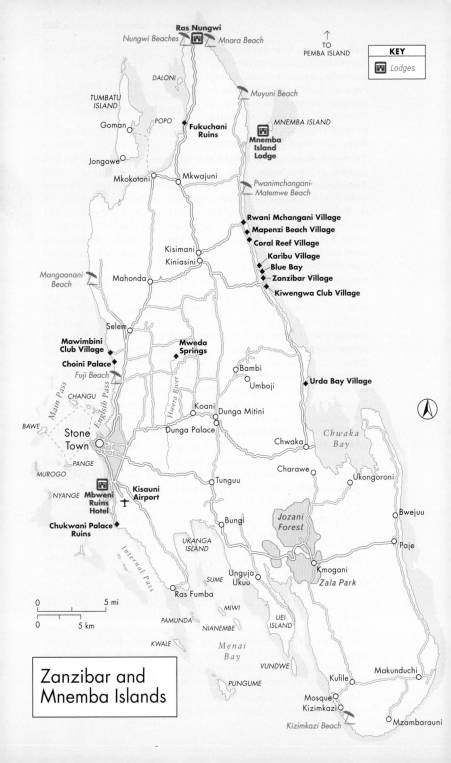

Zanzibar and Mnemba Islands

even more remote. For many years Arabs referred to Pemba as Al Khudra, or the Green Island, and indeed it still is, with forests of king palms, mangos, and banana trees. The 65-km-long (40-mi-long) island is less famous than Unguja except among scuba divers, who enjoy the coral gardens with colorful sponges and huge fans. Archaeology buffs are also discovering Pemba, where sites from the 9th to the 15th centuries have been unearthed. At Mtambwe Mkuu coins bearing the heads of sultans were discovered. Ruins along the coast include ancient mosques and tombs. In the 1930s Pemba was famous for its sorcerers, attracting disciples of the black arts from as far away as Haiti. Witchcraft is still practiced, and, oddly, so is bullfighting. Introduced by the Portuguese in the 17th century, the sport has been improved by locals, who rewrote the ending. After enduring the ritual teasing by the matador's cape, the bull is draped with flowers and paraded around the village.

Beyond Pemba, smaller islands in the Zanzibar Archipelago range from mere sandbanks to Changu, once a prison island, now home to the giant Aldabra tortoise, and Mnemba, a private retreat for guests who pay hundreds of dollars per day to get away from it all. To the west of Pemba, Misali Island reputedly served as a hideout for the notorious Captain Kidd, which makes visitors dream of buried treasure. In reality it is the green sea turtles that do most of the digging.

WHEN TO GO

June through October is the best time to visit Zanzibar because the temperature averages 26°C (79°F). Spice tours are best during harvest time, July and October, when cloves (unopened flower buds) are picked and laid out to dry. Zanzibar experiences a short rainy season in November, but heavy rains can fall from March until the end of May. Temperatures soar during this period, often reaching over 30°C (90°F). Most travelers come between June and August and from mid-November to early January. During these periods many hotels add a surcharge.

Zanzibar observes Ramadan for a month every year. During this period Muslims are forbidden to eat, drink, or smoke between sunrise and sunset. Although hotels catering to tourists are not affected, many small shops and restaurants are closed during the day. If you plan to arrive during Ramadan, aim for the end, when a huge feast called the Eid al-Fitr (which means "end of the fast") brings everyone out to the streets.

GETTING HERE AND AROUND

There are no direct flights from the United States. Generally you need to connect through a city on the mainland, the easiest being Dar es Saalam. From Dar es Saalam to Stone Town, there are regular flights in small twin-engine aircraft operated by Precision Air and Coastal Air. The flight takes around 20 minutes. From Nairobi and Mombasa, you can fly to Stone Town on Kenya Airways.

You can also hop between the two main islands of Zanzibar. Zan Air, a local charter company, flies between Stone Town and Chake Chake three times a week. The flights take 20 minutes, and give you a spectacular aerial view of the islands and the coral reefs. Coastal Air flies every day except Saturday from Dar es Salaam to Stone Town to Chake

Chake. You'll have to exercise patience when flying with the local airlines because schedules are flexible and very often flights are delayed.

Visitors from the United States and Europe require visas to enter Tanzania. Zanzibar is a semiautonomous state within Tanzania, so you don't need a separate visa to visit, but you do need to show your passport.

Bikes can be rented from shops near Darajani Market. Mopeds and motorcycles are another great way to get about the island.

Several hydrofoil ferries travel between Dar es Salaam and Stone Town. The fastest trips, lasting about 75 minutes, are on hydrofoils operated by Sea Express and Azam Marine. Sea Express has daily departures from Dar es Salaam at 7:30, 10, noon, 2:30, and 4:30, with returns at 7, 10, noon, 2:30, and 4:30. Azam Marine departs from Dar es Salaam at 8, 1:15, and 4, returning at 7, 1:30, and 4.

Tickets can be purchased on the spot or in advance from the row of offices next to the port in Dar es Saalam. Timetables and prices are displayed on boards outside each office. Tickets for nonresidents range from $40 for first class (Tsh 65,000) to $35 (Tsh 60,000) for second class. The harbor is quite busy so keep an eye on your possessions and if you don't want help from a porter, be firm.

Whether you arrive by plane or ferry, you will be approached by taxi drivers. Be sure to agree on a price before getting in, as taxis do not have meters. The fare to Stone Town should be around Tsh 11,000 (around $10–$15). Your driver may let you out several blocks before you reach your hotel because the streets are too narrow. Ask the driver to walk you to the hotel. Be sure to tip him if he carries your luggage.

DAY TOURS

Spice tours are a very popular way to see Zanzibar. Guides take you to farms in Kizimbani or Kindichi and teach you to identify plants that produce cinnamon, turmeric, nutmeg, and vanilla. A curry luncheon will undoubtedly use some of the local spices. Any tour company can arrange a spice tour, but the best guides are those who work for Mr. Mitu, a renowned guide who has his own agency and a battalion of guides trained by him. The average price for a spice tour is $20, including lunch. Most depart around 9:30 AM from Stone Town.

Fisherman Tours is an experienced operator based in Stone Town that offers general city tours. There are many types of tours available. John da Silva, a local artist, gives tours of the architecture in Stone Town. If you cannot reach Mr. Da Silva or Mr. Mitu on the below numbers, inquire at a local tour operator or at the tourist information center as to where you can get hold of them.

A trip on an Arab dhow is a must. Dhow Safaris offer picnic excursions to a nearby sandbank and sunrise and sunset cruises. The Zanzibar Serena offers all sorts of excursions. They might be a bit pricier than most, but you can be sure you're getting excellent guides and service. Monarch Travel Services also provide transfers and tours. And if you're into deep-sea fishing, check Deep Sea Fishing Zanzibar, which has two professionally rigged boats.

HEALTH AND SAFETY

Visitors to Zanzibar are required to have a yellow-fever-vaccination certificate; some Web sites also recommend polio, Hepatitis A, and typhoid vaccinations. You should also talk with your doctor about a malaria prophylactic. The best way to avoid malaria is to avoid being bitten by mosquitoes, so make sure your arms and legs are covered and that you wear plenty of mosquito repellent. Antihistamine cream is also quite useful for when you do get bitten, to stop the itch. Always sleep under a mosquito net; most hotels and guesthouses provide them. The sun can be very strong here, so make sure to slather yourself with sunscreen as well. Drink bottled water, and plenty of it—it will help you avoid dehydration. Avoid raw fruits and vegetables that may have been washed in untreated water.

Although the best way of experiencing Stone Town is to wander around its labyrinthine streets, you should always be on your guard. Don't wear jewelry or watches that might attract attention, and keep a firm grasp on purses and camera bags. Leave valuables in the safe at your hotel. Always take a taxi when traveling at night.

Muggings have been reported at Nungwi and other coastal resorts, so never carry valuables onto the beach.

As Zanzibar is a largely conservative, Muslim state, it is advisable for women to dress modestly.

Homosexuality is frowned upon in Zanzibar, and displays of public affection can be prosecutable.

MONEY MATTERS

There are handy currency exchange booths in Stone Town that offer good rates. The best rates are at Forex Bureau around the corner from Mazson's Hotel on Kenyatta Road, and the Malindi Exchange across from Cine Afrique. Mtoni Marine Center, also in Stone Town, will give a cash advance on your Visa or MasterCard. It charges a commission as well as a processing fee. Currency-exchange offices can also be found on Pemba in Chake Chake and in Wete. Most people will except U.S. dollars, but be aware of the exchange rate and make sure you are not being overcharged. ■TIP→ **Be very careful when using ATMs. Make sure you use one at a reputable bank, and check to make sure the bank is open— cards get swallowed all the time. Avoid the airport's ATM; it is omnivorous.**

TELEPHONES

The regional code for Zanzibar is 024. ■TIP→ **Telephone numbers seem to lack consistency, so we've listed them as they appear in promotional materials.**

VISITOR INFORMATION

The free tourist magazine, *Swahili Coast,* found in hotels and shops, lists cultural events, as well as tide tables that are very useful for divers. There is a tourist information center north of Stone Town. Although not very useful for information about the city, it does book rooms in inns in other parts of the island.

ESSENTIALS

Airlines Coastal Aviation (⊕ www.coastal.cc). **Fly540** (⊕ www.fly540.com). **Precision Air** (⊕ www.precisionairtz.com). **Zan Air** (⊕ www.zanair.com).

Airports Zanzibar Airport (⊕ www.zanzibar-airport.com).

Day Tours Fisherman Tours (✉ Vuga Rd., near Majestic Cinema, Stone Town ☎ 024/2555–8791). **John da Silva** (✉ Stone Town ☎ 024/2555–2123). **Mr. Mitu** (✉ Stone Town ☎ 024/223–1020). **The Original Dhow Safaris** (✉ Stone Town ☎ 024/223–2088 ⊕ www.dhowsafaris.com). **Monarch Travel Services** (✉ Stone Town ✐ infomonarch@zanlink.com). **Deep Sea Fishing Zanzibar** (✉ Stone Town ⊕ www.deep-sea-fishing-tanzania.com).

Emergencies Zanzibar Medical and Diagnostic Center (✉ Vuga Rd., near Majestic cinema, Stone Town ☎ 024/223–1071; 0777/750–040 or 0777//413–714 24-hour emergency hotline).

Ferries Azam Marine (☎ 022/212–3324 in Dar es Salaam; 024/223–1655 in Zanzibar). **Sea Express** (✉ Sokoine Dr. ☎ 024/223–4690).

Visitor Info Zanzibar Tourist Information Center (☎ 024/223–3485). **Zanzibar Tourist Corporation** (☎ 024/223–8630 ⊕ www.zanzibartouristcorporation. com).

EXPLORING

The sights in Stone Town are all minutes from one another so you'll see them all as you walk. However, the old part of town is very compact and maze-like and can be a bit disconcerting, especially if you're a female traveler(s). Hiring a guide is a great way to see the city without stress and provides information about the sights you'll see. Many tour operators offer a guided walking tour for approximately US$20–US$25. Ask your hotel for guide suggestions, or ⇨ *see Day Tours above for tour guide recommendations.*

Anglican Cathedral. This was the first Anglican cathedral in East Africa and its crucifix was carved from the tree under which explorer David Livingstone's heart was buried in the village of Chitambo. Built in 1887 to mark the end of the slave trade, the cathedral's high altar was constructed on the site of a whipping post. Nothing of the slave market remains, although nearby are underground chambers in which slaves were forced to crouch on stone shelves less than 2 feet high. Ask to take the stairs up to the tower, which affords a bird's-eye view of Stone Town. ✉ *Off Creek Rd.* ☎ *No phone* ✐ *Tsh 1,000* ☉ *Daily 8–6.*

Beit al-Sahel. This structure was known as the People's Palace, but for a long time the name was a bitter irony. It was here that sultans and their families lived from the 1880s until the revolution of 1964. It now exhibits collections of furniture and clothing from the days of the sultans. A room is dedicated to Princess Salme, daughter of Sultan Said, who eloped with a German businessman in the 19th century. On the grounds outside are the tombs of Sultan Said and two of his sons. ☒ *Mizingani Rd.* ☏ *No phone* 🎟 *US$3* ⊘ *Tues.–Sat. 10–8.*

Beit el-Ajaib. Known as the House of Wonders because it was the first building in Zanzibar to use electric lights, this four-story palace is still one of the largest buildings in the city. Built in the late 1800s for Sultan Barghash, it was bombarded by the British in 1886, forcing the sultan to abdicate his throne. Today you'll find cannons guarding the beautifully carved doors at the entrance. Check out the marble-floored rooms, where you'll find exhibits that detail the country's battle for independence. ☒ *North of Old Fort* ☏ *No phone* 🎟 *US$2* ⊘ *Weekdays 9–6, weekends 9–3.*

Darajani Market. This gable-roofed structure built in 1904 houses a sprawling fruit, fish, meat, and vegetable market. Goods of all sorts—colorful fabrics, wooden chests, and all types of jewelry—are sold in the shops that line the surrounding streets. To the east of the main building you'll find spices laid out in colorful displays of beige, yellow, and red. On Wednesday and Saturday there's an antiques fair. The market is most active in the morning between 9 and 11. ☒ *Creek Rd., north of New Mkunazini St.* ☏ *No phone* 🎟 *Free* ⊘ *Daily 8–6.*

Dhow Harbor. The scent of cloves hangs heavy in the air as stevedores load and unload sacks of the region's most valuable crops. Every day you'll spot dhows arriving from the mainland with deliveries of flour and other goods not available on the islands. Fishermen deposit their catch here early in the morning. This is a seedy area, so be cautious. ☒ *Malindi St., north of Malawi St.*

Forodhani Gardens. Newly revamped in 2009 by the Aga Khan Foundation, this pleasant waterfront park is a favorite spot for an evening stroll both for locals and tourists. Dozens of venders sell freshly grilled fish under the light of gas lanterns. There's also a children's playground. ☒ *Mizingani St.*

Hamamni Baths. Built in the late 19th century by Sultan Barghash, these public baths still retain the grandeur of a past era. Although they are now closed, you can get the key from the shopkeeper next door (don't forget to pay him the entrance fee) and explore the maze of marble-floored rooms leading to the ornately tiled tubs. ☒ *Hamamni St.* ☏ *No phone* 🎟 *Tsh 500.*

Old Dispensary. With intricately carved wood balconies that make it resemble a wedding cake, this former dispensary shines again after being renovated by community groups. Built at the turn of the last century, it was donated to the city by an Indian merchant named Tharia Topan. Today it houses shops, galleries, and a small café. ☒ *Mizingani Rd., near Malindi Rd.* ☏ *No phone* 🎟 *Free* ⊘ *Daily 9–6.*

★ **Old Fort.** Built by the Portuguese in 1560, this bastioned fortress is the oldest structure in Stone Town. It withstood an attack from Arabs in 1754. It was later used as a jail, and prisoners who were sentenced to death met their ends here. It has undergone extensive renovation and today is headquarters for many cultural organizations, including the Zanzibar International Film Festival. Performances of traditional dance and music are staged here several times a week. The Neem Tree Café is a good place to stop for lunch. ⊠ *Creek Rd. and Malawi Rd.* ☎ *No phone* ☎ *Free* ☉ *Daily 10–6.*

St. Joseph's Cathedral. Built by French missionaries more than a century ago, this ornate church is based on the basilica of Notre Dame de la Garde, in Marseilles, France. It's now one of the city's most recognizable landmarks, with twin spires that you'll see as you arrive in Stone Town. ⊠ *Cathedral St. near Gizenda St.* ☎ *No phone.*

WHERE TO EAT

Zanzibar was the legendary Spice Island, so it's no surprise the cuisine here is flavored with lemongrass, cumin, and garlic. Cinnamon enlivens tea and coffee, while ginger flavors a refreshing soft drink called Tangawizi. Zanzibar grows more than 20 types of mangos, and combining them with bananas, papayas, pineapples, and passion fruit makes for tasty juices. When it comes to dinner, seafood reigns supreme. Stone Town's fish market sells skewers of kingfish and tuna. Stop by in the early evening, when the catch of the day is hauled in and cleaned. Try the prawn kebabs, roasted peanuts, and corn on the cob at the outdoor market at Forodhani Gardens (but not if you have a sensitive tummy). Try the vegetarian Zanzibar pizza for breakfast; it's more like an omelet.

Gratuities are often included in the bill, so ask the staff before adding the usual 10% tip. Credit cards are not widely accepted, so make sure you have enough cash. Lunch hours are generally from 12:30 to 2:30, dinner from 7 to 10:30. Dress is casual for all but upscale restaurants, where you should avoid T-shirts, shorts, and trainers.

$$$
SEAFOOD
✕**Archipelago.** The breezy, open layout of this BYOB restaurant adds to the casual feel. You'll find tourists and locals alike dining upon the fresh seafood. Check out the dry-erase board for the daily specials. They also serve breakfast and lunch. ⚠ **You will have to climb up a flight of stairs to get here.** ⊠ *Hurumzi St., Stone Town* ☎ *024/223–0171* ▭ *No credit cards* ☉ *Daily 6–10:30* PM.

$
ECLECTIC
✕**Mercury's.** As you might expect, this trendy waterside hangout, named after Queen lead singer Freddie Mercury born just a couple of blocks away, is one of Zanzibar's vibiest places. There are great seafood, pizzas, pasta, and steaks, and the wooden terrace overlooking the ocean is ideal for those sunset drinks. ⊠ *Hurumzi St., Stone Town* ☎ *024/223–3076* ☉ *Daily 10* AM*–midnight* ▭ *No credit cards.*

$$
AFRICAN
✕**Monsoon Restaurant.** For great Swahili food check out this atmospheric restaurant. The inside is decorated in a North African vibe. There are low tables with cushions for sitting on the floor. If you'd rather have views of the ocean and Fordhani Gardens, choose the veranda instead. Some nights there's traditional Tarab music. Check out the chalkboard by the front door for the daily specials. ⊠ *Hurumzi St., Stone Town* ☎ *024/223–3076* ☉ *Daily 10* AM*–midnight* ▭ *No credit cards.*

$$$–$$$$
SEAFOOD
✕**Tower Top.** With stunning views past the city's minarets to the harbor where dhows are setting out to sea, this rooftop restaurant is a great place to watch the sun sink into the Indian Ocean. It holds only about 20 people, who dine on fish or chicken accompanied by spice-scented rice while reclining on soft cushions. On weekends traditional music

and dance accompany the delicious food. You'll feel more a part of the scene if you wear something loose-fitting, perhaps even one of the local caftans known as *khanzus*. Dinner only. ⊠ *236 Hurumzi St., Stone Town* ☎ *024/223–2784* ⊕ *www.236hurumzi.com* ⚲ *Reservations essential* ▭ *No credit cards.*

WHERE TO STAY

Lodging reviews have been abbreviated in this book. For expanded reviews, please go to Fodors.com.

BEACH RESORTS

¢ **Mbweni Ruins Hotel.** Ten minutes from the airport and Stone Town, this historic, great-value-for-the-money hotel was once an Anglican Girls' School for slave-trade orphans. **Pros:** hotel has its own beach; great historic atmosphere; runs own excursion, free flight specials. **Cons:** 10 minutes from Stone Town. ⊠ *Mbweni* ☎ *223–5478* ⊕ *www. mbweni.com* ⤳ *13 rooms* ⚬ *In-room: safe. In-hotel: restaurant, bar, pool* ▭ *AE, DC, MC, V* ⦿*BP.*

$$–$$$ **Ras Nungwi.** You may ask yourself, "Where exactly am I going?" But the hour-plus drive from the airport through local towns and over bumpy roads will be worth it once you arrive. **Pros:** gorgeous beach; away from the madding crowds; good food. **Cons:** an hour's drive from Stone Town. ⊠ *Nungwi Peninsular, Nungwi* ☎ *024/223–3767* ⊕ *www. rasnungwi.com* ⤳ *32 rooms* ⚬ *In-room: safe, Internet. In-hotel: restaurant, bar, pool, spa, shop* ▭ *MC, V* ☽ *Closed in Apr. and May* ⦿*MAP.*

IN STONE TOWN

$$$$ **236 Hurumzi.** Tucked away in Stone Town, this small hotel, once the home of one of the richest men in Zanzibar, was the brainchild of two New Yorkers. **Pros:** authentic Zanzibar; historic ambience; huge rooms. **Cons:** lots and lots of wooden stairs; some rooms have no sea views or a/c. ☎ *255/77/742–3266* ⊕ *www.236hurumzi.com.com* ⤳ *9 rooms, 7 suites* ⚬ *In-room: a/c (some). In-hotel: restaurant, bar, Wi-Fi hotspot* ▭ *MC, V* ⦿*BP.*

Fodor'sChoice ★

$–$$ **Beyt al Chai.** Also known as the Stone Town Inn, this former tea house recalls days gone by. **Pros:** unpretentiously authentic; excellent location; children under 2 free. **Cons:** basic; breakfast not great. ☎ *0774/444–111* ⊕ *www.stonetowninn.com* ⤳ *6 rooms* ⚬ *In-room: safe. In-hotel: restaurant* ▭ *MC, V* ⦿*BP.*

$$$$ **The Zanzibar Serena Inn.** On one side of Shangani Square, on the fringe of Stone Town, this breathtakingly beautiful hotel is the result of the exquisite restoration of two of Zanzibar's historic buildings: the old Telekoms building, an original colonial-era building, and the Chinese doctors' residence, where several local Chinese doctors practiced their traditional medicine. ■**TIP→** It's worth paying an extra US$50 per night to get a prime room with a huge balcony directly overlooking the beach. **Pros:** gorgeous location; superb historical ambience; exclusivity. **Cons:** pricey; often fully booked; beach not great. ☎ *024/223–3051* ⊕ *www.*

Fodor'sChoice ★

serenahotels.com ⇆ *51 rooms* ⚐ *In-room: a/c, safe, Wi-Fi. In-hotel: 3 restaurants, bar, pool* ▤ *MC, V* ⎽⎺⎼ *FAP.*

MNEMBA ISLAND, OFF ZANZIBAR

Fodor's Choice
★

For the ultimate beach escape where time stands still, where sand, sea, and horizon melt into each other, where there is exclusivity, total relaxation, and impeccable food and service, it would be hard to find anywhere in the world as alluring as Mnemba Island Lodge on &Beyond's privately owned Mnemba Island; the guest list includes royalty, celebrities, pop stars, business tycoons, and honeymooners. You'll be transported from Zanzibar by 4x4 and speedboat to this ultimate desert island, and as you arrive the "Wow!" factor immediately kicks in. Your huge beach house Swiss Family Robinson deluxe—one of only 10 on the island—hidden between strips of coastal forest faces a turquoise sea that would have challenged even the palette of Van Gogh. Coconut matting covers the walls and floors of your bedroom, dressing room, en-suite bathroom, and covered veranda furnished with handmade Zanzibari furniture. A feature of this superlative lodge is its imaginative use of recycled glass. Check out the blue glass-bead shower curtain, your soap dish, or your champagne flute. Diving and snorkeling off a pristine coral reef just a few feet from shore is a perfect 10, and if you've always wanted to dive, then this is the place to fulfill that dream with two experienced dive masters and state-of-the-art equipment. The cooing of doves will soothe even the most savage beast as the tiniest antelopes in the world, the rare *suni*, scamper happily past you while you sit on the beach under your private canopy and sip sundowners. Mix with fellow guests from all over the world or dine alone a few feet from the soft surf under pulsing stars by glowing lantern light. Heaven can't be better than this. Make sure you book well in advance, as Mnemba Island is a legendary and much-sought-after destination.

WHEN TO GO

June through October is the best time to visit. There is a short rainy season in November, but heavy rains can fall from March until the end of May. Temperatures soar during this period, often reaching over 30°C (90°F).

GETTING HERE AND AROUND

There's a direct flight from Johannesburg twice a week on 1time. Most other flights come in from Dar es Salaam and are daily on Precision Air, Fly540, or ZanAir. The flight is 20 minutes from Dar and five hours from Johannesburg. ⇨ *See Zanzibar's Getting Here and Around section, above, for airline contact information.*

TIMING

If you can, plan a week here to take everything in and, most important, relax.

South Africa

WELCOME TO SOUTH AFRICA

TOP REASONS TO GO

★ **Big Game.** You're guaranteed to see big game—including the Big Five—both in national parks and at many private lodges.

★ **Escape the Crowds.** South Africa's game parks are rarely crowded. You'll see more game with fewer other visitors than almost anywhere else in Africa.

★ **Luxury Escapes.** Few other sub-Saharan countries can offer South Africa's high standards of accommodation, service, and food amid gorgeous surroundings of bush, beach, mountains, and desert.

★ **Take the Family.** All the national parks accept children (choose a malaria-free one if your kids are small), and many private lodges have fantastic children's programs.

★ **Beyond the Parks.** Visit Cape Town, one of the most beautiful and stylish cities in the world; the nearby stunning Winelands; the inspiring scenery of the Garden Route; the vibrant port city of Durban; and glorious, soft white-sand beaches.

1 Kruger National Park. A visit to Kruger, one of the world's great game parks, may rank among the best experiences of your life. With its amazing diversity of scenery, trees, amphibians, reptiles, birds, and mammals, Kruger is a place to safari at your own pace and where you can choose between upscale private camps or simple campsites.

2 Sabi Sands Game Reserve. The most famous and exclusive of South Africa's private reserves, this 153,000-acre park is home to dozens of private lodges, including the world-famous Mala Mala and Londolozi. With perhaps the highest game and leopard density of any private reserve in Southern Africa, the Sabi Sands fully deserves its exalted reputation.

ZIMBABWE

Messina

Kruger
National
Park

1

Pietersburg

MPUMALANGA

MOZAMBIQUE

Pilanesberg
National Park

Sabi Sands
Game Reserve

2

Nelspruit

🏵 PRETORIA

Soweto   Johannesburg

Mkuze
Game
Reserve

SWAZILAND

Phinda
Private
Reserve

Itala Game Reserve

Thanda Game Reserve

Ulundi   **3**

Hluhluwe-
Umfolozi
Game Reserve

Drakensberg
Park

Bloemfontein

Richards Bay

LESOTHO

Pietermaritzburg

DRAKENSBERG MOUNTAINS

Durban

Margate

Umtata

EASTERN CAPE

INDIAN OCEAN

East London

Grahamstown

Shamwari
Game Reserve

0 ————————— 200 mi

0 ————————— 200 km

GETTING ORIENTED

South Africa lies at the very foot of the continent, where the Atlantic and Indian oceans meet. Not only geographically and scenically diverse, it's a nation of more than 47 million people of varied origins, cultures, languages, and beliefs. Its cities and much of its infrastructure are thoroughly modern—Johannesburg could pass for any large American city. It's only when you venture into the rural areas or see the huge satellite squatter camps outside the cities or come face-to-face with the Big Five that you see an entirely different South Africa.

5

3 KwaZulu-Natal Parks. Zululand's Hluhluwe-Umfolozi is tiny—less than 6% of Kruger's size—but delivers the Big Five plus all the plains game. It has about 1,250 species of plants and trees—more than you'll find in entire countries. Mkuze and Itala are even smaller, but worth a visit, and if you're looking for the ultimate in luxury, stay at Phinda or Thanda private reserves.

4 Kgalagadi Transfrontier Park. Together with its neighbor, Botswana's Gemsbok National Park, this park covers more than 38,000 square km (14,670 square mi)—one of very few conservation areas of this magnitude left in the world. Its stark, desolate beauty shelters huge black-maned Kalahari lions among other predators and provides brilliant birding, especially birds of prey.

GREEN LODGING IN SOUTH AFRICA

Being a "green traveler" means minimizing the negative impact on your surroundings. How can you be sure you're traveling green? We've given you a few places you can stay on safari that are ecoconscious. Of course our list is not exhaustive, but it's a starting place.

(above) Djuma Game Reserve; (opposite upper right) Hog Hollow Country Lodge; (opposite bottom left) Whale-watching in Walker Bay

Only two hours from Cape Town, **Grootbos Private Nature Reserve** (☏ 028/384–8000 ⊕ *www.grootbos.com*) is home to the largest private fynbos garden in the world. Set on 2,500 acres of Western Cape landscape overlooking Walker Bay, Grootbos offers up-close observation of Protea, fynbos, milkwood forests, and tropical rain forests as well as aquatic life including penguins, dolphins, seals, and Southern Right Whales in early spring. Luxury accommodations include private cottages with fireplaces and sundecks, and exquisite cuisine is enhanced by vegetables and herbs grown on the premise. The reserve's foundation works to educate and employ the community with a variety of conservation, research, and sustainable living projects.

FIND YOUR CAUSE

The African Conservation Foundation (⊕ *www.africanconservation.org*) was established in 1999 to work as link between like minded conservation organizations with the goal of sharing resources and information. If you're looking for an organization to support and/or volunteer with, the Web site has a comprehensive list of available organizations.

Djuma comprises three separate lodges, of which **Vuyatela Bush Lodge** (☎ 013/735–5118 ⊕ www.djuma.com) is the most outstanding—and naturally, the most expensive. Djuma has access to more than 22,000 acres in the Sabi Sand Reserve, which is in itself noteworthy. The game-viewing is among the best there is, and everything at Vuyatela is owner run, so attention to detail is paramount. To lessen the impact on the environment, the camp was built with local labor and there was no heavy machinery used. In keeping with their philosophy of community involvement, the owners of Djuma established a day-care center called N'wa Tumberi in the neighboring Shangaan community that has been received favorably. The lodge also includes an aquarium and a boma, as well as the opportunity for walking safaris. ⇨ *See Luxury Lodges, in Sabi Sands Game Reserve for more information about the camp.*

Just outside Plettenberg Bay, **Hog Hollow Country Lodge** (☎ 044/534–8879 ⊕ www.hog-hollow.com) is a beautiful oasis run by Andy Fermor and Debbie Reyneke, a conscientious couple dedicated to employing local people. The lodge, in a private reserve, has views of the surrounding valleys and Tsitsikamma Mountains. Personalized service is one of the hallmarks of a stay at Hog Hollow. The main lodge and 12 cottages straddle a central dam, creating a serene hideaway that blends with the landscape and indigenous forest. The house includes a pool overlooking the Matjes River gorge, and one of the outdoor lounges has a grand old fig tree sprouting up through its wooden deck, providing an excellent perch for bird-watchers. Hike through the surrounding forest or take a quick drive to Keurbooms Beach and Nature's Valley, both just 10 minutes from Hog Hollow.

GREEN QUESTIONS TO ASK YOUR OPERATOR

If you're serious about being an ecotourist, shouldn't the tour operator you pick be ecologically conscious as well? Make sure to find a tour operator who feels as passionate about being green as you do and has the actions to prove it, that is, cooperates with the local community, a nonprofit partner, etc. How do you find this out? We've got a few question suggestions that should help you find the greenest operator out there.

■ Are the lodges on the itineraries solar powered?

■ Do the safari guides, rangers, and trackers belong to tribes from the region in which you're traveling?

■ Do the chefs and porters hail from the surrounding area?

■ Have local materials been used in building your safari lodge?

■ Does the menu in the dining room where you take meals use local ingredients?

5

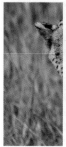

By Kate
Turkington

Since 1994, when Nelson Mandela spearheaded its peaceful transition to democracy, South Africa has become one of the fastest-growing tourist destinations in the world. And it's not difficult to see why. The country is stable and affordable, with an excellent infrastructure; friendly, interesting, amazingly diverse people; and enough stunning sights, sounds, scenery, and attractions to make even the most jaded traveler sit up and take notice. And nearly everybody speaks English—a huge bonus for international visitors.

South Africa has always teemed with game. That's what drew the early European explorers, who aimed to bring something exotic home with them. After all, as Pliny the Elder, one of Africa's earliest explorers, wrote almost 2,000 years ago, *ex Africa semper aliquid novi*—out of Africa always comes something new. Sometimes it was a giraffe, a rhinoceros, a strange bird, or an unheard-of plant.

In the latter half of the 19th century, Dr. Livingstone, Scotland's most famous Christian missionary, opened up much of the interior on his evangelizing expeditions, as did the piratical Englishman Cecil John Rhodes, who famously made his fortune on the Kimberley diamond mines and planned an unsuccessful Cape-to-Cairo railway line. About the same time, lured by the rumors of gold and instant fortunes, hundreds of hunters came to the lowveld to lay their hands on much-sought-after skins, horns, and ivory. Trophy hunters followed, vying with one another to see how many animals they could shoot in one day—often more than 100 each.

Paul Kruger, president of the Transvaal Republic (a 19th-century Boer country that occupied a portion of present-day South Africa), took the unprecedented visionary step of establishing a protected area for the wildlife in the lowveld region; in 1898 Kruger National Park was born.

FAST FACTS

Size 1,221,037 square km (471,442 square mi)

South Africa Pretoria (administrative capital); Cape Town (legislative capital); Bloemfontein (judicial capital)

Number of National Parks 22: Addo Elephant, Agulhas, Augrabies Falls, Bontebok, Camdeboo, Golden Gate Highlands, Karoo, Kruger, Mapungubwe, Marakele, Mokala, Mountain Zebra, Namaqua, Table Mountain, Tankwa Karoo, Tsitsikamma, West Coast, and Wilderness National Parks; Ais/Richtersveld and Kgalagadi Transfrontier Parks; Knysna National Lake Area; uKhahlamba/Drakensberg Park.

Number of Private Reserves Hundreds, including Sabi Sands and KwaZulu-Natal's Phinda and Thanda.

Population Approximately 47.9 million.

Big Five The gang's all here.

Language South Africa has 11 official languages: Afrikaans, English, Ndebele, North and South Sotho, Swati, Tsonga, Tswana, Venda, Xhosa, and Zulu. English is widely spoken.

■ **Time** SAST (South African Standard Time), seven hours ahead of North American Eastern Standard Time.

5

South Africa has 22 national parks covering deserts, wetland and marine areas, forests, mountains, scrub, and savanna. Hunting safaris are still popular but are strictly controlled by the government, and licenses are compulsory. Although hunting is a controversial issue, the revenue is substantial and can be ploughed into sustainable conservation, and the impact on the environment is minimal. Increasingly, wildlife conservation is linked with community development; many conservation areas have integrated local communities, the wildlife, and the environment, with benefits for all. Londolozi, MalaMala, Phinda, and Pafuri Camp are internationally acclaimed role models for linking tourism with community-development projects.

Although the "**Big Five**" was originally a hunting term for those animals that posed the greatest risk to hunters on foot—buffalo, elephants, leopards, lions, and rhinos—it is used today as the most important criterion for evaluating a lodge or reserve. But let the lure of the Big Five turn your safari into a treasure hunt and you'll miss the overall wilderness experience. Don't overlook the bush's other treasures, from desert meerkats and forest bush babies to antelopes, the handsome caracal, and spotted genets. Add to these hundreds of birds, innumerable insects, trees, flowers, shrubs, and grasses. Don't forget to search for the "**Little Five**": the buffalo weaver, elephant shrew, leopard tortoise, lion ant, and rhinoceros beetle. A guided bush walk may let you see these little critters and more.

PLANNING

WHEN TO GO

In the north, summers are sunny and hot (never humid), with short afternoon thunderstorms. Winter days are bright and sunny, but nights can be frosty. Although November through January is Cape Town's most popular time, with glorious sunshine and long, light evenings, the best weather is in February and March. Cape winters (May–August) are unpredictable with cold, windy, rainy days interspersed with glorious sun. The coastal areas of KwaZulu-Natal are warm year-round, but summers are steamy and hot. The ocean water is warmest in February, but it seldom dips below 17°C (65°F).

GETTING HERE AND AROUND

Place names in South Africa are in flux. The names in this book were accurate at time of writing, but even if names are different by the time of your trip, don't worry; all of South Africa will be coping with these large-scale changes and will undoubtedly use both names for a while. Some street and road sighs are signposted alternately in English and Afrikaans.

AIR TRAVEL

When booking flights, check the routing carefully, as South Africa–bound flights from United States cities have refueling stops en route, and sometimes those stops can be delayed. Currently only South African Airways and Delta provide direct service from the United States to South Africa, but flights routed through Europe may be more pleasant because they give you an interim stop to stretch your legs.

In peak season (midsummer and South African school vacations), the Johannesburg can be particularly busy, so allow an extra hour for domestic flights. If you are returning home with souvenirs, leave time for a V.A.T. inspection before you join the line for your international flight check-in.

If you are visiting a game lodge deep in the bush, you will be arriving by light plane—and you will be restricted in what you can bring. Excess luggage can usually be stored with the operator until your return. Don't just gloss over this: charter operators take weight very seriously, and some will charge you for an extra ticket if you insist on bringing excess baggage *(⇨ Charter Flights, below)*.

AIRPORTS

Most international flights arrive at and depart from Johannesburg's O.R. Tambo International Airport (sometimes abbreviated O.R.T.I.A. by safari companies), 19 km (12 mi) from the city. Several international flights departing from Cape Town are also routed via Johannesburg. Cape Town International is 20 km (12½ mi) southeast of the city, and Durban's King Shaka International Airport is 35 km (23 mi) north of the city. If you are traveling to or from either the Johannesburg or Cape Town airport (and, to a lesser extent, Durban), be aware of the time of day. Traffic can be horrendous between 7 and 9 in the morning and between about 3:30 and 6 in the evening.

Just 40 km (25 mi) outside Johannesburg, Lanseria International Airport is closer to Sandton than O.R. Tambo and handles some domestic flights and some charter flights to safari camps.

International Airports Cape Town International Airport (*CPT* ☎ *021/937–1200*). **Durban King Shaka International Airport** (*DUR* ☎ *032/436–6000*). **Lanseria International Airport** (*HLA* ☎ *011/367–0300*). **O.R. Tambo International Airport** (*JNB ORTIA* ☎ *011/921–6262*).

FLIGHTS

South Africa's international airline is South African Airways (SAA). Several major United States carriers also fly to South Africa. Flight times from the U.S. East Coast range from 15 hours (from Atlanta to Johannesburg on Delta) to almost 20 hours (on Delta, via Amsterdam). About 18 hours is the norm.

Three major domestic airlines have flights connecting South Africa's principal airports. SA Airlink and SA Express are subsidiaries of SAA, and Comair is a subsidiary of British Airways. Low-cost carriers include Kulula.com, Mango, and 1time.

Airlines Delta (☎ *800/241–4141* ⊕ *www.delta.com*). **South African Airways** (☎ *800/521–4845* ⊕ *www.flysaa.com*). **United** (☎ *800/538–2929*).

Domestic Airlines 1time (⊕ *www.1time.aero*). **British Airways/Comair** (☎ *011/921–0222* ⊕ *www.comair.co.za*). **Kulula** (☎ *086/158–5852* ⊕ *www.kulula.com*). **Mango** (☎ *011/359–1222, 021/936–2848, or 086/116–2646* ⊕ *ww6.flymango.com*). **South African Airways/SA Airlink/South African Express** (☎ *011/978–1111 or 011/978–5577* ⊕ *www.flysaa.com*).

CHARTER FLIGHTS

Charters are common throughout Southern Africa. These aircraft are well maintained and are almost always booked by your lodge or travel agent. The major charter companies run daily shuttles from O.R. Tambo to popular tourism destinations, such as Kruger Park. Keep in mind that you probably won't get to choose the charter company you fly with. The aircraft you get depends on the number of passengers flying and can vary from very small (you will sit in the co-pilot's seat) to a much more comfortable commuter plane.

Due to the limited space and size of the aircraft, charter carriers observe strict luggage regulations: luggage must be soft-sided and weigh no more than 57 pounds (and very often less).

Federal Air, based at Johannesburg Airport, is the largest charter air company in South Africa. Sefofane is a Botswana-based fly-in charter company that will take you anywhere there's a landing strip from its base in Jo'burg's Lanseria Airport.

Charter Companies Federal Air (☎ *011/395–9000* ⊕ *www.fedair.com*). **Sefofane** (☎ *011/701–3700* ⊕ *www.sefofane.com*).

CAR TRAVEL

South Africa has a superb network of multilane roads and highways; however, distances are vast, so guard against fatigue, which is an even bigger killer than alcohol. Toll roads, scattered among the main routes, charge anywhere from R10 to R60. South Africans drive on the left-hand side of the road. Wearing seat belts is required by law, and the legal blood-alcohol limit is 0.08 mg/100 ml, which means about one glass of wine puts you at the limit. It is illegal to talk on a handheld mobile phone while driving. South Africans can be aggressive and reckless drivers, and accidents are common. You can drive in South Africa for up to six months on any English-language license. ⚠ **Unfortunately, carjackings can and do occur with such frequency that certain high-risk areas are marked by permanent carjacking signs** (⇨ *Safety).*

GASOLINE

■ TIP→ **Credit cards are not accepted anywhere for fueling your tank, but nearly all gas stations are equipped with ATMs.** Huge 24-hour service stations are positioned at regular intervals along all major highways in South Africa. There are no self-service stations, so be sure to tip the attendant R2–R3. Check when booking a rental car as to what fuel to use. Gasoline is measured in liters and is more expensive than in the U.S.

PARKING

In the countryside parking is mostly free, but you will almost certainly need to pay for parking in cities. You'll find informal parking guards in most cities; they also wear brightly colored vests or T-shirts. They don't get paid much (in fact some pay for the privilege of working a spot), so they depend on tips. You'll get the most out of these guys if you acknowledge them when you park, ask them politely to look after your car, and then pay them a couple of rand when you return and find it's safe.

RENTAL CARS

It's common to rent a car for at least part of your trip. Rental rates are similar to those in the U.S., but some companies charge more for weekend rentals. Cars with automatic transmissions and air-conditioning are available but can be expensive. Some companies quote prices without insurance, some include 80% or 90% coverage, and some quote with 100% protection.

The major international companies all have offices in tourist cities and at international airports, and their vehicle types are the same range you'd find at home. There's no need to rent a 4x4 vehicle, as all roads are paved, including those in Kruger National Park.

In order to rent a car you need to be 23 years or older and have held a driver's license for three years. Younger international drivers can rent from some companies but will pay a penalty. You need to get special permission to take rental cars into neighboring countries (including Lesotho and Swaziland). You cannot take rental cars into Zimbabwe. Most companies allow additional drivers, yet some charge.

"The direct eye contact with one of the most majestic mammals alive was just awe inspiring. [It was a] true sense of connection with nature." —jspiegel, Fodors.com member.

CAR-RENTAL INSURANCE

In South Africa it's necessary to buy special insurance if you plan on crossing borders into neighboring countries, but CDW and TDW (theft-damage waiver) are optional on domestic rentals. Any time you are considering crossing a border with your rental vehicle, you must inform the rental company ahead of time to fulfill any paperwork requirements and pay additional fees.

Local Agencies Car Mania (☎ 021/447–3001 ⊕ www.carmania.co.za). **Europcar** (☎ 086/113–1000 or 011/479–4000 ⊕ www.europcar.co.za). **Maui Motorhome Rental** (☎ 011/396–1445 or 021/982–5107 ⊕ www.maui.co.za). **Tempest Car Hire** (✉ O.R. Tambo International Airport ☎ 011/578–0160 ⊕ www.tempestcarhire.co.za). **Value Car Hire** (☎ 021/386–7699 ⊕ www.valuecarhire.co.za).

Major Agencies Alamo (☎ 877/222–9075 ⊕ www.alamo.com). **Avis** (☎ 800/331–1084 ⊕ www.avis.com). **Budget** (☎ 800/527–0700 ⊕ www.budget.com). **Europcar** (☎ 086/113–100 or 011/479–4000 ⊕ www.europcar.co.za). **Hertz** (☎ 800/654–3001 ⊕ www.hertz.com). **National Car Rental** (☎ 877/222–9058 ⊕ www.nationalcar.com).

Emergency Services General emergency number (☎ 112 from mobile phone; 10111 from landline).

HOTELS

Most hotel rooms come with private bathrooms that are usually en suite, but they may, very occasionally, be across the corridor. You can usually choose between rooms with twin or double beds. A full English breakfast is often included in the rate, particularly in more traditional hotels. In most luxury lodges the rate usually covers the cost of dinner, bed, and breakfast, whereas in game lodges the rate includes everything but alcohol—and some include that. A self-catering room is one with kitchen facilities.

CAMPS AND LODGES

Accommodations range from fairly basic huts to the ultimate in luxury at most of the private camps. The advantage of a private lodge (apart from superb game-viewing) is that often everything is included: lodging, meals, beverages including excellent house wines, game drives, and other activities. You'll also be treated like royalty. (Indeed, you may well brush shoulders with royals and celebs of all kinds.) Note that there are no elevators in any safari lodging facility in Kruger.

Most national parks have self-catering accommodations (you buy and prepare your own food): budget huts from R350 per couple per night and much more expensive (but worth it) cottages in the more remote and exclusive bush camps that range from R600 to R1,100. Visit the South African National Parks Web site to get information and book accommodations. ■TIP➔ **Bookings open every September 1 for the following year. Make sure you book well in advance and, if possible, avoid July, August, and December, which are South African school vacations.**

Contacts South Africa National Parks (☎ 012/428–9111 ⊕ www.sanparks. org).

WHAT IT COSTS IN SOUTH AFRICAN RAND					
	¢	$	$$	$$$	$$$$
Safari Camps and Lodges	under R2,000	R2,000–R5,000	R5,001–R8,000	R8,001–R12,000	over R12,000
Hotels	under R500	R500–R1,000	R1,001–R2,000	R2,001–R3,000	over R3,000
Dining	under R50	R50–R75	R76–R100	R101–R125	over R125

Lodging prices are for a standard double room in high season, including 14% tax.

RESTAURANTS

South Africa's cities and towns are full of dining options, from chain restaurants like the popular Nando's to chic cafés. Indian food and Cape Malay dishes are regional favorites in Cape Town, while traditional smoked meats and sausages are available countrywide. In South Africa dinner is eaten at night and lunch at noon. Restaurants serve breakfast until about 11:30; a few serve breakfast all day. If you're staying at a game lodge, your mealtimes will revolve around the game drives—usually coffee and rusks (similar to biscotti) early in the morning, more coffee and probably muffins on the first game drive, a huge brunch in the late morning, no lunch, tea and something sweet in the late afternoon before the evening game drive, cocktails and snacks on the drive, and a substantial supper, or dinner, at about 8 or 8:30.

Many restaurants accustomed to serving tourists accept credit cards, usually Visa and American Express, with MasterCard increasingly accepted.

Most restaurants welcome casual dress, including jeans and sneakers, but draw the line at shorts and a halter top at dinner, except for restaurants on the beach.

COMMUNICATIONS

INTERNET

Most hotels and lodges have Internet, but unless you have business in South Africa, leave the laptop at home and take memory cards for your vacation photos. You can check e-mail for a few rand either in the comfort of your hotel or at a public Internet café.

PHONES

There are toll-free numbers in South Africa. There's also something called a share-call line, for which the cost of the call is split between both parties.

CALLING WITHIN SOUTH AFRICA

Local calls (from landline to landline) are very cheap, although all calls from hotels attract a hefty premium. Calls from a mobile phone or from a landline to a mobile are relatively expensive. South Africa has two types of pay phones: coin-operated phones, which accept a variety of coins (and are being phased out), and card-operated phones. Cards are available at newsstands, convenience stores, and telephone company offices. When making a phone call in South Africa, always use the full 10-digit number, including the area code, even if you're in the same area.

For directory assistance in South Africa, call 1023. For operator-assisted national long-distance calls, call 1025. For international operator assistance, dial 10903#. These numbers are free if dialed from a Telkom (landline) phone but are charged at normal cell-phone rates from a mobile—and they're busy call centers.

CALLING OUTSIDE SOUTH AFRICA

When dialing out from South Africa, dial 00 before the international code. So, for example, you would dial 001 for the United States.

MOBILE PHONES

Cell phones are ubiquitous and have quite extensive coverage; South African uses GSM phones. There are four cell-phone service providers in South Africa—Cell C, MTN, Virgin Mobile, and Vodacom—and you can buy these SIM cards, as well as airtime, in supermarkets for as little as R10 for the SIM card (if you purchase SIM cards at the airport, you will be charged much more). Cell phones also can be rented by the day, week, or longer from the airport on your arrival, but this is an expensive option. A text message costs a fraction of the cost for making an actual call.

5

Language Barrier

If you are traveling in South Africa, you may want to be aware of a few phrases that may not mean what you think—or logically what they are meant—to mean.

If a South African tells you she will meet you at the restaurant "just now" or "now now," this does not mean that she will meet you immediately. It means she will meet you at some vague point in time in the future, which could be 20 minutes or could be two hours. In other words, you probably want to determine an exact time. Also, if a South African tells you something is "lekker," that's a good

thing: "lekker" can mean anything from cool to sexy.

Another word to note is the term *colored* (spelled *coloured*). While its usage is extremely offensive to Americans, the term is widely used in South Africa to describe South Africans of mixed race, often descended from imported slaves, the San, the Khoekhoen, and European settlers. Over the years the term *coloureds* has lost any pejorative connotations. Most coloureds don't regard themselves as black Africans, and culturally they are extremely different.

EMERGENCIES

Europ Assistance offers professional evacuation in the event of emergency. If you intend to dive in South Africa, make sure you have DAN membership, which will be honored by Divers Alert Network South Africa (DANSA).

General Emergency Contacts Ambulance (☎ 10177). **DANSA** (☎ 0800/020-111; 010/209-8112 Emergency hotline ⊕ www.dansa.org). **Europ Assistance** (☎ 0860/635-635 ⊕ www.europassistance.co.za). **General emergency** (☎ 10111 from landline; 112 from mobile phone). **Police** (☎ 10111 ⊕ www.saps.gov.za).

HEALTH AND SAFETY

Although the majority of visitors experience a crime-free trip to South Africa, it's essential to practice vigilance and extreme care. Carjacking is a problem, with armed bandits often forcing drivers out of their vehicles at traffic lights, in driveways, or during a fake accident. Always drive with your windows closed and doors locked, don't stop for hitchhikers, and park in well-lighted places. At traffic lights, leave enough space between you and the vehicle in front so you can pull into another lane if necessary. In the unlikely event you are carjacked, don't argue, and don't look at the carjacker's face. Just get out of the car, or ask to be let out of the car. Do not try to keep any of your belongings—they are all replaceable. If you aren't given the opportunity to leave the car, try to stay calm, ostentatiously look away from the hijackers so they can be sure you can't identify them, and follow all instructions. Ask again, calmly, to be let out of the car.

Many places that are unsafe in South Africa will not bear obvious signs of danger. Make sure you know exactly where you're going; never set out without detailed directions and a good map or GPS. Many cities are ringed by "no-go" areas. Learn from your hotel or the locals which areas to avoid. If you sense you have taken a wrong turn, drive toward a public area, such as a gas station, or building with an armed guard, before attempting to correct your mistake, which could just compound the problem. When parking, don't leave anything visible in the car; stow it all in the trunk—this includes clothing or shoes. As an added measure, leave the glove box open, to show there's nothing of value inside (take the rental agreement with you).

Before setting out on foot, ask a local, such as your hotel concierge or a shopkeeper, which route to take and how far you can safely go. Walk with a purposeful stride so you look like you know where you're going, and duck into a shop or café if you need to check a map, speak on your mobile phone, or recheck the directions you've been given. Lone women travelers need to be particularly vigilant about walking alone and locking their rooms. South Africa has one of the world's highest rates of rape. ⚠ Don't walk while speaking on a cell phone.

EATING AND DRINKING

The drinking water in South Africa is treated and, except in rural areas, is absolutely safe to drink. Many people filter it, though, to get rid of the chlorine, as that aseptic status does not come free. You can eat fresh fruits and salads and have ice in your drinks.

VISITOR INFO

The official South Africa Tourism Web site was given a face left in 2010. Another government-sponsored Web site, SouthAfrica.info, is full of useful but general country information.

⇨ *For Cape Town, Johannesburg, and Durban visitor information, see Visitor Info, in each city's section below.*

Visitor Info SouthAfrica.info (⊕ *www.southafrica.info*). **South African Tourism** (☎ *800/593–1318 in U.S.; 011/895–3000 in South Africa* ⊕ *www.southafrica.net*).

MUST-SEE PARKS

Unfortunately, you probably won't be able to see all of South Africa in one trip. So we've broken down the chapter by **Must-See Parks** (Kruger National Park, Sabi Sands Game Reserve, KwaZulu-Natal Parks, Kgalagadi Transfrontier Park) and **If You Have Time Parks** (Tswalu Kalahari Reserve, Pilanesberg National Park, Kwandwe, Addo Elephant Park, Shamwari Game Reserve) to help you better organize your time. We suggest that you read about *all* of them and then choose for yourself.

KRUGER NATIONAL PARK

There's no getting away from it, and it's worth repeating: visiting Kruger is likely to be one of the great experiences of your life. Founded in 1898 by Paul Kruger, president of what was then the Transvaal Republic, the park is a place to safari at your own pace and choose from upscale private camps or simple campsites.

Game
★★★★★
Park Accessibility
★★★★★
Getting Around
★★★★★
Accommodations
★★★★★
Scenic Beauty
☆★★★★

Kruger lies in the hot lowveld, a subtropical section of Mpumalanga and Limpopo provinces that abuts Mozambique. The park cuts a swath 80 km (50 mi) wide and 320 km (200 mi) long from Zimbabwe and the Limpopo River in the north to the Crocodile River in the south. It is divided into 16 macro eco-zones, each supporting a great variety of plants, birds, and animals, including 145 mammal species and almost 500 species of birds, some of which are found nowhere else in South Africa.

Maps of Kruger are available at all the park gates and in the camp stores, and gas stations are at the park gates and at the major camps. Once in the park, observe the speed-limit signs carefully (there are speed traps): 50 KPH (31 MPH) on paved roads, 40 KPH (25 MPH) on dirt roads. Leave your vehicle only at designated picnic and viewing sites, and if you do come across animals on the road, allow them to pass before moving on. Sometimes you have to be very patient, especially if a breeding herd of elephants is blocking your way. ■TIP→ **Animals always have the right-of-way.** Always be cautious. Kruger is not a zoo; you are entering the territory of wild animals, even though many may be habituated to the sights and sounds of vehicles.

PLANNING
WHEN TO GO
Kruger National Park is hellishly hot in midsummer (November–March), but the bush is green, the animals are sleek and glossy, and the birdlife is prolific, even though high grasses and dense foliage make spotting animals more difficult. Winter in the high season. In winter

(May–September), the bush is at
its dullest, driest, and most color-
less, but the game is much easier
to spot, as many trees are bare,
grasses are low, and animals congregate around the few available
permanent water sources. However, temperatures can drop to
almost freezing at night and in the
very early morning. The shoulder
months of April and October are
also good, and less crowded.

> ### PARK ESSENTIALS
>
> It's worth renting an eight-seater
> *combi* (van) or SUV. Though more
> expensive than a car, they provide
> more legroom, and you'll prob-
> ably have better luck spotting
> and observing game from your
> lofty perch. Always reserve well in
> advance.

GETTING HERE AND AROUND

You can fly to either Kruger Mpumalanga International Airport
(KMIA), at Nelspruit, or Hoedspruit airport, close to Kruger's Orpen
Gate, serve Kruger National Park from either Johannesburg or Cape
Town. You can also drive; if you drive, a 4x4 is not necessary since all
roads are paved.

Airport Information Hoedspruit (*HDS* ⊕ *hoedspruit-hds-airport.webport.com*).
Kruger Mpumalanga International Airport (KMIA) (*MQP* ☎ *27/13–753–7500*
⊕ *www.kmiairport.co.za*).

Car Rentals Avis (☎ *013/750–1015 at KMIA; 015/793–2014 at Hoedspruit*
⊕ *www.avis.co.za*). **Budget** (☎ *013/751–1774 at KMIA; 011/398–0123 at*
Hoedspruit ⊕ *www.budget.co.za*). **Europcar** (☎ *013/751–1855 at KMIA* ⊕ *www.*
europcar.co.za).

South African National Parks (⊕ *www.sanparks.org/parks/kruger/*).

TIMING

How and where you tackle Kruger will depend on your time frame.
With excellent roads and accommodations, it's a great place to drive
yourself. If you don't feel up to driving or self-catering, you can choose
a lodge just outside the park and take the guided drives—but it's not
quite the same as lying in bed and hearing the hyenas prowling round
the camp fence or a lion roaring under the stars.

RESTAURANTS

Food is cheap and cheerful in Kruger's cafeterias and restaurants, and
usually excellent in the private game lodges. Dinner is eaten 7:30-ish,
and it's unlikely you'll get a meal in a restaurant after 9. At private
lodges, dinner is served after the evening game drive, usually around 8.
"Smart casual" is the norm. Many higher-end restaurants close on Monday, and it's always advisable to make reservations at these in advance.

LODGES

Accommodations range from fairly basic in the Kruger Park huts to
the ultimate in luxury at most of the private camps. You may forget
that you are in the bush until an elephant strolls past. The advantage of a private lodge (apart from superb game-viewing) is that often
everything is included—lodging, meals, beverages including excellent
house wines, laundry, game drives, and other activities. Many lodges
and hotels offer special midweek or winter low-season rates. If you're

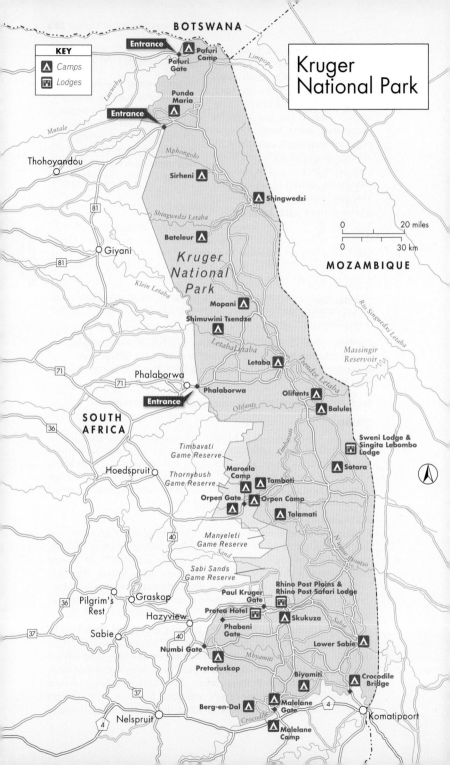

WALKING KRUGER

Kruger's seven wilderness trails accommodate eight hikers each. On three-day, two-night hikes, led by an armed ranger and local tracker, you walk in the mornings and evenings, with an afternoon siesta. You can generally get closer to animals in a vehicle, but many hikers can recount face-to-face encounters with everything from rhinos to lions.

Be prepared to walk up to 19 km (12 mi) a day. No one under 12 is allowed; those over 60 must have a doctor's certificate. Hikers sleep in rustic two-bed huts and share a reed-wall bathroom (flush toilets, bucket showers). Meals are simple (stews and barbecues); you bring your own drinks. In summer walking is uncomfortably hot (and trails are cheaper); in winter, nights can be freezing—bring warm clothes and an extra blanket. Reserve 13 months ahead, when bookings open. The cost is about R3,430 per person per trail.

Bushman Trail. In the southwestern corner of the park, this trail takes its name from the San rock paintings and sites found in the area. The trail camp lies in a secluded valley dominated by granite hills and cliffs. Watch for white rhinos, elephants, and buffalo. Check in at Berg-en-Dal.

Metsi Metsi Trail. The permanent water of the nearby N'waswitsontso River makes this one of the best trails for winter game-viewing. Midway between Skukuza and Satara, the trail camp is in the lee of a mountain in an area of gorges, cliffs, and rolling savanna. Check in at Skukuza.

Napi Trail. White rhino sightings are common on this trail, which runs through mixed bushveld between Pretoriuskop and Skukuza. Other possibilities are black rhinos, cheetahs, leopards, elephants, and, if you're lucky, nomadic wild dogs. The camp is tucked into dense riverine forest at the confluence of the Napi and Biyamiti rivers. Check in at Pretoriuskop.

Nyalaland Trail. In the far north of the park, this trail camp sits among ancient baobab trees near the Luvuvhu River. Walk at the foot of huge rocky gorges and in dense forest. Look for highly sought-after birds: Böhm's spinetail, crowned eagle, and Pel's fishing-owl. Hippos, crocs, elephants, buffalo, and the nyala antelope are almost a sure thing. Check in at Punda Maria.

Olifants Trail. This spectacularly sited camp sits on a high bluff overlooking the Olifants River and affords regular sightings of elephants, lions, buffalo, and hippos. The landscape varies from riverine forest to the rocky foothills of the Lebombo Mountains. Check in at Letaba.

Sweni Trail. East of Satara, this trail camp overlooks the Sweni Spruit and savanna. The area attracts large herds of zebras, wildebeests, and buffalo with their attendant predators: lions, spotted hyenas, and wild dogs. Check in at Satara.

Wolhuter Trail. You'll come face-to-face with a white rhino on this trail through undulating bushveld, interspersed with rocky kopjes, midway between Berg-en-Dal and Pretoriuskop. Elephants, buffalo, and lions are also likely. Check in at Berg-en-Dal.

5

opting for a private game lodge, find out whether it accepts children (many specify kids only over 12) and stay a minimum of two nights, three if you can.

WHERE TO STAY

It's impossible to recommend just one camp in Kruger. One person might prefer the intimacy of Kruger's oldest camp, Punda Maria, with its whitewashed thatch cottages; another might favor big, bustling Skukuza. A great way to experience the park is to stay in as many of the camps as possible. The SANParks Web site (⇨ *See Essentials, above, for contact info*) has a comprehensive overview of the different camps. The bushveld camps are more expensive than the regular camps, but offer much more privacy and exclusivity—but no shops, restaurants, or pools. If you seek the ultimate in luxury, stay at one of the private luxury lodges in the concession areas, some of which also have walking trails.

LUXURY LODGES

The lodges that follow are in private concession areas within Kruger.

$$$ **Singita Lebombo Lodge.** Taking its name from the Lebombo mountain range, Singita Lebombo, winner of numerous international accolades and eco-driven in concept, has been built "to touch the ground lightly." It hangs seemingly suspended on the edge of a cliff, like a huge glass box in space. Wooden walkways connect the aptly named "lofts" (suites), all of which have an uncluttered style and spectacular views of the river and bushveld below. Outdoor and indoor areas fuse seamlessly. Organic materials—wood, cane, cotton, and linen—are daringly juxtaposed with steel and glass. This is Bauhaus in the bush, with a uniquely African feel. Public areas are light, bright, and airy, furnished with cane furniture, crisp white cushions, comfy armchairs, and recliners. Service is superb, as is the food, and nothing is left to chance. You can buy African art and artifacts at the classy Trading Post or enjoy a beauty treatment at the spa. **Pros:** stunning avant-garde architecture; superb food and service. **Cons:** a bit over the top; avoid if you want the traditional safari lodge experience; very, very pricey. ☎ *021/683–3424* ⊕ *www. singita.co.za* ⏎ *15 suites* ⏤ *In-room: a/c, safe, refrigerator, Internet. In-hotel: bar, pool, gym, spa* ⊟ *AE, DC, MC, V* ⏃ *FAP.*

$$$ **Sweni Lodge.** Built on wooden stilts, Sweni is cradled on a low riverbank amid thick virgin bush and ancient trees. More intimate than its sister camp, Lebombo, it has six huge river-facing suites glassed on three sides, wooden on the other. At night khaki floor-to-ceiling drapes lined with silk divide the living area from the bedroom, which has a king-size bed with weighted, coffee-color mosquito netting and a cascade of ceramic beads. Hanging lamp shades of brown netting fashioned like traditional African fish traps, cream mohair throws, and brown leather furniture enhance the natural feel and contrast boldly with the gleam of stainless steel in the living room and bathroom. You can relax in a wooden rocking chair on your large reed-shaded deck while watching an elephant herd drink or spend the night under the stars on a comfy, mosquito-net-draped mattress. **Pros:** tiny, intimate; great location. **Cons:** game not overabundant; dim lighting; all those earth colors

could become a bit depressing.
☎ *021/683–3424* ⊕ *www.singita.
co.za* ↪ *6 suites* ⚅ *In-room: a/c,
safe, refrigerator, Internet. In-hotel:
bar, pool, gym, spa* ⊟ *AE, DC, MC,
V* ⚍*FAP.*

PERMANENT TENTED CAMPS

The camps of Rhino Post Plains
Camp and Rhino Post Safari Lodge
are situated in about 30,000 acres
of pristine bushveld in the Mutlu-
muvi area of Kruger, 10 km (6 mi)
northeast of Skukuza, the heart of
Kruger Park; the area can be easily
accessed by road or air. The concession shares a 15-km (9-mi) boundary with MalaMala, in the Sabi

Sands Game Reserve, and there's plenty of game movement between
the two.

$ 🛏 **Pafuri Camp.** This gorgeous lodge stretches for more than a kilome-
☺ ter along the banks of the Luvuvhu River in Kruger's far north. The
240-square-km (93-square-mi) area embraces an amazing variety of
landscapes and is one of the few places on earth where fever-tree and
baobab forests intermingle. At Crooks Corner, where baddies on the run
of bygone days once lurked, a wide swath of sand stretching as far as the
eye can see links Mozambique, South Africa, and Zimbabwe. There's
great game plus ancient history—more than 1.5 million years ago, early
humans lived here, and the area holds stone-age tools, rock engravings,
and rock paintings. Pafuri also has the best birding in Kruger: this is
the place to spot the rare and elusive Pel's fishing-owl. There's a superb
children's program, and special family accommodations provide privacy
for parents and kids. The tented rooms face the river. **Pros:** one of best
locations in Kruger; terrific biodiversity; family-friendly; adventurous
three-night walking trail. **Cons:** accessible by road, but it's a long drive
to get there. ☎ *011/257–5111* ⊕ *www.safariadventurecompany.com*
↪ *20 tents* ⚅ *In-room: safe. In-hotel: restaurant, bar, pool* ⊟ *AE, DC,
MC, V* ⚍*MAP.*

$ 🛏 **Rhino Post Plains Camp.** Overlooking a water hole amid an acacia
knobthorn thicket deep in the heart of the Timbitene Plain, Plains Camp
has comfortably furnished tents with wooden decks and great views
of the plains. A deck with a bar and plunge pool is great for postwalk
get-togethers, and there's a small tented dining area. The camp is simple, unpretentious, very friendly, and has great food. **Pros:** bang in the
middle of Kruger and easily accessible by road or air; great game; fabulous night drives when everyone else in the Kruger camps is confined
to barracks. **Cons:** surroundings a bit bleak, especially in winter; not
much privacy between tents. ☎ *035/474–1473* ⊕ *www.zulunet.co.za*
↪ *4 tents* ⚅ *In-hotel: bar, pool* ⊟ *AE, DC, MC, V* ⚍*FAP.*

$ ⊡ **Rhino Post Safari Lodge.** This lodge comprises eight spacious suites on stilts overlooking the Mutlumuvi riverbed. Each open-plan suite built of canvas, thatch, wood, and stone has a bedroom, private wooden deck, bathroom with a deep freestanding bath, twin sinks, a separate toilet, and an outdoor shower protected by thick reed poles. **Pros:** eco-friendly; great game; busy water hole. **Cons:** canvas makes the suites very hot in summer and very cold in winter. ☎ *035/474–1473* ⊕ *www.zulunet.co.za* ⇱ *8 suites* ⌂ *In-room: safe. In-hotel: bar, pool, Internet terminal* ▱ *AE, DC, MC, V* ▯◉▯ *FAP.*

NATIONAL PARK ACCOMMODATIONS

Reservations for the following accommodations should be made through **South African National Parks** (⇨ *See Essentials, above, for contact info*). At this writing, some of the national park accommodations in Kruger are undergoing refurbishment, including installation of air-conditioning; if this is an important amenity for you, call or check the Web site to confirm its availability in the accommodation of your choice. ■ TIP➔ **Book your guided game drives and walks when you check in. Opt for the sunset drive. You'll get to see the animals coming to drink plus a thrilling night drive.**

¢   ⊡ **Balule.** On the banks of the Olifants River, Satara's rustic satellite camp differs radically from the others because it really is simple, appealing to those who don't mind roughing it a bit and want to experience the true feel of the bush. There are no shops or restaurants—so bring your own food—and there's no electricity either (only lanterns). Accommodations are in basic three-bed huts with no windows (vents only); the shared bathroom facilities have running water. You must check in at Olifants, 11 km (7 mi) away. **Pros:** intimate; evocative hurricane lamps; captures history and atmosphere of the original Kruger Park. **Cons:** very rustic; no windows or electricity; shared refrigerator; no on-site shop (closest camp is Olifants, 15 minutes away on dirt road). ⇱ *12 campsites, 6 huts.*

¢   ⊡ **Berg-en-Dal.** This rest camp lies at the southern tip of the park, in
℃   a basin surrounded by rocky hills. Berg-en-Dal is known for its white
Fodor'sChoice   rhinos, leopards, and wild dogs, but there's plenty of other game, too. A
★   dam (often nearly dry in winter) by one side of the perimeter fence offers good game-viewing, including a close look at cruising crocodiles and munching elephants. One of the more attractive camps, it has thoughtful landscaping, which has left much of the indigenous vegetation intact, making for more privacy. It has an attractive pool and well-stocked grocery-curio shop, and kids can run around safely here. **Pros:** you can sit on benches at the perimeter fence and watch game—particularly elephants and buffalo—come and go all day; evening wildlife videos under the stars; great food options for those on the go. **Cons:** always crowded (although chalets are well spaced out); very slow service when checking in at reception. ⇱ *62 chalets, 23 family cottages, 2 guesthouses, 70 campsites* ⌂ *In-room: kitchen (some). In-hotel: restaurant, pool, laundry facilities.*

¢   ⊡ **Crocodile Bridge.** In the southeastern corner of the park, this superb small rest camp (it has won several awards for good service) doubles as an entrance gate, which makes it a convenient stopover if you arrive near the park's closing time and thus too late to make it to another camp. Although the Crocodile River provides a scenic backdrop, any sense of being in the wild is quickly shattered by views of power lines and farms on the south side. The road leading from the camp to Lower Sabie is famous for sightings of general game as well as buffalo, rhinos, cheetahs, and lions, but it's often crowded on weekends and holidays and during school vacations. A hippo pool lies just 5 km (3 mi) away. Two of the bungalows are geared toward travelers with disabilities. **Pros:** adjacent to one of best game roads in park; very well run. **Cons:** close proximity to the outside world of roads and farms makes it very noisy. ✍ *20 bungalows, 8 safari tents, 15 campsites ☼ In-room: kitchen (some). In-hotel: laundry facilities.*

¢ 🖬 **Letaba.** Overlooking the frequently dry Letaba River, this lovely camp sits in the middle of elephant country in the central section of the park. There's excellent game-viewing on the roads to and all around the Englelhardt and Mingerhout dams: be careful in the early morning and as the sun goes down that you don't bump a hippo. The camp itself has a real bush feel: all the huts are thatch (ask for one overlooking the river), and the grounds are overgrown with apple-leaf trees, acacias, mopane, and lala palms. The restaurant and snack bar, with attractive outdoor seating, look out over the broad, sandy riverbed. Even if you're not staying at Letaba, stop at the superb elephant exhibit at the Environmental Education Centre and marvel at just how big elephants' tusks can get. Campsites, on the camp's perimeter, offer lots of shade for your tent or trailer. **Pros:** lovely old camp full of trees, flowers, and birds; restaurant deck overlooks Letaba riverbed, where there's always game; interesting environmental center. **Cons:** a long way from the southern entrance gates, so you'll need more traveling time; always busy. ✍ *86 bungalows, 5 huts, 10 guest cottages, 2 guesthouses, 20 safari tents, 45 campsites ☼ In-room: kitchen (some). In-hotel: restaurant, laundry facilities.*

¢ 🖬 **Lower Sabie.** This is one of the most popular camps in Kruger for good reason: it has tremendous views over a broad sweep of the Sabie River and sits in one of the best game-viewing areas of the park (along with Skukuza and Satara). White rhinos, lions, cheetahs, elephants, and buffalo frequently come down to the river to drink, especially in the dry winter months when there is little surface water elsewhere. Long wooden walkways that curve around the restaurant and shop are particularly attractive; you can sit here and look out over the river. Half the safari tents have river views. The vegetation around the camp is mainly grassland savanna interspersed with marula and knobthorn trees. There are lots of animal drinking holes within a few minutes' drive. Don't miss the H10 road from Lower Sabie to Tshokwane, where you'll almost certainly see elephants. **Pros:** great location right on the river; superb game in vicinity; good atmosphere at the camp. **Cons:** always crowded; surly restaurant staff. ✍ *28 huts, 65 bungalows, 24 safari tents, 1 guesthouse, 33 campsites ☼ In-room: kitchen (some). In-hotel: restaurant, pool, laundry facilities.*

¢ 🖬 **Malelane.** Small and intimate, this camp offering privacy and that close-to-the-bush feeling is ideal for backpackers and do-it-yourselfers.

"[This] matriarch [in Kruger National Park] decided that her charges were threatened by our presence! She charged our vehicle. While contemplating my demise, I [snapped] the attached photo." —Linda R. Hansen, Fodors.com member

If you need supplies, a swim, or a bit more sophistication, you can head over to Berg-en-Dal, just a few kilometers away. A bonus is that you're within easy driving distance of good game areas around and toward Lower Sabie. Guided bush drives are also on offer. You check in at Malelane Gate, from which the camp is managed. **Pros:** private and intimate; great for campers and caravans. **Cons:** right on perimeter fence; unattractive surroundings; lots of backpackers and happy campers; no pool. ⇨ *5 bungalows, 15 campsites* ♿ *In-room: kitchen (some).*

¢ **Maroela.** Orpen's small, cozy satellite campsite is just 3 km (2 mi) away from the Orpen Gate. It can be hot, dry, and dusty at any time of the year, but you'll feel close to the bush among thorn and maroela (marula) trees. A small hide (blind) overlooks a water hole, and there's lots of excellent game in the vicinity, including cheetahs, lions, and rhinos. **Pros:** hide (blind) overlooking water hole; good game. **Cons:** only campers and caravans allowed; unattractive surroundings; no pool. ⇨ *20 campsites with power hookups.*

¢ **Mopani.** Built in the lee of a rocky kopje overlooking a lake, this camp in the northern section is one of Kruger's biggest. The camp is a landscaped oasis for birds, people, and a few impalas and other grazing animals amid not very attractive surrounding mopane woodlands. If it's hippos you're after, from your veranda feast your eyes on a cavalcade of these giants frolicking in the lake. Constructed of rough stone, wood, and thatch, the camp blends well into the thick vegetation. Shaded wooden walkways connect the public areas, all of which overlook the lake, and the view from the open-air bar is awesome. The à la carte restaurant (reserve before 6 PM) serves better food than most of the other camps, and the cottages are better equipped and larger than their counterparts elsewhere in Kruger. Ask for accommodations overlooking the lake when you book. Mopani lacks the intimate charm of some of the smaller camps, and the surrounding mopane woodland doesn't attract much game, but it's a really comfortable camp to relax in for a night or two if you're driving the length of the park. **Pros:** lovely accommodation; right on big lake; good restaurant and bar; easy to get bookings. **Cons:** not much game in immediate vicinity. ↗ *45 bunga-lows, 12 cottages, 45 guest cottages, 1 guesthouse ⚿ In-room: kitchen. In-hotel: restaurant, bar, pool, laundry facilities.*

¢ ⊞ **Olifants.** In the center of Kruger, Olifants has the best setting of all the camps: high atop cliffs on a rocky ridge with panoramic views of the distant hills and the Olifants River below. A lovely thatch-sheltered terrace allows you to sit for hours with binoculars and pick out the animals below. Lions often make kills in the river valley, and elephants, buffalo, giraffes, kudu, and other game come to drink and bathe. Try to book one of the thatch rondavels overlooking the river for at least two nights (you'll need to book a year in advance) so you can hang out on your veranda and watch Africa's passing show below. It's a charming old camp, graced with wonderful indigenous trees like sycamore figs, mopane, and sausage—so called because of the huge, brown, sausage-shape fruits that weigh down the branches. The only drawback, particularly in the hot summer months, however, is that it has no pool. **Pros:** hilltop location gives great views of the river below; elephants, elephants, and more elephants; lovely old-world feel; try for riverside accommodation. **Cons:** huts in the middle of the camp have no privacy; high malaria area; no pool. ↗ *107 rondavels, 2 guesthouses ⚿ In-room: kitchen. In-hotel: restaurant, laundry facilities.*

¢ ⊞ **Orpen.** Don't dismiss this tiny, underappreciated rest camp in the center of the park because of its proximity to the Orpen Gate. It may not be a particularly attractive camp—the rooms, arranged in a rough semi-circle around a large lawn, look out toward the perimeter fence, about 150 feet away—but there's a permanent water hole where animals come to drink, and plenty of game is in the vicinity, including cheetahs, lions, and rhinos. The two-bedroom huts are a bit sparse, without bathrooms or cooking facilities (although there are good communal ones), but there are three comfortable family cottages with bathrooms and kitchenettes. And it's a blissfully quiet camp, as there are so few accommodations. **Pros:** permanent water hole; cheetahs and lions usually in vicinity; quiet and relaxing environment. **Cons:** very unattractive camp; close to main gate. ↗ *6 huts, 3 cottages ⚿ In-room: kitchen (some).*

¢ ⊞ **Pretoriuskop.** This large, bare, nostalgically old-fashioned camp, con-
ℭ veniently close to the Numbi Gate in the southwestern corner of the park, makes a good overnight stop for new arrivals. The rocky kopjes and steep ridges that characterize the surrounding landscape provide an ideal habitat for mountain reedbuck and klipspringers—antelope not always easily seen elsewhere in the park. The area's *sourveld*—so named because its vegetation is less sweet and attractive to herbivores than other kinds of vegetation—also attracts browsers like giraffes and kudu, as well as white rhinos, lions, and wild dogs. There's not a lot of privacy in the camp—accommodations tend to overlook each other—but there

is some shade, plus a great swimming pool. **Pros:** great landscaped pool; good restaurant; old-fashioned nostalgic feel; good cheetah country. **Cons:** bleak and bare in winter, barracks-style feel. ⇨ *76 rondavels, 54 bungalows, 4 cottages, 40 campsites, 2 guesthouses* ⌂ *In-room: kitchen. In-hotel: restaurant, pool, laundry facilities.*

¢ **Punda Maria.** It's a pity that few foreign visitors make it to this lovely little camp in the far north end of the park near Zimbabwe, because in some ways it offers the best bush experience of any of the major rest camps. It's a small enclave, with tiny whitewashed thatch cottages arranged in terraces on a hill. The camp lies in *sandveld*, a botanically rich area notable for its plants and birdlife. This is Kruger's best birding camp: at a tiny, saucer-shaped, stone birdbath just over the wall from the barbecue site, dozens of unique birds come and go all day. A nature trail winds through and behind the camp—also great for birding, as is the Punda/Pafuri road, where you can spot lots of raptors. A guided walking tour from here takes you to one of South Africa's most interesting archaeological sites—the stone Thulamela Ruins, dating from 1250 to 1700. Lodging includes two-bed bungalows with bathrooms and, in some cases, kitchenettes, plus fully equipped safari tents. There are also two very private six-bed family bungalows up on a hill above the camp; they're visited by an amazing variety of not-often-seen birds and some friendly genets. Reservations are advised for the restaurant (don't expect too much from the food), and only some of the campsites have power. **Pros:** possibly the most attractive of all the camps; delightful short walking trail in camp; best birding area in Kruger with some endemic species. **Cons:** very far north; game less abundant than the south; cottages very close together. ⇨ *22 bungalows, 2 family cottages, 7 safari tents, 50 campsites* ⌂ *In-room: kitchen (some). In-hotel: restaurant, pool.*

¢ **Satara.** Second in size only to Skukuza, this camp sits in the middle of the hot plains between Olifants and Lower Sabie, in the central section of Kruger. The knobthorn veld surrounding the camp provides the best grazing in the park and attracts large concentrations of game. That in turn brings the predators—lions, cheetahs, hyenas, and wild dogs—which make this one of the best areas in the park for viewing game (especially on the N'wanetsi River Road, also known as S100). If you stand or stroll around the perimeter fence, you may see giraffes, zebras, and waterbucks and other antelope. Despite its size, Satara has far more appeal than Skukuza, possibly because of the privacy it offers (the huts aren't all piled on top of one another) and because of the tremendous birdlife. The restaurant and cafeteria are very pleasant, with shady seating overlooking the lawns and the bush beyond. Accommodations are in large cottages and two- or three-bed thatch rondavels, some with kitchenettes (no cooking utensils). The rondavels, arranged in large circles, face inward onto a central, open, grassy area. Campsites are secluded, with an excellent view of the bush, although they don't have much shade. **Pros:** superb location in middle of park; game galore; good on-site shop and restaurant; great guided sunset drives. **Cons:** not very attractive buildings or immediate surroundings; almost always fully booked. ⇨ *152 rondavels, 10 guest cottages, 3* guesthouses, 97 campsites ⚲ In-room: kitchen (some). In-hotel: restaurant, pool, laundry facilities.

¢ 🗔 **Shingwedzi.** Although this camp lies in the northern section of the
🕓 park, amid monotonous long stretches of mopane woodland, it benefits enormously from the riverine growth associated with the Shingwedzi River and Kanniedood (Never Die) Dam. As a result, you'll probably find more game around this camp than anywhere else in the region—especially when you drive the Shingwedzi River Road early in the morning or just before the camp closes at night (but don't be late—you'll face a hefty fine). The roof supports of thatch and rough tree trunks give the camp a rugged, pioneer feel. Both the à la carte restaurant and the outdoor cafeteria have views over the Shingwedzi River. Accommodations are of two types: A and B. Try for one of the A units, whose steeply pitched thatch roofs afford an additional two-bed loft; some also have fully equipped kitchenettes. The huts face one another across a fairly barren expanse of dry earth, except in early spring, when the gorgeous bright pink impala lilies are in bloom. **Pros:** lovely atmosphere and good accommodation; game-busy river road; pink impala lilies in season; good restaurants. **Cons:** many of the accommodations are grouped in a circle around a big open space that is pretty bleak and bare most of the year and affords little individual privacy; roads south full of mopane trees so not much game. ⤵ 12 huts, 66 bungalows, 1 cottage, 1 guesthouse, 50 campsites ⚲ In-room: kitchen (some). In-hotel: restaurant, pool, laundry facilities.

¢ 🗔 **Skukuza.** It's worth popping in to have a look at this huge camp. More like a small town than a rest camp, it has a gas station, police station, airport, post office, car-rental agency, grocery store, and library. It's nearly always crowded, not only with regular visitors but with busloads of noisy day-trippers, and consequently has lost any bush feel at all. Still, Skukuza is popular for good reason. It's easily accessible by both air and road, and it lies in a region of thorn thicket teeming with game, including lions, cheetahs, and hyenas. The camp itself sits on a bank of the crocodile-infested Sabie River, with good views of thick reeds, dozing hippos, and grazing waterbuck. Visit the worthwhile museum and education center to learn something about the history and ecology of the park. However, if you're allergic to noise and crowds, limit yourself to a stroll along the banks of the Sabie River before heading for one of the smaller camps. **Pros:** plumb in the middle of best game areas in the park; easily accessible; beautifully located right on river; good museum. **Cons:** you don't want to be here when the seemingly never-ending tour and school buses arrive, making it horribly crowded and noisy. ⤵ 198 bungalows, 16 family cottages, 15 guest cottages, 4 guesthouses, 21 safari tents, 99 campsites ⚲ In-hotel: restaurant, pool.

¢ 🗔 **Tamboti.** Kruger's first tented camp, a satellite of Orpen and very close to the Orpen Gate, is superbly sited on the banks of the frequently dry Tamboti River, among sycamore fig and jackalberry trees. Communal facilities make it a bit like an upscale campsite; nevertheless, it's one of Kruger's most popular camps, so book well ahead. From your tent you may well see elephants digging in the riverbed for water just beyond the barely visible electrified fence. Each of the walk-in, permanent tents has its own deck overlooking the river, but when you book, ask for one in the deep shade of large riverine trees—worth it in the midsummer heat. All kitchen, washing, and toilet facilities are in two shared central blocks. Just bring your own food and cooking and eating utensils. Luxury tents have a shower, refrigerator, cooking, and *braai* facilities. **Pros:** lovely location on banks of tree-lined riverbed; tents provide that real "in the bush" feel. **Cons:** food, drink, and cooking supplies not included; always fully occupied; shared bathrooms. ➪ *30 safari tents, 10 luxury tents.*

¢   **Tsendze Rustic Camp Site.** As its name suggests, this new camp is very rustic with no electricity (personal generators are not allowed) and solar-heated warm, not hot, water. It's 7 km (4 mi) south of Mopani Rest Camp. Although the camp itself has some lovely ancient trees, basically it's in the middle of a swath of mopane woodland that doesn't offer much in the way of a variety of game, and what game there is, is difficult to see. However, you should see elephants (often on the tarred road between Tsendze and Mopani) and large herds of buffalo. The area is reputed to be the home turf for some of Kruger's big tuskers. If you're an ardent camper you'll enjoy the intimate bush experience, and if you're a birder you'll be in seventh heaven because what the area lacks in game it makes up for in birds—look out for the endangered ground hornbill. **Pros:** small and intimate; exclusive to campers and caravans; lovely ancient trees; good birding. **Cons:** situated in middle of unproductive mopane woodland so not much game other than elephants and buffalo; noisy when camp is full; no electricity; warm (not hot) water. ➪ *30 campsites.*

BUSHVELD CAMPS

Smaller, more intimate, more luxurious, and consequently more expensive than regular rest camps, Kruger's bushveld camps are in remote wilderness areas of the park that are often off-limits to regular visitors. Access is limited to guests only. As a result you get far more bush and fewer fellow travelers. Night drives and day excursions are available in most of the camps. There are no restaurants, gas pumps, or grocery stores, so bring your provisions with you (though you can buy wood for your barbecue). All accommodations have fully equipped kitchens, bathrooms, ceiling fans, and large verandas, but only Bateleur has air-conditioning and TV, the latter installed especially for a visit by South Africa's president. Cottages have tile floors, cheerful furnishings, and cane patio furniture and are sited in stands of trees or clumps of indigenous bush for maximum privacy. Many face directly onto a river or water hole. There is only a handful of one-bedroom cottages (at Biyamiti, Shimuwini, Sirheni, and Talamati), but it's worth booking a four-bed cottage and paying the extra, even for only two people. The average cottage price for a couple is R900 with extra people (up to five or six) paying R200 each. If you have a large group or are planning a special celebration, you might consider reserving one of the two bush lodges, which must be booked as a whole: **Roodewal Bush Lodge** sleeps 16, and **Boulders Bush Lodge** sleeps 12. Reservations should be made with South African National Parks (➪ *See Essentials, above, for contact info*).

CLOSE UP

South Africa's Tribes

ZULU

The Zulu are the largest tribe in South Africa. They are a patriarchal society, and in a traditional Zulu village there are several households, each with its own cattle herds under the authority of a senior male. The men often have more than one wife, and the "great wife" is usually the mother of his male children. An estimated 10 million Zulu live in the KwaZulu-Natal province, where they migrated more than a thousand years ago. Because of the clashes with the British forces, including the bloody battles of the Anglo-Zulu War (1878), which resulted in the demise of the Zulu Kingdom, Zulus are often stereotyped as being a war-mongering people, but this is far from the case. While the Zulu have historically proven to be highly adept in battle, it's not because of some biological ferocity, but rather an ability to plan and strategize. Today, it's their musical prowess that has had a major impact on popular culture. Kwaito, for example, is a style of music blending dance, hip-hop, and rap music; it's dominated by Zulu musicians. More traditional Zulu music has been incorporated into the music of western musicians, including Paul Simon and the soundtrack for the Broadway musical *The Lion King*. One of the more famous Zulu singing groups today is Ladysmith Black Mambazo, which has toured the world with its popular collection of traditional Zulu anthems.

XHOSA

The Xhosa people have lived in the Eastern Cape Province since the 15th century, when they migrated here from east and central Africa. They are the second most populous tribe in South Africa (about 8 million people), next to the Zulu. A typical Xhosa village is made up of several kraals, or cattle enclosures, surrounded by family huts. In the 18th century, the Xhosa clashed with the Boers over land; both groups were farmers and eventually war broke out over who had dominion over what. Eventually, the Boers and British colonizers united in a policy of white rule, subjugating black Africans through the passage of the Native Land Act of 1913, which confined black Africans to only 13% of the land in South Africa. This laid the foundation for apartheid, which similarly restricted blacks to areas called Homelands. The Homelands were difficult to farm, overcrowded, and disease-ridden, and remain to this day a shameful part of South Africa's apartheid past. It was not until Xhosa tribesman Nelson Mandela was elected president of South Africa in 1994 that the Homelands were abolished.

5

Singita Lebombo Lodge, Kruger National Park

Sweni Lodge, Krugerr National Park

Protea Hotel Kruger Gate, Kruger National Park

Rhino Post Plains Camp, Kruger National Park

¢ ⊞ **Bateleur.** Hidden in the northern reaches of the park, this tiny camp, the oldest of the bushveld camps, is one of Kruger's most remote destinations. Shaded by tall trees, it overlooks the dry watercourse of the Mashokwe Spruit. A raised platform provides an excellent game-viewing vantage point (don't forget to apply mosquito repellent if you sit here at dawn or dusk), and it's only a short drive to two nearby dams, which draw a huge variety of animals, from lions and elephants to zebras and hippos. The main bedroom in each fully equipped cottage has air-conditioning; elsewhere in each cottage there are ceiling fans, a microwave, and a TV. **Pros:** private and intimate; guests see a lot at the camp's hide; no traffic jams. **Cons:** long distance to travel; there's a TV, which can be a pro or a con depending on your point of view. ⟿ 7 *cottages* ⬩ *In-room: no phone, a/c, kitchen, no TV.*

¢ ⊞ **Biyamiti.** Close to the park gate at Crocodile Bridge, this larger-than-average, beautiful, sought-after bush camp overlooks the normally dry sands of the Biyamiti River. It's very popular because it's close to the southern gates, and the game is usually prolific. A private sand road over a dry riverbed takes you to the well-sited camp, where big shade trees attract a myriad of birds and make you feel almost completely cocooned in the wilderness. The vegetation is mixed combretum woodland, which attracts healthy populations of kudu, impalas, elephants, lions, and black and white rhinos. After the stars come out you're likely to hear lions roar, nightjars call, and jackals yipping outside the fence. **Pros:** easily accessible; lots of game; variety of drives in area. **Cons:** difficult to book because of its popularity; may be a bit too close to civilization for some—you can see adjacent sugarcane fields and farms. ⟿ 15 *cottages* ⬩ *In-room: no phone, no a/c, kitchen, no TV.*

¢ ⊞ **Shimuwini.** Birders descend in droves on this isolated, peaceful camp set on a lovely dam on the Letaba River. Towering jackalberry and sycamore fig trees provide welcome shade, as well as refuge to a host of resident and migratory birds. Away from the river, the riverine forest quickly gives way to mopane woodland; although this is not a particularly good landscape for game, the outstandingly beautiful roan antelope and handsome, rare black-and-white sable antelope move through the area. Resident leopards patrol the territory, and elephants frequently browse in the mopane. Be sure to visit the huge, ancient baobab tree on the nearest loop road to the camp—*shimuwini* is the Shangaan word for "place of the baobab," and there are lots of these striking, unusual trees in the surrounding area. Cottages have one, two, or three bedrooms. One disadvantage is that the camp is accessed by a single road, which gets a bit tedious when you have to drive it every time you leave or return to the camp. **Pros:** lovely situation on banks of permanent lake; isolated and tranquil; good chance to spot sable and roan. **Cons:** only one access road so coming and going gets monotonous; game can be sparse. ⟿ 15 *cottages* ⬩ *In-room: no phone, no a/c, kitchen, no TV.*

¢ ⊞ **Sirheni.** The most remote of all the bushveld camps and one of the loveliest, Sirheni is a major bird-watching camp that sits on the edge of the Sirheni Dam in an isolated wilderness area in the far north of the park. It's a long drive to get here but well worth the effort. Because there is permanent water, game—including lions and white rhinos—can often be seen at the dam, particularly in the dry winter months. Keep your eyes open for the resident leopard, which often drinks at the dam in the evening. A rewarding drive for birders and game spotters alike runs along the Mphongolo River. You can watch the sun set over the magnificent bush from one of two secluded viewing platforms at either end of the camp, but be sure to smother yourself with mosquito repellent. **Pros:** permanent water hole attracts lots of animals, especially in winter; really remote. **Cons:** high malaria area; difficult to access; no electrical plug points in accommodation; no cell-phone reception, which can be a pro or con. ⇘ *15 cottages* ⚒ *In-room: no phone, no a/c, kitchen, no TV.*

¢ 🏠 **Talamati.** On the banks of the normally dry N'waswitsontso River in Kruger's central section, this peaceful camp in the middle of a wide, open valley has excellent game-viewing. Grassy plains and mixed woodlands provide an ideal habitat for herds of impalas, zebras, and wildebeests, as well as lions, cheetahs, and elephants. You can take a break from your vehicle and watch birds and game from a couple of raised viewing platforms inside the perimeter fence. The accommodations are well equipped and comfortable, with cane furniture and airy verandas. **Pros:** peaceful; good plains game; couple of good picnic spots in vicinity; bigger camps near enough to stock up on supplies. **Cons:** a bit bland. ⇘ *15 cottages* ⚒ *In-room: no phone, no a/c, kitchen, no TV.*

BUDGET LODGING

¢ 🏠 **Protea Hotel Kruger Gate.** Set in its own small reserve 110 yards from ⟳ the Paul Kruger Gate, this comfortable hotel gives you a luxury alternative to the sometimes bare-bones accommodations of Kruger's rest camps. The hotel has two major advantages: fast access to the south-central portion of the park, where game-viewing is best, plus the impression that you are in the wilds of Africa. Dinner, heralded by beating drums, is served in a *boma*, a traditional open-air reed enclosure around a blazing campfire. Rangers lead guided walks through the surrounding bush, and you can even sleep overnight in a tree house, or you can book a guided game drive (note that all these activities cost extra). Rooms, connected by a raised wooden walkway that passes through thick indigenous forest, have Spanish-tile floors and standard hotel furniture. Self-catering chalets sleep six. Relax on the pool deck overlooking the Sabie River, have a cocktail in the cool bar, or puff on a cheroot in the sophisticated cigar bar while the kids take part in a fun-filled Prokidz program (during school vacations only). **Pros:** good for families; lots of activities from bush walks to game drives (although these cost extra); easily accessible; tree-house sleep-outs. **Cons:** you can't get away from the fact that this is a hotel with a hotel atmosphere. ☎ *013/735–5671* ⊕ *www. proteahotels.co.za* ⇘ *103 rooms, 7 chalets* ⚒ *In-room: no phone, no a/c, no TV, safe, kitchen (some), refrigerator. In-hotel: 2 restaurants, bar, tennis courts, pool, Internet terminal* ☱ *AE, DC, MC, V* ⦿ *MAP.*

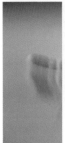

SABI SANDS GAME RESERVE

This is the most famous and exclusive of South Africa's private reserves. Collectively owned and managed, the 153,000-acre reserve near Kruger is home to dozens of private lodges, including the world-famous MalaMala and Londolozi. The Sabi Sands fully deserves its exalted reputation, boasting perhaps the highest game density of any private reserve in Southern Africa.

Game
★★★★★

Park Accessibility
★★★★★

Getting Around
★★★★★

Accommodations
★★★★★

Scenic Beauty
☆☆★★★

Although not all lodges own vast tracts of land, the majority have traversing rights over most of the reserve. With an average of 20 vehicles (from different camps) watching for game and communicating by radio, you're bound to see an enormous amount of game and almost certainly the Big Five, and since only three vehicles are allowed at a sighting at a time, you can be assured of a grandstand seat. The Sabi Sands is the best area for leopard sightings. It's a memorable experience to see this beautiful, powerful, and often elusive cat—the most successful of all feline predators—padding purposefully through the bush at night, illuminated in your ranger's spotlight. There are many lion prides, and occasionally the increasingly rare wild dogs will migrate from Kruger to den in the Sabi Sands. You'll also see white rhinos, zebras, giraffes, wildebeests, most of the antelope species, plus birds galore.

If you can afford it, a splurge on a Kruger SKI ("spend the kids' inheritance") vacation could be the experience of a lifetime. Staying for two or three nights (try for three) at a private game lodge combines superb accommodations, service, and food with equally excellent game-viewing. Exclusivity on game drives (most lodges put only six people in a vehicle, along with a dedicated ranger and tracker) almost guarantees sightings of the Big Five. Words like "elegance," "luxury," and "privacy" are overused when describing the accommodations, but each lodge is unique. One place might have chalets done in modern chic; another, lodges with a colonial feel; and a third, open-air safari tents whose proximity to the bush makes up for what they lack in plushness. At all of them you'll be treated like royalty, with whom you may well rub shoulders.

Many accommodations have air-conditioning, minibars, room safes, ceiling fans, and luxurious en-suite bathrooms. If mainline phone reception is available, there are room telephones. Cell-phone reception is patchy (depending on the area), but never take your cell phone on a game drive (or at least keep it turned off) to avoid disturbing the animals and annoying fellow passengers. All camps have radio telephones in case you need to make contact with the outside world. Chartered flights to and from the camps on shared private airstrips are available, or lodges will collect you from Hoedspruit airport or KMIA.

The daily program at each lodge rarely deviates from a pattern, starting with tea, coffee, and muffins or rusks (Boer biscuits) before an early-morning game drive (usually starting at dawn, later in winter). You return to the lodge around 10 AM, at which point you dine on a full English breakfast or brunch. You can then choose to go on a bush walk with an armed ranger, where you learn about some of the minutiae of the bush (including the Little Five), although you could also happen on giraffes, antelopes, or any one of the Big Five. But don't worry—you'll be well briefed in advance on what you should do if you come face-to-face with, say, a lion. The rest of the day, until the late-afternoon game drive, is spent at leisure—reading up on the bush in the camp library, snoozing, or swimming. A sumptuous afternoon tea is served at 3:30 or 4 before you head back into the bush for your night drive. During the drive, your ranger will find a peaceful spot for sundowners (cocktails), and you can sip the drink of your choice and nibble snacks as you watch one of Africa's spectacular sunsets. As darkness falls, your ranger will switch on the spotlight so you can spy nocturnal animals: lions, leopards, jackals, porcupines, servals (wildcats), civets, and the enchanting little bush babies. You'll return to the lodge around 7:30, in time to freshen up before a three- or five-course dinner in an open-air boma around a blazing fire. Often the camp staff entertains after dinner with local songs and dances—an unforgettable experience. Children under 12 are not allowed at some of the camps; others have great kids' programs (though children under 5 or 6 are not allowed to take part in any activities involving wild animals).

GETTING HERE AND AROUND

Kruger Mpumalanga International Airport (KMIA), at Nelspruit, and Hoedspruit airport, close to Kruger's Orpen Gate, serve Sabi Sands Reserve. You can also drive yourself to the reserve and park at your lodge.

Airport Information Hoedspruit (*HDS ⊕ hoedspruit-hds-airport.webport.com*). **Kruger Mpumalanga International Airport (KMIA)** (*MQP ☎ 27/13–753–7500 ⊕ www.kmiairport.co.za*).

Visitor Info Sabi Sands Reserve (*☎ 012/343–1991 ⊕ www.sabisand.co.za*).

Sabi Sands Game Reserve

KEY
△ Camps
🏠 Lodges

- † Hoedspruit Airstrip
- Djuma Galago △
- Djuma Vuyatela △
- Djuma Bush Lodge 🏠
- Sand River
- Singita Ebony Lodge 🏠
- Lodolozi Private Reserve & Lodges 🏠
- Singita Boulders Lodge 🏠
- Leopard Hills Lodge 🏠
- Mala Mala Main Camp △
- Sable Camp △
- Kruger National Park
- Sabi Sands Game Reserve
- Rattray's on Mala Mala △
- Sand River
- Newington
- 0 — 5 mi
- 0 — 5 km
- Sabi Sabi Selati 🏠
- Sabi Sabi Bush Lodge 🏠
- Kirkman's Camp ◆
- Kruger Mpumalanga Airport †
- Sabi Sabi Earth Lodge 🏠
- Lion Sands Reserve Ivory & River Lodges 🏠 †
- H1-2
- Sabi River
- Entrance
- Paul Kruger Gate ◆
- Skukuza

WHERE TO STAY

LUXURY LODGES

DJUMA PRIVATE GAME RESERVE

Djuma Private Game Reserve. Shangaan for "roar of the lion," Djuma is in the northeast corner of the Sabi Sands Game Reserve. Your hosts are husband-and-wife team Jurie and Pippa Moolman, who are passionate about their work (Jurie has a bachelor's degree in ecology). Although there's a good chance of seeing the Big Five during the bush walk after breakfast and the twice-daily game drives, Djuma also caters to those with special bushveld interests, such as bird-watching or tree identification. Djuma's rangers and trackers are also adept at finding seldom-seen animals such as wild dogs, spotted hyenas, and genets. You'll find none of the formality that sometimes prevails at the larger lodges. For example, members of the staff eat all meals with you and join you around the nighttime fire. In fact, Djuma prides itself on its personal service and sense of intimacy. Your dinner menu is chalked up on a blackboard (try ostrich pâté with cranberry sauce for a starter), as is the evening cocktail menu (how about a Screaming Hyena or African Sunrise?). ☎ 021/424–1037 ⊕ www.djuma.com ⊟ AE, DC, MC, V ⫶❍⫶ FAP.

$ **Bush Lodge.** Sitting in a lush grove of tamboti trees and overlooking a water hole, this homey safari camp contains thatch chalets with rugged wooden furniture and faux-animal-skin fabrics. Don't miss out on a trip to the local villages (the real thing—not tourist traps) of Dixie and Utah, where you'll be introduced to the families of the people looking after you at camp. **Pros:** family-owned and -run for years so boasts a genuine personal feel; floor-to-ceiling windows with great bushveld views; children always welcome; trips to local villages can be arranged. **Cons:** smallish bathrooms; no outdoor showers. ⇨ *8 chalets ⚬ In-room: no phone, a/c, no TV. In-hotel: bar, pool, Internet terminal.*

¢ **Galago.** A delightful and affordable alternative to the upscale lodges, Galago, which means "lesser bush baby" in Shangaan, is a converted U-shaped farmhouse whose five rooms form an arc around a central fireplace. There's a big, shady veranda where you can sit and gaze out over the open plain before cooling off in the plunge pool. You can bring your own food and do your own cooking for less than half the all-inclusive price, or you can bring your own supplies and hire the camp's chef to cook it for you. Game drives and walks are led by your own ranger. This is a perfect camp for a family safari or friends' reunion. **Pros:** real value for money; perfect for family or friends; do-it-yourself in style. **Cons:** hire a cook or you'll spend your time cooking and entertaining. ⇨ *5 rooms ⚬ In-room: no phone, a/c, no TV. In-hotel: pool.*

$ **Vuyatela.** Djuma's vibey, most upscale camp mixes contemporary African township culture with modern Shangaan culture, making it very different from most of the other private camps. Bright colors, trendy designs, hand-painted napkins, and candy-wrapper place mats combine with traditional leather chairs, thatch, and hand-painted mud walls. Look out for some great contemporary African township art, both classic and "naïf" artifacts, and especially for the chandelier made with old Coca-Cola bottles above the dining table. The camp is unfenced, and it's quite usual to see kudu nibbling the lawns or giraffes towering above the rooftops. Accommodations are in beautifully decorated chalets with private plunge pools. For something different in between drives, why not have your hair braided in funky African style at the Comfort Zone, the in-camp spa? **Pros:** amazing African art; the only genuinely innovative and funky lodge in Sabi Sands; legendary hosts; trips to authentic villages. **Cons:** corrugated iron, recycled metals, and in-your-face glitzy township feel not everyone's taste. ⇨ *8 suites ⚬ In-room: no phone, a/c, refridgerator, no TV. In-hotel: bar, gym, spa, Internet terminal.*

LEOPARD HILLS PRIVATE GAME RESERVE

Leopard Hills Private Game Reserve. Owned by the Kruger family, whose distant family member Paul Kruger, president of the former Transvaal Republic, founded Kruger National Park in 1898, this hilltop lodge was built 100 years after the park's founding. Managed and run by the ultra-experienced Duncan and Louise Rodgers, the lodge has grown from its original five suites to the current complex of eight suites, private heated plunge pools, gym and *sala* (outdoor covered deck), library, and traditional Shangaan boma. As with many lodges in the area, Leopard Hills gives back to the community, and its on-site junior school provides an excellent education for the children of lodge staff throughout the

Sabi Sands area. Expect to see the Big Five, take a guided bush walk, fly over the awesome Blyde River canyon in a helicopter, or visit the local village to meet the people and see how they live. ☎ *013/737–6626 or 013/737–6627* ⊕ *www.leopardhills.com* ▭ *AE, DC, MC, V* ❍❘ *FAP.*

$$ 🏠 **Leopard Hills Lodge.** Renowned for its relaxed and informal atmosphere, Leopard Hills is one of the premier game lodges in the Sabi Sands area. Set on a rocky outcrop with panoramic views of the surrounding bushveld, this small lodge offers privacy and luxury. Its main draw is its spectacular game-viewing; during a two-night stay you're almost guaranteed to see the Big Five at close quarters. Rangers are eager to share their knowledge and quick to rush guests off to see big game. The decor has an authentic bush theme, which gels well with the surroundings. Each double room has its own private heated pool (in addition to the main pool) and deck overlooking the bushveld. Bathrooms have his-and-her showers both indoors and out. Attention to detail is apparent in the leopard tracks and similar African motifs that appear in walkways, bedrooms, and bathrooms; check out the ceramic chameleon around the dressing table. **Pros:** very experienced and knowledgeable owners/managers; many rangers are expert photographers and offer great shooting tips; spacious suites. **Cons:** bit of a steep climb to the top of the hill and the main areas. ⬦ *8 suites* ⬧ *In-room: no phone, a/c, safe, refrigerator, no TV. In-hotel: bar, pool, gym, spa, Internet terminal, Wi-Fi hotspot, no kids under 10.*

LION SANDS PRIVATE GAME RESERVE

Lion Sands Private Game Reserve. Separated from Kruger National Park by the Sabie River, the reserve has been owned and operated by the More family for four generations. The reserve was purchased in 1933 as a family retreat and opened to the public in 1978 with two lodges and 10,000 acres of undisturbed wildlife that's available only to its guests. Today, under the watchful eyes of current owners and brothers, Nick and Rob More, the reserve offers guests four different lodging options: the ultraluxe Ivory Lodge, the more economical River Lodge, the once-in-a-lifetime Chalkley Treehouse (yes, it really is a bed on a platform in a tree, but nothing like the tree house in your backyard), and for larger groups the More family vacation home, the 1933 Lodge, complete with personal chef, guide, pool, gym, and wine cellar. The brothers are so committed to keeping the reserve as close to its original state that they employ a full-time ecologist, the only reserve in the Sabi Sands group to do so. Guests of the Lion Sands Private Game Reserve can take direct scheduled flights to the MalaMala Airfield through SA Airlink. ☎ *013/735–5330* ⊕ *www.lionsands.com* ▭ *AE, DC, MC, V* ❍❘ *FAP.*

$$$ 🏠 **Ivory Lodge.** If you seek the ultimate in luxury, privacy, and relaxation, look no further than this gorgeous, exclusive lodge. Suites are really more like villas as each has its own private entrance and a separate sitting room and bedroom that are joined by a breezeway. Superb views overlooking the Sabi River and Kruger beyond are had from every point, especially on the decks, which come equipped with telescopes—you actually never have to leave your suite to catch views of incredible wildlife. The simple, uncluttered, elegant suites are decorated in contemporary African-European style with wood-burning fireplaces,

Fodor's Choice ★

a butler's passage-way where your morning tea is delivered, an indoor and outdoor shower, as well as a freestanding tub to relax in at the end of the day. You'll also have a personal butler and a plunge pool. Relax with intimate dinners and on-the-spot spa treatments, sample some of South Africa's finest wines in the on-site cellar, or head out on a game drive in a private vehicle with your own personal ranger. You won't even know if Brangelina or Ewan is in the next villa. ■ TIP➜ If you're looking for something even more special and over the top, inquire about spending the night at the Chalkley Treehouse. **Pros:** exclusivity; great views from everywhere; attentive staff. **Cons:** suites are so comfortable you might not want to leave them; frequency of meals and abundance of good food may have you crying uncle. ↩ *6 suites ⌂ In-room: a/c, safe, refrigerator, no TV. In-hotel: room service, bar, pool, spa, laundry service, Internet terminal, gym, no kids under 12.*

$$ **River Lodge.** This friendly lodge is set on one of the longest and best stretches of river frontage in Sabi Sands. You can watch the passing animal and bird show from your deck or from the huge, tree-shaded, wooden viewing area that juts out over the riverbank facing Kruger National Park. The guest rooms are comfortable and attractively Africa themed, with honey-color stone floors with pebble inlays, cream wooden furniture, embroidered white bed linens, and lamps and tables of dark indigenous wood. The food is imaginative and tasty (try kudu stuffed with peanut butter with a mushroom-and-Amarula sauce), the young staff cheerful and enthusiastic, and the rangers highly qualified. After an exhilarating game drive, take a leisurely bush walk, go fishing, sleep out under the stars, or relax with a beauty treatment at Lalamuka Spa (*lalamuka* means "unwind" in Shangaan). Public spaces are large and comfortable and lack the African designer clutter that mars some other lodges. There's a resident senior ecologist, plus a classy and interesting curio shop. **Pros:** fabulous river frontage; very friendly atmosphere. **Cons:** chalets built quite close together so not much privacy. ↩ *18 rooms ⌂ In-room: a/c, safe, refrigerator. In-hotel: bar, pool, gym, spa, laundry service, Internet terminal, no kids under 10.*

LONDOLOZI

Londolozi. Formerly a family farm and retreat since 1926, Londolozi today is synonymous with South Africa's finest game lodges and game experiences. (*Londolozi* is the Zulu word for "protector of all living things.") Dave and John Varty, the charismatic and media-friendly grandsons of the original owner, Charles Varty, put the lodge on the map with glamorous marketing, superb wildlife videos, pet leopards and lions, visiting celebrities, and a vision of style and comfort that grandfather Charles could never have imagined. Now the younger generation, brother-and-sister team Bronwyn and Boyd Varty, are bringing their own creative stamp to the magic of Londolozi with a mission to reconnect the human spirit with the wilderness and to carry on their family's quest to honor the animal kingdom. Game abounds; the Big Five are all here, and the leopards of Londolozi are world famous. (You are guaranteed to see at least one.) There are five camps, each representing a different element in nature: Pioneer Camp (water), Tree Camp (wood), Granite Suites (rock), Varty Camp (fire), and Founders

Camp (earth). Each is totally private, hidden in dense riverine forest on the banks of the Sand River. The Varty family lives on the property, and their friendliness and personal attention, along with the many staff who have been here for decades, will make you feel part of the family immediately. The central reception and curio shop are at Varty camp. ☎ 011/280–6655 ⊕ www.londolozi.com ▤ AE, DC, MC, V ⍾ FAP.

$$
☾ **Founders Camp.** This camp takes you back to the early days of Londolozi before ecotourism was invented—when it was more important to shoot a lion than to take the perfect shot of it. The stone-and-thatch chalets sit amid thick riverine bush and are linked to the other chalets by meandering pathways. Each has its own wooden viewing deck and is decorated in classic black-and-cream ticking fabric, with compass safari lamps, military chests, and faded family documents. Relax on the thatch split-level dining and viewing decks that jut out over a quiet backwater of the Sand River, and watch the mammals and birds go by. After your game drive or walk, cool off in the tree-shaded swimming pool, which also overlooks the river. **Pros:** has the first zero-emissions safari vehicles; children welcome. **Cons:** all the lodges are in very close proximity to one another, so it can be noisy. ⇨ 7 chalets ⅗ In-room: a/c, safe, refrigerator, Internet. In-hotel: bar, pool.

$$$ **Granite Suites.** Book all three private suites or just hide yourself away from the rest of the world like the celebrities and royals who favor this gorgeous getaway. Here, it's all about location, location, location. Huge, flat granite rocks in the riverbed, where elephants chill out and bathe, stretch almost to the horizon in front of your floor-to-ceiling picture windows, and the elephant prints and furnishings done in velvets and silvers, grays, and browns echo the shifting colors and textures of the mighty pachyderms. Bathe in your own rock pool. At night, when your suite is lit by scores of flickering candles, you may truly feel that you're in wonderland. **Pros:** among the best-situated accommodation in Sabi Sands with truly stunning views; the candlelit dinners. **Cons:** pricey. ⇨ 3 suites ⅗ In-room: a/c, safe, refrigerator, Internet. In-hotel: bar, pool, no kids under 16.

$$$ **Pioneer Camp.** This is the most secluded of all Londolozi's camps. Three private suites overlook the river and are perfect for getting away from others. If you like, the camp can be adapted into a temporary private bush home for a family group (8 adults, 6 children). Large entrance halls have a modern Ralph Lauren feel, and your floor-to-window glass sliding panels offer great wilderness views. Many of the touches, such as the classic Victorian bathroom are a loving tribute to the early days and legendary characters of Sparta, the original name of the Londolozi property. Channel into a past world through faded sepia photographs, old hunting prints, horse-drawn carts, gleaming silverware, and scuffed safari treasures, taking you back to a time when it took five days by ox wagon to get to Londolozi. In winter, sink deeply into your comfortable armchair in front of your own blazing fireplace; in summer sit outside in your outdoor dining room and listen to Africa's night noises. Keep your ears and eyes open for the resident female leopard as she hunts at night. There are a small, intimate boma, inside and outside dining areas, viewing decks, and a gorgeous S-shaped pool nestling in

the surrounding bush, where after your dip you can laze on padded lie-out chairs and be lulled to sleep by the birdsong. **Pros:** genuine and uncontrived romantic-safari atmosphere; only three suites; intimate. **Cons:** with only three suites it can be hard to book; Ralph Lauren feel not for everyone. *3 suites ☐ In-room: a/c, safe, refrigerator. In-hotel: bar, pool, Internet terminal, no kids under 12.*

$$$ **Tree Camp.** The first Relais & Chateaux game lodge in the world, Fodor's Choice ★ this gorgeous camp, now completely rebuilt and redesigned (think leopards, lanterns, leadwoods, and leopard orchids), is shaded by thick riverine bush and tucked into the riverbank overlooking indigenous forest. Dave Varty has built more than 20 lodges around Africa, and he feels that this is his triumph. The lodge is themed in chocolate and white, with exquisite leopard photos on the walls, airy and stylish interiors, and elegant yet simple furnishings. Huge bedrooms, en-suite bathrooms, and plunge pools continue the elegance, simplicity, and sophistication. From your spacious deck you look out onto a world of cool-green forest dominated by ancient African ebony and marula trees. Treat yourself to a bottle of bubbly from the Champagne Library and then dine with others while swapping bush stories or alone in your private sala. **Pros:** the viewing deck; the ancient forest; state-of-the-art designer interiors. **Cons:** stylishness nudges out coziness. *6 suites ☐ In-room: a/c, safe, refrigerator, Internet. In-hotel: bar, pool, no kids under 16.*

$$ **Varty Camp.** This camp's fire has been burning for more than 80 years, making this location the very soul and center of Londolozi. It's also the largest of Londolozi's camps, centered on a thatch A-frame lodge that houses a dining room, sitting areas, and lounge. Meals are served on a broad wooden deck that juts over the riverbed and under an ancient jackalberry tree. The thatch rondavels, which were the Varty family's original hunting camp, now do duty as a library, a wine cellar, and an interpretive center, where you can listen to history and ecotourism talks—don't miss the Londolozi Leopard presentation. If you're looking for romance, have a private dinner on your veranda and go for a moonlight dip in your own plunge pool. In suites, the pool leads right to the riverbed. All rooms are decorated in African ethnic chic—in creams and browns and with the ubiquitous historic family photographs and documents—and have great bushveld views. Families are welcome, and the fascinating kids' programs should turn any couch potato into an instant wannabe ranger. **Pros:** superb children's programs; meals taken on lovely viewing deck. **Cons:** lots of kids might not be for you; lacks the intimacy of the smaller Londolozi lodges. *2 suites, 8 chalets ☐ In-room: a/c, safe, refrigerator, Internet. In-hotel: bar, pool.*

5

MALAMALA GAME RESERVE

Fodor's Choice
★
MalaMala Game Reserve. This legendary game reserve (designated as such in 1929), which along with Londolozi put South African safaris on the international map, is tops in its field. It delights visitors with incomparable personal service, superb food, and discreetly elegant, comfortable accommodations where you'll rub shoulders with aristocrats, celebrities, and returning visitors alike. Mike Rattray, a legend in his own time in South Africa's game-lodge industry, describes MalaMala as "a camp in the bush," but it's certainly more than that, although it still retains that genuine bushveld feel of bygone days. Both the outstanding hospitality and the game-viewing experience keep guests coming back. MalaMala constitutes the largest privately owned Big Five game area in South Africa and includes an unfenced 30-km (19-mi) boundary with Kruger National Park, across which game crosses continuously. The variety of habitats ranges from riverine bush, favorite hiding place of the leopard, to open grasslands, where cheetahs hunt. MalaMala's animal-viewing statistics are probably unbeatable: the Big Five are spotted almost every day. At one moment your well-educated, friendly, articulate ranger might fascinate you by describing the sex life of a dung beetle, as you watch the sturdy male battling his way along the road, pushing his perfectly round ball of dung with wife-to-be perched perilously on top; at another, your adrenaline will flow as you follow a leopard stalking impala in the gathering gloom. Along with the local Shangaan trackers, whose eyesight rivals that of the animals they are tracking, the top-class rangers ensure that your game experience is unforgettable. ☎ 011/442–2267 ⊕ *www.malamala.com* ▭ *AE, DC, MC, V* ⦿*FAP.*

$
☺
Fodor's Choice
★
🔲 **Main Camp.** Ginger-brown stone and thatch air-conditioned rondavels with separate his-and-her bathrooms are decorated in creams and browns and furnished with cane armchairs, colorful handwoven tapestries and rugs, terra-cotta floors, and original artwork. Public areas have a genuine safari feel, with plush couches, animal skins, and African artifacts. Shaded by ancient jackalberry trees, a huge deck overlooks the Sand River and its passing show of animals. Browse in the air-conditioned Monkey Room for books and wildlife videos, sample the magnificent wine cellar, sun yourself by the pool, or stay fit in the well-appointed gym. The food—among the best in the bush—is delicious, wholesome, and varied, with a full buffet at both lunch and dinner. Children are welcomed with special programs, activities, and goody-filled backpacks; kids under 12 are not allowed on game drives unless they're with their own family group, and children under 5 are not allowed on game drives at all. One guest room is geared toward travelers with disabilities. **Pros:** you'll feel really in the heart of the bush when you look out over the sweeping wilderness views; not as fancy as some of the other camps but you can't beat the authenticity and history; delicious, hearty, home-style cooking; great kids' program; unparalleled game-viewing. **Cons:** rondavels are a bit old-fashioned, but that goes with the ambience. ⇱ *18 rooms* ⚘ *In-room: a/c, safe, refrigerator. In-hotel: bar, pool, gym, children's programs (ages 5–15), Internet terminal.*

"This was the first rhino that I had seen in person. 'HUGE!' was my first impression." —adkinsek, Fodors.com member

$$ **Rattray's on MalaMala.** The breathtakingly beautiful Rattray's merges
Fodor's Choice original bushveld style with daring ideas that run the risk of seeming
★ out of place but instead work wonderfully well. Eight opulent *khayas*
(think Tuscan villas) with spacious his-and-her bathrooms, dressing
rooms, and private heated plunge pools blend well with the surround-
ing bush. Each villa's entrance hall, with art by distinguished African
wildlife artists such as Keith Joubert, leads to a huge bedroom with a
wooden four-poster bed, and beyond is a lounge liberally scattered with
deep sofas, comfy armchairs, padded ottomans, writing desks (for those
crucial nightly journal entries), antique Persian rugs, and a dining nook.
Bird and botanical prints grace the walls. Floor-to-ceiling windows
with insect-proof sliding doors face the Sand River and lead to massive
wooden decks where you can view the passing wildlife. The main lodge
includes viewing and dining decks, an infinity pool, lounge areas, and
tantalizing views over the river. In the paneled library, with plush sofas,
inviting leather chairs, old prints and photographs, and battered leather
suitcases, the complete works of Kipling, Dickens, and Thackeray rub
leather shoulders with contemporary classics and 100-year-old bound
copies of England's classic humorous magazine *Punch*. After browsing
the cellar's impressive fine wines, have a drink in the bar with its huge
fireplace, antique card table, and polished cherrywood bar. **Pros:** accom-
modation so spacious it could house a herd of almost anything; heated
pool; excellent lighting; fascinating library; unparalleled game-viewing.
Cons: Tuscan villas in the bush may not be your idea of Africa. ⤵ 8
villas ⌂ *In-room: a/c, safe, refrigerator, DVD, Internet, pool. In-hotel:
bar, pool, gym, no kids under 16.*

$$ 🏠 **Sable Camp.** This fully air-conditioned, exclusive camp at the southern
Fodor'sChoice   end of Main Camp overlooks the Sand River and surrounding bushveld.
★   With its own pool, library, and boma, it's smaller and more intimate
than Main Camp, but it shares the same magnificent all-around bush
and hospitality experience. **Pros:** small and intimate; privacy guaran-
teed; unparalleled game-viewing. **Cons:** you might like it so much you
never want to leave. ⇨ *7 suites ⚒ In-room: a/c, safe, refrigerator. In-
hotel: bar, pool, gym, Internet terminal, no kids under 12.*

SABI SABI PRIVATE GAME RESERVE

Sabi Sabi Private Game Reserve. Founded in 1978 at the southern end of
Sabi Sands, Sabi Sabi was one of the first lodges, along with Londolozi,
to offer photo safaris and to link ecotourism, conservation, and com-
munity. Superb accommodations and the sheer density of game sup-
ported by its highly varied habitats draw guests back to Sabi Sabi in
large numbers. There's a strong emphasis on ecology: guests are encour-
aged to look beyond the Big Five and to become aware of the birds and
smaller mammals of the bush. ☎ *011/447–7172* ⊕ *www.sabisabi.com*
🖃 *AE, DC, MC, V* ⫴ *FAP.*

$$ 🏠 **Bush Lodge.** Bush Lodge overlooks a busy water hole (lions are frequent visitors) and the dry course of the Msuthlu River. The thatch,
open-sided dining area, observation deck, and pool all have magnificent views of game at the water hole. Thatch suites are connected by
walkways that weave between manicured lawns and beneath enormous
shade trees where owls and fruit bats call at night. All have a deck
overlooking the dry river course (where you may well see an elephant
padding along) and outdoor and indoor showers. Chalets at this large
lodge are older and smaller—although more intimate in a way—but still
roomy; they are creatively decorated with African designs and have a
personal wooden deck. **Pros:** always prolific game around the lodge;
busy water hole in front of lodge; roomy chalets. **Cons:** big and busy
might not be your idea of relaxing getaway. ⇨ *25 suites ⚒ In-room:
a/c, safe, refrigerator. In-hotel: bar, pool, spa, Internet terminal, Wi-Fi
hotspot.*

$$ 🏠 **Earth Lodge.** This avant-garde, eco-friendly lodge was the first to
break away from the traditional safari style and strive for a contempo-
rary theme. It's a cross between a Hopi cave dwelling and a medieval
keep, but with modern luxury. On arrival, all you'll see is bush and
grass-covered hummocks until you descend a hidden stone pathway that
opens onto a spectacular landscape of boulders and streams. The lodge
has rough-textured, dark-brown walls encrusted with orange seeds and
wisps of indigenous grasses. The mud-domed suites are hidden from
view until you're practically at the front door. Surfaces are sculpted
from ancient fallen trees, whereas chairs and tables are ultramodern or
'50s style. Your suite has huge living spaces with a sitting area, mega
bathroom, private veranda, and plunge pool. A personal butler takes
care of your every need, and there's a meditation garden. Dine in a
subterranean cellar or in the boma, fashioned from roots and branches
and lit at night by dozens of lanterns. **Pros:** out-of-the-ordinary avant-
garde, eco-friendly architecture and interior design; warm earth colors.
Cons: don't let your butler become too intrusive; although practical for

guests who don't want to walk to their suites, golf carts seem alien in the bush. ⇛ *13 suites △ In-room: a/c, safe, refrigerator. In-hotel: bar, pool, spa, Internet terminal.*

$$ **Little Bush Camp.** This delightful family camp combines airiness and ☾ spaciousness with a sense of intimacy. At night glowing oil lanterns lead you along a wooden walkway to your comfortable thatch-roof suite decorated in earthy tones of brown, cream, and white. After your action-packed morning game drive—during which you'll see game galore—and your delicious brunch, relax on the wooden deck overlooking the bush, have a snooze in your air-conditioned bedroom, or laze away the time between activities at the pool area. In the evening you can sip a glass of complimentary sherry as you watch the stars—if you're a city slicker, you may never have seen such bright ones. **Pros:** perfect for families. **Cons:** it's popular with families. ⇛ *6 suites △ Inroom: a/c, safe, refrigerator. In-hotel: bar, pool, spa, Internet terminal.*

$$ **Selati Lodge.** For an out-of-Africa experience, you can't beat Selati, Fodor's Choice an intimate, stylish, colonial-style camp that was formerly the private ★ hunting lodge of a famous South African opera singer. The early-1900s atmosphere is created by the use of genuine train memorabilia—old leather suitcases, antique wooden chairs, nameplates, and signals—that recall the old Selati-branch train line that once crossed the reserve, transporting gold from the interior to the coast of Mozambique in the 1870s. At night the grounds of this small, secluded lodge flicker with the lights of the original shunters' oil lamps. Dinner is held in the boma, whereas brunch is served in the friendly farmhouse kitchen. Members of the glitterati and European royalty have stayed at the spacious Ivory Presidential Suite, with its Persian rugs and antique furniture. **Pros:** unique atmosphere because of its old railroad theme; secluded and intimate; Ivory Presidential Suite is superb value for money. **Cons:** some old-timers preferred the camp when it was just lantern-lit with no electricity. ⇛ *8 chalets, 1 suite △ In-room: a/c, safe, refrigerator. In-hotel: bar, pool, no kids under 10.*

SINGITA SABI SAND

Fodor's Choice **Singita Sabi Sand.** Although Singita (Shangaan for "the miracle") offers ★ much the same bush and game experience as the other lodges, nothing is too much trouble here. Its muted, low-key opulence, comforting organic atmosphere, truly spacious accommodations, superb food and wine, and variety of public spaces—quiet little private dining nooks to a huge viewing deck built round an ancient jackalberry tree, comfortable library with TV and Internet, and attractive poolside bar—really do put this gorgeous lodge head and shoulders above the rest of the herd. Whether you fancy a starlit private supper, a riverside breakfast, or just chilling alone in your megasuite, you've only to ask. Forget the usual lodge curio shop and take a ride to the Trading Post where objets d'art, unique handmade jewelry, classy bush gear, and artifacts from all over Africa are clustered together in a series of adjoining rooms and courtyards that seem more like someone's home than a shop. Pop into the wine cellars and learn about the finest South African wines from the resident sommelier, and then choose some to be shipped directly home. If you're feeling energetic, the bush bike rides are great.

5

☎ *021/683–3424* ⊕ *www.singita.* *co.za* ⊟ *AE, DC, MC, V* ❏❘ *FAP.*

$$$ 🏨 **Boulders Lodge.** As you walk
Fodor'sChoice over the wooden bridge spanning
★ a reed- and papyrus-fringed pond,
you'll find yourself in the midst of
traditional Africa at its most luxu-
rious. The terra-cotta colors of the
polished stone floors blend with the
browns, ochers, creams, and rus-
sets of the cow-skin rugs, the hide-
covered armchairs, the hand-carved
tables, the stone benches, and the
carefully chosen artifacts that grace
the surfaces. Tall pillars of woven
reeds, old tree trunks, and stone
walls reminiscent of Great Zimba-

bwe support the huge thatch roof, and from every side there are stun-
ning bushveld views. You're guaranteed to gasp when you walk into
your sumptuous suite. An entrance hall with a fully stocked bar leads
into your glass-sided lounge dominated by a freestanding fireplace.
Earth-colored fabrics and textures complement leather and wicker
armchairs, a zebra-skin ottoman, and desks and tables fashioned from
organic wood shapes, with writing, reading, and watercolor materials.
A herd of impalas could easily fit into the bathroom, which has dark
stone floors, a claw-foot tub, his-and-her basins, and an indoor and
outdoor shower. Every door leads out onto a big wooden deck with
a bubbling horizon pool, inviting sun loungers, and bushveld views.
■TIP→ Request Room 11 or 12, which overlook a waterhole. **Pros:** spa-
cious accommodation; lovely organic, unpretentious bushveld feel; best
food in Sabi Sands. **Cons:** it's quite a walk from some of the rooms to
the main lodge (although transport is available); refuse the crackling
log fire if you're at all congested. ➾ *12 suites* ⌂ *In-room: a/c, safe,
refrigerator. In-hotel: bar, pool, spa, Internet.*

$$$ 🏨 **Ebony Lodge.** If Ernest Hemingway had built his ideal home in the
African bush, this would be it. From the moment you walk into the
main lounge with its genuine antique furniture, leather chairs gleaming with the polish of years of use, old photographs and paintings,
mounted game trophies, and hand-carved doors and windows, you'll be
transported to a past where trendy urban designers had never heard of
the bush, brimming glasses toasted the day's game activities, and deep
laughter punctuated the fireside tales. This is really Old Africa at its
best. Yellow, red, and orange fabrics bring flashes of bright color to the
old club atmosphere and are carried through to the viewing decks over
the river below and into the comfortable dining room. Your room gives
exactly the same feel—beautiful antiques, a claw-foot bathtub, photographs of royalty and original bush camps, lovely lamps and carvings,
splashes of vivid color, a dressing room big enough to swing a leopard
by the tail, and a carved four-poster bed that looks out over the bush
below. Catch the sun or catch up on your journal at the antique desk

Leopard Hills Lodge, Sabi Sands Game Reserve

Bush Lodge, Sabi Sands Game Reserve

River Lodge, Sabi Sands Game Reserve

or on the big inviting deck with pool and stunning views. **Pros:** this is the mother lodge of all the Singita properties, and it shows: maturity, warmth, hospitality, and furniture and fittings antique dealers would kill for; check out the cozy library with its amazing old books and magazines. **Cons:** the beds are very high off the ground—if you've short legs or creak a bit, ask for a stool; mosquito netting in rooms needs a bit of attention. ⤴ *12 suites* ⚒ *In-room: a/c, safe, refrigerator. In-hotel: bar, pool, spa, Internet.*

EXETER PRIVATE GAME RESERVE

$ 🏠 **Kirkman's Kamp.** You'll feel as if you've stepped back in time at this camp. The rooms are strategically clustered around the original 1920s homestead, which, with its colonial furniture, historic memorabilia, and wrap-around veranda, makes you feel like a family guest the moment you arrive. That intimate feeling continues when you sleep beneath a cluster of old photographs above your bed, slip into a leather armchair in front of a blazing log fire, or soak in your claw-foot bathtub in the nostalgia-laden bathroom. Cocoon yourself in your room with its private veranda looking out onto green sweeping lawns, or mingle with the other guests in the homestead where you'll find it hard to believe that you're in the 21st century. You'll see game galore in Sabi Sands (the size of New Jersey), which has the highest density of leopards in the world. Kirkman's is ideal for families and family reunions. **Pros:** more affordable than many other Sabi Sands lodges; one of Sabi Sands' best-loved camps for its old-time nostalgic atmosphere; superb game-viewing; easy road access from Johannesburg. **Cons:** malaria area; gets tour groups; more of a hotel feel than other lodges. ☎ *011/809–4300* ⊕ *www.andbeyond.com* ⤴ *18 cottages* ⚒ *In-room: no phone, safe. In-hotel: bar, pool, Internet terminal* ▭ *AE, DC, V* ⦿ *FAP.*

$$ 🏠 **River Lodge.** Although this is one of Sabi Sands' oldest lodges, it has
Fodor's Choice somehow managed to keep itself something of a secret. Less glamor-
★ ous than many of its more glitzy neighbors, it scores 10 out of 10 for its quite gorgeous location—one of the best in the whole reserve—with lush green lawns sweeping right down to the Sabi River. The main sitting and dining areas have panoramic river views; if you want a quiet game-watching experience you can sink into one of the big comfy sofas on the deck with your binoculars handy, and animals and birds of one kind or another are sure to happen along. If you go out on a game drive, you'll see great game—almost certainly the Big Five—and the experienced rangers and staff, some of whom have been at the lodge for years, will guide, advise, and look after you in a friendly, unfussy way. Your roomy air-conditioned suite (try to sleep with the windows open so you don't miss that lion roaring or hyena whooping) is decorated in soft earth colors and has its own plunge pool. Guests say that there's something about this lodge that melts effortlessly into its surroundings. It's a genuine African-bush ambience. **Pros:** much more affordable than many of its neighbors; unpretentious feel; amazing river views; easy access by road from Johannesburg. **Cons:** malaria area; no triple rooms for guests with children. ☎ *011/809–4300* ⊕ *www.andbeyond.com* ⤴ *8 suites* ⚒ *In-room: no phone, safe. In-hotel: bar, pool, Internet terminal* ▭ *AE, DC, V* ⦿ *FAP.*

KWAZULU-NATAL PARKS

The province of KwaZulu-Natal is a premier vacation destination for South Africans, with some of the finest game reserves in the country, including the Hluhluwe-Imfolozi Game Reserve. The reserve is small compared to Kruger, but here you'll see the Big Five and plenty of plains game, plus an incredibly biologically diverse mix of plants and trees. The nearby Mkuze and Ithala game reserves are even smaller but are still worth a visit for their numerous bird species and game.

Game
☆★★★★
Park Accessibility
★★★★★
Getting Around
★★★★★
Accommodations
★★★★★
Scenic Beauty
☆★★★★

KwaZulu-Natal's best private lodges, including Phinda and Thanda private reserves, lie in northern Zululand and Maputaland, a remote region close to Mozambique. These lodges are sufficiently close to one another and Hluhluwe-Imfolozi Game Reserve to allow you to put together a bush experience that delivers the Big Five and a great deal more, including superb bird-watching opportunities and an unrivaled beach paradise.

WHEN TO GO

Summers are hot, hot, hot. If you can't take heat and humidity, then autumn, winter, and early summer are probably the best times to visit.

GETTING HERE AND AROUND

The Richards Bay airport is the closest to the Hluhluwe-Imfolozi area—about 100 km (60 mi) south of Hluhluwe-Imfolozi and about 224 km (140 mi) south of Ithala. There are daily flights from Johannesburg to Richards Bay; flight time is about an hour. Private lodges will arrange your transfers for you.

Airport Richards Bay Aiport (☎ 035/789–9630).

Car Rentals Avis (☎ 035/789–6555). **Europcar** (☎ 032/436–9500).

HLUHLUWE-IMFOLOZI GAME RESERVE

Reputedly King Shaka's favorite hunting ground, Zululand's Hluhluwe-Imfolozi (pronounced shloo-*shloo*-ee im-fuh-*low*-zee) incorporates two of Africa's oldest reserves: Hluhluwe and Imfolozi, both founded in 1895. In an area of just 906 square km (350 square mi), Hluhluwe-Imfolozi delivers the Big Five plus all the plains game and species like nyala and red duiker that are rare in other parts of the country. Equally important, it boasts one of the most biologically diverse habitats on the planet, a unique mix of forest, woodland, savanna, and grassland. You'll find about 1,250 species of plants and trees here—more than in some entire countries.

The park is administered by Ezemvelo KZN Wildlife, the province's official conservation organization, which looks after all the large game reserves and parks as well as many nature reserves. Thanks to its conservation efforts and those of its predecessor, the highly regarded Natal Parks Board, the park can take credit for saving the white rhino from extinction. So successful was the park at increasing white rhino numbers that in 1960 it established its now famous Rhino Capture Unit to relocate rhinos to other reserves in Africa. The park is currently trying to do for the black rhino what it did for its white cousins. Poaching in the past nearly decimated Africa's black rhino population, but as a result of the park's remarkable conservation efforts, 20% of Africa's remaining black rhinos now live in this reserve—and you won't get a better chance of seeing them in the wild than here.

Until 1989 the reserve consisted of two separate parks, Hluhluwe in the north and Imfolozi in the south, separated by a fenced corridor. Although a road (R618) still runs through this corridor, the fences have been removed, and the parks now operate as a single entity. Hluhluwe and the corridor are the most scenic areas of the park, notable for their bush-covered hills and knockout views, whereas Imfolozi is better known for its broad plains. ☎ *033/845–1002* ⊕ *www.kznwildlife.com* 🖅 *R110 per per person.*

GETTING HERE AND AROUND

If you're traveling to Hluhluwe-Imfolozi from Durban, drive north on the N2 to Mtubatuba, then cut west on the R618 to Mambeni Gate. Otherwise, continue up the N2 to the Hluhluwe exit and follow the signs to the park and Memorial Gate. The whole trip takes about three hours, but watch out for potholes. ⇨ *See Getting Here and Around under KwaZulu-Natal Parks, above, for flight info.*

TIMING

Compared with Kruger, Hluhluwe-Imfolozi is tiny—less than 6% of Kruger's size—but such comparisons can be misleading. You can spend days driving around this park and still not see everything, or feel like you're going in circles. Probably the biggest advantage Hluhluwe has over Kruger is that game-viewing is good year-round, whereas Kruger has seasonal peaks and valleys. Another bonus is its proximity to Mkuze Game Reserve and the spectacular coastal reserves of iSimangaliso Greater St. Lucia Wetland Park. The park is also close enough to Durban to make it a worthwhile one- or two-day excursion.

BUSH WALKS

Armed rangers lead groups of eight on two- to three-hour bush walks departing from Hilltop or Mpila Camp. You rarely spot much game on these walks, but you do see plenty of birds and you learn a great deal about the area's ecology and tips on how to recognize the signs of the bush, including animal spoor. Walks depart daily at 5:30 AM and 3:30 PM (6 and 3 in winter) and cost R200. Reserve a few days in advance at Hilltop Camp reception.

GAME DRIVES

A great way to see the park is on game drives led by rangers. These drives (R250 per person) hold several advantages over driving through the park yourself: you sit high up in an open-air vehicle with a good view and the wind in your face, a ranger explains the finer points of animal behavior and ecology, and your guide has a good idea where to find animals like leopards, cheetahs, and lions. Game drives leave daily at 5:30 AM in summer, 6:30 AM in winter. The park also offers three-hour night drives, during which you search with powerful spotlights for nocturnal animals. These three-hour drives depart at 7, and you should make advance reservations at Hilltop Camp reception.

WILDERNESS TRAILS

The park's **Wilderness Trails** are every bit as popular as Kruger's, but they tend to be tougher and more rustic. You should be fit enough to walk up to 16 km (10 mi) a day for a period of three days and four nights. An armed ranger leads the hikes, and all equipment, food, and baggage are carried by donkeys. The first and last nights are spent at Mndindini, a permanent tented camp. The other two are spent under canvas in the bush. While in the bush, hikers bathe in the Imfolozi River or have a hot bucket shower; toilet facilities consist of a spade and toilet-paper roll. Trails, open March–December, are limited to eight people and should be reserved a year in advance (R3,952 per person per trail).

Fully catered two- or three-night **Short Trails** involve stays at a satellite camp in the wilderness area. You'll sleep in a dome tent, and although there's hot water from a bucket shower, your toilet is a spade.

If that sounds too easy, you can always opt for one of the four-night **Primitive Trails.** On these treks hikers carry their own packs and sleep out under the stars, although there are lightweight tents for inclement weather. A campfire burns all night to scare off animals, and each participant is expected to sit a 90-minute watch. A ranger acts as guide. The cost is R2,685 per person per trail.

A less rugged wilderness experience can be had on the **Bushveld Trails,** based out of the tented Mndindini camp, where you're guaranteed a bed and some creature comforts. The idea behind these trails is to instill in the participants an appreciation for the beauty of the untamed bush. You can also join the Mpila night drive if you wish. Participation is limited to eight people and costs about R2,390 per person per trail.

WHERE TO STAY

Hluhluwe-Imfolozi offers a range of accommodations in government-run rest camps, with an emphasis on self-catering (only Hilltop has a restaurant). The park also has secluded bush lodges and camps, but

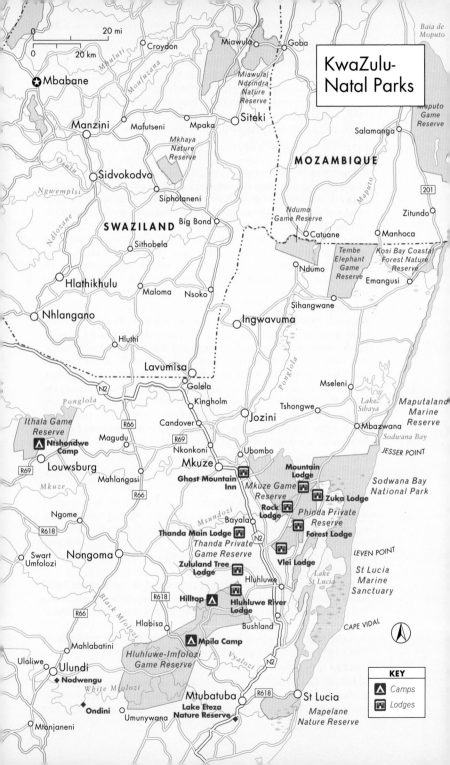

most foreign visitors can't avail themselves of these lodgings, as each must be reserved in a block, and the smallest accommodates at least eight people. Conservation levies are R120 per person.

¢ 📷 **Hilltop Camp.** It may be a government-run camp, but this delightful lodge in the Hluhluwe half of the park matches some of South Africa's best private lodges. Perched on the crest of a hill, it has panoramic views over the park, the Hlaza and Nkwakwa hills, and Zululand. Thatch and ocher-color walls give it an African feel. Scattered across the crown of the hill, self-contained chalets have high thatch ceilings, rattan furniture, and small verandas. If you plan to eat all your meals in the restaurant or sample the evening *braai* (barbecue), forgo the more expensive chalets with fully equipped kitchens. If you're on a tight budget, opt for a basic rondavel with two beds, a basin, and a refrigerator; toilet facilities are communal. An à la carte restaurant, an attractive pub, a convenience store, and a gas station are on-site. Go for a stroll along a forest trail rich with birdsong, or take a bottle of wine to Hlaza Hide and join the animals as they come for their sundowners. **Pros:** floodlit water hole; great views; lovely little forest trail great for a stroll. **Cons:** surly, unhelpful staff; cottage needs a face-lift; cleaning of rooms not up to scratch. ☎ *033/845–1000* ⊕ *www.kznwildlife.com* ⇆ *20 rondavels, 49 chalets* ঙ *In-room: kitchen (some). In-hotel: restaurant, bar, Internet terminal* ▤ *AE, DC, MC, V.*

$ 📷 **Hluhluwe River Lodge.** Overlooking False Bay Lake and the Hluhluwe ⟳ River flood plain, this luxurious, good-value, spacious, family-owned lodge set in indigenous gardens is the ideal base for visiting the game reserves and the iSimangaliso Greater St. Lucia Wetland Park. After a day spent game-viewing, canoeing, bird-watching, boating, fishing, or walking in the pristine sand forest, you can relax in a terra-cotta-color A-frame chalet with cool stone floors, wood and wicker furniture, and cream-and-brown decor and furnishings. Alternatively, sit out on your wooden deck overlooking the bush, the floodplain, and the lake. This lodge is the only one with direct access to the lake, and as you chug along through bird-filled papyrus channels decorated with water lilies en route to the broad expanses of the main body of water, you might easily feel as though you're in Botswana's Okavango Delta. Water activities are dependent on the seasonal rains, so check with the lodge in advance. The food is excellent—wholesome country cooking with lots of fresh vegetables and good roasts. There are two family chalets available and children three and under stay free. **Pros:** only 25 minutes from Hluhluwe-Imfolozi; boat trips (seasonal) reminiscent of Botswana's Okavango Delta; great for families; fun mountain- and quad-bike trails. **Cons:** lots of kids in holiday times; activities cost extra. ☎ *035/562–0246* ⊕ *www.hluhluwe.co.za* ⇆ *12 chalets* ঙ *In-room: a/c. In-hotel: restaurant, bar, pool, Internet terminal* ▤ *AE, DC, MC, V* ⦿ *MAP.*

¢ 📷 **Mpila Camp.** In the central Imfolozi section of the park, Mpila is humbler than the classy Hilltop Camp and more reminiscent of some of Kruger's older camps. Choose among one-room chalets sharing communal facilities, two- and three-bedroom cottages, chalets, an en-suite safari tent, or three secluded lodges. Gas is available, but you can only buy curios and sodas at the camp shop, so stock up with groceries before you arrive. Be sure to book your bush walks and game drives on arrival, as they work on a first-come, first-served basis. **Pros:** game comes right to your door (watch out for hyenas stealing your braai meat); lovely location. **Cons:** churlish staff; poor lighting; no mosquito mesh on windows; no electricity from 10 PM to 8 AM. ☎ *033/845–1000* ⊕ *www.kznwildlife.com* ⤳ *2 cottages, 14 chalets, 14 safari tents, 3 lodges* ⚘ *In-room: kitchen (some)* ⊟ *AE, DC, MC, V.*

¢ ⬚ **Zululand Tree Lodge.** About 16 km (10 mi) from the park, this lodge lies in a forest of fever trees on the 3,700-acre Ubizane Game Reserve, a small park stocked with white rhinos and plains game. It makes a great base from which to explore Hluhluwe, Mkuze, and St. Lucia. Built of thatch and wood, the open-sided lodge sits on stilts overlooking the Mzinene River. Rooms are in separate cottages, also on stilts, along the riverbank. The rooms themselves are small but tastefully decorated with mosquito nets covering old-fashioned iron bedsteads made up with fluffy white duvets, African-print cushions, wicker, and reed matting. If you want the experience of sleeping alfresco, fold back the huge wooden shutters dividing the bedroom from the open deck. A qualified ranger will take you for a bush walk or a game drive (which is included in your stay) through the small reserve or a little farther afield for a game drive in nearby Hluhluwe-Imfolozi. At the nearby Illala Weavers you can buy superb handwoven Zulu baskets. **Pros:** bird's-eye views over lovely game-filled surroundings; very friendly and attentive staff; authentic Zulu baskets available at nearby Illala Weavers. **Cons:** food not much to write home about. ☎ *035/562–1020* ⤳ *24 rooms* ⚘ *In-hotel: restaurant, bar, pool* ⊟ *AE, DC, MC, V* ⦿ *MAP.*

MKUZE GAME RESERVE

This 88,900-acre reserve in the shadow of the Ubombo Mountains, between the Mkhuze and Msunduzi rivers, makes up the northwestern spur of the iSimangaliso Greater St. Lucia Wetland Park, now a World Heritage site. (The park itself is one of the most important coastal and wetland areas in the world with five interlinked ecosystems: a marine system, a coastal dune system, lake systems, swamps, and inland savanna woodlands. It is this often-pristine diversity that makes it both important and amazingly beautiful.) Mkuze is famous for its birds: more than 400 bird species have been spotted here, including myriad waterfowl drawn to the park's shallow pans in summer. Several blinds, particularly those overlooking Nsumo Pan, offer superb views. Don't miss out on the amazing 3-km (2-mi) walk through a spectacular rare forest of towering, ancient fig trees, some as big as 82 feet tall and 39 feet around the base. Although only a fraction of Kruger's size, this is the place to find rhinos; there's a healthy population of both black and white rhinos. You won't find lions, buffalo, or elephants, but the low-lying thornveld supports lots of other game, including zebras, giraffes, kudus, and nyalas. The reserve is 48 km (30 mi) north of Hluhluwe-Imfolozi. ■TIP→ There are variant spellings of Mkuze in the area; you may also see Mkuzi or Mkhuzi. ☎ *035/573–9004* ⊕ *www.kznwildlife.com* ⤳ *R35 per vehicle, R35 per person* ⊙ *Daily 6–6.*

"This giraffe was photographed during my first day on safari. A beautiful animal in the perfect location. I was hooked." —wlbox, Fodors.com member

WHERE TO STAY

¢ ⚘ **Ghost Mountain Inn.** Swaths of scarlet bougainvillea run riot in the lush gardens of this family-owned country inn near Mkuze. It was here that Rider Haggard wrote some of his adventure stories, inspired perhaps by the mysterious lights and elusive flickering flames that give the mountain its spooky name. Rooms, each with a small veranda, are tastefully furnished in understated creams and browns with interesting historical prints. Large, invitingly restful public areas have terracotta tiles and comfortable cane furniture, and the cozy African lounge makes you feel like you've slipped back to the past. Don't miss the enthusiastic Zulu dancing before a succulent barbecue under the stars. At first light, wander down to the lake and watch the waterbirds wake up, or, later in the day, sit in the blind and watch them come home to roost. There's an excellent curio shop. The friendly staff can arrange tours to the neighboring game reserves and cultural sights or will fix you up to go bird-watching or fishing. **Pros:** good value for money; friendly staff. **Cons:** hotel-like atmosphere; tour buses overnight here. ☎ *035/573–1025* ⊕ *www.ghostmountaininn.co.za* ⇥ *50 rooms* ♿ *In-room: a/c. In-hotel: restaurant, bar, tennis courts, pool, Internet terminal* ▭ *AE, DC, MC, V* ⏀ *BP.*

ITHALA GAME RESERVE

In northern KwaZulu-Natal Province, close to the Swaziland border, Ithala (sometimes spelled "Itala"), at 296 square km (114 square mi), is small even compared with the relatively compact Hluhluwe-Imfolozi. Its size and its dearth of lions are probably why this delightful park 221 km (137 mi) northwest of Hluhluwe-Imfolozi is usually bypassed, even by South Africans—although they clearly don't know what they're missing. The other four of the Big Five are here—it's excellent for black and white rhinos—and the park is stocked with cheetahs, hyenas, giraffes, and an array of antelopes among its 80 mammal species. It's also an excellent spot for birders. The stunning landscapes and the relaxed game-viewing make this area a breath of fresh air after the Big Five melee of Kruger.

> **SELF-GUIDED TRAILS**
>
> An unusual feature of Ithala is its self-guided walking trails, in the mountainside above Ntshon-dwe Camp. The trails give you a chance to stretch your limbs if you've just spent hours cooped up in a car. They also let you get really close to the euphorbias, acacias, and other fascinating indigenous vegetation that festoon the hills. Ask at the camp reception for further information.

The reserve, founded in 1972 and run by KZN Wildlife, is a rugged region that drops 3,290 feet in just 15 km (9 mi) through sandstone cliffs, multicolor rocks, granite hills, ironstone outcrops, and quartz formations. Watered by nine small rivers rising in its vicinity and covered with rich soils, Ithala supports a varied cross section of vegetation, encompassing riverine thicket, wetland, open savanna, and acacia woodland. Arriving at its Ntshondwe Camp is nothing short of dramatic. The meandering road climbs from open plains to the top of a plateau dotted with granite formations, which at the last minute magically yield the rest camp at the foot of pink and russet cliffs.

☏ *033/845–1002* ⊕ *www.kznwildlife.com* ✉ *R40 per per person, R30 per vehicle.*

GETTING HERE AND AROUND
If you're headed to Ithala from Durban, drive north on the N2 to Empangeni, and then head west on the R34 to Vryheid. From here cut east on the R69 to Louwsburg. The reserve is immediately northwest of the village, from which there are clear signs. The journey from Durban takes around five hours and from Hluhluwe-Imfolozi about 2½ hours. Roads are good, and there are plenty of gas stations along the way.

WHERE TO STAY
Although Ithala has several exclusive bush camps, these are booked up months in advance by South Africans, making the chalets at its main camp the only practical accommodations for foreign visitors. Two people sharing a two-bed unit at Ntshondwe will pay about R460 per person per night.

¢   **Ntshondwe Camp.** In architecture, landscaping, and style, this beauti-
Fodor's Choice   ful government-run rest camp, 69 km (43 mi) from Vryheid, comes
★   closer than any other in the country to matching the expensive private lodges. Built around granite boulders and vegetation lush with acacias, wild figs, and giant cactuslike euphorbias, airy chalets with steep thatch roofs blend perfectly with the surroundings. Its two-, four-, and six-bed units can accommodate a total of 200 guests. Each self-catering chalet has a spacious lounge simply furnished with cane

chairs, a fully equipped kitchen, and a large veranda surrounded by indigenous bush. Keep an eye open for eagles soaring above the pink and russet sandstone cliffs. A magnificent game-viewing deck juts out over a steep slope to provide views of a water hole and extensive panoramas of the surrounding valleys. Take a guided game drive (R190) or guided walk (R175), hike a self-guided trail, or follow one of the well-laid-out drives with markers at points of interest. Picnic at one of the many scenic picnic spots, all of which have barbecue facilities and toilets. A gas station, a store (with great curios), and a good restaurant are all on the premises. **Pros:** tarred road access; guided game drives or self-drive; spectacular surroundings. **Cons:** it's a busy conference and wedding venue. ☎ *033/845–1000 or 034/983–2540* ⊕ *www.kznwildlife.com* ⬚ *39 chalets* ⚒ *In-room: kitchen. In-hotel: restaurant, bar, pool* ▤ *AE, DC, MC, V.*

> **WORD OF MOUTH**
>
> "If someone is serious about conservation should give Phinda his thumbs up. This is a successful story of restoring misused farm land into a wildlife reserve with one of the biggest reintroduction of game in Africa, Phinda was restocked with lion, rhino, buffalo, elephant, leopard, giraffe and other big game. Their cheetah reintroduction is probably the most successful ever done."
> —PacoAhedo

PHINDA PRIVATE GAME RESERVE

Established in 1991, this eco-award-winning flagship &Beyond (formerly CCAfrica) reserve is a heartening example of tourism serving the environment with panache. *Phinda* (*pin*-duh) is Zulu for "return," referring to the restoration of 54,360 acres of overgrazed ranchland in northern Zululand to bushveld. It's a triumph. You may find it impossible to believe the area wasn't always the thick bush you see all around you. The Big Five have established themselves firmly, and Phinda can claim a stunning variety of five different ecosystems: sand forest (which grows on the fossil dunes of an earlier coastline), savanna, bushveld, open woodland, and verdant wetlands.

Phinda can deliver the Big Five, although not as consistently or in such numbers as most lodges in Mpumalanga. Buffalo, leopards, lions, cheetahs, spotted hyenas, elephants, white rhinos, hippos, giraffes, impalas, and the rare, elusive, tiny Suni antelope are all here, and rangers provide exciting interpretive game drives for guests. Birdlife is prolific and extraordinary, with some special Zululand finds: the pink-throated twin spot, the crested guinea fowl, the African broadbill, and the crowned eagle. Where Phinda also excels is in the superb quality of its rangers, who can provide fascinating commentary on everything from local birds to frogs. It's amazing just how enthralling the love life of a dung beetle can be! There are also Phinda adventures (optional extras) down the Mzinene River for a close-up look at crocodiles, hippos, and birds; big-game fishing or scuba diving off the deserted, wildly beautiful Maputaland coast; and sightseeing flights over Phinda and the highest vegetated dunes in the world. ☎ *011/809–4300* ⊕ *www.phinda.com.*

WHERE TO STAY

For all reservations, contact **&Beyond** (☏ *011/809–4300* ⊕ *www.phinda. com* ▭ *AE, DC, MC, V* ⫮ *FAP*).

$$ **Forest Lodge.** Hidden in a rare sand forest, this fabulous lodge overlooks a small water hole where nyalas, warthogs, and baboons frequently come to drink. The lodge is a real departure from the traditional thatch structures so common in South Africa. It's very modern, with a vaguely Japanese Zen feel, thanks to glass-paneled walls, light woods, and a deliberately spare, clean look. The effect is stylish and very elegant, softened by modern African art and sculpture. Suites use the same architectural concepts as the lodge, where walls have become windows, and rely on the dense forest (or curtains) for privacy. As a result, you'll likely feel very close to your surroundings, and it's possible to lie in bed or take a shower while watching delicate nyalas grazing just feet away. **Pros:** magical feeling of oneness with the surrounding bush; light and airy, Zulu-Zen decor. **Cons:** being in a glass box could make some visitors nervous; not for traditional types. ⇨ *16 suites* ⟁ *In-room: a/c. In-hotel: pool, Internet terminal.*

Fodor's Choice ★

$$ **Mountain Lodge.** This attractive thatch lodge sits on a rocky hill overlooking miles of bushveld plains and the Ubombo Mountains. Wide verandas lead into the lounge and bar, graced with high ceilings, dark beams, and cool tile floors. In winter guests can snuggle into cushioned wicker chairs next to a blazing log fire. Brick pathways wind down the hillside from the lodge to elegant split-level suites with mosquito nets, thatch roofs, and large decks overlooking the reserve. African baskets, beadwork, and grass matting beautifully complement the bush atmosphere. Children are welcome, although those under five are not allowed on game drives and 6- to 11-year-olds are permitted only at the manager's discretion. **Pros:** great mountain views; very family-friendly. **Cons:** rather bland decor; pricey if you take the kids (pricey even if you don't take the kids). ⇨ *25 suites* ⟁ *In-room: a/c. In-hotel: bar, pool, Internet terminal.*

$$ **Rock Lodge.** If you get tired of the eagle's-eye view of the deep valley below from your private veranda, you can write in your journal in your luxurious sitting room or take a late-night dip in your own plunge pool. All of Phinda's activities are included—twice-daily game drives, nature walks, riverboat cruises, and canoe trips along the Mzinene River. Scuba diving, deep-sea fishing, and spectacular small-plane flights are extras. Don't miss out on one of Phinda's legendary bush dinners: hundreds of lanterns light up the surrounding forest and bush, and the food is unforgettable. **Pros:** Olé! If you fancy Mexico in the bush, then this hits the spot; your own plunge pool; great views. **Cons:** could be seen as inappropriately funky by Old Africa hands; stay away if you suffer from vertigo. ⇨ *6 suites* ⟁ *In-room: a/c. In-hotel: bar, pool.*

$$ **Vlei Lodge.** Accommodations at this small and intimate lodge are nestled in the shade of the sand forest and are so private it's hard to believe there are other guests. Suites—made of thatch, teak, and glass—have a distinct Asian feel and overlook a marshland on the edge of an inviting woodland. The bedrooms and bathrooms are huge, and each suite has a private plunge pool (one visitor found a lion drinking from his) and outdoor deck. The lounge-living area of the lodge has two fireplaces on opposite glass walls, a dining area, and a large terrace under a canopy of trees, where breakfast is served. The bush braai, with its splendid food and fairy-tale setting, is a memorable occasion after an evening game drive. **Pros:** superb views over the floodplains—you can lie on your bed and watch the ever-changing show of game; lovely warm romantic feel. **Cons:** you're so cosseted and comfortable you'll be hard put to make all those game drives; lots of mosquitoes and flying insects. *6 suites* In-room: a/c. In-hotel: bar, pool.

$$$$ **Zuka Lodge.** An exclusive, single-use lodge for a family or small group of friends, Zuka (*zuka* means "sixpence" in Zulu) is a couple of miles from the bigger lodges. Thatch cottages overlook a busy water hole, and you'll be looked after by the camp's personal ranger, host, butler, and chef. Children are welcome. **Pros:** exclusivity; it's like having your own private holiday retreat; gives you the feeling of immediate celebrity status. **Cons:** this exclusivity comes at a high price; choose your fellow guests carefully—you're on your own here. *4 cottages (which must be rented as one unit)* In-room: a/c. In-hotel: bar, pool, Internet.

THANDA PRIVATE GAME RESERVE

23 km (14 mi) north of Hluhluwe, 400 km (248 mi) north of Durban.

Located in a wildly beautiful part of northern Zululand, multi-award-winning Thanda is one of KwaZulu-Natal's newer game reserves. Like its neighbor Phinda did in the '90s, the 37,000-acre reserve is restoring former farmlands and hunting grounds to their previous pristine state, thanks to a joint venture with local communities and the king of the Zulus, Goodwill Zweletini, who donated some of his royal hunting grounds to the project. Game that used to roam this wilderness centuries ago has been reestablished, including the Big Five. *Thanda* (tan-duh) is Zulu for "love," and its philosophy echoes just that: "for the love of nature, wildlife, and dear ones." Rangers often have to work hard to find game, but the rewards of seriously tracking lions or rhinos with your enthusiastic and very experienced ranger and tracker are great. Because its owner is passionately committed not only to the land but also to the local people, there are many opportunities to interact with them. Don't miss out on Vula Zulu, one of the most magical and powerful Zulu experiences offered in South Africa. After exploring the village, including the chief's *kraal* (compound) and the hut of the *sangoma* (shaman), where you might have bones thrown and read, you'll be treated to the Vula Zulu show, a memorable blend of narration, high-energy dance, song, and mime that recounts Zulu history. The lodge can also arrange golf, scuba diving, snorkeling, whale-watching, and fishing expeditions. *011/469–5082 www.thanda.com.*

Hilltop Camp, Hluhluwe Game Reserve,

Impala Camp, Hluhluwe Game Reserve

Interior of Chalet, Hilltop Camp, Hluhluwe GR

Left: Rock Lodge; Right: Phinda Zuku Lodge, Phinda Private Game Reserve

Mountain Lodge, Phinda Private Game Reserve

Top: Vlei Lodge; Bottom; Forest Lodge

GETTING HERE AND AROUND

Road transfers from Richards Bay and Durban airports can be arranged with the reserve.

WHERE TO STAY

For all reservations, contact **Thanda**. Both the tented camp and the main lodge have kids' programs and a customized junior-ranger course. (☎ *011/469–5082* ⊕ *www.thanda.com* ▤ *AE, DC, MC, V* ⍾⎢*FAP*).

$$ ⛺ **Thanda Main Lodge.** There's a palpable feeling of earth energy in this
☺ magical and exquisite lodge that blends elements of royal Zulu with an eclectic pan-African feel. Beautiful domed, beehive-shaped dwellings perch on the side of rolling hills and overlook mountains and bushveld. Inside, contemporary Scandinavian touches meet African chic—from the "eyelashes" of slatted poles that peep out from under the thatch roofs to the embedded mosaics in royal Zulu red and blue that decorate the polished, honey-color stone floors. Creative light fixtures include chandeliers made of handcrafted Zulu beads and lamps of straw or filmy cotton mesh. A huge stone fireplace divides the bedroom area from the comfortable and roomy lounge. Each chalet has a different color scheme and is decorated with beaded, hand-embroidered cushions and throws. Dip in your personal plunge pool after an exciting game drive, sunbathe on your private deck, or commune with the surrounding bushveld in your cool, cushioned *sala* (outdoor covered deck). Later, after a meal that many a fine restaurant would be proud to serve, come back to your chalet to find a bedtime story on your pillow, marshmallows waiting to be toasted over flickering candles, and a glass of Amarula cream. Or dine alone in your private boma by the light of the stars and the leaping flames of a fragrant wood fire. The spacious, uncluttered public areas—dining decks, bomas, library, and lounge—are decorated in restful earth tones accented by royal Zulu colors, beads from Malawi, Ghanaian ceremonial masks, and Indonesian chairs. **Pros:** luxury unlimited; superb food and service; kids will love the junior-ranger program; late-night snacks and drinks await you in your room. **Cons:** a bit over the top—some might say it's Hollywood in the bush; very near to the main road. ⤳ *9 chalets* ⚷ *In-room: a/c. In-hotel: bar, pool, spa, children's programs (ages 5–15), Internet terminal.*

$ ⛺ **Thanda Tented Camp.** Perfect for a family or friends' reunion, this
☺ intimate camp deep in the bush brings you into close contact with your surroundings. You might wake up in your spacious safari tent with en-suite bathroom and private veranda to find a warthog or nyala grazing outside. The camp has its own vehicle, ranger, and tracker, and a huge sala with pool and sundeck. **Pros:** opportunities to learn stargazing; perfect for small (adults only) reunions or celebrations. **Cons:** not for the nervous type; only four tents so hope for pleasant fellow guests. ⤳ *4 tents* ⚷ *In-hotel: bar, pool, spa, no kids under 16.*

KGALAGADI TRANSFRONTIER PARK

If you're looking for true wilderness, remoteness, and stark, almost surreal landscapes and you're not averse to forgoing the ultimate in luxury and getting sand in your hair, then this amazing, uniquely beautiful park within the Kalahari Desert is for you.

Game
☆★★★★

Park Accessibility
☆☆★★★

Getting Around
★★★★★

Accommodations
☆★★★★

Scenic Beauty
★★★★★

In an odd little finger of the country jutting north between Botswana in the east and Namibia in the west lies South Africa's second largest park after Kruger. Kgalagadi was officially launched in 2000 as the first transfrontier, or "Peace Park," in Southern Africa by merging South Africa's vast Kalahari Gemsbok National Park with the even larger Gemsbok National Park in Botswana. The name Kgalagadi (pronounced kala-hardy) is derived from the San language and means "place of thirst." It is now one of the largest protected wilderness areas in the world—an area of more than 38,000 square km (14,670 square mi). Of this awesome area, 9,600 square km (3,700 square mi) fall in South Africa, and the rest in Botswana. Passing through the Twee Rivieren Gate, you will encounter a vast desert under enormous, usually cloudless skies and a sense of space and openness that few other places can offer.

The Kgalagadi Transfrontier is less commercialized and developed than Kruger. The roads aren't paved, and you will come across far fewer people and cars. There is less game on the whole than in Kruger, but because there is also less vegetation, the animals are much more visible. Also, because the game and large carnivores are concentrated in two riverbeds (the route that two roads follow), the park offers unsurpassed viewing and photographic opportunities. Perhaps the key to really appreciating this barren place is in understanding how its creatures have adapted to their harsh surroundings to survive—like the gemsbok, which has a sophisticated cooling system allowing it to tolerate extreme changes in body temperature. There are also insects in the park that inhale only every half hour or so to preserve the moisture that breathing expends.

The landscape—endless dunes punctuated with blond grass and the odd thorn tree—is dominated by two *wadis* (dry riverbeds): the Nossob (which forms the border between South Africa and Botswana) and its tributary, the Auob. The Nossob flows only a few times a century, and the Auob flows only once every couple of decades or so. A single road runs beside each riverbed, along which windmills pump water into man-made water holes, which help the animals to survive and provide good viewing stations for visitors. There are 82 water holes, 49 of which are along tourist roads. Park management struggles to keep up their maintenance; it's a constant battle against the elements, with the elements often winning. Similarly, the park constantly maintains and improves tourist roads, but again it's a never-ending struggle. A third road traverses the park's interior to join the other two. The scenery and vegetation on this road change dramatically from the two river valleys, which are dominated by sandy banks, to a grassier escarpment. Two more dune roads have been added, and several 4x4 routes have been developed. From Nossob camp a road leads to Union's End, the country's northernmost tip, where South Africa, Namibia, and Botswana meet. Allow a full day for the long and dusty drive, which is 124 km (77 mi) one-way. It is possible to enter Botswana from the South African side, but you'll need a 4x4. The park infrastructure in Botswana is very basic, with just three campsites and mostly 4x4 terrain.

The park is famous for its gemsbok and its legendary, huge, black-maned Kalahari lions. It also has leopard, cheetah, eland, blue wildebeest, and giraffe, as well as meerkat and mongoose. Rarer desert species, such as the desert-adapted springbok, the elusive aardvark, and the pretty Cape fox, also make their home here. Among birders, the park is known as one of Africa's raptor meccas; it's filled with bateleurs, lappet-faced vultures, pygmy falcons, and the cooperatively hunting red-necked falcons and gabar goshawks.

The park's legendary night drives (R110) depart most evenings about 5:30 in summer, earlier in winter (check when you get to your camp), from Twee Rivieren Camp, Mata Mata, and Nossob. The drives set out just as the park gate closes to everyone else. You'll have a chance to see rare nocturnal animals like the brown hyena and the bat-eared fox by spotlight. The guided morning walks—during which you see the sun rise over the Kalahari and could bump into a lion—are also a must. Reservations are essential and can be made when you book your accommodations.

WHEN TO GO

The park can be superhot in summer and freezing at night in winter (literally below zero, with frost on the ground). Autumn—from late February to mid-April—is perhaps the best time to visit. It's cool after the rains, and many of the migratory birds are still around. The winter months of June and July are also a good time. It's best to make reservations as far in advance as possible, even up to a year or more if you want to visit at Easter or in June or July, when there are school vacations.

GETTING HERE AND AROUND

Upington International Airport is 260 km (162 mi) south of Kgalagadi Transfrontier Park; many lodgings provide shuttle service from the airport, or you can rent a car at the airport; if you reserve a car through an agency in Upington, you can pick it up from the Twee Rivieren Camp. If you drive from Johannesburg you have a choice of two routes: either via Upington (with the last stretch a 60-km [37-mi] gravel road) or via Kuruman, Hotazel, and Vanzylrus (with about 340 km [211 mi] of gravel road). The gravel sections on both routes are badly corrugated, so don't speed.

Kgalagadi (except on the 4x4 routes). However, a 4x4 will give you greater access in the park and, as you sit higher up, better game-viewing.

FOOD AND DRINK

You can buy Styrofoam coolers at Pick 'n' Pay in Upington (or at any large town en route to the park) and then leave them behind for the camp staff when you exit the park. Pack ice and frozen juice boxes to keep your perishables chilled between camps. Ziplock bags are indispensable for keeping dust out of food (and for storing damp washcloths and swimsuits). You're not allowed out of your vehicle between camps, so keep your snacks and drinks handy inside the passenger area and not in the trunk.

VISITOR INFORMATION

There is a daily conservation fee, but Wild Cards, available at the gates or online, are more economical for stays of more than a few days. Reservations for all accommodations, bush drives, wilderness trails, and other park activities must be made through South African National Parks.

ESSENTIALS

Airport Information Upington International Airport (☎ 054/337–7900).

Visitor Info Kgalagadi Transfrontier Park (✉ *Park reception at Twee Rivieren Camp* ☎ 054/561–2000). **South African National Parks** (☎ 012/428–9111 Pretoria; 021/552–0008 Cape Town ⊕ www.sanparks.org).

WHERE TO STAY

LUXURY LODGING

$ **!Xaus Lodge.** If you want to experience one of South Africa's most Fodor's Choice beautiful and isolated parks without hassle, then this luxury lodge ★ owned by the Khomani San and Mier communities and jointly managed with SANParks is the place for you. You'll be picked up in a 4x4 from Twee Rivieren, fed, watered, taken on game drives and desert walks, and introduced to the local San. Located deep in the desert 32 km (20 mi) from the Auob River road along a track that crosses the red dunes of the Kalahari, this enchanting lodge overlooks an amazingly scenic pan. The twin-bed, en-suite chalets perch on sand dunes overlooking a water hole; each chalet has a private deck. A fan will keep you cool in summer, and a gas heater, hot-water bottle, and warm sheets will help you stay warm on winter nights. A welcome swimming pool is set in a deck

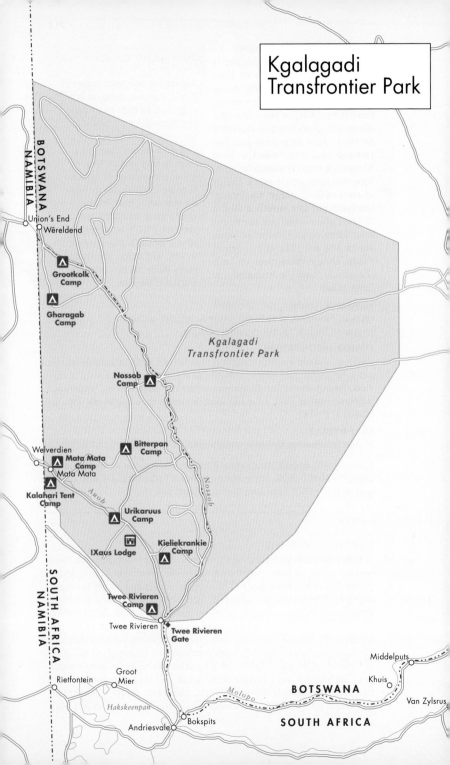

CLOSE UP

San Culture and Language

Also called the /Xam, the hunter-gatherer San (Bushmen) have a culture that dates back more than 20,000 years, and their genetic origins are more than 1 million years old, contemporary humans' oldest. Fast-forward a few years—about 2,000 years ago, to be inexact—when Korana or Khoi (Khoe) herders migrated south, bringing their livestock and settling along the Orange (Gariep/Garieb), Vaal, and Riet rivers. During the 18th and 19th centuries, the Griquas—thought to be part Khoi and part slave—moved into the Northern Cape with their cattle and sheep.

At one time 20 to 30 languages pertaining to various clans flourished, but colonialism brought with it devastating results for the San's native tongue.

It lost out to Tswana and Afrikaans. In the nick of time in the 1870s, British doctor Wilhelm Bleek, who spoke /Xam, and Lucy Lloyd recorded the last activities of /Xam culture and tradition. (Some of these records can be found at the McGregor Museum in Kimberley.)

Still, thousands of Northern Cape residents today acknowledge an ancestral connection to the largest San or /Xam group of the 18th and 19th centuries. The two biggest remaining groups are the !Xu and Khwe, who live at Schmidtsdrift, 80 km (50 mi) from Kimberley. Among the best-known groups in South Africa today are the Khomani San, some of whom still speak the ancient Nu.

overlooking the pan. The attractive rustic furniture and eye-catching artwork throughout this delightful, unique lodge are all made by local craftspeople and artists. Activities include game drives in an open safari vehicle, walks with San trackers, and a chance to watch San artists at work. At night the stars and planets are bright and clear; a telescope brings ancient tradition and modern technology together as the San interpret for you their legends of the night sky. But !Xaus (pronounced kaus) comprises so much more than its activities: it is solitude, peace, and silence as you "listen" to day turn into night, plus interaction with the cheerful and willing staff, the majority of whom come from the surrounding local communities. Negotiations are ongoing to establish a private airstrip nearby. **Pros:** unique wilderness setting; only private lodge in area; opportunities to interact with the local people. **Cons:** very long (almost an hour) roller-coaster approach road through dunes; game not abundant around lodge. ☎ *021/701–7860* ⊕ *www.xauslodge. co.za* ⌦ *12 chalets* ⌂ *In-room: no a/c. In-hotel: restaurant, bar, pool, Internet terminal* ▭ *AE, DC, MC, V* ℃ *FAP.*

NATIONAL PARK ACCOMMODATIONS

Accommodations within the park are in three traditional rest camps and several highly sought-after wilderness camps (try to reserve these if possible), which are spread around the park. All of the traditional rest camps have shops selling food, curios, and some basic equipment, but Twee Rivieren has the best variety of fresh fruit, vegetables, milk, and meat, and is the only camp with a restaurant. Twee Rivieren is also the only camp with telephone and cell-phone reception (although

!Xaus Lodge, Kgalagadi Transfrontier Park.

cell-phone reception quickly disappears as you head into the dunes) and 24-hour electricity; the other camps have gas and electricity, but the electricity runs only part of the day, at different times in each camp.

For all national park accommodations, contact South African National Parks (⇨ *See Essentials, above, for contact info*), or you can reserve directly through the park if you happen to be there and would like to stay a night or add another night onto your stay.

REST CAMPS

¢ ▦ **Mata Mata.** This camp, 120 km (74 mi) from Twee Rivieren on the Namibian border, has good game-viewing due to the proximity of the water holes. The camp's facilities are not as modern as those at Twee Rivieren, although there is a small shop stocking basics and a swimming pool. **Pros:** you're allowed to drive into Namibia without visas for a certain distance; great water holes; giraffes galore. **Cons:** dry and dusty year-round; unattractive barracks-like buildings. ⤳ *13 chalets* ⌂ *In-room: kitchen. In-hotel: pool.*

¢ ▦ **Nossob.** In the central section of the park, this camp is on the Botswana border, 166 km (103 mi) from Twee Rivieren. Basic brick chalets come with an outside braai and real bush atmosphere and sleep three to six people. Guesthouses have showers but no tubs. Most of the chalets are less than 50 yards from the fence, and there's also a stunning blind overlooking the water hole. You can see game without even leaving camp, but watch out for marauding jackals here; although they're not dangerous or aggressive, they're always on the lookout for unattended food. A small shop sells the basics. There's no electricity in the camp, and the generators are turned off at 11. **Pros:** this is the place to see predators, particularly lions; predator information center. **Cons:** barren, unattractive camp; no phone reception. ⌦ *15 chalets, 1 cottage, 2 guesthouses* ⌂ *In-room: kitchen. In-hotel: pool.*

¢ ⛺ **Twee Rivieren.** On the Kgalagadi's southern boundary, this camp is home to the park's headquarters. It's the biggest of the camps and has the most modern facilities; all units have fully equipped kitchens, and the camp shop here is the best. You can choose from a couple of types of accommodations, from a two-bedroom, six-bed family cottage to a bungalow with two single beds and a sleeper couch. Try for units 1–16, which look out over the dunes. Take a guided morning walk *and* a night drive—worth every penny. There are educational exhibits on the Kalahari's animal and plant life. From Upington to Twee Rivieren is 260 km (161 mi) on a relatively good road; only the last 52 km (32 mi) are gravel. **Pros:** modern, well-equipped chalets; on-site grocery store; not-to-be-missed guided morning and night drives; 24-hour electricity. **Cons:** the biggest and noisiest camp in the area. ⌦ *1 cottage, 30 bungalows* ⌂ *In-room: a/c, kitchen, no TV. In-hotel: restaurant, bar, pool.*

CAMPING

There is a limited number of campsites (R165) at Mata Mata (20), Nossob (20), and Twee Rivieren (24). All campsites have a braai and access to electricity and water, and there are communal bathroom facilities and a basic communal kitchen. Before you arrive, be sure to arm yourself with the "blue camping plug"—available from any camping–caravanning shop—and a long extension cord. Try to find a shady spot.

WILDERNESS CAMPS

Kgalagadi is the first national park to provide accommodation deep in the wilderness, where several unfenced wilderness camps with their own water holes for game-viewing put you deep in the heart of the Kalahari. These enchanting camps are very popular, so make your reservations well in advance—a year ahead, if possible. Each camp is slightly different, but all have the same facilities and are similarly priced. All have an equipped kitchen with a gas-powered refrigerator, solar-powered lights, gas for hot water, and a deck with braai facilities. You do need to supply your own water and firewood.

As all of these camps are unfenced (which is part of their desirability and charm), you should *never* walk outside your accommodation at night—you don't want to come face-to-face with a hungry lion or scavenging hyena!

¢ ⛺ **Bitterpan.** This camp overlooks an enormous expanse of sand and a water hole, where you can watch game come and go from your deck or from the communal areas. Four double cabins with their own bathrooms border a narrow walkway that leads to a large communal kitchen, dining room, and braai area. Bitterpan is accessible only by 4x4, and only guests here may use the road from Nossob to Urikaruus. **Pros:** spectacular game-viewing from your accommodation; spectacular desert scenery; only four cabins. **Cons:** 4x4s only; no children under 12; communal kitchen and eating area (cross fingers you share the camp with amenable visitors); it's a long drive to get here from any starting point; guests have to bring their own drinking water and firewood. ⌐ *4 cabins* ⏷ *In-hotel: no kids under 12.*

¢ **Gharagab.** Although you'll need a 4x4 to negotiate the two-track road to Gharagab, it's worth every dusty mile for the chance to feel like you're the only person on earth. Situated in the far northern region of the park close to the Namibian border, this camp provides stunning elevated views of Kalahari dunes and the thornveld savanna. Although the game isn't as abundant as in the Grootkolk area, you're likely to have unusual or even rare sightings, such as a honey badger, eland, or an aardvark, and the feeling of splendid isolation is unforgettable. You may never again feel this alone. Each long tent built on wooden stilts has a kitchen, bedroom, and bathroom, plus a wooden deck (with a braai) overlooking a water hole. **Pros:** you've probably never experienced solitary wilderness such as this. **Cons:** 4x4s only; no children under 12; not much in the way of big game; guests must bring their own drinking water and firewood. ⌐ *4 cabins* ⏷ *In-room: kitchen. In-hotel: no kids under 12.*

¢ **Grootkolk.** Surrounded by camelthorn trees and close to the Nossob River bed, this lovely camp has good game-viewing, with lions, cheetahs, hyenas, and lots of antelope, including oryx and springbok. All four well-sited rustic desert cabins have a good view of the water hole, which is spotlighted for a couple of hours every night. Although the road to Grootkolk is heavily corrugated, you can negotiate it with a two-wheel-drive vehicle. **Pros:** spotlighted water hole; sublime wilderness; ceiling fans in the cabins. **Cons:** 4x4s or 2x4s only; no children under 12; chalets are made from canvas and sandbags, so if you prefer something more substantial, stay away. ⌐ *4 cabins* ⏷ *In-room: kitchen. In-hotel: no kids under 12.*

¢ **Kalahari Tent Camp.** Many visitors say that this good game-viewing camp overlooking the Auob River bed and water hole is one of the most beautiful places in the park, so try to stay for more than one night. Your accommodation consists of a large walk-in tent with a spacious and attractive bedroom, shower, and toilet. There's a separate, fully equipped kitchen tent, also suitable as a dining room, and the terrace between these two tents has excellent views over the riverbed and its wildlife. At night, look out for jackals, lions, a resident family of meerkats, and spare-wheel-cover-eating hyenas around the tents—just be sure to stay in your tent at night and avoid walking around. The secluded honeymoon unit has a king-size bed and a bath and shower. The camp is near the Mata Mata shop and gas station. **Pros:** near Mata Mata, which has a shop and gas; excellent game; family-friendly; lovely honeymoon tent; ceiling fans in the tents. **Cons:** guests must bring their own drinking water and firewood. ⌐ *10 tents, 4 family tents, 1 honeymoon tent* ⏷ *In-room: kitchen. In-hotel: pool.*

¢ **Kieliekrankie.** Perched high on a big sand dune only 8 km (5 mi) from the game-rich Auob River road, this small camp overlooks seemingly infinite red Kalahari sands, creating an amazing sense of space and isolation. To be among the red dunes at full moon is an unforgettable experience. The four cabins have stunning views over the desert and come with a kitchen tent, bedroom, bathroom, and deck with braai.

Situated in the Twee Rivieren region, the camp can be easily reached with a two-wheel-drive vehicle. **Pros:** easily accessible with a sedan; you can start your game drives before residents of the other camps reach the area so you have the game to yourself for a while; the red Kalahari sands are unforgettable. **Cons:** no children under 12; guests must bring their own drinking water and firewood. ⤴ *4 cabins* ⌂ *In-room: kitchen. In-hotel: no kids under 12.*

¢ 🏠 **Urikaruus.** Four cabins with kitchens, bedrooms, and bathrooms are built on stilts among camelthorn trees overlooking the Auob River. You'll easily spot game as it comes to drink at the water hole close to the cabins. On-site wardens will help you interpret the spoor you find around your cabin. Set in the Mata Mata region, Urikaruus is accessible by two-wheel-drive vehicles. **Pros:** accessible with a sedan; stunning location; game to yourself on early-morning and late-afternoon drives; cabins have their own kitchen. **Cons:** no children under 12; guests must bring their own drinking water and firewood. ⤴ *4 cabins* ⌂ *In-room: kitchen. In-hotel: no kids under 12.*

IF YOU HAVE TIME

Although we've gone into great detail about the must-see parks in South Africa, there are many others to explore if you have time. Here are a few good ones to consider.

TSWALU KALAHARI RESERVE

300 km (186 mi) northwest of Kimberley, 270 km (168 mi) northeast of Upington.

☾ **Tswalu Kalahari Reserve.** Near the Kgalagadi Transfrontier Park is the malaria-free Tswalu Kalahari Reserve, which at 900 square km (347 square mi) is the biggest privately owned game reserve in Africa; it's the perfect place to photograph a gemsbok against a red dune and an azure sky. Initially founded as a conservation project by the late millionaire Stephen Boler primarily to protect and breed the endangered desert rhino, it's now owned by the Oppenheimer family. Today it spreads over endless Kalahari dunes covered with tufts of golden veld and over much of the Northern Cape's Korannaberg mountain range. Its initial population of 7,000 animals has grown to more than 12,000, and it's now home to lion, cheetah, buffalo, giraffe, and many species of antelope. It's the best place in Africa to see rhino—the reserve has more than 50 white and 20 black rhinos, which have amazingly adapted to living in the desert. Other rare species include roan and sable antelope, black wildebeest, and mountain zebra. There's not so much game as in some of Mpumalanga's private reserves because the land has a lower carrying capacity (the annual rainfall is only about 9¾ inches). But when you do see the animals, the lack of vegetation makes sightings spectacular. And the fact that only about three open-sided game vehicles traverse an area two-thirds the size of the entire Sabi Sands makes your escape all the more complete.

This is one of the most child-friendly game reserves in Southern Africa. Children are welcomed and well catered to, with lots of freedom and special activities. ☎ 086/187–9258 ⊕ www.tswalu.com.

GETTING HERE AND AROUND

It's easiest to fly to Kimberley or Upington and be picked up from there by the lodge. Daily flights are available from Johannesburg, Durban, and Cape Town with Airlink and Federal Air. Road transfers from Kimberley or Upington can be arranged, or you can book a charter flight from Johannesburg.

WHERE TO STAY

The emphasis at **Tswalu** is on exclusivity, which is why the entire reserve can accommodate no more than 30 people at a time. Nothing is left wanting at this exclusive Relais & Châteaux property. Children 12 and under stay free with adults, and there are discounted rates for older kids. ☎ 011/274–2299 ⊕ www.tswalu.com ▤ AE, DC, MC, V ⍩ FAP.

$$ 🏨 **The Motse.** Tswalu's main lodge is made up of freestanding thatch-and-stone suites clustered around a large main building with a heated natural-color pool and a floodlighted water hole. The decor—in keeping with the unusual and unique Tswalu experience—is minimalist and modern, echoing the landscape in colors and textures. **Pros:** special children's room and babysitting services and nannies available; unique desert landscape; same great wildlife as Tarkuni; wonderful library with rare books. **Cons:** no elephants. ⇆ 8 suites ᗌ In-room: a/c. In-hotel: restaurant, bar, pool, gym, spa, Wi-Fi hotspot.

$$$$ 🏨 **Tarkuni.** In a private section of Tswalu, Tarkuni is an exclusive, self-contained house decorated similarly to Motswe and offering a comparable level of luxury. Perfect for small groups and families, Tarkuni sleeps 10 and comes with its own chef, game vehicle, and tracker. The food is almost as memorable as the scenery, and every meal is served in a different location: on a lantern-lighted dune or alongside a crackling fire in the lodge's boma. Apart from guided walks and drives, horseback trails (not included in the rate) that you traverse with a qualified guide offer close encounters with wildlife. Two sets of bunk beds, plus an adjoining nanny's quarters, are geared toward children. **Pros:** this is excellent value for money, and if there are 10 of you, it works out to be far more affordable than most other luxury lodges; a children's paradise; black-maned Kalahari lions, wild dogs, cheetah, and one-third of South Africa's endangered desert black rhino population; if you're a fan of TV's *Meerkat Manor,* you'll be in a seventh heaven. **Cons:** no elephants. ⇆ 1 house ᗌ In-room: a/c. In-hotel: restaurant, bar, pool, Internet terminal.

ADDO ELEPHANT NATIONAL PARK

72 km (45 mi) north of Port Elizabeth.

Smack in the middle of a citrus-growing and horse-breeding area, Addo Elephant National Park is home to more than 500 elephants, more than 400 buffalo, 48 black rhino, hundreds of kudu and other antelopes, and 21 lions. At present the park has about 420,000 acres, but it's expanding all the time and is intended to reach a total of about 600,000 acres.

But Addo is a work in progress: not all of the land is contiguous, and parts of the land are not properly fenced in yet. The most accessible parts of the park are the original, main section and the Colchester, Kabouga, Woody Cape, and Zuurberg sections. The original section of Addo still holds most of the game and is served by Addo Main Camp. The Colchester section, in the south, which has one SANParks camp, is contiguous with the main area but is not properly fenced yet so there's not much game there. The scenic Nyati section is separated from the main section by a road and railway line; there are two luxury lodges in the Nyati section, and the game-viewing is excellent (but exclusive to guests staying in the lodges). Just north of Nyati is the mountainous Zuurberg section, which doesn't have a large variety of game but is particularly scenic, with fabulous hiking trails and horse trails. It is also the closest section of the park to Addo Elephant Back Safaris.

You can explore the park in your own vehicle, in which case you need to heed the road signs that claim DUNG BEETLES HAVE RIGHT OF WAY . . . seriously. Addo is home to the almost-endemic and extremely rare flightless dung beetle, which can often be seen rolling its unusual incubator across the roads. Watch out for them (they're only about 2 inches long, but they have the right-of-way—as well as sharp spines that can puncture tires), and watch them: they're fascinating.

Instead of driving you could take a night or day game drive with a park ranger in an open vehicle from the main camp. A more adventurous option is to ride a horse among the elephants. Warning: no citrus fruit may be brought into the park, as elephants find it irresistible and can smell it for miles. ☏ *No phone* ⊕ *www.addoelephantpark.com* ✉ *R130* ⊙ *Daily 7–7 (may vary with seasons).*

GETTING HERE AND AROUND

The closest airport to Addo Elephant Park is Port Elizabeth (PLZ) airport. Flights arrive daily from all of South Africa's main cities via South African Airways, SA Airlink, and the budget airlines Kulula and 1time. Flights from Cape Town take one hour and from Johannesburg 1½ hours.

Traveling by car is the easiest and best way to tour this area as there's no public transport. Some roads are unpaved but are in decent condition. Most lodges will organize airport transfers for their guests.

⌚ **Addo Elephant Back Safaris.** This company lets you get up close and personal with a small group of trained African elephants. You get to do a short elephant ride and then go for a scenic walk through the bush with them. You can touch them, feed them, and watch them as they bathe themselves with sand, water, or both (i.e., mud). The whole experience lasts about two to three hours and includes a meal either before or after the safari. You can also arrange for a fly-in day-trip from Port Elizabeth. ☏ *086/123–3672* ⊕ *www.addoelephantbacksafaris.co.za* ✉ *R875* ⊙ *Visits by appointment only.*

Schotia Safaris. If you're short on time or budget, Schotia offers a good value, family-run, no-frills safari experience taking place in a privately owned wildlife reserve bordering the eastern side of Addo. Due to its small size (4,200 acres) and the fact that it's very densely stocked (more

"Addo Elephant Park: [these elephants were lined up] all in a row, drinking water in an orderly way. Small to big." —JAK, Fodors.com member

than 2,000 animals and 40 species) you're almost guaranteed to see a wide variety of wildlife—lion, giraffes, hippos, white rhinos, crocodiles, zebras, and all kinds of buck. The popular Tooth and Claw safari (R660) starts at 2:30 PM and includes a game drive and a tasty, generous buffet dinner served in an attractive open-air area with roaring fires. After dinner you're taken on a short night drive back to the reception area—keep your eyes peeled for some unusual nocturnal animals. There's also the option of going on a morning game drive into Addo, with lunch, and then the Tooth and Claw safari for R1,320. Other packages include one or two nights' accommodation on the reserve. Although you may see other vehicles during your drive, tours are very good value and well run, and the guides are excellent. The Tooth and Claw half-day safari can be done easily as a day-trip from Port Elizabeth, as it's only a 45-minute drive away. A transfer from PE is R200. ☎ 042/235–1436 ⊕ www.schotia.com.

WHERE TO STAY

¢ 🍴 **Addo Elephant National Park Main Camp.** One of the best SANParks rest camps, this location has a range of self-catering accommodations, such as safari tents, forest cabins, rondavels, cottages, and chalets, and a shop that sells basic supplies as well as souvenirs. An à la carte restaurant with reasonable prices is open for all meals, and a floodlighted water hole is nearby. Prices are calculated according to a complicated SANParks formula, which works by unit price, not per person, and is anything from R480 for up to two people sharing to R2,315 for four people sharing (luxury chalets). Camping rates are R150 for up to two people. Note that these are the minimum rates even if there's only one person booking the accommodation. There's also a conservation levy, which is paid per person per day in the park. **Pros:** great value; you get to enter the game area before the main gates open and go on night drives. **Cons:** the shop has only basic supplies; the rondavels have shared cooking facilities. ☎ *012/428–9111* ⊕ *www.addoelephantpark.com* ➪ *30 chalets, 5 tents, 2 cottages, 2 guesthouses, 10 campsites, 10 cabins, 6 rondavels, 20 caravan sites* ⌂ *In-room: a/c (some), kitchen, no TV (some)* ▤ *AE, DC, MC, V* ⏼*EP.*

$$ 🏠 **Gorah Elephant Camp.** A private concession within the main section of Addo, this lodge has accommodations in spacious, luxurious tents with thick thatch canopies that are furnished in colonial-era antiques. Each tent has an en-suite bathroom with shower and a private deck with views. The lodge itself, a gracious old farmhouse dating from 1856, overlooks a watering hole, so it's possible to watch elephants, buffalo, and other animals from your lunch table or the veranda. Everything is understated yet seriously stylish, including the swimming-pool area, and the cuisine and service are outstanding. There's no electricity (although solar lamps are more than adequate), and dinner is served by romantic candlelight, either on the veranda or in the splendid dining room. The lodge operates two game drives a day, and the Web site has interesting updates on the animals viewed on recent game drives. **Pros:** the food and service are top-notch; guests are not required to sit together at meals. **Cons:** the wind can make the tents noisy at night; rooms do not have bathtubs. ☎ *044/501–1111* ⊕ *www.hunterhotels.com* ➪ *11 tents* ⌂ *In-room: safe, no TV. In-hotel: restaurant, room service, pool, laundry service, Internet terminal, Wi-Fi hotspot, no kids under 10* ▤ *AE, DC, MC, V* ⏼*AI.*

¢ 🏠 **Hitgeheim Country Lodge.** This lovely lodge is set on a steep cliff overlooking the Sundays River and the town of Addo. Classically decorated rooms graced with lovely antiques are in separate thatch buildings, all with verandas overlooking the river. The bathrooms are spacious and luxuriously appointed with large tubs and enormous shower stalls. Some rooms have indoor and outdoor showers. Birds frolic in the natural vegetation that has been allowed to grow up to the edge of the verandas, and tame buck often wander around the garden. Hitgeheim (pronounced *hitch*-ee-hime) is situated on an eco-reserve and you can go for walks to observe birdlife and perhaps view some of the 11 indigenous antelope species found here. The food is fabulous, and most guests opt to stay for the six-course dinners (R325, guests only), although simpler dinner options can be tailor-made to your preferences. The lodge has its own game-viewing vehicle and guide, which can be

Fodor's Choice
★

5

booked at an extra cost, and can also organize elephant-back riding and day-trips to the nearby Big Five game reserves. **Pros:** personal touches, such as a turndown service and luxury bath products by the South African company Charlotte Rhys; friendly and helpful owners. **Cons:** not for independent travelers, as the owners like to arrange your activities for you; the restaurant is not open to nonguests. ☎ *042/234–0778* ⊕ *www.hitgeheim-addo.co.za* ↝ *8 chalets* ⚄ *In-room: a/c, no phone, safe, refrigerator, no TV. In-hotel: restaurant, bar, pool, laundry service, Internet terminal* ☱ *AE, DC, MC, V* ◉ *BP.*

$ ⊡ **Nguni River Lodge.** Within the scenic Nyati section of Addo and close to the main game area is this stylish lodge notable for its unusual decor. Each room takes its name and theme from a particular color pattern of the indigenous Nguni cattle. Stone, thatch, rough metal sculptures, and, of course, the skins of Nguni cattle work together to produce a funky contemporary interpretation of African architectural styles and legends. Indoor and outdoor showers and private plunge pools increase the living space of the already quite large rooms, and the enormous bathrooms have huge circular tubs. You'll see animals from your room and the open-air reception areas, which look out onto a natural watering hole. The food is cooked mostly on open fires and could best be described as fusion cuisine with an African twist. Two game drives per day are included. You leave your car at the reception just off the tarred road and are taken to the lodge in a 4x4, which means you don't need to drive on bumpy gravel roads. **Pros:** it's tranquil and secluded; you don't have to do your own driving on dirt roads. **Cons:** Internet reception is available only at the reception; the fireplaces in the rooms aren't operational. ☎ *042/235–1022 reservations* ⊕ *www.ngunilodges.co.za* ↝ *8 rooms* ⚄ *In-room: safe, no TV. In-hotel: restaurant, bar, laundry service, Internet terminal, no kids under 8* ☱ *AE, DC, MC, V* ◉ *AI.*

$$ ⊡ **River Bend Country Lodge.** Situated on a 34,594-acre private con-
☺   cession within the Nyati section of Addo, River Bend perfectly balances the idea of a sophisticated, comfortable country house with all the facilities of a game lodge. The spacious public rooms, filled with antiques and comfy couches, are in a beautifully renovated farmhouse and outbuildings. The guest rooms are in individual cottages with private verandas dotted around the lovely gardens; some have outdoor showers and each is uniquely decorated with a different color scheme. In addition to the usual game drives, you can tour the adjacent citrus farm and a small game sanctuary, where you may see animals not found in Addo—giraffes, white rhinos, blue wildebeest, nyala, and impala. There's also a safari villa that sleeps six. **Pros:** kids are welcome, and there's an enclosed playground; the food is excellent, especially the seven-course dinner menu. **Cons:** decor is more English colonial than African; only the honeymoon suite has a plunge pool. ✉ *Box 249, 6105* ☎ *042/233–8000* ⊕ *www.riverbendlodge.co.za* ↝ *8 suites* ⚄ *In-room: a/c, safe, refrigerator, DVD. In-hotel: restaurant, room service, bar, pool, spa, laundry service, Internet terminal, Wi-Fi hotspot* ☱ *AE, DC, MC, V* ◉ *AI.*

SHAMWARI GAME RESERVE

45 km (72 mi) from Port Elizabeth.

In the Eastern Cape, Shamwari Game Reserve is, in every sense of the word, a conservation triumph. Unprofitable farmland has been turned into a successful tourist attraction, wild animals have been reintroduced, and alien vegetation has been, and is still being, eradicated. The reserve is constantly being expanded and now stands at about 62,000 acres. Its mandate is to conserve not only the big impressive animals but also small things: the plants, buildings, history, and culture of the area. Shamwari has been named the World's Leading Conservation Company and Safari Lodge at the World Travel Awards for the past 12 years, and wildlife manager Dr. Johan Joubert, now the wildlife director for the Mantis Group, was voted one of South Africa's top 10 conservationists by the Endangered Wildlife Trust in 1999. ☎ *041/407–1000* ⊕ *www.shamwari.com.*

☉ Part of the reserve has been set aside as the **Born Free Centres** (there's
Fodor's Choice one in the northern part and one in the southern part of the reserve).
★ Here African animals rescued from around the world are allowed to roam in reasonably large enclosures for the rest of their lives, as they cannot safely be returned to the wild. Although these are interesting tourist attractions, the main purpose is educational, and about 500 local schoolchildren tour the centers every month. ⊕ *www.bornfree.org.*

GETTING HERE AND AROUND

The closest airport to Shamwari Game Reserve is Port Elizabeth (PLZ) airport, about 72 mi (45 km) away. Small and easy to navigate, the airport is served daily by South African Airways, SA Airlink, Kulula, and 1time. Flights arrive from Cape Town (1 hour) and Johannesburg (1½ hours). From here it's best to rent your own car, as there isn't any reliable public transport. If you are flying into Port Elizabeth and visiting only Shamwari, it may be easier to arrange an airport transfer with the reserve. As with all of the luxury game reserves, it's advised that you arrive by midday so you can check in and have lunch before the afternoon game drive.

WHERE TO STAY

$$ 🏕 **Bayethe Tented Lodge.** Huge air-conditioned safari tents under thatch create characterful, comfortable accommodations, and private decks with plunge pools overlook the Buffalo River. One tent is wheelchair accessible. Suites, which are separated from the other rooms by the reception area and a walk of a hundred yards or so, are huge and impressive. Gleaming light wood floors, fireplaces, and an enormous deck with the most beautiful loungers all contribute to a sense of restrained style and opulence. As at all the lodges at Shamwari, you sit with your game ranger and other guests for breakfast and dinner. **Pros:** each tent has an amazing outside shower and hammock for napping; tents have fabulous bathrooms; the king-size beds have 400-thread-count sheets

that immediately make you feel relaxed and pampered. **Cons:** dinner includes a barbecue every second night; there's no Wi-Fi. ☎ *041/407–1000* ⊕ *www.shamwari.com* ⇴ *12 tents* ⌂ *In-room: safe, refrigerator, no TV (some). In-hotel: bar, pool, laundry service, Internet terminal, no kids under 12* ▤ *AE, DC, MC, V* ⏍ *AI.*

$$ ⛺ **Eagles Cragg.** Very different from the other Shamwari options, this

Fodor's Choice sleek, modern lodge makes use of light wood, pale sandstone, and

★ stainless-steel finishes. It's light and airy and spacious. All rooms have indoor and outdoor showers and private decks with plunge pools. Glass walls fold away to bring the feel of the bush into the room. You may also spot a movie star along with the wildlife; a number of celebrities have stayed here. As with all the lodges at Shamwari, breakfast and dinner are taken communally with your guide and other guests. Dinner alternates between a traditional South African braai cooked on open fires and an à la carte menu. **Pros:** a carefully selected choice of top local wines and spirits is included; the rooms are enormous. **Cons:** the reception areas are very large and can feel impersonal; rooms can be chilly in winter. ☎ *041/407–1000* ⊕ *www.shamwari.com* ⇴ *9 suites* ⌂ *In-room: a/c, safe, refrigerator, no TV. In-hotel: bar, spa, laundry service, Internet terminal, no kids under 16* ▤ *AE, DC, MC, V* ⏍ *AI.*

$$ ⛺ **Lobengula Lodge.** Rooms are set around a central lawn and pool area but face outward for privacy. Thatch roofs and earth tones are part of the African decor. All rooms have outdoor and indoor showers and open onto a private veranda. Two rooms and the suite have private plunge pools. Meals are served around a fireplace, and you may choose wines from the extensive cellar. **Pros:** there are only six rooms, so it feels very exclusive; service is top-notch. **Cons:** only three rooms have private pools; meals are taken communally with other guests and your ranger. ☎ *041/407–1000* ⊕ *www.shamwari.com* ⇴ *6 suites* ⌂ *In-room: safe, refrigerator. In-hotel: bar, pool, gym, spa, laundry service, Internet terminal, no kids under 16* ▤ *AE, DC, MC, V* ⏍ *AI.*

KWANDWE PRIVATE GAME RESERVE

38 km (24 mi) northeast of Grahamstown.

Fodor's Choice Kwandwe Private Game Reserve is tucked away in the Eastern Cape,

★ near the quaint, historic cathedral city of Grahamstown. More than a decade ago, the area was ravaged farmland and goat-ridden semidesert. Today it is a conservation triumph—more than 55,000 acres of various vegetation types and scenic diversity, including rocky outcrops, great plains, thorn thickets, forests, desert scrub, and the Great Fish River— that's home to more than 7,000 mammals, including the Big Five. Your chances of seeing the elusive black rhino are very good, and it's likely you'll see game you don't always see elsewhere, such as the black wildebeest, the black-footed cat, caracal, Cape grysbok, and many rare and endangered birds. Kwandwe is also known for its nocturnal animals, so it's worth opting for a night drive, during which you stand a pretty good chance of unusual sightings like aardwolf, aardvark, porcupine, genet, and other creatures of the night.

Kwandwe means "place of the blue crane" in Xhosa, and you may well see South Africa's national bird on any of your thrilling game drives. If you come in winter, you'll see one of nature's finest floral displays, when thousands of scarlet, orange, and fiery-red aloes are in bloom, attended by colorful sunbirds. ☎*011/809–4300* ⊕*www. kwandwereserve.co.za.*

GETTING HERE AND AROUND

Kwandwe is a 20-minute drive from Grahamstown, and air and road shuttles are available from Port Elizabeth, which is a two-hour drive.

WHERE TO STAY

There are four great places to stay within the reserve; guests can choose between classic colonial or modern chic. You'll be cosseted, pampered, well-fed, and taken on some memorable wildlife adventures. Kwandwe is a member of the prestigious Relais & Châteaux group. All the lodges listed here have cable TV in a communal area as well as a safari shop, and massages are available upon request. The child-friendly lodges have movies and games. In the single-use lodges, these are hidden away in a cupboard, so you can keep their existence a secret from your brood unless a rainy day makes them essential.

$–$$ **Ecca Lodge.** This classy lodge combines understated modern elegance with Scandinavian chic. High, white, open-raftered, wooden ceilings top paneled walls, and the furnishings complement and enhance the views outside the huge windows and viewing decks. Orange cushions echo the flowering aloes, soft greens repeat the surrounding wilderness, and the pillars of rough-hewn rock with russet-colored rugs at their base recall the kopjes and wildflowers that dot the reserve. Your bedroom may qualify as one of the biggest you will ever sleep in. Keep the curtains facing your king-size bed open at night so that you're woken by a dazzling dawn. Chill by the rim-flow lodge pool, or just hang out at your private plunge pool with only the birds and the sounds of the wilderness to keep you company. You'll dine in a big airy dining room with an interactive kitchen. Watch the chef whip up *bobotie* (spicy minced meat with savory custard topping)—the house special—toss a pancake or three, or stir some succulent sauce. If you find time, watch videos or read in the library or games room, or just sit on your massive wraparound deck and listen to the silence. **Pros:** superb guides; attentive well-trained local staff; a must-see community center and village. **Cons:** temperamental showers that ricochet between scalding hot and freezing cold; no tea and coffee in the rooms. ☎*011/809–4300* ⊕*www. kwandwereserve.co.za* ⇄ *6 rooms* ⚐ *In-room: safe, refrigerator, no TV. In-hotel: pool, children's programs (ages 0–12), laundry service, Internet terminal, Wi-Fi hotspot* ⊟ *AE, DC, MC, V* ⦿*FAP.*

$$$

Fodor's Choice

★

Great Fish River Lodge. If you have an artistic eye, you'll immediately notice how the curving thatch roof of the main buildings echoes the mountain skyline opposite. Steps lead down to the public areas—dining room, comfortable lounges, and library—that sprawl along the banks of the Great Fish River. Floor-to-ceiling windows bathe the stone walls, Persian rugs, fireplaces, deep armchairs, bookcases, and old prints and photographs in clear light. At night the stars provide a dazzling display as lions call over the noise of the rushing river. All the spacious en-suite bedrooms overlook the river, and you'll be hard put to tear yourself away from your personal plunge-pool-with-a-view to go chasing game. The lodge is permeated with a comfortable colonial ambience—the 21st century has never seemed so far away. **Pros:** spectacular river views; unusual habitats (it's not often you find lions clambering up and down rocky outcrops); ultrafriendly staff. **Cons:** avoid if you're a bit unsteady as there are lots of tricky steps. ☎ *011/809–4300* ⊕ *www.kwandwereserve.co.za* ⟿ *9 suites* ⚱ *In-room: safe, refrigerator, no TV. In-hotel: room service, bar, laundry service, Internet terminal, Wi-Fi hotspot, no kids under 12* ▤ *AE, DC, MC, V* ⊠ *FAP.*

$$$

Melton Manor. Slightly bigger than Uplands, the Manor accommodates up to eight guests and offers the same superb service and exclusivity. It's a farmhouse in contemporary style with handmade clay chandeliers, cowhide rugs, vintage ball-and-claw armoires, and huge bathrooms with claw-foot tubs. Built around a small central lawn with a swimming pool, the four spacious rooms look outward into the bush for privacy. You have your own chef and game ranger, and you call the shots. This is a great option for families, as you can take the little ones on game drives or leave them behind with babysitters. It's also a good deal for three couples traveling together (and a great deal for four). **Pros:** exclusivity deluxe; great food. **Cons:** as you're in your own group you miss out on the opportunity to meet other lodge guests. ☎ *011/809–4300* ⊕ *www.kwandwereserve.co.za* ⟿ *4 rooms* ⚱ *In-room: no TV. In-hotel: bar, pool, laundry service, Internet terminal, Wi-Fi hotspot* ▤ *AE, DC, MC, V* ⊠ *FAP.*

$$$$

Uplands Homestead. If you're a small family or a bunch of friends and want to have a genuine, very exclusive, out-of-Africa experience, then stay at this restored 1905 colonial farmhouse. There are three spacious en-suite bedrooms with balconies furnished in early Settlers style, and you'll have your own tracking and guiding team, plus a dedicated chef. The game experience is excellent, and you'll have memorable moments sitting around a blazing log fire as you swap fireside tales in the evening. Try one of Kwandwe's specialist safaris that range from learning about carnivore research to walking trails and excursions revealing the colorful past of this area, which is steeped in cultural, military, and archaeological history. **Pros:** perfect for that special family occasion or friends' reunion. **Cons:** you're in very close proximity to other guests, so it can be a bummer if you don't mesh well. ☎ *011/809–4300* ⊕ *www.kwandwereserve.co.za* ⟿ *3 rooms* ⚱ *In-room: no TV. In-hotel: bar, pool, laundry service, Internet terminal* ▤ *AE, DC, MC, V* ⊠ *FAP.*

AFRICAN MUSIC & DANCE

Talking drums echo in the forests and over the plains. The pounding of hands on taut animal-skin–covered logs is heard and interpreted by tribes' versed in jungle telegraphy. This form of dialogue is outlawed, but the art survives and modern African music is born. The beat is the essential component of the music, and by extension, of African dance.

African music and dance are all about conveying moods and emotions. They're also an integral part of ritual and ceremony. Rhythm is the key. Interlocking rhythms follow a time-honored, prescribed pattern. Drumming as a spiritual release and a team-building exercise has now become cool in Europe and the United States. African singing is easily recognized for its polyphony, where several parts, or voices, take turns producing wonderful harmonies. African choirs, like the Soweto Gospel Choir (above), are world-famous. Praise-singers are common in ceremonies where high-ranking African dignitaries are present. Dance is polycentric—different parts of the body are used independently—and conveys images of love, war, coming of age, welcome, and rites of passage.

Musicologists lament that traditional forms of indigenous music and dance are being replaced by Western genres, but fortunately, African rhythms are eternal.

THE SOUNDS OF AFRICA

When you think traditional African music, think percussion (drums and xylophones), strings (the mouth bow), and winds (horns and whistles). You should also think of trumpets, guitars, pianos, or saxophones, as these have been absorbed into African jazz.

DJEMBE DRUMS

Djembe drums, originally from Mali, come in various sizes and are copied and manufactured all over the world.

TALKING DRUMS

These drums are among the oldest instruments in West Africa. They are typically hourglass-shaped, with goat- or lizard-skin drum heads. The two heads are joined by strings or thongs, and their sound can be manipulated. The player, who puts the drum under his shoulder and beats the drum with a stick, can also tighten or loosen the connectors to create a sound similar to speech. Messages can thus be conveyed over considerable distances.

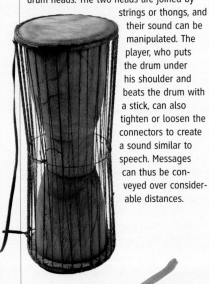

MBIRA

The *mbira*, or thumb-piano, has been played for more than 1,000 years at religious and social events. It consists of 22 to 28 metal keys or strips mounted atop a resonating box or shell.

KHOISAN MOUTH BOW

Derived from the hunting bow of the Kalahari Bushmen, the instrument dates back more than 40,000 years. You can still find them—usually as tourist souvenirs—all over the continent.

KUDU HORN

Made from the horn of the male greater kudu antelope, this instrument was originally used in hunting. Today you'll probably hear it only when you're called to meals at your safari lodge.

CONCERTINA

Though the concertina arrived with European settlers, it was absorbed into township music, as well as Boeremusiek (Afrikaans folk music). Present-day Afrikaans dance bands use the instrument in *sakkie-sakkie*, a style of music that accompanies sakkie, a South African dance.

MARIMBAS

Marimbas, or African xylophones, are found all over Southern and East Africa; the bigger the instrument, the deeper the sound. Originally part of the Lozi and Chopi tribal traditions in Zambia and Mozambique, they're now used in everything from pop songs to national anthems.

PENNYWHISTLE

The tin or pennywhistle, once used by cattle herders, is now an integral part of African music, specifically *kwela* (street music with jazz undertones).

MUSICIANS

Music and political activism have always gone hand in hand in South Africa. Under Apartheid, black music was ignored by music companies and radio stations, though it continued to thrive underground. American swing jazz had a huge influence on the music community in the 1950s, which soon evolved into an African jazz form known as *mbaqanga*, or "home-made."

In the 1960s, radio exposure forced the government to restrict lyrics and censor all songs considered subversive. This resulted in many jazz musicians leaving the country, among them Hugh Masekela and Miriam Makeba. After the collapse of Apartheid in the '90s, many of the exiled artists finally returned home. Today South Africa's Yvonne Chaka Chaka is one of the country's best known vocalists, singing everything from disco to R&B; her fans call her Princess Africa.

LADYSMITH BLACK MAMBAZO
Formed in 1964 by Joseph Shabalala, the Grammy-award–winning vocal group (*above*) came to world prominence when it joined Paul Simon on his 1986 album *Graceland*. The group performed at Nelson Mandela's inauguration in 1994 and continues to record and perform today, spreading a message of peace, love, and harmony.

MIRIAM MAKEBA
The late Miriam Makeba (*below*) began her professional career in the 1950s when she joined the Manhattan Brothers and later started her own, all-female group, the Skylarks. Her international hits "Pata Pata" and "The Click Song" focused world attention on South Africa's Apartheid policy. She performed with Harry Belafonte and Paul Simon and became known worldwide as Mama Africa.

HUGH MASEKELA
After much musical success in the 1950s, Masekela (*left*) fled South Africa in 1961 and studied music in London and New York. He had several hits in the United States, including "Grazin' in the Grass," which sold four million copies in 1968. Maseleka has performed with everyone from Louis Armstrong to Paul Simon and is considered by many to be a master of African music.

AFRICAN DANCING

Gumboot dancers perform during a New Year's eve carnival in Johannesburg, South Africa

Wherever groups of people come together in Africa, be it at weddings, funerals, or parties, you can be sure that there will be dancing. It's an essential part of the African psyche, one that is a form of expression and release for many Africans. The South Africa protest dance, the *toi-toi*, is synonymous with marches and strikes. Dancing is also synonymous with rhythm, and rhythm means drums. The drum symbolizes life and emotion; it beats as the heart of the community.

GUMBOOT DANCING

Gumboot dancing started in the late 1800s as a form of communication between mine workers. Today this ground-stomping dance is a spectacular art form that's performed all over Southern Africa. The dance is a specialty of Black Umfolozi, a troupe from Zimbabwe, and "Gumboots," a track from Paul Simon's *Graceland* album, featured South Africa's Boyoyo Boys.

KWAITO DANCING

The 1990s and the release of Nelson Mandela saw the creation of *kwaito*, a form of hip-hop music created on computers and synthesizers. It's widely known as the voice of the ghetto. The hugely popular kwaito dance, a kind of synchronized group tap-dancing, soon followed.

South Africa's leading kwaito group, Mandoza, performs before thousands of fans on the sand at Durban's North Beach

5

IN FOCUS AFRICAN MUSIC & DANCE

GATEWAY CITIES

South Africa's two hub cities are Johannesburg and Cape Town. It's almost certain that you will arrive and leave the country from one of these two cities. Make the most of your time in transit—there's a lot you can do in 24 hours, or even less.

JOHANNESBURG

Johannesburg epitomizes South Africa's paradoxical make-up—it's rich, poor, innovative, and historical. Traders hawk *skop* (boiled sheep's head, split open and eaten off newspaper) in front of polished glass buildings, as taxis jockey for position in rush hour. *Sangomas* (traditional healers) lay out herbs and roots next to the pavement tents of roadside barbers, and you never seem to be far from a woman selling *vetkoek* (dollops of deep-fried dough), beneath billboards advertising investment banks or cellphones.

Jo'burg was born as a mining camp, and its downtown area—the oldest part—is a jumbled grid of one-way streets heading in opposite directions reflecting its hasty start to life. While the city center is experiencing a revival, it's not somewhere that all visitors choose to visit close up. The attractions in or close to the city center include the Nelson Mandela Bridge, MuseuMAfrica and the SAB World of Beer in the Newtown area, the Johannesburg Art Gallery, the Standard Bank Gallery and Diagonal Street in the downtown area, and Constitution Hill, the Civic Theatre, and the Johannesburg Planetarium in Braamfontein.

PLANNING

WHEN TO GO

Jo'burgers boast that they enjoy the best climate in the world: not too hot in summer (mid-September–mid-April), not too cold in winter (mid-April–mid-September) and not prone to sudden temperature changes. Summer may have the edge, though: it's when the gardens and open spaces are at their most beautiful.

GETTING HERE AND AROUND

O.R. Tambo International Airport (formerly Johannesburg International Airport) is linked to the city by a fast highway, which is always busy but especially before 9 AM and between 4 and 7 PM. The Gautrain, a high-speed train, connects O.R. Tambo to Sandton in 12 minutes (and is planned to connect Johannesburg and Pretoria in 2011) Magic Bus offers private transfers to all major Sandton hotels (R350 per vehicle, plus R40 per person) as well as shared transfers elsewhere in Johannesburg. The journey takes 30 minutes to an hour, longer in rush-hour traffic. Airport Link will ferry you anywhere in Johannesburg in a Toyota Camry or Mercedes minibus for R365 per person. Legend Tours and Transfers offers prearranged shared-ride transfers starting from R490 from O.R. Tambo. Wilro Tours runs from the airport to Sandton (R645 for three people, plus R250 if you arrive between 9 PM and 6 AM). In addition, scores of licensed taxis line up outside the airport terminal. By law they must have a working meter. Expect to pay about R250–R450 for a trip to Sandton. Negotiate a price before you get in a taxi.

Most hotels offer transfers. Prices vary, depending on where you are staying, but plan on R350–R400 ($35–$40) for a ride from the airport to Sandton hotels, and about R275 or R300 ($28–$30) for a hotel or guesthouse in Rosebank or Melrose. Most will allow you to add the charge to your bill, so you needn't worry about paying in cash.

It's virtually impossible to see anything of the Johannesburg area without a car. Your best bet is to rent one, decide what you want to see, and get a good road map or rent a GPS navigator. If you're reluctant to drive yourself, book a couple of day or half-day tours that will pick you up from where you're staying or from a central landmark.

Shared minibus taxis form the backbone of Jo'burg's transportation for ordinary commuters, but you should avoid using them since they're often not roadworthy, drivers can be irresponsible, and it's difficult to know where they're going without consulting a local. Car taxis, though more expensive, are easier to use. They have stands at the airport and the train station, but otherwise you must phone for one. Ask the taxi company how long it will take the taxi to get to you. Taxis should be licensed and have a working meter. Meters start at R10 and charge R10 per km. Expect to pay about R350 to the airport from town or Sandton and about R200 to the city center from Sandton.

⇨ *For information on airlines or roadside assistance or national car-rental companies, see the Planning section at the beginning of the chapter.*

TIMING

If you have only one day in Jo'burg, take a tour of Soweto and visit the Apartheid Museum, then stop by Constitution Hill if you have a chance. Spend the evening having dinner at an African-style restaurant, such as Moyo. If you have a second day, focus on what interests you most: perhaps a trip to the Cradle of Humankind, where you can explore the sites of some of the world's most significant paleontological discoveries; a trip to Cullinan, where you can visit a working diamond mine; or a fun day or two at Sun City.

TOURS

Several companies offer general-interest tours of Johannesburg, some of which are customizable. Expect to pay over R1,000 for a full-day tour, double that for a single-person tour. Small-group tours tend to be more expensive than larger group tours.

A hop-on, hop-off tour (R180; valid 12 hours) with Tour Network is a good way to see Johannesburg's main sights in a day, with plenty of stops along the way. Tours leave several times a day from Montecasino, Fourways. Africa Explore offers full-day and half-day tours; the full package (from R1040 per person per day on a group tour to R1,885 per person for a single-person tour) includes the Kromdraai Gold Mine, Sterkfontein Caves, and the Rhino and Lion Park.

Tours of Soweto are offered by many of the *above* operators as well as Jimmy's Face to Face Tours. Information on Soweto tours can also be obtained from the Soweto Tourism Association and ⊕ *www.soweto. co.za*, a private initiative of tour operator KDR Travel.

SAFETY AND PRECAUTIONS

Johannesburg is notorious for being a dangerous city—it's quite common to hear about serious crimes such as armed robbery and murder. Even South Africans fear it, regarding it as some Americans regard New York City: big and bad. That said, it's safe for visitors who avoid dangerous areas and take reasonable precautions. △ **Never, ever visit a township or squatter camp on your own.** Carjacking is so prevalent that there are permanent street signs marking those areas that are most dangerous. Order a car service or transportation from your hotel for trips in and around the city. △ **It's inadvisable to drive yourself in and around the city, as certain areas are known carjacking spots.**

VISITOR INFORMATION

The helpful Gauteng Tourism Authority has information on the whole province, but more detailed information is often available from local tourism associations—for example, the Soweto Accommodation Association lists more than 20 lodgings. The Johannesburg Tourism Company has a good Web site, with information about Johannesburg and up-to-date listings of events happening around the city. The City of Johannesburg's Web site lists local events, news, service advisories, and more.

ESSENTIALS

Airport Transfers Airport Link (☎ *011/792–2017 or 083/625–5090* ⊕ *www. airportlink.co.za*). **Legend Tours and Transfers** (☎ *021/704–9140* ⊕ *www. legendtours.co.za*). **Magic Bus** (☎ *011/548–0822 or 011/394–6902* ⊕ *www. magicbus.co.za*). **Wilro Tours** (☎ *011/789–9688* ⊕ *www.wilrotours.co.za*).

General Interest Tours Africa Explore (☎ *011/917–1999* ⊕ *www.africa-explore.co.za*). **JMT Tours and Safaris** (☎ *010/233–0073* ⊕ *www.jmttours.co.za*). **Johannesburg Tourism Company** (☎ *011/342–4316* ⊕ *www.joburgtourism. com*). **Palaeo-Tours** (☎ *011/214–0700* ⊕ *www.palaeotours.com*). **Tour Network** (☎ *011/447–0432*). **Springbok Atlas** (☎ *011/396–1053* ⊕ *www.springbokatlas. com*). **Wilro Tours** (☎ *011/789–9688* ⊕ *www.wilrotours.co.za*).

Taxis Maxi Taxi (☎ *011/648–1212*). **Rose Taxis** (☎ *011/403–9625 or 011/403–0000* ⊕ *www.rosetaxis.com*). **Safe Cab** (☎ *086/166–5566*).

Township Tours Jimmy's Face to Face Tours (☎ *011/331–6109* ⊕ *www. face2face.co.za*). **Soweto.co.za** (☎ *011/326–1700* ⊕ *www.soweto.co.za*).

Visitor Info City of Johannesburg (⊕ www.joburg.org.za). **Gauteng Tourism Authority** (☎ 0860/428–8364 ⊕ www.gauteng.net). **Soweto Accommodation Association** (☎ 011/936–8123).

EXPLORING

The Greater Johannesburg metropolitan area is massive—more than 1,600 square km (635 square mi)—incorporating the large municipalities of Randburg and Sandton to the north. Most of the sights are just north of the city center, which degenerated badly in the 1990s but is now being revamped.

About 20 km (12 mi) to the south of downtown Johannesburg lies the vast township of Soweto, where you can take a township tour and visit the Hector Pieterson Museum.

FAMOUS RESIDENTS

What other place on Earth can boast of having had two Nobel laureates living within a block of each other? For most of his adult life, Anglican Archbishop Desmond Tutu lived on Vilakazi Street, in Johannesburg's Orlando West neighborhood. For most of that time, his close neighbor would have been an attorney named Nelson Rolihlahla Mandela, had he not spent most of *his* adult life incarcerated on Robben Island. The archbishop's home is a gray, two-story affair, which is not open to the public, but you can visit the nearby Mandela house, which became a museum in 1997.

To the south, in Ormonde, are the Apartheid Museum and Gold Reef City; the sprawling township of Soweto is farther to the southwest. Johannesburg's northern suburbs are its most affluent. Rosebank and Sandton are the city's shopping meccas.

■TIP→ If you only have 24 hours, spend the evening at Newtown, and the next day take any one of the numerous half-day or full-day tours on offer.

Fodor's Choice ★ **Apartheid Museum.** The Apartheid Museum takes you on a journey through South African apartheid history—from the entrance, where you pass through a turnstile according to your assigned skin color (black or white), to the myriad historical, brutally honest, and sometimes shocking photographs, video displays, films, documents, and other exhibits. It's an emotional, multilayered journey. As you walk chronologically through the apartheid years and eventually reach the country's first steps to freedom, with democratic elections in 1994, you experience a taste of the pain and suffering with which so many South Africans had to live. A room with 121 ropes with hangman's knots hanging from the ceiling—one rope for each political prisoner executed in the apartheid era—is especially chilling. ⊠ *Northern Pkwy. and Gold Reef Rd., Ormonde* ☎ *011/309–4700* ⊕ *www.apartheidmuseum.org* ☞ *R50* ⊗ *Tues.–Sun. 10–5.*

Fodor's Choice ★ **Cradle of Humankind.** This World Heritage Site stretches over an area of about 470 square km (181 square mi), with about 300 caves. Inside these caves, paleoanthropologists have discovered thousands of fossils of hominids and other animals, dating back about 4 million years. The most famous of these fossils are Mrs. Ples, a skull more than 2 million years old, and Little Foot, a skeleton more than 3 million years old. Although the Cradle does not have the world's oldest hominid fossils, it does have the most complete fossil record of human evolution of anywhere on earth and has produced more hominid fossils than anywhere else.

Archaeological finds at the Cradle of Humankind include 1.7 million-year-old stone tools, the oldest recorded in southern Africa. At Swartkrans, near Sterkfontein, a collection of burned bones tells us that our ancestors could manage fire more than 1 million years ago.

Not all the fossil sites in the Cradle are open to the public, but a tour of the Sterkfontein Caves and the visitor center provides an excellent overview of the archaeological work in progress, and a trip to Maropeng, a much larger visitor center 10 km (6 mi) from the Sterkfontein Caves, provides even more background. Special tours to fossil sites with expert guides can be booked at either of the visitor centers.

Public transport to the Cradle of Humankind area is limited, so using a rental car or transfer with a tour company is best, and some hotels in the area arrange transport on request. The Cradle of Humankind is about a 90-minute drive northwest of Johannesburg and is relatively well signposted once you get off the N1 highway at the 14th Avenue off-ramp. **Maropeng Visitor Centre** (☎ *014/577–9000* ⊕ *www.maropeng. co.za*) provides information about the various sites in the Cradle of Humankind.

☟ **Gold Reef City.** This theme park lets you step back in time to 1880s Johannesburg and see why it became known as the City of Gold. One of the city's most popular attractions (avoid it on public holidays or weekends), it has good rides that kids will enjoy and is based on the real history of Jo'burg. In addition to riding the Anaconda, a scary roller coaster on which you hang under the track, feet in the air, you can (for an additional fee) descend into an old gold mine and see molten gold being poured, or watch a gumboot dance, a riveting dance developed by black miners. The reconstructed streets are lined with operating Victorian-style shops and restaurants. And for those with money to burn, the large, glitzy Gold Reef Village Casino beckons across the road. ⊠ *Gold Reef Rd., 6 km (4 mi) south of city center, Ormonde* ☎ *011/248–6800* ⊕ *www.goldreefcity.co.za* ⊠ *R140* ☉ *Wed.–Sun. (except for school holidays) 9:30–5; mine tours 10–4 every hour.*

Hector Pieterson Memorial and Museum. Opposite Holy Cross Church, a stone's throw from the former homes of Nelson Mandela and Archbishop Desmond Tutu on Vilakazi Street, the Hector Pieterson Memorial and Museum is a crucial landmark. Pieterson, a 12-year-old scholar, was the first victim of police fire on June 16, 1976, when schoolchildren rose up to protest their second-rate Bantu (black) education system. The memorial is a paved area with benches for reflection, an inscribed stone and simple water feature; inside the museum are grainy photographs and films that bring that fateful day to life. Small granite blocks in the museum courtyard are a tribute to the 350 children among the more than 500 people who died during this violent time. ⊠ *Khumalo and Phela Sts., Orlando West* ☎ *011/536–2253* ⊕ *www.joburg.org.za* ⊠ *R25* ☉ *Mon.–Fri. 10–5, Sat. and Sun. 10–4:30.*

WHERE TO EAT

Jo'burgers love eating out, and there are thousands of restaurants scattered throughout the city to satisfy them. Some notable destinations for food include Melrose Arch, Parkhurst, Sandton, the South (for its Portuguese cuisine), Melville, and Chinatown in the CBD (Central Business District). Try asking locals what they recommend; eating out is the most popular form of entertainment in Johannesburg, and everyone has a list of favorite spots, which changes often. Also check out the restaurants recommended on the official Johannesburg Web site (⊕ *www. johannesburg.gov*). Smart-casual dress is a good bet. Many establishments are closed on Sunday nights and Monday.

$$$$
STEAKHOUSE

✕**The Butcher Shop and Grill.** This is a good place for hungry meat lovers. It specializes in prime South African meat aged to perfection by Alan Pick, the butcher-owner. An operating butchery features prominently in the restaurant, and special cuts can be ordered for the meal or to take home. Kudu, springbok, ostrich, and other game are often on the specials list, and only the most tender cuts are served. For lighter choices, try the chicken or linefish. Jelly and custard pudding is a favorite with regulars. There's an excellent wine cellar. ⊠ *Nelson Mandela Sq., Shop 30, Sandton* ☎ *011/784–8676* ⊕ *www.thebutchershop.co.za* ▭ *AE, DC, MC, V.*

$$$
AFRICAN

✕**Gramadoelas at the Market Theatre.** Crossing the threshold here is like stepping into a strange old museum: African artifacts and mirrors litter the huge room. Established in 1967, Gramadoelas has hosted an impressive list of guests including Nelson Mandela, Elton John, the Queen of England, Bill and Hillary Clinton, and many others. The restaurant specializes in South African fare, but does have a few dishes from farther north in the continent. Try *umngqusho* (beans and whole corn) or, if you're feeling adventurous, *mogodu* (unbleached ox tripe) or *masonja* (mopane worms, or large, edible caterpillars). Traditional Cape Malay dishes include *bredie* (lamb casserole in a tomato sauce) and bobotie (a spicy casserole of minced lamb with savory custard topping). Meat lovers will like the selection of game meats such as the kudu (antelope) panfried with dried fruit and spices. The popular buffet is available most evenings for R250. ⊠ *Market Theatre, Margaret Mcingana St., Newtown* ☎ *011/838–6960* ⊕ *www.gramadoelas.co.za* ▭ *AE, DC, MC, V* ⊗ *Closed Sun. No lunch Mon.*

$$$$
ITALIAN
Fodor'sChoice
★

✕**La Cucina di Ciro.** This is one of the best Italian restaurants in Johannesburg. The owner and chef, Ciro, says the cuisine is "very much my own," which means you can find truly inventive dishes on his seasonally changing menu. The pasta is made on the premises. His most popular dishes are the duck and the variety of homemade pasta dishes, especially the seafood pasta. Be warned: Ciro will chat with complete strangers as if they've been friends for years. La Cucina di Ciro serves breakfast, lunch, and dinner. ⊠ *43 7th Ave., Parktown North* ☎ *011/442–5187* ⊕ *www.lacucinadiciro.co.za* ⌲ *Reservations essential* ▭ *AE, DC, MC, V* ⊗ *Closed Mon.*

5

$$$$
CONTINENTAL
Fodor'sChoice
★

✕**Linger Longer.** Set in the spacious grounds of a grand old home in Wierda Valley, in the business center of Sandton, Linger Longer has an air of gracious elegance. The wooden floors, colored walls, and striped curtains give this restaurant a Wedgewood-like quality. Though upscale, this restaurant has a warm atmosphere, and the

WORD OF MOUTH

"I think so highly of a restaurant very close to Sandton called Linger Longer that I have even called from the USA to book a table. It is rather formal and expensive, but a wonderful experience." —Zambezi

hospitable staff and personal service of chef Walter Ulz attract local and international diners. The menu is varied and includes an array of seasonal specials. Start with the prawn firecracker, followed by the Asian split duck or the lamb rack cooked with crushed *chermoula*, a North African spice mix. The delicious porcini ravioli is the best choice on the vegetarian main menu, and the trio of sorbets is a nice finale. There's also a good wine list. ✉ *58 Wierda Rd., Wierda Valley, Sandton* ☎ *011/884–0465* ⌖ *Reservations essential* ▭ *AE, DC, MC, V* ☉ *Closed Sun. No lunch Sat.*

$$$$
AFRICAN
Fodor'sChoice
★

✕**Moyo.** From the food and decor to the music and live entertainment, Moyo is strongly African in theme. The focus of the rich and varied menu is pan-African, incorporating tandoori cookery from northern Africa, Cape Malay influences such as lentil bobotie, Moroccan-influenced tasty *tagines* (stews with lamb, chicken, fish, or seven vegetables), and ostrich burgers and other dishes representing South Africa. Diners are often entertained by storytellers, face painters, and musicians. The restaurant has four locations (in Johannesburg at Melrose Arch in Melrose North and at Zoo Lake in Parkview, outside Cape Town at the Spier wine estate, and in Durban at the uShaka Pier). At night or in wintertime, Melrose Arch is the best bet of the two Jo'burg outposts. In summer and during the day, the Zoo Lake and Spier branches are nicest. ✉ *Melrose Arch, Shop 5, High St., Melrose North* ☎ *011/684–1477* ⊕ *www.moyo.co.za* ⌖ *Reservations essential* ▭ *AE, DC, MC, V.*

$$$
AFRICAN
★

✕**Wandie's Place.** Wandie's isn't the only good township restaurant, but it's the best known and one of the most popular spots in Jo'burg. The decor is eclectic township (a bit makeshift), and the walls are adorned with signatures and business cards of tourists who have crossed its path. The waiters are smartly dressed in bow ties, and the food is truly African. Meat stews, *imifino* (a leafy African dish), sweet potatoes, beans, corn porridge, traditionally cooked pumpkin, chicken, and tripe are laid out in a buffet in a motley selection of pots and containers. The food is hot, the drinks are cold, and the conversation flows. You may end up here with a tour bus, but it's big enough to cope, and Wandie's now has an on-site guesthouse in case the alcohol flows too much. It's not that difficult to find, and parking is safe, but it's probably better to organize a visit on a guided trip. ✉ *618 Makhalamele St., Dube* ☎ *011/982–2796* ⊕ *www.wandies.co.za* ▭ *AE, DC, MC, V.*

WHERE TO STAY

Many of the hotels are linked to nearby malls and are well policed. Boutique hotels have sprung up everywhere, as have bed-and-breakfasts. Hotels are quieter in December and January, and their rates are often cheaper over this period. Generally, the busy months in Jo'burg are from June to August. Most, if not all, of the good hotels are now in the northern suburbs.

Lodging reviews have been abbreviated in this book. For expanded reviews, please go to Fodors.com.

$$ ⬚ **Clico.** This small, upmarket guesthouse in central Rosebank is a 60-year-old Cape Dutch house with a gracious garden and offers perhaps the best value in an area known for expensive accommodation. **Pros:** 24-hour manned security and CCTV cameras; free Wi-Fi throughout the hotel; the restaurant serves breakfast daily, and lunch and dinner are available upon request. **Cons:** constant noise and dust from construction of the nearby Gautrain rail network; some of the on-site parking spaces are difficult to negotiate; noise from the pool activity travels to the suites. ⊠ *27 Sturdee Ave., at Jellicoe Ave., Rosebank* ☎ *011/252–3300* ⊕ *www.clicoguesthouse.com* ⌁ *9 suites, including 1 room with kitchen* ♿ *In-room: safe, refrigerator, Wi-Fi. In-hotel: pool, laundry service, Internet terminal* ▤ *DC, MC, V* ¶◎¶ *BP.*

$ ⬚ **Crowne Plaza Johannesburg–The Rosebank.** Following a major upgrade in May 2009, this hotel now carries the Crowne Plaza insignia. **Pros:** hip nightspot; great spa and gym. **Cons:** popular with partying locals; toilets in deluxe suites lack privacy. ⊠ *Tyrwhitt and Sturdee Aves., Rosebank* ☎ *011/448–3600* ⊕ *www.therosebank.co.za* ⌁ *318 rooms, 24 suites.* ♿ *In-room: safe, Wi-Fi. In-hotel: 2 restaurants, room service, bar, pool, gym, spa, laundry service, Internet terminal, Wi-Fi hotspot, parking (paid)* ▤ *AE, DC, MC, V* ¶◎¶ *BP.*

$$$ ⬚ **InterContinental Johannesburg O.R. Tambo Airport.** A few paces from international arrivals and adjacent to the car-rental park, this is a good choice for those who have a one-night layover. **Pros:** ideal for those who want to bypass Johannesburg; excellent paid-access arrivals facility with Internet, showers, and pressing facilities free to Diners Club cardholders; great runway views from gym and pool. **Cons:** at the airport; large and impersonal. ⊠ *O.R. Tambo Airport, opposite Terminal 3, Kempton Park* ☎ *011/961–5400* ⊕ *www.intercontinental.com* ⌁ *138 rooms, 2 suites* ♿ *In-room: safe, Internet, Wi-Fi. In-hotel: restaurant, room service, bar, pool, gym, spa, laundry service, Wi-Fi hotspot, parking (paid)* ▤ *AE, DC, MC, V* ¶◎¶ *BP.*

$$ ⬚ One of Johannesburg's newest additions, built for the FIFA 2010 World Cup, this convenient and classy hotel is a minute away from the new Gautrain station (O.R. Tambo is 12 minutes away by the Gautrain) and only a few minutes' walk from Sandton's business district and shopping centres. **Pros:** location, location, location; classy, with all amenities, excellent accommodation. **Cons:** unattractive surroundings. ⌂ *P.O. 653148, Sandton, Johannesburg 2196* ⊠ *Corner Rivonia Rd. and West St., Sandton, Johannesburg2196* ☎ *11/286–1000* ⊕ *www.radissonblu. com* ⌁ *216 rooms* ♿ *In-room: a/c, safe, Internet. In-hotel: restaurant, bar, pool, spa, gym,* ▤ *MC, V* ¶◎¶ *BP.*

5

$$$$ 🖼 **The Saxon.** In the exclusive suburb of Sandhurst, adjacent to the
Fodor's Choice commercial and shopping center of Sandton, the Saxon has repeat-
★ edly received awards for its excellence. **Pros:** possibly the most exclusive address in Gauteng; exceptionally high security; good for business
travelers or high-profile folk who'd rather not see anyone else in the
corridors. **Cons:** some might find the atmosphere a bit snooty; children under 14 not welcome in restaurant. ⊠ *36 Saxon Rd., Sandhurst*
☎ *011/292–6000* ⊕ *www.thesaxon.com* ⇨ *53 suites* ⚷ *In-room: DVD,
Internet, Wi-Fi, pools (some). In-hotel: restaurant, room service, bar,
pools, gym, spa, laundry service, Internet terminal, Wi-Fi hotspot, parking (free)* ⊟ *AE, DC, MC, V* ⏏⚬⎮*BP.*

NIGHTLIFE

Johannesburg comes alive after dark, and whether you are a 24-hour
visitor, rebellious punk rocker, or a suave executive in search of a classy
lounge, there is always something to do. The best place to find out
what's going on is in the "Tonight" section of the **Star** (⊕ *www.tonight.
co.za*), Johannesburg's major daily.

SHOPPING

Whether you're after designer clothes, the latest books or DVDs, high-
quality African art, or glamorous gifts, Johannesburg offers outstanding shopping opportunities. At the city's several markets, bargaining
can get you a great price, although it's not as expected here as in other
countries.

The **African Craft Market**, between the Rosebank Mall and the Zone, has
a huge variety of African crafts from Cape to Cairo, all displayed to
the background beat of traditional African music. ⊠ *Cradock Ave. and
Baker St., Rosebank* ☎ *011/880–2906* ◷ *Daily 9–5.*

Rosebank's **Rooftop Market** has become a Sunday tradition in the city.
More than 600 stalls sell African and Western crafts, antiques, books,
food, art, trinkets, CDs, jewelry, and clothes. Frequently, African musicians, dancers, and other entertainers delight the crowds. ⊠ *Rosebank
Mall, 50 Bath Ave., Rosebank* ☎ *011/442–4488* ◷ *Sun. 9–5.*

CAPE TOWN

If you visit only one place in South Africa, make it Cape Town. Whether
you're partaking of the Capetonian inclination for alfresco fine dining
(the so-called "Mother City" is home to many of the country's best
restaurants) or sipping wine atop Table Mountain, you sense—cor-
rectly—that this is South Africa's most urbane, civilized city.

Here elegant Cape Dutch buildings abut ornate Victorian architecture
and imposing British monuments. In the Bo-Kaap neighborhood, the
call to prayer echoes through cobbled streets lined with houses painted
in bright pastels, while the sweet tang of Malay curry wafts through
the air. Flower sellers, newspapers hawkers, and numerous markets
keep street life pulsing, and every lamppost advertises another festival,
concert, or cultural happening.

But as impressive as Cape Town's urban offerings are, what you'll ultimately recall about this city is the sheer grandeur of its setting—the

"[This] person [was] waiting to sell his goods to a tourist. The colors were so vivid and alive."
—larrya, Fodors.com member

mesmerizing beauty of Table Mountain rising above the city, the stunning drama of the mountains cascading into the sea, and the gorgeous hues of the two oceans. Francis Drake wasn't exaggerating when he said this was "the fairest Cape we saw in the whole circumference of the earth," and he would have little cause to change his opinion today.

A visit to Cape Town is often synonymous with a visit to the peninsula beneath the city, and for good reason. With pristine white-sand beaches, hundreds of mountain trails, and numerous activities from surfing to paragliding to mountain biking, the accessibility, variety, and pure beauty of the great outdoors will keep nature lovers and outdoor adventurers occupied for hours, if not days. You could spend a week exploring just the city and peninsula.

Often likened to San Francisco, Cape Town has two things that the City by the Bay doesn't—Table Mountain and Africa. The mountain, or tabletop, is vital to Cape Town's identity. It dominates the city in a way that's difficult to comprehend until you visit. In the afternoon, when creeping fingers of clouds spill over Table Mountain and reach toward the city, the whole town seems to shiver and hold its breath. Meanwhile, for all of its bon-vivant European vibe, Cape Town also reflects the diversity, vitality, and spirit of the many African peoples who call this city home.

THE WINELANDS

No stay or stopover in Cape Town would be complete without a trip to the historic Cape Winelands, which lie in the city's backyard. They produce fine wine amid the exquisite beauty of purple mountains, serried vines, and elegant Cape Dutch estates. By South African standards, this southwestern region of the Cape is a settled land, with a sense of continuity lacking in much of the rest of the country. Here farms have been handed down from one generation to another for centuries, and old-name families like the Cloetes and Myburghs have become part of the fabric of the region. But the whole Western Cape is an alluring province: a sweep of endless mountain ranges, empty beaches, and European history dating back more than three centuries and anchored by Cape Town in the southwest. The cultures of the indigenous Khoekhoen and San people—the first inhabitants of this enormous area—also contribute to the region's richness. In less than two hours you can reach most of the province's highlights from Cape Town—including the wine centers of Stellenbosch, Franschhoek, and Paarl—making the city an ideal base from which to explore. If your time is limited in the Cape Town area, you might want to join one of the many tours to the Winelands. (⇨ *See Cape Town Tours in Cape Town Essentials, below.*)

PLANNING

GETTING HERE AND AROUND

It should take about 20 minutes to get from the airport to the city; during rush hour it can easily be double that. There is no scheduled public transport to or from the airport, but private operators abound. Metered taxis and shuttle services (usually minivans) are based inside the domestic baggage hall and outside the international and domestic terminals and can also be phoned for airport drop-offs. Rates vary depending on the operator, number of passengers, destination, and time of arrival.

One person going into the city center alone pays about R280 in a metered taxi; a group of up to four will usually pay the same rate. ⚠ Reports of overcharging are common, so check the fare first. Touch Down Taxis is the only officially authorized airport taxi. Look for the ACSA symbol on the vehicles.

Private transfer companies include Shawn Casey Taxi Service, which charges a fixed rate for to four passengers but must be booked ahead. For single travelers, a prearranged shared shuttle with Legend Tours and Transfers or Magic Bus is the most economical, costing about R165–R200 per person. For the ultimate luxury ride you can hire a six-seat Lincoln stretch limo from Cape Limousine Services. A surcharge of up to R50 is sometimes levied from 10 PM until early morning, and some shuttles charge more for arrivals than for departures to cover waiting time.

All major car-rental companies have counters at Cape Town International, and driving to the City Bowl or V&A Waterfront is straightforward in daylight.

A car is by far the best way to get around Cape Town, particularly in the evening, when public transportation closes down. Cape Town's roads are excellent, but they are unusual in a few respects and can be a bit confusing. Signage is inconsistent, switching between Afrikaans and English, between different names for the same road (especially highways), and between different destinations on the same route. Sometimes the signs simply vanish. ⚠ Cape Town is also littered with signs indicating CAPE TOWN instead of CITY CENTRE, as well as KAPSTAAD, which is Afrikaans

for Cape Town. Good one-page maps are essential and freely available from car-rental agencies and tourism information desks. Among the hazards are pedestrians running across highways, speeding vehicles, and minibus taxis. Roadblocks for document and DWI checks are also becoming more frequent.

The main arteries leading out of the city are the N1, which bypasses the city's Northern Suburbs en route to Paarl and, ultimately, Johannesburg; and the N2, which heads out past Khayelitsha and through Somerset West to the Overberg and the Garden Route before continuing on through the Eastern Cape to Durban. Branching off the N1, the N7 goes to Namibia. The M3 splits off from the N2 near Observatory, leading to the False Bay side of the Peninsula via Claremont and Constantia; it's the main route to the False Bay towns like Muizenberg. Rush hour affects all major arteries into the city from 7 to 9, and out of the city from 4 to 6:30.

Taxis are expensive compared with other forms of transportation but offer a quick way to get around the city center. Don't expect to see the throngs of cabs you find in London or New York. Your best bet is to summon a cab by phone or head to one of the major taxi stands, such as at Greenmarket Square or either end of Adderley Street (near the Slave Lodge and outside the train station). For lower rates at night, try prebooking the Backpacker Bus, a shuttle service on Adderley Street. Expect to pay R50–R70 for a trip from the city center to the Waterfront. Lodging establishments often have a relationship with particular companies and/or drivers, and this way you will be assured of safe, reliable service.

(⇨ *For information on airlines or roadside assistance or national car-rental companies, see the Planning section at the beginning of the chapter.*)

EMERGENCIES

There are several numbers you can call for general emergencies, including Vodacom mobile networks. Metrorail has its own security/emergency number. If you get lost on Table Mountain, call Metro Medical Emergency Services, and for all sea emergencies, call the National Sea Rescue Institute (NSRI).

HEALTH AND SAFETY

There's no reason for paranoia in Cape Town, but there are a few things to look out for. Aside from busy nightlife zones like Long Street, avoid the City Bowl at night and on Saturday afternoons and Sundays, when it's very quiet. Street kids and roving teens are blamed for much of the petty crime, but sophisticated crime syndicates are often involved, and many of Cape Town's fraudsters are smartly dressed. Cell phones can be snatched from car seats through open windows and even out of people's hands while in use. Watch your pockets at busy transportation interchanges and on trains. Pick a crowded car; if you suddenly find yourself alone, move to another one. Public transportation collapses after dark. Unless you're at the Waterfront or are in a large group, use metered taxis. Better still, rent a car, but don't leave valuables visible and don't park in isolated areas. Despite thousands of safe visits every year, Table Mountain, which couldn't look less threatening, has been the location of several knife-point robberies in daylight. The point is, never be completely off guard.

Poor signage is an issue in Cape Town, especially in the black townships, where most streets still have numbers rather than names and many streets are not signed at all. Carry a good map, and visit township attractions only as part of an organized tour with a reputable operator. Women and couples are strongly advised not to walk in isolated places after dark. If you want to walk somewhere in the evening, make sure you do so in a large group, stay vigilant at all times, and keep flashy jewelry and expensive cameras hidden, or better yet, at the hotel.

MONEY MATTERS

Most shops, restaurants, hotels, and B&Bs in Cape Town take credit cards, but you need cash to buy gas. ■ TIP→ **Don't even think about changing money at your hotel.** The rates at most hotels are outrageous, and the city has plenty of banks and *bureaux de change* (exchange counters) offering better rates; most are open during business hours (weekdays and Saturday mornings).

TOURS

Numerous companies offer guided tours of the city center, the peninsula, the Winelands, and any place else in the Cape (or beyond) that you might wish to visit. They differ in type of transportation used, focus, and size. The following list provides an idea of what is generally available and points out some of the more unique offerings. For comprehensive information on touring companies, head to one of the Cape Town Tourism offices; alternately, ask for recommendations at your hotel.

The Waterfront Boat Company offers trips on a range of boats, from yachts to large motor cruisers. A 1½-hour sunset cruise from the V&A Waterfront costs about R200 and includes a glass of bubbly. Tigger 2 also runs boats from the Waterfront to Clifton 4th beach or Table Bay. Drumbeat Charters runs a variety of trips in the Hout Bay area, ranging from sunset cruises to full-day crayfishing expeditions. A trip from Hout Bay to Seal Island with Drumbeat Charters costs R60 for adults, R25 for kids. ■ TIP→ **The only boat trip to actually land on Robben Island is the museum's ferry.**

Many companies offer bus and car tours. For shared group tours, expect to pay R350–R500 for a half-day trip and about R500–R800 for a full-day tour (the smaller and more personalized the tour, the higher the price). Private tours can cost much more.

The hop-on/hop-off red City Sightseeing bus is a pleasant way to familiarize yourself with Cape Town; a day ticket costs R120, and there are two routes to choose from. The Red Route runs through the city, and you can get on and off at major museums, the V&A Waterfront, Table Mountain Cableway, Two Oceans Aquarium, and other attractions. The Blue Route takes you farther afield—to Kirstenbosch National Botanic Gardens, Hout Bay, and Camps Bay, to name a few destinations. Tickets are available at the Waterfront outside the aquarium or on the bus.

Fly from the V&A Waterfront for a tour of the city and surrounding area on a three- to six-seat chopper. Most operators charge between R700–R2,200 for a 20-minute trip, and R2,100–R3,000 for 50 minutes in the air. Custom tours can also be arranged, and the price varies according to how many people are flying.

Several companies offer walking tours of Cape Town, from the V&A Waterfront to Bo-Kaap, covering important historical attractions, architecture, and highlights of modern-day Cape Town.

Pamphlets for a self-guided walking tour of city-center attractions can be picked up at Cape Town Tourism.

VISITOR INFORMATION

Cape Town Tourism is the city's official tourist body, providing information on tours, hotels, restaurants, rental cars, and shops. It has a coffee shop and Internet café. The staff make hotel, tour, and travel reservations. From October to March, the office in town is open weekdays 8–6, Saturday 8:30–2, and Sunday 9–1; from April to September, it's open weekdays 8–5:30, Saturday 8:30–1, and Sunday 9–1. The branch at the Waterfront is now run by Cape Town Routes Unlimited (CTRU) but offers the same services and is open daily 9–9.

5

ESSENTIALS

Airport Transfers Cape Limousine Services (☎ 021/785–3100). **City Hopper** (☎ 021/386–0077). **Legend Tours and Transfers** (☎ 021/704–9140 ⊕ www.legendtours.co.za). **Magic Bus Airport Transfers** (☎ 021/505–6300 ⊕ www.magicbus.co.za). **Marine Taxis** (☎ 021/434–0434). **Shawn Casey Taxi** (☎ 082/954–4867). **Touch Down Taxis** (☎ 021/919–4659).

Boat Tours Drumbeat Charters (☎ 021/791–4441 ⊕ www.drumbeatcharters. co.za). **Tigger 2 Charters** (☎ 021/790–5256 ⊕ www.tigger2.co.za). **Waterfront Boat Company** (☎ 021/418–0134 ⊕ www.waterfrontboats.co.za).

Bus and Car Tours African Eagle Day Tours (☎ 021/464–4260 ⊕ www. africa-adventure.org/a/africaneagle). **Cape Point Route** (☎ 021/782–9356 ⊕ www.capepointroute.co.za). **Cape Sidecar Adventures** (☎ 021/434–9855 ⊕ www.sidecars.co.za). **Coffeebeans Routes** (☎ 021/424–3572 ⊕ www. coffeebeansroutes.com). **Friends of Dorothy** (☎ 021/465–1871 ⊕ www. friendsofdorothytours.co.za). **Grassroute Tours** (☎ 021/464–4269 ⊕ www. grassroutetours.co.za). **Hylton Ross Tours** (☎ 021/511–1784 ⊕ www.hyltonross. co.za). **iKapa Tours & Travel** (☎ 021/510–8666 ⊕ www.ikapa.co.za). **Western Cape Action Tours** (☎ 021/448–5760 ⊕ www.dacpm.org.za).

Emergency Services Ambulance (☎ 10177). **Metro Medical Emergency Services** (☎ 021/937–0300). **Metrorail** (☎ 0800/210–081). **National Sea Rescue Institute** (☎ 021/449–3500). **Police** (☎ 10111). **Police, fire, and ambulance services** (☎ 107 from landline). **Vodacom emergency services** (☎ 112 from mobile phone).

Exchange Services American Express (✉ Ground fl., Sahara House, Thibault Sq., Cape Town Central ☎ 021/425–7991 ✉ Shop 11A, Alfred Mall, Waterfront ☎ 021/419–3917 ⊕ www.amex.co.za).

Helicopter Tours Civair Helicopters (☎ 021/419–5182 ⊕ www.civair.co.za). **NAC/Makana Aviation** (☎ 021/425–3868 ⊕ www.nacmakana.com).

Taxis **Backpacker Bus** (☎ 021/439–7600 ⊕ www.backpackerbus.co.za). **Excite Taxis** (☎ 021/448–4444). **Marine Taxis** (☎ 021/434–0434). **Sea Point Taxis** (☎ 021/434–4444). **Unicab** (☎ 021/486–1600).

Visitor Info Cape Town Routes Unlimited (⊠ Shop 107, Clock Tower Centre, South Arm Rd., Waterfront ☎ 021/405–4500 ⊕ www.tourismcapetown.co.za). **Cape Town Tourism** (⊠ The Pinnacle Building, Burg and Castle Sts., Cape Town Central ☎ 021/487–6800 ⊕ www.tourismcapetown.co.za).

Walking Tours Cape Town on Foot (☎ 021/462–4252 ⊕ www.wanderlust. co.za). **Footsteps to Freedom** (☎ 021/671–6878 or 083/452–1112 ⊕ www. footstepstofreedom.co.za). **Ilios Travel** (☎ 021/697–4056 ⊕ www.ilios.co.za). **Tana Baru Tours** (☎ 021/424–0719 or 073/237–3800).

EXPLORING

ⓒ   **Boulders Beach.** This series of small coves lies among giant boulders
Fodor's Choice   on the southern outskirts of Simon's Town. Part of Table Mountain
★   National Park, the beach is best known for its resident colony of African penguins. You must stay out of the fenced-off breeding beach, but don't be surprised if a wandering bird comes waddling up to you to take a look. Penguin-viewing platforms, accessible from either the Boulders Beach or Seaforth side, provide close-up looks at these comical birds. When you've had enough penguin peering, you can stroll back to Boulders Beach for some excellent swimming in the quiet coves. This beach is great for children because it is so protected, and the sea is warm(ish) and calm. It can get crowded in summer, though, so go early. Without traffic, it takes about 45 minutes to get here from town, less from the Southern Suburbs. ⊠ *Follow signs from Bellvue Rd., Simon's Town* ☎ *021/786–2329* ⊕ *www.sanparks.org* ☎ *R35* ☉ *Daily, Dec. and Jan. 7 AM–7:30 PM; Feb., Mar., Oct., and Nov. 8–6:30; Apr.–Sept. 8–5.*

★   **Greenmarket Square.** For more than a century this cobbled square served as a forum for public announcements, including the 1834 declaration abolishing slavery, which was read from the balcony of the Old Town House, overlooking the square. In the 19th century the square became a vegetable market as well as a popular watering hole, and you can still enjoy a drink at an open-air restaurant or hotel veranda while watching the crowds go by. Today the square has a great outdoor market (⇨ *Shopping*), and is flanked by some of the best examples of art-deco architecture in South Africa. A beautiful example of urban Cape Dutch architecture, the **Old Town House** (☎ *021/481–3933* ⊕ *www.iziko.org. za/michaelis* ☎ *Free* ☉ *Weekdays 10–5, Sat. 10–4*) is now home to the extensive **Michaelis Collection**. This 17th-century collection of Dutch paintings includes evocative etchings by Rembrandt, as well as changing exhibits. ⊠ *Greenmarket Square, Cape Town Central.*

ⓒ   **Kirstenbosch National Botanic Gardens.** Spectacular in each season, these
Fodor's Choice   world-famous gardens showcase stunning South African flora in a mag-
★   nificent setting, extending up the eastern slopes of Table Mountain and overlooking the sprawling city and the distant Hottentots Holland Mountains. No wonder the gardens are photographed from every angle. They aren't just enjoyed by out-of-town visitors; on weekends Cape-tonians flock here with their families to lie on the lawns and read their

"After a day of [enduring the] constant baying from the colony of Jackass Penguins, this one decided to get away from the crowd for a quiet stroll on the beach." —Stacy Freeman, Fodors.com member

newspapers while the kids run riot. Walking trails meander through the gardens, and grassy banks are ideal for a picnic or afternoon nap. The plantings are limited to species indigenous to Southern Africa, including fynbos—hardy, thin-leaved plants that proliferate in the Cape. Among these are proteas, including silver trees and king proteas, ericas, and *restios* (reeds). Magnificent sculptures from Zimbabwe are displayed around the gardens, too. A visitor center by the conservatory houses a restaurant, bookstore, and coffee shop. Unfortunately, muggings have become increasingly more common in the gardens' isolated areas, and women are advised not to walk alone in the upper reaches of the park far from general activity. ⊠ *Rhodes Dr., Newlands* ☎ *021/799–8783* ⊕ *www.sanbi.org* ✉ *R35* ☉ *Apr.–Aug., daily 8–6; Sept.–Mar., daily 8–7.*

Long Street. The section of Long between Orange and Wale streets is lined with magnificently restored Georgian and Victorian buildings. Wrought-iron balconies and fancy curlicues on these colorful houses evoke the French Quarter in New Orleans. In the 1960s, Long Street played host to bars, prostitutes, and sleazy hotels, but today antiques dealers, secondhand bookstores, pawnshops, the Pan-African Market, and funky clothing outlets make this the best browsing street in the city. Lodgings here range from backpackers' digs to the more exclusive Grand Daddy. At the mountain end is Long Street Baths, an indoor swimming pool and old Turkish *hammam* (steam bath). ⊠ *Cape Town Central.*

Fodor's Choice

★

Robben Island. Made famous by its most illustrious inhabitant, Nelson Mandela, this island, whose name is Dutch for "seals," has a long and sad history. At various times a prison, leper colony, mental institution, and military base, it is finally filling a positive, enlightening, and empowering role in its latest incarnation as a museum.

Declared a World Heritage site on December 1, 1997, Robben Island has become a symbol of the triumph of the human spirit. In 1997 around 90,000 made the pilgrimage; in 2006 more than 300,000 crossed the water to see where some of the greatest South Africans spent much of their lives. Visiting the island is a sobering experience, which begins at the modern Nelson Mandela Gateway to Robben Island, an impressive embarkation center that doubles as a conference center. Interactive exhibits display historic photos of prison life. Next make the journey across the water, remembering to watch Table Mountain recede in the distance and imagine what it must have been like to have just received a 20-year jail sentence. Boats leave on the hour (every other hour in winter), and the crossing takes 30 minutes.

Tours are organized by the Robben Island Museum. (Other operators advertise Robben Island tours but just take visitors on a boat trip *around* the island.) As a result of the reconciliation process, most tour guides are former political prisoners. During the 2½-hour tour you walk through the prison and see the cells where Mandela and other leaders were imprisoned. You also tour the lime quarry, Robert Sobukwe's place of confinement, and the leper church. Due to increased demand for tickets during peak season (December–January), make bookings at least three weeks in advance. Take sunglasses and a hat in summer. **■ TIP→ You are advised to tip your guide only if you feel that the tour has been informative.** ✉ *Waterfront* ☎ *021/413–4220; 021/413–4263 for ticket sales* 🌐 *www.robben-island.org.za* *R200* ⏲ *Sept.–Apr., boats depart from the Nelson Mandela Gateway daily 9–3; May–Aug., daily 9–noon; last boat generally leaves the island at 6* PM *in summer and 4* PM *in winter (opening times and boat departures can vary, so phone ahead to check).*

★ **Table Mountain.** Along with Victoria Falls on the border of Zimbabwe and Zambia, Table Mountain is one of Southern Africa's most beautiful and impressive natural wonders. The views from its summit are awe-inspiring. The mountain rises more than 3,500 feet above the city, and its distinctive flat top is visible to sailors 65 km (40 mi) out to sea. It's possible to climb the mountain, thought it'll take two to three hours, depending on your level of fitness. There is no water along the route; you *must* take at least 2 liters (½ gallon) of water per person. Table Mountain can be dangerous if you're not familiar with the terrain. Many paths that look like good routes down the mountain end in treacherous cliffs. Do not underestimate this mountain. It may be in the middle of a city, but it is not a genteel town park. Wear sturdy shoes or hiking boots; always take warm clothes, such as a Windbreaker, and a mobile phone; and let someone know of your plans. Also be aware that in light of occasional muggings here, it's unwise to walk alone on the mountain. It's recommended that you travel in a group or, better yet, with a guide. Consult the staff at a Cape Town Tourism office for more guidelines. Another way to reach the summit is to take the cable car, which affords fantastic views. Cable cars depart from the Lower Cable Station, which lies on the slope of Table Mountain near its western end; the station is a long way from the city on foot, and you're better off traveling by car, taxi, or rikki. ⊠ *Table Mountain Aerial Cableway, Tafelberg Rd.* ☎ *021/424–8181* ⊕ *www.tablemountain.net* 🖪 *R165 round-trip, R85 one-way* ⊙ *Hrs vary so it's best to check when you arrive, but usually daily 8:30–7:30.*

Two Oceans Aquarium. This aquarium is considered one of the finest in the world. Stunning displays reveal the marine life of the warm Indian Ocean and the icy Atlantic. It's a hands-on place, with a touch pool for children and opportunities for certified divers to explore the vast, five-story kelp forest or the predator tank, where you share the water with a couple of large ragged-tooth sharks (*Carcharias taurus*) and get a legal adrenaline rush (R570, R445 with own gear). If you don't fancy getting wet, you can still watch the feeding in the predator tank every day at 3. But there's more to the aquarium than just snapping jaws. Look for the endangered African penguins, also known as jackass penguins because of the awkward braying noise they make; pulsating moon jellies and spider crabs; and a new frog exhibit. ⊠ *Dock Rd., Waterfront* ☎ *021/418–3823* ⊕ *www.aquarium.co.za* 🖪 *R94* ⊙ *Daily 9:30–6.*

Fodor's Choice ★

5

WHERE TO EAT

Dining in Cape Town and its suburbs can offer a truly global culinary experience, since Cape chefs are now showing the same enthusiasm for global trends as their counterparts worldwide. French and Italian food has long been available here, but in the last decade, with the introduction of Thai and Pan-Asian flavors, locals have embraced the chili. Kurdish, Pakistani, Persian, Ethiopian, Lebanese, and regional Chinese cuisines are now easily available, and other Asian fare is commonplace. Sushi is ubiquitous. If there is a cuisine trend it is toward organic produce and healthful dishes made with foams rather than creams. A number of restaurants operate in historic town houses and 18th-century wine estates, and many include heritage dishes on their menus.

$$ ⨯ **Africa Café.** Tourist oriented it may be, but it would nevertheless be
AFRICAN a pity to miss out on this vibrant restaurant in a historic 18th-century former home, with its African decor and city views. Fresh-fruit cocktails accompany a communal feast, with dishes originating from Ethiopia to Zambia, from Kenya to Angola. There are no starters or entrées, but rather a tasty series of patties, puffs, and pastries accompanied by addictive dips, along with dishes like Bostwanan *seswaa masala*, a game-meat curry traditionally served at weddings and funerals, and an East African *mchicha wa nazi* (spinach cooked in a coconut milk sauce). Vegetarian dishes are plentiful, including the Soweto *chakalaka* (a fiery cooked-vegetable relish). Poppy-seed cake with vanilla ice cream is the prix-fixe dessert. The cost of this colorful prix-fixe abundance is R245 per person. Wines from Cape estates are available, or you can ask for *umqomboti* beer, brewed from sorghum or millet. ⊠ *Heritage Square, 108 Shortmarket St., Cape Town Central* ☎ *021/422–0221* ⊕ *www. africacafe.co.za* ⊟ *AE, DC, MC, V* ⊙ *Closed Sun. No lunch.*

$$$$ ⨯ **Aubergine.** Aubergine's timber-and-glass interior matches chef-owner
ECLECTIC Harald Bresselschmidt's classic-with-a-twist cuisine. A beaded Strelitzia
Fodor's Choice flower in the entrance hall is a clue to what will come: South African
★ produce, prepared with strong classical methods that echo the Austrian

Sip and Spoeg Like an Expert

South Africa has numerous growing areas that yield a huge selection of very different wines. One of the best ways to find your way around the enormous selection is to buy one of the local magazines, such as the monthly *Wine* magazine (R25), devoted to the subject.

AH, BUT YOUR LAND IS BEAUTIFUL

When it comes to South African terroir, think sun, sea, and soil. While Northern Hemisphere farmers work hard to get as much sunlight onto their grapes as possible, local viticulturists have to deal with soaring summer temperatures (this is why the cooling influence of the two oceans is so welcome). South Africa also has some of the world's oldest soil, and there's a mineral element to its wines, a quality that's most prominent in the top-end Sauvignon Blancs like those produced by Cape Point Vineyards, Steenberg, and Springfield.

YOU CAN'T LEAVE WITHOUT TRYING PINOTAGE

In 1920s, a professor at Stellenbosch University decided to create a truly South African varietal. He crossed Pinot Noir (a tricky grape to grow) with Cinsaut (a vigorous and very hardy grape)—he liked the idea combining the drama queen with a pragmatic, no-nonsense type—and came up with Pinotage. Though it's had its ups and downs, including being accused—by everyone from critics to connoisseurs—of being bitter and rubbery, strides are being made to express the grape's character. One example is the coffee Pinotage. It's been on the market for just a few years and is hugely popular because it's a ballsy, bold wine. There's a distinct mocha flavor to the wine that's a combination of the soil and the wine-making technique. A good example of this is the Diemersfontein Carpe Diem Pinotage, which retails for R120. Other Pinotages to keep an eye out for: Stellenzicht golden triangle Pinotage (R79), Spier Private

Collection Pinotage (R148), or Kanonkop Pinotage (R170).

HUNDREDS AND THOUSANDS TO CHOOSE FROM

Wines that have helped put South
Africa on the map include Chenin
Blanc, Sauvignon Blanc, and
Bordeaux-style red blends of Cabernet
Sauvignon, Merlot, and Cabernet
Franc. South African red blends have
done well at international competi-
tions, and the quality rivals some
of the world's best producers. Until
recently, Chenin Blanc was something
of a Cinderella varietal. It accounts
for the bulk of South African white
wine plantings but, because of its
versatility, was largely overlooked.
Luckily, this has shifted and there are
now more than 100 Chenin Blancs out
there demanding attention and com-
manding top prices.

■ Good Sauvignon Blancs: Alexander-
fontein Sauvignon Blanc (R30), Springfield Estate Life from Stone Sauvignon
Blanc (R53), or Cape Point Vineyards
Sauvignon Blanc (R110).

■ Great Red Blends: Stellenrust Time-
less (R89), Rustenberg John X Merri-
man (R120), or Kanonkop Paul Sauer
(+/- R175).

■ Great Chenin Blancs: Kleine Zalze
barrel fermented Chenin Blanc (R49),
Rudera Robusto Chenin Blanc (R95), or
Ken Forrester The FMC Chenin Blanc
(R230).

A ROSÉ BY ANY OTHER NAME

Though it legally can't be called
champagne, Methode Cap Classique,
South Africa's version of the bubbly, is
made in exactly the same way. You'd
be unwise to pass on an offer of Gra-
ham Beck Brut Blanc de Blancs (R169)
or Villiera Brut Tradition (R75).

NAME-DROPPING

There are some iconic South African
wines you really should try before
you leave the country. Of course, the
list of such wines varies depending
on who you talk to, but keep an eye
out for:

■ Kanonkop Pinotage (R210) or Paul
Sauer (R259)

■ Meerlust Rubicon (R219)

■ De Toren Fusion V (R220)

■ Vergelegen V (R750)

■ Steenberg Sauvignon Blanc Reserve
(R85)

■ Hamilton Russell Chardonnay (R195)
and Pinot Noir (R250)

■ Cape Point Isliedh (R130)

■ Jordan Chardonnay (R95)

■ Springfield Méthode Ancienne Cabernet Sauvignon (R230)

■ Boekenhoutskloof Cabernet Sauvignon (R170)

■ Boplaas Vintage Reserve Port
(R365)

■ Potential future icons include Colu-
mella and Palladius, both made by
Eben Sadie, and Raats Family Vineyard
Cabernet Franc.

5

chef's roots, surprises and requires a closer look. This is serious cuisine. You may notice yourself sitting more upright than usual—not because of stuffiness or any pretentious formality, but out of respect for the food. There is a superb wine selection, and servers double as sommeliers. The fish on the menu is line-caught—never frozen. Yellowtail (a fleshy local catch) is poached in saffron and served with a beetroot sorbet and fennel salad. Heartier options include pork and pancetta pralines with cumin cabbage and blue-cheese wontons. The highly recommended surprise du chef selection of minidesserts might include melon soup with wine gelée and rhubarb sorbet, chocolate fondant with cherry ragout, crème brûlée, magnificent apricot linzer tartlet, and passion-fruit ice-parfait with deep-fried chocolate. Showered with every award possible, the Cinq à Sept (served between 5 and 7 in the evening) is unexpectedly affordable. ⊠ *39 Barnet St., Gardens* ☎ *021/465–4909* ⊕ *www. aubergine.co.za* ⌂ *Reservations essential* ▭ *AE, DC, MC, V* ☉ *Closed Sun.; no lunch Mon., Tues., and Sat.*

$$ ✕ **Bizerca Bistro.** Here, it's all about the food, and diners will encounter superb cuisine in a monochromatic bistro setting. The raw Norwegian salmon salad is enlivened by ginger and soy flavors before being dressed in a sauce of finely minced shallots in butter with reduced meat stock. The braised pig trotter with a seared scallop and truffle oil is a triumph. Served off the bone and encased in a crispy caul-fat envelope, it delivers taste and texture. Culinary magic transforms chicken into a dish that invokes the best childhood memories of when chicken tasted wholesome and delicious. The dish is served with corn, coriander polenta, asparagus, and tomato salsa. A red-pepper sauce is the final flavor accent. Atmosphere at lunch is better than dinner. ⊠ *Jetty St., Foreshore* ☎ *021/418–0001* ⊕ *www.bizerca.com* ⌂ *Reservations essential* ▭ *MC, V* ☉ *Closed Sun. No lunch Sat.*

FRENCH
Fodor's Choice
★

$$$$ ✕ **Haiku.** This is still the best Pan-Asian restaurant in town, and it's worth putting up with the waiting lists, multiple seatings, and a complex menu of dim sum, sushi, and wok-fried items. A tip: allow your server to order for you, though we do suggest starting with steamed scallop *siu mai* (a traditional Chinese dumpling) with salmon roe for tongue fireworks. The Peking duck with paper-thin pancakes is delicious. Grills include mint lamb chops served with dry red chilies and garlic. On the sushi menu, the salmon roses—thin sashimi curls filled with mayonnaise and topped with pink caviar—are outstanding. Four kitchens mean that dishes arrive when ready. Although this provides the freshest dining experience, it may mean fellow diners watch while you eat, or vice versa. The owners of Haiku also own Bukhara, the excellent Indian restaurant above it. There's a minimum per person of R170. ⊠ *33 Burg St., Cape Town Central* ☎ *021/424–7000* ⊕ *www.haikurestaurant.com* ⌂ *Reservations essential* ▭ *AE, DC, MC, V* ☉ *No lunch Sun.*

ASIAN
★

$$ ✕ **Panama Jack's.** In this raw-timber structure in the heart of the docks, about 3 mi north of other V&A venues, the music is loud, the tables are crowded, and the decor is nonexistent, but nowhere in town will you find bigger crayfish. Your choice, made from large open tanks, is weighed before being grilled or steamed. Expect to pay upwards of R530 per kilogram for this delicacy and a whopping R1,150 a kilogram

SEAFOOD

for the scarce and endangered wild abalone, which is being poached nearly to extinction. Large prawns range in price from R255 for 10 to about R77 each for Mozambique langoustines. There is plenty of less expensive seafood as well, and daily specials such as baby squid and local line-caught fish are competitively priced. It can be difficult to find this place at night, so you may want to come for lunch, which is far more affordable, if it's your first visit. ⊠ *Quay 500, Waterfront* ☎ *021/447–3992* ⊕ *www.panamajacks.net* ⊟ *AE, DC, MC, V* ⊗ *No lunch Sat.*

WHERE TO STAY

Finding lodging in Cape Town can be a nightmare during peak travel season (December–January), as many of the more reasonable accommodations are booked up. It's worth traveling between April and August, if you can, to take advantage of the "secret season" discounts that are sometimes half the high-season rate. If you arrive in Cape Town without a reservation, head for the Tourism Office, which has a helpful accommodations desk.

Hotels in the city center are a good option if you're here on business or are here for only a short stay. During the day the historic city center is a vibrant place. At night, though, it's shut up tight (though this is changing slowly as more office buildings are converted into apartment complexes); night owls may prefer a hotel amid the nonstop action of Long Street or the Waterfront. Hotels and bed-and-breakfasts in the Southern Suburbs, especially Constantia, offer unrivaled beauty and tranquility and make an ideal base if you're exploring the peninsula. You'll need a car, though, and plan on 25–45 minutes to get into town. Atlantic Coast hotels provide the closest thing in Cape Town to a beach-vacation atmosphere despite the cold ocean waters.

Keep in mind that international flights from the United States and Europe arrive in the morning and return flights depart in the evening. Because most hotels have an 11 AM checkout, you may have to wait for a room if you've just arrived; if you're leaving, you will be hauled kicking and screaming out of your room hours before your flight. Most hotels will try to accommodate you, but they often have no choice in peak season. Many small luxury accommodations either do not permit children or have minimum-age restrictions.

The most reliable source of good B&B establishments is **South African Accommodation** (⊕ *www.bookabed.co.za*). The **Portfolio of Places** (☎ *021/689–4020* ⊕ *www.portfoliocollection.com*) brochure includes guesthouses, B&Bs, villas, and more. If you don't like tiptoeing around someone's house or you want to save money, consider renting a fully furnished apartment, especially if you're staying two or more weeks. **CAPSOL Property & Tourism Solutions** (☎ *021/438–9644* ⊕ *www.capsol. co.za*) has around 1,500 high-quality, furnished, fully stocked villas and apartments on its books. **Cape Stay** (☎ *021/674–3104* ⊕ *www.capestay. co.za*) has a wide selection of accommodations to suit different needs.

Hotel reviews have been abbreviated in this book. For expanded reviews, please go to Fodors.com.

$$$$ 🏨 **Cape Grace.** The recent refurbishment of Cape Town's beloved Cape

Fodor'sChoice Grace has transformed this storied hotel's look from period French

★ to a mélange of indigenous and foreign influences that have come to epitomize the region. **Pros:** mountain and harbor views from all rooms; spa; complimentary shuttle within city center; child-friendly; excellent waterfront location. **Cons:** lacks the intimacy of a boutique hotel. ⊠ *West Quay Rd., Waterfront* ☎ *021/410–7100* ⊕ *www.capegrace. com* 🛏 *120 rooms* ♿ *In-room: DVD, Internet, Wi-Fi. In-hotel: restaurant, room service, bar, pool, gym, spa, children's programs (infant–16), laundry service, Internet terminal, Wi-Fi hotspot, parking (free)* ⊟ *AE, DC, MC, V* ⊠ *BP.*

¢ 🏨 **Daddy Long Legs Boutique Hotel.** Independent travelers with artistic

★ streaks love this place. **Pros:** loads of dash without cash; the hotel has had lots of positive global media coverage, and your chums will be impressed that you stayed here. **Cons:** small rooms; Long Street is noisy until late into the night. ⊠ *134 Long St., Cape Town Central* ☎ *021/422–3074* ⊕ *www.daddylonglegs.co.za* 🛏 *13 rooms* ♿ *In-room: no phone, no TV (some), Wi-Fi. In-hotel: bar, laundry service, Wi-Fi hotspot* ⊟ *AE, DC, MC, V.*

$$ 🏨 **More Cape Cadogan.** Declared a national monument in 1984, this

★ lovely space is housed in a Georgian and Victorian building that dates back to the beginning of the 19th century. **Pros:** minutes from the busy and popular Long and Kloof streets; beautiful, historic accommodations; apartments available for those who want to self-cater. **Cons:** traffic noise (hooting minibus taxis at nearby intersection). ⊠ *5 Upper Union St., Gardens* ☎ *021/480–8080* ⊕ *www.capecadogan.co.za* 🛏 *8 rooms, 4 suites, 1 villa* ♿ *In-room: safe, refrigerator, Internet. In-hotel: restaurant, room service, pool, laundry service, Internet terminal, Wi-Fi hotspot, parking (free)* ⊟ *AE, DC, MC, V* ⊠ *BP.*

$$$$ 🏨 **Mount Nelson Hotel.** This distinctive pink landmark is the grande

Fodor'sChoice dame of Cape Town. **Pros:** the most glamorous hotel in town; guests

★ include movie stars and diplomats; everyone in Cape Town knows it. **Cons:** breakfast and lunch restaurant overlooks guests at the pool; Friday nights in the Planet Bar are legendary, and the main building is abuzz until late. ⊠ *76 Orange St., Gardens* ☎ *021/483–1000* ⊕ *www. mountnelson.co.za* 🛏 *145 rooms, 56 suites* ♿ *In-room: safe, DVD, Wi-Fi. In-hotel: 2 restaurants, room service, bar, tennis courts, pools, gym, spa, laundry service, Internet terminal, Wi-Fi hotspot, parking (free)* ⊟ *AE, DC, MC, V* ⊠ *BP.*

¢ 🏨 **Townhouse Hotel.** Its proximity to government buildings and its easygoing atmosphere (not to mention extremely competitive rates) make the Townhouse a popular choice, especially for the business traveler. **Pros:** near Long St., St. George's Cathedral, and the Castle; helpful staff. **Cons:** not a great area to walk around in at night; parking is costly (about R40 per day) and slightly challenging as it's in a nearby building accessed by one-way roads. ⊠ *60 Corporation St., Cape Town Central* ☎ *021/465–7050* ⊕ *www.townhouse.co.za* 🛏 *104 rooms* ♿ *In-room: a/c, safe, Wi-Fi. In-hotel: restaurant, room service, bars, pool, gym, laundry service, Internet terminal, Wi-Fi hotspot, parking (free)* ⊟ *AE, DC, MC, V.*

SPORTS AND THE OUTDOORS

SHARK DIVING

Seeing great white sharks hunting seals around False Bay's Seal Island is one of the most exhilarating natural displays you're likely to witness. And if witnessing it all from a boat is not thrill enough, you can get in the water (in a cage). Run by marine biologists, **Apex Predators** (☎ *082/364–2738* ⊕ *www.apexpredators.com*) runs small trips (R1,700) out of Simon's Town during season (April–September). If the great whites aren't around, try the Ocean Predator Trip, in which you free dive (no cage) with makos and blues.

5

BEACH ESCAPES

So you've had your fill of exploring the bush, tracking animals and birds, immersing yourself in wilderness. Now maybe you've got time to head for the beach. Summer is the best time to catch a tan, but people also head to Durban in winter as well as in summer.

DURBAN

Though Durban is South Africa's most vibrant city as well as Africa's busiest port, it also has some of the most accessible, beautiful, and safe beaches in the world. The sand and inviting water temperatures extend all the way up the Dolphin (North) Coast and beyond, as well as south from Durban, down the Hibiscus Coast and into the Eastern Cape. Even in winter (April through September), the weather is particularly pleasant and you'll be able swim.

Durban's beachfront extends for about 12 km (7½ mi) from South Beach, at the base of Durban Point, all the way past North Beach and the Suncoast Casino to Blue Lagoon, on the southern bank of the Umgeni River. The section of beachfront between South Beach and the Suncoast Casino is particularly safe, as police patrol often. It's lovely to take a stroll along here early or late in the day, when it's less busy, just don't walk here late at night. Walk out onto one of the many piers and watch surfers tackling Durban's famous waves. Of any place in Durban, the Beachfront most defines the city.

PLANNING

GETTING HERE AND AROUND

Durban's new international airport, King Shaka International Airport, at La Mercy on the north coast, is about 17 km (11 mi) from Umhlanga and about 32 km (20 mi) from Durban. The most inexpensive transfer into Durban and back is the Airport Shuttle Service, which costs R70 and departs a half hour to 45 minutes after incoming flights arrive and leaves the city center every hour. Its drop-off points are flexible within the city and include the Hilton Hotel and South Sun Elangeni, but it's likely to drop you anywhere central if you request it first. Call ahead and the bus will pick you up at any hotel in the city; there's no need to reserve for the trip into Durban. If you want to go farther afield, call the Magic Bus or catch a cab from outside the terminal building.

⇨ *For airline contact information see Air Travel, at the beginning of the chapter.*

Durban is relatively easy to find your way around because the sea is a constant reference point. Downtown Durban is dominated by two parallel one-way streets, Dr. Pixley Kaseme Street (West Street) going toward the sea and Anton Lembede Street (Smith Street) going away from the sea, toward Berea and Pietermaritzburg; together they get you in and out of the city center easily. Parking downtown is a nightmare; head for an underground garage whenever you can.

Avis, Budget, Europcar, and Tempest have rental offices at the airport. The cheapest car costs about R300 per day, including insurance and 200 km (125 mi) free, plus R1.50 per kilometer (per half mile), or about R400 for the weekend. Avis offers unlimited mileage to international visitors, as long as you can produce your return ticket as proof.

Colorfully decorated rickshaws are unique to Durban—you won't find them in any other South African city. Though their origins lie in India, these two-seat carriages with large wheels are all over the city and are pulled exclusively by Zulu men dressed in feathered headgear and traditional garb. The rickshaw runners ply their trade all day, every day, mostly along the Golden Mile section of the beachfront. The going rate is R20 per person for about 15 minutes, and R8 for a photo (don't assume you can take a picture without paying for the privilege). While it's worth doing because it will be memorable and you won't have the opportunity anywhere else—negotiate the rate before climbing on.

Taxis are metered and start at R5, with an additional R9 to R10 per kilometer (per half mile); after-hours and time-based charges apply. Fares are calculated per vehicle up to four passengers. Expect to pay about R50 from City Hall to North Beach and R200 to Durban International Airport. The most convenient taxi stands are around City Hall, in front of the beach hotels, and outside Spiga d'Oro on Florida Road in Morningside. Some taxis display a "for-hire" light, whereas others you simply hail when you can see they're empty; they are easy to find, or your hotel or restaurant will call one for you. If you're headed to the Indian Market on a weekend, consider having your taxi wait for you, as it can be difficult to flag a taxi in this neighborhood.

MONEY MATTERS

There are plenty of ATMs in and around Durban—at shopping centers, large attractions like Suncoast and uShaka, and even some of the smaller supermarkets. Most bank branches exchange money, and the airport and uShaka have money exchanges, as do Rennies and the AmEx foreign-exchange bureau. Shops in the bigger malls like Gateway, Pavilion, Musgrave, and La Lucia often take traveler's checks. Though you will need cash at the markets, don't carry too much. Use credit cards where you can.

SAFETY AND PRECAUTIONS

Durban has not escaped the crime evident in every South African city. Particularly in the city center but also elsewhere, smash-and-grab thieves roam the streets, looking for bags or valuables in your car, even while you're driving. While there's no need to be fearful, be observant wherever you go. Hire a guide to take you around Durban, don't wander around the city center or outside your hotel alone at night, and keep expensive cameras and other possessions concealed. The Durban Beachfront (with recently upgraded security features), Umhlanga, and the outlying areas are safe to explore on your own, though you'll need a taxi or car to get between them.

TOURS

The city's tourism office, Durban Tourism, has a series of city walking tours for R100 per person. Tours depart from the Tourist Junction weekdays at 9:30 and return at 1:30, but you need to book in advance, as the tour guide arrives only if reservations have been made. Durban Tourism offers other tour options as well; a comprehensive list of tour options is on its Web site.

Sightseeing cruises around Durban Bay are also popular. Your hotel should be able to assist in recommending tour companies, and most will tailor a trip for you, although there may be a minimum charge for small parties.

VISITOR INFORMATION

The Tourist Junction, in the restored Old Station Building, houses a number of tourist-oriented companies and services, where you can find information on almost everything that's happening in Durban and KwaZulu-Natal. Among the companies represented are Durban Tourism, the city's tourism authority; an accommodations service; a KwaZulu-Natal Nature Conservation Service booking desk; regional KwaZulu-Natal tourist offices; and various bus and transport companies. It's open weekdays 8–4:30 and weekends 9–2. Sugar Coast Tourism (covering the Umhlanga and nearby Umdloti areas), is open weekdays 8:30–4:45 and Saturday 9–1.

ESSENTIALS

Airport Airports Company South Africa (☎ 011/921-6262 ⊕ www.acsa.co.za). **King Shaka International Airport** (☎ 032/436-6000).

Airport Transfers Airport Shuttle Service (☎ 031/465-5573). **Magic Bus** (☎ 031/263-2647).

Rental Companies Avis (☎ 086/102-1111 ⊕ www.avis.co.za). **Budget** (☎ 0861/016-622 ⊕ www.budget.co.za). **Europcar** (☎ 0861/131-000 ⊕ www.europcar.co.za). **Tempest Car Hire** (☎ 0861/836-7378 ⊕ www.tempestcarhire.co.za).

Tour Operators Durban Tourism (☎ 031/304-4934 ⊕ www.zulu.org.za). **Isle of Capri** (☎ 031/337-7751). **Sarie Marais Pleasure Cruises** (☎ 031/305-2844).

Visitor Info Sugar Coast Tourism (✉ Shop 1A Chartwell Centre, 15 Chartwell Dr., Umhlanga ☎ 031/561-4257). **Tourism KwaZulu-Natal** (☎ 031/366-7500 ⊕ www.zulu.org.za). **Tourist Junction** (✉ 160 Monty Naicker Rd. [Pine St.], City Centre, Durban ☎ 031/304-4934).

EXPLORING

To get the most from your visit, get ready to explore the Central Business District (CBD), which includes the Indian District; the Beachfront; and Berea and Morningside. If you're concerned about safety within the CBD, book tours through Tourist Junction.

KwaZulu-Natal Sharks Board. Most of the popular bathing beaches in KwaZulu-Natal are protected by shark nets maintained by this shark-research institute, the world's foremost. Each day, weather permitting, crews in ski boats check the nets, releasing healthy sharks back into the ocean and bringing dead ones back to the institute, where they are dissected and studied. One-hour tours are offered, including a shark dissection (sharks' stomachs have included such surprising objects as a boot, a tin can, and a car license plate!) and an enjoyable and fascinating audiovisual presentation on sharks and shark nets. An exhibit area and good curio shop are also here. You can join the early morning trip from Durban harbor to watch the staff service the shark nets off Durban's Golden Mile. Depending on the season, you will more than likely see dolphins and whales close at hand. Booking is essential for trips to the shark nets, and a minimum of six people is required; no one under age six is allowed. ■ TIP➡ Book well in advance for this—it may turn out to be a highlight of your trip. No kids under 6. ⊠ *1a Herrwood Dr.* ☎ *031/566–0400* ⊕ *www.shark.co.za* 🖼 *Presentation R35, boat trips R250* ☻ *Presentation Tues., Wed., and Thurs. at 9 and 2, Sun. at 2. Boat trips to shark nets, daily (weather dependent) 6:30–8:30* AM.

uShaka Marine World. This aquatic complex combines the uShaka Sea World aquarium and the uShaka Wet 'n Wild water park. The world's fifth largest aquarium and the largest in the Southern Hemisphere, **uShaka Sea World** has a capacity of nearly 6 million gallons of water, more than four times the size of Cape Town's aquarium. The innovative design is as impressive as the size. You enter through the side of a giant ship and walk down several stories, past the massive skeleton of Misty, a Southern Right whale that died near Cape Town after colliding with a ship, until a sign welcomes you to the BOTTOM OF THE OCEAN. Here you enter a "labyrinth of shipwrecks"—a jumble of five different fake but highly realistic wrecks, from an early-20th-century passenger cruiser to a steamship. Within this labyrinth are massive tanks, housing more than 200 species of fish and other sea life and the biggest variety of sharks in the world. On land, there are dolphin and seal shows, and there are several activities offered for an additional fee.

The extensive **uShaka Wet 'n Wild** water fun park comprises slides, pools, and about 10 different water rides. The intensity ranges from toddler to adrenaline junkie. Durban's moderate winter temperatures make it an attraction pretty much all year round, though it's especially popular in summer. ■ TIP➡ Avoid it on public holidays and call ahead during the winter as hours can change. ⊠ *1 Bell St., Point* ☎ *031/328–8000* ⊕ *www.ushakamarineworld.co.za* 🖼 *Sea World R99, Wet 'n Wild R99, combo ticket R130* ☻ *Daily 9–5.*

WHERE TO EAT

Durban offers some superb dining, provided you eat to its strengths. Thanks to a huge Indian population, it has some of the best curry restaurants in the country. Durban's other great gastronomic delight is fresh seafood, especially prawns brought down the coast from Mozambique. Apart from the food, some of the dining locales—including many with spectacular sea views—are among the best in the world.

$–$$
MEDITERRANEAN

✕ **Bean Bag Bohemia.** One of the city's most intimate and popular restaurants, Bean Bag serves a mix of cosmopolitan and Mediterranean food. It's abuzz with Durban's young and trendy, especially late at night, when you can get a good meal after a movie or the theater. Cocktails and lighter meals are served at the downstairs bar, where live musicians often play jazz. Up rickety wooden stairs at the main restaurant, a popular starter is the meze platter, with Mediterranean snacks such as hummus, baba ghanoush (an eggplant spread), olives, and pita. It's well known for its vegetarian meals, but dishes such as lamb shank and duck are also good. Finish your meal with the baked pecan-praline cheesecake and then relax on the terrace. ✉ *18 Lilian Ngoyi (Windermere) Rd., Morningside* ☎ *031/309–6019* ⊕ *www.beanbagbohemia. co.za* ▭ *AE, DC, MC, V.*

$$–$$$
SEAFOOD
★

✕ **Cargo Hold.** You might need to book several months in advance to secure a table next to the shark tank here, but if you do it'll be one of your most memorable dining experiences ever. You can enjoy a trio of carpaccios—smoked ostrich, beef, and salmon—while 13-foot ragged-tooth and Zambezi sharks drift right by your table. Aside from the array of fish dishes like sesame-seared tuna and kingklip à la Cargo (grilled kingklip topped with mussels poached in a passion-fruit-and-bourbon cream sauce), Cargo Hold also serves meat dishes like oxtail, and rosemary-and-rock-salt leg of lamb. The restaurant is done up like a shipwreck; of three floors, two have tank frontage (the view of the shark tank from the bottom floor is best, so ask for this when booking). The restaurant is part of the building known as the Phantom Ship. Access to the ship costs R20, though this is refunded if you dine in Cargo Hold. ✉ *1 Bell St., Point* ☎ *031/328–8065* ✍ *Reservations essential* ▭ *AE, DC, MC, V.*

$$–$$$
ECLECTIC
★

✕ **Havana Grill & Wine Bar.** The sea views and good food combine to make this one of Durban's finest restaurants. It offers spectacular sea vistas (ask for a table with a view when making your reservation) and minimalist Afro-Cuban decor, with richly upholstered chairs, some leather couches, and antelope horns on the walls. Steak—aged on meat hooks in a giant fridge—and seafood are both specialties. Try Havana's tasting platter for starters (minimum of two people sharing): nachos; jalapeño poppers stuffed with cheese; grilled calamari; and spring rolls. For mains, consider the Lamb Tanganyika, which is rubbed with toasted cumin and coriander and served with a rich gravy, or line fish (likely sailfish, dorado, or Cape salmon) served in five different ways: grilled with lemon butter; topped with fresh pesto and fettuccine; with a coriander dipping sauce and wasabi-infused mash; in a Thai green coconut curry; and in an Asian red curry. There's a good basic wine list as well as a walk-in cellar from which special bottles can be ordered.

✉ Shop U2, Suncoast Casino & Entertainment World, North Beach ☎ 031/337–1305 ⊕ www.havanagrill.co.za ⚞ Reservations essential ▭ AE, DC, MC, V.

WHERE TO STAY

Hotel reviews have been abbreviated in this book. For expanded reviews, please go to Fodors.com.

$$$
★

Quarters on Florida. Four converted Victorian homes comprise the city's most intimate boutique hotel, on Florida Road; an additional, newer, 17-room property up the road is called Quarters on Avondale. **Pros:** tastefully appointed rooms; on-site restaurants; close to restaurants and nightlife of Florida Road. **Cons:** despite efforts, street-facing rooms are noisy; no pool; limited off-street parking. ✉ *101 Florida Rd., Morningside* ☎ *031/303–5246* ⊕ *www.quarters.co.za* ⤤ *17 rooms* ⚿ *In-room: a/c, safe, refrigerator, Internet. In-hotel: restaurant* ▭ *AE, DC, MC, V* ⦿ *CP.*

$$

Southern Sun Elangeni. One of the best hotels on the beachfront, this 21-story high-rise overlooks North Beach and is a two-minute drive from the city center. **Pros:** tour and travel desk; friendly staff; tastefully decorated rooms; great on-site restaurants; discounted weekend rates. **Cons:** not for travelers who prefer an intimate hotel experience; breakfast not included in price during peak times. ✉ *63 Snell Parade, Beachfront* ☎ *031/362–1300* ⊕ *www.southernsun.com* ⤤ *449 rooms* ⚿ *In-room: safe, refrigerator (some), Internet. In-hotel: 3 restaurants, room service, bars, pools, gym* ▭ *AE, DC, MC, V.*

$$–$$$

Suncoast Hotel and Towers. Situated adjacent to the Suncoast Casino, the hotel is a stone's throw from the beach. **Pros:** closest hotel to Moses Mabhida Stadium; fantastic spa; access to beautiful beach (albeit with a R5 fee). **Cons:** adjacent to casino; smallish rooms. ✉ *20 Battery Beach, Beachfront* ☎ *031/314–7878* ⊕ *www.southernsun.com* ⤤ *165 rooms* ⚿ *In-room: safe, refrigerator, Wi-Fi. In-hotel: restaurant, room service, bar, pool, gym, spa* ▭ *AE, DC, MC, V* ⦿ *BP (suites only).*

BEACHES

The sea near Durban, unlike that around the Cape, is comfortably warm year round: in summer the water temperature can top 27°C (80°F), whereas in winter 19°C (65°F) is considered cold. The beaches are safe, the sand is a beautiful golden color, and you'll see people swimming all year round. All of KwaZulu-Natal's main beaches are protected by shark nets and staffed with lifeguards, and there are usually boards stating the wind direction, water temperature, and the existence of any dangerous swimming conditions. Directly in front of uShaka Marine World, **uShaka Beach** is an attractive public beach. The **Golden Mile,** stretching from South Beach all the way to Snake Park Beach, is packed with people who enjoy the waterslides, singles' bars, and fast-food joints. A little farther north are the **Umhlanga beaches,** and on the opposite side of the bay are the less commercialized but also less accessible and safe beaches on **Durban's Bluff.** Another pretty beach and coastal walk, just north of the **Umhlanga Lagoon,** leads to miles of near-empty beaches backed by virgin bush. Please note: you should not walk alone on deserted beaches or carry any jewelry or other valuables, and you should never walk at night.

MAPUTALAND COASTAL FOREST RESERVE

300 km (186 mi) from Richards Bay.

GETTING HERE AND AROUND

Visitors fly into Richards Bay from Johannesburg and are picked up by the lodge, which will make all the flight and pickup arrangements. If you'd like to drive instead of flying, the lodge can arrange a car service to get you to and from Johannesburg. You could drive yourself, but it's really an unnecessary waste of time as you won't be able to use the vehicle once you're on the property. Plus, you'd need to rent a 4x4 as the last part of the road is very bumpy and muddy.

WHEN TO GO

The loggerhead and leatherback turtle egg-laying season goes from November through early March. During these months rangers lead after-dinner drives and walks down the beach to look for turtles, and you can expect to cover as much as 16 km (10 mi) in a night. From a weather standpoint, the best times to visit the lodge are probably spring (September–October) and autumn (March–May). In summer the temperature regularly soars past 38°C (100°F), and swimming during winter is a brisk proposition. August is the windiest month, and it's in summer that the turtles come ashore to dig their nests and lay their eggs—an awesome spectacle.

EXPLORING

Maputaland Coastal Forest Reserve. Expect great swaths of pale, creamy sand stretching to far-off rocky headlands; a shimmering, undulating horizon where whales blow. Watch out for pods of dolphins leaping and dancing in the morning sun. If you're here in season (November–early March), one of nature's greatest and most spiritually uplifting experiences is waiting for you—turtle tracking. Nothing, not photographs, not wildlife documentaries, prepares you for the size of these creatures. On any given night, you might see a huge, humbling leatherback, 2 meters long and weighing up to 1,100 pounds, drag her great body up through the surf to the high-water mark at the back of the beach. There she will dig a deep hole and lay up to a 120 gleaming white eggs, bigger than a golf ball but smaller than a tennis ball. It will have taken her many, many years to achieve this moment of fruition, a voyage through time and across the great oceans of the world—a long, solitary journey in the cold black depths of the sea, meeting and mating only once every seven years, and always coming back to within 100 meters of the spot on the beach where she herself had been born. And if your luck holds, you might even observe the miracle of the hatchlings, when perfect bonsai leatherback turtles dig themselves out of their deep, sandy nest and rush pell-mell toward the sea under a star-studded sky.

WHERE TO STAY

Hotel reviews have been abbreviated in this book. For expanded reviews, please go to Fodors.com.

$ 🏠 **Rocktail Beach Camp.** This family-friendly, rustic camp lies behind Fodor'sChoice the dunes fronting the Indian Ocean in lush coastal forest. It's a brisk ★ 20-minute walk to the golden beach that sweeps in a gentle arc several miles to the north. **Pros:** great place to relax; children's playroom. **Cons:** 20-minute walk to the beach. ☎ *011/257–5111* ⊕ *www.safariadventurecompany.com* ➷ *17 chalets* ⚴ *In-hotel: bar, pool* ▤ *AE, DC, MC, V* ⫯⊙⫯ *FAP.*

$ 🏠 **Thonga Beach Lodge.** Dramatically sited, this lovely beach lodge makes Fodor'sChoice the best of its unique situation. **Pros:** Robinson Crusoe deluxe; privacy ★ and tranquility; discover different (all magical) ecosystems. **Cons:** difficult to get to, so pricey. ☎ *035/474–1473* ⊕ *www.isibindi.co.za* ➷ *12 chalets* ⚴ *In-hotel: bar, pool, Internet terminal* ▤ *MC, V* ⫯⊙⫯ *FAP.*

5

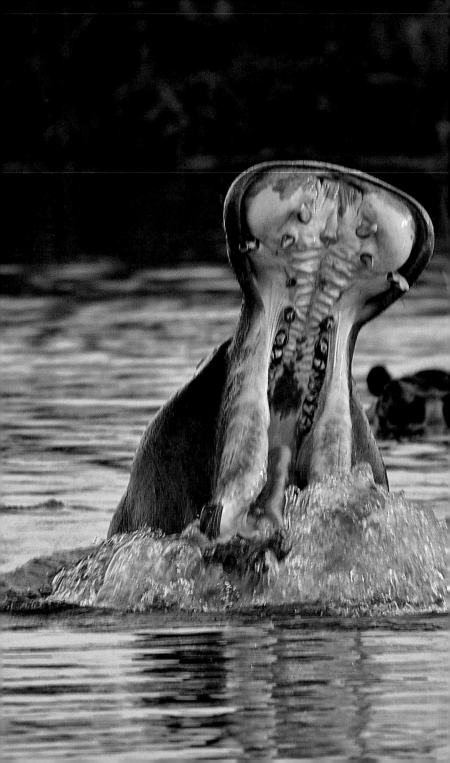

Botswana

WELCOME TO BOTSWANA

TOP REASONS TO GO

★ **The Okavango Delta.** Whether you are drifting dreamily in a *mokoro* through the crystal-clear, papyrus-fringed channels, or walking among ancient trees on one of the many islands, your everyday world is guaranteed to fade from your consciousness.

★ **Big Game.** You won't find huge herds as in Serengeti, but you will come face-to-face with more critters than you ever knew existed. And there won't be hordes of other visitors blocking your view or diluting the experience.

★ **Birding.** Marvel at more than 900 species—many endemic—that crowd the game reserves. A sighting of a Pel's fishing owl, one of the world's rarest birds, will have Audubon twitching in his grave.

★ **Walking with the Bushmen.** Far from being lifeless, deserts are miracles of plenty, you just have to be in the right company—that of the Kalahari Bushmen. Listen to their dissonant music, watch them dance a dance as old as time, and then listen to the stars sing.

1 The Okavango Delta. The Okavango Delta is formed by the Okavango River, which descends from the Angolan highlands and then fans out over northwestern Botswana. It's made up of an intricate network of channels, quiet lagoons, and reed-lined backwaters. There *is* big game, but it's more elusive and difficult to approach than in the game reserves.

2 Moremi Game Reserve. In the northwestern sector of the Okavango lies the spectacular reserve where the life-giving waters of the Okavango meet the vast Kalahari. Teeming with game and birds, it is one of Africa's greatest parks, and, unlike the Masai Mara or Kruger Park, with hardly any people. You'll love the Garden of Eden atmosphere even if you do encounter the odd snake or two.

ANGOLA

Kwando Reserve

Sepupa

Moremi Game Reserve

OKAVANGO DELTA

Maun

Toteng

NAMIBIA

Ghanzi

Tshootsha

Kule

KALAHARI

Tshane

Tsabong

SOUTH AFRICA

0   100 mi

0   100 km

3 Chobe National Park.
Huge herds of game roam this 11,700-square-km (4,500-square-mi) park that borders the Chobe River in northeast Botswana. Although it's one of Africa's great game reserves, its lack of roads and often almost inaccessible conditions—especially in the rainy season—mean you'll need a 4x4 to tackle it on your own.

ZAMBIA

Chobe
Kasane
Kachikau
CHOBE
Chobe National Park
3
ZIMBABWE
Nxai Pan
Makgadikgadi Pan
Mopipi
Ntwetwe Pan
Sowa Pan
Francistown
Central Kalahari Game Reserve
Selebi Phikwe
Serowe
Mashatu Game Reserve
Mahalapye
SOUTH AFRICA
D E S E R T
Molepolole
Mochudi
GABORONE ✪
Kanye
Lobatse

GETTING ORIENTED

Botswana is roughly the size of France or Texas, and nearly 18% is reserved for conservation and tourism. The Moremi Game Reserve, the first such reserve in Southern Africa created by an African community on its own tribal lands, is a major draw. One hundred kilometers (62 mi) west of Victoria Falls in Botswana's northeast corner is Chobe National Park, known for its elephants. The wide and tranquil Chobe River is surrounded by a natural wilderness of floodplain, dead lake bed, sand ridges, and forest. Downstream it joins the mighty Zambezi on its journey through Zimbabwe and Mozambique. Upstream, where it's known as the Linyanti, it forms the border between Botswana and Namibia. In this area the Linyanti Reserve, which borders Chobe National Park, is a huge private concession, as is the Kwando Reserve, to the west.

4 Kwando Reserve.
This 2,300-square-km (900-square-mi) private reserve northwest of Chobe and Linyanti has more than 80 km (50 mi) of river frontage. It stretches south from the banks of the Kwando River to the Okavango Delta. It's an area crisscrossed by thousands of ancient game trails traversed by wildlife that move freely between the Okavango Delta, Chobe, and the open Namibian wilderness to the north.

6

GREEN LODGINGS IN BOTSWANA

Botswana's fragile ecosystem is made up of more than 15,000 square km (5,791 square mi) of waterways. Make sure you're doing your part to preserve this vast area by checking into an eco-conscious lodge. Our list of options is a good place to start.

(above) Duba Plains; (opposite top right) Chief's Camp; (opposite bottom right) Nxabega Okavango Safari Camp

Chief's Camp (☎ 11/438–4650 ⊕ www.sanctuarylodges. com) is in the exclusive Mombo Concession of the Okavango Delta's Moremi Game Reserve. The area is home to the rare white rhino and is the only area in Botswana where these animals can be seen in their natural environment. The lodge was built with wood from commercially grown forests using the skills of local builders. Also, the limited number of suites is part of the camp's commitment to low-impact tourism. The camp works in partnership with the nonprofit Friends of Conservation in an effort to involve the local community in the running of the camp. *See Luxury Lodging, in Moremi Game Reserve, for more information about the camp.*

DID YOU KNOW?

Wondering where Nxabega Okavango Safari Camp got its interesting name? *Nxabega* (pronounced Na-becka) means "Place of the Giraffe" in the language of the Bayei, who live nearby in the most remote parts of the delta.

Needless to say, giraffe aren't the only animals here. The Okavango has lion, elephant, antelope, hippo, and many other species.

MORE GREEN LODGES IN BOTSWANA

Arguably the Okavango Delta's most remote camp, **Duba Plains** (☎ 11/807–1800 ⊕ www.dubaplains.com) is built on an island that can be reached only by plane. Shaded by ebony, fig, and garcinia trees, and surrounded by vast plains—which are flooded from about May to early October, depending on the rains—the camp is ideal for true wilderness buffs. The camp is in the Kwedi Reserve, a massive wildlife sanctuary that has been ceded by the Botswana Government and the Tawana Land Board to the people who live in the north of the delta. The aim is that the local people benefit from the wildlife that tourists come to see in their "backyard," so to speak. Annual payments are made to a trust called the Okavango Community Trust, which represents the interests of all the people living in the five villages to the north of the Okavango. *See Permanent Tented Camps, in the Okavango Delta for more information about the camp.*

Set on the edge of the Okavango Delta in a private wildlife concession on the southwestern border of the Moremi Wildlife Reserve, **Nxabega Okavango Safari Camp** (☎ 11/809–4300 ⊕ www.andbeyond.com) is made up of nine classic safari tents on raised platforms with private verandas. The camp overlooks wetlands, delta channels, and grassy floodplains, which host lion, leopard, elephant, and buffalo, as well as several unique bird species; African ebony and strangler figs shade the main camp. Boat excursions and bush walks are offered, and the staff will even arrange wilderness picnics or breakfast in bed. &Beyond, which runs Nxabega Camp, promotes sustainable development in the region through the nonprofit Africa Foundation. Projects include building classrooms, libraries, and clinics, as well as offering jobs to the local Tswana people. *See Permanent Tented Camps, in the Okavango Delta for more information about the camp.*

BE SENSITIVE TO CULTURES AND CUSTOMS

- You'll often receive service with a smile, but service with speed is a different story.

- Be clear on the tipping protocol of your tour operator and/or lodges. Paying too little or too much can be viewed as disrespectful of a person's work ethic and way of life.

- Always ask before taking photos (i.e., locals), and make sure there's adequate distance between you and the subject (i.e., wildlife).

- No revealing clothing, especially in African cities, as this is offensive to the Muslim majority.

- Behave appropriately at religious sites.

- Keep the binoculars for safari use only. They aren't necessary in cities or near military personnel or national landmarks.

6

By Kate
Turkington

More than half a century ago Botswana was a Cinderella among nations. Then the Fairy Godmother visited and bestowed upon her the gift of diamonds. The resulting economic boom transformed Botswana into one of Africa's richest countries (as measured by per capita income). In 1966 the British Protectorate of Bechuanaland was granted independence and renamed Botswana, and the first democratic president, the internationally respected Sir Seretse Khama, guided his country into a peaceful future.

Where other nations' celebrations quickly turned sour, Botswana's independence brought an enduring tide of optimism. The country sidestepped the scourge of tribalism and factional fighting that cursed much of the continent and is considered one of Africa's most stable democracies. The infrastructure is excellent, and the country's extremely safe. Another big bonus is that nearly everybody speaks English—a legacy from when Botswana was a British colony.

Although cities such as Gaborone (pronounced *ha*-bo-ronee), the capital, have been modernized, Botswana has little in the way of urban excitement. But outside the cities it's a land of amazing variety: the Kalahari Desert is in stark contrast to the lush beauty of the Okavango Delta, one of Botswana's most magnificent and best-known regions. Botswana is passionate about conservation, and its legendary big game goes hand-in-hand with its admirable conservation record. Once a hunting mecca for the so-called Great White Hunters (i.e., Ernest Hemingway), most shooting now is with cameras, not rifles. A few proclaimed hunting areas still exist, but they are strictly and responsibly government controlled.

Botswana's policy of low-impact, high-cost tourism ensures the wilderness remains pristine and exclusive. Nearly 18% of the country's total land area is proclaimed for conservation and tourism. The Moremi Game Reserve, for example, was the first such reserve in Southern

Africa to have been created by an African community (the Batawana people) on its own tribal lands.

The great rivers—the Chobe, the Linyanti and the Kwando—are teeming with herds of elephants and packs of wild dogs, otherwise knows as the elusive "painted wolves" of Africa. The Savuti Channel, which was dry for decades, is now flowing again and is a mecca for water birds. The golden grasses of the Savuti plains are still home to huge prides of lions which hunt under skies pulsing with brilliant stars. Then there are the vast white pie-crust surfaces of the Makgadikgadi Pans (the nearest thing on earth to the surface of the moon), once a mega inland lake where flamingoes still flock to breed and strange prehistoric islands of rock rise dramatically from the flaky, arid surface.

If you'd like to meet some of the most fascinating people, the stark and desolate Central Kalahari Game Reserve is home to the fastest-disappearing indigenous population on earth, the Kalahari Bushmen.

> **TIPPING IN BOTSWANA**
>
> Though the national currency is the pula, you can use U.S. dollars or euros as tips. Your information folder at each lodge will give helpful suggestions on whom and what to tip.

PLANNING

WHEN TO GO

The best time to visit Botswana is in the autumn and winter months (April through September), though it's also the most expensive. In the delta during the winter months the water has come in from the Angolan highlands, and the floodplains, channels, lakes, and inland waterways are literally brimming with sparkling, fresh water. Elsewhere, as it's the dry season, the grass and vegetation are sparse, and it's much easier to see game, which often have no choice but to drink at available water holes or rivers. But be warned: it can be bitterly cold, particularly early in the morning and at night. Dress in layers (including a thigh-length thick jacket, hat, scarf, and gloves), which you can discard or add to as the sun goes up or down.

During the green season (October–February), aptly named as it's when the bush is at its most lush and is populated with lots of baby animals, you'll find great economy deals offered by most of the lodges, but, and this is a big but, it's very hot—temperatures can reach up to 35°C (95°F). If you're a birder (Botswana has more than 400 species of birds), this is the best time to visit because all the migratory birds have returned. Unless you're in a lodge with air-conditioning, can stand great heat, or are a keen bird-watcher, stick with fall and winter.

FAST FACTS

Size At 581,730 square km (224,607 square mi), it's roughly the size of France or Texas.

Capital Gaborone.

Number of National Parks Six. Chobe National Park (including the Savuti and Linyani areas); Mokolodi Nature Reserve; Moremi Game Reserve; Okavango Delta; Central Kalahari Game Reserve; Kgalagadi National Park.

Number of Private Reserves As new private reserves and concessions are established regularly, it's difficult to estimate. Private reserves can be found in all the following areas: Okavango Delta, Moremi Wildlife Reserve, Chobe, Linyanti, Savuti, Selinda, Kwando, Kalahari, the Tuli Block, Makgadikgadi Pans.

Population 2 million.

Big Five The gang's all here.

Language The national language is Setswana, but English is the official language and is spoken nearly everywhere.

Time Botswana is on CAST (Central African standard time), which is two hours ahead of Greenwich Mean Time and seven hours ahead of North American Eastern Standard Time.

GETTING HERE AND AROUND

AIR TRAVEL

AIRPORTS

In this huge, often inaccessible country, air travel is the easiest way to get around. Sir Seretse Khama Airport, 15 km (9½ mi) from Gaborone's city center, is Botswana's main point of entry. Kasane International Airport is 3 km (2 mi) from the entrance to Chobe National Park, and small but very busy Maun Airport is 1 km (½ mi) from the city center of this northern safari capital. All three are gateways to the Okavango Delta and Chobe; they're easy to find your way around in and rarely crowded.

Airports Kasane International Airport (☎ 625–0161). **Maun Airport** (☎ 686–0762). **Sir Seretse Khama Airport** (☎ 391–4518).

FLIGHTS

Air Botswana has scheduled flights from Johannesburg to Gaborone and Maun on a daily basis. The airline also flies Johannesburg to Kasane on Monday, Wednesday, and Friday. SA Express Airways also has daily flights between Johannesburg and Gaborone.

Mack Air, Northern Air, Sefofane Air, Swamp Air, and Delta Air/Synergy Seating fly directly between Johannesburg's Grand Central Airport, adjacent to O.R. Tambo, and Maun on private charters.

Airlines Air Botswana (☎ 395–1921 ⊕ www.airbotswana.co.bw). **Delta Air/Synergy Seating** (☎ 686–0044). **Mack Air** (☎ 686–0675). **Northern Air** (☎ 686–0385). **SA Express Airways** (☎ 11/978–5577 in South Africa; 397–2397 in Botswana). **Sefofane Air** (☎ 686–0778). **Swamp Air** (☎ 686–0569).

CHARTER FLIGHTS

Air charter companies operate small planes from Kasane and Maun to all the camps. Flown by some of the youngest-looking pilots in the world, these flights, which your travel agent will arrange, are reliable, reasonably cheap, and average between 25 and 50 minutes. Maximum baggage allowance is 12 kilograms (26 pounds) in a soft sports/duffel bag (no hard cases allowed), excluding the weight of camera equipment (within reason). Because of the thermal air currents over Botswana, and because most flights are around midday, when thermals are at their strongest, flights can sometimes be very bumpy—take air-sickness pills if you're susceptible to motion sickness; then sit back and enjoy the fabulous bird's-eye views. You're sure to spot elephants and hippos from the air.

CAR TRAVEL

All the main access roads from neighboring countries are paved, and cross-border formalities are user-friendly. Maun is easy to reach from South Africa, Namibia, and Zimbabwe, but the distances are long and not very scenic. Gaborone is 360 km (225 mi) from Johannesburg via Rustenburg, Zeerust, and the Tlokweng border post. Driving in Botswana is on the left-hand side of the road. The "Shell Tourist Map of Botswana" is the best available map. Find it at Botswana airports or in airport bookstores.

Forget about a car in the Okavango Delta unless it's amphibious. Only the western and eastern sides of the delta panhandle and the Moremi Wildlife Reserve are accessible by car; but it's wisest to always take a 4x4 vehicle. The road from Maun to Moremi North Gate is paved for the first 47 km (29 mi) up to Serobe, where it becomes gravel for 11 km (7 mi) and then a dirt road.

It's not practical to reach Chobe National Park by car. A 4x4 vehicle is essential in the park itself. The roads are sandy and/or very muddy, depending on the season.

CUSTOMS AND DUTIES

⇨ *For information on what you can and cannot bring into Namibia, see Customs and Duties, in the On Safari chapter.*

HEALTH AND SAFETY

There are high standards of hygiene in all the private lodges, and most hotels are usually up to international health standards. But malaria is rife, so don't forget to take those antimalarials. Botswana has one of the highest AIDS rates in Africa (approximately one in three are HIV positive) but also one of Africa's most progressive and comprehensive programs for dealing with the disease. All the private lodges and camps have excellent staff medical programs; you're in no danger of contracting the disease unless you have sex with a stranger. As in most cities, crime is prevalent in Gaborone, but simple safety precautions such as locking up your documents and valuables and not walking alone at night will keep you safe. On safari, there is always potential danger from wild animals, but your ranger will brief you thoroughly on the do's and don'ts of encountering big game.

The American embassy is in Gaborone, the country's capital city.

Most safari companies include medical insurance in their tariffs, but if not or there's a major problem, you can contact Medical Rescue International, which has 24-hour emergency help.

Embassies U.S. Embassy (✉ *Government Enclave, Embassy Dr., Gaborone* ☎ *395–3982*).

Emergencies Police (☎ *999*). **Ambulance** (☎ *997*). **Fire** (☎ *998*). **Medical Rescue** (☎ *911*).

Emergency Services Medical Rescue International (☎ *390–1601*).

MONEY MATTERS

The pula and the thebe constitute the country's currency; one pula equals 100 thebe. You will need to change your money into pula, as this is the only legally accepted currency. However, most camp prices are quoted in U.S. dollars.

There are no restrictions on foreign currency notes brought into the country as long as they are declared. Travelers can carry up to P10,000 (about US$1,600), or the equivalent in foreign currency, out of the country without declaring it. Banking hours are weekdays 9–3:30, Saturday 8:30–11. Hours at Barclays Bank at Sir Seretse Khama International Airport are Monday–Saturday 6 AM–10 PM.

COMMUNICATIONS

Botswana phone numbers begin with the 267 country code, which you don't dial within the country. (There are no internal area codes in Botswana.)

PASSPORTS AND VISAS

All visitors, including infants, need a valid passport to enter Botswana for visits of up to 90 days.

HOTELS AND LODGES

Most camps accommodate 12 to 16 people, so the only traffic you'll encounter among the delta's waterways is that of grazing hippos and dozing crocodiles. Even in the northern part of Chobe, where most vehicles are, rush hour consists of buffalo and elephant herds trekking to the rivers. Prices are highest June through October. Check with individual camps for special offers.

A word about terminology: "Land camps" are in game reserves or concessions and offer morning and evening game drives. If you're not in a national park, you'll be able to go out for night drives off-road with a powerful spotlight to pick out nocturnal animals. "Water camps" are deep in the Okavango Delta and often accessible only by air or water.

Many camps offer both a land and a true water experience, so you get the best of both worlds.

There is little or no local cuisine in Botswana, so the food is designed to appeal to a wide variety of visitors. Nevertheless, it is very tasty. Most camps bake their own excellent bread, muffins, and cakes and often make desserts such as meringues, éclairs, and homemade ice cream. And you'll find plenty of tasty South African wine and beer. Don't expect TVs or elevators, even at very expensive camps.

Most lodging prices are quoted in U.S. dollars, and you can use dollars as tips wherever you stay. The average price per person per night at private lodges is US$500–US$1,000, which includes accommodations, all meals, soft drinks, and good South African wine. Camps arrange transfers from the nearest airport or airstrip.

■ TIP→ It's important to note that there are few budget lodging options available in Botswana, and most of the camps we write about fall into the "luxury" category.

⇨ *For information on converters and electricity while on Safari, see Electricity, in the On Safari chapter.*

WHAT IT COSTS IN U.S. DOLLARS				
¢	$	$$	$$$	$$$$
Hotels under $500	$500–$600	$600–$700	$700–$800	over $800
Dining under P50	P50–P75	P75–P100	P100–P125	over P125

All prices refer to an all-inclusive per-person rate including tax, assuming double occupancy.

VISITOR INFO

Visit Botswana Tourism's Web site for tour operator and travel agency information. To be listed on the Web site, these organizations must satisfy and adhere to the high standards demanded by Botswana Tourism.

Contacts Botswana's Department of Tourism (☎ 395–3024 ⊕ www. botswana-tourism.gov.bw).

MUST-SEE PARKS

You'd probably like to see all of Botswana, but we know that's not always possible. So we've broken down the chapter by **Must-See Parks** (Okavango Delta, Moremi Game Reserve, Chobe National Park, and Kwando Reserve) and **If You Have Time Parks** (Linyanti and Central Kalahari Game Reserves) to help you better organize your time. We suggest, though, that you read about all of them and then choose which one is best for you.

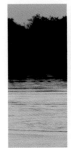

THE OKAVANGO DELTA

Game
★★★★★

Park Accessibility
☆☆★★★

Getting Around
☆★★★★

Accommodations
★★★★★

Scenic Beauty
★★★★★

There's no place on earth like the Okavango. The world's largest inland delta, the Okavango was formed by the Okavango River, which floods down from the Angolan highlands once a year and fans out into northwestern Botswana in a meandering complex network of papyrus-lined channels, deep still pools (where crocodiles and hippos lurk), secret waterways (where reeds and grasses almost meet over your head), palm-fringed islands, and natural lagoons.

This watery network covers an area of more than 15,000 square km (5,791 square mi), think a little smaller than Israel or half the size of Switzerland. The lily-studded crystal-clear water is so pure that you can drink it.

This vast area is sometimes referred to as the Swamps, but this gives a false impression because there are no murky mangroves or sinister everglades here. It's just open, tranquil waters where you'll discover an unparalleled experience of being in one of the world's last great wilderness areas. Often, the only way to get around this network of waterways is by boat.

The *mokoro*, a canoelike boat synonymous with the Okavango, was introduced to the delta in the mid-18th century, when the Bayei tribe (the River Bushmen) moved down from the Zambezi. The Bayei invented the mokoro as a controllable craft that could be maneuvered up- or downstream. These boats were traditionally made from the trunks of the great jackalberry, morula, and sausage trees. Today, because of the need to protect the trees, you may find yourself in the modern equivalent: a fiberglass canoe. Either way, a skilled poler (think gondolier) will stand or sit at the rear of the narrow craft guiding you through the delta's waterways—he will be on full alert for the ubiquitous and unpredictable hippos but may be a bit more laid-back when it comes to the mighty crocs that lie in the sun. (Powerboats are an option in deeper waters.) Bird-watching from these boats is a special thrill: the annual return of thousands of gorgeous carmine bee-eaters to the delta in August and September is a dazzling sight, as is a glimpse of the huge ginger-color Pel's fishing owl, the world's only fish-eating owl and one of its rarest birds. ■TIP➔ Don't miss the chance to go on a guided walk on one of the many islands.

A HAZARDOUS HERBIVORE

They may look cute and harmless, but it's been said that hippos cause more human deaths than any other large animal in Africa. Though they are not threatening creatures by nature and quickly retreat to water at any sign of danger, the trouble occurs when people get between a hippo and its water.

Although most camps are now both land- and water-based, in a water camp—usually an island surrounded by water—you'll almost certainly see elephants, hippos, crocs, and red lechwes (a beautiful antelope endemic to the Swamps), and you may catch a glimpse of the rare, aquatic sitatunga antelope. You'll almost certainly hear lions but may not always see them; if you're very lucky, you may see a pride swimming between islands. On the other hand, if you are in a land-and-water camp, you will see lots of game. Remember that you'll see plenty of animals elsewhere in Botswana. You're in the delta to experience the unforgettable beauty.

GETTING HERE AND AROUND

You'll fly into Maun and then be transferred by your tour operator to a small plane that will bring you to an airstrip in the delta. Distance from the airstrip to camps varies, but the longest would be 20–25 minutes and this is often an exciting game drive through the bush. Roads are bumpy but you are in a game vehicle.

WHERE TO STAY

LUXURY LODGES

$$$$ ⊡ **Jao Camp.** Spectacular Jao (as in "now"), a pure Hollywood-meets-Africa fantasy, is on a densely wooded island in a private concession bordering the Moremi Wildlife Reserve. Land and water activities are available, depending on the seasonal water levels, so you can take a day or night game drive in an open 4x4, glide in a mokoro through rippling meadows of water lilies, chug along hippo highways in a motorboat, or go on a guided walk. You'll see lots of predators, especially lions, which live here in the highest concentration in the country, according to a recent wildlife census. Accommodations are individual spacious tents with superb views over the vast floodplains. Private bath facilities include an indoor and outdoor shower, flush toilet, and Victorian clawfoot tub. Rare African artifacts decorate the multitiered wood interior of the main building. The food is delicious and the standard of service is superb. **Pros:** African fantasy deluxe; superb service; gorgeous views. **Cons:** lots of steps; game not always on tap. ☏ *11/807–1800* ⊕ *www. wilderness-safaris.com* ➴ *9 tents* ♿ *In-room: no phone, no a/c, no TV.*

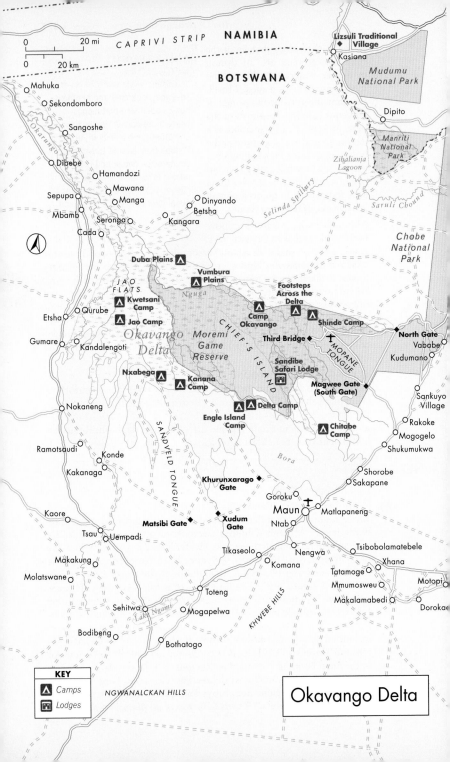

In-hotel: bar, pool, spa ⊟ *MC, V* ☉ *FAP.*

$$$$ ⛺ **Vumbura Plains.** If it's old-style African safari ambience you're looking for, then this camp is not for you. These state-of-the-art buildings are all about space, shape, light, and texture on a grand scale. Public areas are decorated with rag rugs, beaded beanbag chairs, fiberglass coffee tables (that resemble

giant pebbles), and some exquisite indigenous African artwork. The art deco–style carved wooden bar divides the lounge area from the dining area, which is decorated with dry hollow palm trunks and hanging lamps that mimic the local "sausage" trees. Sip your coffee or after-dinner drinks in deep padded armchairs by firelight on the deck as frogs pipe and fireflies dance. ⚠ There are many steps and long up-and-down boardwalks between the widely spaced rooms. If this seems a bit challenging, you may want to stay someplace else. Each en-suite room has a huge wooden outside deck, with comfortable lie-out chairs, a sala (thatched, outdoor daybed area), and plunge pool, and the enclosed living spaces have floor-to-ceiling windows and mesh doors that capture every source of light, from the early rays of dawn to the blazing sunset. Curl up with a book in your cushioned, sunken lounge, snooze in your king-size bed, or cool off in the emperor-size, leaf-patterned shower. Softly blowing gauzy white curtains divide the sleeping, living, and bathroom areas, and the decor of cream, grey, soft browns, and moss green echoes the pebble and stone theme of the main lodge. ■ TIP➜ Don't miss out on the superb curio shop; it's one of the best in Botswana. **Pros:** Manhattan in the bush; great game. **Cons:** not for the traditionalist; rooms have an open floor plan, and the showers are divided from the rest of the room by a glass beaded curtain. ☎ *11/807–1800* ⊕ *www.vumbura.com* ↪ *2 7-room camps* ♿ *In-room: no phone, no a/c, no TV. In-hotel: bar, pool* ⊟ *MC, V* ☉ *FAP.*

$$$ ⛺ **Delta Camp.** This enchanting camp is set deep on an island in the
♿ Okavango. Reed chalets, each with a private bathroom, are furnished with wood furniture and upturned mokoros; they look like something straight out of *The Swiss Family Robinson.* Each chalet faces northeast to catch the first rays of the sun as it rises above the palm trees, and below your windows are shallow, bird-filled pools, with deep waterways only paces from your front door. Family-owned for many years, the camp has an intimate, relaxed atmosphere; the goal here is to experience the tranquility of the environment. Activities include guided mokoro trails into the maze of waterways and game walks on adjacent islands with a professional licensed guide. A major conservation plus for Delta Camp: motorboats are not used as the emphasis is on preserving the pristine purity of the environment. This adds immeasurably to the relaxed, peaceful atmosphere that pervades this lovely camp. **Pros:** splendid isolation; no noises from motor boats. **Cons:** if you want to go power boating, this is not the place; comfortable but not luxurious accommodation. ☎ *686–1154* ⊕ *www.lodgesofbotswana.com* ↪ *7*

chalets ⚊ *In-room: no phone, no a/c, no TV* ▤ *MC, V* ⊙⏐ *FAP.*

$$$$ ⊞ **Kwetsani Camp.** Perched on high wooden stilts amid a forest canopy on a small island surrounded by enormous open plains, Kwetsani is one of the loveliest of the delta camps. The public areas overlooking the floodplains are built around huge, ancient trees, with a giant jackalberry dominating the bar. Each spacious room, made of canvas, wood, and slatted poles, is set like a child's building block in the middle of a large wooden deck built high into the trees. Polished wooden floors; coir mats; cane armchairs; butlers' tables with tea, coffee, and biscuits; billowing mosquito nets; twinkling ostrich-egg lamps; and indoor and outdoor showers all contribute to a warm, homey atmosphere. After enjoying a game drive or mokoro trip, end your day with a sundowner (cocktail) party by the lagoon lighted by flickering lanterns, with entertainment by the best in local talent—snorting hippos, whooping hyenas, and keening waterbirds. **Pros:** gorgeous views; genuine delta feel. **Cons:** game sporadic; don't expect to see lions. ☎ *11/807–1800* ⊕ *www. kwetsani.com* ➔ *6 rooms* ⚊ *In-room: no phone, no a/c, no TV. In-hotel: bar, pool* ▤ *MC, V* ⊙⏐ *FAP.*

$$$$ ⊞ **Sandibe Safari Lodge.** A land and water camp run by &Beyond, San-
★ dibe clings to the edge of a pristine channel of the Santantadibe River. Go fishing, take a mokoro ride through tunnels of interlacing papyrus, walk on a palm-studded island, or track big game in an open-sided vehicle. Watch out for some Okavango-specific animals: the aquatic tsessebe antelope—the fastest antelope—and the secretive sitatunga. The camp has a fairy-tale feel, as if a giant fashioned an idyllic tiny village out of adobe and thatch and set it down amid an enchanted forest full of birds. It'll be difficult to tear yourself away from your honey-color cottage with its huge carved bed covered with a woven leather bedspread to walk to the main lodge with its "curtains" of tattered russet bark wafting in the breeze. After a splendid dinner, enjoy a nightcap around a crackling fire under a star-studded sky. **Pros:** beautiful, stylish accommodation; great food. **Cons:** very small personal viewing decks; public areas can be cold in winter. ☎ *11/809–4300* ⊕ *www.sandibe. com* ➔ *8 cottages* ⚊ *In-room: no phone, no a/c, no TV. In-hotel: bar, pool* ▤ *MC, V* ⊙⏐ *FAP.*

PERMANENT TENTED CAMPS

$$ ⊞ **Camp Okavango.** Most people involuntarily draw a breath when
★ they walk from the airstrip into this sprawling campsite. Its location on remote Nxaragha (Na-*ka*-ra) Island in the heart of the permanent delta makes it accessible only by plane or water. Built by an eccentric American millionaire many years ago (she used to jet off to Los Angeles to get her hair done), this water camp combines style, comfort, and a year-round water wilderness experience. Huge trees arch over an outdoor lounge with sweeping lawns leading down to the water, where hippos snort all night. Your tent, with private bathroom, is built

"Obviously not happy with our encroachment, this hippo signals that we should move away before his splashing turns into a charge." —hslogan, Fodors.com member

on a raised wooden platform that overlooks the delta. It's set among groves of ancient trees and is so well separated that you might believe you're the only one in camp. Common areas with worn flagstones have comfortable colonial-style furniture, and elegant dinners are served in the high-thatch dining area, where an original sycamore fig mokoro is suspended over the long wooden dining table. A camp highlight: chilled drinks from a bar set up in the middle of a lagoon tended by a wading barman. **Pros:** a truly authentic water camp. **Cons:** no game-viewing by road; unlikely to see much game other than elephants and hippos. ☎ *11/394–3873* ⊕ *www.desertdelta.com* ⇱ *11 tents* ♿ *In-room: no phone, no a/c, no TV. In-hotel: bar, pool* ▭ *MC, V* ⏍ *FAP.*

$$$$ 🏕 **Chitabe Camp.** Bring lots of film to this exclusive reserve that borders the Moremi Wildlife Reserve; you'll want to take pictures of everything. Spacious, comfortable tents on stilts are connected by raised wooden walkways that put you safely above the ground and give you a Tarzan's-eye view of the surrounding bush. You'll sleep in a luxurious, East African–style tent with wooden floors, two comfortable single beds, woven palm furniture, wrought-iron washstands, and a private bath. A separate thatch dining room, bar, and lounge area, also linked by wooden walkways, looks out over a floodplain. Unfortunately, there are no vistas of water. The camp lies within the Botswana Wild Dog Research Project's research area, which has up to 160 dogs in packs of 10 to 12, so you're almost certain to see these fascinating "painted wolves." The area has a variety of habitats, from marshlands and riverine areas to open grasslands and seasonally flooded plains. Although it's on one of the most beautiful islands in the delta, it's not really a water camp because it doesn't offer water activities. **Pros:** very good chance to

Vumbura Plains

Kwetsani   Jao

see wild dogs. **Cons:** water activities dependent on season. ☎ *11/807–1800 ⊕ www.wilderness-safaris.com ↝ 8 tents at Main Camp, 4 tents at Trails Camp △ In-room: no phone, no a/c, no TV. In-hotel: bars, pool, Internet terminal ⊟ MC, V ⊘ FAP.*

$$$$ 🏕 **Duba Plains.** This tiny camp deep in the delta is nestled upon an island
Fodor's Choice shaded by huge trees and surrounded by horizon-touching plains that
★ are seasonally flooded—usually from late April to early October. When the water is high, the game competes with the camp for dry ground, and lions and hyenas become regular dusk-to-dawn visitors. You can watch hundreds of buffalo, leopards, lions, cheetahs, elephants, hippos, lechwes (a type of antelope), and the most beautiful of all the antelopes—the sable—from one of only two 4x4 open-game vehicles in the reserve. The Duba lion prides are among the few to hunt by day—they have a taste for buffalo—and if you're really lucky, you might find yourself and your vehicle bang in the middle of one of these spectacular hunts. The area is also a birder's paradise, with an abundance of waterfowl. En-suite tents with ceiling fans and gleaming Rhodesian teak furniture complement stupendous views. There's a comfy lounge and small bar in the public area and a poolside gazebo as well as a bird blind tucked behind the camp. **Pros:** some of the delta's best game-viewing with lions hunting by day; far way from other camps so there's little chance of traffic jams around the animals. **Cons:** renovations ongoing as we went to press. ☎ *11/807–1800 ⊕ www.dubaplains.com ↝ 6 rooms △ In-room: no phone, no a/c, no TV. In-hotel: bar, pool ⊟ MC, V ⊘ FAP.*

$$$$ 🏕 **Eagle Island Camp.** You'll find this camp deep in the central delta on Xaxaba (pronounced ka-*ka*-ba) Island, which is surrounded by pristine waterways, tall palm trees, and vast floodplains. At dawn and dusk hippos chortle, birds call, and hyenas whoop. Activities here are water based. You'll glide through high, emerald-green papyrus tunnels in a mokoro; go powerboating on wide lagoons; or enjoy sundowners as you float silently in your mokoro as the sun sets in a blaze of red and gold. Or have a front-row seat for the same nightly spectacle—a sunset—in the Fish Eagle Bar, which juts out over the water. Large walk-in tents are decorated in traditional African style with four-poster beds and lamps fashioned out of Botswana baskets and carved African pots. Sit out on your huge veranda, or snooze in the inviting canvas hammock. Dine in style in the elegant dining room where old photographs add to the classic safari ambience. The main viewing deck overlooks vast expanses of water complete with dozing hippos. **Pros:** gorgeous views of the delta; genuine delta water experience. **Cons:** this is a water camp, so no game drives. ☎ *21/483–1600 ⊕ www.orient-express-safaris.com ↝ 15 tents △ In-room: no phone, a/c, no TV, safe. In-hotel: bar, pool, Internet terminal ⊟ MC, V ⊘ AI.*

$$$ 🏕 **Kanana Camp.** The simple natural charm of Kanana makes you feel part of the delta, not cocooned away from it. Game drives, mokoro-ing, boating, and bush walks (there are resident Pel's fishing owls on nearby islands) are all part of the experience, but a visit to the Thapagadi Lagoon is a must. The lagoon is home to a fantastic heronry, where open-billed maribou and yellow-billed storks nest with all kinds of herons, cormorants, pelicans, darters, and egrets—you'll never forget

6

Botswana's Tribes

Bayei local people act as guides punting tourists around in mokoros canoes in the marshes of the Okavango delta

TSWANA

The largest tribal group in Botswana, the Tswana comprise just over half the country's population and mainly live in the eastern part of the country; many Tswana also live in South Africa. Also known as the Batswana, they live mainly in thatch-roof *rondavels* made of mud and cow dung. They are pastoralists and are tied to the land and their cattle, which are used in negotiating marriages and other rites of passage. Though the tribal structure of the Tswana has changed in modern times, they remain family oriented and still live in villages with the *kgosi* (chief) as the primary decision-maker. As Botswana has prospered from diamond mining, Tswana society has become more modernized, with many tribe members leaving the family at a young age to seek work in the cities. A large number of Tswana also speak English in addition to their tribal language.

BAYEI (RIVER BUSHMEN)

The Bayei, also known as the River Bushmen, live along the tributaries of the Okavango and Chobe rivers in northern and central Botswana. African oral history states that the Bayei came to the region in the 18th century from Central Africa. One of the tribe's great leaders then married one of the women of the San tribe, perhaps as a means of negotiating peace or perhaps to incorporate the tribe into the matrilineal society.

The Bayei are expert fishermen, and they use nets and traps to fish along the waterways and floodplains. The mokoro, a dug-out canoe carved from tree trunks, is also an essential part of their daily life, serving as both transportation along the rivers and an important tool for fishing. The Bayei also farm tobacco and wild corn.

the sounds of this avian community. Safari tents (where tea and coffee are brought at dawn by a cheerful staff member) with wooden decks overlook dense reed beds and a papyrus-thick floodplain. Cane furnishings and dark wood cabinetry are complemented by colorful rugs and a white curtain, which separates the gaily decorated bathroom from the bedroom. You'll fall asleep to the sound of hippos munching, squelching, and splashing outside your tent and awake to tumultuous birdsong. Public areas are built around a massive ancient fig tree, where green pigeons feast as you enjoy imaginative food on the dining deck. **Pros:** superb birding in the nearby heronry. **Cons:** no pool. ☎ *686–0375* ⊕ *www.kerdowneybotswana.com* ⤴ *8 tents* ⌂ *In-room: no phone, no a/c, no TV. In-hotel: bar, no children under 10* ⊟ *MC, V* ⍩ *FAP.*

$$$$ ⬚ **Nxabega Okavango Safari Camp.** Renowned for its beauty, Nxabega (pronounced *na*-becka) is in the very heart of the delta and offers both a water and a land experience. Because it's a private concession, you can take a night drive in an open vehicle and spot big predators as well as the small nocturnal ones like civets (black-and-white badger-looking creatures), bush babies (similar to furry, flying squirrels), and genets (small spotted cats). There's a resident naturalist to complement the team of knowledgeable and friendly &Beyond–trained guides. En-suite safari tents are on raised teak platforms, each with a private veranda overlooking the water and bush. The main lodge is made of thatch and wood; the high-roofed and paneled dining room has an almost medieval banquet-hall feel. The food is excellent but don't worry, you'll lose some of those extra calories by taking a guided walk on one of the nearby islands to track game and spot birds. **Pros:** guests have the opportunity to experience game drives and water excursions. **Cons:** no sweeping views of the delta. ☎ *11/809–4300* ⊕ *www.andbeyond.com* ⤴ *9 tents* ⌂ *In-room: no phone, no a/c, no TV. In-hotel: bar, pool, shop* ⊟ *MC, V* ⍩ *FAP.*

$$$$ ⬚ **Shinde Camp.** Ker & Downey's oldest camp, and possibly its loveliest, lies in a vast palm-dotted area in the heart of the northern delta. Surrounded by lagoons and waterways encrusted with white, yellow, and purple water lilies, and home to hundreds of birds, it's also home to lots of game. Your large tent, outfitted with cane and Rhodesian teak furniture, has polished wooden floors both inside and outside on your viewing deck. Spacious bathrooms have flower-painted ceramic sinks, and a sturdy door leads to a separate outside toilet. A spiraling wooden ramp connects the dining area, built high in the trees at the top of the lodge, with a lookout deck and lounge in the middle and a boma under huge old trees at the bottom. If you want even more exclusivity and private pampering, opt for Shinde Enclave, which accommodates up to six guests with a private guide and waiter. **Pros:** perfect for those looking for the out-of-Africa experience; energy-giving ancient trees; superb birdlife. **Cons:** lots of steps. ☎ *686–0375* ⊕ *www.kerdowneybotswana. com* ⤴ *8 tents* ⌂ *In-room: no phone, no a/c, no TV. In-hotel: bar, pool, no children under 10* ⊟ *MC, V* ⍩ *FAP.*

6

MOREMI WILDLIFE RESERVE

Game
★★★★★
Park Accessibility
☆☆★★★
Getting Around
☆★★★★
Accommodations
★★★★★
Scenic Beauty
☆★★★★

Prolific wildlife and an astonishing variety of birdlife characterize this reserve, which has become well known because it's the first in Southern Africa to be proclaimed by the local people (the Batawana) themselves. As there are no fences, the big game—and there's lots of it—can migrate to and from the Chobe Park in the north.

Sometimes it seems as if a large proportion of Botswana's 70,000 elephants have made their way here, particularly in the dry winter season. Be prepared to check off on your game list lions, cheetahs, leopards, hyenas, wild dogs, buffalo, hippos, dozens of different antelopes, zebras, giraffes, monkeys, baboons, and more than 400 kinds of birds.

GETTING HERE AND AROUND
Self-driving is possible in the Moremi, but a 4x4 is essential because road conditions are poor (sometimes impassable in the rainy season) and distances from cities are long. Unless you have lots of time, are a really experienced 4x4 driver and camper, and are prepared for only limited camping facilities, we would recommend you stick to an all-inclusive fly-in package.

WHEN TO GO
If you're a birder, choose the hot summer months (November–April) because dozens of returning migrants flock here in the thousands. The return of the Carmine bee-eaters and Woodland kingfishers is a dazzling sight, as are the hosts of wading water birds, from storks of all kinds to elegant little sandpipers. Although during the South African school vacations (July and December) there are more vehicles than normal, traffic is mostly light, and in the Moremi, unlike many of Africa's other great reserves, you'll often be the only ones watching the game. Winter (May–October) is the best game-viewing time as the vegetation is sparse and it's easier to spot game. Also, because there's little or no surface water, animals are forced to drink at the rivers or permanent water holes. However, during the other months—known as the green

season—you'll often get fantastic offers by individual lodges, with greatly reduced rates. But be warned, summer temperatures can soar to the mid-30s centigrade and over, so make sure your lodge of choice has a pool and a/c, or at least a fan.

WHERE TO STAY

National-park lodging is better than in the old days, with new ablution blocks at the camp sites. But remember, you have to bring all your own supplies and drinking water, and roads are very bad, especially in the wet season. The camping sites are not fenced and lions, hyenas, and all sorts of game frequent them. If you're an overseas visitor, we suggest you stick to the private lodges. They might be pricey, but they're worth every penny.

LUXURY LODGING

$$$ ★ **Chief's Camp.** Located in the exclusive Mombo Concession of the Okavango Delta's Moremi Game Reserve, the area is home to the rare white rhino and is the only area in Botswana where these animals can be seen in their natural environment. The main lodge sits under a canopy of jackalberry, sausage, and rain trees. The lodge was built with wood from commercially grown forests using the skills of local builders. Also, the limited number of suites is part of the camp's commitment to low-impact tourism. Chief's Camp works in partnership with the nonprofit Friends of Conservation in an effort to involve the local community in the running of the camp. **Pros:** always has repeat customers; great friendly atmosphere; chance to see white rhinos. **Cons:** can be difficult to book because of the exclusivity and limited number of suites. ☎ 11/438–4650 ⊕ www.sanctuary.retreats.com ⇆ 12 suites ⚭ In-room: no phone, no a/c, no TV. In-hotel: bar, pool ☰ MC, V ⏚ FAP.

$$$$ Fodor's Choice ★ **Mombo Camp and Little Mombo.** On Mombo Island, off the northwest tip of Chief's Island, this legendary camp is surrounded by wall-to-wall game. Although there is plenty of surface water in the area (marshes and floodplains), it's strictly a land-activity camp. The camp has exclusive use of a large area of Moremi, so privacy is assured. Its great wildlife, including all of the large predators, has made this area one of Botswana's top wildlife documentary locations—*National Geographic* and the BBC have both filmed here. The stunning camp has identical guest rooms divided into two distinct camps: Mombo has nine rooms, Little Mombo only three. These camps are among the best known, most expensive, and most sought after in Botswana, so be sure to book months in advance. Each spacious room is built on a raised wooden platform with wonderful views over the open plains (you're almost guaranteed to see game as you sit there), and although the en-suite rooms have a tented feel, they are ultraluxurious. The dining room, lounge, and bar are also built on big wooden decks overlooking the magnificent animal-dotted savanna. The atmosphere is friendly, and the personal attention, food, and guides all excellent. **Pros:** brilliant game-viewing; one of the best safari lodges in Botswana. **Cons:** very, very pricey; often fully booked. ☎ 11/807–1800 ⊕ www.mombo.co.za

6

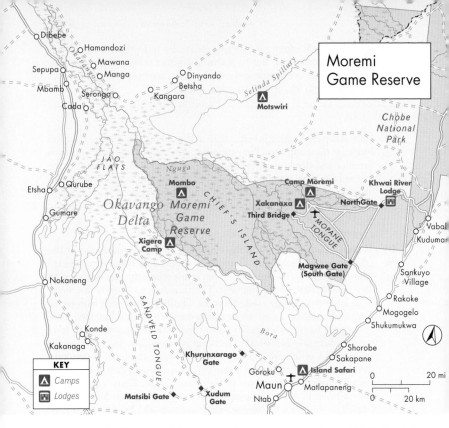

12 rooms ⚬ In-room: safe, no phone, no a/c, no TV. In-hotel: bar, pool ⊟ MC, V ⦿ FAP.

$$$$ 🛏 **Xigera Camp.** The cry of the fish eagle permeates this exceptionally
⟳ lovely camp (pronounced *kee*-jer-ah), which is set on the aptly named
★ Paradise Island amid thickets of old trees in one of the most beautiful
parts of the reserve. Spacious rooms of timber and canvas are built on a
high wooden platform overlooking a floodplain. Reed walls separate the
sleeping area from the spacious dressing room, which in turn leads into
a reed-floored shower and separate toilet; you can also shower under
the stars. Raised wooden walkways connect rooms to the main lodge,
which sprawls beside a lagoon where a small wooden bridge joins the
island to the mainland. At night this bridge becomes a thoroughfare for
lions and hyenas, and it's not uncommon to see one of these nocturnal
visitors walk by as you sip your postprandial drink by the blazing fire.
The food is varied and excellent, and the staff is ultrafriendly and attentive. **Pros:** lovely setting; camp bridge often has lions crossing, which
some may view as a con; very good food; indoor and outdoor showers.
Cons: less intimate than some smaller camps. 🖀 *11/807–1800* ⊕ *www.
xigera.com* *10 rooms ⚬ In-room: no phone, no a/c, safe, no TV. In-
hotel: bar, pool ⊟ MC, V ⦿ FAP.*

Mombo Camp

Mombo

Xigera

PERMANENT TENTED CAMPS

$$ ⛺ **Camp Moremi.** You get the best of both water and land at Camp Moremi. You'll see lions, elephants, giraffes, zebras, all kinds of antelopes, and often the elusive leopard, cheetah, and wild dog. The rare Pel's fishing owl regularly plummets down to the shallow pool below the Tree Lodge to snag a fish. Bird-watching is excellent throughout the year; ask for a powerboat ride to the heronries on nearby lagoons. Huge African ebony trees, home to two-legged, four-legged, winged, and earthbound creatures, dominate the campsite on the edge of a lovely lagoon. From the high viewing platform in the trees you can look out on a limitless horizon as the sun sets over the smooth, calm waters. Tastefully decorated, comfortable tents are well spaced to ensure privacy. Camp Moremi's timber-and-thatch tree lodge has a dining area, bar, lounge, library, and sundeck with great views of Xakanaxa Lagoon. **Pros:** excellent location in great game area; well established with ancient trees; Pel's fishing owl known to frequent camp. **Cons:** tents are comfortable but not ultraluxurious. ☎ *11/394–3873* ⊕ *www.desertdelta. com* 🛏 *11 tents* ⚹ *In-room: no phone, no a/c, no TV. In-hotel: bar, pool* ▤ *MC, V* ◎ *FAP.*

$$$$ ⛺ **Khwai River Lodge.** As you sit on the wooden deck jutting out over the clear delta waters, munching brunch or chilling out, you may just forget the outside world. Floating water lilies, tiny bejeweled kingfishers dipping and swooping in front of you, and the sounds of gently lapping water relax even the most driven work junkie. Bigger than some of the other safari lodges and one of the oldest, Khwai is renowned for its personal attention and friendly service. The location, 8 km (5 mi) northwest of the north gate of the Moremi Wildlife Reserve, means

"At Vumbura camp, the resident elephant was quite friendly and curious."
—Kim Freedman, Fodors.com member

that you will see lots of game, not only on your drives but also from the lodge itself. The excitement of seeing a hippo or elephant stroll past the viewing deck outside your deluxe tent is not something you'll easily forget. The lodge is also the stuff of bird-watchers' dreams. **Pros:** genuine delta experience; romantic bar with fabulous sunset views. **Cons:** Moremi Reserve is a bumpy 25-minute drive away. ☎ *21/483–1600* ⊕ *www.orient-express-safaris.com* ⤴ *15 tents* ⌂ *In-room: no phone, a/c, safe, no TV. In-hotel: bar, pool* ▤ *MC, V* ⦿ *FAP.*

$$$$
Ⓒ
Fodor's Choice
★

⬚ **Xakanaxa Camp.** For a genuine bush-camp experience—no unnecessary frills—it would be hard to beat this old-fashioned camp (pronounced ka-*kan*-ah-ka). From the moment you walk through the rustic reception area, a feeling of unpretentious warmth and relaxation envelops you; it's no wonder that visitors return again and again. Each spacious tent has wooden floors, plenty of storage space, a huge comfy bed, reading lamps, a megasize bathroom under the stars (read: no roof), and a viewing deck. Lighting at night is *au naturel* (candles, hurricane lamps, and flashlights), although there's electricity during the day. The staff, many with more than 10 years of experience, get everything right, from their attentive service to the superb, wholesome, home-cooked food. Even the resident croc, who sunbathes under her very own sign "BEWARE CROCODILE," has been here since she was a tiny whippersnapper. Wooden-decked public areas sprawl along the water, and elephants and hippos wander past your tent most nights. **Pros:** authentic, unpretentious, out-of-Africa experience; heaps of return guests; superb value for money. **Cons:** the only bad thing we can say is that it's not drop-dead luxury. ☎ *11/463–3999* ⊕ *www.xakanaxa-camp.com* ⤴ *12 tents* ⌂ *In-room: no phone, no a/c, no TV. In-hotel: pool* ▤ *MC, V* ⦿ *FAP.*

CHOBE NATIONAL PARK

This 12,000-square-km (4,500-square-mi) reserve is the second largest national park in Botswana, and it has four very different ecosystems: Serondela in the extreme northwest with fertile plains and thick forests; the dry Savuti Channel in the west; the Linyanti Swamps in the northwest; and the arid hinterland in between.

The whole area, however, is home to a shifting migratory population of more than 40,000 elephants. In addition to spotting Chobe's great pachyderm herds, you should see lions, leopards, hyenas, wild dogs, impalas, waterbucks, kudus, zebras, wildebeests (gnus), giraffes, and warthogs. Watch closely at the water holes when prey species come down to drink and are most vulnerable—they are so palpably nervous that you'll feel jumpy, too. Lions in this area are often specialized killers; one pride might target giraffes, another zebras, another buffalo, or even young elephants. But lions are opportunistic killers, and you could see them pounce on anything from a porcupine to a lowly scrub hare. Birdlife along the river is awesome and the major must-sees are the slaty egrets, rock pratincoles, pink-throated longclaws, and lesser gallinules.

The northern section of the park comprises riverine bush devastated by the hordes of elephants coming down to the perennial Chobe River to drink in winter. Fortunately, the wide sweep of the Caprivi floodplains, where hundreds of buffalo and elephants graze silhouetted against almost psychedelic sunsets, softens this harsh, featureless landscape where it faces neighboring Namibia.

A SUNSET CRUISE

A sunset sundowner cruise on the Chobe River is an unforgettable experience. If your own lodge offers this experience, you'll most likely be in a smallish boat, but if they don't, try to avoid the big, noisy "Booze Cruise" excursions sold by the travel companies in the area. Instead, opt for a smaller boat with an experienced local guide and boatman.

Chobe can be crowded, unlike the rest of Botswana, because there are simply too many vehicles on too few roads, particularly in the dry season. One of the quieter parts of the park is around the Ngwezumba River, an area of forests and pans in the more remote middle of the park; the drawback here is that game is harder to find.

In the southwestern part of the park lies the fabled Savuti (also spelled Savute) area, famous for its predators. Savuti offers a sweeping expanse of savanna brooded over by seven rocky outcrops that guard a relic marsh and the now-flowing Savuti Channel. Savuti is dramatically different from elsewhere in Botswana; there are open spaces, limitless horizons, wide skies, and unending miles of waving tall grass punctuated by starkly beautiful dead trees—the legacy of the relentless drought. Because of exceptional rains and an above-average flood in 2010, the Savuti Channel is now flowing again, attracting thousands of plains animals and attendant predators. Your chances of seeing wild dogs are high. Like Chobe National Park overall, Savuti is famed for its elephants, but the female of the species is less often seen here, for Savuti is the domain of the bull elephant: old grandfathers, middle-aged males, and feisty young teenagers. The old ones gaze at you with imperturbable dignity, but it's the youngsters who'll make your adrenaline run riot as they kick up the dust and bellow belligerently as they make a mock charge in your direction.

And while you're in the Savuti area looking for leopards and the tiny acrobatic klipspringer antelopes, be sure to pay a visit to the striking rock paintings, early humans' attempts to represent the wildlife all around. In summertime thousands of migrating zebras and wildebeests provide the equivalent of fast food for the lion prides, hungry hyenas, and cheetahs which follow the herds. The Cape buffalo herds also arrive in summer along with thousands of returning bird migrants. The raptors are spectacular. You'll see falcons, eagles, kestrels, goshawks, ospreys, and sparrow hawks. In the northwest of the park are the Linyanti Swamps, also famous for their game concentrations, and in particular wild dogs.

GETTING HERE AND AROUND

You can fly straight to Kasane from Johannesburg where your lodge will meet and transfer you. Most lodges are 10 minutes from the airstrip.

WHEN TO GO

You can see game elsewhere in Botswana (although not in these numbers), so you should visit May through September to find out why this place is unique.

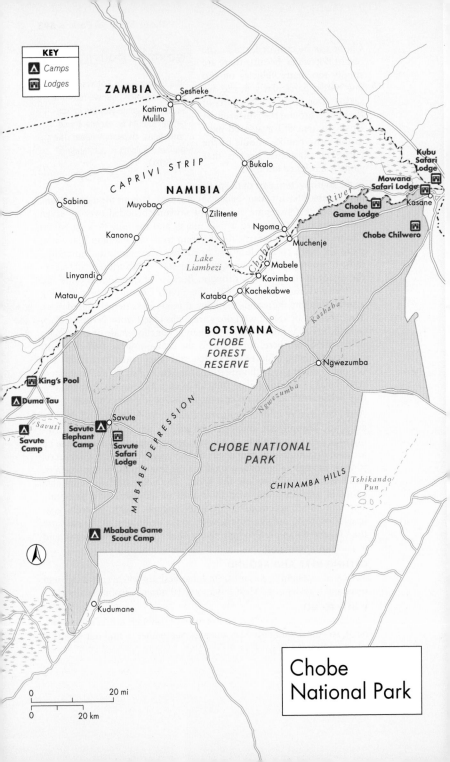

KEY
- △ Camps
- 🏠 Lodges

ZAMBIA · Sesheke

Katima Mulilo

CAPRIVI STRIP

NAMIBIA · Bukalo

Sabina · Muyoba · Zilitente

Kanono

Lake Liambezi

Ngoma

Muchenje

Kubu Safari Lodge

Mowana Safari Lodge

Kasane

Chobe Game Lodge

Chobe Chilwero

Linyandi

Matau

Mabele

Kavimba

Kataba · Kachekabwe

Chobe River

Kashaba

BOTSWANA
CHOBE FOREST RESERVE

Ngwezumba

King's Pool

Duma Tau

Savuti

Savute

Savute Elephant Camp

Savute Camp

Savute Safari Lodge

MBABABE DEPRESSION

Ngwezumba

CHOBE NATIONAL PARK

CHINAMBA HILLS

Tshikando Pan

Mbababe Game Scout Camp

Kudumane

0 _____ 20 mi

0 _____ 20 km

Chobe National Park

WHERE TO STAY

LUXURY LODGES

$$$$ ☂ **Chobe Chilwero River Lodge.** Easily accessible from both the Zimbabwe
☾ and Zambian side of Vic Falls, this lodge is perched on a small hill on
the border of Chobe National Park (Chilwero means "high view" in
Setswana, the national language). Its 15 spacious thatch cottages are
the ultimate in luxury: en-suite bathrooms with sunken baths, private
gardens with hammocks, and viewing decks with stunning vistas of the
Chobe River. Catch up on the real world (if you can bear to!) in the
communications center, or pamper yourself with an in-room beauty
treatment. All the Chobe activities are available, from walking safaris
and fishing to game drives, canoeing, day trips to the nearby Vic Falls,
and the must-not-miss sunset cruises. Although you're not really in a
wilderness area, the privacy and exclusivity of the lodge will persuade
you that you are miles away from civilization. **Pros:** lovely views; intimate atmosphere. **Cons:** situated near busy town, which means you are
not in the bush. ☎ *11/438–4650* ⊕ *www.sanctuaryretreats.com* ➲ *15
cottages* ☾ *In-room: no phone, no a/c, safe, no TV, Internet. In-hotel:
bar, pool, spa, laundry facilities, shop* ▤ *MC, V* ⦿ *FAP.*

$$ ☂ **Chobe Game Lodge.** The only permanent lodge in Chobe National
☾ Park, this grand old dame—Liz Taylor and Richard Burton got married
for the second time here in the '70s—still offers one of Botswana's most
sophisticated stays, although the feel is more hotel-like than lodgelike.
Terra-cotta tiles, Rhodesian teak furniture, tribal artifacts, and the ubiq-
uitous beautiful handwoven Botswana baskets give the feel of Africa.
The solid Moorish-style buildings—with their graceful high arches and
barrel-vaulted ceilings—insulate the not-so-intrepid traveler from too-
close encounters of the animal kind: baboon mothers have been known
to teach their young how to turn a doorknob! The gorgeous gardens
are a riot of color and attract lots of small fauna. Don't miss out on
the well-run daily activities from game drives to river cruises. An early-
morning canoe ride is also a must. **Pros:** well-run operation; lovely
views and gardens. **Cons:** hotel-like atmosphere; lots of tour groups.
☎ *11/394–3873* ⊕ *www.desertdelta.com* ➲ *46 rooms, 4 suites* ☾ *In-
room: no phone, a/c, safe, no TV. In-hotel: bar, pool, gym, Internet
terminal, library* ▤ *MC, V* ⦿ *FAP.*

$$$$ ☂ **Kubu Safari Lodge.** If you want to escape the real world for a while,
☾ then this small, quiet attractive lodge on the banks of the Chobe, which
prides itself on its seclusion, is right for you; it has no phones, radios,
or TV. Situated where Botswana, Namibia, Zimbabwe, and Zambia
meet, the 11 en-suite thatch chalets are on stilts and are unpretentiously
but comfortably furnished in earth tones. After your Chobe National
Park game drive or boat cruise, come back and take a leisurely saunter
around the Kubu Lodge Nature Trail—be on the lookout for dozens
of birds and the endemic Chobe bushbuck—or go next door to the
Crocodile Farm and eyeball Nelson, one of the oldest and biggest crocs
in captivity. **Pros:** very affordable; quiet. **Cons:** could be too quiet for
someone looking for excitement after the game drive. ☎ *31/762–2424*
⊕ *www.afrizim.com* ➲ *11 chalets* ☾ *In-room: no phone, no a/c, no TV.
In-hotel: restaurant, bar, pool, shop* ▤ *MC, V* ⦿ *FAP.*

6

¢ 🖼 **Mowana Safari Lodge.** Built round an 800-year-old baobab tree situated among lovely private gardens on the banks of the Chobe River, you'll find this lodge just 8 km (5 mi) from the entrance to Chobe National Park. Like its older sister, Chobe Safari Lodge, farther downstream, this lodge is more like a hotel than a safari lodge. That's not to say that you still won't get your full safari experience; you'll just be a bit cocooned away from the actual wilderness. Pleasantly decorated with an ethnic African theme, all 104 air-conditioned rooms overlook the river, on which you'll probably spend a fair amount of time boating, bird-watching, game-viewing, canoeing, and fishing. Morning, evening, and night drives are available, but because the river roads are few and many game vehicles use the same roads, your game-viewing can become rather crowded. You can take a short flight or helicopter ride over the nearby Victoria Falls, go white-water rafting on the Zambezi, or try a host of other activities. Children under 12 stay free if sharing with parents. **Pros:** great location; excellent excursions. **Cons:** big and bustling, more like a hotel than a lodge. ☎ 625–0300 ⊕ *www.afrizim. com* ⟲ *104 rooms* ⚄ *In-room: no phone, a/c, safe, refrigerator, no TV. In-hotel: bar, pool, shop* ☰ *MC, V* ⧖ *FAP.*

$$ 🖼 **Savute Safari Lodge.** As your small plane arrives at this attractive lodge, you can see the wide swath the dry riverbed makes through the surrounding countryside. The exterior of the main building and the safari suites are traditional thatch and timber; however, when you enter your suite, it's like walking out of Africa into a Scandinavian design center—blond wood, comfortable furniture in primary colors, gaily colored rugs, and lots of glass. Outside on your spacious deck it's back to Africa; by full moon watch the gray, ghostly shapes of elephants drinking from the water hole in front of the camp, or if the moon is not yet full, marvel at the stars. When you're not watching the abundant game, there's a large, elegant dining room where you can enjoy scrumptious late-morning brunches and candlelight silver-service dinners, a lounge with a huge fireplace, and an upstairs viewing deck. **Pros:** elephants galore; good wilderness feel. **Cons:** Scandinavian-inspired decor may not be to everyone's taste. ☎ 11/394–3873 ⊕ *www.desertdelta.com* ⟲ *12 suites* ⚄ *In-room: no phone, a/c, safe, no TV. In-hotel: bar, pool* ☰ *MC, V* ⧖ *FAP.*

PERMANENT TENTED CAMPS

$$$$ 🖼 **Savuti Camp.** This intimate camp has only seven walk-in tents, which are raised on stilts above the dry Savuti Channel. If you have an elephant phobia, don't even think about coming here, because all day and often all night long, elephants pass in front of the camp and in front of the tents on their way to and from the water hole directly in front of the dining area, pub, plunge pool, and viewing decks. This camp is also home to the legendary "woodpile hide"—a small enclosure at the water hole, which you hide in to watch the pachyderms a few feet away. You will feel part of the herd and feel protected from it. It's an amazing thrill to be nose-to-knee with elephants galore. Because the water hole is the only permanent water in the area, there's superb game-viewing all year round—particularly in winter—with lions, leopards, cheetahs, wild dogs, and hyenas. You'll have a good chance of also seeing roan

"We watched in awe as a leopard dragged the freshly killed impala, crossing just a few feet in front of our vehicle and headed for a clump of trees, where he could safely enjoy the meal." —wwhatmough, Fodors.com member

and sable antelopes—perhaps the most stately and beautiful of all the species. Your comfortable tent has a bathroom and shower, hand basin and flush toilets. If an elephant wanders past your tiny viewing deck (and one will), just stay still and enjoy the view, because it may be the best you ever get at such close quarters—and the best photograph, too. **Pros:** the woodpile hide is an amazing place to watch game. **Cons:** very dry and hot in the summer. ☎ *11/807–1800* ⊕ *www.wilderness-safaris. com* ⇥ *7 tents* ⌂ *In-room: no phone, no a/c, safe, no TV. In-hotel: bar, pool* ⊟ *MC, V* ⧓ *FAP.*

$$$$ ⌂ **Savute Elephant Camp**. In the semiarid Savuti region, splendid, spacious, air-conditioned, twin-bedded tents are elegantly furnished with cane and dark wood furniture, an impressive bed canopy with mosquito net, and a roomy bathroom with his-and-her sinks. For cold winter mornings and evenings, there's even a built-in heater. Your private viewing deck overlooking one of the busiest elephant water holes in the world has comfortable chairs and an inviting hammock. As the camp is in Chobe National Park, night drives and walking are against regulations, but you'll still see plenty of game and birds during the day. If you can manage to be here at full moon, the sight of hundreds of great, gray shapes gleaming in the moonlight is truly unforgettable. **Pros:** great location; great game sightings almost a guarantee. **Cons:** not very original decor, especially if you are staying at other Orient Express properties. ✉ *Chobe National Park* ⌖ *Orient-Express Safaris, Box 786432, Sandton 2146, South Africa* ☎ *21/483–1600* ⊕ *www. orient-express-safaris.com* ⇥ *12 tents* ⌂ *In-room: no phone, a/c, safe, no TV. In-hotel: bar, pool, no kids under 8* ⊟ *MC, V* ⧓ *FAP.*

Savuti Camp

Savuti Camp

Savuti Camp

KWANDO RESERVE

Game
★★★★★

Park Accessibility
☆☆★★★

Getting Around
☆★★★★

Accommodations
☆☆★★★

Scenic Beauty
☆☆★★★

This 2,300-square-km (900-square-mi) private concession has more than 80 km (50 mi) of river frontage. It stretches south from the banks of the Kwando River, through open plains and mopane forests to the Okavango Delta.

6

It's an area crisscrossed by thousands of ancient game trails traversed by wildlife that move freely between the Okavango Delta, Chobe, and the open Namibian wilderness to the north. As you fly in to the reserve, you'll see this web of thousands of interlacing natural game trails—from hippo highways to the tiny paths of smaller animals. This should clue you in to Kwando's diverse animal life: wall-to-wall elephants, crowds of buffalo, zebras, antelope of all kinds including roan and sable, wild dogs, lions, and wildebeests. Participants on one night drive came upon a running battle between a pack of 14 wild dogs and two hyenas who had stolen the dogs' fresh kill. The noisy battle ended when a loudly trumpeting elephant, fed up with the commotion, charged the wild dogs and drove them off. There's a sheer joy in knowing you are one of very few vehicles in a half-million acres of wilderness.

Kwando is a great place to take children on safari. The safari starts with a safety briefing, and kids get their own tents next to mom and dad (or you can share). Kids learn to track and take plaster casts of spoor, sit up in the tracker's seat on the vehicle to follow game, cook marshmallows over the boma fire, tell stories, catch and release butterflies, and make bush jewelry. Kids can eat on their own or with you, and if you want an afternoon snooze, they'll be supervised in a fun activity. The program's available at both Kwando camps; the price is the same per night as for an adult.

GETTING HERE AND AROUND

Guests fly directly into Kwando Reserve from Maun; the flight takes about 35–40 minutes. You'll be landing on a rough dirt airstrip, and transfer to lodges will take between 10 and 30 minutes.

WHEN TO GO

Visit May through September.

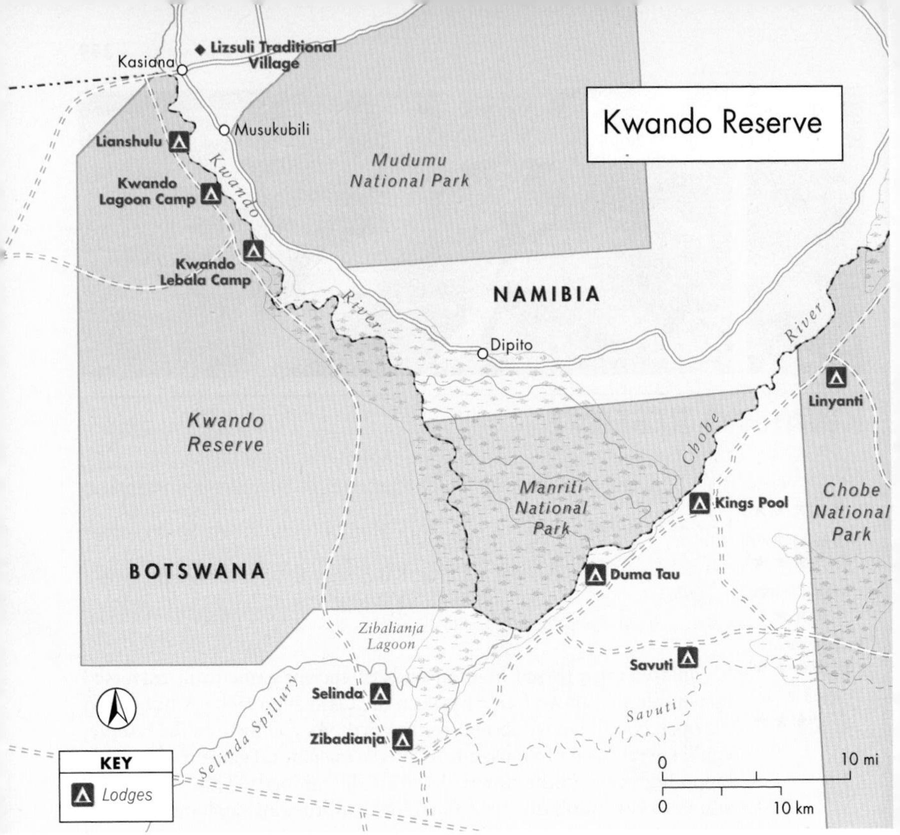

WHERE TO STAY

LUXURY LODGING

$$$$ Fodor's Choice ★ **Kwando Lagoon Camp.** The camp perches on the banks of the fast-flowing Kwando River, quite literally in the middle of nowhere. Comfortable walk-through tents with private bathrooms and verandas nestle on grassy slopes under the shade of giant jackalberry trees that are hundreds of years old. After a night spent next to one of these mighty trees, a major source of natural energy, people say you wake up rejuvenated, your body buzzing with new life. From the thatch dining and bar area you can watch herds of elephants only yards away as they come to drink and bathe, or hippos snoozing in the sun. You might also spot a malachite kingfisher darting like a bejeweled minijet over the water. Go for a morning or evening game drive, drift along the river in a small boat, or go spinner- or fly-fishing for tiger fish and bream. The emphasis in the camp is on informality, simplicity, and soaking up the wilderness experience. **Pros:** exclusivity: unforgettable river views. **Cons:** too close to nature for some; rustic but very comfortable. *686–1449 www.kwando.co.za 8 tents In-room: no phone, no a/c, no TV. In-hotel: bar, pool DC, MC, V FAP.*

$$$$ Fodor's Choice ★ **Kwando Lebala Camp.** Lebala Camp is 30 km (18 mi) south of Lagoon Camp and looks out over the Linyanti wetlands. The secluded tents, built on raised teak decks, are magnificent. All have private bathrooms

Kwando Lebala Camp

Kwando Lebala Camp

Kwando Lagoon Camp

with Victorian claw-foot tubs. If you want to get even closer to nature, bathe in your own outdoor shower or just sit on your sundeck and look out at the endless vistas. On morning or evening game drives you'll see loads of game, and if you fancy a freshly caught fish supper, try your hand at spinner fishing. **Pros:** superb predator viewing. **Cons:** very remote location makes it difficult to get to. ☎ *686–1449* ⊕ *www. kwando.co.za* ⤵ *8 tents* ⚬ *In-room: no phone, no a/c, no TV. In-hotel: pool* ⊟ *DC, MC, V* ⦿ *FAP.*

IF YOU HAVE TIME

By all means, do your Big Five–big park thing, but if you can make or take the time, these following parks and areas will entice you into their quite unforgettable uniqueness.

THE CENTRAL KALAHARI GAME RESERVE

One of the biggest conservation areas in the world, this huge area has its own unique beauty that's only enhanced by its vastness, emptiness, grandeur, and desolation. You won't see the prolific game of Chobe or Moremi, but there's unusual wildlife, such as the elusive brown hyena, the stately gemsbok, elegant kudus, African wild cats, leopards, and porcupines. And if you're very lucky, you may spot the huge, black-maned Kalahari lions, which dwarf their bush counterparts. Deception Valley—so-called because from a distance a dry riverbed appears to run deep and full—lies on the northern border of the reserve.

GETTING HERE AND AROUND

While self-drives are possible here, we don't advise it. Instead, fly in from Maun. Your lodge can and will arrange all your transportation to and from the airstrip for you in an open-sided game vehicle.

WHEN TO GO

Summers are very hot and winters very cold. The shoulder seasons (April and September) are the best.

WHERE TO STAY

¢   🏨 **Deception Valley Lodge.** This striking thatch-and-stone lodge is the
★   only lodge in the Central Kalahari and is worth visiting for this reason alone. Built entirely by hand by the desert-dwelling Naru people, the main lounge has deep-red sofas and kilims with wooden sliding doors leading out onto a wraparound deck, which faces a busy water hole. You'll sleep in a large thatch bungalow where the roomy lounge has polished wooden floors, more kilims, wrought iron, wood chairs, a deep comfy sofa, and framed bushman memorabilia. Your bedroom will have a hand-carved headboard, crisp white linens, and plump duvets. There's a separate en-suite bathroom with a claw-foot bath and outside shower. Enjoy delicious food (try the tender oryx fillet marinated in Worcestershire sauce, olive oil, and herbs) including homemade bread and rolls, before sitting out under the blazing desert stars for a nightcap. Although you'll be taken on game drives and birding expeditions, the absolute highlight of your stay at this unique lodge will be a walk with the bushmen themselves. Dressed in skins and thong sandals, with their

bows and arrows over their shoulders, and carrying spears and digging sticks, they'll lead you through the dry grass and bush on a three-hour walk through one of the most remote areas on earth. You'll be shown how to trap a bird or animal, how to make fire, which plants and trees will heal and sustain you, and at the end of the walk, they will dance and sing for you. This is pure magic. **Pros:** if you're looking for solitude, this is the place as it's the only lodge in the area; great curio shop. **Cons:** there's game here, but not always easy to find. ☎ 11/234–9997 ⊕ *www. islandsinafrica.com* 📮 *5 chalets* ⚠ *In-room: no phone, no a/c, no TV. In-hotel: bar, pool, library* ▭ *DC, MC, V* ⊙ *AI.*

THE MAKGADIKGADI PANS

These immense salt pans in the eastern Kalahari—once the bed of an African superlake—provide some of Botswana's most dramatic scenery. Two of these pans, Ntetwe and Sowa, the largest of their kind in the world, have a flaky, pastrylike surface that might be the nearest thing on earth to the surface of the moon. In winter these huge bone-dry surfaces, punctuated by islands of grass and lines of fantastic palm trees, dazzle and shimmer into hundreds of dancing mirages under the beating sun. In summer months the last great migration in Southern Africa takes place here: more than 50,000 zebras and wildebeests with predators in their wake come seeking the fresh young grass of the flooded pans. Waterbirds also flock here from all over the continent; the flamingoes are particularly spectacular.

You can see stars as never before, and if you're lucky, as the San/Bush-men say, even hear them sing. Grab the opportunity to ride 4x4 quad bikes into an always-vanishing horizon; close your eyes and listen as an ancient San/Bushman hunter tells tales of how the world began in his unique language—the clicks will sound strange to your ears—or just wander in wonder over the pristine piecrust surface of the pans.

GETTING HERE AND AROUND
Just like the Central Kalahari Game Reserve, self-drives are possible here, but we don't advise it. Instead, have your lodge arrange your transportation. Flights from Maun take about 40 minutes and don't be shocked when you land on a dirt airstrip in the middle of the bush. Your transportation to and from the lodge and on all game drives will be in an open-sided vehicle.

WHEN TO GO
Visit May through September.

WHERE TO STAY
LUXURY LODGING
$$$$ 🏠 **Jack's Camp.** If you're bold-spirited, reasonably fit, and have kept
★ your childlike sense of wonder, then Jack's is for you. A cross between a Fellini movie, a Salvador Dalí painting, and *Alice in Wonderland,* this camp doesn't offer the cocooned luxury of some of the Okavango camps; it offers a more rugged, pioneer feel reminiscent of a 1940s-style safari. East African safari tents on wooden decks set in a palm grove have ancient Persian rugs, antique brass-hinged storage boxes, teak and canvas furniture, hot and cold running water, a flush toilet, and

6

indoor and outdoor showers. Meals are taken under a huge acacia tree or in a large, open-sided tent. The camp's highly qualified rangers are respected throughout Botswana for their love and commitment to this amazing area. You won't find the Big Five here, but you will find unique desert-adapted animals and plants like the brown hyena, meerkats, salt bushes, and desert palms. Remember though, this is the Kalahari Desert. It's hot, hot, hot in summer, and freezing cold in winter. **Pros:** exclusivity and isolation. **Cons:** no shaded walkways; the desert locale can be dusty; blisteringly hot in summer, freezing in winter. ☎ *11/447–1605* ⊕ *www.jacks-camp.com* 🔊 *10 tents* ⚄ *In-room: no phone, no a/c, no TV. In-hotel: bar* ⊟ *MC, V* ⦿*FAP.*

MASHATU GAME RESERVE

Mashatu offers a genuine wilderness experience on 90,000 acres that seem to stretch to infinity on all sides. There are wall-to-wall elephants—breeding herds often with tiny babies in tow—as well as aardvarks, aardwolves (a type of hyena), lots of leopards, wandering lions, and hundreds of birds. All the superb rangers are Batswana—most were born in the area, and some have been here for more than 15 years. Their fund of local knowledge seems bottomless.

GETTING HERE AND AROUND

Mashatu is an easy five-hour drive from Johannesburg and Gaborone. You'll be met at Pont Drift, the South African/Botswana border post, where you leave your car under huge jackalberry trees at the South African police station before crossing the Limpopo River by 4x4 vehicle or cable car—depending on whether the river is flooded.

If you'd rather fly, South African Airlink flies daily from O.R. Tambo International Airport, Johannesburg, to Polokwane, where you can pick up a self-drive or chauffeur-driven car from Budget Rent a Car for the just-under-two-hour drive to Pont Drift, the South African/Botswana border post.

WHEN TO GO

Summers are very hot, and winters very cold. The shoulder seasons (April and September) are the best.

ESSENTIALS

Airlines South African Airlink (☎ *011/978–1111* ⊕ *www.flyairlink.co.za*).

Car Rentals Budget Rent a Car (☎ *011/398–0123*).

EXPLORING

The reserve is located in an area known as the Tuli Block. This ruggedly beautiful corner of northeastern Botswana is very easily accessible from South Africa and well worth a visit. Huge, striking red-rock formations, unlike anywhere else in Botswana, mingle with acacia woodlands, riverine bush, hills, wooded valleys, and open grassy plains. Be sure to visit the Motloutse ruins, where ancient baobabs stand sentinel over Stone Age ruins that have existed here for more than 30,000 years, as majestic black eagles soar overhead.

Still relatively unknown to foreign travelers, the Tuli Block is home to huge elephant herds, the eland—Africa's largest and highest-jumping antelope—zebras, wildebeests, leopards, and prolific bird life. Try to catch a glimpse of the elusive and diminutive klipspringer antelope perching on top of a rock zealously guarding his mountain home. Gareth Patterson, southern Africa's "Lion Man," lived here alone with three young lions over a period of years, successfully reintroducing them to the wild after having brought them down from Kenya after George "Born Free" Adamson was brutally murdered there by poachers. If the Limpopo River is full, you will be winched into Botswana over the river in a small cage—a unique way of getting from one country to another. If the river is dry, you'll be driven over in an open-sided game vehicle.

WHERE TO STAY

LUXURY LODGING

$$
★ **Mashatu Main Camp.** A sister camp to South Africa's world-famous Mala Mala Camp, the professionalism of the staff here is so unobtrusive you only realize later how superbly and sincerely welcomed, entertained, and informed you have been during your stay. Accommodations are in tasteful family suites where earth-patterned and earth-colored fabrics pick up and enhance the terra-cotta floor tiles. Comfort is assured by heaters in the cold winter months and air-conditioning in the hot summer ones. The thatched outdoor dining area overlooks a large water hole where elephants, zebras, wildebeests, and other Mashatu regulars drink. **Pros:** game galore, particularly lions and leopards; superb service and guiding. **Cons:** suites are lacking personal viewing decks. ☎ *011/442–2267* ⊕ *www.mashatu.com* ↘ *14 suites* ♨ *In-room: no phone, a/c, safe, no TV. In-hotel: bar, pool, shop* ▭ *AE, DC, MC, V* ⦿ *FAP.*

PERMANENT TENTED CAMPS

¢ **Mashatu Tent Camp.** This small and intimate camp offers the same excellent service as Main Camp but with a firsthand bush experience. The camp is deep in the wilderness, and as you lie in your tent and listen to a lion's roar, a hyena's whoop, or a leopard's cough, you'll feel part of the heartbeat of Africa. Seven spacious tents with carpeted floors, each with a tiny veranda overlooking the surrounding bush, provide an unparalleled back-to-nature feeling. A fenced walkway leads to an en-suite bathroom where the stars are your roof. Knowledgeable, local rangers will open your ears and your eyes to the environment: on one night game-drive guests saw a male leopard up a tree jealously guarding his impala kill from a female leopard who was hoping for a slice of the action, while a hopeful hyena lurked nearby. There's plenty of water in the vicinity, so the game is also plentiful—once two guests were trapped in their tent when a pride of lions killed a zebra outside it. This camp may not be for everyone; but for something truly different, real, and very special, a stay here won't soon be forgotten. **Pros:** true wilderness experience; splendid isolation. **Cons:** very close to nature; don't come here if you are fearful of critters big or small. ☎ *011/442–2267* ⊕ *www. mashatu.com* ↘ *8 tents* ♨ *In-room: no phone, no a/c, no TV. In-hotel: bar, pool, shop, no kids under 12* ▭ *AE, DC, MC, V* ⦿ *FAP.*

LINYANTI RESERVE

The Linyanti Reserve, which borders Chobe National Park, is one of the huge concession areas leased to different companies by the Department of Wildlife and National Parks and the Tawana Land Board; concessions can be leased for up to 15 years. It's a spectacular wildlife area comprising the Linyanti marshes, open floodplains, rolling savanna, and the Savuti Channel. Because it's a private concession, open vehicles can drive where and when they like, which means superb game-viewing at all hours of the day.

Basic choices for viewing wildlife are game drives (including thrilling night drives with spotlights), boat trips, and walks with friendly and knowledgeable Motswana guides. Even in peak season there is a maximum of only six game vehicles driving around at one time, allowing you to see Africa as the early hunters and explorers might have first seen it. The Savuti Channel, once a huge river but dry now for more than two decades, has starred in several *National Geographic* documentaries, and it's not hard to see why. Take lots of pictures, and for once you won't bore your friends with the results: hundreds of elephants drinking from pools at sunset, hippos and hyenas nonchalantly strolling past a pride of lions preparing to hunt under moonlight, and thousands of water and land birds everywhere.

GETTING HERE AND AROUND

Flights from Maun take about 40 minutes; don't be shocked when you land on a dirt airstrip in the middle of the bush. Your transportation to and from the lodge and on all game drives will be in an open-sided vehicle.

WHEN TO GO

Summers are very hot, and winters very cold. The shoulder seasons (April and September) are the best.

WHERE TO STAY

PERMANENT TENTED CAMPS

$ **Duma Tau.** This classy camp, with imaginatively decorated and furnished raised tent chalets under thatch and overlooking the water, lies at the very heart of the concession. The spacious chalets have African fabrics; clever cane furniture decorated with plaited reeds, brass, and local beadwork; an indoor shower and another on your outside deck so you can wash as you view; and personal touches such as a guinea-fowl feather or dried seedpod placed artistically among your towels. The food is simple but superb. Before you set out on your early-morning game drive, try a plate of piping-hot porridge, a Danish straight from the oven, or a freshly baked muffin. **Pros:** great predator viewing. **Cons:** public areas can be cold in winter. ☎ *11/807–1800* ⊕ *www.dumatau. com* ↻ *8 chalets* △ *In-room: no phone, no a/c, no TV. In-hotel: bar, pool* ⊟ *MC, V* ⎮◎⎮ *FAP.*

$$$$ **King's Pool.** The centuries-old giant leadwood tree, which dominates
★   the spacious main deck that overlooks the Linyanti River, gives you a clue about your classic, yet understated, out-of-Africa–like accommodation. Everything about this camp is on a regal scale—a modern-day tribute to the European royalty who used to hunt in this area. There's

"Wild dogs are endangered; there are only about 800 left in Botswana. We [saw] a pack of 7 adults and 4 puppies getting ready to go on a hunt. This puppy was very interested in our jeep!" —DAleffi, Fodors.com member

even a small gym facing the river where you can work off some of the yummy food before taking a river cruise (only when the water is high), a guided bush walk, a fishing trip, or a visit to the sunken blind (a must in the dry season) where you're eye-level with splashing elephant feet. The massive hand-carved door of your megasize thatch and canvas–ceiling chalet leads into an entrance hall, bedroom with four-poster bed, a sitting area with earth-color couches and armchairs splashed with orange and red cushions, and a huge bathroom with his and her basins and tiled showers. Don't miss the fascinating curio shop with classy artifacts from all over Africa. **Pros:** classy and comfortable. **Cons:** very grand—you may prefer something simpler. ☎ *11/807–1800* ⊕ *www. wilderness-safaris.com* ⇨ *9 chalets* ⚴ *In-room: no phone, a/c, safe, no TV. In-hotel: bar, pool* ▭ *MC, V* ⑂ *FAP.*

GATEWAY CITY

Many visitors to Botswana will find themselves with a layover in Johannesburg before or after their safari. It's a massive metropolitan area—more than 1,300 square km (800 square mi)—that epitomizes South Africa's paradoxical make-up—it's rich, poor, innovative, and historical all rolled into one. Most of the sights and many of the city's good hotels and major malls are in the northern suburbs: Melville (closest to the city center), Greenside, Parkhurst, Sandton, and Rosebank, among many others. Some notable destinations for food include Melrose Arch, Parkhurst, Sandton, the South (for its Portuguese cuisine), Melville, and Chinatown in the CBD (Central Business District).

For some ideas and suggestions to help determine where you should stay, eat, and if you have time, some sights to visit, *See Johannesburg Under Gateway City in Chapter 5 South Africa.*

If you don't fly from Johannesburg, your first entry into Botswana will probably be by air into Maun, the gateway to the delta. At best, you'd only spend a night here, though most visitors are picked up at Maun airport immediately upon arrival by their respective tour operators and whisked away to their lodges by charter planes.

MAUN

The little town of Maun serves as the gateway to the Okavango Delta and the Moremi Game Reserve. And, despite the city's rapid development in the last decade, it has kept the feel of a pioneer border town. The name comes from the San word *maung,* which means the "place of short reeds," and Maun became the capital of the Tawana people in 1915; it's now Botswana's fifth-largest town. Although there are now shopping centers and a paved road to Gaborone, Botswana's capital, cement block houses and mud huts still give Maun a rural feel, especially as goats and donkeys litter the roads.

The town spreads along the banks of the Thamalakane River, and it's possible to take mokoro trips into the delta directly from Maun. It's also a good base from which to explore by road the Tsolido hills and the Makgadigadi Pans.

The bustling airport is claimed to be one of the busiest small airports in the world, with planes of all sizes taking off and coming in at all hours of the day, delivering tourists to and from the tourist camps in the delta and Moremi. Maun itself is by no means a tourist destination—at best you'd probably stay a night or even two before setting off further afield. There are three supermarkets so you can stock up on supplies if you are setting off on a road trip, but in general, most camps are accessible only by air, so you'll probably see only the Maun airport.

GETTING HERE AND AROUND
A local taxi is your best bet for getting around as there is no public transportation. Taxis are usually available outside Maun airport. It's possible to hire a fully equipped 4x4 for camping, but generally speaking, you are better off and safer (the roads in the delta are sometimes impassable) to fly between Maun and the tourist camps. Make sure your tour package includes all local flights.

SAFETY AND PRECAUTIONS
Crime has increased in recent years, so take good care of your belongings and utilize your hotel's safe. Don't walk alone at night. If you must leave the hotel, have the concierge or front desk call a taxi for you.

TIMING
Most people will be here only a night, if not just a few hours, so use the time to relax or stock up on supplies at one of the local groceries if you're self-driving.

Continued on page 414

(top) Weaving pandanu vegetal carpets. (bottom) Botswana basket.

AFRICAN ARTS & CULTURE
by Kate Turkington

African art is as diverse as its peoples. If you're a collector, an artist, or just an admirer, you'll find everything from masks and carvings to world famous rock art, hand-painted batiks, and hand-woven cloths.

African art is centered on meaning. Its sculptures, carvings, and masks symbolize the powerful spirit world that underpins most African societies. Christianity and the Westernization of many African communities has stifled much of the traditional craftsmanship by imposing new themes and, in the past, denigrating traditional religions. Fortunately, wooden masks—some genuine, some not, some beautiful, some seriously scary—wire and bead tribal necklaces, beadwork, woven baskets, and much, much more continue to be big sellers all over Southern and East Africa.

If you're looking for something a little funky or unique, check out the handmade bead-and-wire animals, birds, cars, and mobiles for sale along South Africa's roads and in Tanzania's markets.

TYPES OF CRAFTS AND ART

High-quality crafts abound, from handwoven cloths in East Africa, to stunning soapstone and wood carvings at Victoria Falls, hand-woven baskets in Botswana and Zululand, leatherwork, pottery and embroidery in Namibia, and jewelry just about everywhere.

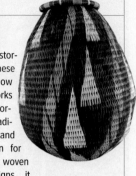

BOTSWANA BASKETS

Once used for storage purposes, these baskets are now sought-after works of art that incorporate many traditional designs and patterns. Known for the intricately woven geometric designs, it can take up to six weeks to make a basket. Zulu baskets, from South Africa's KwaZulu province, can be made of brightly colored wire or grass and palm coils. For either type, expect to pay anywhere from US$20 to US$300.

MASKS

Masks were often worn by tribal elders in rites of passage (birth, initiation, weddings, and funerals) and can range from frightening depictions of devils and evil spirits, to more gentle and benign expressions. A few dollars will buy you a readily available tourist mask; an authentic piece could run you hundreds, sometimes thousands of U.S. dollars.

BEADWORK

Each color and pattern has meaning. Green is for grass or a baby, red is for blood or young women, and white is for purity. By looking at a women's beadwork you can tell how many children she has (and what sex), how old she is or how long she's been married. Beading is used in headdresses, necklaces, rings, earrings, wedding aprons, barrettes, and baskets. Expect to pay US$10 for a Zulu bracelet or US$200 for a Masai wedding necklace.

WEAVING

The striking red handmade robes of East Africa's Masai people are a fine example of a centuries-old African weaving tradition. Fabrics, like kekois and Masai cloaks, are usually made of cotton. Handpainted or batik cloths are more expensive than factory printed ones. A cotton kekoi will cost you US$15, a red Masai cloth US$20, a batik US$30.

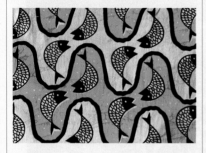

ROCK ART

Engravings (made by scratching into a rock's surface), paintings, and finger paintings are found all over sub-Saharan Africa, particularly in South Africa. The rock paintings in the Drakensburg Mountains in Kwa-Zulu Natal, are regarded as the world's finest. Central Namibia has the world's largest open-air art gallery at Twyfelfontein where thousands of paintings and engravings line the sides of the rocks and mountain. Materials came from the immediate environment: ocher (red iron-oxide clay) for red, charcoal for black, and white clay for white. Many images illustrate the activities and experiences of the African shamans. The shamans believed that when an image was drawn, power was transferred to the people and the land.

WIRECRAFT FIGURES

Wire-and-bead animals and all kinds of previously unimagined subjects are now contemporary works of art. First made and sold in South Africa, you can now buy them just about anywhere. A palm-sized critter usually sells for US$10, but a nearly-life-sized animal can cost up to US$450; you'd pay three times more in a European or U.S. gallery. Tip: Beaded key rings (US$5) make great easy-to-pack gifts.

PAINTING

Painting in acrylics is a fairly recent medium in Africa. Keep an eye out for Tinga Tinga paintings (above) at curio shops or stalls in Kenya and Tanzania. Prices range from $10 to $50; you can expect to pay upwards of $100 online. The semi-impressionistic wildlife paintings of Keith Joubert are particularly sought-after. The Everard Read Gallery (☎ 021/418–4527 in Cape Town, 011/788–4805 in Johannesburg ⊕ www.everardread.co.za) specializes in wildlife paintings and sculpture, including the work of Joubert.

SMART SHOPPING TIPS AND WHERE TO SHOP

So where should you buy all of this amazing handiwork? And what do you do when you've found that piece you want to take home? Read on for helpful tips and locations across our Safari coverage.

KENYA

What Nairobi lacks in safety and charm, it makes up for in its abundance of curios. The widest and best selection is at the curio stalls around the city market on Muindi Mbingu St. Bargain for masks, drums, carvings of all kinds, batiks and the famous brightly-colored kekoi cloths. Semiprecious stones can be found at Kimathi Jewellers (⌧ Norwich Union House, Kimathi St. ☎ 02/224–754). Adelphi Leather Shop (E Jubilee Insurance Exchange Bldg., Kaunda St. ☎ 02/228–925) specializes in exclusive handcrafted articles using local leather. In Mombasa, Malindi, and Lamu, ask at your accommodation where the best markets are.

TANZANIA

For some of the best Masai jewelry, batiks, Tinga Tinga paintings and Makonde carvings, check out the curio shops between the clock tower and India Rd in Arusha. One of the city's largest dealers in tanzanite, Cultural Heritage (⌧ Dodoma Rd. ☎ 27/250–8698), has in-house artisans producing beautiful jewelry plus souvenirs galore. If you're in Dar es Salaam, head to the Slipway (⌧ Slipway Road Junction ☎ 22/260–0893 ⊕ www.slipway.net), a converted boatyard on the Msasani Bay that has four restaurants and a traditional market. Get

AFRICAN BEADS

Small discs, dating from 10,000 B.C., made from ostrich eggshells are the earliest known African beads. The introduction of glass beads came with the trade from around 200 B.C. Subsequently, European and Arab traders bartered beads for ivory, gold, and slaves. In many African societies, beads are still highly prized for both everyday and ceremonial ornamentation.

ready to bargain for everything from beaded leather sandals and wire animals to jewelry and carved figures. There are plenty of shopping opportunities in Zanzibar as well. If you're in Stone Town, head to Kenyatta Road which has numerous shops including Memories of Zanzibar (☎ 24/223–9376 ⊕ www.memories-zanzibar.com) and Zanzibar Secrets (☎ 24/223–4745). Memories has great deals on tanzanite jewelry, kangas, carved wooden animals, and all sort of gifts that make great souvenirs and presents. The shopping at Zanzibar Secrets is a little more exclusive as its clothing, jewelry, beaded purses, and beautiful lighting fixtures won't be found at many other places on the island.

SOUTH AFRICA

Art lovers should make sure to include Johannesburg in their trip. Excellent galleries abound, including the Everard Read Gallery (⊠ 6 Jellicoe Ave., Rosebank ☎ 011/788–4805), which specializes in wildlife paintings and sculpture; the Kim Sacks Gallery (⊠ 153 Jan Smuts Ave., Rosebank ☎ 011/447–5804), which has a superb collection of authentic African art; and the African Craft Market (⊠ Rosebank Mall, 33 Bath Ave. ☎ 011/880–2906), which has an amazing selection of arts and crafts from all over Africa. Cape Town's V&A Waterfront is a shopper's paradise, and you can buy some of the best wine in the world along the Cape Winelands.

BOTSWANA

Handmade woven baskets are the best buy here. Find them in your safari lodge shop or at the Gaborone Mall (⊠ Queen's St., Gaborone), in the middle of the city.

NAMIBIA

Windhoek's Post Street Mall has an impressive array of crafts and curios (check out the irresistible Herero dolls) as does the Namibia Craft Centre (⊠ 40 Tal St., Windhoek ☎ 061/242–2222), next to the Warehouse Theatre. You'll have gemstones on the soles of your shoes if you visit House of Gems (⊠ 131 Stübel St., Windhoek ☎ 061/225–202), where you can see gemstones sorted, cut, faceted, and polished. Tourmalines, a local specialty,

TIPS

■ Local markets, roadside stalls, and cooperatives often offer the cheapest, most authentic crafts.

■ Safari lodge shops can be pricey, but stock really classy souvenirs (often from all over Africa) and cool safari gear.

■ A universal rule for bargaining is to divide the seller's first price by half, then up it a bit.

■ If possible, carry your purchases with you. Try to get breakables bubble-wrapped and pack securely in the middle of your main suitcase. Pack smaller purchases in your carry-on.

■ Mail your dirty clothes home or donate them to a local charity so you'll have more room for purchases.

■ Only ship home if you've bought something very big, very fragile, or very expensive.

are a best buy item here. Or treat yourself to a stunning Namibian karakul leather jacket or coat at Nakara, which has locations in Windhoek and Swakopmund (☎ 061/224–209 in Windhoek, 064/405–907 in Swakopmund ⊕ www.nakara-namibia.com). If you do go to Windhoek, head to Independence Avenue. It's a major shopping destination and where you'll find Nakara.

VIC FALLS

If you're staying on the Zambian side of the Falls, be sure to cross the historic bridge over the Zambezi to visit the craft market on the Zimbabwe side. You'll find some of Africa's finest carvings here, from masks and tableware to chess sets and soapstone sculptures. The market opens at 9 am and stays open late; it's just behind Livingstone Way, the town's main street. Bargaining is essential and U.S. dollars are eagerly accepted. Make sure you have small bills ($1, $5, $10); you do not want to get change in Zimbabwe banknotes.

A MODEL MOTSWANA

The Batswana (singular: Motswana) are renowned for their courtesy and dignity. A perfect role model is the now world-famous Motswana lady detective, Patience Ramotswe of *The No. 1 Ladies' Detective Agency* series—published by Random House—by Alexander McCall Smith, who introduced millions of readers all over the world to the unchanging wisdom of a solid, traditional society. These book were made into popular TV series for BBC and HBO in 2009.

Fans can now follow in Mma Ramotswe's footsteps by taking a half- or full-day walking tour of her favorite haunts throughout Gaborone, Botswana's capital. You'll visit her house in Zebra Drive, as well as Tlokweng Road Speedy Motors (owned by Mma Ramotswe's eventual husband, JLB Matekoni), the village of Mochudi, and sometimes, if available, a visit to the Orphan Farm, where her two adopted children were living. And, of course, you'll sample her favorite red bush tea. Tours can be arranged through African Insight (⊕ *www.africainsight. com*), and prices range from BWP450 to BWP780.

ESSENTIALS

Banks **Barclays Bank** (✛ *Opposite Shoprite, slightly west of Riley's* ☎ *686–0210*).

Standard Chartered Bank (✛ *Opposite Shoprite, slightly west of Riley's* ☎ *686–0209*).

Medical Assistance **Delta Medical Centre** (✉ *Old Mall, Tshekotseko Rd.* ☎ *686–1411* ⊕ *www.deltamedicalcentre.org*). **General** (☎ *911*). **MediRescue** (☎ *686–1831*).

Rental Cars **Avis** (✉ *Maun Airport* ☎ *686–0039* ⊕ *www.avis.com*). **Maun Self Drive 4x4** (☎ *686–2429* ⊕ *www.maunselfdrive4x4.webs.com*).

Taxis **Atol Taxis** (☎ *686–4770*).

WHERE TO EAT

¢   ✕**Hillary's Coffee Shop.** If you've time for a cup of coffee and a quick
CAFÉ   snack in between flights or before you set out on safari, leave the airport and head toward the Bull&Bush. You'll find the coffee shop behind the offices of Okavango Wilderness Safaris. Hillary has run this coffee shop for years, and everything you eat here is home baked, including the best breakfast options in Maun. Grab a sandwich or a salad and be sure to try her homemade whole-wheat bread. ✉ *Just before the Avis Rent-a-Car office on Mathiba Rd.* ☎ *686–1610* 🗏 *MC, V.*

¢   ✕**Sports Bar and Restaurant.** This is one of Maun's liveliest eateries and
STEAKHOUSE where you can get a really good pizza and good spare ribs. Friday night is party night with live music and game rangers, expats and local yuppies dancing their hearts out. It's a bit out of town so you will need transport. ✉ *Shorobe Rd., Sedie* ☎ *267/686–2676* 🗏 *MC, V.*

¢   ✕**The Power Station.** This is a small complex of offices, shops, a craft
ECLECTIC center, and even a small theater. Also there's a small restaurant that

is especially good for light meals, salads, and juices. ⊠ *Mophane Rd.* ☎ *267/686–2037* ⊟ *MC, V.*

WHERE TO STAY

Lodging reviews have been abbreviated in this book. For expanded reviews, please go to Fodors.com.

¢ ⊞ **Audi Lodge.** This lively tented camp offers a budget option for the Okavango Delta. **Pros:** affordable lodging; excellent service and staff; good value excursions. **Cons:** noisy; not much privacy; only four en-suite tents. ⊠ *12 km from Maun on Shorobe Rd.* ☎ *267/686–0599* ⊕ *www.okavangocamp.com* ⇨ *22 tents, 1 self-catered house* ⟁ *In-room: no a/c, no phone (some). In-hotel: restaurant, bar, golf, pool* ⊟ *MC, V.*

¢ ⊞ **Riley's Hotel.** A Maun institution, this comfortable modern hotel, on the banks of the Thamalakane River, is a far cry from the seven dusty rooms built by the legendary Harry Riley in the middle 1930s. **Pros:** central location; clean and comfortable. **Cons:** bland hotel-like rooms; indifferent service. ⊠ *Riverside Rd.* ☎ *267/686–0204* ⊕ *www.crestahospitalityco.za* ⇨ *51 rooms* ⟁ *In-room: a/c, TV, phone. In-hotel: restaurant, bar, pool* ⊟ *AE, DC, MC, V.*

¢ ⊞ **Thamalakane Lodge.** Situated en route to Moremi Game Reserve, this lovely lodge sits on the bank of the Thamalakane River. **Pros:** very affordable; brilliant service and good restaurant; closest accommodation to Moremi Game Reserve. **Cons:** if you're not en route to Moremi it's a bit out of the way, but worth the 15-minute drive from Maun. ⊠ *Shorobe Rd.* ☎ *27–(0)21–782–5337* ⊕ *www.thamalakane.com* ⇨ *18 chalets, 3 tents* ⟁ *In-room: no phone (some), no a/c, safe (some). In-hotel: restaurant, room service, bar* ⊟ *MC, V.*

BEACH ESCAPES

Looking for a little R&R after your safari? Botswana may not be a coastal country, but it's close proximity to South Africa's coast provides many opportunities for sun, sand, and smiles.

Just (762 km) 474 mi southeast from Botswana's capital Gaborone, Durban's accessible, beautiful, and safe beaches make it a great escape for this landlocked country (as well as for South Africa). Plus, there are daily flights between Gaborone and Durban, though you will probably have to do a stopover in Johannesburg, making it a quick escape as well.

If you love exploring untouched beaches, fishing, scuba diving, snorkeling, and walking, Maputaland Coastal Forest Reserve will be the perfect beach getaway after your safari. The reserve is 300 km (186 mi) from Richard's Bay; it's a 1½-hour flight from Johannesburg to Richard's Bay.

See Beach Escapes in Chapter 5 South Africa for information on places to eat, stay, and visit.

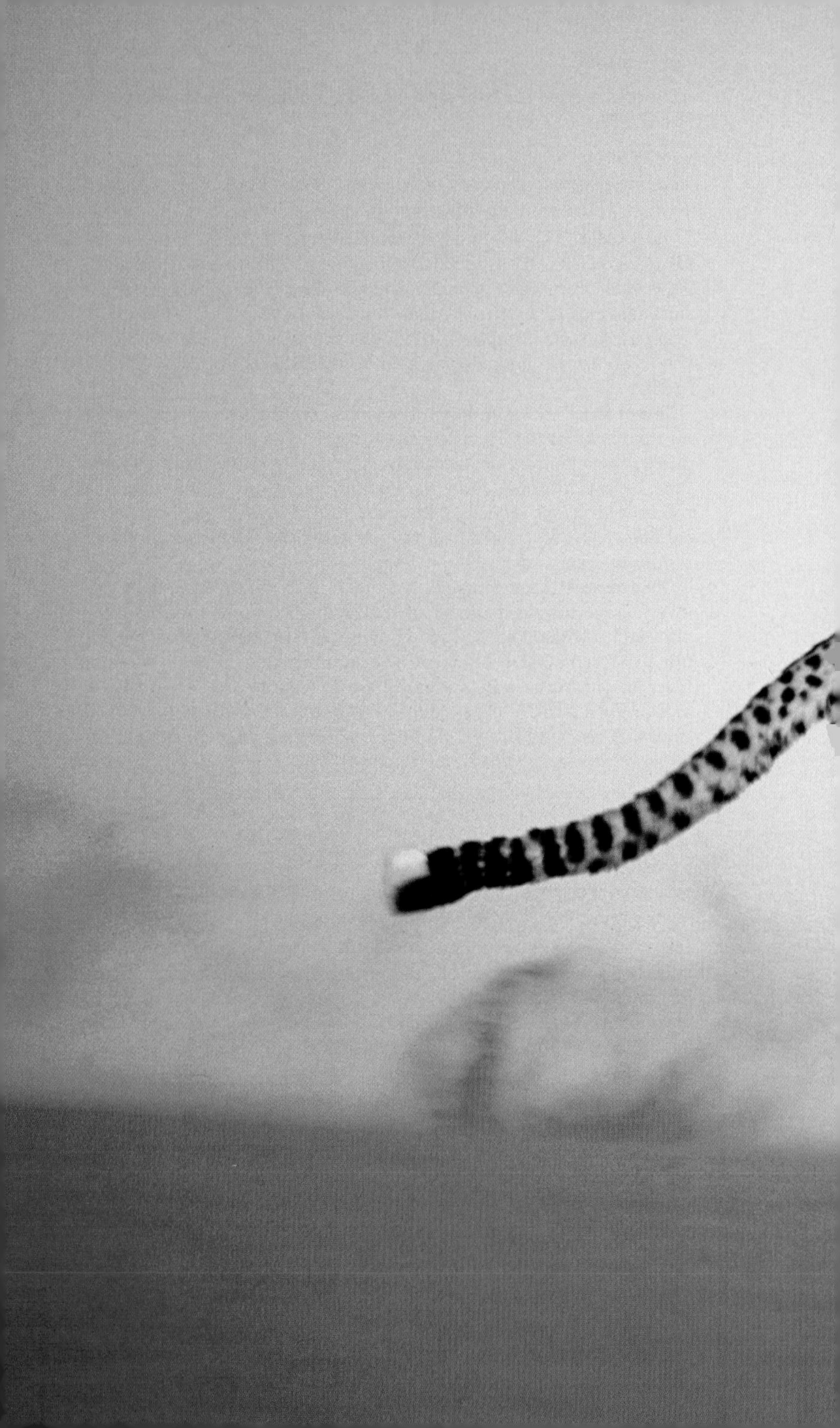

Namibia

WELCOME TO NAMIBIA

TOP REASONS TO GO

★ **The world's oldest living desert.** The Namib is everything you might imagine a "real" desert to be.

★ **A memorable drive.** The road from Swakopmund to Walvis Bay is one of the most beautiful and unusual routes in the world.

★ **Water-hole wonders.** Arm yourself with binoculars, drinks, a picnic, and patience. Open your car windows and wait for the game to come. You won't be disappointed.

★ **Ride the Desert Express.** During this two-day train journey between Windhoek and Swakopmund, you'll stop to walk in the desert, visit the world's biggest outdoor rock-art gallery, watch lions being fed, and view a spectacular desert sunset (or sunrise).

★ **Etosha National Park.** One of Africa's largest and most spectacular game parks, Etosha has cheap and cheerful self-catering accommodations, an excellent road network, and superb game-viewing.

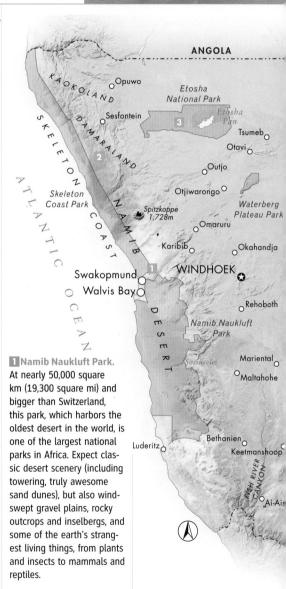

1 Namib Naukluft Park. At nearly 50,000 square km (19,300 square mi) and bigger than Switzerland, this park, which harbors the oldest desert in the world, is one of the largest national parks in Africa. Expect classic desert scenery (including towering, truly awesome sand dunes), but also windswept gravel plains, rocky outcrops and inselbergs, and some of the earth's strangest living things, from plants and insects to mammals and reptiles.

GETTING ORIENTED

ZAMBIA
○ Katima Mulilo

C A P R I V I   S T R I P

Grootfontein
○

K A U K A U V E L D

○ Gobabis   BOTSWANA

N A M A L A N D

SOUTH
AFRICA

○ Karasburg

R i v e r

0 ————————— 100 mi
0 ————————— 100 km

Namibia is a big country, four times as large as the United Kingdom and bigger than Texas, but its excellent road network means you can get around very easily. The country is bordered by the icy Atlantic on the west, the Kalahari Desert on the east, the Kunene River to the north, and the Orange River to the south. Although South Africa, Botswana, and Angola are its immediate neighbors, if you're traveling by road, it's easiest to access Namibia from South Africa. By all means drive yourself, but punctuate this self-drive with a fly-in safari into one of the more remote lodges on the Skeleton Coast or Damaraland. This way you'll get to see Namibia's true vastness and remoteness.

7

2 **Damaraland.** Situated in northwest Namibia, Damaraland is a different desert from Namib. It's barren and inhospitable, but there is life, and plenty of it, including *Welwitschia mirabilis*, reputed to be the world's longest-living plants; colorful lichen fields; camelthorn trees; candelabra euphorbias; salt bushes; and the ubiquitous shepherd's tree. And, of course, there are the amazing desert elephants.

3 **Etosha National Park.** Regarded as one of Africa's great national parks, Etosha is dominated by Etosha Pan: a landscape of white, salty plains. The numerous water holes make this park ideal for game-viewing. If you're looking to do a self-drive, this is the place to come—the roads are good, and there are plenty of affordable accommodations.

GREEN LODGINGS IN NAMIBIA

Plenty of lodges and camps in Namibia are eco-conscious, but we've chosen a few properties to help you start your search. We hope reading about these places will help you on your path toward green travel.

(above) Wolwedans Private Camp; (opposite above) The Sossusvlei; (opposite bottom) Skeleton Coast Camp

---

Located in the serene and secluded NamibRand Nature Reserve, **Wolwedans Private Camp** (☎ *061/230–616* ⊕ *www.wolwedans.com*) gives its guests up-close access to the surrounding desert habitat. The reserve is a reflection of the diversity of the Namib Desert with its steep mountain ranges, vast savannahs, glorious red sand dunes, and clay pans. Here you might possibly see the oryx, as well as more than 100 bird species, including the rare dune lark. The reserve is sparsely developed and off-limits to large vehicles such as tour buses and 4x4s. What's more, a percentage of your park entry fee goes directly into conserving the integrity of the reserve. The camp itself is made up of just two en-suite doubles that share a library, kitchen, chef, and numerous outdoor spaces from which to enjoy the views.

DID YOU KNOW?

Namibia's four coastal zones are considered a refuge for a number of endangered species, including the African Penguin. Other endangered species in the country include the Wild Dog, Black Rhino, and Oribi and Puku antelope. There are only about 100 Puku, which are found in Botswana's Chobe River and Namibia's Linyati marshes.

MORE ECOLOGICALLY CONSCIOUS CAMPS

Skeleton Coast Camp (☎ *27/11/807–1800* ⊕ *www. wilderness-safaris.com*) hosts fly-in safaris in one of the most remote wilderness areas in Africa. Visitors to the camp—built on an island just a few miles in from the coast—are privy to 660,000 acres of pristine, uninhabited coastline. Many areas are accessible only on foot as vehicle tracks can damage the natural environment. Nature hikes are a large part of any stay and include views of unique plants like *lithops* and *Welwitschia*. Wilderness Safaris, which runs the camp, also operates the Wilderness Wildlife Trust. The trust has some interesting projects, including the Skeleton Coast Lichen Research Project, which assesses the long-term impact of human activity on the Namib Desert's lichen communities and aims to increase recovery rates; lichen is vital to the Skeleton Coast's ecology. ⇨ *See Permanent Tented Camps in the Skeleton Coast under If You Have Time for more information about the camp.*

Set on Namibia's Skeleton Coast between Khorixas and Torra Bay, this beautiful 10-tent camp manages to integrate conservation and community development with the tourist mission of the camp. With the assistance of the Integrated Rural Development & Nature Conservation (IRDNC), the World Wildlife Fund (WWF), and other sustainable development organizations, **Wilderness Damaraland Camp** (☎ *27/11/807–1800* ⊕ *www.wilderness-safaris.com)* has included local indigenous tribes in the protection and management of wildlife and the land surrounding the camp, giving them an income, training, and the feeling of ownership in the community. Elephant, black rhinoceros, oryx, kudu, springbok are just a few species that might be spotted at Damaraland Camp. There are also opportunities to visit the nearby Twyfelfontein engravings, one of the most unique rock art sites in Southern Africa, which provide evidence of human habitation of life at Twyfelfontein more than 6,000 years ago. ⇨ *See Permanent Tented Camps, in Damaraland for more information about the camp.*

MINIMIZE YOUR FOOTPRINT

- Never litter.

- Stay in locally owned accommodation that benefits the local community.

- Buying shells or coral from street vendors encourages ocean destruction.

- Don't drive off-road: Namibia's "empty" landscapes are incredible fragile habitats that cars can scar for hundreds of years.

- Purchase local products whenever possible.

- Use water sparingly.

- Turn off all lights when not in use.

- Don't feed wild animals.

- If you're camping, don't leave anything behind. Use only biodegradable soap or toothpaste.

- Don't take anything with you from the environment, whether it's a flower, a rock, or impala horns from a carcass you've found lying in the bush.

- You're a guest in Africa. The people and creatures you see were here long before you arrived, and they will be here long after you depart.

By Lee
Middleton

Many countries in Africa boast teeming wildlife and gorgeous scenery, but few others, if any, can claim such limitless horizons; such untamed wilderness; such a pleasant climate; so few people (fewer than two per square mile); the oldest desert in the world; a wild, beautiful coastline; one of Africa's greatest game parks; plus—and this is a big bonus—a well-developed infrastructure and tourist facilities that are among the best in Africa. Welcome to Namibia.

A former German colony, South West Africa, as it was then known, was a pawn in the power games of European politics. Although the Portuguese navigators were the first Europeans to arrive, in 1485, they quickly abandoned the desolate and dangerous Atlantic shores of the "Coast of Death," as they called it. By the late 1700s British, French, and American whalers were using the deepwater ports of Lüderitz and Walvis (Whalefish) Bay, which the Dutch, now settled in the Cape, then claimed as their own. A few years later, after France invaded Holland, England seized the opportunity to claim the territory, together with the Cape Colony. Then it became Germany's turn to throw its hat into the ring. In the wake of its early missionaries and traders, Germany claimed the entire country as a colony in 1884, only to surrender it to the South African forces fighting on the Allied side during World War I. South Africa was given a League of Nations mandate to administer the territory after the war, and despite a 1978 UN resolution to revoke the mandate, South Africa held on to Namibia for 10 years. A bitter and bloody bush war with SWAPO (South West African People's Organization) freedom fighters raged until Namibia finally won its independence on March 21, 1990, after 106 years of foreign rule. Although most of the earlier colonial influences have now vanished, everywhere you go in Namibia today you'll find traces of the German past—forts and castles, place names, cuisine, and even German efficiency.

Often called the "Land God Made in Anger" because of its stark landscapes, untamed wilderness, harsh environment, and rare beauty, Namibia was carved out by the forces of nature. The same continuous geological movements produced not only spectacular beauty but also great mineral wealth: alluvial diamonds, uranium, platinum, lead, zinc, silver, copper, tungsten, and tin—still the cornerstone of Namibia's economy. Humans have lived here for thousands of years; the San (Bushmen) are the earliest known residents, although their hunting-gathering way of life is now almost extinct. Today most Namibians work in agriculture, from subsistence farms to huge cattle ranches and game farms.

Namibia prides itself on its conservation policies and vision. More and more, wildlife conservation is symbiotically linked with community development; in many conservation areas, local communities, the wildlife, and the environment have been successfully integrated. Wilderness Damaraland Camp, for example, is an internationally acclaimed role model in linking tourism with community development projects. Hunting, a controversial issue for many people, is carefully controlled so that the impact on the environment is minimal and the revenue earned is substantial and can often be ploughed back into sustainable conservation.

PLANNING

WHEN TO GO

Namibia has a subtropical desert climate with nonstop sunshine throughout the year. It's classified as arid to nonarid, and, generally speaking, it gets wet only in the northwest and then only during the rainy season (October–April), which is the hottest season. The south is warm and dry, although temperatures vary dramatically between night and day, particularly in the desert, where the air is sparkling, and pollution practically unheard of. Days are crystal clear and perfect for traveling. Elsewhere the weather is clear, dry, crisp, and nearly perfect, averaging 25°C (77°F) during the day, but in the desert areas it can drop to freezing at night, especially in winter. (Bring warm clothes for after the sun goes down.)

The climate can be breathtakingly varied along the Skeleton Coast because of the Atlantic and its cold Benguela current, which makes the night cool and damp and brings thick morning coastal fog. Days are usually bright and sunny, and during the summer, extremely hot, so dress in layers.

Etosha's best season is winter (May–September), when the weather is cooler, the grass shorter, and game easier to see. But if you can stand the heat, consider a summer visit to see the return of thousands of waterbirds, as well as the tens of thousands of animals to the lush feeding grounds around Okuakuejo.

FAST FACTS

Size Namibia covers 824,292 square km (318,259 square mi).

Capital Windhoek.

Number of National Parks 20: Ai-Ais & Fish River Canyon, Etosha National Park, Kaudom National Park, Mamili National Park, Mudumu National Park, Namib-Naukluft National Park, Skeleton Coast Park, and Waterberg National Park are among the most visited.

Number of Private Reserves There are almost 200 privately owned game reserves.

Population Slightly more than 2 million.

Big Five In Etosha you can see all of the Big Five.

Language English is the official language, but it's usually spoken as a second language. Afrikaans is spoken by many residents of various races, and there is a large population of German-speaking people. The most widely spoken indigenous languages are Kwanyama (a dialect of Owambo), Herero, and a number of Nama (San) dialects.

Time Namibia, like Botswana, is on CAST (Central African standard time), which is two hours ahead of Greenwich Mean Time and seven hours ahead of North American Eastern Standard Time (six hours during eastern daylight saving time).

GETTING HERE AND AROUND

AIR TRAVEL

Namibia's main point of entry is Hosea Kutako International Airport, near Windhoek. The smaller Eros Airport handles local flights and charters. Once in the country you can make use of scheduled flights or charter flights that service all domestic destinations. Walvis Bay—the nearest airport for Namib Naukluft and the Skeleton Coast—now has a small international airport with flights to and from Windhoek, Johannesburg, and Cape Town.

The national carrier is Air Namibia, which operates international flights between Windhoek and London, Frankfurt, Johannesburg, and Cape Town, and internal flights to most of Namibia's major tourist destinations. South African Airways (SAA) operates links to Johannesburg and Cape Town. Air Botswana links Maun with Windhoek, and SA Express Airways flies between Johannesburg or Cape Town and Walvis Bay.

All camps in Etosha National Park have their own landing strip. Have your tour operator arrange charters or fly-in safaris for you. Air Namibia flies directly to Mokuti on the regularly scheduled flight between Windhoek and Victoria Falls. Chartered flights and fly-in safaris also use the Ongava airstrip.

Airlines Air Botswana (☎ 27/11390–3070/Johannesburg ⊕ www.airbotswana. co.bw). **Air Namibia** (☎ 061/299-6111 ⊕ www.airnamibia.com.na). **SA Express Airways** (☎ 27/11978–5577/Johannesburg). **South African Airways** (☎ 27/11978–5313/Johannesburg ⊕ www.flysaa.com).

CAR TRAVEL

Driving to Namibia from South Africa is possible, and there's an excellent road network for all in-country tourist attractions, but be warned that the trip is tiring and time-consuming because of the huge distances involved. The Trans-Kalahari Highway links Johannesburg to Windhoek and Gaborone. From Johannesburg to Windhoek on this road it's 1,426 km (884 mi). To allow free access to game, there are no fences in the Kalahari, so don't speed, and look out for antelope as well as donkeys and cows on the road. You can also drive from Johannesburg to Windhoek (1,791 km [1,110 mi]) via Upington, going through the Narochas (Nakop) border post (open 24 hours). This is a good route if you want to visit the Augrabies Falls and Kgalagadi Transfrontier Park in South Africa first. You can also drive from Cape Town to Namibia along the N7, an excellent road that becomes the B1 as you cross into Namibia at the Noordoewer border post (open 24 hours). It's 763 km (473 mi) from Cape Town to Noordoewer, 795 km (493 mi) from Noordoewer to Windhoek. Border posts are efficient and friendly—make sure you have all your paperwork to hand over. You will need a current international driver's license.

Coming from Botswana, Namibia is popularly entered at the Buitepos on the Trans-Kalahari Highway if coming from Gaborone, or through Ngoma on the Caprivi Strip if coming from the Okavango Delta. Border posts are not open 24 hours, and opening times should be confirmed before traveling. Cross-border charges (CBCs) must be paid by all foreign-registered vehicles entering Namibia, and cost about N$180 per vehicle (more for buses and motor homes). Tourists driving a rental car must also pay the CBC and will receive a CBC certificate for every entry into Namibia.

To reach Etosha National Park you can drive from Windhoek, via Otjiwarongo and Tsumeb, and arrive at the park on its eastern side by the Von Lindequist Gate (near Namutoni Rest Camp), 106 km (66 mi) from Tsumeb and 550 km (341 mi) north of Windhoek. Alternatively, you can drive from Windhoek via Otjiwarongo and Outjo and come in the Anderson Gate, south of Okaukuejo, 120 km (74½ mi) from Outjo, 450 km (279 mi) north of Windhoek. The latter is the more popular route. Both drives are long, hot, and dusty, so you might want to fly to your camp's landing strip if you're short on time.

If you're not staying at a private lodge that provides transportation, you will need to rent your own vehicle. Air-conditioning is a must at any time of the year, as are spare tires in good condition. You can pick up rental cars at the town nearest whichever park you are visiting or at Etosha itself, but it's better to book them before you leave home. For driving on the main roads, a two-wheel-drive vehicle is fine. In some areas, though, including parts of the Namib Naukluft Park and Damaraland, four-wheel drive is essential. In Etosha a two-wheel-drive car is fine; don't exceed the speed limit of 60 KPH (37 MPH). Always check the state of the roads with the nearest tourist office before you set off, and never underestimate the long distances involved. Don't drive at night unless you absolutely have to. Roads are unlighted, and animals like to bed down on the warm surfaces. If you hit an animal, even a small one, it could be the end of you and your vehicle, not to mention the critter. Never speed on gravel roads (80 KPH [50 MPH] is reasonable). It's very easy to skid or roll your vehicle—at least one tourist per year dies this way. And make sure you have plenty of water and *padkos,* Afrikaans for "road food." Finally, keep in mind that gas stations only accept cash, and can be few and far between.

Automobile Associations Automobile Association of Namibia (AAN) (✉ *Windhoek* ☎ *061/224–201*).

TRAIN TRAVEL

The Desert Express travels between Windhoek, the capital of Namibia and Swakopmund, the country's premier coastal resort. The train departs from Windhoek on Fridays and from Swakopmund on Saturdays. Longer journeys to Etosha are also available.

Train Information Desert Express (✉ *Windhoek Railway Station, Bahnhof St., Windhoek* ☎ *061/298–2600* ⊕ *www.desertexpress.com.na*).

COMMUNICATIONS

PHONES

The country code for Namibia is 264. When dialing from abroad, drop the initial 0 from local area codes.

CALLING WITHIN NAMIBIA

Namibian telephone numbers vary and are constantly changing; many have six digits (not including the area and country code), but some have fewer or more digits.

CALLING OUTSIDE NAMIBIA

You can use public phones for direct international calls. Buy Telecards in different denominations from post offices and telecom offices.

MOBILE PHONES

There's cell-phone reception in all major towns. Enable your own for international roaming before you leave home, or buy a local SIM card when you arrive (a much cheaper option, and very easy to do). The two major cell networks are MTC, and the newer and, at the time of writing, much cheaper Leo. A SIM card will cost around N$10–N$20, and the prepaid rate varies from about N$1–N$3 per minute. Airtime is available in most supermarkets, convenience stores, and some bookshops.

CUSTOMS AND DUTIES

⇨ *For information on what you can and cannot bring into Namibia, see Customs and Duties, in the On Safari chapter.*

HEALTH AND SAFETY

Malaria is endemic in the east, north, and northeast, so antimalarials are essential. Never venture into the desert without water, a sun hat, and sunblock. AIDS is a major problem, as elsewhere in Africa; do not have sex with a stranger. In towns, don't walk alone at night, and lock your valuables, documents, and cash in the hotel or lodge safe. In game

"[T]he stark beauty [of the Namibian desert] was beyond words. The Deadvlei trees have stood for almost a thousand years, and we were speechless when we saw them." —jeep61, Fodors.com member

areas, never walk after dark unless accompanied by an armed guide. Because there is comparatively little traffic, self-driving visitors are often tempted to speed. Don't. Gravel roads can be treacherous.

Be sure you have comprehensive medical insurance before you leave home. There's a high standard of medical care in Namibia. Consult your hotel or the white pages of the telephone directory under medical practitioners. If you get sick, go to a private clinic rather than a government-run one.

Windhoek and Otjiwarongo both have excellent private clinics. Both cities have a Medi-Clinic, and Windhoek also has the Roman Catholic Hospital.

Embassies U.S. Embassy (⊠ *14 Lossen St., Windhoek* ☎ *061/295–8500*).

Emergency Services International SOS (☎ *112 from mobile phone* ☎ *061/230–505 Windhoek* ☎ *064/463–676 Swakopmund* ☎ *081/128–5501 Tsumeb* ☎ *064/400–700 Walvis Bay*). **Netcare 911** (☎ *061/223–330*).

Hospitals Roman Catholic Hospital (⊠ *92 Stubel St., Windhoek* ☎ *061/270–2911*). **Medi-Clinic** (⊠ *Heliodoor St., Eros Park, Windhoek* ☎ *061/22–2687* ⊠ *Son St., Otjiwarongo* ☎ *067/303–734 or 067/303–735*).

HOURS OF OPERATION

Shops in Windhoek and Swakopmund are generally open 9–5, though some close for lunch and then stay open a bit later into the evening. Banking hours are 8:30–3:30 Monday–Friday, and 8:30–noon on Saturday. Restaurants vary but usually operate noon–3 and 6–10, although cafés frequently stay open all day. Nightclubs stay open late; the closing hour usually depends on the number of customers. Even on public holidays many shops will be open—only banks, government offices, and business premises will close.

MONEY MATTERS

Namibia's currency is the Namibian dollar, which is linked to the South African rand. (Namibia's currency cannot be used in South Africa, except unofficially at border towns.) At this writing, the Namibian dollar was trading at about N$7 to US$1. *Bureau de change* offices at the airports often stay open until late.

There are main branches of major banks near or in the city center of Windhoek, Swakopmund, and Walvis Bay, plus several easy-to-find ATMs. Ask at your accommodation for more information. Major credit cards are accepted everywhere but at street markets, with Visa being the preferred card. South African rand are accepted everywhere. In more rural or remote areas, carry Namibian dollars or South African rand. In Windhoek, Swakopmund, and the larger towns there are plenty of banks and ATMs. Note that gas stations take only cash.

RESTAURANTS

You won't find much truly Namibian food (although local venison, seafood, and Namibian oysters are superb); cuisine is mainly European, often German, though international variety and standards increasingly are found in the larger towns. Lodges usually serve good home-style cooking—pies, pastries, fresh vegetables, lots of red meat, mouthwatering desserts, and the traditional braai. Because of its past as a German colony, Namibia is known for its lager. South African wine, which is excellent, is readily available. ⇨ *For information on South African wine, see Sip and Spoeg Like an Expert, in South Africa chapter.*

HOTELS AND LODGES

Namibia's private camps, lodges, and other accommodations are often up to high international standards. Even deep at tented camps, there are en-suite bathrooms and private verandas, but don't expect TV. Most private lodges are all-inclusive (Full American Plan), including transfers, meals, activities, and usually drinks. Camps offer at least two activities a day.

At the national park camps, self-catering (with cooking facilities) accommodations are basic, clean, comfortable, and much cheaper than private lodges outside the park. In Etosha each camp has a restaurant with adequate food; a shop selling basic foodstuffs and curios; a post office; a gas station; and a pool. Most rooms have private toilets, baths or showers, air-conditioning, a refrigerator, and a *braai* (barbecue). Linens are provided. Some bigger bungalows have a full kitchen.

In Windhoek and Swakopmund, a large array of lodging, from large upmarket hotels to intimate boutique hotels and family-run B&Bs, are yours to choose from. All urban lodging rates include breakfast, but rarely any other meals.

⇨ *For information on converters and electricity while on Safari, see Electricity, in the What to Pack section of the On Safari chapter.*

WHAT IT COSTS IN NAMIBIAN DOLLARS				
¢	$	$$	$$$	$$$$
Safari Camps and Lodges	under N$1,300	N$1,300–N$2,300	N$2,300–N$3,500	N$3,500–N$5,000	over N$5,000
Restaurants	under N$60	N$60–N$100	N$100–N$140	N$140–N$180	over N$180
Hotels	under N$500	N$500–N$1,000	N$1,001–N$2,000	N$2,001–N$3,000	over N$3,000

Most safari prices refer to an all-inclusive per-person rate excluding tax (a few only operate on a half-board rate), assuming double occupancy. Hotel rates refer to double occupancy excluding tax.

PASSPORTS AND VISAS

All nonnationals, including infants, need a valid passport to enter Namibia for visits of up to 90 days. Business visitors need visas.

VISITOR INFO

The Namibia Tourism Board (NTB) can provide a free map and a free copy of Welcome to Namibia—Official Visitors' Guide, which gives useful information plus accommodation lists, but does not provide detailed personalized advice. It's open weekdays 8–5. For more hands-on assistance, check out the Tourist Information centers (all run by different agencies, from the City of Windhoek to private companies) located in Windhoek and Swakopmund. Namibia Wildlife Resorts offers information on accommodation in the national parks, which you can also book through them.

Visitor Information Leading Lodges Tourist Information Center (✉ 117 Independence Ave. ☎ 061/375–300). **Namibia Tourism Board** (NTB ✉ 39 Post Street Mall, Channel Life Tower, 1st Fl., Windhoek ☎ 061/290–6000 ⊕ www.namibiatourism.com.na). **Namibia Wildlife Resorts** (NWR ✉ 189 Independence Ave., opposite Zoo Park, Windhoek ☎ 061/285–7200 ⊕ www.nwr.com.na). **Tourist Information Bureau** (✉ Post St. Mall ☎ 061/290–2092 or 061/290–2596 ⊕ www.cityofwindhoek.org.na ✉ Independence Ave., opposite Kalahari Sands and Casino).

MUST-SEE PARKS

You probably won't be able to see all of Namibia in one trip, so we've broken down the chapter by **Must-See Parks** (Namib Naukluft Park, Damaraland, Etosha National Park) and **If You Have Time Parks** (the Skeleton Coast and the Caprivi Strip) to help you organize your time. We suggest that you read about *all* of them and then choose for yourself.

NAMIB NAUKLUFT PARK

Game
☆☆☆★★

Park Accessibility
☆★★★★

Getting Around
☆★★★★

Accommodations
★★★★★

Scenic Beauty
★★★★★

Namib Naukluft Park, south of Walvis Bay, is the fourth-largest national park in the world and is renowned for its beauty, isolation, tranquility, romantic desert landscapes, and rare desert-adapted plants and creatures.

Covering an area of 12.1 million acres, it stretches 400 km (248 mi) long and 150 km (93 mi) wide, along the southern part of Namibia's coastline from Walvis Bay to Lüderitz, and accounts for a tenth of Namibia's surface area. The Namib Desert is considered the world's most ancient desert, at more than 55 million years old. To examine the park properly, it's best to think of it as five distinct areas: the northern section—between the Kuiseb and Swakops rivers—synonymous with rocky stone surfaces, granite islands (inselbergs), and dry riverbeds; the middle section, the 80-million-year-old heart of the desert and home of Sesriem Canyon and Sossusvlei, the highest sand dunes in the world; Naukluft (meaning "narrow gorge"), some 120 km (74½ mi) northwest of Sesriem, which has wall-to-wall game and birds and is the home of the Kuiseb Canyon; the western section, with its lichen-covered plains, prehistoric plants, and bird sanctuaries of Walvis Bay and Sandwich Harbour; and the southern section, where, if you're traveling up from South Africa by road, it's worth having a look at Duwisib Castle, 72 km (45 mi) southwest of Maltahöhe beside the D286—an anachronistic stone castle built in 1909 by a German army officer who was later killed at the Somme. The park's southern border ends at the charming little town of Lüderitz.

The kind of wildlife you'll encounter will depend on which area of the park you visit. In the north look out for the staggeringly beautiful gemsbok (oryx), the quintessential desert antelope, believed by some to be the animal behind the unicorn myth. These animals are amazingly well adapted for the desert; they obtain moisture from roots, tubers, and wild melons when water is scarce, and although oryx body temperatures can soar, specialized blood vessels in their nostrils keep their brains cool. Also visible are springboks, spotted hyenas, black-backed jackals, and the awesome lappet-face vultures, the biggest in Africa.

In Naukluft you'll see the most game, more than 50 species of mammals, including leopards, caracals, Cape and bat-eared foxes, aardwolves, and klipspringers. There are almost 200 species of birds, from the startlingly beautiful crimson-breasted boubou shrike to soaring falcons and buzzards. You'll notice huge haystacks weighing down tall trees and telephone poles. These are the condominiums of the sociable weavers, so called because they nest communally, sometimes with thousands of fellow weavers.

You'll be able to observe some of the earth's strangest creatures in the sand dunes: the dune beetle, which collects condensed fog on its back into a single droplet that it then rolls down its back into its mouth; the golden mole (thought until recently to be extinct), which "swims" beneath the sand, ambushing beetles and grubs on the surface; the sidewinding adder; and the sand-diving lizard that raises one foot at a time above the hot sand in a strange stationary dance.

Don't overlook the amazing desert-adapted plants. Ask your guide to point out a dollar bush (so called because its leaves are dollar size) or an ink bush, both of which can survive without rain for years; the gold, frankincense, and myrrh of the Commiphora plants; the Namib's magic plant, the nara melon, still harvested and eaten by the locals; and the baffling geophytes, plants that disguise themselves as stones. Watch for withered-looking desert lichens—if you pour a tiny drop of water onto one it will seemingly rise from the dead. Last, but by no means least, is the mind-boggling *Welwitschia mirabilis,* the Namib's most famous, and the world's oldest, living plant.

GETTING HERE AND AROUND

At its closest, the Namib-Naukluft is approximately 200 km (124 mi) from Windhoek and can be accessed by many roads, major and minor. Entry permits for the park, including Sossusvlei and Sandwich Harbour, are required, and can be obtained from the Ministry of Environment Tourism offices in Windhoek, Swakopmund, or Sesriem. The park is split into four sections: Sesriem and Sossusvlei; Namib; Naukluft; and Sandwich Harbour. Entrance is between sunrise and sunset only. The distance between Sesriem and Sossusvlei is 65 km (40 mi), the last 5 km of which require a 4x4. The dunes are easily accessible by foot from the sedan car park. Sandwich Harbour is accessible only with a 4x4, and an experienced guide is highly recommended.

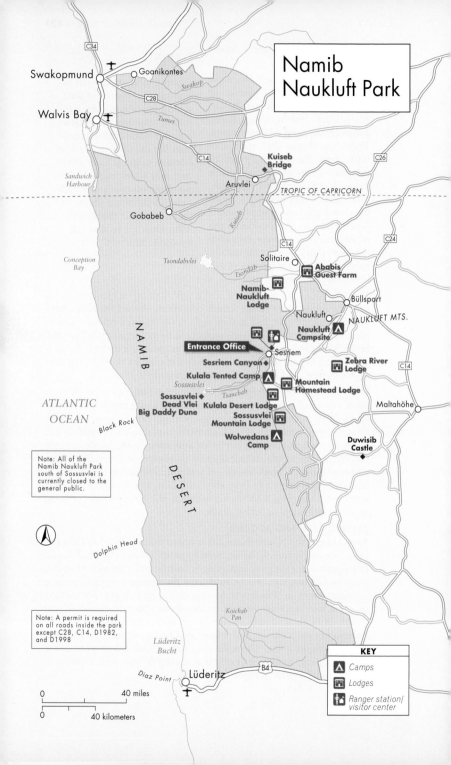

Namib Nraukluft Park

Swakopmund
C34
Goanikontes
Swakop
C28
Walvis Bay
Tumes
C14
Kuiseb
Bridge
Aruvlei
C26
Sandwich Harbour
TROPIC OF CAPRICORN
Gobabeb
Conception Bay
Tsondabvlei
Tsondab
Solitaire
C14
Ababis Guest Farm
C24
Namib-Naukluft Lodge
Büllsport
Naukluft
NAUKLUFT MTS.
Naukluft Campsite
Entrance Office
Sesriem
Zebra River Lodge
C14
Sesriem Canyon
Kulala Tented Camp
Mountain Homestead Lodge
N A M I B
Sossusvlei
Tsauchab
Maltahöhe
Sossusvlei Dead Vlei Big Daddy Dune
Kulala Desert Lodge
Sossusvlei Mountain Lodge
ATLANTIC OCEAN
Black Rock
Wolwedans Camp
Duwisib Castle
Note: All of the Namib Naukluft Park south of Sossusvlei is currently closed to the general public.
D E S E R T
Dolphin Head
Koichab Pan
Note: A permit is required on all roads inside the park except C28, C14, D1982, and D1998
Lüderitz Bucht
Diaz Point
Lüderitz
B4

0   40 miles
0   40 kilometers

KEY
△ *Camps*
▣ *Lodges*
▮ *Ranger station/ visitor center*

WHEN TO GO

Temperatures can be extremely variable, with days generally hot (sometimes exceeding 104°F [40°C]) and nights that can descend to freezing. Given these extremes, the dunes are best visited early in the morning, especially in the summer (September–March). The park is open throughout the year, and in winter one can visit the dunes during the day, though note that it can still get warm, especially when climbing the dunes.

SAFETY AND PRECAUTIONS

Stay on existing roads and tracks, and always have plenty of water available (at least a liter per person in case the car breaks down and it takes time for help to arrive). The lichen and gravel plains are extremely fragile and tire tracks can last for hundreds of years. Avoid disturbing nesting raptors if mountain climbing. Campsites have very limited facilities, which are mostly concentrated in the northern section of the park. You must be fully independent when camping. Bring firewood, water, and food. Always carry water, sunblock, and a hat, regardless of the season. If traveling in an open vehicle, always take a thick jacket (i.e., a wind breaker) as the wind while driving can be freezing (even in summer in the early morning before sunrise). At Sesriem Canyon there are ablution blocks with potable water. Private camping sites at guest farms or lodges also often have water. Always be sure to inquire ahead of time and make use of dedicated camping sites. Community camping sites may not always have water, so if you plan to visit these, bring water for washing up and cooking as well as for drinking.

TIMING

Those only intending to visit Sossusvlei should plan on at least two nights so as to have an entire day to climb the dunes and visit Dead Vlei; climbing the dunes should be done very early in the morning to avoid the heat. If you're planning to hike the Namib Naukluft Trail as well, five days total should suffice.

EXPLORING

Sesriem and Sossusvlei. Even if you're not a romantic, the Sossusvlei's huge, star-shaped desert dunes, which rise dramatically 1,000 feet above the surrounding plains and sprawl like massive pieces of abstract sculpture, are guaranteed to stir your soul and imagination. The landscape has continuously shifting colors—from yellow-gold and ocher to rose, purple, and deep red—that grow paler or darker according to the time of day. The dunes have their own distinctive features, ranging from the crescent-shaped barchan dunes—which migrate up to 2 or 3 yards a year, covering and uncovering whatever crosses their path—to the spectacular, stationary star-shaped dunes, formed by the multidirectional winds that tease and tumble the sands back and forth. Park gates open an hour before sunrise, so if you can, try to be among the dunes as the sun comes up—it's a spectacular sight.

TOP ATTRACTIONS

Big Daddy Dune. If you're in good shape, you can hike to the top of Big Daddy, the highest sand dune in the world at 360 meters (1,181 feet). But it's tough going: more than an hour of very hot trudging and wading through ankle- and sometimes knee-deep sand to climb the major route up to Dead Vlei (where ghostly skeletons of ancient trees jut up from a flat, sandy, dried-up lake) and Big Daddy (the hub of Sossusvlei) from the parking area. If you don't feel up to any physical exertion at all, then sit in the shade of camelthorn trees at the bottom of the dunes and watch the birdlife, or focus your binoculars on the distant climbers. ✤ *70 km (43 mi) from the Sesriem gate* ☉ *Sunrise to sunset.*

Sesriem Canyon. About 4 km (2½ mi) from Sesriem Gate, your entry point to Sossusvlei, is Sesriem Canyon, named after the six *rieme* (thongs) that were tied to the buckets of the early Dutch settlers when they drew up water from the canyon. A narrow gorge of about 1 km in length, the Sesriem Canyon is the product of centuries of erosion. Plunging down 30–40 meters at its end are a series of pools that fill with water during the rains. If you have time, cool off in the pools, easily reached by steps in the rock. ✤ *Near entry to Sossusvlei* ☉ *Sunrise to sunset.*

Elim Dune. If you're fairly fit, it's well worth climbing the towering Elim Dune, the nearest sand dune to Sesriem, about 5 km (3 mi) away; it will take you more than an hour, but the superb views of the surrounding desert and gravel plains are infinitely rewarding. Be warned: dune climbing is exhausting, so make discretion the better part of valor. If you're driving yourself, check with your car-rental company for distances and times, which can vary according to the state of the roads. Keep in mind that a 4x4 will give you more access and better viewing, and with a 4x4 you can park just below Dead Vlei. ✤ *5 km (3 mi) from Sesriem* ☉ *Sunrise to sunset.*

WHERE TO STAY

LUXURY LODGES

$$$$ ▦ **Kulala Desert Lodge.** In the heart of the Namib and set on a 91,000 acre wilderness reserve that borders the Namib Naukluft Park, this lodge offers magnificent views of the famous red dunes of Sossusvlei, superb mountain scenery, and vast open plains. Tented, thatch-roofed chalets (*kulala*) sit on a wooden platform overlooking the dry riverbed. In summer you can request a bedroll from reception to sleep on your roof under the stars. The veranda at the main lodge overlooks a water hole and is the perfect place to watch or photograph the magnificent desert sunset. Activities include desert excursions, morning and evening game drives, trips to Sossusvlei, birding, and guided walks. For an

additional fee you can splurge on a hot-air balloon trip or helicopter ride over the desert—a once-in-a-lifetime opportunity. **Pros:** located on a 91,000-acre reserve, this is the lodge closest to the dune belt at Namib Naukluft Park; great guides. **Cons:** decor can seem stark to some; if you choose the half-board option you must pay for activities and extras like bottled water. ☎ *27/11807–1800 in South Africa* ⊕ *www.safariadventurecompany.com* ⇆ *19 chalets* ♿ *In-room: no phone (some), no a/c, safe (some), no TV. In-hotel: bar, pool, laundry, parking (free)* 🖃 *AE, DC, MC, V* ¶◎¶ *MAP, AI.*

$$–$$$
Fodor's Choice
★

🏨 **Sossusvlei Mountain Lodge.** This gorgeous glass and stone lodge has a spectacular setting in the NamibRand Nature Reserve. Its ultraluxurious desert villas, facing a vast golden-yellow plain with misty mountains on the horizon, are built of natural rock and look out over a plain ringed by peaks. Huge desert-facing suites have private patios and sundecks and big open fireplaces to keep you warm on chilly desert nights. Shower in your megasize bathroom (even your toilet has an incomparable view) or outside in your own little walled garden. You can lie in bed and watch the stars through the skylight overhead or climb up to the observatory behind the lodge. It has its own state-of-the-art telescope through which an astronomer-ranger will guide you through the heavens. The food is as creative as the lodge itself—try tandoori-baked *kingklip* (a delicious Southern African fish) served with mango salsa—and there's a super wine cellar. You can explore the area on an eco-friendly quad bike, go for guided nature walks or drives, spot some native desert birds and animals, or just sit and gaze at the incredible views. **Pros:** lodge planetarium with resident astronomers; more than the usual activities available including guided or unguided nature walks, expeditions to San caves to view paintings, and quad biking; fantastic service. **Cons:** excursions into Sossusvlei are at an additional cost. ☎ *27/11809–4300* ⊕ *www.sossusvlei-namibia.com* ⇆ *10 villas* ♿ *In-room: a/c, safe (some), refrigerator (some), no TV (some).* ♿ *In-hotel: pool, bar, laundry service (free), Internet terminal* 🖃 *MC, V* ¶◎¶ *FAP.*

$$$
🏨 **Wolwedans Private Camp.** This simple wood and canvas camp, in the serene and secluded NamibRand Nature Reserve, gives its guests up-close access to the surrounding desert habitat. The reserve is a reflection of the diversity of the Namib Desert with its steep mountain ranges, vast savannahs, glorious red sand dunes, and clay pans. Here you might possibly see the oryx, as well as more than 100 bird species including the rare dune lark. The reserve is sparsely developed and off-limits to large vehicles such as tour buses and 4x4s. What's more, a percentage of your park entry fee goes directly into conserving the integrity of the reserve. The camp itself is made up of just two en-suite doubles that share a library, kitchen, chef, and numerous outdoor spaces from which to enjoy the views. **Pros:** beautiful, private, and intimate location with outdoor salas and decks to enjoy the views; fully equipped kitchen and open-plan design; guided activities include drives, flights, walks, and hot-air ballooning. **Cons:** you won't meet any other guests; some activities are at extra charge. ☎ *061/230–616* ⊕ *www.wolwedans.com* ⇆ *2 rooms* ♿ *In-room: no a/c, kitchen (some), refrigerator (some), no TV.*

7

In-hotel: restaurant, room service, bar, pool, laundry service, Internet terminal, Wi-Fi hotspot, parking (free) ▤ *AE, DC, MC, V* ⏐◎⏐ *FAP.*

PERMANENT TENTED CAMPS

$$$$ ⌕ **Kulala Tented Camp.** Although this small, stylish camp calls itself a "tented" camp, only the walls of your unit are actually made of canvas: your roof is thatch and your floor and deck are wood. As the camp faces west, don't miss the opportunity to sit out on your personal rooftop deck to watch a spectacular Namibian sunset (you can also request a bedroll to sleep under the stars up there). You won't find much big game here, but spotting springbok and ostrich skittering over the stark landscape, catching a glimpse of the dramatic desert oryx, and listening to the barking geckos as the sun goes down are all memorable experiences. Take a guided trip to Sossusvlei, go walking with a knowledgeable guide in the surrounding desert, or treat yourself (go on; it's expensive but the experience of a lifetime) to a dawn hot-air balloon ride. **Pros:** main lodge area has a beautiful sundeck and pool with views of the valley and mountains; camel rides, quad bikes, and helicopter flights also available at extra cost. **Cons:** no a/c can make for a hot stay in summer. ☎ *27/11807–1800 in South Africa* ⊕ *www.safariadventurecompany. com* ⇲ *9 tented chalets* ⚒ *In-room: no phone, no a/c, safe, no TV. In-hotel: bar, pool* ▤ *AE, DC, MC, V* ⏐◎⏐ *MAP, AI.*

BUDGET ACCOMMODATIONS

$ ⌕ **Ababis Guest Farm.** Ostriches and cows rub unlikely shoulders at this intimate, historic guesthouse at a farm on the northern side of the Naukluft Mountains, near the tiny town of Solitaire. It was established in 1898 as an outpost of the German Imperial Stud Farm at Nauchas. Today it's an ideal base for exploring the area, whether on foot or by 4x4—although it's a day-long trip to Sossusvlei and back. With long hikes and short strolls around the farm, the area is ideal for hikers. There are seven en-suite rooms with private verandas, and the English-and-German-speaking hosts will escort you on game drives, to nearby San paintings, or to the Naukluft plateau. You'll dine well on home-cooked food, and there's a surprisingly good wine selection. **Pros:** charming, homey environment; self-guided hikes and walking. **Cons:** 4x4 excursions at extra cost; far from Sossusvlei. ☎ *063/683–080* ⊕ *www.ababis-guestfarm.com* ⇲ *7 rooms* ⚒ *In-room: no phone, a/c (some). In-hotel: restaurant, bar, pool, laundry, Wi-Fi, parking (free)* ▤ *MC, V* ⏐◎⏐ *MAP.*

$$ ⌕ **Mountain Homestead Lodge.** In one of the most dramatic settings in Africa, exquisitely appointed rock, timber, and thatch bungalows cling to the side of a mountain with spectacular views of the desert as it stretches away to the horizon. After the bumpy 20-km (12½-mi) drive to the dunes, you'll enjoy breakfast under spreading camelthorn trees at the foot of Sossusvlei before returning to camp at midday via the Sesriem Canyon. You can then cool off in your private plunge pool as you watch the sun set over awesome desert scenery to the calls of barking geckos. **Pros:** superb location to see Sossusvlei dunes without having to travel large distances; each room has a private plunge pool. **Cons:** diesel generator can be quite loud at night; not a great environment for

Kulala Desert Lodge

Sossusvlei Wilderness

Sossusvlei Mt Lodge

solo travelers. ☎ *061/246–788* ⊕ *www.deserthomestead-namibia.com* ⤷ *9 bungalows ⚭ In-room: no phone, no a/c, safe (some), no TV. In-hotel: restaurant, bar, pool, laundry service* ☰ *AE, DC, MC, V* ⦿ *MAP.*

$ 🏨 **Namib Naukluft Lodge.** Resembling children's building blocks set down by a giant hand in the middle of nowhere, this pinkish-brown desert-toned lodge sits in the midst of a wide plain of desert, backed by gorgeous granite hills. Awesome views go with the territory. You can choose to sit on your private veranda and watch the fiery desert sunset, sip a sundowner by the pool, or enjoy a meal in the open-air restaurant. The lodge will arrange outings and activities for you—don't miss out on an easy walk in the world's oldest desert. **Pros:** shuttle available from Windhoek and Swakopmund to the lodge; friendly service; stunning location. **Cons:** relatively long drive to Sossusvlei; no-frills accommodation, but views make up for it. ☎ *061/372–100* ⊕ *www.namib-naukluftlodge.com* ⤷ *16 rooms ⚭ In-room: a/c. In-hotel: restaurant, bar, pool, laundry* ☰ *AE, DC, MC, V* ⦿ *BP, MAP.*

$ 🏨 **Sossusvlei Lodge.** If you want to be on the spot when the park gates open at first light, then this hotel right at the Sesriem entrance is the right choice for you. Its decor—in shades of terra-cotta, burnt sienna, and apricot—blends perfectly with the desert surroundings. You may feel like a well-to-do Bedouin in your spacious and luxurious tented room, imaginatively constructed of concrete, ironwork, canvas, and leather. After a hot, dusty day in the desert, it's wonderful to wallow in the swimming pool, which faces the dunes, and later gaze at the dazzling brilliance of the night skies. There's a good restaurant serving light meals. **Pros:** great, convenient location for early-morning drives; many of the rooms have a good view on the water hole. **Cons:** some might feel the style verges on a housing development; no bathtubs. ☎ *063/693–223* ⊕ *www.sossusvleilodge.com* ⤷ *45 rooms ⚭ In-room: no phone, a/c, safe, no TV. In-hotel: restaurant, room service, bar, pool, laundry service* ☰ *AE, MC, V* ⦿ *MAP.*

$ 🏨 **Zebra River Lodge.** From this delightful lodge, where personal atten-
☺ tion and friendly service are outstanding (the lodge gets lots of repeat visitors), you can drive yourself to Sesriem and Sossusvlei (90 km [56 mi] to the gate) or to Naukluft, or take a full-day excursion with Rob Field, the friendly and knowledgeable owner (book this when you reserve your room). The comfortable and unpretentious lodge has its own canyon, hiking trails, perennial springs, and superb cooking. The nine guest rooms all have views of the plunge pool and green garden. **Pros:** incredibly friendly hosts; the farm is of international importance for its fossils and birds with more than 118 species seen on the property. **Cons:** far from Sossusvlei; activities are at additional cost. ☎ *063/693–265* ⊕ *www.zebrariver.com* ⤷ *9 rooms ⚭ In-room: no phone, no a/c, no TV. In-hotel: restaurant, bar, pool, laundry, Internet terminal, parking* ☰ *MC, V* ⦿ *FAP.*

The Sossusvlei salt pans.

THE NAMIBIA DUNES

by Kate
Turkington

Be prepared for sand like you've never seen it before: in dunes that roar, rumble, and ramble. We guarantee the sight will stir your soul and imagination.

Namibia's dunes, which rise dramatically more than 1,000 meters (3,281 feet) above the surrounding plains, are said to be the world's highest. But don't think that if you've seen one sandy ridge you've seen them all. Expect great variety here. There are crescent-shaped dunes that migrate up to 2 or 3 meters (7 to 10 feet) a year, covering and uncovering whatever's in their path. There are also fossil dunes made of ancient sand that solidified millions of years ago, and star-shaped dunes formed by multidirectional winds teasing and tumbling the sand.

Amid this unique landscape live some of the world's strangest, most well-adapted creatures. The golden mole, for instance, spends its life "swimming" under the sand, popping up to the surface to grab unwary insects. Certain types of beetles collect condensed droplets of water on their backs and then roll the liquid down to their mouths; still other beetles dig trenches to collect moisture. As its name suggests, the side-winding adder moves itself from side to side over the sand, while, contrary to its name, the sand-diving lizard stands motionless, one foot raised, as if in some ancient ritual dance. And then there's the quintessential desert antelope: the beautiful gemsbok (oryx), which is believed by some to be the animal behind the unicorn myth.

WHERE DID THE DUNES COME FROM?

The formation and structure of sand dunes is extremely complex, but basically there are three prerequisites for dunes: plenty of loose sand, plenty of wind, and a flat surface with no obstacles like trees or mountains to prevent dunes building up. Namibia has these three things in abundance.

A MILLION GRAINS OF SAND FOR YOU TO EXPLORE

Gemsbok in the desert dunes of Namib-Naukluft Park.

WHERE ARE THE DUNES?

Enormous Namib-Naukluft Park—renowned for its isolated, romantic desert scapes—stretches 400 km (250 mi) along the southern part of Namibia's coastline, from Walvis Bay to Lüderitz, and accounts for a tenth of the country's surface area. Sossusvlei, the 80-million-year-old heart of the desert, is in the middle section of the park. It's a great entry point from which you can start your adventures. This desert is thought to be the oldest desert in the world. Although its geological base area is relatively stable, the dunes themselves are continuously sculpted by the desert winds.

DUNE EXPLORER

Sure, you could explore the dunes on your own, but you really can't beat the know-how of an experienced guide; ask your lodge to arrange this. Look to climb "Big Daddy," a dune that's as tall as a seven-story building, or Dune 7 (about 1,256 feet) or Dune 45 (557 feet). You could also just climb to the halfway point of Big Daddy or simply sit in the shade at the bottom of a dune and watch the distant climbers exert themselves.

WHEN TO GO

Sunset and sunrise are the best times to visit (be at the gates of Sesriem when it opens at 5 AM or camp in the park), because the colors of the dunes change in spectacular fashion from yellow-gold and ocher to rose, purple, and deep red. Keep in mind that midday temperatures can peak at over 40°C (104°F) in summer.

THE SLOW PACE

Sip sundowners as the sun sinks, go hot-air ballooning at dawn, or simply marvel at the life that is found in this harsh environment. You won't see big game, but you will see a wealth of unique birds, insects, plants, and geological formations. Whatever you do, make sure you take a moment to appreciate the soul-searing and soul-searching silence.

ADRENALINE JUNKIES WELCOME

(top) Preparing to sandboard. (bottom) Sandboarding.

Looking for some excitement? Adrenaline junkies can try their hand (or feet) at skydiving, dune-buggying, paragliding, sandboarding or dune-boarding (for the more advanced). The less adventurous (but romantic) can take day, moonlight, sunrise or sunset horseback or camel rides through the riverbeds and up into the moonlike landscape.

If you have time for just one thing, make it sandboarding because it will certainly get your heart pumping. Once you are ferried up the dunes by quad bike, your operator will arm you with the necessary equipment: a sandboard—a flat piece of hardboard, a safety hat, gloves, and elbow guards. It's also a good idea to wear long pants and long sleeves to avoid a sandburn. Beginners should head to the smaller dunes to practice (i.e. sliding down on your stomach) to get the feel of it. As you get better and more adventurous, head to the top of a high dune, but be advised, you can reach speeds of up to 80 kph (50 mph). Once you get the hang of this, try standing up. Hey, if Cameron Diaz survived, so will you.

If you get really advanced, there's always dune-boarding. You use all the same gear as sandboarding, except your board is similar to a regular surfboard on which you stand up and "surf" down the dunes.

DAMARALAND

Game
☆☆★★★

Park Accessibility
☆☆☆☆★

Getting Around
☆☆☆★★

Accommodations
☆☆☆★★

Scenic Beauty
★★★★★

Stretching 600 km (370 mi) from just south of Etosha to Usakos in the south and 200 km (125 mi) from east to west, this stark, mountainous area is inland from Skeleton Coast National Park.

You can drive into Damaraland from the park via the Springbokwater Gate or drive from Swakopmund to Uis, where you can visit the Daureb Craft Centre and watch the craftspeople at work, or make it part of your customized safari. A good base for touring southern Damaraland is the little town of Khorixas. From here you can visit the Organ Pipes, hundreds of angular rock formations, or watch the rising or setting sun bathe the slopes of Burnt Mountain in fiery splendor. You'll find yourself surrounded by a dramatic landscape of steep valleys; rugged cliffs of red, gray, black, and brown; and towering mountains, including Spitzkoppe (Namibia's Matterhorn, which towers nearly 2,000 feet above the plains), where Damara guides will show you the Golden Snake and the Bridge—an interesting rock formation—and the San paintings at Bushman's Paradise. There are more spectacular rock paintings at Brandberg Mountain, especially the famous White Lady of Brandberg at Tsisab Gorge, whose depiction and origin have teased the minds of scholars for decades. (Is she of Mediterranean origin? Is "she" really a "he" covered in white initiation paint?)

Other stops of interest are the Petrified Forest, 42 km (25 mi) west of Khorixas, where the corpses of dead trees lie forever frozen in a bed of sandstone. The first UNESCO World Heritage Site in Namibia, Twyfelfontein, 90 km (56 mi) west of Khorixas, is also the biggest outdoor art gallery in the world, where thousands of rock paintings and ancient rock engravings are open to the sky. It's extremely rare for this many paintings and engravings to be found at the same site. As you approach, you'll see scattered boulders everywhere—a closer examination will reveal thousands of rock paintings and engravings. Get yourself a local knowledgeable guide when you arrive, and try to give yourself a full day here; start early (it's hard to pick out some of the art in full sunshine), bring binoculars, wear sturdy shoes, and bring water (at least a gallon) and a hat.

Northern Damaraland consists of concession areas that have been set aside for tourism, with many tourist operators working hand in hand with the local communities. This is a desert of a different kind from the classic sand dunes of the Namib. It's a landscape of almost unsurpassed rugged beauty formed by millions of years of unending geological movement. Vivid brick-red sediments complement gray lava slopes punctuated by black fingers of "frozen" basaltic rock creeping down from the jagged rocky horizons. Millions of stones, interspersed with clumps of silvery-gray shrubs and pioneer grasses, litter the unending slopes, hillsides, and mountain faces. There seem to be as many rocks, huge and small, as there are grains of sand on the beaches of the windswept, treacherous Skeleton Coast, some 90 km (56 mi) to the west. But there is life, and plenty of it, in this seemingly inhospitable landscape, including dozens of *Welwitschia mirabilis* plants that can live for up to 1,000 years. Stop at a 500-year-old "youngster" and consider that when this plant was a newborn, Columbus was sailing for the New World and the Portuguese to Namibia.

The landscape is also dotted with colorful lichen fields, dark-green umbrella-shaped camelthorn trees, candelabra euphorbias raising their prickly fleshy arms to the cloudless sky, saltbushes, and the ubiquitous shepherd's tree. Also here is the *moringa* tree—the "enchanted" tree, so-called because according to San legend, the god of thunder, not wanting moringa trees in heaven, pulled them all up and threw them out. They fell upside down into the earth, looking like miniature baobab trees. In the middle of this rocky desert rubble is Slangpost, a small, verdant oasis in the middle of what seems to be nowhere (not even the mountains have a name in this part of the world; they're referred to simply as the "no-name mountains"). Look out for traces of the amazing desert elephants (sometimes called the desert-adapted elephants), their huge footprints trodden over by the healthy herds of goats and sheep belonging to the local Damara farmers. Your best chance of seeing the elephants is along the surprisingly green and fertile dry Huab River bed, where they browse on the large seedpods of the Ana tree and whatever else they find edible. The great gray shapes silhouetted against the dry river's sandy mounds ringed by mountains and sand dunes is an incredible sight.

The Kaokoveld, north of Damaraland, although enticing because it is pristine and rarely visited, is also inhospitably rugged. Self-drives are for the really intrepid, do-it-yourself explorer.

GETTING HERE AND AROUND
One can access Damaraland from the coast (Swakopmund and Walvis Bay) by traveling via Henties Bay and Uis on the C35, or further up the coast, accessing the park from Springbokwater on the C39. Coming from Windhoek, drive via Omaruru (C33) and Uis (C36) to Damaraland. From the north, travel via Kamanjab (C35) and Outjo (C39) to Khorixas. Good gravel roads can be traveled between attractions. The area is extremely fragile, and vehicles must always stay on existing

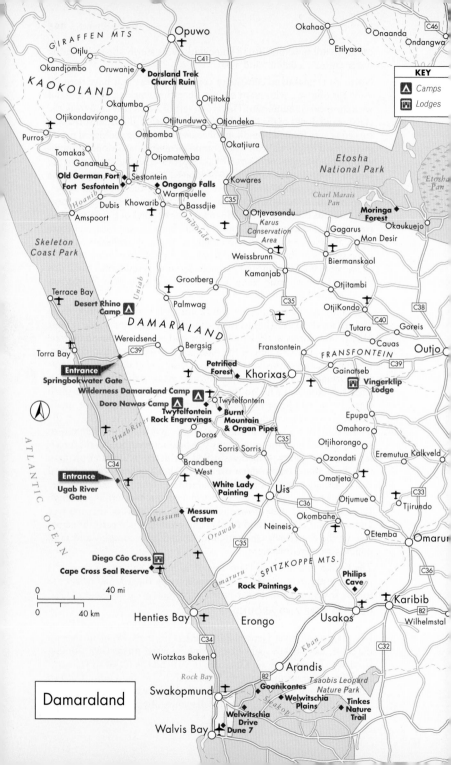

roads/tracks. It is not advised to travel on to smaller tracks without the company of an experienced Namibian guide, as tourists frequently loose their way in these parts.

WHEN TO GO

The area can be visited throughout the year. However, during the rainy season (January–April), roads and tracks may be difficult to negotiate, or not accessible at all due to flooding. Come May the area has a special splendor with waves of green grass growing on the plains and hills. From May to September the days will be cooler and more bearable, but nights can be very cold, especially for the camper. From October to December nights can be cool and days very hot.

SAFETY AND PRECAUTIONS

Do not travel faster than 80 KPH (50 MPH) on gravel roads. Always fill up your tank when a gas station is available (e.g., Kamanjab, Outjo, Khorixas, and Uis). Smaller towns such as Palmwag and Sesfontein may not have gas available, so it's also advisable to take additional gas in a can if you plan to travel long stretches between places where gas is not available. Always bring sufficient water.

TIMING

Four days is a suggested minimum, especially if you plan to visit Burnt Mountain, the Organ Pipes, Twyfelfontein, and the Petrified Forest, which can easily take a full day or a day and a half to explore. A half-day or full-day drive (offered by one of the lodges around Twyfelfontein Area) to view the desert-adapted elephant and other wildlife in the Huab River is also a highlight. Additionally, a day trip to the Welwitschia plains and Messum Crater is worthwhile.

7

WHERE TO STAY

LUXURY LODGES

$$$$ ☷ **Damaraland Camp.** A joint community venture with the local *riemvasmakers* (thong makers), this desolate camp is on the Huab River in central Damaraland, midway between Khorixas and the coast. Perched on a raised wooden platform, the views from the gorgeous and spacious adobe-style, thatch unit take in a landscape of craggy beauty formed by millions of years of unending geological movement. You'll drive with an experienced ranger in an open 4x4 to see the famous *Welwitschia* and track desert elephants. After a day in the desert, cool off in the natural rock pool and watch the desert birds, or relax with a drink in the adobe and thatch lodge, where stunning and surreal views are the name of the game. **Pros:** one of Namibia's most pristine wilderness areas; solar powered and using eco-building techniques; impressive community-based responsible tourism model. **Cons:** game drives are additional for those on half-board basis; rough entrance road means leaving your 2x4 vehicle in a parking area about 45 minutes away on arrival. ☏ *27/11807–1800 South Africa ⊕ www.wilderness-safaris.com* ↪ *10 tents ⌂ In-room: no phone, no a/c, safe, no TV. In-hotel: bar, pool, parking (free) no kids under 6* ▭ *AE, DC, MC, V* ⑩ *MAP, AI.*

$$$$ ☷ **Doro Nawas Camp.** Set amid stony slopes, rugged boulders, the distant Entendeka Mountains, and the pink and russet sandstone cliffs

Doro Nawas

Vingerklip Lodge

Damaraland Camp

of Twyfelfontein to the south (where you can visit some of the most famous San rock paintings and engravings in the world), this is classic Damaraland. What's more, this camp may be your best bet to see the long-legged desert elephants. You'll stay in a sturdy en-suite stone, canvas, and thatch unit with an indoor and outdoor shower. You can relax in the pool after a day's activities, or climb up to the roof area of the main building to sip sundowners or watch the blazing stars. **Pros:** guided walking trails; great community based responsible tourism model; amazing location close to rock art at Twyfelfontein. **Cons:** half-board clients must pay for guided trips to see the elephants. ☎ *27/11807–1800 South Africa* ⊕ *www.safariadventurecompany.com* ⇥ *16 chalets* �& *In-room: no phone, no a/c, no TV. In-hotel: restaurant, pool, parking (free)* ⊟ *AE, DC, MC, V* ¶⊙¶ *MAP, AI.*

PERMANENT TENTED CAMPS

$$$$ ⬚ **Desert Rhino Camp.** If it's rhinos you're after, especially the rare black
★ rhino, then this remote tented camp, formerly Palmwag Rhino Camp, in the heart of the private 1 million–acre Palmwag Reserve is a must. Because there are freshwater springs everywhere, you'll see not only the desert-adapted black rhino, but plenty of other game, too, including desert elephants, giraffes, zebras, kudu, and possibly lions, leopards, and cheetahs. The camp collaborates with the Save the Rhino Trust, and one of the highlights of your stay will be tracking the rare black rhino on foot. (If this is not your idea of fun, go tracking in an open vehicle instead.) You'll likely feel very close to the desert in your spacious tent with en-suite bathroom, flush toilet, and hot water on demand for your bucket shower. **Pros:** amazing educational experience on rhinos and their ecology; evening meals taken together by the fire pit allow guests to mingle. **Cons:** some visitors could find this experience overly rustic. ☎ *27/11807–1800 South Africa* ⊕ *www.wilderness-safaris.com* ⇥ *8 tents* �& *In-room: no phone, no a/c, no TV, safe. In-hotel: restaurant, bar, laundry, parking (free), no kids under 6* ⊟ *MC, V* ¶⊙¶ *AI.*

BUDGET ACCOMMODATION

$ ⬚ **Vingerklip Lodge.** In a dramatic locale in Damaraland's Valley of the Ugab Terraces, this lodge is set against the backdrop of a mighty stone finger pointing toward the sky. Take time while you're here to listen to the silence. The 360-degree views from the Sundowner Terrace are magnificent. The friendly and knowledgeable staff organizes tours to the well-known sights in the vicinity such as the petrified forest, a Himba village, and the rock engravings at Twyfelfontein. Bungalows cling to the side of a rocky hill and are clean and comfortable, but it's the remarkable views that you'll always remember. **Pros:** drop-dead gorgeous views; great food. **Cons:** rooms are not huge; service can vary. ☎ *061/255–344* ⊕ *www.vingerklip.com.na* ⇥ *22 bungalows* �& *In-room: no phone, no a/c, no TV, safe. In-hotel: restaurant, bar, pool, laundry, parking (free)* ⊟ *MC, V* ¶⊙¶ *MAP.*

ETOSHA NATIONAL PARK

Game
★★★★★

Park Accessibility
★★★★★

Getting Around
★★★★★

Accomodations
★★★★★

Scenic Beauty
★★★★★

This photogenic, startlingly beautiful park takes its name—meaning Great White Place—from a vast flat depression that was a deep inland lake 12 million years ago. The white clay pan, also known as the Place of Mirages, covers nearly 25% of the park's surface.

Although it's usually dry, in a good rainy season it floods and becomes home to many waterbirds, including tens of thousands of flamingos that feed on the blue-green algae of the pan. Although the park is never crowded with visitors like some of the East African game parks, the scenery here is no less spectacular: huge herds that dot the plains and gather at the many and varied water holes, the dust devils and mirages, and terrain that changes from densely wooded thickets to wide-open spaces and from white salt-encrusted pans to blond grasslands.

The game's all here—the Big Five—large and small, fierce and gentle, beautiful and ugly. But one of Etosha's main attractions is not the numbers of animals that you can see (more than 114 species), but how easily you can see them. The game depends on the natural springs that are found all along the edges of the pan, and as the animals have grown used to drinking at these water holes for decades, they are not put off by vehicles or game-seeking visitors. On the road from the Von Lindequist Gate, the eastern entrance to Etosha, to the well-restored white-wall German colonial fort that is now Namutoni Rest Camp, look out for the smallest of all African antelopes, the Damara dik-dik. If you see a diminutive Bambi sheltering under a roadside bush, that's it. The Namutoni area and the two Okevi water holes—Klein Namutoni and Kalkheuwel—probably provide the best chances to see leopards. Don't miss the blackface impala, native to Etosha, one of the rarest of antelopes and an endangered species. Bigger and more boldly marked than its smaller cousin, the impala, you'll find it drinking in small herds at water holes all over the park.

The real secret of game-watching in the park is to settle in at one of the many water holes, most of which are on the southern edges of the pan, and wait. And wait. Each water hole has its own unique personality and characteristics. Even if the hole is small and deep, like Ombika, on the western side, you'll be amazed at what may arrive. Old Africa hands maintain that you should be up at dawn for the best sightings, but you can see marvelous game at all times of day; one visitor was lucky enough to see a leopard and her cubs come to drink

PARK ESSENTIALS

The park gates are open from sunrise to sunset, and the daily entrance fee is N$80 for foreign visitors and N$10 for a passenger vehicle with fewer than 10 seats. You pay for your vehicle entry permit and for any balance remaining on your prebooked accommodations (which include personal entry fees) at the reception of the rest camp closest to the gate through which you enter.

at high noon. The plains, where you'll likely spot cheetahs, are also home to huge herds of zebras and wildebeests, and you may see the silhouettes of giraffes as they cross the skyline in stately procession. Watch out for herds of springbok "pronking"—pronking is when these lovely little antelopes bounce and bound high into the air as they run. Zoologists argue over the reason for this behavior. Some say it is to avoid predators, others that it is to demonstrate agility, strength, and stamina; most visitors like to believe that pronking is just for fun. Salvadora, a constant spring on the fringe of Etosha Pan near Halali, is a favorite watering point for some of these big herds. Watch out also for the stately eland, Africa's largest antelope. As big as a cow, although more streamlined and elegant, this antelope can jump higher than any other African antelope—amazing when you consider its huge size. And where there's water, there's always game. Predators, especially lions, lurk around most of the water holes looking for a meal. Plan to spend at least half a night sitting on a bench at the floodlighted Okaukuejo water hole. You really are within spitting distance of the game. Bring a book, write in your journal, or just sit while you wait. You may be amazed at the variety of animals that come down to drink: black and white rhinos, lions, jackals, and even the occasional leopard. This is a particularly good place to look out for black rhinos, which trot purposefully up to drink and in so doing scare all but the bravest of other game away. Groot Okevi water hole, close to Namutoni, is also good for black rhinos.

Don't overlook the more than 340 dazzling varieties of birds—the crimson-breasted boubou is particularly gorgeous—and watch for ostriches running over the plains or raptors hunting silently overhead. There are many endemics, including the black-faced and bare-cheeked babblers, violet woodhoopoe (look for them in Halali camp), Rüppell's parrot, Bradfield's swift, and the white-tailed shrike (which you can see hopping happily around on the lawns at Namutoni camp).

The park is huge—22,270 square km (8,598 square mi), 300 km (186 mi) wide and 110 km (68 mi) long. Rest camps in the park were renovated in 2007. The western part is still mostly undeveloped and not

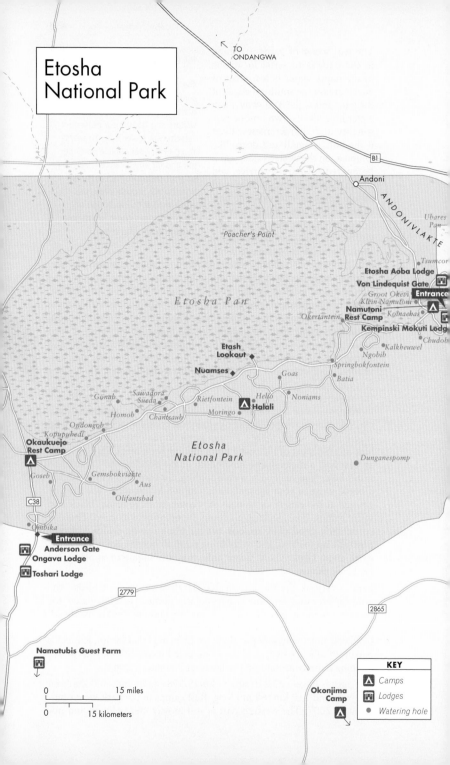

accessible, so stick to the other parts; there's plenty to see. If you prefer to visit the park on one of the many safaris offered by various tour companies, make sure you choose one with an open vehicle or pop-top with few passengers—you probably don't want to find yourself in an air-conditioned 75-seater bus. That said, the best way to see the park is to drive yourself so you can stop at your leisure (don't exceed the 60 KPH speed limit, and stick to marked roads). A two-wheel-drive car is fine, as the roads are good, but the higher up you sit, the better your view, so opt for the more expensive *combis* (vans) or 4x4s if possible. In addition to patience, you'll need drinks, snacks, field guides to the animals and birds, binoculars, and your camera. There are more than 40 water holes, with Rietfontein, Okaukuejo, Goas, Halali, Klein Namutoni, and Chudob regarded as the best for game-watching and taking pictures, but nothing is certain in the bush. Keep your eyes and ears open, and you may come across game at any time, in any place. Arm yourself with the MET map of Etosha (available in the camps), which shows the names and locations of the water holes and indicates which roads are open.

Be aware of the trees, shrubs, and plants as well. Just east of Okaukuejo is the legendary Haunted or Ghost Forest, where moringa trees have morphed into twisted, strange, and grotesque shapes: you may feel as if you're in Snow White's forest or deep in Middle Earth.

GETTING HERE AND AROUND

Tourists coming from the Oshakati area via the B1 can access the park through King Nehale Gate (northeast); coming from the Tsumeb also via the B1 through the Von Lindequist Gate (east), and coming from Outjo via the C38 through the Anderson Gate (south) from sunrise to sunset. Tourists may not drive in the park after sunset or before sunrise, and thus need to allow time to arrive at their respective rest camps if moving around close to these times. Namibia Wildlife Resorts (NWR) also offers guided night-drives, which can be booked directly at the camps. If you are staying at Onkoshi, you need to report to reception at Namutoni to be transferred to Onkoshi, as guests may not travel with their own vehicle along this section of road.

WHEN TO GO

The best time to visit is from April to September, when the temperatures are cooler, and the increasingly thirsty animals gather at water holes, making it easiest to see them (the driest time of year when this will be the case is August to September). May to August is the coolest time of year, and nights can be downright freezing—be sure to bring adequate warm clothes for night drives. Bird-watchers will want to visit in the summer (November to March) when the migratory birds (both intra-African and Palaearctic) flock in the park's many habitats after the summer rains. The main Etosha Pan can become a huge expanse of shallow water filled with flamingos, wildfowl, and waders.

SAFETY AND PRECAUTIONS

Motorists are not allowed to travel faster than 60 KPH (37 MPH) inside the park, nor are they allowed to exit their vehicles unless they are at the rest camps or toilets. Always be on the lookout for animals, which can cross the road at random, and often are concealed by bushes before emerging. Refrain from making noise and getting too close to any animals, especially elephants, as they could panic and charge your car.

TIMING

Two to three days will allow you to visit the eastern and central parts of the park, as well as Okaukuejo. There are numerous water holes to visit, but that's best done in the early morning and late afternoon when the animals are more active and temperatures are cooler.

WHERE TO STAY

If you wish to stay inside Etosha itself you can lodge at one of the NWR rest camps (book months in advance, especially for the peak periods of July to September and around Christmas and Easter, though you may want to avoid the crowds at these times). The rest camps of Halali, Namutoni, and Okaukuejo have pools, grocery-curio-liquor stores, gas stations, and restaurants serving breakfast, lunch, and dinner. There are also numerous full-service private lodges and guest farms near the park.

LUXURY LODGES

$$$$ ★ **Ongava Lodge.** On the southern boundary of Etosha close to the Anderson Gate, this lodge has its own surrounding game reserve. Each unit features its own plunge pool, sala (a covered open-air pavilion), outdoor shower and bath with magnificent views, and wood decks, which cling to the side of a steep, rocky outcrop. Some units overlook a couple of busy water holes. The stunning main area has stone floors and sweeping thatch roofs, as well as myriad spots from which to gaze at the never-ending plains beyond. Take a guided walk and sneak up on some zebras and wildebeests, go rhino tracking, or sit in a hide at the water hole just before sunset and listen to the soft twittering calls of hundreds of sand grouse as they come to drink. Lions often stray in from Etosha and join the evening party. If you want to be more on the wild side, you can stay at Ongava Tented Camp, a small, intimate site nestled deep in the bush. You'll sleep in a walk-in tent on a slate base under a thatch awning with a private bathroom. After a day spent game-watching, it's great to cool off in the outside shower or in the plunge pool. If you want even more exclusivity and luxury, opt for Little Ongava, which has three gorgeous suites. **Pros:** great location by the entrance of Etosha; large luxurious rooms; great wildlife viewing from the lodge water hole; guided walks include white rhino tracking. **Cons:** pool on the small side. ☎ *27/11807–1800/South Africa* ⊕ *www.wilderness-safaris.com* ⤶ *13 units, 1 family room, 6 tented units, 3 suites* ⚬ *In-room: no phone, a/c (some), safe, no TV. In-hotel: bar, pool, laundry, parking (free), no kids under 6* ▭ *AE, DC, MC, V* ⧉ *AI.*

$$$–$$$$ **Okonjima Camp.** Located about halfway between Windhoek and Etosha, this camp is an excellent stopover point on your way to the

park. Nestled among the Omboroko Mountains, this lovely but very busy lodge is also home to the environmental-award-winning Africat Foundation (⊕ *www.africat.org*), which has rehabilitated and cared for leopards and cheetahs for many years. You can get a close look at these magnificent cats feeding, and there are also guided San and Bantu walking trails. A bonus is the spacious hide, within walking distance of your thatched room, where you can sit and watch some of the smaller animals and hundreds of birds. In addition to lodging in the farmhouse with either garden or mountain views, there's a villa that sleeps up to 12, a suite that sleeps four, and a bush camp of eight thatch chalets with a canvas "front wall" that can be lifted during the day so you can enjoy the view. If you're looking for ultimate exclusivity, treat yourself to the gorgeous bush suite. **Pros:** numerous activities including hyena tracking, self-guided walking trails, and bird-watching; outside and inside fireplaces; kitchen facilities are available. **Cons:** some of the garden rooms are small and dark; rehabilitation project not always on view for guests. ☎ *067/687–032 or 067/687–034* ⊕ *www.okonjima.com* ⇋ *20 rooms, 2 villas* ⚊ *In-room: no phone, a/c (some), safe, no TV, refrigerator (some). In-hotel: restaurant, bar, pool, laundry service, Internet terminal, Wi-Fi hotspot, parking (free), no kids under 12* ⊟ *AE, DC, MC, V* ❧ *FAP.*

BUDGET LODGINGS

$ **Etosha Aoba Lodge.** This small, family-owned, ultrafriendly lodge is
★ 10 km (6 mi) east of the Von Lindequist Gate—about a 30-minute drive from the park. After a hot, dusty day in the park, you can slip into crisp white bed linens in your cool thatch chalet, or sip a cocktail on your mini-veranda while listening to the noises of the night. The owners emphasize excellent cuisine made with fresh, local produce; you'll dine under the thatch roof of the main building. Most visitors have their own vehicles, but the lodge can arrange trips into the park for you. The lodge gets many repeat visitors. **Pros:** lodge is set in a beautiful natural forest; great night drive with "bush observatory" for budding astronomers; fabulous food (three-course dinner is N$165). **Cons:** rooms are on the small side; doesn't cater to the "super luxury" set. ☎ *067/229–100* ⊕ *www.etosha-aoba-lodge.com* ⇋ *12 chalets* ⚊ *In-room: no phone, a/c (some), safe, refrigerator (some), no TV. In-hotel: restaurant, bar, pool, laundry, parking (free), Internet terminal* ⊟ *MC, V* ❧ *BP.*

$$ **Kempinski Mokuti Lodge.** Since this lodge is in its own park a stone's throw from the Von Lindequist Gate, you may well wake up and find an antelope or warthog munching the grass outside your room. Despite being one of Namibia's largest lodges, the rooms are smallish and rather sparsely furnished, but you'll be out most of the day game-viewing. You can take a walk, either guided or on your own, and be quite safe. Follow the paths, and you may come face-to-face with a giraffe or any number of gorgeous birds. Don't miss the amazing reptile park, where you can meet pythons, scorpions, tortoises, and the odd crocodile. To catch sight of the bigger game, take an early-morning or afternoon tour into Etosha from the lodge. Air Namibia flies to and from Mokuti five days a week. **Pros:** stone's throw from Etosha gate; all the amenities of a big hotel, including tennis and billiards. **Cons:** rooms lack views and the character of a smaller lodge. ☎ *061/388–400* ⊕ *www.kempinski.*

com ↬ *90 rooms, 8 suites, 8 family units* ⏃ *In-room: a/c, safe (some), refrigerator (some). In-hotel: 2 restaurants, room service, bars, tennis courts, pools, gym, spa, laundry service, Internet terminal, parking (free)* ⊟ *MC, V* ⦿ *BP.*

¢ ⌂ **Namatubis Guest Farm.** About 15 km (9 mi) from Outjo on the Okaukuejo road to Etosha, Namatubis is an oasis in the surrounding dry countryside. You'll find pastel-color chalets with tile floors and Namibian rugs surrounded by

green lawns and multicolor carpets of flowers and shrubs. The food is good farm-style cooking; choose either the superb steak, venison, chicken pie, or a decadent brandy pancake. You can also take day excursions from the lodge to the Vingerklip rock formation, Twyfelfontein, or the Petrified Forest and still be back in time for dinner. **Pros:** beautiful garden with indigenous plants; disabled access; self-guided walking trails. **Cons:** no organized game drives or other activities offered. ☎ *067/313–061* ⊕ *www.namatubis.com* ↬ *30 chalets* ⏃ *In-room: no phone, no a/c, refrigerator (some), no TV. In-hotel: restaurant, bar, pool, parking (free)* ⊟ *AE, DC, MC, V* ⦿ *MAP.*

¢ ⌂ **Toshari Lodge.** Situated 25 km (15½ mi) south of Etosha's Anderson
☼ Gate and previously called the Etosha Gateway Lodge, this pleasant and affordable lodge makes a great base for exploring the park. If you're fed up with self-driving, then let an experienced guide take you on the lodge's 7½-hour drive in an open game vehicle with a great picnic included (30 people maximum; six people max per vehicle). Cheerful well-appointed double rooms with fans and mosquito nets are set among green lawns and old mopane and seringa trees. The restaurant serves excellent home-cooked food and has a good wine list specializing in fine Cape wines. You can also dine in the *boma* (a traditional open-air enclosure) under the unbelievably brilliant Namibian stars. Kids under 6 stay free with their parents. **Pros:** convenient location; friendly helpful staff; clean comfortable rooms with air-conditioning, great campsite, walking trails, and water hole. **Cons:** not a luxury lodge; due to proximity to the main road between Outjo and the Anderson Gate, some traffic noise can be heard in the campsites (though not the rooms). ☎ *067/333–440* ⊕ *www.etoshagateway-toshari.com* ↬ *28 chalets, 3 family rooms, 4 luxury rooms* ⏃ *In-room: no phone, a/c, refrigerator (some), no TV. In-hotel: restaurant, bar, pool, laundry facilities* ⊟ *MC, V* ⦿ *BP.*

NATIONAL PARKS ACCOMMODATIONS

¢ ⌂ **Halali.** Etosha's smallest NWR camp with self-catering and non-self-catering chalets as well as a campsite has undergone a renovation that has vastly improved most of the chalets (though the cheapest category is still very small). If you're a bird-watcher, this place merits a giant check mark on your list. Rare violet wood hoopoes and bare-cheeked

CLOSE UP

Namibia's Tribes

HERERO

The Herero came to Namibia during the 17th century from East Africa. They are traditionally pastoralists; cattle playing a major role in their nomadic lifestyle. Today, though, most Herero are farmers or merchants in Namibia's urban hubs; some have also become professionals. Herero women are known for their stylish dress—full-length colorful gowns and unique, wide-brimmed hats. Ironically, this style of dress was adopted from missionaries that introduced German colonial rule to Namibia in the early part of the 20th century. The Herero–German War (1904–07) was a cruel episode in the history of Southern Africa as German military policy was to annihilate or confine Herero to labor camps so Europeans could establish farms. Issues regarding the treatment of the Herero during this time are still being battled out in the legal system: the German government has issued an official apology, but the Herero feel they deserve more for the death of an estimated 65,000 tribe members, and are seeking financial reparations through the international courts.

HIMBA

The Himba, a matriarchal tribe closely related to the Herero, are famous for covering their faces and hair with a light mixture of ochre, herbs, and animal fat to shield them from the hot sun. They wear very little clothing due to the harsh desert climate. The tribe lives mainly in the Kunene region of northern Namibia and, like the Herero, the Himba are a nomadic people who breed cattle as well as goats. Himba women do most of the work in the tribe—they bear children, take care of the children, tend to the livestock, and even build homes. In the 1980s and '90s, Himba culture was endangered due to severe draught and the war in nearby Angola. Recently they had to battle modernization with a proposed hydroelectric dam, which threatened to flood their homesteads and destroy their pastures. However, with help from the international community, the Himba have successfully blocked the dam and managed to maintain control of their land and their traditions.

7

babblers frequent the camp, and if you walk up the rocky path to the pleasant floodlighted water hole and are prepared to sit and wait, there's a good chance you'll spot lions, elephants, and black rhinos. Halali, which is roughly halfway between Okuakuejo and Namutoni, is in the only area of the park with hills. Halali offers its own game drives, and its small convenience store is useful, even if the stock is somewhat limited and costly. **Pros:** prime location in the middle of Etosha; good restaurant; one of the quieter and less trafficked camps. **Cons:** mosquito nets are not all in great shape; electricity can go out, which renders a/c useless. ☎ *061/285–7200* ⊕ *www.nwr.com.na* ⇆ *61 chalets* ⚒ *In-room: no phone, a/c, kitchen (some), refrigerator (some), no TV. In-hotel: restaurant, bar, pool* ☰ *MC, V* ⫶⃝*BP.*

$ ☐ **Namutoni Rest Camp.** On the eastern edge of the park and resembling something out of the novel and films *Beau Geste,* this restored colonial fort with its flying flag and graceful palm trees is the most picturesque of the national-park camps. Hearing the bugle call from the watchtower at sunrise and sunset, you almost expect to see the French Foreign Legion come galloping over the horizon. The historic rooms are tiny—the troops didn't live all that well—so if it's comfort rather than history you're after, don't choose a fort room; opt instead for one of the fully equipped bush chalets, built at a respectful distance from the fort so as not to destroy the ambience. A recent renovation has left the spacious chalets gorgeous and well equipped, with nice touches like patios and outdoor showers. Directly behind the fort is a floodlighted water hole for game-viewing. **Pros:** great location with access to the northeast section of the park where the flamingo colony at Fischer's Pan is found; two restaurants, a gas station, and good shop; daily game drives available. **Cons:** car park is a bit of a hike; camp water hole not one of the best in the area; only camp sites are self-catering. ☎ *061/285–7200* ⊕ *www. nwr.com.na* ⇆ *20 bush chalets, 24 rooms* ⚒ *In-room: no phone, a/c, refrigerator, no TV. In-hotel: 2 restaurants, pool* ☰ *MC, V* ⫶⃝*BP.*

$ ☐ **Okaukuejo.** On the western side of Etosha, this is the biggest and noisiest national-park camp, and the staff could certainly do with a few workshops on how to deal with the public in a pleasant way. But its floodlighted water hole—regarded as one of the finest in Africa—more than makes up for any inconvenience. Climb the spiral staircase to the top of the round tower for a good view of the surrounding countryside, and then settle down to an all-night game-watching vigil. Recently renovated, pleasantly furnished, and spotlessly clean accommodations range from a premier water-hole chalet, water-hole and bush chalets, and double rooms, some of which have self-catering facilities. There is also a campsite. There are mail facilities at the camp, as well as a restaurant, gas station, and store to stock up on provisions. **Pros:** famously great water hole; can sit on your deck and view the water hole from certain chalets. **Cons:** this popular camp can be busy and noisy; service can vary. ☎ *061/285–7200* ⊕ *www.nwr.com.na* ⇆ *35 water-hole chalets, 25 bush chalets, 40 double rooms, 2 family chalets* ⚒ *In-room: no phone, a/c, kitchen (some), refrigerator, no TV. In-hotel: restaurant, pool, parking* ☰ *MC, V* ⫶⃝*BP.*

Ongava Lodge

Halali

Namutoni

IF YOU HAVE TIME

While we've gone into great detail about the must-see parks in Namibia, there are still other places worth exploring if you have time.

THE SKELETON COAST

This wildly beautiful but dangerous shore, a third of Namibia's western coastline, stretches from the Ugab River in the south to the Kunene River, the border with Angola, in the north. The Portuguese seafarers who explored this area in the 15th century called this treacherous coast with its cold Benguela current and deadly crosscurrents the "Coast of Death." Its newer, no-less-sinister name, the Skeleton Coast, testifies to innumerable shipwrecks, lives lost, bleached whale bones, and the insignificant, transient nature of humans in the face of the raw power of nature. Still comparatively unknown to tourists, this region has a stark beauty and an awesomely diverse landscape—gray gravel plains, rugged wilderness, rusting shipwrecks, desert wastes, meandering barchan dunes, distant mountains, towering walls of sand and granite, and crashing seas. You'll rarely see more than a handful of visitors in this inaccessible and rugged coastal area. This is not an easy ride, as distances are vast, amenities scarce or nonexistent, and the roads demanding. Don't exceed 80 KPH (50 MPH) on the gravel roads, and never drive off the road on the ecologically vulnerable salt pans and lichen fields: the scars left by vehicles can last for hundreds of years and do irreparable damage.

Skeleton Coast National Park extends along this rugged Atlantic coast and about 40 km (25 mi) inland; the 200-km (125-mi) stretch of coast from Swakopmund to the Ugab River is named National West Coast Tourist Recreational Area. You can drive along a coastal road right up to Terrace Bay, and for the first 250 km (155 mi) from Swakopmund north to Terrace Bay you'll find not sand dunes but glinting gravel plains and scattered rocks. Stop and sift a handful of gravel: you may well find garnets and crystals among the tiny stones. In other places the plains are carpeted with lichens—yellow, red, orange, and many shades of green. In the early morning these lichen fields look lushly attractive, but during the heat of midday they seem dried up and insignificant. But don't whiz by. Stop and pour a drop of water on the lichens and watch a small miracle as they unfurl and come alive. If you're a birder, the salt pans on the way from Swakopmund to Henties Bay are worth a visit; you might spot a rare migrant wader there. The famous Namibian oysters are farmed here in sea ponds—don't leave Namibia without tasting these. The surreal little seaside holiday town of Henties Bay is like a deserted Hollywood back lot in winter, but in summer is full of holidaying Namibian fisherfolk from Swakopmund, Windhoek, and Tsumeb hoping to catch kabeljou and steenbras.

You'll smell the hundreds of thousands of Cape fur seals (*Arctocephalus pusillus pusillus*) at the Cape Cross seal colony, north of Henties Bay, long before you get there, but stifle your gags and go goggle at the seething mass on land and in the water. If you visit in late November or early

December, you can ooh and aah at
the furry baby seal pups, as well as
the marauding jackals looking for
a fast-food snack. Farther north the
dunes begin, ending in the north at
the Kunene River, Namibia's border
with Angola. This northern stretch
of coast from the Ugab River to the
Kunene River is managed by the

government as a wilderness area and accounts for a third of Namibia's
coastline. But if it's lush green pastures and abundance of game you
want, then this raw, rugged, harsh, and uncompromising landscape is
not for you. What you will find are dramatically different scenery—big
skies and unending horizons—an absence of tourists ("crowds" around
here means one or two vehicles), and some wildlife: brown hyenas,
springbok, oryx, jackals, and, if you're really lucky, a cheetah or rhino.
The sight of a majestic oryx silhouetted against towering sand dunes
or a cheeky jackal scavenging seal pups on the beaches is extremely
rewarding. The best activity, however, is just concentrating on the freedom, beauty, and strange solitude of the area.

GETTING HERE AND AROUND

You can drive (a 4x4 gives you more flexibility) from Swakopmund
north through Henties Bay via the Ugab Gate, with its eerie painted
skulls and crossbones on the gates, or from the more northerly Springbokwater Gate. You must reach your gate of entry before 3 PM. Always
stick to the marked roads and avoid driving on treacherous salt pans.
Look out for an unusual wreck lying next to the road between the Ugab
River and Terrace Bay; it's an abandoned 1960s oil rig, now home to
a huge colony of cormorants.

The Uniab River valley, between Torra Bay and Terrace Bay, is your best
chance of spotting big game such as rhino and occasionally elephants.
Once you get to Terrace Bay, 287 km (178 mi) north of Henties Bay,
that's the end of your car trip. It's the last outpost. If you want to
explore further, then a fly-in safari is your only option.

Many parts of the Skeleton Coast can be visited only with a dedicated
operator, and the lengths of tours vary. If you intend to spend time only
in Torra Bay or Terrace Bay, two to three days will suffice. Bear in mind
that this coastline does not conform to the usual "beach holiday" image:
Namibia's beaches are wild and desolate, offering a welcome respite
from the hot inland areas during summer months and a wonderful
destination for fishermen.

The C34 road runs parallel to the coast, and then a rough track continues up past Torra Bay to the ranger (Ministry of Environment and
Tourism) station. Driving the C34 is straightforward, although fog can
make the surface slick, and the road is mostly gravel, so keep speeds
below 80 KPH (49 MPH). You can purchase your entry permit either at
the Ugab or Springbokwasser Gates. There are several short detours to
points of interest, but off-road driving is strictly prohibited.

7

From Portugal to the Skeleton Coast

More than 500 years ago, a daring little band of Portuguese sailors, inspired by the vision of their charismatic leader, Prince Henry the Navigator—who, contrary to what you might expect from his name, never left his native land—set sail from the School of Navigation at Sagres, the farthest western point of Europe, to find fame, fortune, and new lands for the Crown. Facing unknown dangers and terra incognita (the maps of the time were little more than fanciful sketchbooks filled with dragons and warnings that "here be monsters"), the intrepid sailors pushed back the edges of the known world nautical mile by mile until they entered the waters of the southwest coastline of Africa on tiny, frail caravels. In 1485, Captain Diego Cão and his battered crew finally dropped anchor off a desolate beach thousands of miles from home and safety. There, on the lonely windswept sands, they erected a cross both in honor of their heavenly king, whom they credited with protecting and directing them during their arduous journey, as well as to King John I, their earthly monarch. North of Swakopmund, as you marvel at thousands upon thousands of the Cape fur seals at Cape Cross, you can see a replica of that cross (the original is in the Berlin Oceanographic Museum). Sadly, the courageous Captain Cão never made it home: he is buried nearby on a rocky outcrop.

WHEN TO GO

The northern Skeleton Coast experiences the same weather year-round: moderate temperatures with mist, wind, and hardly any rain. For anglers, the best time to visit is November to March. For the inland Kaokoveld, the dry winter season from May to August is best. The rainy summer months of January to March can bring extremely high temperatures and flash floods.

WHERE TO STAY

LUXURY LODGES

$$$$

Fodor's Choice ★

Serra Cafema. This astonishingly different and dramatically sited camp in the extreme northwest of Namibia on the Angolan border is the most remote camp in Southern Africa. After a dry, dusty, but magnificently beautiful drive from the airstrip, you are guaranteed to gasp with awe as you first catch sight of the camp from a high sand dune. Built amid a grove of ancient albida trees on the banks of the wide Kunene River, it seems like a desert mirage. Only the nomadic Himba people share this area, and a visit to a local village is an eye-opening experience and one of the highlights of a stay here. Another day, ride a quad bike over the billowing sand dunes and spot the Atlantic from a high vantage point. Although tents (on raised platforms) are luxurious and have private bathrooms, don't come here if you aren't tough. The flight from Windhoek is long and bumpy, and the terrain harsh and demanding, but the experience—staying by a wide river in the midst of the oldest desert in the world—is almost surreal. This is one-of-a-kind Africa. Stay for three nights to make the most of the experience: go walking, boating, birding, or quad biking; do a nature drive; or just sit by the rushing river and contemplate. **Pros:** surreal remote wilderness area (malaria-free zone); gorgeous camp and rooms with views of Kunene River; a wealth of activities beyond game drives. **Cons:** you may find yourself torn between activities and relaxing in your lovely tent; not a lot of wildlife; arduous travel to get here. ☎ *27/11807–1800/ South Africa ⊕ www.wilderness-safaris.com ⤵ 8 tents ⚐ In-room: no phone, no a/c, safe, no TV. In-hotel: bar, pool, laundry, no kids under 6 ⊟ AE, DC, MC, V ⑩ AI.*

PERMANENT TENTED CAMPS

$$$–$$$$ 🏠 **Skeleton Coast Camp.** If you long for a remote wilderness area, consider a four-day safari into this desolate camp, which is built on a small island in the dry Khumib riverbed, among 660,000 acres of the northern part of Skeleton Coast National Park. You sleep under canvas in an elegantly furnished tent on a raised wooden deck with your own smaller deck and awesome desert view, and eat in the open-air dining room under an ancient leadwood tree. Guests can visit an authentic Himba settlement, picnic beside the crashing Atlantic, and drive through oryx-studded plains and shifting sand dunes with their desert birds. The days are long—beginning after breakfast as the morning mists drift from the coastline and ending after sunset—but they are packed so full of excitement and beauty that your head will still be spinning as you fall into your comfortable bed after a splendid dinner. Departures are from Windhoek every Wednesday and Saturday. **Pros:** access to extremely isolated and unique landscape and ecosystem; desolate beauty. **Cons:** can only pay in US$, with minimum stay of three nights; water shortages in the area mean no long showers, and hot water may not be so hot in the early morning; overall experience can be too rustic for some. ☎ *27/11807–1800/South Africa ⊕ www.wilderness-safaris.com ⤵ 6 tents ⚐ In-room: no phone, no a/c, safe, no TV. In-hotel: bar, laundry facilities, no kids under 8 ⊟ AE, DC, MC, V ⑩ AI.*

NATIONAL PARKS ACCOMMODATION

$ 🏠 **Terrace Bay.** An isolated outpost and government resort and the northernmost point in the park to which you can drive, this may well be the most remote spot on earth you ever visit. Surrounded by gravel plains, it's a popular spot for anglers and people who want to get to know the desert. Don't miss the surprising Uniab River delta—a lush green oasis in a miniature canyon a couple of miles from Terrace Bay. It's also a good stop if you're going on into Damaraland. The accommodations, once part of a diamond-mining operation, are simple and basic, though each bungalow has a refrigerator, shower, and toilet. The four-room family chalet has all the modern conveniences, including air-conditioning and a fully equipped kitchen. Breakfast and dinner are provided, and there's a small shop that stocks basic groceries, beer, wine, and some fishing equipment. The resort does not accommodate day visitors. **Pros:** the angling is awesome, so be sure to bring a permit and your rod; remote desolate coast. **Cons:** rooms are clean and comfortable but nothing special; activities for nonfishermen are limited. ☎ *061/285–7200 ⊕ www.nwr.com.na ⤵ 20 rooms, 1 family chalet ⚐ In-room: no phone, no a/c, refrigerator, no TV. In-hotel: restaurant, bar, pool, beachfront ⊟ MC, V ⑩ MAP.*

7

CAPRIVI STRIP

This lovely unspoiled area—one of Namibia's best-kept secrets—lies in northeast Namibia (and is sometimes simply referred to as northeast Namibia) at the confluence of the Zambezi and Chobe rivers, and serves as a gateway to Zimbabwe's Victoria Falls and Botswana's Chobe National Park. Because it's relatively unknown as a tourist area, you'll get the feeling here that you are truly alone with nature.

Think of the Caprivi Strip as a long finger of land at the top of the country pointing eastward for 450 km (280 mi) toward Zimbabwe and Zambia; in many ways, because of its rivers, marshes, and forests, the area is much more like those countries than the rest of Namibia. This part of Namibia is the closest thing to Botswana's Okavango Delta, and it shelters much of the same game: elephants, the aquatic lechwe and the rare sitatunga antelope, the uncommon roan and sable antelopes, and, hardly ever seen in Namibia, big buffalo herds. However, you're unlikely to see predators.

This corridor of land became strategically important when Germany annexed South West Africa (now Namibia) in 1884. The British, concerned about further German colonial expansion up into Africa, struck a deal with Khama, a local Bechuana king, and formed the British Protectorate of Bechuanaland (now Botswana). The Caprivi Strip was part of the deal. It was then shuttled back and forth between Britain and Germany until it finally passed into the hands of South Africa at the end of World War II. However, its troubles were far from over, and during the Namibian struggle for independence, the area became the scene of bitter fighting between Sam Nujoma's freedom fighters (Sam Nujoma became the first president of Namibia in 1990) and the South African Defence Force (SADF). Today, the game that was scared away is back, the area is once again peaceful, and it's a relatively little-known and little-visited destination by overseas tourists. If you've seen your Big Five and your classic desert and are looking for somewhere offbeat, then this is a great destination.

You've got to be fairly determined to get here because the journey can be circuitous, to say the least. You can fly in to Katima Mulilo, the vibey little main town (which is closer to Gaborone, Botswana; or Lusaka, Zambia; than it is to Windhoek), pick up a vehicle, and drive. Visit the Caprivi Art Centre near the African market, where you'll find beautifully crafted baskets, carvings, and handmade pottery. There's a main road across the strip, the B8, but it's relatively busy with commercial traffic to and from Zambia and Botswana. Or you can fly into Livingstone in Zambia, cross the Sesheke border (over the Zambezi River), and continue by road and river to your chosen lodge. (To give you some idea: to get to Susuwe Island Lodge, you fly from Johannesburg into Livingstone, then take a small plane to the Namibian immigration post at Katimo Mulilo, then fly to the Immelman airstrip nearby, the once infamous Doppies SADF forward base, and travel by road and river to the lodge.) However you get here, the destination is well worth every last mile for a remote, water-wilderness experience. Your best bet is to choose a lodge and then let it make all your travel arrangements for you.

Neither the Caprivi Strip's Mudumu National Park or Mahango National Park is easily accessible—particularly in the wet season—but if you're a do-it-yourself adventure type, you might enjoy a visit to either park. You'll see plenty of game, including hippos, elephants, buffalo, roan and sable antelope, kudu, zebra, and maybe even wild dogs. Mahango is great for bird-watching, with more species than any other Namibian park.

GETTING HERE AND AROUND

The B8 road from Katima Mulilo to Kasane is paved, and the Namibia/Kasane Bridge has been renovated. Kasane immigration in town is open from 7:30–4:30. Roads from Katima Mulilo to Victoria Falls and through Gaborone to Johannesburg are all paved and in good condition. The Seseheke Bridge between Namibia and Zambia opened in 2004, completing the TransCaprivi Highway, and linking the port of Walvis Bay with Zambia's capital Lusaka. The Wenela Border Post is open from 6 to 6. Immigration and customs facilities are also available at Lianshulu Lodge, open from 8 to 5. The Ngoma border is open from 7 to 6. Day trips can be taken across the border in Chobe National Park.

■ TIP➔ A 4x4 vehicle is required for some of the parks. One can travel on the main roads by sedan car.

WHEN TO GO

For bird-watchers the best time to visit is summer (December–February), but be forewarned that the heat and humidity can be unbearable. Toward the end of summer, the Zambezi, Chobe, and Linyanti Rivers usually flood, making access to Lake Liambezi and the Mamili National Park difficult. Access will be by 4x4, and will require negotiating completely submerged roads. Otherwise, the Caprivi can be visited for most of the year, but inquire at the lodge you're interested in how negotiable their roads are during the rainy season (November–April/May). The winter months of April to October are great for game-viewing, and far more pleasant what with the cooler temperatures and lack of rainfall.

TIMING

To explore Caprivi from east to west and to enjoy its peace and quiet, at least a week should be set aside.

WHERE TO STAY

LUXURY LODGES

$$$$ ⊡ **Impalila Island Lodge.** At the crossroads of four countries—Namibia, Botswana, Zambia, and Zimbabwe—this all-inclusive lodge is famous for its hospitality, accommodations, food, and activities. Raised wood-and-thatch chalets, furnished with polished local mukwa wood, open onto wide verandas overlooking the Mambova Rapids at the confluence of the Zambezi and Chobe rivers. The main thatched dining and bar area is built around two huge baobab trees. After your day's activities, relax on the wooden deck and boast about your tiger-fishing skills, or tick off your mammal and bird lists. Don't miss a guided boat trip to the banks of Botswana's Chobe National Park for game-viewing, or a tranquil *mokoro* (canoe) trip in the papyrus-fringed channels. **Pros:** great food; with more than 450 bird species, this place is wonderful for birders; fantastic river safaris in Chobe National Park. **Cons:** game

drives into Chobe must be prearranged at extra cost. ☎ *061/401–047/ Windhoek; 27/11234–9997/South Africa* ⊕ *www.islandsinafrica.com* ⌂ *8 chalets* ⌂ *In-room: no phone, no a/c, safe, no TV. In-hotel: bar, pool, laundry (free), no kids under age 8* ☐ *AE, DC, MC, V* ⍩ *AI.*

$$$$ ⊞ **Lianshulu Lodge.** This lovely lodge, which sprawls under huge jack-alberry and mangosteen trees along the banks of the Kwando River, bordering Botswana, was one of the first private lodges to be built inside a national park—Mudumu National Park. Considered for many years one of the best lodges in Namibia, it offers a splendid water-wilderness experience—from chugging down the Kwando in a double-decker pontoon, sipping sundowners as the boat dodges hippos and crocs, to tiger-fishing, game cruises, and superb birding with more than 400 recorded species. A night cruise on the river is particularly exciting. Accommodation is in beautiful and spacious reed, brick, and thatch units (en-suite); the food is outstanding; and the personal service memorable. You can visit the nearby Lizauli traditional village, built and managed by the local community. Because an immigration official lives at the lodge, you can easily cross into Botswana. **Pros:** beautiful views of Kwando River and Lianshulu Lagoon from lodge and chalets; lovely features include fireplaces, a library, and split wooden decks. **Cons:** generator noise may be audible from some rooms. ☎ *27/11807–1800/South Africa* ⊕ *www.wilderness-safaris.com* ⌂ *10 chalets, 1 family unit* ⌂ *In-room: no phone, no a/c, safe, no TV. In-hotel: restaurant, bar, pool, laundry, parking (free), no kids under age 6* ☐ *AE, DC, MC, V* ⍩ *MAP, AI.*

$$$$
Fodor's Choice
★

⊞ **Ntwala Island Lodge.** East of Susuwe Island Lodge is the breathtaking, daringly beautiful Ntwala Island Lodge. Only 80 km (50 mi) upstream from Victoria Falls, the four art deco–meets-Africa chalets are built on an untouched Namibian cluster of small islands linked by floating wooden walkways. You can fly in from Namibia or Botswana, but there's also a road option. Drive to Kasane in Botswana, and then board a small boat that skirts rapids and dodges hippos as it takes you to your very own Treasure Island. A gray, mosaic-edge, kidney-shaped pool surrounded by white sand shimmers outside your cream-color, tile-roof chalet, just a couple of yards from the rushing Zambezi. The braying of trumpeter hornbills, the liquid notes of the robins, and the startled calls of francolins greet you. The chalets are spectacular by any standard, with huge rooms, circular wooden canopies echoing the circular bed platforms, carved half-moon chests, handwrought light fittings of metal feathers, and bathrooms big enough to host a party. Freestanding canvas and wooden screens are topped by metal Prince-of-Wales's feathers, matching the metal curlicued towel rails and bath accessories trolley. Try your hand at tiger-fishing, marvel at the industry of the reed cormorants as they continuously crisscross the sky carrying nesting material to their heronry, or watch the sunset herds of elephants and buffalo, the unique Chobe bushbuck, a group of impala, and if you're really lucky, in the dry season, some thirsty lions. **Pros:** known as the most luxurious and intimate of the Islands in Africa lodges; huge beautiful rooms with private plunge pools, outdoor showers, and great views; each suite has its own boat and guide. **Cons:** aluminum building materials at the main lodge can rob the luxurious "African feeling" for some; insects at night can be irritating (the consequence of the proximate river). ☎ *061/401–047 Windhoek; 27/11234–999/South Africa* 🌐 *www.islandsinafrica.com* ⇨ *4 luxury suites* ☝ *In-room: no phone, no a/c, safe, refrigerator, no TV. In-hotel: bar, pool, laundry (free), no kids under 12* ▭ *DC, MC, V* 🍴 *AI.*

$$$$ **Susuwe Island Lodge.** This is classic Africa, a solid structure of wood and stone built before the designer-chic lodge invasion. This six-chalet lodge is at the eastern end of the Caprivi Strip (before the strip broadens and widens on its way to Botswana) on a small island in a teak forest in the Bwabwata National Park. Here, the deep, clear waters of the Kwando River lap the island's edges, and swamp boubous whistle their melodious calls. Take the time to climb to the highest viewing deck—up in that bird-rich canopy your inner spirit will be restored. A brass lizard, frozen in time, scurries up a wooden stair rail, while a long-lashed giraffe with bead earrings adorns the outside of one door. Two mokoros act as bookcases; a tiny, tiled elephant watches you from a corner of the stone floor; and in your emperor-size chalet, you'll find candles in carved logs, faded kilims, and a personal plunge pool beside the rushing river. This river trip is one you won't likely forget. Though elephants are around, this is not Big Five country; it's a place to unwind, which is a perfect way to end a safari. **Pros:** more than 8,000 elephants and other exciting game inhabit this area, which is a mix of savanna, wetlands, and woodlands; game drives, boat cruises, and walks are all included; each suite has its own lounge, private plunge pool, and river-facing deck. **Cons:** some game-viewing vehicles lack canvas canopies. ☎ *061/401–047/ Windhoek; 27/11234–999/South Africa* 🌐 *www.islandsinafrica.com* ⇨ *6 chalets* ☝ *In-room: no phone, no a/c, safe, no TV. In-hotel: restaurant, pool, bar, laundry (free), no kids under 12* ▭ *AE, DC, MC, V* 🍴 *AI.*

7

BUDGET LODGINGS

¢ **Zambezi Lodge.** Just 2 km (1 mi) from Katimo Mulilo, this is the town's best hotel, where the rooms spread along the banks of the Zambezi River amid colorful bougainvillea bushes and flame trees. But far from the traditional sounds of Africa, the sounds you are most likely to hear are rap, hip-hop, and hard rock from the radios in the Zambian riverside villages just across the river. It's a convenient stopover offering recently renovated, clean, comfortable, tiled rooms with windows and double doors facing the river. (Look for the Cape clawless otters playing in the river.) Food is quick and palatable, but don't hold your breath for something special. Short cruises on the river are available. **Pros:** conveniently located 20 minutes from the airport; modern conveniences like satellite TV, a/c, and room service. **Cons:** though clean and comfortable, this outlet of the Protea chain lacks the charm of a smaller hotel. ☎ *66/251–500* 🌐 *www.proteahotels.com* ⇨ *42 rooms* ☝ *In-room: a/c. In-hotel: restaurant, pool, room service, Wi-Fi hotspot, laundry, parking (free)* ▭ *DC, MC, V* 🍴 *BP.*

WATERBERG PLATEAU PARK

This lovely game reserve, established in 1972 when several rare and endangered species were introduced from other areas of Namibia and South Africa, is one of the most peaceful and relatively unknown wilderness areas in Namibia. About 91 km (56 mi) east of Otjiwarongo, it's also an ideal stopover on the way from Windhoek to Etosha. The plateau is a huge, flat-top massif rising abruptly from the surrounding plain and offering superb views of the park, the outstanding rock formations, and the magnitude of the plateau itself. Edged with steep-sided, rugged, reddish-brown cliffs, the plateau is covered with red Kalahari sand that supports a range of dry woodland vegetation, from the red syringa trees and Kalahari apple leaf to the kudu bush. You're not allowed to drive yourself, but game-viewing tours operate every morning and evening from the beautifully landscaped Bernabé de la Bat Rest Camp (book in advance through the NWR; you can join a tour even if you're not a guest of the camp). Although you won't see the big numbers of game that you'll find in Etosha, you could spot the rare roan and sable antelope, Cape buffalo, white and black rhinos, giraffes, hyenas, leopards, and cheetahs. But game-spotting is not an exact science, so there are no guarantees. The park is a wonderful place to hike, whether on the much-sought-after, three-day accompanied Waterberg Wilderness Trail (book through the NWR at the Waterberg Camp [formerly the Bernabé de la Bat Rest Camp] in advance) or on a short 3-km (2-mi) walk round camp.

GETTING HERE AND AROUND
The park is located about 300 km (186 mi) northeast of Windhoek. Visitors can't drive up onto the plateau in their own vehicles, but can explore on foot on self-guided wilderness trails. Daily guided game drives (about four hours) include visits to fantastic hides on the plateau that offer excellent views of water-hole life. Daily game drives can be booked at the Waterberg Camp.

WHEN TO GO
The park can be visited throughout the year. During the rainy season (December–April) the last stretch of road (which is gravel) must be negotiated very carefully as the surface can be slippery when wet.

SAFETY AND PRECAUTIONS
Do not feed the animals, and keep your belongings safely away from inquisitive baboons. Lock your bungalow when leaving, as baboons may try to enter an unlocked room. Bring warm clothing for winter weather—game drives in the early morning or late afternoon can be very chilly—even in summer, and especially when it has rained.

TIMING
There are hikes of differing lengths, so inquire how much time you will need for your chosen route from NWR. If not hiking, then a minimum stay of two nights is recommended so you'll have one whole day to climb the mountain, go on a game drive, relax at the pool, and explore the walking-trails around the camp.

"As the sun began to descend over the edge of the Waterberg Plateau, a golden light glazed these two grazers. One was cautious, the other sprung."—Britton Upham, Fodors.com member

WHERE TO STAY

NATIONAL PARKS ACCOMMODATIONS

Waterberg Camp. Previously known as Bernabé de la Bat Rest Camp, this recently renovated NWR property is located on the escarpment's wooded slopes. Take a dip in the camp's natural-spring-fed swimming pool at the foot of the towering sandstone cliffs or the new pool bar, then relax in front of your bungalow and watch the sun set over the plateau. Surrounding the camp is one of the largest varieties of plant species in Southern Africa. It's best to book accommodations in advance at NWR in Windhoek, although you can take a chance (particularly in the low season) and book when you arrive at the park office between 8 AM and sunset. Camping is also available. There is a restaurant and small shop selling basic groceries and drinks; and should the shop fail to deliver, there's a grocery store in town. **Pros:** guided game drives on the plateau where you can see rare animals; beautiful self-guided walks on the plateau and nature trails in the cap. **Cons:** self-catering kitchens are not all well stocked. ☎ 061/285–7200 ⊕ www.nwr.com.na ⋟ 23 *bush chalets, 34 rooms, 8 premier chalets, 2 family chalets* ⚘ *In-room: no phone, no a/c, kitchen (some), refrigerator (some), no TV. In-hotel: restaurant, bar, pool* ▭ *DC, MC, V* ⦿ *BP.*

GATEWAY CITY

It's very likely that you'll have to take a connecting flight through Windhoek, Namibia's capital city, on route to your safari destination. In fact you may have to spend an overnight here. The following information will help you plan where to stay and eat and what to visit.

WINDHOEK

The pleasant if provincial little capital city of Windhoek lies almost exactly in the center of the country and is surrounded by the Khomas Highland and the Auas and Eros mountains. With its colonial architecture, sidewalk cafés, shopping centers, and shady parks, it is by no means a hardship to spend a day or two here. Settled by the Germans in the 1890s, this is an easy town to explore on foot (though summers are blisteringly hot). Main sights, which are clustered around the downtown area, include the national gallery (where you can often purchase works in the temporary exhibits), the remarkably good craft center, and some old German architecture. The city has a population of about 250,000 and growing, most of which resides in the largely black township of Katutura. If you have a few free hours, a visit to the Katutura makes an interesting half-day expedition that gives visitors at least an idea of how the majority of urban Namibians live. Windhoek is also home to the country's brewing industry—a holdover from its days as a German colony—and visits to breweries of all sizes are possible.

GETTING HERE AND AROUND

Namibia's main point of entry is Hosea Kutako International Airport. It's a small, bustling, modern airport that's a scenic 45-km (28-mi) drive from Windhoek. The smaller Eros Airport handles local flights and charters. Once in the country you can make use of scheduled flights or charter flights that service all domestic destinations.

Licensed shuttle companies (look for a sticker that shows they are registered with the NTB) offer service from Hosea Kutako International Airport to Windhoek's city center; the pickup and drop-off point is at the taxi stand on Independence Avenue, next to the Tourist Information Center. Expect to pay N$250–N$300 each way. Many larger hotels run a courtesy shuttle service to and from the airport. "Radio taxis" (taxis with radio contact to the dispatch) are available, but negotiate the price before you get in. Check on current fares at the airport information counter.

Intercape Mainliner runs buses between Windhoek and Swakopmund, as do other smaller and reliable shuttle services. Information on these is available at the Tourist Information Center in both cities.

If you're only in Windhoek for 24 hours or so, you won't need a car. It's an easy city to walk around in, and taxis are available everywhere. Always negotiate with the driver before getting into the taxi. Hotels also provide shuttle service.

WORD OF MOUTH

"Windhoek is a pleasant city to stroll. There are some modest attractions, such as the Kudu Statue and a fountain surrounded by meteorite fragments. The tourist office will give you a walking map and arrange more distant excursions if you're interested. The German influence is still very strong with even grocery store items labeled in German. That also means there's good beer."
—Marija

That said, if you plan to drive to Swakopmund or any of the parks, you can rent a car here. Gas is on sale in all towns, but if you are planning a long journey between towns, fill up in Windhoek before you leave.

If you've got three days or so to spare and you're headed to or from the coastal resort of Swakopmund, then consider traveling on the Desert Express. The train departs from Windhoek on Friday around midday, and from Swakopmund on Saturday around 3 PM, arriving the next day around 10:30 AM. Your first stop on the outward journey from Windhoek is Okapuka Ranch, where you'll watch lions being fed, after which you get back on the train and enjoy a splendid dinner yourself. The train parks in a siding for the night, then leaves early in the morning so you can catch a spectacular sunrise over the desert. Later, you get a chance to walk in the Namib when the train stops in the dunes between Swapkopmund and Walvis Bay. If you do the return journey, you'll be taken to see the San rock paintings at Spitzkoppe. The train has 24 air-conditioned, small but comfortable cabins with en-suite facilities. Longer journeys to Etosha are available. One way fares from Windhoek to Swakopmund start at N$2,320 per person sharing, and are all-inclusive of meals and activities.

African Extravaganza specializes in shuttle services, scheduled safaris, charter tours and fly-ins, self-drive options, day excursions, and transfers. But as Windhoek is a small town, easy to walk around in, your best bet is to stay in the city and see what's going on there. Ask your hotel concierge or guesthouse owner for up-to-date information, or check out the Tour and Safari Association Web site (⊕ *www.tasa.na*) for a comprehensive list of registered operators describing their specialties.

HEALTH AND SAFETY

If you need medical attention in Windhoek, consider the Medi-Clinic, an excellent private clinic, or the Roman Catholic Hospital. Ask at your accommodation for the nearest pharmacy.

Pickpockets work the city center, particularly the markets and the Post Street Mall. Lock your valuables away in the hotel safe, and carry only what you need. Never travel with expensive jewelry. Don't walk alone at night, and stick to well-lighted areas.

VISITOR INFORMATION

The very helpful Tourist Information Bureau (run by the City of Windhoek) at the Post Street Mall provides information on Windhoek and environs; it's open weekdays 7:30–1 and 2–4:30. It also operates a kiosk on Independence Avenue next to the main taxi stand and opposite the Kalahari Sands and Casino. Also on Independence Avenue is the Tourist Information Center run by the Leading Lodges of Africa; here you can book accommodation, car rentals, and get advice about travel throughout the country. There is also a luggage storage facility and a small café with Wi-Fi.

The head office of the Namibia Wildlife Resorts (NWR) is also on Independence Avenue. Here you can get information on NWR lodging in all the parks, and make bookings. Finally, the Namibia Tourism Board (NTB) has general information on Windhoek as well as the rest of Namibia, but is not tailored to individual consultation. It's open weekdays 8–5.

Additionally, Windhoek City Tours now has a bus tour on the ubiquitous double-decker red buses that ply cities from London to Tokyo. Leaving twice daily at 9:30 and 2:30, the bus (N$185) is a pleasant zero-effort way to get your bearings and catch all the major sights in about two hours, with live commentary. Tickets and information are available at the Leading Lodge's Tourist Information Center on Independence Avenue.

ESSENTIALS

Airports Eros Airport (☎ 061/295–5527). Hosea Kutako International Airport (☎ 061/295–5600 or 061/540–271).

Bus Line Intercape Mainliner (☎ 061/227–847 or 061/227–521 ⊕ www.intercape.co.za).

Car Rentals Avis (☎ 061/233–166 ⊕ www.avis.co.za). Budget (☎ 062/540–150 ⊕ www.budget.co.za). Hertz (☎ 062/540–118 ⊕ www.hertz.co.za).

Hospitals Roman Catholic Hospital (✉ 92 Stubel St. ☎ 061/270–2911). Medi-Clinic (✉ Heliodoor St., Eros Park ☎ 061/222–687).

Tour Operator African Extravaganza (☎ 061/372–100 ⊕ www.african-extravaganza.com).

Train Contacts Desert Express (✉ Windhoek Railway Station, Bahnhof St., Windhoek ☎ 061/298–2600 ⊕ www.namibweb.com/desertexpress.html).

Visitor Info Namibia Tourism Board (NTB ✉ 39 Post Street Mall, Channel Life Tower, 1st Flr., Windhoek ☎ 061/290–6000 ⊕ www.namibiatourism.com.na). Namibia Wildlife Resorts (NWR ✉ 189 Independence Ave., Windhoek ☎ 061/285–7200 ⊕ www.nwr.com.na). Tourist Information Bureau (✉ Post St. Mall ☎ 061/290–2092 or 061/290–2596 ⊕ www.cityofwindhoek.org.na ✉ Independence Ave., opposite Kalahari Sands and Casino). Tourist Information Center (✉ 117 Independence Ave., Windhoek ☎ 061/375–300

⊕ *www.leadinglodges.com)*. **Windhoek City Tours** (⊠ *117 Independence Ave., Windhoek* ☎ *081/129–2935)*.

EXPLORING

TOP ATTRACTIONS

❽ **Namibia Crafts Centre.** On Tal
★ Street in the old breweries building behind the Kalahari Sands and Casino hotel, the Namibia Crafts Centre boasts some truly beautiful

WORD OF MOUTH

"Be certain to visit the Namibian Craft Centre; there's a good selection of crafts at reasonable prices. The centre has a small café on an open-air balcony, which is very good." —canadian_robin

and unique pieces of work. Dozens of stalls showcase the work of more than 1,500 rural craftspeople, and include items such as particularly fine woven baskets, striking and original beadwork, distinct Caprivian pots, handmade contemporary jewelry, and much more. Be sure to check out the Omba Arts Trust stall, where changing exhibits of truly stunning work done by women from disadvantaged communities can be viewed and purchased. ⊠ *40 Tal St.* ☎ *061/242–2222* ⊙ *Weekdays 9–5:30, weekends 9–1:30.*

★ **National Gallery.** This small but lovely museum features contemporary Namibian art. The somewhat ho-hum permanent exhibit downstairs features German-Namibian painters from the 20th century. Head upstairs, where cool contemporary lithographs by young Namibian artists line the walls, and regularly changing temporary exhibits feature very good work by Namibian and other African artists, most of which is for sale. A small café and shop adjoin. ⊠ *Corner of John Meinart St. and Robert Mugabe Ave.* ☎ *061/231–160* ⊕ *www.nagn.org.na* ✉ *Suggested donation N$20* ⊙ *Tues.–Fri. 8–5.*

Post Street Mall. At this open-air market known for its colorful sidewalk displays of curios, crafts, and carvings of all kinds, international tourists and businesspeople rub shoulders with Herero women in full traditional Victorian dress. Keep an eye out for the meteorites mounted on slender steel columns. These meteorites hit the earth during the Gibeon meteorite shower, which rained down some 600 million years ago, the heaviest such shower known on earth. A fairly large curio market with the usual carvings and beadwork is also found here. ⊠ *Post St.* ⊙ *Mon.–Sat. 9–5.*

WORTH NOTING

Alte Feste Museum. Literally the "old fort," the oldest existing building in Windhoek (1890) once garrisoned the first contingent of German colonial troops. Now this somewhat decrepit edifice serves as the National Museum's historical display center, with exhibits from the colonial and postcolonial periods, including numerous military items and an interesting section on Namibia's first democratic election and important patriots of the Namibian revolution. A somewhat flashier exhibit on Namibian rock compiled in cooperation with the University of Cologne is the most recent addition. ⊠ *Robert Mugabe Ave.* ☎ *061/276–800* ⊕ *www.natmus.cul.na* ✉ *Free* ⊙ *Daily summer 9–6, winter 9–5.*

Bushman Art Gallery. This souvenir and curio shop on bustling Independence Avenue distinguishes itself from the rest with its fairly sizable collection of cult objects (religious, ceremonial, drums, etc.) and domestic utensils of local bushman and Himba tribes (not for sale). A large assortment of other carvings and antiques from around Africa adorn the walls and display cases. ⊠ *187 Independence Ave.* ☏ *061/228–828 or 061/229–131* ⊕ *www.bushmanart-gallery.com* ⊟ *Free* ⊙ *Daily 9–5.*

Camelthorn Brewing Company. Lovers of the brew can enjoy a 1½-hour tour of Windhoek's only commercial microbrewery, with tastings of all five of their standard ales, including the Cream of the Crop Bavarian style, and local favorite, Liquid Gold. ⊠ *76 Nickel St., Prosperita* ☏ *061/411–250 or 081/407–6244* ⊕ *www.camelthornbrewing.com* ⊟ *N$50 (includes tasting)* ⊙ *Mon.–Fri. 9–5.*

Christuskirche. The Lutheran Christ Church is a good representation of German colonial architecture—a mixture of art nouveau and neo-Gothic dating from 1896. Although the church is sometimes locked, you can obtain a key from the nearby church office at 12 Fidel Castro Street (down the hill from the church). ⊠ *Robert Mugabe Ave.* ☏ *061/288–2627* ⊙ *Church office weekdays 7:30–1.*

Katutura. Created in the late 1950s for the forced evictions of blacks from the town center, Windhoek's vast African township now houses an estimated 60% of the city's population and makes for an interesting trip. Be sure to visit the Oshetu Market ("our market"), where northern Namibian fare like mopane worms and dried patties of a type of local spinach are sold, and whose bustling meat market includes a barbeque area where the adventurous can try succulent slices of all types of roasted meat, dipped by locals in a mixture of salt and chili. Most tours will include a visit to Penduka, an NGO (a non-governmental organization set up by the UN) to empower women. Here you can meet the women who have learned to manufacture beads and fabrics for sale. ■TIP➔ Be sure to go with a guide who can both navigate the dirt roads and provide commentary on what you're seeing; Tojuwe Safaris are one of several companies that run tours. ⊠ *Katutura* ☏ *061/309–013* ⊕ *www.tojuwesafaris.com* ⊟ *Tours N$400–500 per person* ⊙ *Tours last 3–4 hrs.*

National Museum of Namibia-Owela Display Centre. With displays on everything from archeology to natural history to ethnology, this rather musty but endearing museum makes up in information (on densely formatted placards) for what it lacks in style. The exhibit on the San, including refreshingly critical commentary on the bushman as a constructed concept, and a discussion on the exploitation of that concept, is worth noting. ⊠ *18 Luderitz St.* ☏ *061/276–800* ⊕ *www.natmus.cul.na* ⊟ *Suggested donation N$20* ⊙ *Daily 8–5.*

Tintenpalast. The handsome circa-1912 *Palace of Ink* is fronted by beautiful formal gardens. Formerly the administration offices of the German colonial government, the two-story building now houses the National Assembly. One-hour tours are given weekdays at 9, 10, and 3. Nearby is the **Office of the Prime Minister,** decorated in mosaics, indigenous woods, and murals. Security guards will give informal tours on request. ⊠ *Robert Mugabe Ave.* ☏ *061/288–2590* ⊟ *Free* ⊙ *Mon.–Fri. 9–5.*

WHERE TO EAT

$$–$$$ ✕ **Am Weinberg.** Located in one of Windhoek's older homes (built in
CONTINENTAL 1901), this good-value fine-dining establishment has fabulous views of
the city from an unexpectedly relaxed and homey vantage—think warm
mustard-color walls, slate tile floors, and hurricane lamps. The food
is upscale European, with French and Italian classics, such as homemade gnocchi in Gorgonzola and divine French onion soup. The mains
focus, however, is on perfectly cooked steaks and game meat, such
as the herb-crusted springbok loin. There are also a few fish options,
including a delicious and rich Marseilles-style bouillabaisse. The wine
list befits an ex-wine estate, but mark-ups are significant. Early arrivals
can enjoy sundowners from the bar on a lower terrace that enjoys great
views. ✉ *13 Jan Jonker Rd., Klein Windhoek* ☎ *061/236–050* ⊕ *www.
amweinberg.com* ▤ *MC, V.*

$ ✕ **Craft Café.** This bustling café with lovely outdoor seating serves up
CAFÉ generous portions of delicious and (mostly) healthy fare, including
huge open-faced sandwiches on fresh bread, gorgeous salads, quiches,
and freshly squeezed fruit and vegetable juices. It's not all good for
you, though: delightful cakes and sweet treats are also baked fresh
daily, and all manner of smoothies and milkshakes can be had. Conveniently located upstairs at the Craft Centre, the café's shaded balcony
underneath a fig tree is a great place to take a load off. ✉ *40 Tal St.*
☎ *061/249–974* ⊕ *www.craftcafe-namibia.com* ▤ *MC, V.*

$–$$ ✕ **Fusion Restaurant.** Located in the quiet suburban neighborhood of
AFRICAN Windhoek West, Fusion offers first-timers a gentle introduction to
dishes from a variety of African cuisines. Softening and melding flavors from traditional recipes, the chef makes dishes like the delicious
Senegalese Bourakhe—a lamb and prawn stew in spinach with pea-
nut butter—extremely accessible to Western palates. The food here is
lovingly presented, and the atmosphere and service are friendly and
unpretentious. A gallery of local art (for sale), and a huge garden complete the picture. ✉ *Corner Simpson St. and Beethoven, Windhoek West*
☎ *081/214–8404* ⊕ *www.fusionnamibia.com* ▤ *MC, V.*

$–$$ ✕ **The Gourmet.** The massive menu at this popular and conveniently
ECLECTIC located eatery ensures something for everyone. You'll find German specialties like schnitzels and *spätzelpan* next to a huge selection of pizzas,
the ever-popular steaks and game meats, some tasty vegetarian options, a
huge array of sweet and savory crepes, and even a few pan-African dishes
(the Malawian *msamba* veggie dish is great). Located in the old (very
German) Kaiserkrone Hotel just off the Post Street Mall in a lovely leafy
courtyard, The Gourmet may not be exactly gourmet, but it is a good-
value favorite among locals and tourists alike. ✉ *Kaiserkrone Centre,
Post Street Mall* ☎ *061/232–360* ▤ *AE, DC, MC, V* ⊘ *Closed Sunday.*

$$–$$$ ✕ **Joe's Beerhouse.** Tuck into generous portions of German and Namib-
ECLECTIC ian food at this popular Windhoek institution. Venison is a specialty
♨ (try the kudu steak or gemsbok fillet), but if the Teutonic urge strikes,
opt for the sauerkraut and pork fillet. Vegetarian food is also available. Although the interior is fun-filled with Joe's personal collection of
memorabilia, it's also pleasant to sit outside in the boma by a roaring
fire and quaff *glüwein* (mulled wine) or a local lager. There's a great play

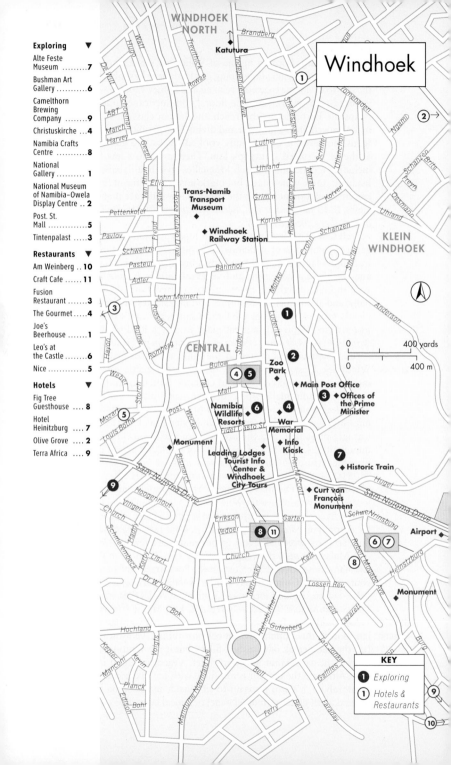

Windhoek

WINDHOEK NORTH

KLEIN WINDHOEK

CENTRAL

Trans-Namib Transport Museum

Windhoek Railway Station

Zoo Park

Main Post Office

Offices of the Prime Minister

War Memorial

Namibia Wildlife Resorts

Monument

Info Kiosk

Leading Lodges Tourist Info Center & Windhoek City Tours

Curt von François Monument

Historic Train

Airport

Monument

Katutura

0   400 yards
0   400 m

KEY

❶ *Exploring*

① *Hotels & Restaurants*

area for kids. ✉ *160 Nelson Mandela Ave.* ☎ *061/23–2457* ⊕ *www.joesbeerhouse.com* ⌂ *Reservations essential* ▭ *AE, DC, MC, V.*

$$$–$$$$ ✕ **Leo's at the Castle.** Doubtless the
CONTINENTAL most pricey restaurant in town, Leo's is also arguably Windhoek's only true fine-dining establishment. Literally in a castle on a hill, Leo's small chandelier-dazzled dining

room has fabulous views across the city. Inside, it's all champagne and taupe elegance, with red roses in simple sterling vases, and sepia prints of early-20th-century photographs of the castle. The cuisine is haute all the way: pigeon breast in honey sherry, oryx loin on a mushroom ragout in a juniper cream sauce, and the like, all gorgeously prepared and presented. The seasonal menu is not large but focuses on meat, with a couple fresh fish and vegetarian options. The wine list is an impressive tome. In warm weather, the outside seating is its own delight. ✉ *22 Heinitzburg St. (at the Hotel Heinitzburg)* ☎ *061/249–597* ⊕ *www.heinitzburg.com* ⌂ *Reservations essential* ▭ *AE, DC, MC, V.*

$$–$$$ ✕ **Nice.** Windhoek's newest and hippest place to wine and dine is the
ECLECTIC restaurant showcase for the Namibian Institute of Culinary Education. With an emphasis on local ingredients and a multitude of influences, trainees supervised by head chefs produce delicious fare, such as the tart and tasty pickled fish fillet on lentils with sour cream, or oryx loin with onion marmalade, polenta, and broccoli. Simpler fare like fish-and-chips can also be had, and the desserts are excellent. The gorgeous space—multiple rooms with crimson red walls, rough wood floors, and lots of open space and light—is elegant cool all the way, and bodes well for the future of Namibian cuisine. ✉ *2 Mozart St. (corner Hosea Kutako Dr.)* ☎ *061/300–710* ⊕ *www.nice.com.na* ▭ *AE, DC, MC, V.*

WHERE TO STAY

Lodging reviews have been abbreviated in this book. For expanded reviews, please go to Fodors.com.

$$ ▦ **Fig Tree Guesthouse.** This small and lovely guesthouse is very centrally located on Robert Mugabe Avenue, just a 5- to 10-minute walk from downtown Windhoek. **Pros:** all rooms have fridges and microwaves; rooms have printers; small intimate B&B in convenient central location. **Cons:** not many rooms so can get fully booked in season; rooms lack a view and some can be a bit dark. ✉ *11 Robert Mugabe Ave.* ☎ *061/400–966* ⊕ *www.figtreeguesthouse.com.na* ⤳ *6 rooms* ⌂ *In-room: a/c, safe (some), refrigerator (some), Wi-Fi (free). In-hotel: restaurant, bar, pool, gym, laundry service, Internet terminal, Wi-Fi hotspot, parking (free)* ▭ *DC, MC, V* ⊘ *Closed Dec. 17–Jan. 11* ▯⃝↾ *BP.*

$$$ ▦ **Hotel Heinitzburg.** This is your chance to stay in a turn-of-the-20th-
Fodors Choice century castle, a white fort with battlements set high on a hill and
★ commissioned by a German count for his fiancée in 1914. **Pros:** lavishly decadent interior styling; great personalized service; 5-minute drive from city center. **Cons:** rooms don't have tons of natural light (it's a castle after all); Wi-Fi is not free. ✉ *22 Heinitzburg St.* ☎ *061/249–597*

7

⊕ *www.heinitzburg.com* 🛏 *16 rooms* ⟨ *In-room: a/c, safe (some), refrigerator (some), Wi-Fi. In-hotel: restaurant, room service, bar, pool, laundry service, Wi-Fi hotspot, parking (free)* ⊟ *AE, DC, MC, V* ⟨○⟩ *BP.*

$$ **Olive Grove.** Located about a 10-minute drive north of the city center, this elegant guesthouse is incredibly popular for its stylish simplicity and great service. **Pros:** great food; helpful and friendly staff. **Cons:** must drive to city center; downstairs "patio" rooms lack views and can be a bit dark; pool is for plunging only. ⊠ *20 Promenaden Rd.* ☎ *061/239–199* ⊕ *www.olivegrove-namibia.com* 🛏 *12 rooms* ⟨ *In-room: a/c, safe (some), refrigerator (some), Wi-Fi. In-hotel: restaurant, bar, pool, spa, laundry service, Internet terminal, Wi-Fi hotspot, parking (free)* ⊟ *DC, MC, V* ⟨○⟩ *BP.*

$$ **Terra Africa.** The feeling of being in someone's home starts upon entering the lounge decorated with African art and strewn with magazines by a fireplace, and continues thanks to the personalized and friendly service here. **Pros:** extremely friendly and helpful staff; charming pool and garden area; homey comforts like a fireplace in the lounge. **Cons:** rooms vary significantly in size and view; must drive to city center. ⊠ *6 Kenneth McArthur St., Olympia* ☎ *061/252–100* ⊕ *www.terra-africa.com* 🛏 *10 rooms* ⟨ *In-room: a/c, safe (some), refrigerator (some), Wi-Fi. In-hotel: restaurant, bar, pool, laundry service, Internet terminal, Wi-Fi hotspot, parking (free)* ⊟ *DC, MC, V* ⊘ *Closed Dec. 22–Jan. 3* ⟨○⟩ *BP.*

BEACH ESCAPE

You don't come to Namibia for beaches, but if you do fancy a dip in the freezing Atlantic waters, Swakopmund, the country's only real beach resort, is your best bet.

SWAKOPMUND

Although the desert continues to sweep its remorseless way toward the mighty Atlantic and its infamous Skeleton Coast, humans have somehow managed to hang on to this patch of coastline, where Swakopmund clings to the edge of the continent. The first 40 German settlers, complete with household goods and breeding cattle, arrived here with 120 German colonial troops on the *Marie Woermann* in the late 19th century. Today, instead of the primitive shelters that the early settlers built on the beach to protect themselves from sand and sea, stands Swakopmund, or Swakops, as the resort town is affectionately known. There's something surreal about Swakops. On the one hand, it's like a tiny European transplant, with its seaside promenade, sidewalk cafés, fine German colonial buildings, trendy bistros, friendly and neat-as-a-pin pensions, and immaculate boarding houses and hotels. On the other hand, this little town is squashed between the relentless Atlantic and the harsh desert, in one of the wildest and most untamed parts of the African continent—something you might understandably forget while nibbling a chocolate torte or sipping a good German beer under a striped umbrella.

Swakops makes for a different, unique beach escape because of its history and surreal surroundings. It's one of the top adventure centers in Africa, second only to Victoria Falls in Zimbabwe. Adrenaline junkies can try their hand (or feet) at skydiving, sandboarding, kayaking, dunebuggying, paragliding, or wave-skipping in a light aircraft. The less adventurous (but romantic) can take day, moonlight, sunrise, or sunset horseback or camel rides through the riverbeds and up into the moonlike landscape. The curious can partake in one of the fabulous "little five" living desert tours through the dunes that represent the northern extent of the Namib-Naukluft (⇨ *see Essentials below*). There are also lots of curio shops and commercial art galleries, making Swakops great for shopping, and the dining options are improving all the time.

GETTING HERE AND AROUND

The closest airport, handling domestic and international flights, is about a 45-minute drive from Swakopmund at Walvis Bay. ⇨ *For more information on flights and carriers, see Air Travel in the Planning section, above.*

Intercape Mainliner runs buses between Windhoek and Swakopmund. The Town Hoppers shuttle service also runs a daily shuttle between Windhoek and Swakopmund for N$220 one-way. For an additional fee, they will provide door-to-door pickup and/or drop-off. There are no reliable bus services within Swakopmund for visitors.

If you have the time, it's worth renting a car to drive from Windhoek to Swakopmund. It's a very scenic and easy four-hour drive, about 368 km (228 mi) on the B1, a good paved road. Once in Swakopmund, it's easy to find your way around. With a car, you'll also be able to visit the Cape Cross seal colony and drive farther north toward the Skeleton Coast, or drive 30 km (19 mi) south to Walvis Bay, where numerous outdoor activities originate. (⇨ *For more information on Walvis Bay, see Walvis Bay section below.*) A two-wheel-drive vehicle is fine, but if you intend on visiting Sandwich Harbour or Sossusvlei in Namib Naukluft Park, then a 4x4 will give you more access and better viewing (and is essential for Sandwich Harbour).

If you arrange to rent a car in advance at any of the reliable agencies, you'll be met at Walvis Bay Airport. The car-rental agencies also have offices in Swakopmund.

⇨ *For more information on train travel between Windhoek and Swakopmund, see Windhoek's Getting Here and Around section, above.*

WHEN TO GO

Keep in mind that the town is packed with vacationing Namibians and South Africans at Christmas, New Year's, and Easter, so avoid these times if you can. The sea keeps temperatures relatively comfortable year round, and positively chilly outside of summer.

SAFETY AND PRECAUTIONS

Swakops is a very safe little town, but you should always be aware of potential pickpockets. Lock your valuables away in the hotel safe, and carry only what you need. Never travel with expensive jewelry. Don't walk alone at night, and stick to well-lighted areas.

Cottage Private Hospital is a private clinic. Ask at your accommodation about the nearest pharmacy.

TIMING

Swakopmund is both a pleasant place in itself, and also offers a surprising array of activities and good shopping, as well as some culinary variety if you've been on safari for awhile. Visitors generally stay two nights, but three to four nights is better if you really want to partake in a few of the outdoor activities for which this area is famous (several of which happen in Walvis Bay, which is a 40-minute drive south), as well as relax and stroll around the town itself.

VISITOR INFORMATION

Namib-I, the tourist information center, provides excellent national and local information, maps, and more.

ESSENTIALS

Airport Walvis Bay Airport (☎ 064/20-0077).

Bus Line Intercape Mainliner (☎ 061/227-847 ⊕ www.intercape.co.za).

Car Rentals Avis (✉ Swakopmund Hotel and Entertainments Centre, 2 Theo-Ben Guribab Ave. ☎ 064/40-2527). **Hertz** (✉ GIPF Building, Sam Nujoma Ave. ☎ 064/46-1826). **Town Hoppers Shuttle** (✉ Shop 4, Tobias Hainyeko St. ☎ 064/407-223 or 081/210-3062). **Crossroads 4x4 Hire** (✉ 3 Moses Garoëb St. ☎ 064/403-777).

Emergency Contacts Ambulance/Hospital (☎ 064/41-2400). **Police** (☎ 064/402-431).

Hospital Cottage Medi-Clinic (✉ Franziska van Neel St. ☎ 064/412-200).

Visitor Info Namib I (✉ 28 Sam Nujoma Ave. [corner of Hendrik Witbooi St.] ☎ 064/40-4827).

EXPLORING

TOP ATTRACTIONS

Kristall Galerie. This sizable gallery houses the largest known quartz-crystal cluster in the world—an awesome natural wonder more than 520 million years old and weighing 14,000 kilograms. Numerous smaller but no less beautiful chunks of Namibian minerals and gems, including a wide variety of quartz crystals, rainbow tourmalines, and other semiprecious stones, are also on display. Some great souvenirs can be had in the adjoining large gift shop and high-end jewelry boutique. ✉ Corner of Tobias Hainyeko and Theo-Ben Guribab Ave. ☎ 064/406-080 ⊕ www.kristallgalerie.com ☑ N$20 ⊗ Mon.-Sat. 9-4:45.

⟳ **The Living Desert Snake Park.** With more than 25 species of Namibian snakes, lizards, chameleons, and scorpions, this small museum will excite herpetologists large and small. Several of Southern Africa's most dangerous snakes can be seen in the flesh here, including the black mamba and puff adder. Snake feedings take place on Saturdays at 10. ✉ Sam Nujoma Ave. (corner of Otavi Bahnhof) ☎ 064/405-100 or 081/128-5100 ☑ N$30 ⊗ Mon.-Fri. 9-5, Sat. 9-1.

★ **Swakopmund Dunes.** Though you may have already visited higher or more visually stunning dunes, the Swakop dunes have the unique distinction of being the subject of a truly fascinating tour that introduces visitors to the numerous—and normally invisible—creatures thriving in this surreal ecosystem. Chris Nel, the operator of Living Desert Namibia tours, is a passionate and well-informed character who tends to leap out of the moving 4x4 to catch the desert's perfectly camouflaged lizards, geckos, and snakes. A visit here is a unique, educational, and often humorous experience. ✉ Swakopmund Dunes ☎ 064/405-070 or 081/127-5070 ⊕ www.livingdesertnamibia.com.

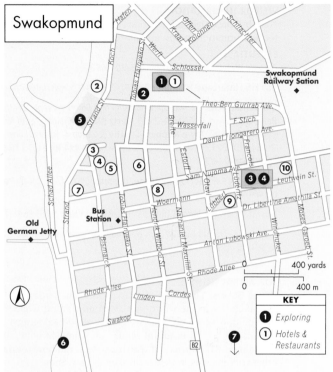

WORTH NOTING

Old Station Building. Probably Swakops's most notable landmark, the gorgeous, historic Old Station Building was built in 1901. Declared a national monument in 1972, this magnificent example of German colonial architecture came to life again in the early 1990s, when it was restored and renovated in a style evoking the charm and nostalgia of the old railway days. Don't miss the huge bustling lobby—a remnant of the building's former life as a railway station. Today, the building houses the Swakopmund Hotel and Entertainment Centre, which includes a movie theater, casino, spa, and two restaurants. ⊠ *2 Theo-Ben Gurirab Ave.*

Sam Cohen Library. As in Windhoek, there are lots of historic German buildings dating to the turn of the 20th century, most of them in perfect condition. The railway station, the prison, the Woermann House, the Kaserne (barracks), the Lutheran church, and the district court look more like illustrations from some Brothers Grimm fairy tale than the working buildings they once were. You can usually purchase a book with detailed information about these buildings from the Sam Cohen Library, which is worth a visit for its impressive collection of Africana books, archives of old newspapers (many in German), and vast photo collection (though note the N$50 users' fee to browse the archives). ⊠ *Sam*

Nujoma St. (corner of Windhuker St.) ☎ *064/402–695* 🖻 *Free (N$50 browsing fee)* ☉ *Weekdays 8–1 and 3–5, 2nd Sat. of the month 9–1.*

Swakopmund Museum. The largest private museum in Namibia, this old and somewhat musty building down by the lighthouse houses a surprisingly large and varied collection of items. Displays on everything from natural history, archeology, and ethnology to the German colonial period may be a bit dated in presentation, but are nonetheless informative and worth a look. ⊠ *Strand St. (just below the lighthouse)* ☎ *064/402–046* ⊕ *www.swakopmund-museum.de* 🖻 *N$25* ☉ *Daily 10–5.*

BEACHES

Though Namibia is hardly a beach destination, if you really want some sand and sun time, head to The Mole and adjacent Palm Beach, Swakops's most popular beaches (in front of the lighthouse). Keep in mind that this is not Mauritius or the Caribbean: the sea can be treacherous, and the temperature usually runs in the lower 50s. Both of these beaches are a short walk from the center of town, and there are numerous cafés and restaurants along here to stop for a quick drink or bite to eat. Since the beach is sheltered by a breakwater, its calm waters attract crowds, especially on the weekends; if you do swim out, beware of the strong currents just off the breakwater. There's a paved walkway that heads north along the beach if you need to stretch your legs. You can also head to the jetty at the southern end of the beach for a stroll. The southern side of the jetty is for walkers, while the northern side is reserved for fishing.

SHOPPING

African Art Jewellers. A cut above the rest, the original and African-inspired designs and materials used by this fine jeweler are worth checking out. ⊠ *1 Hendrik Witbooi St.* ☎ *064/405–566* ☉ *Mon.–Fri. 8:30–1 and 2–6, Sat. 8:30–1.*

Art Africa. A lovely emporium of high-quality crafts and curios from all over Namibia, as well as other parts of Africa. Items include rural art, contemporary jewelry, ceramics, leather products, masks, baskets, and funky whimsical crafts. ⊠ *Shop 6, The Arcade* ☎ *064/463–454* ⊕ *www.artafrica.com.na* ☉ *Mon.–Fri. 8:30–6, Sat. 8:30–1 and 4–6, Sun. 10–6.*

Die Muschel. This beautiful book and coffee shop in the center of Swakopmund, specializes in gorgeous coffee table books of African landscapes, people, and animals, as well as a great selection of field guides, maps, and other books about Namibia and Southern Africa. ⊠ *Corner of Brauhaus Arcade and Tobias Hainyeko St.* ☎ *064/402–874* ⊕ *www.muschel.iway.na* ☉ *Mon.–Fri. 8:30–6, Sat. 8:30–1 and 4–6, Sun. 10–6.*

Peter's Antiques. This store has been described as the best shop in Africa for its superbly eclectic collection of pieces from all over sub-Saharan Africa. Those not in the market are still welcome to browse the shop like a museum. ⊠ *24 Tobias Hainyeko St.* ☎ *064/405–624* ⊕ *www.peters-antiques.com* ☉ *Weekdays 9–1 and 3–6, Sat. 9–1 and 5–6, Sun. 5–6.*

WHERE TO EAT

$–$$
GERMAN
★

✕**The Brauhaus.** A Swakopmund institution, the original Brauhaus burned to the ground in 2009 in an electrical fire, but the current edifice is an exact replica of its predecessor, minus many of the beloved beer steins and other decorative memorabilia. The beer is flowing once again, and the big wooden tables invite long sit-downs over hearty lunches and dinners featuring dishes like schnitzel, bratwurst, and rosti (similar to a potato pancake). The German fare is excellent but if goulash and sauerkraut don't do it for you, there is a large selection of steaks and game meat, as well as seafood and even a few pasta and vegetarian options. A lively gathering place on Saturday afternoons, this is the place to mingle with the (mostly Germanic) locals. ⊠ *The Arcade 22, Sam Nujoma Ave.* ☎ *064/402–214* ⊕ *www.swakopmundbrauhaus. com* ▤ *MC, V* ☾ *Closed Sundays, except from mid–Dec. to mid–Jan.*

¢
CAFÉ

✕**Café Anton.** This is a good place to take a break after perusing the curio market around the lighthouse. Sit on the palm-shaded terrace overlooking the lighthouse and the sea and watch the world go by while you eat a breakfast of scrumptious home-baked cake or pastry, or enjoy a late afternoon tea with hazelnut triangles or croissants. The chocolate-drenched Florentiner cookies are divine, and the Black Forest cake is made exactly as it is in Germany. A small selection of light lunch options like toasted sandwiches and soups is served until 2 PM. ⊠ *Schweizerhaus Hotel, 1 Bismarck St., overlooking the Mole* ☎ *064/400–331* ▤ *AE, DC, MC, V.*

$–$$
ECLECTIC

✕**De Kelder.** Located in the small Klimas Building shopping complex, this otherwise homey restaurant brings to mind an old-world auntie with its decor of blue and white china, huge wooden spoons, and Dutch paintings, not to mention its generous portions of rich comfort food. A fairly massive dinner menu has something for everyone (including vegetarians), but the unifying theme here is a love of rich sauces, melted cheese, and a dash of bacon. The calamari *fritti* is wonderfully tender, and the *kabeljou de kelder* (a local fish served with ham, pineapple, mushrooms, and cheese) is seafood's answer to a Hawaiian pizza. ⊠ *Tobias Hainyeko St.* ☎ *402–433 or 081/129–4206* ▤ *MC, V* ☾ *Closed Sun.*

$$$$
SUSHI

✕**Haiku.** For those returning from days and nights book-ended by the ubiquitous bounty of meat that is safari cuisine, this sushi joint will offer a delightful though costly alternative. The owners take pains to import the majority of their grocery ingredients from Japan and also have nonlocal fish flown in on a regular basis. Inventive combinations and rolls like the white-pearl starter (crab mixed with sushi rice with a ponzu wasabi sauce) and the black-dragon roll (spicy tuna with mango and avo) are recommended. Portions are not large, but everything is fresh and lovingly prepared. ⊠ *37 Tobias Hanyeko St.* ☎ *064/406–406* ▤ *MC, V* ☾ *Closed Mon.*

$$–$$$
CONTINENTAL
★

✕**Hansa Hotel Main Restaurant.** If you're looking for a special-occasion dinner and you appreciate good, rich food such as venison, steak, and Namibian seafood delicacies, then you can't do better than this rather formal, highly rated restaurant with an excellent wine list. Start with the game consommé with marrow dumplings before moving on to the giant prawns in honey-lemon butter or the springbok loin. Your surroundings are a perfectly restored 1905 German colonial building (the hotel itself has earned plenty of accolades). ✉ *3 Hendrik Witbooi St.* ☎ *064/414–200* ⊕ *www.hansahotel.com.na* ⌨ *Reservations essential* ⊟ *AE, DC, MC, V.*

$$ ✕ **The Tug.** It's all about location at the Tug, which, as its name suggests, SEAFOOD is actually an old tugboat that has been raised up and moored next to the jetty. Swakops is known for its fresh seafood, which is quite good here; if you're not in the mood for something fishy, opt for the venison or ostrich stir-fry. Try to reserve a sea-view table so you can watch the ocean crashing just beneath you, but call two weeks in advance to avoid disappointment. The outside deck is also a coveted location for a summer sundowner. ✉ *The Strand* ☎ *064/402–356* ⌨ *Reservations essential* ⊟ *AE, DC, MC, V.*

WHERE TO STAY

Several of the lodging establishments listed do not have air-conditioning, but because of the cool climate, this is actually standard practice in the smaller guesthouses. They all have fans for use in summer, and it is rarely so hot that the average person would consider a/c necessary. For much of the year, having a heater indoors is more of an issue.

Lodging reviews have been abbreviated in this book. For expanded reviews, please go to Fodors.com.

$ 🏨 **Central Guest House.** This charming and extremely conveniently located old house is an owner-managed B&B with six rooms. **Pros:** personalized and helpful service; convenient location; lovely old house **Cons:** exterior is a bit stark; Internet is not free; rooms lack any particular view. ✉ *Corner of Lüderitz and Lutwein Sts.* ☎ *064/407–189* ⊕ *www.guesthouse.com.na* ⇌ *6 rooms* ⌂ *In-room: no a/c, safe, refrigerator (some), Wi-Fi. In-hotel: restaurant, laundry service, Internet terminal, Wi-Fi hotspot, parking (free)* ⊟ *V* ❖ *BP.*

$ 🏨 **Cornerstone Guesthouse.** Walking into Cornerstone one is struck by
★ the lovely manicured garden and the pleasantly homey (and exceedingly clean) ambience. **Pros:** great breakfast; personalized friendly service; lovely garden. **Cons:** one room looks onto parking area instead of garden; often fully booked. ✉ *40 Hendrik Witbooi St.* ☎ *064/462–468* ⊕ *www.cornerstoneguesthouse.com* ⇌ *6 rooms* ⌂ *In-room: no phone (some), no a/c, safe (some), refrigerator (some), Wi-Fi. In-hotel: restaurant, laundry service, Internet terminal, Wi-Fi hotspot, parking (free)* ⊟ *MC, V* ❖ *BP.*

$$ 🏨 **Hansa Hotel.** This old-world grand dame gives guests a Belle Epoque–
★ era feeling with the hushed solicitude, gleaming brass, thick carpets, and manicured garden. **Pros:** lovely extras like a house library with a great selection of books; gorgeous old bar with a fireplace; amazing restaurant. **Cons:** could be a bit stuffy for the younger crowd; lacks the intimacy of a boutique hotel or guesthouse. ✉ *3 Hendrik Witbooi St.* ☎ *064/414–200* ⊕ *www.hansahotel.com.na* ⇌ *58 rooms* ⌂ *In-room: a/c, safe (some), kitchen (some), refrigerator (some), DVD (some), Wi-Fi. In-hotel: restaurant, room service, bars, laundry service, Internet terminal, Wi-Fi hotspot, parking (free)* ⊟ *AE, DC, MC, V* ❖ *BP.*

$$ 🏨 **Swakopmund Boutique Hotel.** This new three-story boutique hotel by the beach—with its tones of silver, champagne, and taupe, and modern art and orchid displays—is all contemporary elegance and comfort. **Pros:** many of the rooms have a partial sea view; amazing roof bar with great sunset views. **Cons:** not all rooms have Wi-Fi access. ⊠ *4 Sam Nujoma Ave.* ☎ *064/417–100* ⊕ *www.swkboutiquehotel.com* ⤶ *21 rooms* ⚏ *In-room: a/c, safe (some), refrigerator (some), DVD (some), Wi-Fi (some). In-hotel: restaurant, bar, laundry service, Internet terminal, Wi-Fi hotspot, parking (free)* ⊟ *AE, MC, V* ⑪ *BP.*

$$$ 🏨 **Swakopmund Hotel and Entertainment Centre.** At this hotel within the ☾ 1901 Old Station Building, the huge bustling lobby is a reminder of the building's previous incarnation as a railway station. **Pros:** conveniences of a large hotel with numerous facilities; lovely lobby architecture and pleasant (though unheated) pool. **Cons:** lack of real character or intimacy; often used as a business or conference center; nonsmoking rooms exist, but those sensitive to smoke may smell occasional smoke. ⊠ *2 Theo-Ben Gurirab Ave.* ☎ *064/410–5200* ⊕ *www.legacyhotels.co.za* ⤶ *90 rooms* ⚏ *In-room: a/c, safe (some), refrigerator (some), Wi-Fi. In-hotel: 2 restaurants, room service, bars, pool, gym, spa, laundry service, Internet terminal, Wi-Fi hotspot, parking (free)* ⊟ *AE, DC, MC, V* ⑪ *BP.*

SPORTS AND THE OUTDOORS

Africa's second adventure-activity capital after Livingstone, Swakopmund is the departure point for all manner of tours that make use of its surreal location between the dunes and the sea. Daytime, moonlight, sunrise, and sunset horseback rides are possible with Okakambe Trails. Desert Explorers, Outback Orange, and the Swakopmund Skydiving Club can organize skydiving over the dunes, sandboarding, and quadbike (ATV) trips. The Living Desert Tour is highly recommended, as is a 4x4 day trip to Sandwich Harbour, with its rich birdlife and spectacular views. Numerous sea-based tours are also available but most depart from Walvis Bay (⇨ *below*). Finally, Namib Tracks & Trails can organize all manner of trips, including day trips a bit farther afield to sights like the amazing rock formations and bush paintings at Spitzkoppe or the seal colony at Cape Cross.

Tour Operators Desert Explorers (⊠ *Nathaniel Maxuilili St.* ☎ *064/406–096* ⊕ *www.namibiadesertexplorers.com*). **Living Desert Tour** (☎ *064/405–070 or 081/127–5070* ⊕ *www.livingdesertnamibia.com*). **Namib Tracks & Trails** (⊠ *14A Sam Nujoma Ave.* ☎ *064/416–820*). **Okakambe Trails** (⊠ *11 km [7 mi] east of Swakopmund on the B2 to Windhoek, next to the camel farm* ☎ *064/402–799*). **Outback Orange** (⊠ *44 Nathaniel Maxuilili St.* ☎ *064/400–968* ⊕ *www.outback-orange.com*). **Swakopmund Skydiving Club** (⊠ *5 km east of Swakopmund on the B2, near the airport turn-off* ☎ *064/405–671* ⊕ *www.skydiveswakopmund.com*).

WALVIS BAY

One of Southern Africa's most important harbor towns, the once industrial Walvis Bay has recently developed into a seaside holiday destination with a number of pleasant lagoon-front guesthouses and several good restaurants—including one of Namibia's best. The majority of water activities advertised in Swakopmund actually depart from Walvis's small waterfront area, and there's an amazing flamingo colony residing in Bay's 3,000-year-old lagoon.

GETTING HERE AND AROUND

About 15 km (9 mi) east of town, the Walvis Airport serves the region (including Swakopmund) and has direct flights to South Africa. The major car-rental companies are located at the airport. Thirty kilometers (18 mi) from Swakopmund, the drive takes about 40 minutes on the B2. The town itself lacks attractions, and most visitors will head straight to the Walvis Bay lagoon. Here you'll find the majority of accommodations, the waterfront, from where almost all activities—both sea- and land-based—depart, and a handful of restaurants. Most everything in the lagoon area is within walking distance.

WHEN TO GO

Like Swakopmund, Walvis Bay enjoys a mild climate thanks to the cold Atlantic. Although most of the local Christmas and Easter holidaymakers head to Swakops, the overflow can spill out here, so it's best to avoid these times of year.

SAFETY AND PRECAUTIONS

Be sure to turn your lights on when driving between Walvis and Swakops, even in the daytime. Locals say that the way light reflects between the dunes and the sea impairs depth perception.

TIMING

Most of Walvis's activities, including bird-watching, boat tours, and 4x4 day trips to Sandwich Harbour, depart relatively early. As such, spending the night before such an activity is certainly worthwhile. Given the new accommodations and restaurants in town, if time allows and you plan on participating in more than one activity, two nights would not be wasted.

WHERE TO EAT

$–$$

FRENCH

Fodor's Choice

★

✕ **Lyon des Sables.** Located in an old church close to "downtown" Walvis Bay, this unexpected gem is arguably Namibia's finest restaurant and a reason in itself to visit Walvis Bay. Owned and run by two Frenchmen, this former church is the perfect place to worship at the altar of excellent cuisine. Genius combinations of texture and flavor using the freshest ingredients result in a sublime culinary experience. The seared tuna starter with a pine nut pesto and balsamic reduction topped with hazelnut crumble, and the kingklip with marinated artichokes and oyster cream sauce are highly recommended. Keep an eye out for specialty-themed nights, like "sushi Wednesdays." The funky decor— purple walls and a sort of retro-hip vibe—great cocktails and wine list, and friendly efficient service complete the picture. Save room for des-

Seal colonies can be found all around Walvis Bay, particularly at Pelican Point.

sert. ✉ *Corner of Theo Ben Gurirab St. and 10th Rd.* ☎ *064/221–220* ✍ *lyondessables@gmail.com* 🟰 *MC, V* 🕙 *Closed Sun.*

$–$$ ✕ **The Raft.** Brought to you by the builders of The Tug in Swakopmund,
SEAFOOD The Raft enjoys a similarly spectacular view from its perch out over beautiful Walvis Bay Lagoon. Divided into two parts—bar to the right, restaurant to the left—this warm and friendly establishment is the place to be in Walvis Bay. The menu is massive, with the usual array of seafood, red meat (including many game options), and the requisite pasta and vegetarian options (pizzas and burgers available at the bar only). At the time of writing, the menu was undergoing a revamp, in recognition of Walvis's food bar being raised from a standard of decent filling food to truly fine cuisine. Expect a slightly pared down menu, new homemade pastas, and sides like couscous and grilled veggies (instead of the standard parboiled rice and french fries). ✉ *Esplanade, on the lagoon* ☎ *064/204–877* ⊕ *www.theraftrestaurant.com* 🟰 *DC, MC, V.*

WHERE TO STAY

Lodging reviews have been abbreviated in this book. For expanded reviews, please go to Fodors.com.

$$$ 🏠 **Egumbo Lodge.** This gorgeous new guesthouse is located in a large thatch roof, nine-room home. **Pros:** gorgeous decor; great location on the lagoon; amazing wine and whiskey collection. **Cons:** only a few rooms have lagoon views. ✉ *42 Kovambo Nujoma Dr. (on the lagoon)* ☎ *064/207–700* ⊕ *www.egumbolodge.com* ⤳ *9 rooms* ⚒ *In-room: no phone (some), no a/c, safe (some), refrigerator (some), Wi-Fi (some, free). In-hotel: restaurant, room service, bar, pool (heated), laundry* *service (free), Internet terminal, Wi-Fi hotspot, parking (free)* ⊟ *AE, MC, V* ⦿*BP.*

$$ ⚏ **Protea Hotel Pelican Bay.** This outlet of the Protea chain has a great location on the lagoon, and all 50 rooms enjoy lagoon views. **Pros:** great location with amazing views of the lagoon; all the amenities of a larger hotel, including free airport shuttle. **Cons:** rooms lack character and intimacy with decor faintly reminiscent of an expensive nursing home. ✉ *The Esplanade on the lagoon* ☎ *064/214–000* ⊕ *www.proteahotels. com/pelicanbay* ⇆ *50 rooms* ♿ *In-room: a/c, safe (some), DVD (some) kitchen (some), refrigerator (some), Wi-Fi (some). In-hotel: 2 restaurants, room service, bar, gym, spa, laundry service, Internet terminal, Wi-Fi hotspot, parking (free)* ⊟ *AE, DC, MC, V* ⦿*BP.*

SPORTS AND THE OUTDOORS

Sun Sail Catamarans (☎ *081/124–5045* ⊕ *www.sailnamibia.com*) has daily departures at 8:15 to Pelican Point. During the four- to five-hour cruise you'll likely see seals, dolphins, numerous sea birds, and whales (in season). Fresh oysters, sparkling wine, and snacks are served on board. **Catamaran Charters** (☎ *064/200–798* ⊕ *www.namibiancharters. com*) also runs a seal and dolphin cruise on a 45- or 60-foot catamaran. The four-hour cruise, which sets sail at 8:30 AM, visits Pelican Point and the lighthouse, with almost guaranteed dolphin and seal sightings along the way. Keen fishermen should check out **Pelican Boat Fishing** (☎ *064/207–644* ⊕ *www.pelican-tours.com*) to organize a day of fishing for large game fish and sharks. **Sandwich Harbour 4x4** (☎ *064/207–663* ⊕ *www.sandwich-harbour.com*) runs an excellent day trip to the dunes that includes a hearty lunch (with oysters and sparkling wine). Expect to drive over the dunes as if it was a series of roller coasters. They also run bird-watching trips and combination trips (a boat trip and the dunes, or kayaking and the dunes). If you just want to peacefully paddle the calm waters of Walvis Bay, enjoying the scenery and up-close encounters with marine and bird life, try **Eco-Marine Kayak Tours** (☎ *064/203–144 or 081/129–3144* ⊕ *www.emkayak.iway.na*). Their five-hour trips start at 7:45 and can be combined with a Sandwich Harbour tour.

7

Victoria Falls

WELCOME TO VICTORIA FALLS

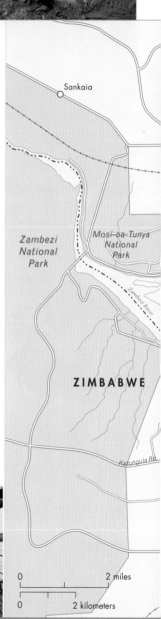

TOP REASONS TO GO

★ **A World-Class Phenomenon.** Not only can you experience Victoria Falls and the Batoka Gorge from every angle—the sheer size of this wonder fosters the delightful illusion of exclusivity.

★ **The Adrenaline Rush.** Looking for an adventure to get your heart pounding? From bungee jumping to elephant back riding and skydiving, Victoria Falls truly has it all.

★ **Perfectly Indulgent Relaxation.** Massages are offered on the banks of the Zambezi River, sumptuous food is served wherever you turn, and there are few sights on earth that rival watching the spray of the Falls fade from rainbow to starlight whilst you enjoy cocktails at the end of the day.

★ **Intact Africa.** The heart of the Dark Continent proudly showcases a region governed by people who have lived here for centuries, proudly utilizing the very latest in ecotourism and benefiting from environmentally conscious development.

1 Livingstone, Zambia. Named after the famous Dr. David Livingstone, the town was established in 1900, 6 mi (10 km) north of the Falls. Its main street, Mosi-oa-Tunya Road, still boasts examples of classic colonial buildings. The recently publicized political unrest in Zimbabwe has caused many tourists to choose Livingstone rather than Victoria Falls as a base for exploration of the area.

2 Victoria Falls, Zimbabwe. The town of Victoria Falls hugs the Falls on the Zambezi's southwestern bank. The view of the Falls and the gorge is pretty spectacular from Zimbabwe. At one time, the town was the principal tourist destination for the area. The town of Victoria Falls continues to be perfectly safe, and the general atmosphere has greatly improved as tentative stability returns to the area.

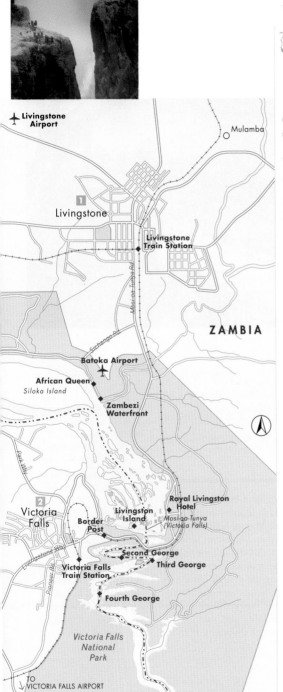

GETTING ORIENTED

Victoria Falls is in Southern Africa and physically provides a natural border between Zambia and Zimbabwe. Each country has a national park that surrounds the Falls (Mosi-oa-Tunya National Park in Zambia and Victoria Falls National Park in Zimbabwe), as well as a town (Livingstone in Zambia and Victoria Falls in Zimbabwe) that serves as the respective tourist center for each country. The fissure currently framing the Falls stretches over a mile, roughly from northwest to southeast. Livingstone lies to the north and the town of Victoria Falls immediately to the south of the Falls. The official border between the countries is within walking distance of the compact town of Victoria Falls but around 10 km (6 mi) from Livingstone. The stretch between the Falls border and town center on the Livingstone side should not be attempted on foot, because of the dangers of wandering elephants, the African sun, and the occasional opportunistic thief.

8

GREEN LODGINGS IN ZIMBABWE AND ZAMBIA

Staying green in the area surrounding Victoria Falls is especially important because of the recent political instability that has plagued Zimbabwe. Check out these properties to get an idea of what's available—you might even book yourself a room.

(above) Matetsi Water Lodge; (opposite top right) Islands of Siankaba; (opposite bottom left) Islands of Siankaba.

About 25 mi upstream from Victoria Falls lays **Matetsi Water Lodge** (☏ 27/11/809–4314 ⊕ *www.andbeyond. com*), which is at the center of the Matetsi Game Reserve, the largest private game reserve in Zimbabwe and the single biggest rangeland for Africa's surviving elephants. The lodge employs local people and works with them on an ongoing project to catalog the traditional use of plants. The fact that there are no fences between Matetsi and bordering Botswana's Chobe National Park and the Okavango Delta means that wildlife can roam freely across borders, which creates a rich sanctuary here for all manner of creatures.

CARBON OFFSETS

Take trains over flying. If you must fly, try to take a nonstop flight. You can calculate your CO_2 footprint using several online Web sites. Atmosfair (⊕ www.atmosfair.de), Better World Club (⊕ www.betterworldclub.com), and NativeEnergy (⊕ www.nativeenergy.com) all have tools that will calculate your emissions for individual flights, as well as provide you with ideas on how to offset them.

ANOTHER GREEN LODGE IN ZIMBABWE

Victoria Falls Safari Lodge (☎ *013/4–3211* ⊕ *www.victoria-falls-safari-lodge.com*) features elegant, luxury, award-winning architecture, and every imaginable convenience while instilling a sense of respect and care for the wildlife and the environment in every guest. The hotel has been winning awards for environmental consciousness and social responsibility since its inception in 1993. The lodge maintains a strict natural vegetation policy—95% of all plants are indigenous species, new trees are planted annually, and electricity and water are conserved aggressively. The lodge also takes responsibility for keeping Victoria Falls clean and helped set up the Vic Falls Anti-Poaching Unit, which it continues to support administratively and financially.

GREEN LODGES IN ZAMBIA

Islands of Siankaba (☎ *03/32–7490* or *01/26–0279* ⊕ *www.siankaba.net*) is about 48 km (30 mi) upstream from Victoria Falls. Awarded the Environmental Certificate by the Environmental Council of Zambia in 2002, shortly before its opening, the lodge is on two forested islands in the Zambezi River. A suspension bridge links the two islands and leads to an overhead walkway in the tree canopy that connects the elevated chalets to the lodge's restaurant. The walkways protect the islands' delicate riverine environment. The lodge was constructed with mostly commercially grown, nonindigenous pine. Where local wood was used, the lodge planted hardwood saplings to replace them. Electricity is drawn from the Victoria Falls hydroelectric plant, and river water is recycled and treated on-site for use in the camp. Local tribes are employed by the lodge, where sunset cruises, mokoro rides, guided nature walks, white-water rafting, and bungee jumping are all on the menu.

Sindabezi Island
(☎ *03/32–7450* or *03/32–7468* ⊕ *www.tongabezi.com*) is the Zambezi's most environmentally friendly property. The island makes use of recycled wood chips and solar power for heating, all the gray water is recycled, and the chalets are constructed mainly from sustainable forests. There's a strict 10-guest limit and each of the island's chalets is raised on a wooden deck built artistically around the existing trees—they are all completely open to the river with spectacular private views (curtains drop down at night). There is absolutely no electricity on the island, and hot water is provided on demand. If your party takes Sindabezi exclusively, the guide, boat, and land vehicle are at your disposal. Dinner is served by lantern and candlelight on a sandbank or wooden deck under the stars.

8

Updated by Sanja Cloete-Jones

Roughly 1,207 km (750 mi) from its humble origins as an insignificant spring in northern Zambia, the Zambezi River has grown more than a mile wide. Without much warning the river bends south, the current speeds up, and the entire mass of water disappears into a single fissure. More than 1 million gallons of water rushes over a vertical, 328-foot-high drop in the time it takes an average reader to reach the end of this paragraph. The resulting spray is astounding, the brute force forming a cloud of mist visible 64 km (40 mi) away on a clear day.

The settlements of Livingstone in Zambia, and Victoria Falls in Zimbabwe both owe their existence to the Zambezi and the Falls. Though they are located in different countries and intriguingly diverse in character, they function almost like two sides of one town. Crossing the border is a formality that generally happens with minimum fuss. Although the Zimbabwean town of Victoria Falls has escaped the political strife that has dogged the country in recent years, Livingstone, on the Zambian side is determined to remain the favored destination. Zambia spoils guests with an overabundance of top-class safari lodges along the Zambezi, and this strong competition has resulted in an emphasis on personalized service, which enables you to tailor your visit.

On the other hand, Zimbabwe is slowly rebuilding itself and severe shortages of basic necessities are becoming a thing of the past. The relative absence of large numbers of travelers is a luxury in itself, and this area currently provides excellent value for money.

The region as a whole deserves its reputation as an adventure center and offers adrenaline-inducing activities by the bucketful. The backdrop for any of these is stunning, and the safety record nothing less than spectacular.

PLANNING

WHEN TO GO

If you're at all sensitive to heat and humidity, visit from May through August, when it is dry and cool, with pleasant days and cool to cold nights. Although the winter bush can resemble a wasteland, with short brown stubble and bare trees, it does improve game-viewing, and most other adventure activities are more comfortable in the cooler weather. This is also the time when the mosquitoes are less active, although it remains a malaria area year-round, and precautions should always be taken.

The rainy season starts sometime around late October and generally stretches well into April. As the heavens open up the bug population explodes with mosquitoes, and the harmless but aptly named stink bug seemingly runs the show for brief periods of the day. Of course, the abundance of insect life also leads to great bird-watching. Although the rain showers tend to be of the short and spectacular kind, they can interfere with some activities, especially if your visit to the area is brief. Try to arrange excursions for the early hours of the day, as the rain generally falls in the late afternoon.

Peak flow for Victoria Falls occurs in late April and May, when rafting and visiting Livingstone Island might not be possible. If your visit coincides with school vacations in South Africa, the area can become quite crowded.

HEALTH AND SAFETY

It's always a good idea to leave ample space in your luggage for common sense when traveling to Victoria Falls. Wild animals abound throughout this area (even in the center of town) and must be given a lot of physical space and respect. You must also remember that Zimbabwe and Zambia are relatively poor. Both countries have tourism police, but opportunistic thieving still happens occasionally. Although crime in this area is generally nonviolent, losing your money, belongings, or passport will result in spending the remainder of your trip with various officials in stuffy, badly decorated offices instead of sitting back on the deck of your sunset cruise with drink in hand.

As for the water, it is always advisable to drink bottled water, although the tap water in Zambia is generally considered safe. Should you develop any stomach upset, be sure to contact a physician, especially if you are running a fever, in

WHEN IN ROME...

Fearing a few weeks without your Budweiser? No worries. There are a couple great local brews for you to try on both sides of the Falls: Mosi in Zambia and Zambezi in Zimbabwe. Both are crisp, light, and thirst-quenching beers. What about after your meal? Order an Amarula on ice. Not unlike Baileys Irish Cream, this liquor is made from the fruit of the marula tree, a well-documented delicacy for elephants.

8

"At the end of our safari, we went to Victoria Falls. . . . The thundering roar of the falls and the many rainbows were like nothing I had ever seen."—Pam Record, Fodors.com member

order to rule out malaria or a communicable disease. Do remember to mention your visit to a malaria area to your doctor in the event of illness within a year of leaving Africa.

Finally, confirm that your insurance covers you for a medical evacuation should you be involved in a serious accident, as the closest intensive-care facilities of international standard are in South Africa.

HOTELS

It is advisable to make both flight and lodge reservations ahead of time. Lodges tend to have all-inclusive packages; hotels generally include breakfast only. All hotels and lodges quote in U.S. dollars but accept payment in other major currencies at unfriendly exchange rates. It might be best to take an all-inclusive package tour because meals can be exorbitantly expensive. A 10% service charge is either included or added to the bill (as is the value-added tax) in both countries, which frees you to include an extra tip only for exceptional service. Although air-conditioning can be expected in the hotels, lodges tend to have fans.

■ TIP➜ Travel with a sarong (locally available as a chitenge), which you can wet and wrap around your body, guaranteeing a cooler siesta.

RESTAURANTS

In Zimbabwe, game meat can be found on almost any menu, but it's something of a delicacy in Zambia; superior free-range beef and chicken are available everywhere. The local bream, filleted or whole, is excellent, and the staple starch, a thick porridge similar to polenta—*sadza* in Zimbabwe and *nsima* in Zambia—is worth a try; use your fingers to eat it (you'll be given a bowl for washing afterward). Adventurous? Try *macimbi* or *vinkuvala* (sun-dried mopane worms) . . . in the flood season the brave also enjoy *inswa* (flash-fried flying ants).

Meals are taken at regular hours, but during the week, restaurants close around 10. Dress is casual, but Africa easily lends itself to a little bling, and you'll never be out of place in something more glamorous.

WHAT IT COSTS IN U.S. DOLLARS				
	¢	$	$$	$$$	$$$$
Restaurants	under $5	$5–$10	$11–$15	$16–$25	over $25
Hotels	under $50	$50–$100	$101–$200	$201–$350	over $350

Restaurant prices are per person for a main course at dinner, a main course equivalent, or a prix-fixe meal. Hotel prices are for a standard double room in high season, including 17.5% value-added tax (VAT) in Zambia and 15% VAT in Zimbabwe and service charge.

PASSPORTS AND VISAS

You'll need a valid passport and visa to enter **Zambia**. Nationals of any country not on the Zambian Immigration Referred Visa list can simply purchase a visa upon entering the country. At press time a standard U.S. single-entry visa costs US$50, and a single-entry and transit visa cost the same. Day-trip visas cost US$20 (often included in the cost of prebooked activities, so check with your booking agent). If you plan to return to Zambia in the near future, you will need a multiple-entry visa, or you'll have to buy another visa upon your return. Multiple-entry visas and visas for nationals from countries on the referred visa list (⊕ *www.zambiaimmigration.gov.zm*) can be purchased only at Zambian Missions abroad and not on arrival.

It's possible to buy point-of-entry visas for **Zimbabwe** for US$30 for a single entry. If you leave Zimbabwe for more than 24 hours, you will need to buy another to reenter (unless you bought a double-entry visa for US$40). Visas can be purchased from a Zimbabwean embassy before departure (application for multiple-entry visas can only be lodged here), but it will almost certainly be more trouble and generally cost more than buying them at the border.

8

LIVINGSTONE, ZAMBIA

This marvelous old town, once the government capital of Northern Rhodesia (now Zambia), boasts a wealth of natural beauty and a surplus of activities. After a few decades of neglect it has recently recast itself as Zambia's tourism and adventure capital. There's a tangible whiff of the past here: historic buildings outnumber new ones, and many local inhabitants live a life not unlike the one they would have experienced 100 years ago. Livingstone handles the surge of tourists with equal parts grace, confidence, African mischief, and nuisance.

Many visitors to this side of the Falls opt to stay in one of the secluded safari-style lodges on the Zambezi River. The Zambian experience sprawls out along the many bends of the large river and time ticks in a very deliberate African manner.

GETTING HERE AND AROUND

South African Airways, Comair/ British Airways, and 1time regularly fly from Johannesburg into Livingstone International Airport, 5 km (3 mi) out of town. The flight is a comfortable hop, under two hours in duration, and the airport is small and friendly, with helpful staff to speed you on your way.

DID YOU KNOW?

The uttering of the popular phrase "Dr. Livingstone, I presume?" may never have happened. Although Livingstone did meet John Rowlands (the person reported to have uttered the phrase) in Tanzania in 1871, the famous quote is widely considered a figment of Rowlands's imagination. Mr. Rowlands was fond of a good story—he also told people that he was American (which he wasn't) and that his name was Henry Stanley (which it wasn't).

FAST FACTS

Size 752,618 square km (290,587 square mi).

Number of National Parks 19. Kafue National Park; Lower Zambezi National Park; Mosi-oa-Tunya National Park (Victoria Falls National Park).

Population 13.5 million.

Big Five The gang's all here.

Language Zambia has between 70 and 80 recorded languages, of which 42 are main dialects. Luckily English is the official language, and it is widely spoken, read, and understood.

Time Zambia is on CAST (Central African standard time), which is two hours ahead of Greenwich Mean Time and seven hours ahead of North American Eastern Standard Time; it's the same as South Africa.

■TIP→ If at all possible, don't check your luggage in Johannesburg and always lock suitcases securely, as luggage theft in South Africa is an everyday occurrence.

There's a perfectly reasonable traffic code in Zambia. Unfortunately, not many people have ever heard of it. You would do well to leave the driving to your local guides or negotiate an all-inclusive rate with a taxi driver recommended by your hotel or lodge for the duration of your stay. Note that taxis are generally not allowed to cross the border, so if you want to visit Zimbabwe, you will have to book a tour that includes transfers. Once at the border, it is feasible to walk into and around Victoria Falls town or rent a bicycle.

If you insist on renting a car, you should know that some of the roads have more potholes than tar. You don't necessarily need a 4x4, but it's not a bad idea, especially if you want to go off-road at all. Voyagers operate from the Day Activity Center near the Zambezi Sun lodge. Hemingway's rents out Toyota Hilux Double Cabs (similar to the Toyota Tacoma), fully equipped with tents and other camping equipment—you can even hire a driver! Costs start from US$180 for an unequipped vehicle.

■TIP→ If you plan to add the popular Kafue and Lower Zambezi camps to your trip, you should book your transfers together with your accommodation through a travel agent or with your camp reservations, as air-transfer companies change hands and/or minds quite often in Zambia. A travel agent or camp will also assure that connection times work to your best advantage if they are responsible for the transfers.

MONEY MATTERS

Zambia's currency is the Zambian *kwacha*, which comes in denominations of ZK50, ZK100, ZK500, ZK1,000, ZK5,000, ZK10,000, ZK20,000, and ZK50,000 bills, necessitating carrying huge wads of notes. The kwacha is theoretically divided into 100 *ngwees*, but as you can buy nothing for one kwacha, an ngwee exists in name only, and any bill including ngwees will simply be rounded off. At the time of writing, the conversion rate was about ZK4,800 to US$1.

Kwacha and U.S. dollars are welcome everywhere. It's a good idea to travel with plenty of small U.S. bills for tips and small purchases. Make sure you have only "big headed" dollars, as the older, "small headed" ones are no longer accepted. ⚠ Small denominations are often not exchanged for the same rate as larger denominations at the bureaux de change. Official banks have standard exchange rates across the board for all notes. International banks along Mosi-oa-Tunya Road have ATMs and exchange services. Banking hours are generally weekdays 8–2 (although some do open the last Saturday of the month). Bank ATMs accept only Visa.

⚠ You may be invited to do a little informal foreign exchange by persuasive street financiers. Resist the temptation—it's not worth the risk of being ripped off or arrested. There are many reputable exchange bureaus throughout town, though they are sometimes flooded with dollars and low on kwacha, generally toward the end of the month. MasterCard and Visa are preferred by business owners and banks to American Express or Diners Club. Business owners always prefer cash to credit cards, and some smaller hotels levy fees up to 10% to use a credit card.

Zambia has a 17.5% VAT and a 10% service charge, which is included in the cost or itemized on your bill.

Tipping is less common in Zambia since service charges are included, but it's appreciated. Small notes or 10% is appropriate. Gas-station attendants can be tipped, but tip a taxi driver only on the last day if you have used the same driver for a number of days.

Electricity and voltage are the same in Zambia and South Africa. ⇨ *For more information, see Electricity in Travel Smart South Africa.*

SAFETY AND PRECAUTIONS

For minor injuries, a test for malaria, or the treatment of non-life-threatening ailments, you can go to the Rainbow Trust Mwenda, Southern Medical, or Shafik clinic. For serious emergencies, contact SES (Specialty Emergency Services). There are a number of pharmacies in town including Health and Glow Pharmacy, Link Pharmacy, and Musamu Pharmacy. Pharmacies are generally open weekdays 8–8, Saturday 8–6, and Sunday 8–1.

Homosexuality is technically illegal in Zambia, although it is widely accepted and presents no real problem.

TELEPHONES

Telephone rates in Zambia are much cheaper and more stable than those in Zimbabwe. Check numbers very carefully, as some are Zimbabwean mobile phones. Zambia and Zimbabwe now both have cell coverage, and there are certain areas where the networks overlap and mobile telephones work in both countries. If you have any trouble dialing a number, check with a hotel or restaurant owner, who should be able to advise you of the best and cheapest alternative. International roaming on your standard mobile phone is also an option, as coverage is quite extensive. Alternatively, you could purchase a local SIM card with pay-as-you-go fill-ups. Pay phones are not an option, and the costs of all telephone calls out of the country can be exorbitant.

The country code for Zambia is 260. When dialing from abroad, drop the initial 0 from local area codes and cell-phone numbers. Note that all telephone numbers are listed as they are dialed from the country that they are in. Although the number for operator assistance is 100, you will be much better off asking your local lodge or restaurant manager for help.

VISITOR INFORMATION

Although the Zambia National Tourist Board (next to the museum; open weekdays 8–1 and 2–5, Saturday 8–noon) is very helpful and friendly, you might be better off visiting Jollyboys (behind the Livingstone Museum; open daily 7 AM–10 PM) for comprehensive and unbiased advice.

> ### CHOBE: A GREAT DAY TRIP
>
> If it is serious game-viewing you desire, join a one-day excursion to Chobe National Park in Botswana with **Bushtracks** (☎ *213/32-3232* ⊕ *www.gotothevictoriafalls.com*). The trip costs US$185 and includes transfers from Livingstone, a morning boat cruise, lunch with a drink, and an afternoon game drive. Bushtracks is also your best bet for a visit to the Mukuni Village (US$37). Reservations must be in writing and prepaid for both.

ESSENTIALS

Airlines 1time Airlines (☎ *0213/32-2744* ⊕ *www.1time.aero*). **Comair/British Airways** (☎ *0213/32-2827* ⊕ *www.british-airways.com*). **South African Airways** (☎ *0213/32-3031* ⊕ *www.flysaa.com*).

Car Rental Companies Hemingway's (☎ *0213/32-0996 or 0977/86-6492* ⊕ *www.hemingwayszambia.com*). **Voyagers** (☎ *0213/32-2753* ⊕ *www.voyagerszambia.com*).

Embassies U.S. Embassy (✉ *United Nations Ave. and Independence Rd., Lusaka* ☎ *0211/25-0955* ⊕ *zambia.usembassy.gov*).

Internet Access Jollyboys (✉ *34 Kanyanta Rd.* ☎ *213/32-4229* ⊕ *www.backpackzambia.com*).

Emergency Services General emergencies (note all emergencies 112 from cell phones only) (☎ *999*). **Police** (☎ *991*). **Fire** (☎ *993*). **SES** (☎ *213/32-2330 from landline; 0977/74-0307 from cell phone*).

Hospitals Rainbow Trust Mwenda Medical Centre (✉ *1907 Kabila St.* ☎ *213/32-3519*). **Shafik clinic** (✉ *49 Akapelwa St.* ☎ *213/32-1130*). **Southern Medical Centre** (✉ *House 9, 1967 Makombo Rd.* ☎ *213/32-3547*).

Visitor Info Zambia National Tourist Board (✉ *Tourist Centre, Mosi-oa-Tunya Rd.* ☎ *213/32-1404* ⊕ *www.zambiatourism.com*). **Jollyboys** (✉ *34 Kanyanta Rd.* ☎ *213/32-4229* ⊕ *www.backpackzambia.com*).

EXPLORING

Sights below appear on the Livingstone map.

☼ **Batoka Gorge.** Just below the Falls, the gorge forms an abyss between the countries with edges that drop away from the cliffs of both Zambia and Zimbabwe. Each successive sandstone gorge is numbered in sequence

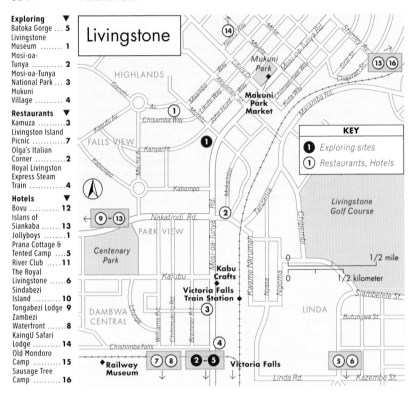

starting from the youngest (First Gorge to the Fifth Gorge), followed by Songwe Gorge and finally the official Batoka Gorge; it is common for all these gorges to be referred to collectively as The Gorge or Batoka Gorge. Batoka Gorge is more than 120 km (75 mi) long with vertical walls that are an average of 400 feet high (the Zambezi river water levels fluctuates up to 65 feet between the wet and dry season). Batoka lies mostly within the Hwange Communal Land and is covered with mopane and riparian forests that are interspersed with grassland. On the Zambian side, the gorge is surrounded by the Mosi-oa-Tunya National Park, which contains a tropical rain forest that thrives on the eternal rainfall from the Falls. Victoria Falls National Park in Zimbabwe surrounds the other side of the gorge. Operators from both countries offer excursions to what is reputed to be the world's best one-day white-water rafting, with rapids rated between Class I and Class VI (amateurs can do only Class V and down commercially) that have been given evocative nicknames like "The Ugly Sisters" and "Oblivion." If you're "lucky" enough to experience what locals call a "long swim" (falling out of the raft at the start of a rapid and body surfing through), your definition of the word *scary* will surely be redefined. The walk in and out of the gorge is quite strenuous on the Zimbabwe side, but as long as you are reasonably fit and looking for adventure, you need no experience. On the Zambian side though, operators use a cable car to transport you from the bottom of the gorge to your waiting transportation (and beverage) at the top. Also on the Zambian side, travelers can walk down into the Boiling Pot (the first bend of the river after the Falls) in the First Gorge. It's an easy walk down and slightly more challenging walk out of the gorge (lots of steps), but even young children enjoy it—be sure to carry extra sun protection and water.

Livingstone Museum. The country's oldest and largest museum contains history, ethnography, natural history, archaeology sections, and materials ranging from newspaper clippings to photographs of Queen Elizabeth II dancing with Kenneth Kaunda (Zambia's first president) to historical information dating back to 1500. Among the priceless David Livingstone memorabilia is a model of the mangled arm bone used to identify his body and various journals and maps from the period when he explored the area and claimed the Falls for the English queen. ⊠ *Mosi-oa-Tunya Rd., between civic center and post office* ☎ *213/32–3566* ⊠ *US$8* ⏱ *Daily 8:30–4:30* ⏱ *Closed Christmas and New Years Day.*

Fodor's Choice
★

Mosi-oa-Tunya (Victoria Falls). Literally translated as "the Smoke that Thunders," the Falls more than lives up to its reputation as one of the world's greatest natural wonders. Words can never do these incredible Falls justice, and it's a difficult attraction to fully appreciate in a single visit, as it's constantly changing. Though the Zimbabwean side offers famously panoramic views, the Zambian side of the Falls features the Knife Edge bridge, which allows guests to stand virtually suspended over the Boiling Pot (the first bend of the river after the Falls), with the deafening water crashing everywhere around you. From around May through August the Falls are a multisensory experience, and there may be too much spray to see the bottom of the gorge. In high season the entire experience can be summed up in two words: power shower! Prepare to get soaked. If you stand with your back to the sun, you'll be surrounded by a symphony of rainbows. A network of paths leads to the main viewing points; some are not well protected, so watch your step and wear sensible shoes, especially at high water, when you are likely to get dripping wet. You will have dramatic views of the full 1½ km (1 mi) of the ironstone face of the Falls, the Boiling Pot directly below, the railway bridge, and Batoka Gorge. During low water levels, it's possible to take a guided walk to Livingstone Island and swim in the **Devils Pool,** a natural pond right on the lip of the abyss. ⊠ *Entrance off Mosi-oa-Tunya Rd., just before border post* ☎ *No phone* ⊠ *US$20* ⏱ *Daily 6–6, later at full moon.*

Mosi-oa-Tunya National Park. This park is a quick and easy option for viewing plains game. In fact, you are almost guaranteed to spy white rhinos. You can also visit the Old Drift graveyard, as the park marks the location of the original settlement of Livingstone. The park's guides are very knowledgeable, and while you're free to explore on your own, the roads do get seriously muddy in the rainy season, and a guide who knows where to drive becomes a near-necessity. ⊠ *Sichanga Rd.,*

8

off Mosi-oa-Tunya Rd., 3½ km (2 mi) from Livingstone ☎ *No phone* 💳 *US$10* ⊘ *Daily 6–6.*

☺ **Mukuni Village.** Fascinated by the history, customs, and traditions of the area? Local guides can escort you on an intimate visit inside a house and explain the customs of the village. This is not a stage set but a very real village, so your tour will be different depending on the time of day. It is customary to sign in the visitors' book and to pay a small fee to your guide. **Bushtracks** (☎ *213/32–3232* ⊕ *www.gotothevictoriafalls. com*) conducts organized visits. ⊘ *Daily 6–6.*

WHERE TO EAT

$–$$
INDIAN

✕ **Kamuza.** The Moghuls themselves might declare a meal here a feast. Spicy but not hot, the curries are lovingly prepared from ingredients imported from India. The chicken *tikka masala* is a house specialty, and the handmade saffron *kulfi* is an inspired dessert at the end of another hot day in Africa. ✉ *Ngolide Lodge, 110 Mosi-oa-Tunya Rd.* ☎ *213/32–1091* 💳 *MC, V* ⊘ *No dinner Mon.*

$$$$
ECLECTIC
☺
Fodor'sChoice
★

✕ **Livingstone Island Picnic.** Available throughout the year whenever the water levels are low enough, this is a spectacular, romantic dining option. Livingstone Island is perched right on the edge of the void, where you'll dine at a table dressed with linen and gleaming silver on a delicious organic lunch (with salads) with drinks served by attentive waiters. You get there by boat (two engines, just in case). Brunch and afternoon tea are US$60 and US$90, respectively, and lunch is US$115, including transfers. The trips are run by Tongabezi Lodge, and there is a maximum of 16 guests. ✉ *Livingstone Island* ☎ *213/32–7450* 💳 *MC, V* ⊘ *Closed a couple of months around Feb.–June, depending on water levels. No dinner.*

$–$$
ITALIAN
☺

✕ **Olga's Italian Corner.** This restaurant delivers a double whammy. Not only does it serve genuine homemade Italian food prepared from fresh local ingredients, it's also part of an NGO project that trains and benefits the local youth. Open six days a week, Olga's features homemade croissants and muffins with Italian espresso for breakfast and seasonal delights for lunch and dinner. All the Italian pastas and pizzas are prepared on the premises and served with flavorful sauces made to order. ✉ *20 Mokambo Rd.* ☎ *213/32–4160* w*www.olgasproject.com* 💳 *No credit cards* ⊘ *Closed Tues.*

$$$$
SOUTH AFRICAN
Fodor'sChoice
★

✕ **Royal Livingstone Express.** Walking the long stretch of red carpet alongside Locomotive 156 while it blows steam and rumbles in preparation for the journey is undeniably exciting and romantic. Dinner guests are seated in either the Wembley or Chesterfield dining carriage (both exquisitely restored) while the historic steam train pulls you through a bustling, charming, shanty town, over the Sinde River Bridge, and then back through Mosi-oa-Tunya National Park at sunset. The gourmet dinner is beautifully presented and meticulously prepared, offering guests no fewer than five set courses (special dietary requests can be catered to with advance notice). And yes, the train gives right-of-way to giraffes, elephants, and any other plains game who might decide to cross the tracks during dinner! ✉ *Km 0 of the Mulebezi line on*

Zambia's Tribes

BEMBA

Originally from the Luba and Lunda states of the Democratic Republic of Congo's Katanga Province, the Bemba people farmed the soil until it became infertile and then moved on, eventually establishing their modern-day settlement in Zambia's northern provinces. Chibemba (the Bemba language) is widely spoken throughout Zambia, with Bemba clans accounting for 20% of the population.

The Bemba are also known as the forest people, and they live in grass-roofed huts in villages comprised of several generations of extended family. Bemba women traditionally oversee agriculture, while the Bemba men are involved in trade and the running of the village. Folklore remains a large part of Bemba culture, and clans often name themselves after regional flora and fauna, such as the Royal Crocodile Clan whose main chief is called "The Great Tree." Many Bemba legends incorporate a belief in the supernatural or magical powers of the Bemba god who lives in the sky and controls things such as weather and fertility.

CHEWA/NYANJA

Historically from Nigeria and Cameroon by way of the Congo, the Chewa or Nyanja tribes today live in Zambia, Malawi, and Zimbabwe. Famous for intricate masks and secret societies called Nyau, Chewa men often dress as animals or mask themselves as ancestors and participate in dance ceremonies in which they enter a trance and perform intricate movements. Land rights are inherited through the mother in this tightly knit matrilineal society. The Chewa are also revered for their agricultural prowess and most engage in tobacco and maize farming. ChiChewa (or Nyanja) emerged as a distinct language in the 16th century.

8

Mosi-oa-Tunya Rd. ☎ *213/32–3232* ⊕ *www.royal-livingstone-express. com* ⚠ *Reservations essential* ☰ *MC, V* ☉ *Closed Mon. and Tues.*

WHERE TO STAY

CLOSE TO VICTORIA FALLS

¢ 🏠 **Bovu.** The vibe of California and Marrakesh in the '60s and '70s is
alive and well at this collection of thatch huts and campsites along the
banks of the Zambezi, 52 km (32 mi) upstream of the Falls. Take a
good book or an excellent companion. Accommodations are basic but
somehow quite perfect, each with gorgeous river views, and there are
hot showers and flush toilets. The kitchen is the heart of the island, and
the emphasis is on wholesome organic food ($–$$). Vegetarian diners
are always catered to, and coffee is taken fabulously seriously. Whether
you are taken for a swim in a shallow section of small rapids naturally
protected from crocodiles or hippos (this is the theory) or on a sunrise
canoe trip, every day will hold natural wonder. Warning: "island time"
operates here and anything goes, so the staid or conservative are likely
to find it unsuitable. The best way to reach Bovu is by guided *mokoro*
trip run by BUNDU (⊕ *www.bunduadventures.com*). Don't forget to
check out the hat collection behind the bar in the main camp and add
your own to the mix. **Pros:** Bovu is *the* Zambian chill-out zone; a great
way to combine an educational canoe trip with a basic overnight camp;
the perfect balance between comfort and a real commune with nature.
Cons: this might be too basic for travelers who like their little luxuries;
meals, fishing, and transfers are charged separately; guests have to bring
their own towels and linens. ✉ *52 km (32 mi) upstream from Victoria
Falls, on Zambezi River* ☎ *097/872–5282* ⊕ *www.junglejunction.info*
⤢ *8 huts* ⚘ *In-room: no phone, no TV. In-hotel: restaurant, bar, laundry
facilities, laundry service, some pets allowed* ☰ No credit cards Ⓞ *EP.*

¢ 🏠 **Jollyboys.** When the *New York Times* includes a backpacker lodge on
the same list as two five-star resorts, your curiosity should be tweaked.
The entire design of this small establishment is user-friendly, inviting,
and certainly aimed at both private relaxation and easy interaction
with other travelers. Superbly maintained and professionally run, the
lodge offers a variety of room types to suit every budget and need.
There are eight unisex dorms varying from three to 16 beds, 10 private
rooms with shared bathrooms, five private en-suite rooms and one
executive suite with a private kitchen. The suite, five en-suite rooms,
and two eight-bed dorms also have air-conditioning. The restaurant
(¢– $) serves the usual hamburger but also has a number of surprises
on the menu, including a full roast on Sundays and exotic vegetarian
soups made from local sweet potatoes and Indian spices. The swimming
pool is large, and there is a public Jacuzzi as well. You can entertain
yourself with board games or explore the extensive library that has
information on absolutely everything you could ever need in Zambia
and all neighboring countries. **Pros:** very central location; free daily
transfers to the Falls. **Cons:** it's a backpackers' lodge, so it's pretty basic;
the location right in the middle of town might not be exactly where
you'd like to spend your holiday. ✉ *Kanyanta Rd., Livingstone* ☎ *213/*

324–229 ⊕ *www.backpackzambia. com* ⟿ *24 rooms* ∆ *In-room: safe (some), kitchen (some), refrigerator (some), Wi-Fi. In-hotel: restaurant, bar, pool, laundry service, Internet terminal, Wi-Fi hotspot, parking (free), some pets allowed, no kids under 12* ⊟ *No credit cards* ⊙ *EP.*

$$ ⊡ **Prana Cottage & Tented Camp.**
ʘ Taking its name from the Sanskrit for breathing, this exclusive camp offers the perfect opportunity for taking just that, a breather. Guests have their choice: stay in the main house or in one of the beautiful, well-appointed, en-suite tents. Spread out along one of the highest points in the region, the camp overlooks the surrounding bush. Plenty of staff are on hand to look after you and take care of the cooking, cleaning, and booking all of the area's adventure activities for you. Prana also hosts yoga retreats, and you can enjoy various treatments like shiatsu massage and individual yoga classes on the property. The camp can sleep 17 adults, plus three children in total with the Cottage (which is rented exclusively for US$300 per night) sleeping six adults and three children. **Pros:** this is privately owned and managed, and is the best value for an exclusive stay in the area. You are assured of personal attention and the luxury of being completely off the beaten track yet only 10 minutes from Livingstone and 10 minutes from the entry to Mosi-oa-Tunya Park at the Falls. **Cons:** transfers must be booked for every activity if you do not hire a car. ⊠ *Off Mosi-oa-Tunya Rd., Livingstone* ☎ *213/32–7120* ⊕ *www.pranazambia.com* ⟿ *5 tents, 3 rooms* ∆ *In-room: no phone, a/c (some), safe (some), kitchen (some), refrigerator (some). In-hotel: bar, pool, laundry service, parking (free)* ⊟ *No credit cards* ⊙ *BP.*

$$$$ ⊡ **River Club.** With split-level rooms that cling to the edge of the great Zambezi, the River Club puts a modern spin on a Victorian house party. The view from the infinity pool seems unbeatable, until you watch the sun set from your claw-foot tub. Clever cooling mists of water draw flocks of birds to the massage tent, and the library begs for a glass of port and a serious book. History clings to the structure, built to the plans of the original house, but decorations have been lovingly collected from past and present. You could spend an entire day reading interesting anecdotes, old maps, *Punch* cartoons, and updates about the River Club's support of the local village. A candlelight dinner is followed by croquet on the floodlighted lawn before you retire to your partially starlit room. You approach the lodge from the river—purely for the spectacular effect—but it necessitates negotiating some steep stairs. If you think you'll struggle, ask to be transferred by vehicle. **Pros:** beautiful location with stunning views of the Zambezi; a/c and enclosed rooms are pluses for those who don't want to give up too many modern conveniences. **Cons:** colonial decor may not be Zambian enough for some travelers; 20-minute drive from town for any activities that

8

are not in-house. ⊠ *About 18 km (11 mi) upstream from Victoria Falls town, on Zambezi River* ☎ *213/32–7457* ⊕ *www.theriverclubafrica. com* ⌂ *10 rooms* ⚒ *In-room: safe, a/c. In-hotel: restaurant, room service, bar, spa, pool, laundry service, Internet terminal, parking (free), no kids under 8* ⊟ *MC, V* ⁑ *AI.*

$$$$ ⊡ **The Royal Livingstone.** This high-volume, high-end hotel has an incredibly gorgeous sundowner deck, arguably on the best spot on the river, just upstream from the Falls. The attractive colonial safari-style buildings recall a bygone era of elegance and splendor. Set amid sweeping green lawns and big trees, the Royal boasts some fantastic views, although passing guest traffic makes for a lack of real privacy. The decor of the 17 residences, each with approximately 10 guest rooms, as well as the public rooms is deliberately colonial and ostentatious. Food is beautifully prepared ($$$–$$$$) from a blend of fresh local and exotic imported ingredients. The Royal contributes to a truly noteworthy number of local charities and environmental efforts. This resort is tremendously popular and can be extremely busy, especially during peak times, but the staff is always friendly and helpful. Each room has a dedicated butler to take care of the individual needs of every guest. ■**TIP**➔ Vervet monkeys are an entertaining nuisance, so hang on to your expensive cocktail. **Pros:** Location, location, location; the level of service here is definitely that of a five-star international hotel; rooms have air-conditioning, satellite TV, and fantastic snacks; there is direct access to the Falls via a resort gate that opens onto the eastern cataract. **Cons:** volume of people can lead to problems, omissions, and errors, with service standards struggling to match the high costs; if you're traveling from other intimate safari properties, this big hotel might feel very impersonal. ⊠ *Mosi-oa-Tunya Rd., Livingstone* ☎ *213/32–1122* ⊕ *www.suninternational.com* ⌂ *173 rooms* ⚒ *In-room: safe, refrigerator. In-hotel: 3 restaurants, room service, bars, pool, spa, children's resort programs (ages 2–12), laundry service, Internet terminal, Wi-Fi hotspot, parking (free)* ⊟ *AE, MC, V* ⁑ *BP.*

$$$$
Fodor's Choice
★   ⊡ **Tongabezi Lodge.** If you're looking for a truly African experience, Tongabezi Lodge won't disappoint. Never formal, flagrantly romantic, this lodge is designed to complement and frame the Africa you have come to see without ever trying to upstage it. At Tongabezi, standard rooms are spacious cream-and-ocher rondavels featuring private verandas that can be enclosed in a billowing mosquito net. Three suites are built into a low cliff and incorporate the original riverine forest canopy, one suite hugs the water with a private deck extending over the river, and the Nuthouse breaks with Tongabezi tradition as it's entirely enclosed and also has an exclusive plunge pool. King size beds set into tree trunks and covered by curtains of linen netting, oversize sofas in the sitting areas, and large claw-foot bathtubs on the private decks are all unashamedly indulgent. Every room has a local guide who acts as a personal valet and caters to your every whim. Room service is ordered via antique telephone, and the lodge has an in-house holistic therapist. The lodge offers various meal options, including a romantic candlelit san pan (pontoon boat) floating on the Zambezi with waiters delivering each course by canoe, as well as a number of private decks and the

eclectic Lookout. **Pros:** Tongabezi is the original open-fronted lodge; the property is owner-run, so lots of thought goes into every aspect of your stay; management is extremely environmentally and community aware. **Cons:** the use of local materials for building and decoration might not meet the standard expectations of guests; individual itineraries are arranged for all guests, making it only possible to interact with other guests should they wish to—of course some might count this as a pro. ⊠ *About 19 km (12 mi) upstream from Victoria Falls, on Zambezi River* ☎ *213/32–7450 or 213/32–7468* ⊕ *www.tongabezi.com* ⬠ *5 suites, 6 cottages* ⟳ *In-room: safe, Wi-Fi in main areas. In-hotel: restaurant, room service, bar, laundry service, Internet terminal, Wi-Fi hotspot, parking (free), no kids under 7* ⊟ *MC, V* ⫯⃝ *AI.*

$$ 🏠 **Waterfront.** There's a hive of happy activity here ranging from opportunistic monkeys relieving unsuspecting tourists of their lunch to serious late-night boozing, and in between adventure enthusiasts (hangover optional) are being whisked off to do their thing at all hours of the day. Curiously, the spacious rooms where families can stay are reached only via a steep exterior wooden staircase, but this is also a popular spot for camping. The recent addition of a professional chef tasked with updating the general pubfare ($–$$) to a standard that will match the fabulous location is promising. **Pros:** great location right on the river with beautiful sunsets; many of the adventure activities in the area are managed from the Waterfront, so this is an excellent choice for travelers who like socializing and one-stop convenience. **Cons:** can be very noisy as it caters to campers; food can be inconsistent. ⊠ *Sichanga Rd., just off Mosi-oa-Tunya Rd., Livingstone* ☎ *213/32–0606* ⊕ *www.safpar.net* ⬠ *21 chalets, 24 adventure village tents, campsites accommodating 86 campers* ⟳ *In-room: no phone, no TV. In-hotel: restaurant, no room service, bar, 2 swimming pools, laundry service, Internet terminal, Wi-Fi hotspot, parking (free)* ⊟ *MC, V* ⫯⃝ *BP.*

ZAMBIAN SAFARI CIRCUIT

$$$ 🏠 **KaingU Safari Lodge.** KaingU Safari Lodge is a small camp comprised
↻ of a family house with two bedrooms and four classic en-suite safari tents. The tents are raised on rosewood decks to provide ideal views over the myriad channels and islands formed by the Kafue River. It's also very remote—situated in the southern reaches of the Kafue National Park. This combination of intimacy and seclusion lends an undeniable flavor of mystery and discovery to your stay. The thatched boma has a lounge, bar, and dining room, where the hosted dinner conversations cover all topics. Big game is not an everyday occurrence, but the lodge's guiding team is particularly fine-tuned to the many different wildlife stories constantly unfolding in the bush. Two activities are included every day, and the selection ranges from chilled-out river safaris to serious birding excursions. The natural splendor of deepest Zambia takes precedence—at this camp even the swimming pool is a wholly natural Jacuzzi in the rapids of the Kafue! From each nightly rate, $10 is paid into a registered Community and Conservation Trust. **Pros:** Africa untouched in all its glory; the owners have a true commitment to environmental and community development. **Cons:** transfers from Lusaka take 5–6 hours; the area does not have an abundance of big game. ⊠ *South Kafue, 400 km*

8

north of Victoria Falls ☎ 097/784–
1653 ⊕ *www.kaingu-lodge.com*
↝ *1 Family house, 4 luxury tents
under thatch* ⚒ *In-room: no phone,
no a/c, no TV. In-hotel: restaurant,
room service, bar, pool, children's
programs (ages 2–11), laundry
facilities, laundry service, Internet terminal, parking (free)* ▭ *No
credit cards* ⍾ *AI.*

\$\$\$\$
Fodor's Choice
★

"We went on the Zambezi Queen
for three nights end of December,
and it might very well be one of
the very best safaris and African
experiences I've ever had. They
offer wonderful excursions out
on small speed boats for game/
bird viewing, fishing, off to a restaurant; the food onboard is really
nice). We saw—some very close-
up—many animals in a way we've
never experienced before. Sitting
in a speed boat watching a herd
of elephants swimming past, protecting their little ones even under
water, trunks up as periscopes.
And the crocodiles, hippos, buffalos, and the abundance of birds.
it was awesome!" —LauraLS

🛏 **Old Mondoro Camp.** The legend
of a great white-maned lion that
used to call this area its home
lives on in the name of this camp,
which is Shona for the "king of
cats." If you're looking for an African adventure of the original epic
variety and love the opportunity
to take lots of pictures, then you
need to stay at Old Mondoro. The
gin-and-tonics are cold, and the
game-viewing sizzles with sightings
of wild-dog dens and leopards in
trees. Old Mondoro is decorated in old-school-safari style with canvas
bucket showers and hand basins all lit by romantic lanterns. Tents are
open (with canvas flaps at night) to maximize views of the surrounding
floodplains, woodlands, and complex maze of waterways and hippo
paths. The smell of fresh homemade bread introduces a back-to-basics
bushveld kitchen repertoire that includes generous portions of hearty,
flavorful meals. The entire experience manages to be marvelously satisfying without any fuss or complication. This is deliberately not a
supercharged, over-the-top new safari palace where the design of the
establishment completely usurps the natural environment and all local
flavors are lost. **Pros:** great game drives led by top-notch wildlife guides;
one of the few places to see wild dogs; best walking area in the Lower
Zambezi. **Cons:** the open rooms have only canvas flaps to ward off the
wild at night, and this might be too daring for some. ⊠ *Old Mondoro
is a 1-hr motorboat ride or a 2-hr game drive from Chiawa Camp. Jeki
Airstrip is only a 30-minute game drive away from Old Mondoro and
can be reached in a 2-hr flight from Livingstone or a 40-minute flight
from Lusaka* ☎ *211/261–588* ⊕ *www.oldmondoro.com* ↝ *4 tents* ⚒ *In-
room: no phone. In-hotel: restaurant, room service, bar, laundry service,
Internet terminal, parking (free), no kids under 12* ▭ *MC, V* ⊗ *Closed
Nov.–May 1* ⍾ *AI.*

\$\$\$\$
🛏 **Sausage Tree Camp.** There is no formal dress code, but this camp offers
the perfect backdrop for throwing practicality to the wind and dressing
up for dinner. All the hallmarks of the genuine safari experience including beautiful bush views, great creature sightings and dining alfresco by
lamplight are perfectly balanced by a splendidly chic minimalist design
that focuses on space and pure white fabrics. Sausage Tree Camp is a

very satisfying and perfectly decadent bush retreat. Sumptuous fabrics by night and lion from canoe by day. Simply bliss! △ **The closest airstrip is Jeki, and this is two hours from Livingstone and 40 minutes from Lusaka in a small aircraft. Sausage Tree Camp is a one-hour drive from Jeki.** **Pros:** gorgeous food and the services of a private *muchinda* (butler) to attend to every detail of your stay; the complimentary Mohini body-care products are infused with perfectly balanced Ayurvedic herbs. **Cons:** its remote location makes it very expensive and time-consuming to reach; if you don't like small aircraft transfers, avoid coming here. ⊠ *Lower Zambezi National Park* ☎ *211/84–5204* ⊕ *www.sausagetreecamp.com* ↝ *5 tents, 3 suites* ⚭ *In-room: no phone, refrigerator (some). In-hotel: restaurant, room service, bar, pool, laundry service, Internet terminal, parking (free), no kids under 8* ▤ *MC, V* ☉ *Closed Nov. 15–Mar.* ⅋ *AI.*

SPORTS AND THE OUTDOORS

Livingstone can compete with the best as far as indulging the wildest fantasies of adrenaline junkies and outdoor enthusiasts goes. You can reserve activities directly with the operators, let your hotel or lodge handle it, or book through a central booking agent. **Safari Par Excellence** (☎ *213/32–1629* ⊕ *www.safpar.net*) offers elephant-back safaris, game drives, river cruises, canoeing, and rafting as well as trip combinations, which are a good option if your time is limited or you just want to go wild. Discounted prices for combinations are available.

BOATING

Truly the monarch of the river, the **African Queen** (☎ *213/32–0058* ✍ *reservations@livingstonesadventure.com*) —no relation to the movie—is an elegant colonial-style riverboat. Sunset cruises offer the maximum style and splendor. Costs start at US$55 for a 90-minute sunset cruise.

BUNGEE JUMPING

Bungee jumping off the 346-foot-high Victoria Falls Bridge with **Zambezi Adrenaline Company** (☎ *213/32–4231* ✍ *bungi@zamnet.zm*) is a major adrenaline rush, with 65 feet and three seconds of free fall and a pretty spectacular view. The jump costs from US$115, but it's also worth getting the photo and video (US$50), complete with *Top Gun* music track.

CANOEING

A gentle canoeing trip on the upper Zambezi is a great opportunity to see birds and a variety of game. Many of the lodges upriver have canoeing as an inclusive activity, but trips are also run by a number of companies, which are all reputable. **Bundu Adventures** (☎ *213/32–4407* ⊕ *www.bunduadventures.com*) offers custom-made canoe trips that range from half-day outings to multiday excursions, with costs starting at US$100.

ELEPHANT-BACK RIDING

♻ **Elephant-Back Safaris.** Fancy the idea of meandering through the bush along the shores of the Zambezi courtesy of your own ellie? Very lucky clients might even have the opportunity to ride through the river! Not only does this operation keep clients happy enough to forget their sore thighs the next day, it also has the elephants happy enough to keep

8

having babies! Trips with **Safari Par Excellence** (☏ *213/32–1629* ⊕ *www.safpar.net*) cost US$160 for a ride.

FLYING

Batoka Sky (☏ *213/32–0058* ⊕ *www.livingstonesadventure.com*) offers weight-shift Aerotrike twin-axis microlighting (flying jargon for what resembles a motorized hang glider) and helicopter flights over

the Falls and through the gorges. There's a minimum of two passengers for helicopters. You are issued a flight suit (padded in winter) and a helmet with a headset, before you board the microlight, but you may not bring a camera for safety reasons. Batoka Sky has been operating since 1992, and has a 100% microlighting safety record. Flights are booked for early morning and late afternoon and are dependent on the weather. Prices are US$120–US$260, depending on length of flight and aircraft. Your transfer and a day visa, if you are coming from Victoria Falls, are included. The Helicopter Gorge picnic (US$365) includes lunch and drinks for a minimum of six people.

HORSEBACK RIDING

You can take a placid horseback ride through the bush along the banks of the Zambezi with **Chundukwa Adventure Trails** (☏ *213/32–7452* ✉ *chundukwa@zamnet.zm*). If you are comfortable enough to keep your cool while riding through the African hinterland, you may want to book a horseback bush trail. Cost is U$55 for 1½ hours; US$95 for a half day (8 AM–noon).

JETBOATING

♻ If you want some thrills and speed but rafting seems a bit daunting, or you can't face the walk in and out, you'll probably enjoy jetboating with **Jet Extreme** (☏ *213/32–0058* ⊕ *www.livingstonesadventure.com*). A new cable-car ride, included in the cost of the jetboat ride (US$95 for 30 minutes), means no more strenuous walking out of the gorge. Jetboating can be combined with a rafting excursion, as the jetboat starts at the end of the rafting run, or with a helicopter trip out of the gorge. ■TIP➔ The rafting and helicopter must be booked separately, although big operators like Safari Par Excellence and Livingstone's Adventure offer combinations. Children over seven can jetboat if they are accompanied by an adult.

RAPPELLING AND SWINGING

For something completely different, **Abseil Zambia** (☏ *213/32–1188* ✉ *theswing@zamnet.zm*) has taken some specially designed heavy-duty steel cables, combined them with various pulleys and rigs, one dry gorge, and a 100% safety record to entertain both the fainthearted and the daring. The full day (US$85) is a great value, as it includes lunch, refreshments, and as many repeats of the activities as you like. ⚠ Keep in mind that you will have to climb out after the gorge swing and the rappel. A half day (US$75) is advised during the hot months of October–December. Work up an appetite for more daring drops by starting

Continued on page 520

The first European to set eyes on the Falls was the explorer and missionary Dr. David Livingstone in the mid-1850s. Overcome by the experience he named them after the English queen, Victoria.

VICTORIA FALLS

Expect to be humbled by the sheer power and majesty. Expect to be deafened by the thunderous noise, drenched by spray, and overwhelmed at the sight. Expect the mighty swath of roaring, foaming Victoria Falls—spanning the entire 1-mile width of the Zambezi River—to leave you speechless.

On a clear day the spray generated by the Falls is visible from 31 mi (50 km) away—the swirling mist rising above the woodland savanna looks like smoke from a bush fire inspiring their local name, Mosi-Oa-Tunya, or the "Smoke that Thunders." The rim of the Falls is broken into separate smaller falls with names like the Devil's Cataract, Rainbow Falls, Horseshoe Falls, and Armchair Falls.

The Falls, which are more than 300 feet high, are one of the world's seven natural wonders and were named a UNESCO World Heritage Site in 1989. Upon seeing Victoria Falls for the first time Dr. David Livingstone proclaimed, "Scenes so lovely must have been gazed upon by angels in their flight." Truer words were never spoken.

updated by
Sanja Cloete-Jones

WATCH OUT

Unlike other great waterfalls, the Zambezi has no rapids to warn of the approaching drop. One moment you'll be in calm placid waters; the next you'll be hurtling over the edge.

FALLS FACTS

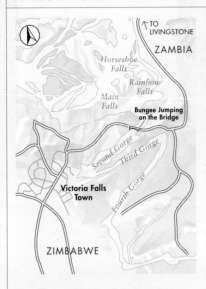

FORMATION OF THE FALLS

A basaltic plateau once stood where the Falls are today. The whole area was once completely submerged, but fast-forward to the Jurassic Age and the water eventually dried up. Only the Zambezi River remained flowing down into the gaping 1-mile-long continuous gorge that was formed by the uneven cracking of the drying plateau. The river charges through the ancient gorges creating some of the world's best commercial white water rapids.

WHEN TO GO

The Falls are spectacular at any time, but if you want to see them full, visit during the high water season (April–June) when more than 2 million gallons hurtle over the edge every second. The resulting spray is so dense that, at times, the view can be obscured. Don't worry though, the frequent gusts of wind will soon come to your aid and your view will be restored. If you're lucky to be there during a full moon, you might be able to catch a moonbow or lunar rainbow (a nighttime version of a rainbow) in the spray. The rest of the year offers its own charms with dry season only activities like visiting Livingstone's Island, swimming in the Devil's Pool, and walking along the bottom of the Falls.

TO ZIM OR TO ZAM

Honestly? BOTH sides are great, but if you have to choose one, take the following into consideration: The Zambian side has more than four times the physical Falls frontage of Zimbabwe, but you're mostly looking across the gorge which means that Zimbabwe offers four times the visual display. Zimbabwe definitely has the most spray, the most rainbows, the best flat stone pathways for easy access, and the only views of the incredible Devil's Cataract. Rain forests with exotic flowers can be enjoyed on the Zimbabwe side year round and on the Zambian side during high water. Adventure seekers will love the Zam side's steep steps, the trail into the Boiling Pot, the slick Knife Edge bridge, and, during low water season visits to Livingstone Island, swimming in the Devil's Pool.

CROSSING THE FALLS

Built in 1905, Victoria Falls Bridge is one of the few useful remnants of the Colonial era. An important link in former South African Prime Minister Cecil John Rhodes's dream of creating the Cape-to-Cairo railway—it was never finished—the bridge continues to provide a convenient link between Zimbabwe and Zambia. It also offers a knockout view of the Falls and the Zambezi River raging through the Gorge, plus the added bonus of watching adrenaline junkies taking the 364-foot bungee plunge.

EXTREME SPORTS

Bungee jumping off Victoria Falls Bridge above the Zambezi River

Victoria Falls is renowned for the excess of adventure activities that can be organized on either side. It's best to arrange activities through your hotel, or a safari adventure shop, but if you want to go it alone, know that some operators only serve one side of the Falls and operators have a tendency to come and go quickly.

■ Bungee jumping with **Zambezi Adrenaline Company** (☎ 213/32-4231 ✉ bungi@zamnet.zm) is a major adrenaline rush, with 65 feet and three seconds of free fall and a pretty spectacular view. The jump costs from US$115, but it's also worth getting the photo and video (US$50), complete with the *Top Gun* music soundtrack.

■ If you fancy an elephant-back safari on your own elephant for a couple of hours in the morning or evening then **Safari Par Excellence** (☎ 213/32-1629 ⊕ www.safpar.com) will take you over the Falls on board.

■ **Batoka Sky** (☎ 213/32-0058 ⊕ www.livingstones adventure.com) will put you in a helicopter or microlight plane.

■ If you want some thrills and speed but rafting seems a bit daunting, go jetboating with **Jet Extreme** (☎ 213/32-0058 ⊕ www.livingstoneadventure.com). A cable-car ride, included in the cost of the jetboat ride, will save strenuous walking out of the gorge.

■ The easiest way to organize combinations that will satisfy your every adventure whim must be through **Jollyboys** (☎ 213/32-4229 ⊕ www.backpackzambia.com) on the Zambian side and **Backpackers Bazaar** (☎ 13/4-2208 ⊕ www.zimtravelagent.com) in Zimbabwe. Both offer a wealth of knowledge, insiders tips, and can work out an itinerary that will suit your budget and satisfy your thirst for adventure. Activities included kayaking, rappelling, gorge swinging, and of course, white water rafting. The Zambezi River offers the world's very best rapids rated from Class 6 (which is not commercially operated) and down.

on the zip line (or flying fox). You run off a ramp while attached to the line, and the sensation is pure freedom and surprisingly unscary, as you are not moving up or down. Next rappel down into the 175-foot gorge, and, after you climb out, try it again facing forward. It's called a rap run. You're literally walking down the cliff face. End the day with the king of adrenaline activities, a whopping 175-foot,

3½-second vertical free-fall swing into the gorge (US$55 for one swing). Three-two-one—hoooo-ha!

RAFTING AND RIVERBOARDING

Safari Par Excellence (☎ *213/32–1629* ⊕ *www.safpar.net*) offers rafting excursions to Batoka Gorge that cost US$120 for a morning trip or US$145 for a full-day trip. The cable car transports rafters out of the gorge, so you only have to climb down. You can also do a combination helicopter-and-rafting trip. Bring secure shoes, dry clothes for the long drive home, a baseball cap to wear under your helmet, and plenty of sunscreen. You can also decide to try riverboarding (from US$155), in which you hop off the raft onto a body board and surf suitable rapids.

SHOPPING

Kubu Crafts (✉ *133 Mosi-oa-Tunya Rd.* ☎ *213/32–0320* ⊕ *www. kubucrafts.com*), a stylish home-decor shop, features locally made furniture in hardwood and wrought iron. There's also a selection of West African masks and weavings and the work of numerous local artists, including prints of the late Stephen Kapata's fantastic oil paintings. Local curios are attractively displayed and screened for quality. Kubu Crafts also provides both fair employment and training opportunities for the community.

Although the park at the entrance to the Falls has stalls where you can find stone and wood carvings and simple bead and semiprecious-stone jewelry, the real gem of an African bazaar lies in the center of town, at **Mukuni Park Market** (✉ *Mosi-oa-Tunya Rd. and Libala Dr.* ☎ *No phone*). ■ TIP→ This is the place to try your hand at bargaining. You'll be quoted top dollar initially, but shop around and watch the prices drop to roughly one-third of the original quote. Look out for individual and unusual pieces, as it is occasionally possible to find valuable antiques. The market is open daily approximately 7–6.

VICTORIA FALLS, ZIMBABWE

Victoria Falls started with a little curio shop and slowly expanded until the 1970s, when it became the mecca around which the tourist phenomenon of Victoria Falls pivoted. The political problems following independence have been well documented in the world press and certainly took their toll.

There has been significant poaching in Zambezi National Park to the northwest. (If you really want to have the African game experience, take a day trip to Chobe National Park, only 70 km [44 mi] away in Botswana.) The country is currently regaining political stability, and the town of Victoria Falls enjoys the happy coincidence of being a curio shopper's paradise inside a national park. This means you can literally buy an elephant carving while watching the real McCoy march past the shop window. The town is extremely compact. Almost all the hotels are within walking distance, and the Falls themselves are only 10 minutes away on foot. The main road that runs through town and goes to the Falls in one direction and to the airport in the other is called Livingstone Way. Park Way is perpendicular. Most of the shops, banks, and booking agents can be found on these two streets, and this part of town is also where most of the hawkers operate. ■TIP➔ **Give these vendors a clear berth, as their wares are cheap for a reason (the boat cruise is substandard, it's illegal to change money, etc.).**

GETTING HERE AND AROUND

Tourists are slowly returning to Victoria Falls. If you choose to fly in and out of Victoria Falls Airport, most hotels will provide free shuttle service; book in advance.

Hotels can summon reputable taxis quickly and advise you on the cost. Tipping is not mandatory, but change is always appreciated.

8

FAST FACTS

Size 390,757 square km (150,872 square mi).

Number of National Parks 10. Hwange National Park; Victoria Falls National Park.

Population 11.6 million.

Big Five The gang's all here.

Language Zimbabwe has three official languages; English, ChiShona, and SiNdebele. Although the number of native English speakers is small, it is widely understood and used.

Time Zimbabwe is on CAST (Central African standard time), which is two hours ahead of Greenwich Mean Time and seven hours ahead of North American Eastern Standard Time; it's the same as South Africa.

MONEY MATTERS

Zimbabwe's currency used to be the Zimbabwe dollar, but now foreign currency is the only acceptable method of payment. Carry U.S. dollars in small denominations and stick to U.S. dollars for all activity payments to both the Zimbabwean- and the Zambian-based operators (all activities are quoted in U.S. dollars). Credit card facilities are not readily available and MasterCard can only be used across the border in Zambia.

SAFETY AND PRECAUTIONS

The political situation in Zimbabwe is currently fairly stable, but the damage from the lengthy dictatorship and internal strife is still very apparent. Prices have stabilized and the basic goods have reappeared on the shelves, but the tourist capital of Victoria Falls has by no means regained its status as a prime international destination. All the activities, shopping, and dining options on offer on the Zimbabwean side can also be enjoyed across the border in Zambia—without any of the uncertainty and potential for sudden political and economical upheavals that could result in cancellations, substandard service, or threats to visitors' safety. ■ TIP→ Until the rule in Zimbabwe has proven itself completely stable and the industry on the road to recovery, we recommend concentrating on Zambia and only venturing into Zimbabwe with reputable Zambian tour operators.

MARS (Medical Air Rescue Services) is on standby for all emergencies. Dr. Nyoni is a trauma specialist and operates a hospital opposite the Shoestring Lodge. Go to Victoria Falls Pharmacy for prescriptions.

Male homosexuality is illegal in Zimbabwe—female homosexuality is not mentioned in law—and same-sex relationships receive no recognition. Attitudes are improving, but it's advisable to be extremely circumspect.

Beware of street vendors. They'll try to rip you off in ways that will make the crime channel seem naive.

TELEPHONE

The country code for Zimbabwe is 263. When dialing from abroad, drop the initial 0 from local area codes. Ask a hotel or restaurant manager for exact telephone numbers and costs, should you wish to make any telephone calls from within Zimbabwe.

VISITOR INFORMATION

In Zimbabwe, the Victoria Falls Publicity Association is fairly well stocked with brochures. Its open weekdays 8–1 and 2–4 and Saturday 8–1. You could also choose to seek advice from one of the many safari companies in town.

ESSENTIALS

Airlines Air Zimbabwe (☎ *013/4–4316* ⊕ *www.airzimbabwe.aero*). **Comair-British Airways** (☎ *013/4–2053 or 013/4–2388* ⊕ *www.british-airways.com*). **South African Airways** (☎ *04/738–922* ⊕ *www.flysaa.com*).

Airport Victoria Falls Airport (✉ *Livingstone Way* ☎ *013/4–4250*).

Embassies U.S. Embassy (✉ *172 Herbert Chitepo Ave., Box 4010, Harare* ☎ *04/25–0593* ⊕ *harare.usembassy.gov*).

Emergency Services Police (☎ *013/4–4206 or 013/4–4681*). **MARS** (✉ *West Dr., opposite Shoestring* ☎ *013/4–4646*).

Visitor Info Victoria Falls Publicity Association (✉ *412 Park Way* ☎ *013/44–202* ✍ *vfpa@mweb.co.zw*).

EXPLORING

Ⓒ **Victoria Falls Bridge.** A veritable monument to Cecil Rhodes's dream of completing a Cape-to-Cairo rail line, this graceful structure spans the gorge formed by the Zambezi River. It would have been far easier and less expensive to build the bridge upstream from the Falls, but Rhodes was captivated by the romance of a railway bridge passing over this natural wonder. A net was stretched across the gorge under the construction site, which curiously prompted the construction workers to go on strike for a couple of days. They resumed work only when it was explained that they would not be expected to leap into it at the end of every workday. Although the workers did not share the current adrenaline-fueled obsession with jumping into the abyss, the net probably had a lot to do with the miraculous fact that only two people were killed during construction. The bridge was completed in only 14 months, and the last two cross-girders were defiantly joined on April 1, 1905.

To get onto the bridge, you first have to pass through Zimbabwean immigration and customs controls, so bring your passport. Unless you decide to cross into Zambia, no visa is necessary.

Depending on crowds, the simple procedure can take from five minutes to a half hour. The border posts are open daily from 6 AM to 10 PM, after which the bridge is closed to all traffic. From the bridge you are treated to a fabulous view of the river raging through Batoka Gorge, as well as a section of the Falls on the Zambian side. An added bonus is watching the bungee jumpers disappear over the edge. ✉ *Livingstone Way.*

8

Zimbabwe's Tribes

NDEBELE

The Ndebele people (called Matabele by the British who could not pronounce Ndebele) are distant cousins of the Zulu. A tribe of warriors, their history is filled with intrigue, betrayal, victories, and forced resettlements. They battled the Shona for a territory now known as Matabeleland which makes up the west and southwest region of modern-day Zimbabwe.

Ndebele women are known for their colorful beaded dress in striking geometric patterns and contrasting colors. Beaded ornamentation on female Ndebele symbolizes their status in society; the older a woman gets, the more ornamentation she wears. The Isingolwani, a colorful necklace made of grass and cotton, is the typical ornamentation of married women and has been incorporated into Western designs. The Ndebele have struggled to keep their heritage alive. They live in wards, with the chief, or *ikozi*, holding authority over each ward. Extended families make up the *umuzi*, or residential unit. Initiation into adulthood for Ndebele women entails being secluded in the home and taught to be a homemaker. This is followed by a coming-out ceremony where the woman displays herself wearing traditional dress. Once initiation is completed an Ndebele woman is considered eligible for marriage.

SHANGAAN

The original Shangaan people took their name from the Zulu warrior Soshangane. A large empire known as the Gaza stretched throughout Zimbabwe and Mozambique and incorporated some of the conquered Tsonga people. Although about 6 million Shangaan people can be found in various regions across Southern Africa, a large concentration reside in east-southern Zimbabwe. They live in rondavels and are a largely agricultural society. Shangaan society is patrilineal, with many men taking more than one wife, and the extended family living together. When minerals were discovered in Southern Africa, many Shangaan became laborers in the diamond and gold mines. This shift has caused the rural traditions of the tribe to fade somewhat. With the introduction of Christianity to Africa, many Shangaan converted, though some still practice the animist worship of their ancestors. This can involve the practice of animal sacrifice or ritual offerings, especially in rural settlements. There are as many as five variants of the language of the Shangaan, called Xichangana.

☺ **Victoria Falls National Park.** Plan to spend at least two hours soaking in the splendors of this park. Bring snacks and water, and supervise children extremely well, as the barriers are by no means safe. Babies and toddlers can be pushed in a stroller. If you visit the Falls during

the high-water peak, between April and June, you'd do well to carry a raincoat or umbrella (you can rent them at the entrance) and to bring along a waterproof, disposable camera because you *will* be drenched in the spray from the Falls, which creates a permanent downpour. Be prepared for limited photo opportunities due to the mist. ■TIP→ Leave expensive cameras, cell phones, and wristwatches in your hotel or lodge safe.

The constant drizzle has created a small rain forest that extends in a narrow band along the edge of the Falls. A trail running through this dripping green world is overgrown with African ebony, Cape fig, Natal mahogany, wild date palms, ferns, and deep red flame lilies. A fence has been erected to keep non-fee-paying visitors at bay. Clearly signposted side trails lead to viewpoints overlooking the Falls. The most spectacular is **Danger Point,** a perilous rock outcropping that overlooks the narrow gorge through which the Zambezi River funnels out of the **Boiling Pot,** but be careful, as this viewpoint is hazardously wet and precarious. In low-water months (September–November) most of the water goes over the Falls through the **Devil's Cataract,** a narrow and mesmerizingly powerful section of the Falls visible from **Livingstone's statue.** Around the full moon the park stays open late so you can see the lunar rainbow formed by the spray—a hauntingly beautiful sight. Early morning and late afternoon are popular visiting times, as you can see the daylight rainbows most vividly then. A booklet explaining the formation and layout of the Falls is available from the Victoria Falls Publicity Association for a small fee. ⊠ *Off Livingstone Way* ☎ *No phone* 🖃 *US$30* ☺ *Daily 6–6; open later around full moon.*

WHERE TO STAY

It's important to know that the current political climate is causing prices to constantly rise. Getting an all-inclusive package tour is by far the best bet in this area. Electricity and voltage are the same in Zimbabwe and South Africa.

$$$ 🛏 **Ilala Lodge.** The lodge's elegant interior design is tempered with thatch
☺ roofs, giving it a graceful African look. Dining outside under the night
★ sky at the Palm Restaurant ($$$), with the Falls thundering 300 feet away, is a particularly enticing way to while away a Zimbabwean evening. The Palm also serves a great terrace lunch overlooking the bush. Guest rooms are hung with African paintings and tapestries and filled with delicately caned chairs and tables and with dressers made from old railroad sleepers. French doors open onto a narrow strip of lawn backed by thick bush. Unlike most hotels in town, Ilala Lodge has no fence around it, so at night it's not uncommon to find elephants browsing

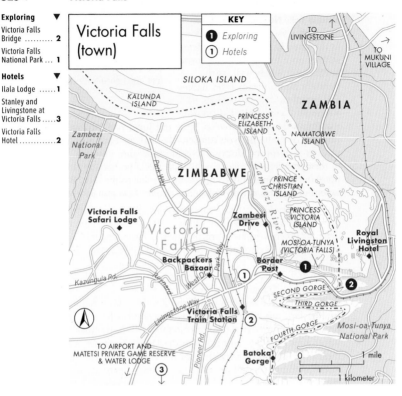

Victoria Falls
(town)

KEY
❶ Exploring
① Hotels

outside your window or buffalo grazing on the lawn. **Pros:** great central location; family-friendly; only 10 minutes from the Falls by foot. **Cons:** the location in the center of town can ruin expectations if you are keen on the peace of the African bush; the noise from the helicopters and microlights can be disturbing. ⊠ *411 Livingstone Way* ☎ *013/4–4737* ⊕ *www.ilalalodge.com* ⌁ *32 rooms, 2 suites* ⌂ *In-room: safe, TV, Internet (some), Wi-Fi (some). In-hotel: restaurant, room service, bar, pool, laundry service, Wi-Fi hotspot, some pets allowed* ▭ *V* ⦿ *BP.*

$$$$

Fodor'sChoice
★

🏨 **Stanley and Livingstone at Victoria Falls.** It's almost surreal to step from the surrounding bushveld into the meticulously composed rooms of this small hotel, which is set on a 6,000-acre private game reserve. Public rooms are luxuriously furnished in colonial style with some spectacular antiques and have verandas overlooking a water hole where elephants and other animals come to drink. The suites are large with Victorian flourishes, dark wood furnishings, wall-to-wall carpeting, heavy drapes, and an expensive chocolate on your pillow at night. The bathrooms are a calming study in white tile, green marble, and gold trim. Service is personal but slightly more casual than the decor would lead you to expect. The rate includes game drives and all on-site activities except elephant rides and transfers to the airport or to town. **Pros:** rooms have air-conditioning; 10 minutes outside town; unbelievably over-the-top and decadently indulgent decor. **Cons:** the design of this lodge owes very little to Africa, and once you close your door you could very well be almost anywhere in Europe; you might find yourself wanting to use words like "mahvelous" a lot! ✛ *Off Ursula Rd., 13 km (8 mi) south of Victoria Falls town* ☎ *013/4–1003* ⊕ *www. stanleyandlivingstone.com* ⇨ *16 suites* ⅋ *In-room: phone, safe, refrigerator, DVD. In-hotel: restaurant, room service, bar, pool, laundry service, no kids under 12* ▭ *MC, V* ⓧ *AI.*

$$$ 🛏 **Victoria Falls Hotel.** Hotels come and go, but this landmark built in 1904 has retained its former glory as a distant, stylish outpost in empire days, while pandering to today's modern tastes, needs, and wants. Such grandeur can be a little overwhelming, and especially surprising if you've just been on safari. The hotel's manicured lawns are perched on the Falls' edge, with a view of the bridge, and soothing sounds permeate the gardens (and the rooms if you leave the windows open). Cool cream walls form the backdrop for elegant mahogany and wicker furniture. In the bathroom an old-fashioned drench shower will wash away the most stubborn African dust. Halls are filled with sepia-tone photos from throughout the hotel's history and animal trophies so old they are going bald. After checking your e-mail in the E-Lounge and visiting the salon, you can dine and dance at the elegant Livingstone Room ($$$$). Two far less formal restaurants include the Terrace ($–$$), with an à la carte menu, daily high tea, and a beautiful view of the bridge; and Jungle Junction (US$30), which has a huge barbecue buffet and traditional dancers. **Pros:** one of the very best views of the Falls—it does not come closer than this! **Cons:** hotel is slightly run down following the Zimbabwean political crises. ✉ *2 Mallet Dr.* ☎ *013/4–4751* ⊕ *www. africansunhotels.com* ⇨ *161 rooms* ⅋ *In-room: phone, a/c, safe, no TV, Wi-Fi. In-hotel: 3 restaurants, room service, 2 bar, 2 tennis courts, pool, spa, laundry service, Internet terminal, Wi-Fi hotspot, parking (free)* ▭ *V* ⓧ *BP.*

8

The Seychelles

9

WELCOME TO THE SEYCHELLES

TOP REASONS TO GO

★ **Splashing in Solitude:** Home to the world's most beautiful (and empty) beaches, Seychelles' tropical waters are one big playground for snorkeling, diving, fishing, and kayaking.

★ **Unspoiled Nature:** Jungle-clad granite islands have become seabird sanctuaries, where the abundance of winged creatures will blow your mind and you can look a giant tortoise in the eye.

★ **Island Hopping:** From "busy" Mahé to the empty beaches of coralline Denis to the über-luxury of private-island resorts to the entirely undeveloped nature sanctuary of Aldabra—every island offers something different and unforgettable.

★ **Creole Culture:** Old French Victorian mansions, colorful gardens, a cuisine that blends Indian, French, and Southeast Asian influences—the friendly Seychellois culture is a lovely and unique melting pot.

1 **Mahé.** Home to the International Airport, the capital of Victoria, and by far the largest (in population and size) and most developed island, "busy" Mahé is still slow paced and charming by almost any definition. Mahé's size means dramatic views of forest-cloaked granite cliffs, and numerous empty bays and beaches. Many fine restaurants have emerged, mostly along popular Beau Vallon, which is the only place in Seychelles where motorized water sports are allowed.

2 **Praslin.** Seychelles' second largest island, Praslin is much quieter than Mahé, with accommodation tending toward smaller and often homier resorts and guest houses. Home to the Vallée de Mai, the World Heritage site protecting the famous Coco de Mer palm, Praslin also is a stepping-off point for numerous day-trips to other smaller islands.

North I.

Labriz
Silhouette

INNER ISLANDS

Ste. Anne

Round I.

VICTORIA ✪

Cerf

1

Mahé

Seychelles
Bank

Aride

Curieuse

Cousin

Round I.

Cousine

Praslin

La Digue

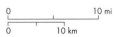

3 La Digue. This tiny charmer takes one back in time. With almost no motor traffic, everyone on La Digue gets around on foot or bicycle, which is the perfect way to take in the lovely old Creole-French homes, and gorgeous wild beaches, including the famous Anse Source d'Argent. For those seeking an unpretentious, laid-back beach lifestyle, this is your island.

Frégate

GETTING ORIENTED

The three most popular islands in the Seychelles archipelago are Mahé, Praslin, and La Digue. Home to 98% of the Seychelles' population, these three are clustered in Seychelle's northeast area known as the Inner Island group. Mahé and Praslin are Seychelles' largest islands (nearby Silhouette Island is larger than La Digue, but less populated), and all three are granitic (versus coral). The Inner Islands also include other popular islands to visit, such as Denis, Bird, Silhouette, and North. Southwest of the Inner Islands lie the other island groups: Amirantes, Alphonse, Farquhar, and Aldabra. Barring a handful of private-island resorts, these islands are mostly uninhabited and accessible only by boat.

9

```
0 _____ 10 mi
0 _____ 10 km
```

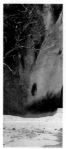

By Lee Middleton

Unique. A word overused in tourism, but one that truly describes the Seychelles. One hundred and fifteen coral and granite islands rising from the Indian Ocean, this pristine hideaway of white-sand beaches, majestic granite cliffs, palm-fringed jungles, and astonishing azure waters is a mostly uninhabited paradise. Trading in exclusivity, luxury, and undeveloped natural environments, the Seychelles is an ideal beach escape for those who can afford all that gorgeous privacy.

With its countless perfect beaches and secluded coves fringed by sea-sculpted granite boulders, the Seychelles is a favored backdrop for fashion shoots and once-in-a-lifetime dream vacations. It has earned its reputation as an exclusive and costly destination, but in recent years, numerous locally owned guesthouses and two- and three-star hotels have opened their doors, making these islands more accessible. However, if ultraluxurious pampering, breathtaking style, and total privacy on some of the world's most stunning beaches are what you seek, Seychelles has them in spades, but not on a budget.

Beyond the luxury resorts—and really the basis for their existence—the Seychelles claims some of the world's best-preserved tropical habitats. Originally a huge granite shard attached to India's west coast, some event—probably a volcanic eruption or meteor impact—caused what would become the Seychelles to break free and begin its northward drift. Over time, that single mass became a shimmering line of islands, transformed by their isolation, 1,600 km (994 mi) from mainland Africa in the middle of the Indian Ocean.

Known as the Galápagos of the Indian Ocean, most of the islands were never settled by people (though many served as notorious pirate hideouts), and thus remain as nature intended, with important populations of rare plants, birds, and animals, including the heartbreakingly beautiful ferry tern, the gentle giant tortoise, and the bizarrely suggestive Coco de Mer—once thought to be the fruit of the Tree of Knowledge. On the islands where human-introduced predators like cats and rats have been removed, astonishing populations of seabirds thrive, allowing visitors a view onto what the first explorers might have seen.

Those first explorers were probably seafarers hailing from Austronesia, followed by Arab traders. The first European to pass through was Portuguese Admiral Vasco da Gama in 1502, followed by the English in 1609. A transit point for trade between Africa and Asia, the islands were used by pirates until 1756, when the French took control, laying down their "Stone of Possession" (visible today at the museum in Mahé) and naming the islands after Jean Moreau de Séchelles. Britain and France fought over the islands through the late 18th to early 19th centuries, with Britain finally gaining control in 1814. Achieving independence from Britain in 1976, the Seychelles today is a true success story of people who claim origins from all over the world and live together with an unusual and inspiring degree of harmony in diversity.

PLANNING

WHEN TO GO

Seychelles has two seasons: the cool southeast monsoon (May–September), and the hot northwest monsoon (October–April). During the cool season, breezes prevail, skies can be partly cloudy, temperatures are lower, and the sea less than perfect for diving and snorkeling. The hot northwest monsoon brings crystalline waters, incredible heat, and occasional but serious rainstorms, interspersed with perfect blue skies. The cusp months of November and April are optimal, with the best of both on offer. The super busy (and far more expensive) high seasons fall from July to August, and Christmas to New Year's.

GETTING HERE AND AROUND

AIR TRAVEL

The International Airport is located on Mahé, 8 km (5 mi) south of Victoria. If you're coming from safari, you can catch flights departing from both Nairobi and Johannesburg twice a week (Kenya Airways, Air Seychelles, and Emirates operated). If you're coming directly to the Seychelles from the U.S., it's often cheapest (and necessary) to route through Europe; look for cheaper airfares direct from Rome, London, and Paris. Airlines with international routes include Air Seychelles, Emirates, Qatar, and Air France. Many cheaper fares route through Dubai or Abu Dabi.

The domestic terminal at Mahé will handle departures for all flights within Seychelles—i.e., the almost hourly 15-minute flight (€73 one-way) to Praslin—and any of the other private islands (there is no airport on La Digue). Domestic flights are handled by Air Seychelles and the Island Development Company (the latter handles the outer islands and Desroches Island). Luggage limits are 20kg (44 lbs). Many private islands use the privately chartered Helicopter Seychelles, a service that links any of the islands with a helipad.

Contacts Air France (☎ 322–414, 800/237–2747 in the U.S. ⊕ www. airfrance.com). **Air Seychelles** (☎ 381–000, 800/677–4277 in the U.S. ⊕ www.airseychelles.com). **Emirates** (☎ 292–799, 800/777–3999 in the U.S. ⊕ www.emirates.com). **Helicopter Seychelles** (☎ 385–858 ⊕ www. helicopterseychelles.com). **Island Development Company** (☎ 224–640 ✎ idc@seychelles.sc). **Kenya Airways** (☎ 322–989, 866/536–9224 in the U.S. ⊕ www.kenya-airways.com). **Qatar** (☎ 224–518, 877/777–2827 in the U.S. ⊕ www.qatarairways.com).

BOAT AND FERRY TRAVEL

Travel by boat between Mahé, Praslin, and La Digue is easy and relatively cheap. The Cat Coco ferry connects Mahé and Praslin, and takes about the same time as the flight (factoring in the need to arrive 45 minutes before a flight). About 50 minutes one-way, the ferry runs three times a day (only twice on Sundays), for €40 one-way (€45 in the upper air-con lounge). Children under 12 pay half. Book through the ferry or a travel agent at least a day in advance during high season. Free shuttles to and from the airport are sometimes available.

To get to La Digue, take the Inter-Island Ferry from Praslin. Seven departures daily in each direction run from about 7 AM to 5 PM and take about 30 minutes (€10). The ride can be a bit bumpy during the southeast monsoon. Children under 8 travel for €5. Book ahead through your hotel or tour operator. Cat Coco will soon run ferries from Mahé direct to La Digue.

Contacts Cat Cocos Catamaran (☎ 324–843 or 324–844 ⊕ www.catcocos. com). **Inter-Island Ferry Co** (☎ 232–329 ⊕ www.seychelles.net/iif).

BUS TRAVEL

The bus system in Mahé and Praslin is surprisingly good and cheap, saving you from needing to rent a car if you don't mind the usual vagaries of public transport. Destinations and routes are usually marked on the front of the bus (always double check with the driver). There is a flat fee of Rs5 for any ride. Bus stops are painted on the road in places with no shoulder, or indicated by signs and small shelters. You can call the Seychelles Public Transport Corporation (SPTC) hotline to get the Mahé route and schedule information Monday to Friday from 8 to 4, and the Seychelles Tourism Board's head office also provides copies of the maps and schedule for Mahé.

On La Digue, most people get around by bicycle. See La Digue section for contacts.

Contacts Seychelles Taxi Operators (✉ Mahé ☎ 323–895 ✎ taxi@seychelles. net). **Seychelles Public Transport Corporation** (☎ 325–252 hotline, 280–227 head office ⊕ www.sptc.sc).

CAR TRAVEL

Having your own car is the only way to fully explore all of Mahé's charms. Even if most of your holiday will be spent lazing on beaches and enjoying your resort's offerings, at least a day exploring this beautiful island—particularly the far southern reaches—is highly worthwhile. Though the paved roads are good, the combination of left-hand driving, numerous tourists in rental cars, and Mahé's frequently steep roads with hairpin bends and no shoulder (the road literally drops off into ditches) can be nerve-wracking. The main rule of the road: drive slowly. On Praslin a car could also be handy, though the frequent shuttle services offered by many resorts to the islands' other "main" beaches and a decent public bus service (also present on Mahé) renders the need for your own wheels less keen. None of the other islands offer car rentals. Numerous car rental agencies are located both at the international terminal of the airport, as well as at points around the island. Most agencies can arrange delivery/drop-off at your hotel or the jetties for a small fee. Prices are fairly standard: the cheapest you're likely to find on Mahé is about €50 a day for a hatchback, and about €10–€15 more per day in Praslin. You can book at the airport, through a tour operator, or from your hotel. Most companies will accept your national license.

Contacts Aventure (⊠ Amitié, Praslin ☎ 233–805 ⬧ resa@aventure-carhire. com). **Avis** (Seychelles International Airport, Victoria ☎ 224–511 or 514–512 ⊕ www.avis.com.sc). **Capricorn Car Rental** (⊠ Bay St. Anne, Praslin ☎ 581–110 ⬧ capcorn@seychelles.net). **Hertz** (⊠ Seychelles International Airport, Victoria ☎ 322–447 ⊕ www.seychelles.net/hertz). **Omega Cars** (Seychelles International Airport, Victoria ☎ 376–932 or 521–821 ⊕ www.omegacarhire.com). **Palm Cars** (⊠ Seychelles International Airport, Victoria ☎ 361–221 or 521–221 ⬧ palm-cars@seychelles.sc).

TAXI TRAVEL

Independently owned taxis operate on Mahé and Praslin (as do a handful on La Digue) and can (sometimes) be hailed from the street, at designated taxi stands, or by phoning (most reliable). They are expensive, however, and it's advised to request a metered ride. The first kilometer is Rs25, after that Rs23. There is no night or weekend charge, and each piece of luggage is an additional Rs10. Following are sample approximate fares from the airport to: Victoria, Rs230; Beau Vallon, Rs400; to Anse Soleil, Rs415. If there is no meter, agree on a price before getting in. You can also organize a half-day fixed rate "tour" with a taxi driver. A normal rate would be about €150 for five to six hours. All hotels have numbers of reliable drivers.

HEALTH AND SAFETY

Free of malaria, venomous snakes and spiders, or other nasties, the worst you're likely to deal with in Seychelles is a sunburn or sprained ankle. The public health system in Seychelles is good by African standards, and small clinics with a nurse available are dotted around Mahé. Tourists are advised to go to the hospital in Victoria for anything serious. The hospital's pharmacy can also dispense prescriptions, though it's best to bring any needed prescription meds with you. Praslin also has a small hospital at Bay St. Anne, and a clinic at Grand Anse. There is a small hospital on La Digue. There are only two decompression chambers in Seychelles, one at the Mahé hospital, and the other on Silhouette Island. Other than Silhouette, the outlying islands have little in the way of medical resources. Tap water on the main islands is safe to drink, but most people stick to bottled water or water treated by the resort. Food is well prepared and clean, though sometimes the Creole spices can affect sensitive stomachs. Most important for those traveling from a yellow-fever country—i.e., much of Africa—you absolutely must have proof of vaccination before entering Seychelles. Health insurance with an evacuation policy is advised, as should anything serious happen, you'd want to be evacuated to South Africa or beyond.

Generally speaking, Seychelles is a safe place. However, most hotels provide a safe in your room or at reception, and it's wise to use it. When out and about, use common sense: don't leave valuables visible in a car in remote or quiet places, and if you go hiking alone or in just a pair, be alert to strangers. That said, violent crime is practically unheard of.

Emergency Contacts Emergency Fire, Police, Ambulance (☎ 999).

MONEY MATTERS

The currency in use is the Seychelles rupee (Rs). The exchange rate was US$1 to Rs12.9 at the time of writing. The days when tourists were strictly obliged to use foreign exchange are blessedly over. Although tourist prices are often quoted in euros, you can always pay in rupees at the current exchange rate. ATMs (which accept foreign cards) are available at the airports, in Victoria, and scattered around the larger towns on all three main islands. The most reliable bank for foreign cards is MCB (Barclays also has ATMs, but some do not accept foreign cards). Foreign exchange offices are fairly plentiful on Mahé, and exist on Praslin and La Digue in the touristy areas. Almost all hotels, restaurants, shops, and even small curio stalls take major credit cards, with a preference for Visa and MasterCard. Banks are open Monday to Friday 8:30–2 and Saturday 9–11; they do not close for lunch.

RESTAURANTS

The international dining scene in Seychelles has undergone a massive transformation in the last few years, and complaints of paying top dollar for sub-par food should be a thing of the past. That said, prices are on the high side, but bear in mind that everything but seafood and some produce is imported. Most hotels have their own restaurant (to which nonguests are usually welcome), often serving buffet meals of both international and Creole cuisine; a few of the finest à la carte restaurants are in hotels. Mixing Indian, Southeast Asian, and French influences and using the copious fresh seafood, fruits, and spices of Seychelles, Creole food is a real treat for those who enjoy spice. Octopus is used abundantly and is extremely good in all forms (salads and coconut curries); red snapper is a favorite grilled fish; and the adventurous could try a fruit bat curry. A number of good restaurants—mostly Italian, French, and seafood or Creole—have emerged in the tourist areas around Mahé and Praslin, and serve as a welcome alternative to the hotel buffets. Most breakfast buffets start at 7 (until 10:30), but early departures can usually be accommodated. Lunch is typically served between noon and

3, and dinner from 7 to 10. The private islands and some upscale resorts will sometimes offer a more flexible dining schedule.

HOTELS

The variety of hotels has exploded in the past few years, and no longer is it the case that Seychelles offers only super exclusive (and super expensive) accommodation. From ultraluxurious private island resorts to five-star global hotel brands to an increasing market of three-star hotels and guest houses, and even some B&Bs and self-catering units, there are plenty of choices. Almost all hotel rates include breakfast; many are on a half-board system (MAP), and a few (mostly the private islands) operate on a full-board system (FAP or AI). Most half- and full-board plans include a buffet dinner (vs. the à la carte menu, if there is one at your hotel). If staying near a tourist destination where there are plenty of restaurant choices (such as Beau Vallon in Mahé, or Cote d'Or in Praslin), it may be better value (and more interesting) to take only the B&B option. All hotels accept credit cards. The star rating system that you'll find on the island is determined by the Seychelles' Tourism board.

WHAT IT COSTS IN DOLLARS					
		$	$$	$$$	$$$$
Restaurants	under Rs200	Rs200–Rs 260	Rs260–Rs 390	Rs390–Rs 515	over Rs515
Hotels	under €150	€150–€300	€300–€500	€500–€1,000	over €1,000

Restaurant prices are based on the median main course price at dinner. Hotel prices are for two people in a standard double room in high season, excluding service and 12% tax.

VISITOR INFORMATION

The only tourist information body in the Seychelles is the generally very good Seychelles Tourism Board (STB). The head office is in Victoria, with smaller offices at the jetties in Praslin and La Digue. The Web site is also tremendously helpful when planning a trip, and includes copious and updated information from logistics to accommodation to activities. Maps of the walking trails in Mahé are usually available at the Victoria office, as are free maps of the main islands, and the quite useful "Seychelles in your pocket" bilingual guide (for purchase). The largest tour operator in Seychelles is Mason's Travel. You can book any kind of tour imaginable with their helpful staff, and note that their hotel rates are almost always more competitive.

Contacts Seychelles Tourism Board (✉ Independence Ave., Victoria ☎ 671–300 Mahé, 232–669 Praslin, 234–393 La Digue ⊕ www.seychelles. travel). **Mason's Travel** (✉ Michel Building, Revolution Ave., Victoria ☎ 288–888 ⊕ www.masonstravel.com).

MAHÉ

Mahé is the archipelago's largest island at 27 km by 8 km (17 mi by 5 mi). Home to 90% of the country's population of 87,000, it displays an amazing ethnic diversity, with descendents of European colonists and African slaves living harmoniously with later settlers from Arabia, India, and China.

Mahé also displays the magnificent geology and verdant landscapes of the whole country with its own 3,200-foot granite peaks, virgin mist forests, and more than 65 exceptional beaches, making it the perfect one-stop island for a short visit. Mahé is the main transport hub for transfers to other islands in the archipelago, many of which can be visited on a long day-trip. Tours of the capital Victoria or the whole island are enjoyable and educational, but many visitors may prefer to spend their time simply soaking in the tropical ambience on the sugar-white beaches. North Mahé, home to famous Beau Vallon Beach, is more populous than other parts of the island, though its wide range of hotels and restaurants remains discreet and tasteful. In contrast, the farther south you go, the quieter it gets, with some of the most beautiful beaches and Creole villages found around Anse Intendance and Anse Forbans.

GETTING HERE AND AROUND

The domestic terminal at Mahé handles all flights anywhere else in Seychelles, and the helipad is also at the airport. The Cat Coco ferry goes to Praslin three times a day (twice on Sunday). The 50-minute trip costs €40–€45 for adults. Cat Coco will soon run ferries to La Digue. Having your own car is the best way to explore all of Mahé's nooks and crannies (⇨ *See Car Travel, above, for car rental info*). But if the narrow roads and left-hand driving put you off, have your hotel call you a taxi or take the public bus. A flat fee of Rs5 will get you anywhere on the island. Timetables and maps are available at the terminus in Victoria, or call the SPTC line. Buses ply each route once an hour from 6 AM until 7 PM.

SAFETY AND PRECAUTIONS

Generally speaking, Mahé is a very safe destination and violent crime is practically unheard of. Still, it's best to avoid tempting petty theft: resist leaving cameras in open view in cars, or purses and cell phones unattended on beaches while swimming. If hiking in Morne Seychellois Park, do not leave valuables in sight in your car; better yet, leave them at the hotel.

TIMING

Many visitors base themselves on Mahé for the duration of their visit to the Seychelles, merely taking day-trips to the other islands. If you plan to spend much time on other islands, bear in mind that Mahé is one of the most interesting islands, and excluding time to laze on the beach or go diving and snorkeling, three days could easily be filled with exploring Victoria, hiking one of the numerous inland or coastal trails, visiting the cluster of art galleries and Creole villages around Anse Soleil, and discovering your own empty beach.

ESSENTIALS

Banks and Currency Exchange Barclays Bank (✉ *Independence Ave., Victoria* ☎ *383–838* ⊕ *www.barclays.com/africa/seychelles*). **Mauritius Commercial Bank (MCB)** (✉ *Manglier St., Victoria* ☎ *284–555* ⊕ *www.mcbseychelles.com*). **Nouvobanq** (✉ *Victoria House, State Ave., Victoria* ☎ *293–000* ⊕ *www.nouvobanq.sc*).

Emergency Contacts Mahé Police (✉ *Revolution Ave., Victoria* ☎ *288–000*).

Hospitals Victoria Hospital (✉ *Mont Fleuri, Mahé* ☎ *388–000*).

Taxis Luc Pouponneau (☎ *510–570*). **Mike Mein** (☎ *525–798*).

EXPLORING MAHÉ

9

VICTORIA

Seychelles' tiny capital, Victoria, is a bustling town and the nerve center of the Seychelles. Sheltered under the granite massifs on Mahé's northeast side, this town whose streets are lined with endemic palms is a hodgepodge of Creole-style houses, Indian shops, and British relics. The streets are clean and new buildings are going up all the time, though the variety of items for sale can be somewhat limited. This is the commercial center of Seychelles, all the banks have branches here, and if you need to buy anything (souvenirs or otherwise), this is your best bet. The nearby harbor is where boats of all types dock for travel to many other islands at the inter-island quay (aka wharf), and at the deepwater quay you'll find large cruise ships and cargo vessels. The funny smell in the air may be from the tuna processing plant, also quayside.

TOP ATTRACTIONS

Seychelles National Botanical Gardens. Victoria's botanical gardens at Mont Fleuri on the outskirts of town were planted more than a century ago, and the comprehensive collection of native Mascarene plants and exotic imports stretches over five acres. The abundant palms—including

Mahé

Shark Bank

North Pt.

Mt. Howard ▲

Glacis

Sunset
De Quincy Village

Beau Vallon Bay

Aurore

Sainte Anne
Marine National Park

Saint Anne

Beau Vallon

Beau Vallon

Bel Ombre

Perseverance

Beacon I.

Moyenne

Danzil
Pascal Village

Port I.

Inter-Island Quay

Round I.

Long I.

Mt. Le Niol ▲

VICTORIA

Seychelles National
Botanical Gardens

Romainville

Cerf I.

Baie Ternay
Marine
National Park

Morne Seychellois
National Park

Victoria
Hospital

Eden

Cerf Passage

Pt. Matoopa

Morne
Seychellois ▲

Conception

Port Launay

La Misère

Cascade

Seychelles
International
Airport

Anonyme

Suète I.

Port Launay
Marine
National Park

Port
Glaud

Grande
Anse

Soleil I.

Thérèse I.

INDIAN OCEAN

Anse
aux Pins

La Marine

0   4 mi
0   4 km

Boileau Bay

Anse
Boileau

Brûlée ▲

1

Michael Adams
Studio

Anse à
la Mouche

Anse Forbans

Anse Royale

Anse Soleil

5

6

9

2 12

Anse Royale
Bay

Petite Anse

7 8   Nautica

Baie
Lazare

10 11

Takamaka

13

Anse Intendance

Quatre
Bornes

Lighthouse

KEY

1 *Exploring sites*

1 *Restaurants, Hotels*

Beaches

Dive sites

the rare Coco de Mer—are the most important local species, and there is a fine assortment of orchids in and outside of an orchid house (open 8–2). Watch out for the native Aldabra tortoises (some over 150 years old) and the flying foxes (large fruit-eating bats), which roost in the palm fronds. ✉ *Mont Fleuri, Victoria* ☎ *670–500* 💰 *Rs100* ⏰ *Daily 8–5.*

Sir Percy Selwyn Selwyn-Clarke Market. Built in the 1840s in glorious early-Victorian style (and renovated in 1999), this national landmark, which is also Victoria's main market, is the place to buy the freshest fruit and fish and the most pungent spices. The market is a colorful place to browse for souvenirs and is particularly lively on Saturday mornings (closed Sundays). ✉ *Market St., Victoria* ⏰ *Mon.–Fri. early morning–4:30* PM*; Sat. early morning–1* PM*; closed Sun.*

WORTH NOTING

Bicentennial Monument. Erected in 1978, the monument commemorated the 200th anniversary of the founding of Victoria. This simple white structure depicting three pairs of extended wings was designed by artist Lorenzo Appiani, an Italian who made his home in Seychelles. ✉ *Independence Ave., Victoria.*

National Museum of History. Established in 1964, the national museum houses artifacts relating to traditional lifestyles of the pre-colonial peoples, plus items such as the oldest known map of the islands, drawn in 1517. On the frumpy side, the museum is nonetheless worth visiting for its informative displays, such as an extremely interesting section on the slave trade and its influences on Seychelles. ✉ *Francis Rachel St., Victoria* ☎ *321–333* 💰 *Rs15* ⏰ *Mon., Tues., Thurs., and Fri. 8:30–4:30; Wed. 8:30–noon; Sat. 9–1; closed Sun. and public holidays.*

Victoria Clock. The clock tower, known to the locals as Lorloz, is the symbolic heart of the city. Now surrounded by the high-rise signs of modern Mahé, this diminutive Big Ben replica was erected in 1903 to memorialize Queen Victoria; locals have been using it to set their own watches ever since. ✉ *Corner of Albert St. and Independence Ave., Victoria.*

ELSEWHERE ON THE ISLAND

Domaine de Val des Près (The Craft Village). This traditional colonial homestead, one of very few left in the Seychelles, is now the center of a crafts village showcasing aspects of traditional Creole culture in the Seychelles. Explore a collection of buildings, including Grann Kaz, the family plantation home built in 1870, with its period furniture and large shaded veranda. The surrounding servant cottages now host artisans producing a range of souvenirs. ✉ *Anse Au Cap* ☎ *225–240 or 376–100* ⏰ *Mon.–Sat. 9–5.*

Le Jardin Du Roi Spice Garden. From its elevated position above Anse Royale, the spice garden is a renovated plantation where vanilla, citronella, cinnamon, nutmeg, and other endemic plants are grown. Its Spice Shop trades in (surprise!) spices and crafts, and other buildings such as a very small museum can be visited. It's wise to book ahead at the popular open-air restaurant, which offers great food and views.

9

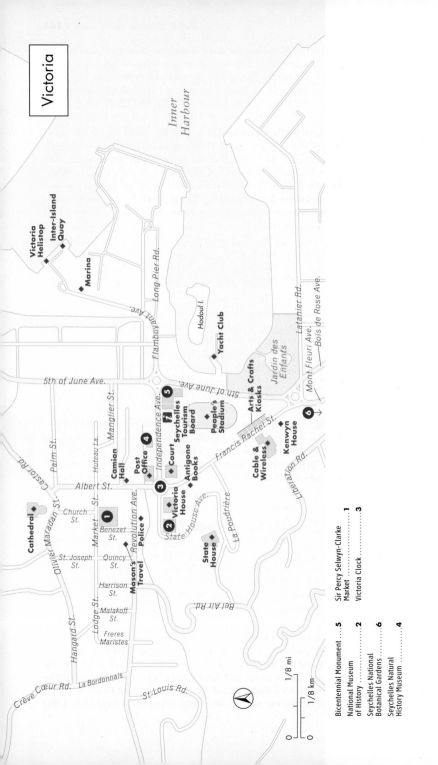

Victoria

Inner Harbour

Victoria Helistop

Inter-Island Quay

Marina

Long Pier Rd.

Flamboyant Ave.

Hodoul I.

Yacht Club

5th of June Ave.

Mangtier St.

Palm St.

Huteau La.

Seychelles
Tourism Board

5

1

People's
Stadium

5th of June Ave.

Arts & Crafts
Kiosks

Jardin des
Enfants

Latanier Rd.

Bois de Rose Ave.

Mont Fleuri Ave.

6

Court

4
Post
Office

Independence Ave.

3

Antigone
Books

Francis Rachel St.

Cable &
Wireless

Kenwyn
House

Liberation Rd.

Castor Rd.

Camion
Hall

Albert St.

Victoria
House

2

State House Ave.

La Poudrière

Cathedral

*Church
St.*

1
Benezet
St.

Police

State
House

State
St.

Bel Air Rd.

Olivier Maradan St.

*St. Joseph
St.*

*Quincy
St.*

Mason's
Travel

Revolution Ave.

Market St.

Lodge St.

Hangard St.

*Harrison
St.*

*Malakoff
St.*

*Freres
Maristes*

Crève Cœur Rd.

La Bordonnais

St. Louis Rd.

0   1/8 mi

0   1/8 km

Bicentennial Monument **5**

National Museum
of History **2**

Seychelles National
Botanical Gardens **6**

Seychelles Natural
History Museum **4**

Sir Percy Selwyn-Clarke
Market **1**

Victoria Clock **3**

✉ *Domaine de L'Enfoncement, Anse Royale* ☎ *371–313* ✉ *Rs110 (free on Sun.)* ⊙ *Daily 10–5.*

WHERE TO EAT

In Mahé you can indulge in the luxury of an ever-growing stable of true restaurants (not associated with a hotel), many of which are clustered in the Beau Vallon area. A few hotel restaurants are included here because of their exceptional food and willingness to accommodate outside guests; however, always call ahead to dine at hotel restaurants, as they may not be able to take nonguests during high season.

$–$$
CREOLE
Fodor's Choice
★

✕ **Anse Soleil Café.** A favorite toes-in-the-sand, small, family-run, open-air restaurant on one of Mahé's most beautiful beaches, the café serves delicious Creole dishes with an emphasis on seafood, and some meat-and-fries options. The café does a hopping lunch business and can remain busy through dinner. Meals are served family style (big platters of whatever you've ordered to suit your numbers), and casual is king. Try the ginger crab curry—it's legendary. Efficiency isn't always a strong point, so order ahead of your hunger if you've built up an appetite swimming and sunning all day long. ✉ *Anse Soleil* ☎ *361–700* ✍ *No reservations accepted* ☰ *MC, V* ⊙ *Daily noon–8.*

¢–$
CREOLE

✕ **Jardin du Roi.** With soaring views through steep forested hills down to a turquoise slice of Anse Royale, this quaint, open-air restaurant serves fabulous Creole fare. Delicious salads of papaya, golden apple, and mango accompany perfectly grilled fish, subtly spiced curries, and fragrant basmati rice. Crepes, sandwiches, a few vegetarian options, and the homemade ice creams are also great. Come on Sunday from noon to 3 for the Lunch Planteur, a Creole feast that includes all the salads, chutneys, and extras you might expect at a huge family potluck with the home-style cooking to match for Rs289. ✉ *Domaine de l'Enforcement, Anse Royale* ☎ *371–313* ✍ *Reservations essential in season* ☰ *MC, V* ⊙ *Closed Christmas, New Year's, and Easter.*

$$$–$$$$
CREOLE

✕ **Kannel Restaurant.** Gleaming warm wooden tones and screens of metal cutout flowers adorn this elegant yet casual pool-side restaurant which serves lunch and dinner daily. Lunch menus focus on international fare, with excellent salads, pastas, seafood dishes, and wood-oven baked pizzas to choose from. Dinners flaunt the chef's Creole cooking, with exquisite renditions of island favorites, such as a tuna carpaccio with deep-fried okra, grilled job fish (a delicious firm whitefish similar to snapper) over turmeric prawns, heavenly curries served with local chutneys, and the famous bat curry, a spicy curry based on the ubiquitous fruit bats seen all over the islands. Nonhotel guests should be sure to book ahead. ✉ *Four Seasons Resort, Petite Anse, Baie Lazare* ☎ *393–000* ⊕ *www.fourseasons.com* ✍ *Reservations essential* ☰ *AE, MC, V.*

$–$$
ITALIAN

✕ **Le Perle Noire.** Housed in a slightly shabby nautically themed setting just off the beach at Beau Vallon, the black pearl serves extremely tasty and good value dinners. With a focus on seafood, international flavors, and a tendency toward Italian influences, dishes are fresh and perfectly seasoned. Service is friendly and efficient, and there's a kids' menu. The octopus salad in a reduced balsamic sauce, and the Fish Fillet

9

Perle Noire are recommended. The ice cream with coconut caramel is a wonderful (super-sweet) local dessert. ⊠ *Beau Vallon* ☎ *620–220* ☐ *MC, V* ☾ *Closed Sun.*

$$–$$$
THAI
Fodor's Choice
★
✕ **Saffron Restaurant.** If you're craving something different, this Thai restaurant at the Banyan Tree Hotel is a real treat. In a simply elegant dining room of rose and saffron hues graced with Thai silks and sea views to gorgeous Anse Intendance, Saffron serves up delicious and authentic Thai food, including a seafood glass noodle salad, a fabulous red curry duck with lychees, and delicately steamed red snapper in a chili lime sauce. The Thai chef and availability of locally grown Thai produce are no doubt behind the authentic flavors. The Peter Sellers room for private dining is a tribute to the actor who once owned this piece of land. ■ TIP➔ **The Thursday night buffet is extremely popular, so call ahead if you're interested.** ⊠ *Banyan Tree Hotel, Anse Intendance* ☎ *383–500* ⊕ *www.banyantree.com* ⌕ *Reservations essential* ☐ *AE, DC, MC, V* ☾ *Daily 7–10* PM.

¢–$
CAFÉ
✕ **Surfers Beach Restaurant.** This casual and friendly joint is located in a wild and secluded spot just before the southeastern road ends at Anse Forbans. It's a great place to enjoy a very affordable and tasty lunch, dinner, or snack while watching local surfers catch waves. The octopus salad is deliciously tart, and the pizzas and fish dishes are popular. There's plenty for the meat eaters too with tasty burgers, fillet, and lamb. Located on the road right next to the beach under coconut trees and with nothing but the waves and white sand, it's a peaceful place, not to mention the only restaurant in the immediate vicinity; they do a rollicking take-away business. This local favorite is a great spot for surfers and au naturel hipsters to enjoy a drink or three. With an outdoor shower and talk of renting surfboards in the near future, this could become a great all-day escape from busier parts of Mahé. ⊠ *Anse Parnel* ☎ *783–703* ⊕ *www.pwcseychelles.com/surfer/* ☐ *MC, V* ☾ *Closed Tues.*

WHERE TO STAY

In recent years, accommodation in the Seychelles has expanded tremendously, with the majority of development on Mahé. Everything from super-luxurious five-star resorts to self-catering bungalows can now be found; the two- and three-star guest houses will be less glamorous and stylish, but many have the advantage of local ownership, and some enjoy beachfront locations, making them comparatively very good value. The Seychelles Tourism Board Web site (⇨ *See Essentials, above, for contact info*) is a great resource for reviewing the multitude of options.

¢–$
Fodor's Choice
★
▥ **Anse Soleil Beachcomber.** Set on a charming little bay on the island's southwest coast, all the rooms at this gem of a guest house are perched right on the beach among granite boulders with great sea views. The rooms are serviceable and pleasant, and come with the necessary amenities, plus you'll have the sound of waves crashing 5 meters away. Request rooms at either end of the property for a little added privacy (Room 5 in standard, and Room 8 or 10 in superior). The guest-only restaurant overlooks the golden sand and turquoise water, and serves up tasty Creole food, as well as sandwiches and snacks. **Pros:** great value

for money; local place with a friendly philosophy; smack dab on one of Mahé's nicest beaches; free kayaks, snorkeling gear, and Internet. **Cons:** rooms share walls; terraces are visible from the beach and some from the restaurant; Wi-Fi doesn't reach most of the rooms. ⊠ *Anse Soleil* ☎ *361–461* ⊕ *www.beachcomber.sc* ⬠ *14 rooms* ⬠ *In-room: no phone, a/c, safe, refrigerator, no TV (some), Wi–Fi (some). In-hotel: room service, bar, beachfront, water sports, laundry service (by request), Wi–Fi hotspot, parking (free)* ⊟ *MC, V* ⊘ *Closed June* ⎟⊚⎟ *BP.*

¢   ⬠ **Augerine Guesthouse.** A family-run place on Beau Vallon beach, Augerine's recent renovation included a/c and standing fans in all of its pleasant, clean, and comfortable rooms. The junior suites upstairs are huge and have TVs. Though lacking any particular style, the location can't be beat, and the staff is incredibly friendly and helpful. Meals in the Takamaka Restaurant (a 400-year-old Takamaka tree sacrificed to the renovation was turned upside down to support the restaurant's thatched roof) are toes-in-the-sand affairs, with a (small) view of the sea. **Pros:** good value for great beachfront location where all rooms have sea view; friendly service; close to all the Beau Vallon restaurants. **Cons:** rooms are a bit stark; next door to a dive operator that can be noisy. ⊠ *Beau Vallon* ☎ *247–257* ⊕ *www.augerinehotel.com* ⬠ *15 rooms* ⬠ *In-room: a/c, safe, refrigerator, no TV (some). In-hotel: restaurant, bar, beachfront, water sports, laundry facilities, laundry service, Wi-Fi hotspot, parking (free)* ⊟ *AE, DC, MC, V* ⎟⊚⎟ *BP.*

$$$$ ⬠ **Banyan Tree Seychelles.** The only property on Anse Intendance—one

Fodor's Choice   of Seychelles most beautiful beaches—the Banyan Tree Seychelles is

★   arguably the most romantic resort on Mahé. The large, quasi-French Colonial villas ooze luxury and privacy. All have their own pools, outdoor dining salas, and decks—all of which are enclosed so that those inclined can treat their outdoor space with the same abandon as they do the indoors. Two restaurants, including the amazing Saffron, are yours to choose from, but the in-villa dining and beachfront dining (think hurricane lanterns and tikki torches surrounding a table laid with beautiful china and silver, all on the beach with only the moon and stars above) are the height of romance. The infinity pool frequently gets top honors, and the spa, part of the famous Banyan Tree line, is world class. A colonial-elegance-meets-NYC-hipster bar overlooking the sea is the perfect place for a drink, day or night. In keeping with the hotel line's Southeast Asian roots, service is exemplary. **Pros:** absolutely idyllic for honeymooners and those looking for a little romance; great Thai restaurant; amazing beach. **Cons:** not great for children; the free equipment at the activities center could use an upgrade. ⊠ *Anse Intendance* ☎ *383–500* ⊕ *www.banyantree.com* ⬠ *60 rooms* ⬠ *In-room: a/c, safe, refrigerator, DVD (some), Internet, Wi-Fi. In-hotel: 2 restaurants, room service, bars, tennis court, pools, gym, spa, beachfront, diving, water sports, laundry service, Internet terminal, Wi-Fi hotspot, parking (free)* ⊟ *AE, DC, MC, V* ⎟⊚⎟ *BP, MAP.*

9

$$$$ ⬠ **Four Seasons.** The 67 villas at this resort, which opened in 2009, dot

⟳   the forested hillsides of a natural amphitheater overlooking the perfect

Fodor's Choice   bay of Petite Anse. The vegetation and trees were all left in place or

★   replanted so that this gorgeous and very upmarket resort feels like it's

Banyan Tree Seychelles

Four Seasons

been here for years, blending in remarkably well with its surrounds. The villas themselves are breathtaking: spacious, modern, and yet imbued with Creole style and original artworks by Seychellois artists. The water in Petite Anse's protected bay is clear year-round, and offers some of the best snorkeling in the area. An incredibly well-stocked activity center (good-quality kayaks, snorkeling gear, etc.) and kids' programs, along with cooking classes (highly recommended if you're fond of Creole cuisine) and a library, mean you'll never want for things to do. The stunning spa at the top of the hill is probably one of the best places on Mahé for sundowners, not to mention to enjoy fabulous treatments and yoga classes with a view. Both restaurants are excellent, and the hotel's breakfast buffet is unusually tasty (and offers a truly global selection of breakfast options). **Pros:** spectacular villas with private plunge pools; fantastic beach with excellent snorkeling year-round; great activities center, kids' program, and cooking classes. **Cons:** because of hillside arrangement, villas above yours can see into your outside private areas; garden villas closest to beach lack a sea view; buggy service (electric golf carts to get you up and down those hills) can be a bit slow during busy pre-dinner hours, and steep hillsides may discourage walking. ⊠ *Petite Anse, Baie Lazare* ☎ *393–000* ⊕ *www.fourseasons.com* ↩ *67 rooms* ⌂ *In-room: a/c, safe, refrigerator, DVD, Wi-Fi (paid in room). In-hotel: 2 restaurants, room service, bars, pools, gym, spa, beachfront, diving, water sports, children's programs (ages 4–12), laundry service, Internet terminal, Wi-Fi hotspot, parking (free)* ⊟ *AE, DC, MC, V* ⊙| *BP, MAP.*

SHOPPING

Shops in Seychelles resorts tend to stock imported crafts and clothing, plus high-value items like designer watches and diamond jewelry; however, there is a small and interesting selection of locally produced souvenirs for every budget. Black pearls are a specialty and make exquisite rings or necklaces. Look also for the fiery local rum. There are many tourist shops in Mahé's downtown, including a row of kiosks selling sarongs, hats, bags, and certified Coco de Mer seeds on Francis Rachel Street. The larger hotels usually have a small souvenir shop.

Antigone Books. Probably the best bookstore for reads on the Seychelles, this small shop stocks everything from field guides to cook books, travel guides to coffee table books. They also sell novels in English and a small stock of imported newspapers and magazines. The main branch is located in a small shopping arcade in Victoria, but there is also a branch at the International Airport. ⊠ *Victoria House, Francis Rachel St., Victoria* ☎ *225–443* ⊙ *Mon.–Fri. 9–4:30; Sat. 9–noon.*

Kenwyn House. One of Seychelles' best examples of a 19th-century French colonial home, Kenwyn House is a historic monument as well as a duty-free shop and gallery. Built entirely from wood in 1855, this elegant home now houses a jewelry shop featuring South African diamonds and tanzanite, an art gallery, high-end souvenirs from the Indian Ocean region, and a charming—if only sometimes-functioning—coffee shop. ⊠ *Francis Rachel St., Victoria* ☎ *224–440* ⊕ *www.kenwynhouse. com* 🖃 *free* ⊙ *Mon.–Fri. 9–5; Sat. 9–1.*

Michael Adams Studio. Seychelles' best-known artist, Malaysian-born Michael Adams has studied the Seychelles' otherworldly jungle- and seascapes through dreamlike watercolors and silk screens for more than 30 years now. Visit his studio in Anse Soleil to view (and purchase) his unique work, as well as that of his extremely talented children, both of whom are also painters. ⊠ *Anse Aux Poules Bleues* ☎ *361–006* ⊕ *www. michaeladamsart.com* ⊙ *Mon.–Fri. 10–4.*

Nautica. Also featuring handmade maquettes, this Anse Soleil shop can custom-make any vessel of your choice. This is a fun place to browse and visitors should check out the amazingly crafted models of the *CSS Alabama* and *The Constitution,* among many others. Prices start at around €1,350 and go up to €15,000. ⊠ *Anse Soleil* ☎ *421–425 or 713–638* ⊕ *www.nauticaseychelles.com* ⊙ *Daily 9–5:30.*

OUTDOOR ACTIVITIES AND SPORTS

BEACHES

Luxuriating on a magnificent beach under the shade of a swaying palm isn't self-indulgence—it's what you come to the Seychelles for. With more than 65 beaches to choose from, there's something for everyone. Even the busiest beaches won't be packed, and if you have an car, pack a picnic and find your own perfect spot. Beaches with rough currents will be signposted, so watch out for and heed the warnings.

Anse à la Mouche. If you want a calmer experience, head for Anse à la Mouche, a crystal clear bay on the southwest coast of the island, where shallow, calm water reigns year-round. Good for kids.

Anse Forbans. To get away from it all, head to this beach in the southeast. The sea can be rough (it's a favorite spot for surfers), but you may have the whole thing to yourself. The nearby Surfer's Café is a great place for a snack or a drink.

Anse Intendance. This is one of Mahé's most picturesque beaches, and its also the widest, and one of the few places on Mahé where turtles still nest. The large swells make it a favorite for surfers, but swimming can be rough. The Banyan Tree Seychelles dominates the northern side of this beach, but is open to nonguests. If you are organized, you could reserve at one of their excellent restaurants for lunch or dinner.

Anse Soleil. A calm, jade-blue bay fringed with granite boulders borders this great swimming beach. Its golden sands are a popular spot, made more so by the Anse Soleil Café—the only public property on the beach—where you can enjoy a fantastic seafood lunch or dinner.

Beau Vallon. This 3-km (2-mi) crescent on the northwest coast enjoys surf from September to April, as well as many recreation and dining facilities. Mahé's most popular beach, it is the only one where motorized water sports (Jet Skis, waterskiing) are allowed. There are numerous places to eat and water-sport operators to choose from around this beach. It's also a popular beach for an evening run.

Sunset Beach. For great swimming and snorkeling, head to this beach in northwest where turtle sightings are common and sunsets are breathtaking. Enjoy a sundowner at the hotel bar, where drinks come with mouthwatering baked coconut and plantain chips, as well as a perfect sea view.

DIVING AND SNORKELING

Qualified divers can book tanks and a guide to explore rich underwater worlds of coral reefs and abundant sea life. But you don't need to be a certified diver to enjoy the marine life of Seychelles, where shallow reefs and lagoons offer perfect conditions for snorkeling. Ask your hotel for a recommended operator. The best time of year for diving is the hot season (about November to April), when the waters achieve that legendary crystal-clear visibility. Unfortunately, the coral bleaching that affected the entire Indian Ocean in 2002 damaged the majority of the Seychelles' reefs, so don't expect acres of colorful corals. The real thrill of diving in the Seychelles is the abundance of game fish and the rich large marine life—turtles, rays, and huge shoals of fish—centered around Seychelles' unique underwater granite formations.

BEST DIVE SITES

Port Launay Marine National Park. Located on the northwest coast, the Port Launay marine park is famous for its beautiful beaches and whale-shark sightings; the reefs on both sides of the bay provide stellar snorkeling, and in season, the gentle whale sharks can be seen feeding on plankton. Tickets for the marine park must be purchased at the ranger base in Port Launay, which is open daily 9–5. Organized tours normally include the price of the ticket in the total fee. 💳 *Rs200* ⏱ *Daily 9–5.*

Shark Bank. Also on the northwest coast, about 9 km (5 mi) off of Beau Vallon, this dive around a 30-meter granite pillar is famous for— surprise!—shark sightings. Usually divers will encounter reef sharks, though in season whale sharks also abound. Huge brissant rays, barracuda, batfish, and yellow snapper are common. This site is for experienced divers only, as a strong current runs here.

BEST SNORKEL SITES

Bay Ternay Marine National Park. On the northwest coast around the point from Port Launay, the reefs here are excellent for snorkeling. There is no vehicle road to Bay Ternay, so you must go by boat, usually with an organized tour.

Ste. Anne Marine National Park. The first protected marine park in the Indian Ocean, Ste. Anne Marine National Park was established in 1973. Just offshore (a 20-minute boat ride) from Mahé, its boundaries incorporate six islands, one of Seychelles' most important Hawksbill turtle nesting sites, and large sea-grass meadows. The warm, clear, shallow lagoons are perfect for snorkeling and exploring the profusion of marine life from tiny, iridescent tropical fish to colorful corals and swaying anemones. The best way to get here is on one of the many half- or full-day boat trips offered by tour operators on Mahé, or to stay on one of the islands with accommodation.

9

RECOMMENDED OPERATORS

Big Blue Divers. Located in Beau Vallon, these friendly folks have 15 years of experience and more than 75 dive sights to show you. They offer PADI certification, and focus on smaller groups. ⊠ *Beau Vallon* ☎ *261–106 or 248–046* ⊕ *www.bigbluedivers.net.*

Dive Resort Seychelles. Another five-star PADI dive resort, this one is based in the south. Also with more than 15 years of experience in Seychelles, they are well versed in dive sights both in the inner and outer islands. ⊠ *Anse a la Mouche* ☎ *361–361 or 717–272* ⊕ *www. seychellesdiving.net.*

HIKING

Morne Seychellois National Park. If you want to get off the beach and explore some of the enticing lush jungle clinging to the steep cliffs around Mahé, this is the place to come. Seychelles' largest park was created in 1979 and covers an area of about 30 square km (12 square mi), or more than 20% of Mahé, and encompasses its eponymous peak, the highest point in Seychelles at 910 meters (2,985 feet). About 10 km (6 mi) in length and 3 km (1.8 mi) in width, the park is equipped with 12 different trails that can be explored on half- or full-day excursions. Rare orchids, endemic palms, and carnivorous pitcher plants are among the botanical treats. Twelve different trails cover more than 14 km (9 mi) in the park, and maps detailing the trails are available at the head office of the tourism board or at the botanical gardens. Many of the trails are easy and well marked. For the more difficult routes (e.g., Mont Serbert, Congo Rouge, and Les Trois Frères), hikers should definitely enlist the help of a guide. ▨ *Free.*

RECOMMENDED GUIDES

Basil Beaudouin. Mahé's most famous hiking guide, Beaudouin is the Seychelles' answer to Crocodile Dundee. His knowledge is extensive, and he takes good care of his clients, regardless of skill level. ☎ *241–790 or 514–972.*

SAILING

What better way to enjoy an island nation than to hop from one island to the next on a sailboat? Offering visitors the ultimate way to experience the diversity and beauty of the archipelago, a trip on a chartered boat can last a day or a week. Most trips leaving from Mahé will sail around the island itself, anchoring at snorkel spots, and including a bit of actual sailing at some point in the journey (wind providing). Diving, kayaking, and waterskiing may also be offered on your cruise. A week-long liveaboard is a truly special experience—itineraries vary depending on the time of year and sea conditions.

Silhouette Cruises. Offers day- or week-long excursions on a fleet of beautiful liveaboard vessels, including a special whale-shark trip from October to November. ⊠ *Victoria* ☎ *324–026 or 514–051* ⊕ *www. seychelles-cruise.com.*

PRASLIN

Forty kilometers (25 mi) northeast of Mahé, Praslin is just a 15-minute flight or 45-minute ferry ride away. Praslin, at 11 km (7 mi) long and 4 km (2.5 mi) wide, is the second largest island in the Seychelles. First settled as a hideaway by pirates and Arab merchants, the island's original name, Isle de Palmes, bears testament to its reputation as home of the Vallée de Mai UNESCO World Heritage Site: the only place in the world where the famous Coco de Mer, the world's heaviest nut, grows abundantly in the wild.

Praslin's endemic palm forests shelter many rare species, and the island is a major bird-watching destination. Surrounded by a coral reef, majestic bays, and gorgeous beaches, Praslin is much quieter and less developed than Mahé. With few real "sights," the pleasures of Praslin largely involve relaxing in or exploring its stunning beaches and fantastical forests.

WHEN TO GO
The main areas where accommodation is found are Grande Anse on the west, and Cote d'Or (or Anse Volbert) on the east. Due to the nature of Seychelles' wind and weather patterns, the west coast beaches tend to gather seaweed and sea grass from May to September, during which time the Cote d'Or beaches are clear and clean. When the season (and wind) changes from October to April, the west coast clears up, while the east coast waters can be a bit rougher. It is wise to note these differences when deciding where you want to stay.

GETTING HERE AND AROUND
The Cat Coco ferry from Mahé Inter Island Quay (45 minutes) docks at Praslin's main jetty at the Bay St. Anne, which is also the departure point for most day-trip boat excursions (though several other small jetties exist around the island). The Inter Island ferry to and from La

Praslin

KEY

❶ *Exploring sites*

① *Restaurants, Hotels*

Digue, which takes about 30 minutes each way (Rs192 one way), also docks here. The Praslin airport (with flights to Mahé only) is in the west at Amitié, and also houses a landing pad for helicopter flights.

Rental-car agencies have kiosks at the airport. The local agencies have offices in Bay St. Anne, Grand Anse, and Cote d'Or, but you can usually arrange to have them meet you at a jetty or your hotel. The local bus runs two routes, departing about once an hour, one plying the east coast, the other the west. Double-check with the driver which route you are on, as they sometimes fail to change the destination sign. The fare is Rs5. Taxis are available at the airport and Bay St. Anne, as well as around Grand Anse and Cote d'Or. The first kilometer is Rs28, each additional km Rs24.50 in a metered taxi. Luggage is charged at Rs10 per piece. Sample fares from the airport are Cote d'Or, Rs350; Anse Lazio, Rs470; Bay St. Anne jetty, Rs370.

TIMING

Tour operators in Mahé often run day-trips to Praslin to visit the famous Vallée de Mai, but this beautiful island deserves at least a few days of its own. At least half a day is needed to properly appreciate the aforementioned World Heritage Site. And then Praslin is a great spot from which to explore the numerous tiny islands that surround it, including the bird sanctuaries of Cousin and Aride, and gorgeous La Digue (if you're not planning to overnight there). With all of these attractions, Praslin merits a minimum of two nights, and if you want to take it easy and explore Praslin's beaches, at least 4 nights would be needed.

ESSENTIALS

Ferry Service Inter Island Ferry (to La Digue) (✉ *Bay St. Anne* ☎ *232–329 or 232–394*).

Emergency Contacts Praslin Police (✉ *Grande Anse* ✉ Bay St. Anne ☎ *233–251*).

Medical Assistance Bay St. Anne Hospital (✉ *Bay St. Anne* ☎ *232–333 or 233–414*).

Rental cars Amitié Car Hire (✉ *Amitié* ☎ *233–358 or 515–226 lyvonesther@ hotmail.com.* **Prestige Car Hire** (✉ *Grand Anse* ☎ *233–226 or 580–787 lprestige@seychelles.sc).* **Capricorn Car Rental** (✉ *Bay St. Anne* ☎ *581–110 or 510–446 lcapcorn@seychelles.net).* **Aventure** (✉ *Amitié* ☎ *233–805* ✍ *resa@ aventure-carhire.com).*

Visitor and tour info Seychelles Tourism Board (✉ *Bay St.,* Praslin Airport ☎ *232–669 or 233–346* ⊕ *www.seychelles.travel).* **Mason's Travel** (✉ *Bay St.,* Praslin Airport ☎ *288–888* ⊕ *www.masonstravel.com).*

EXPLORING PRASLIN

Aride. A 30- to 45-minute boat trip from Praslin, Aride is one of the most pristine of the Seychelles islands and is known as the "seabird citadel" of the Indian Ocean, with more than a million seabirds breeding here each year. Protected as a reserve since 1967, Aride hosts 18 species of native birds, including the world's only hilltop colony of sooty terns and the only granitic breeding sites for the world's largest colony of lesser noddies. The Seychelles warbler was introduced from Cousin in 1988, as were the Seychelles fody and magpie robin in 2002. Aride also boasts one of the densest populations of lizards on earth, as well as unique endemic plants. A beautiful reef surrounds the island, and in season it is common to see whale sharks and flying fish in the waters just offshore. Visitors to the island must land between 9:30 and 10, but then may spend the whole day on the island if desired. Numerous operators can take you to Aride, and usually include lunch in the trip; inquire at your hotel. Due to weather conditions, Aride sometimes closes to visitors from May to September, when strong winds can prevent boats from landing. ✉ *Aride* ☎ *321–600* ⊕ *www.arideisland.net* ✉ *Rs500* ◷ *Mon.–Fri. 9:30–10 (boat-landing hours).*

Fodor'sChoice
★
Cousin Island. Cousin lies just off the southwest coast of Praslin, about 30 to 45 minutes away by boat. A nature reserve since 1968, Cousin is home to some of Seychelles' rarest birds, including the Seychelles bush warbler and the Seychelles magpie robin, and also serves as the breeding ground for thousands of lesser noddies, ferry terns, and tropic birds. Arriving on this small island, you'll see a sky darkened with the diving silhouettes of thousands of birds, and a visit gives a glimmer of an idea of what the first explorers to Seychelles might have experienced when alighting on these islands. In addition to its magnificent

bird populations, the island is home to giant Aldabra tortoises, as well as being a favorite nesting site for hawksbill turtles. Your hotel can organize a trip to the island with one of the many boat excursion operators; the stop at Cousin will usually be one of three that the boat will make. Be sure to bring your camera (fantastic photo ops of ground-nesting birds), mosquito spray (the mozzies can be thick in the interior), and a hat (they say it's good luck to be pooped on by a bird, but let your hat take the hit). ☒ *Cousin* ☏ *601–100 or 783–119* ⊕ *www.natureseychelles.org* ▨ *Rs500* ☉ *Mon.–Fri. 9:30–noon.*

Curieuse. Once known as Île Rouge on account of its red earth, this rugged island was previously home to a leper colony situated at Anse St. Joseph. The resident doctor's house, which dates back to the 1870s, was converted into an eco-museum and visitor center, and Aldabra tortoises roam freely. Aside from Praslin, Curieuse is the only other island where the coco de mer grows naturally (Coco de Mers have been planted and cultivated elsewhere in the Seychelles). Curieuse also boasts eight different species of mangrove. It is reachable by boat from Praslin, and often serves as a lunch spot on the various boat excursions from Praslin and La Digue. ☒ *Curieuse* ☏ *225–115* ▨ *Rs200* ☉ *Daily 8–5.*

Fodor's Choice ★ **Vallée de Mai National Park.** Located on Praslin's southeastern end, the Vallée de Mai National Park protects some of the last ancient virgin Mascarene forest in the world. This World Heritage Site is also the only place on earth where the unique double coconut or Coco de Mer palms grow wild and abundantly. Some 6,000 specimens bearing the largest nut in the plant kingdom flourish here. This idyllic paradise is also home to the other five species of Seychelles endemic palms, the rare black parrot, fresh-water crabs, giant crayfish, and vanilla orchids. Visitors can take the tarmac road from Bay St. Anne toward Grand Anse for a drive through the park that will introduce them to its charms, but the only real way to experience it is to walk along the very well-maintained nature trails (sandals will suffice) that run through the valley. Allow at least three hours to really explore the park. A nice gift shop where you can buy certified Coco de Mer seeds, and a café with drinks and light meals are on the premises. ☒ *Vallée de Mai* ☏ *321–735* ⊕ *www.sif.sc* ▨ *Rs350* ☉ *Daily 8–5:30.*

WHERE TO EAT

Almost all of Praslin's hotels have a restaurant. The best area for dining is Cote d'Or, which boasts some very good hotel restaurants and most of the island's true stand-alone dining establishments.

$$–$$$
CREOLE
✕ **Beach Bar & Grill.** Serving fabulous Creole-inspired food in a gorgeous setting atop a small rocky outcrop between Grande and Petite Anse Kerlan, Constance Lemuria's elegant beach restaurant is well worth a visit for lunch or dinner. The whitefish ceviche marinated with lemongrass oil and served on a bed of dried coconut and the whole grilled reef fish in a piquant Creole sauce (you can request it extra spicy) are highly recommended. Enjoy the sea breezes that cross from bay to bay, and bird's-eye views of the small reef sharks that sometimes ply the granite boulders below. Nonguests should call ahead to make a reservation.

Cousin Island, a nature reserve since 1968, is home to some of the Seychelles' rarest birds.

⊠ *Anse Kerlan* ☎ *281–091 or 281–281* ⊕ *www.lemuriaresort.com* ▭ *AE, DC, MC, V.*

$$$–$$$$
CREOLE

✕ **Bonbon Plume.** Located on lovely Anse Lazio beach, this outdoor establishment is open for lunch only, but serves fabulous grilled seafood and Creole specialties right on the water's edge. There is a three-course set menu (Rs400), or you can order grilled lobster, fish, scallops, or mussels Seychellois from the à la carte menu (all served with rice, salad, and lentils). A large open-air structure of thatch and wood, the restaurant's best tables are in the sand under umbrellas. Outside of lunch hours, fresh fruit juices, milkshakes, and ice cream are available. ⊠ *Anse Lazio* ☎ *232–136* ▭ *MC, V* ◷ *Daily 12:30–3. Closed June.*

$$$–$$$$
INTERNATIONAL
Fodor's Choice
★

✕ **Café des Arts.** Perhaps Praslin's best restaurant, Café des Arts is a funky, brightly colored haven of divine cuisine, located right on Cote d'Or, one of Seychelles' most beautiful beaches. Though the decor is a fine and festive combination of high-low—mixing elements like coconut-shell lamps with a ceiling swathed in cinnamon-color silks—the food here (dinner only) is all high, meeting the fussiest fine diner's expectations. The octopus gratin with lobster and the tuna carpaccio with a caper, garlic, and olive oil dip are highly recommended. Save room for the desserts, which are fabulously decadent. The cheesy music is forgiven by the excellent and incredibly friendly service. ⊠ *Cote d'Or* ☎ *232–252* ⊕ *www.cafe.sc* ⌲ *Reservations essential* ▭ *AE, MC, V* ◷ *Closed Mon.*

$
INTERNATIONAL

✕ **Coco de Mer Bar and Restaurant.** Set smack dab on Cote d'Or beach, the Village du Pecheur Hotel's restaurant's magical ambience of fairy lights and hurricane lanterns will attract passersby, but the food is what will keep them coming back. An excellent menu of seafood and international

9

dishes, and unpretentious setting makes this one of Praslin's popular eateries. The sea bass and the curried seafood pasta are recommended. ■ TIP➜ Children over 12 only are accommodated. ⊠ *Cote d'Or* ☎ *290–300* ⊕ *www.thesunsethotelgroup.com* ▤ *AE, MC, V.*

$ ✕ **Coco Rouge.** A small family-run restaurant serving authentic Creole
CREOLE cuisine, this casual eatery is popular with locals and offers takeout for both lunch and dinner. Perfectly cooked fish accompanied by delicious Creole salads made from smoked fish, mango, papaya, and breadfruit are the specialties at this extremely friendly and unpretentious establishment. The set dinner menu is very popular and a great value. ⊠ *Bay St. Anne* ☎ *232–228* ▤ *No credit cards* ⊘ *Closed Sun.*

WHERE TO STAY

Compared to Mahé, Praslin's hotels are generally much smaller and less swish: there are only a couple of resorts (at the time of writing, two more were being built), and many of the large hotels are locally owned and enjoy a casual, friendly atmosphere. Most of Praslin's accommodation is clustered either on Cote d'Or (also known as Anse Volbert) on the island's east side, or Grand Anse on the west coast.

¢ ☷ **Britannia Hotel.** Set back about 100 meters (328 feet) from the beach in a residential neighborhood of pretty gardens and a backdrop of forested mountain, Britannia offers prices that reflect its lack of killer views. Big, comfortable, modern rooms with all the amenities and small terraces are mostly situated around a large swimming pool and pleasant garden filled with frangipani trees and hibiscus. The restaurant serves delicious and reasonably priced Creole food with a bit of an Asian bent (nonguests are welcome but should book by 6 PM), and the local staff are very friendly. **Pros:** great value for money; five minutes' walk from Grand Anse; free shuttle three times a week to other popular beaches and dive sites. **Cons:** not on the beach; no real views. ⊠ *Grande Anse* ☎ *233–215* ✉ *Britannia@seychelles.net* ⤵ *12 rooms* ⌂ *In-room: a/c, safe, refrigerator. In-hotel: restaurant, bar, pool, bicycles, laundry service, Internet terminal, Wi-Fi hotspot (free), parking (free)* ▤ *AE, MC, V* ⦿ *BP, MAP.*

¢ ☷ **Chalet Côte Mer.** This small, homey, owner-managed hotel has fantastic value sea-facing rooms. The decor is tropical and not particularly elegant and the standard rooms a bit small, but with these prices and sea views from your balcony, who cares? A great breakfast with homemade jams, fresh bread, and perfect omelets gives you a taste of things to come: the chef, who is also an owner, is French, and his dinner menus are considered excellent value and quality. A new pool overlooks the rocky shore that's great for snorkeling, and the surrounding gardens are beautifully cared for. This conveniently located hotel is just a few minutes' walk from the Bay St. Anne jetty (and a bus stop). **Pros:** gorgeous views and convenient location; great value for money; lovely restaurant where everything is homemade. **Cons:** no actual beach nearby (but you can swim and snorkel); standard rooms are a bit small. ⊠ *Bay St. Anne* ☎ *294–200* ⊕ *www.chaletcotemer.com* ⤵ *7 rooms, 6 apartments* ⌂ *In-room: a/c (some), safe, refrigerator, Wi-Fi (some, free).*

In-hotel: restaurant, room service, bar, pool, gym, beachfront (rocky), water sports, laundry service, Wi-Fi hotspot, parking (free) ⊟ *MC, V* ⊺⊙⊺ *BP, MAP.*

$$ ⊞ **Coco de Mer and Black Parrot Suites.** Located on more than 200 acres of forest and beachfront, this lovely jungle-theme hotel is the only property on Anse Bois de Rose, and every room has beachfront views. Numerous extras like hammocks, mini golf, a library, free shuttle to Anse Lazio, and a guided nature trail make guests feel truly welcome and taken care of (and also makes it a good choice for families). A gorgeous pavilion over the water is a great place for a sundowner, fish feeding, or wedding ceremony. Perched on a granite outcrop and separated from the main hotel by a walkway, the Black Parrot junior suites form the honeymooners section (no kids under 14 on this side). These rooms enjoy a secluded and intimate atmosphere, and all have magnificent views of the sea while also having access to all the facilities at the main hotel. All rooms throughout the property are spacious and modern, with satellite TV and other conveniences. **Pros:** great value for money; sea views from all rooms; Black Parrot suites are wonderfully romantic; lots of activities and free extras like shuttle to Anse Lazio. **Cons:** located on the western side of Praslin, where beach is subject to seaweed May–October; Wi-Fi is not free. ⊠ *Anse Bois de Rose* ☎ *290–555* ⊕ *www.cocodemer.com* ⟿ *40 rooms, 12 suites* ⅛ *In-room: a/c, safe, refrigerator, Wi-Fi (paid). In-hotel: 2 restaurants, room service, bars, tennis courts, pools, gym, spa, beachfront, water sports, bicycles, laundry service, Wi-Fi hotspot (paid), parking (free)* ⊟ *AE, DC, MC, V* ⊺⊙⊺ *BP, MAP.*

$$$–$$$$ ⊞ **Constance Lemuria Resort.** This Relais & Châteaux hotel set on 370 acres of scenic palm groves was one of Seychelles' first five-star resorts and remains a favorite luxury destination. A large hotel with 105 rooms strung along on both Grand Anse Kerlan and Petite Anse Kerlan, the resort developers did a good job of ensuring that the rooms are invisible from the beach, and thus maintained a sense of pristine privacy. Unfortunately, some of the rooms are stacked a bit close together, and though the interiors are beautifully decorated, the exteriors look somewhat utilitarian for a five-star resort. All three restaurants are considered excellent, and with a full service Shiseido spa, great sports facilities, including the only 18-hole golf course in Seychelles, a kids' club, and a very well-stocked activities center, you will never want for things to do here. Enjoy access to Anse Georgette, a famously gorgeous crescent of totally undeveloped white sand; the hotel provides a buggy shuttle service to this private beach throughout the day, or you can walk through the golf course to get there. **Pros:** access to three of Praslin's nicest beaches, including the famous Anse Georgette; the only 18-hole golf course in Seychelles; resort was designed to be mostly invisible from the sea, leaving the beach pristine. **Cons:** one of Seychelles' older hotels, the buildings don't all live up to five-star expectations; service can be a bit spotty. ⊠ *Anse Kerlan* ☎ *281–281* ⊕ *www.lemuriaresort. com* ⟿ *105 rooms* ⅛ *In-room: a/c, safe, kitchen (some), refrigerator, DVD (some), Wi-Fi (free). In-hotel: 3 restaurants, room service, bars, golf courses, tennis courts, pools, gym, spa, beachfront, diving, water sports, bicycles, children's programs (ages 4–12), laundry facilities,*

9

laundry service, Internet terminal, Wi-Fi hotspot, parking (free) ⊟ *AE, DC, MC, V* ⏁ *BP, MAP.*

$$$$ ⌂ **Cousine Island.** With only four villas, this resort is a birder's and naturalist's paradise. Villas in French colonial Seychelles style—all blue and white Chinese porcelain, antique wooden furniture, and lacy white trim—are spacious and well decorated. Unfortunately, tile floors and pedestrian fittings lack the accompanying charm, and some of the structures are in a bit of disrepair, though renovations are in the works. However, these small cracks can be overlooked by the truly breathtaking reality of the island itself. A rehabilitated conservation zone, Cousine is home to more than 100,000 sea birds that wheel and dive through the sky 24 hours a day. Get up close and personal with chicks nesting on low-hanging branches and the nooks of trees, or sitting on the massive pink granite boulders that loom like surreal sculptures all over the island. Totally private powder-white-sand beaches, wonderful and inventive cuisine, and extremely friendly staff complete the experience and ensure many repeat visitors. As if all this weren't enough, all proceeds from the lodge go back into the continued conservation of this sea-bird sanctuary. James Bond fans will be interested to know that you can also rent the *Sun Seeker* yacht, featured in various 007 flicks. **Pros:** an absolute paradise for birders and nature lovers; great food; with only four villas on this private island, total privacy and pampering are the name of the game. **Cons:** the spa and gym are in need of a makeover; a prefab look to some of the structures. ⊠ *Cousine Island* ☎ *321–107* ⊕ *www.cousineisland.com* ⤳ *4 villas* ⌂ *In-room: a/c, safe, refrigerator, Wi-Fi. In-hotel: restaurant, room service, bar, pools, gym, spa, beachfront, water sports, laundry service, Internet terminal, Wi-Fi hotspot* ⊟ *AE, MC, V* ⏁ *FAP.*

$ ⌂ **Indian Ocean Lodge.** Set in a lovely palm- and takamaka-tree-filled garden right on Grand Anse beach, this hotel excels in friendly service and creating a homey atmosphere. The 32 rooms are set in eight units of four rooms each (two upstairs and two downstairs), decorated in a tropical theme, with king-size beds and all the amenities. All rooms have balconies with sea views and can interconnect (great for families). The large open-air restaurant resides under a huge thatch roof, and serves a surprisingly good buffet of both local and international cuisine. **Pros:** good-value hotel with all the amenities on the popular Grand Anse beach; free daily shuttle to Cote d'Or beach; super-friendly staff and management. **Cons:** located on the western side of Praslin, Grand Anse is subject to seaweed accumulation from May–Oct.; Wi-Fi is not free. ⊠ *Grand Anse* ☎ *233–324 or 233–457* ⊕ *www.indianoceanlodge.com* ⤳ *32 rooms* ⌂ *In-room: a/c, safe, refrigerator, Wi-Fi (paid). In-hotel: restaurant, bar, pool, beachfront, laundry service, Wi-Fi hotspot, parking (free)* ⊟ *MC, V* ⏁ *BP, MAP.*

SHOPPING

Praslin's shops mostly offer artisanal crafts and curios and are fairly limited. The unique double-nut Coco de Mer seeds are on sale in the Vallée de Mai Park, but they are part of a strictly controlled quota—if you buy one, make sure that it has a label that authenticates its origins.

Most shops cluster around the Bay St. Anne jetty and the popular Cote d'Or beach.

Black Pearl Praslin Ocean Farm. Located just outside the airport, you'll find black pearls from the Seychelles' black-lip oyster, a specialty of the islands, at the source. ⊠ *Amitié* ☎ *233–150* ☉ *Mon.–Fri. 9–4, Sat. 9–noon.*

La Vallée de Mai Boutique. The souvenir shop at the Vallée de Mai Park sells a certified Coco de Mer nut (about Rs2,700), books about Seychelles natural history, and other souvenirs. ⊠ *Vallée de Mai* ☎ *321–735* ☉ *Daily 9–5.*

OUTDOOR ACTIVITIES AND SPORTS

BEACHES

Anse Bois de Rose, Anse Boudin, and **Anse Kerlan** are all beautiful and display some of the Seychelles' amazing granite formations.

Anse Georgette. This stretch of white sand could certainly contend for Praslin's prettiest beach—a complete lack of development and difficult access keep it so. Unfortunately, road access passes through the Lemuria Hotel, and nonguests must get permission to enter, which is not always an easy task.

Anse Lazio. Praslin's most famous beach is located on the island's northeastern tip. A long strip of golden sand with stunning granite boulders on either end and takamaka trees providing much coveted shade, this calm beach is known for excellent swimming and snorkeling opportunities. Unfortunately, this postcard perfect spot can get extremely crowded, diminishing the magic for some. ■TIP➔ When you arrive, head left and look for a nook at the very end between the boulders. The bus doesn't reach here, so you'll have to drive or walk about 20 minutes from the closest bus stop. Two restaurants operate on either end of the beach.

Cote d'Or Beach (also known as Anse Volbert) is a stunning white-sand beach that frequently appears on best-beach lists. There is a good number of hotels and restaurants nearby. The only downside to this gorgeous strip of sand, probably Praslin's most popular, is that you won't be alone, and you may get hassled by beach boys selling boat trips and the like.

Grand Anse, on the southwest coast, is another large stretch of sand and is lovely from October to March, but it can be the recipient of a lot of mucky sea grass the rest of the year.

BOAT EXCURSIONS

Half- or full-day snorkeling, sailing, and deep-sea fishing excursions are all possibilities. Most tours leave from Bay St. Anne, Cote d'Or, or Grand Anse.

RECOMMENDED TOUR OPERATORS

Creole Charters. Offering fishing and private boat excursions on a 28-foot catamaran, this company's trips typically include visits to Cousin, Aride, and Curieuse islands, complete with snorkeling and a beach BBQ.

Deep-sea fishing on a half- or full-day basis is also offered. ⊠ *Anse Lafarine* ☎ *712–977.*

DIVING AND SNORKELING

Qualified divers can book tanks and a guide to explore the rich underwater environment of coral reefs and abundant sea life at **Cote d'Or** (Anse Volbert). But you don't need to be a certified diver to enjoy the marine life of Seychelles. The shallow reefs and languid lagoons, particularly at **Anse Lazio** and **Anse Possession**, offer perfect conditions for snorkeling. You can while hours away watching the antics of schools of elegant angelfish or bold sergeant majors with their distinctive stripes. Even better, the snorkeling around the small islands of **Curieuse, Ile Cocos, St. Pierre, Sisters**, and **Marianne**, is excellent. Numerous boat excursions offer snorkeling day-trips, usually visiting two to three islands.

RECOMMENDED DIVE OPERATORS

Whitetip Divers. Based at the Paradise Sun Hotel on Cote d'Or, the professionals at Whitetip take guests on dives of up to 20 meters (65 feet) only. Many of the sites are around underwater granite formations. They also organize snorkeling trips by boat. ⊠ *Paradise Sun Hotel, Cote d'Or* ☎ *232–282 or 514–282* ⊕ *www.whitetipdivers.com.*

GOLF

Lemuria Resort Golf Course. Praslin is home to the only 18-hole golf course in the Seychelles. Surrounded by lush forested hills, this is probably one of the world's most beautiful greens. Golfing must be prebooked through the resort, which also rents all necessary equipment and buggies. ⊠ *Anse Kerlan* ☎ *281–230* ⊕ *www.lemuriaresort.com.*

HIKING

With countless secluded bays and forested nooks and crannies, Praslin is ideal for exploration on foot. The island is covered in a network of paths, and due to its small size, any path will lead to the coast within an hour, so there's very little chance of getting lost.

The hauntingly beautiful primeval forest of the **Vallée de Mai** is home to some 6,000 Coco de Mer palm trees and was once believed to be the original Garden of Eden. The well-maintained trails here allow hikers the flexibility of doubling back before completing an entire circuit, but for thorough exploration of the park, it's best to allow three to four hours. The Vallée boasts all six of Seychelles' endemic palm species and many other indigenous trees, and it is the last habitat of the endangered black parrot. A path branching off from the main circular track leads up to a sheltered viewpoint that looks out across the valley, and another small trail leads to a beautiful waterfall. The trails are very well maintained, and sandals will suffice.

LA DIGUE

La Digue is the fourth largest inhabited island of the Seychelles (though only 3 mi long and 1.8 mi wide), and the real deal when it comes to a laid-back tropical paradise. Only 6.4 km (4 mi) from Praslin (about a 15- to 30-minute ferry ride) and 43 km (27 mi) from Mahé (currently there is no direct ferry), little la Digue nonetheless feels a world away.

With no natural harbor, La Digue is protected by a coral reef, which, together with masses of colossal pink granite boulders, encircle and protect the island. Streets here hum the quiet rhythm of local life: a melody of ox-carts and bicycles, paths shaded by flowers and lush vegetation, and old colonial-style houses that speak of times past. Named in 1768 after a ship in the fleet of French explorer Marc-Joseph Marion du Fresne, La Digue's economic mainstays used to be vanilla and coconut oil. The island's fabulous beaches, lush interior, and colonial charm have made tourism its number-one industry today. The island's population of about 2,000 mostly reside in the west coast villages of La Réunion and La Passe.

GETTING HERE AND AROUND

The island's jetty and the majority of hotels are located in La Passe. Large boats (like cruise ships) usually anchor in Praslin's Bay St. Anne, then use smaller craft to tender passengers to the jetty in La Passe. The trip between the islands takes 15 minutes (on the speed boat) or 30 minutes (schooner ferry). There is no airport on La Digue; the only air travel is by helicopter. The best way to get around La Digue is on foot or bicycle—which are readily available for rent—as any part of the island can be reached in less than an hour. Bicycle rentals are about Rs100 per day, with discounts sometimes available for longer rentals. A handful of taxis and even some ox-carts are available in La Passe. The La Digue Public Transport shuttle is a van that covers set routes between the La

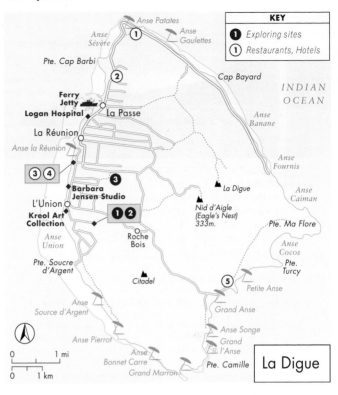

La Digue

Passe jetty and Grand Anse, Belle Vue, and Gros Roche, to correspond
with the arrival and departure of the ferry (Rs7/person). La Digue Island
Lodge also operates a shuttle for its guests (a trip from La Passe to
Grand Anse costs about €10 per person and takes 15 minutes or so).

SAFETY AND PRECAUTIONS

La Digue's east coast is wild, with remote and beautiful pink-granite
sand beaches, but dangerous currents prevail, and care must be taken
anytime you go into the water.

TIMING

Many tour operators offer day-trips to La Digue from Praslin. But on an
island ruled by a pace that encourages one to watch the orchids grow,
you really shouldn't rush your visit, and a minimum of two nights is
recommended. To truly get in the spirit of the place, at least four to
five nights are needed.

ESSENTIALS

Emergency Contacts La Digue Police (⊠ La Passe ☎ 234–251).

Hospitals La Digue Logan Hospital (⊠ La Passe La Digue ☎ 234–255).

Bike rentals Kwikwi (⊠ Anse Réunion ☎ 576–930). **Michelin Bicycle Rental**
(⊠ La Passe ☎ 234–304). **Tati's Bicycle Rental** (⊠ La Passe ☎ 512–111 or
234–346).

Taxis **La Digue Public Transport Shuttle** (✉ *La Passe* ☎ *514–317*). **Jamie Ernesta taxi** (✉ *La Passe* ☎ *511–015*). **Elias Radegonde taxi** (✉ *La Passe* ☎ *513–338*).

Visitor and tour info STB (✉ *La Passe* ☎ *234–393*). **Mason's Travel** (✉ *La Passe* ☎ *288–888*).

EXPLORING LA DIGUE

⇨ *See Praslin, above, for more info on excursions to neighboring islands.*

L'Union Estate. A traditional copra mill still produces coconut oil from the dried flesh of the nut at the L'Union Estate. Stroll around the outside of the majestic Plantation House framed by giant granite boulders, or go horseback riding. The grounds also house a small shipyard where displays (intermittently) show how craftsmen used to build pirogues and fishing boats. The estate is also home to the cemetery of the original settlers of La Digue and provides access to one of the most pristine beaches in Seychelles—the legendary Source d'Argent—among the most photographed beaches on earth.

Plantation House. This architectural gem among the plantation houses remaining in Seychelles. Said to be one of the oldest, it is the focal point of L'Union Estate. Unfortunately at the time of writing, admission into the house was prohibited. ✉ *L'Union* ☎ *234–240* 🖾 *Rs100* 🕓 *Daily 7–6.*

Veuve Nature Reserve. La Digue is the last refuge of the rare black paradise flycatcher, of which there are only about 100 still in existence. Once on the brink of extinction, these rare birds, which the locals call the veuve, or widow, are now protected in this reserve, which is also home to two extremely rare species of terrapin. ✉ *Anse Réunion* ☎ *234–353* 🖾 *Free* 🕓 *Mon.–Fri. 8–4.*

9

WHERE TO EAT

In the spirit of this super-chilled-out island, most of La Digue's restaurants are pretty casual. There are a few great beachside joints, as well as a couple notable hotel restaurants.

$$ ✕ **La Digue Island Lodge Restaurant.** Located along the edge of beautiful
INTERNATIONAL Anse Réunion, the lapping waters on the white sand as well as views of the gorgeous lush garden where massive pandanus palms, fig trees wrapped in orchids, and Indian almonds are lit to lovely effect. Dinners are buffet style with a focus on the international, which means that on any given night there will be some degree of influence from Asian, Middle Eastern, European, and of course, Creole cuisine. Great grilled fish, fresh salads, and reasonable Asian fare can be expected (pastas are not a highlight), though check in advance if there is a theme on the night you intend to go (Saturdays are typically all Creole). Not a fan of buffets? Choose from the à la carte seafood specialties, which are heavy on lobster and prawns (neither usually sourced from the Seychelles). Non-hotel guests are welcome, but large groups must reserve in

Grand Anse is a beautiful beach, but you have to watch out for the dangerous undertow.

advance. When the weather is fine, the beachfront tables, lit by gleaming oil lamps, are extremely romantic and peaceful. ✉ *Anse Réunion* ☎ *292–525* ⊕ *www.ladigue.sc* ▭ *AE, MC, V.*

\$\$ ✕ **Loutier Coco.** The only restaurant on the east side of the island, casual

CREOLE and friendly Loutier Coco serves an extremely tasty lunch buffet of the usual Creole favorites. Expect items like a beautifully spiced octopus curry in coconut milk, delicious grilled fish, roast pork, veggie curries, several piquant salads of mango or papaya, and dessert. Located just off Grande Anse beach, the sand floors, coconut-frond and hibiscus-flower decor, and brightly painted rustic murals invite dining in one's swimsuit. ■TIP➜ **Try to arrive early, as items like the grilled fish tend to dry out a bit towards the end.** Open for lunch only from 12:30–3, and serving drinks from 8–5. If you call a day ahead, you can organize a lobster feast. ✉ *Grande Anse* ☎ *234–243* ▭ *No credit cards.*

WHERE TO STAY

La Digue's accommodation is largely comprised of smaller hotels, guest houses, and an increasing number of self-catering options. Check out the STB's Web site for updated lists of these. There are only two large hotels on the island.

\$\$ ⌂ **La Digue Island Lodge.** The 44 A-frame villas of La Digue's oldest hotel dot Anse Réunion beach are fully equipped with the expected amenities of a large hotel. The simple villas of white painted takamaka wood and thatched latanier leaves are pleasant and comfortable if lacking an overwhelming sense of elegance or pizzazz. With the beach just outside your front door, a large pool overlooking the sea, and great sunset views, chances are you won't spend too much time inside. A spa with a variety of massage treatments, the island's only dive center, and excursions to the nearby smaller islands mean that you never need search far to keep yourself occupied. **Pros:** shuttle to Grand Anse; convenient and well-equipped rooms; pleasant swimming beach with great sunset views. **Cons:** nondescript in style; rooms are on the small side; Internet is not free and located only in reception. ✉ *Anse Réunion* ☎ *292–525* ⊕ *www.ladigue.sc* ⤴ *44 rooms* ⌂ *In-room: a/c, safe, refrigerator, Wi-Fi (some, paid). In-hotel: 2 restaurants, room service, 2 bars, pool, spa, beachfront, diving, laundry service, Wi-Fi hotspot (not free)* ▭ *AE, MC, V* ⏃ *BP, MAP.*

$ 🏨 **Le Domaine L'Orangerie.** The place to stay for those who swoon over elegant Zen style, the hotel's 45 villas are set in an old orange-tree grove (hence the name) and along its granite hills among enormous granite boulders. Overflowing with details like intricate stonework, dangling walls of shells, finely wrought mobiles of driftwood, water features, stone Buddhas graced with flowers and the like, the ambience fuses a Seychelles and Southeast Asian–spa style. Only some villas have sea views, so be sure to request if this is a priority. However, those without sea views enjoy a real romantic jungle perspective, complete with birds chirping and the scents of flowers. Garden villas have kitchens, and the hotel's newly completed beachfront annex will provide a beach bar as well a new, high-end, "gastronomic" French-influenced restaurant. **Pros:** stunning style and elegance; free bicycles; great breakfast. **Cons:** most rooms lack sea views; some of the rooms can be a bit dark; service can lack the down-home island friendliness found in less lofty locations. ✉ *Anse Severe* ☎ *234–444* ⊕ *www.orangeraie.sc* ⤴ *45 villas* ⌂ *In-room: a/c, safe, kitchen (some), refrigerator, Wi-Fi (paid). In-hotel: 2 restaurants, room service, bars, pools, gym, spa, beachfront, bicycles, laundry service, Internet terminal, Wi-Fi hotspot (free)* ▭ *AE, DC, MC, V* ⏃ *EP, BP, MAP.*

OUTDOOR ACTIVITIES AND SPORTS

BEACHES

La Digue is home to some of the world's best beaches, including one of the most photographed, **Anse Source d'Argent** (the film *Cast Away* was filmed here). With its soft white sand, clear turquoise water, and huge granite boulders, it's easy to see why this would be the case. However, the crowds it attracts could outweigh the beach's stunning natural attributes. In either case, it's worth visiting and deciding for yourself. The beach is accessible only through L'Union Estate, for which you must pay the normal entry fee of Rs100.

If you are near Anse Source d'Argent but want more privacy, the neighboring beaches of **Anse Bonnet Carré** and **Anse Pierrot** have the same white sand and shallow waters as their famous neighbor. Each requires a short walk—and these often-deserted beaches are perhaps less photogenic—but you'll definitely see fewer crowds here.

Closer to La Passe, **Anse Réunion** is a long beautiful beach with fine views of neighboring Praslin Island, great for snorkeling and swimming.

9

On La Digue's eastern side, **Grande Anse** and **Petite Anse** are picturesque beaches with huge waves. The sea may look inviting, but there is an extremely strong undertow, so beware. Strong surfers may find good waves, but picnics and sunbathing are the recommended activities here. If you're feeling adventurous, look for a guide at the Loutier Coco restaurant to take you to **Anse Songe** or all the way to **Anse Marron** down at the southern tip of the island. About a 20- to 40-minute walk from Grand Anse, these wild, empty beaches are absolutely gorgeous and are a worthy reward for the adventurous. On the island's northernmost tip, **Anse Patates** and the longer beach of **Anse Gaulettes** have soft white sand and calm seas, making them well suited for swimming and snorkeling.

BOAT EXCURSIONS

⇨ *See Praslin, above, for more info on excursions to neighboring islands.*

Boat trips around La Digue offer opportunities for bird-watching and snorkeling, as well as island-hopping and Creole barbeques. Big-game and deep-sea fishing can also be arranged. Half- and full-day boat trips can be booked in Anse Réunion and La Passe.

RECOMMENDED TOUR OPERATORS

Belle Petra. This catamaran operates from La Digue with half- and full-days trips to the neighboring islands of St. Pierre, Cousin, and Aride, among others. Activities include snorkeling and bird-watching. ⊠ *La Passe* ☏ *234–302 or 716–220.*

Zico 1 Boat Charter. This 9-meter boat can take up to eight people on half- or full-day big game or bottom-fishing excursions. ⊠ *Anse Réunion* ☏ *515–557 or 344–615.*

DIVING AND SNORKELING

La Digue and its neighboring islands are excellent dive destinations. Certified PADI instructors at Anse Réunion are available to introduce divers to the wonderful marine environment that La Digue has to offer: enjoy breathtaking granitic slopes; experience the thrill of diving among a school of reef sharks; and discover the Seychelles' extraordinary underwater life. Not so keen on bottled air? Snorkeling at Anse Réunion, Anse Patates, and Anse Source d'Argent is a simpler way to experience the marvel of the island's underwater world.

RECOMMENDED DIVE OPERATORS

Azzura Pro-Dive Center. The only dive center on La Digue, Azzura is associated with the La Digue Island Lodge, and can organize dive trips and open water to divemaster certification, as well as other excursions like snorkeling and island visits. Popular trips include Marianne for sharks, Anse Marron for tuna and sting rays, and the huge underwater mountain at the north Sister island. Daily dive trips start at 9:15 or 2:30. ⊠ *Anse Réunion* ☏ *292–535* ⊕ *www.ladigue.sc* ☉ *Daily 8:30–5.*

HIKING

The best way to explore tiny La Digue when not on a bicycle is on foot. Numerous trails wend their way through this island paradise, allowing visitors to absorb the atmosphere like locals. From La Passe, take the main track in a southerly direction past the hotels and church to the

L'Union Estate. Though you must pay the entrance fee, if you stay on the track, you will be rewarded with a beautiful walk through massive granite boulders, winding in and out of the forest and along white sand coves, until it ends at **Anse Source à Jean,** a beautiful place to spend the day. If you're feeling adventurous, hire a guide to take you around the island's southern end to **Anse Marron** and then up to **Grand Anse**—a gorgeous though at times tricky walk. Amphibious shoes with a good sole are recommended, as are a hat and plenty of sunscreen.

Eagle's Nest Mountain (*Nid d'Aigle*) is La Digue's tallest peak at more than 305 meters (1,000 feet) above sea level. It's a steep but rewarding climb of about an hour to the top. On the way up Belle Vue, look out for the rare endemic paradise flycatchers and an enormous fruit-bat colony. From Anse Réunion take the first left toward the island's interior. Pass an old house surrounded by high walls ("the chateau"), then turn left down a small pathway past a small group of houses. This track will head up the mountain toward the peak.

RECOMMENDED GUIDES

Leon Morel, hiking guide, works at the Loutier Coco on Grand Anse, and can guide hikers along the coast. Prices start at around Rs500 for two people to walk to Anse Marron. ⊠ *Grand Anse* ☎ *565–436.*

PRIVATE ISLAND RESORTS

Although largely uninhabited, there is a handful of private islands—most with nothing on them other than a single resort—that will blow your mind (and possibly your budget).

$$$–$$$$ ☷ **Denis Private Island Resort.** Discovered in 1773 by Denis de Trobiand, this coralline island was the sight of cotton, maize, and then coconut farming from 1845 to 1982, becoming a resort (for a private individual and his friends) only in 1978. The current owners purchased the island in 1997, entirely rebuilding it in 2006. The end result is a spectacularly elegant and yet unpretentious resort of 25 deluxe cottages on the beach—some are staggered a bit behind the true beachfront units—that boast features like private outside salas with daybeds, gorgeous partially outdoor bathrooms, iPod docks, king-size beds, and private beachfront with sun loungers. The tasteful decor takes an elegant view on the natural theme, and the lack of TVs and Internet in the rooms is intentional: you are here to relax and to (comfortably) commune with nature (a TV and computers with Internet are available in the library). In addition to revamping all of the structures on the island, the owners turned it into a conservation site in 1998, eradicating human-introduced predators, introducing rare endemic birds from nearby islands (including the Seychelles fody, Seychelles warbler, magpie robin, and paradise flycatcher), and attempting to encourage seabirds to use the newly safe (no rats, cats, or dogs) terrain to breed and nest. There are a lovely reef just off the restaurant beach, an excellent dive center, and, of course, postcard-perfect, powder-white-sand beaches. Thanks to the resort's conservation work and isolation, the birdlife is wonderful (though don't expect the insane numbers of seabirds that you'll encounter on islands like Aride

9

or Cousin). The main areas of the lodge itself are beautifully designed, the food is generally excellent, and the service genuinely friendly. **Pros:** nature walks with conservationists and great bird-watching; glorious isolation. **Cons:** not all of the cottages have direct sea views. ☒ *Denis Island* ☎ *288–963 or 295–999* ⊕ *www.denisisland.com* ➯ *25 cottages* ⚲ *In-room: a/c, refrigerator, no TV. In-hotel: restaurant, room service, bar, tennis courts, pool, beachfront, diving, water sports, laundry service, Internet terminal* ☐ *AE, MC, V* ⦿ *FAP.*

$$$ ▥ **Desroches Island.** The only resort on the Amirantes coral island group (and situated within an entire atoll), Desroches will fulfill all your coconut-fringed, white-sand-beach-paradise fantasies. Twenty double villas are located around the main lodge area, which includes the spacious and airy Veloutier Restaurant, a very hip bar with great cocktails, a gorgeous pool area, a small shop, and the reception area—all graced with comfortable couches in whites and beiges, elegant displays of shells, and a convenient Wi-Fi connection. Farther afield, 28 four-bedroom villas are the ideal family or group vacation spot. Each gorgeous villa—styled between Seychelles and Southeast Asia—has its own pool, kitchen, and villa assistant. All villas (family or doubles) lay claim to their own spot of white sand shaded by coconut palms, outdoor showers, and views of tranquil turquoise water (the entire west side of the island is protected from rough seas year-round). Complete the picture with what might be the best activities center in Seychelles—kayaks, surf skis, paddle surfing, surfing, snorkeling, pedalos (a peddle boat), and fly-fishing equipment are all free of charge and of excellent quality. And the motorized sports like diving and deep-sea fishing are reputed to offer some of the finest sites for both pursuits in the Indian Ocean. Guests can visit the tortoises (and babies at the breeding center), the lighthouse at the northern end of the island, or one of several snorkeling locations just offshore. Be sure to take advantage of the picnics delivered to various idyllic beach locations (nothing like returning from a good snorkel to find a picnic laid out with a cooler of ice-cold beer). **Pros:** absolute heaven for active water lovers and fishermen, with an incredible activities center and stunning diving and fishing sites; four-bedroom villas are an opulent yet affordable option for a large group or family; all rooms are 25 meters (82 feet) from the beach. **Cons:** though walled off with vegetation, the villas are spaced close enough together that you wouldn't want to sunbathe nude; the vegetation and wildlife are yet to be rehabilitated, so naturalists won't find an abundance of endemics or seabirds. ☒ *Desroches Island* ☎ *229–003, or 27/137376626 in South Africa* ⊕ *www.desroches-island.com* ➯ *48 villas* ⚲ *In-room: a/c, safe, kitchen (some), refrigerator, no DVD. In-hotel: 2 restaurants, room service, bars, tennis court, pools, gym, spa, beachfront, diving, water sports, bicycles, laundry service, Internet terminal, Wi-Fi hotspot* ☐ *AE, MC, V* ⦿ *AI.*

$$$$ ▥ **North Island Resort.** Operated by Wilderness Safaris, this private island
Fodor's Choice   takes the wow effect to a new level. The only property on Seychelles'
★   third largest granitic island, the resort's breathtaking villas are each the size of most people's houses, and unlike most abodes, boast a private plunge pool, deck, sun pavilion, private butler, and sea views from every angle. With a unique "any menu any venue any time" attitude toward

food, guests are encouraged to culinary whimsy, and are welcome to put chefs to the test if not enticed by the daily gourmet menus. Use of your own golf cart and bicycles allow freedom to roam the island. There is something so wonderfully decadent about cycling to the wilds of West Beach (one of the island's two main beaches) and being able to order a fancy fruit shake or cocktail from the bar, grab a fluffy towel, and nest on one of the comfortable daybeds. If you hang out long enough, you might want to feast on treats from the informal restaurant there—seared tuna, homemade pizzas, grilled veggies, and pork-belly morsels. The fine-dining restaurant on the other beach is gourmet all the way, and set in a magical environment of wood, shells, and water features. Great hiking trails that wind through granite hills and rehabilitated palm forests are thick with fruit bats and other wonders. The total rehabilitation of the island (rats and cats were removed several years back), and introductions of various endangered Seychelles endemic species is the goal at this high-class "Noah's ark." With its own dive and activity center boasting great boat dives, fishing, kayaking, and even surfing, a gorgeous hilltop spa with insane views, beautiful library filled with books about the Seychelles, and incredible wine cellar, you could easily spend a month here if your bank account could handle it. **Pros:** villas that take space, privacy, and comfort to a new level of barefoot luxury (your villa may well have once hosted Hollywood celebrities and heads of state); dining anywhere, anytime, and whatever your appetite craves; all activities are inclusive except full-day deep-sea-fishing charters and spa treatments. **Cons:** you may have to mortgage your house to holiday here. ⊠ *North Island* ☎ *293–100* ⊕ *www.north-island.com* ⇱ *11 villas* ⚒ *In-room: a/c, safe, kitchen, refrigerator, DVD, Internet, Wi-Fi. In-hotel: 2 restaurants, room service, bars, pools, spa, gym, beachfront, diving, water sports, bicycles, laundry service, Internet terminal, Wi-Fi hotspot* ▭ *AE, DC, MC, V* ⎢⊙⎢ *AI.*

9

On Safari

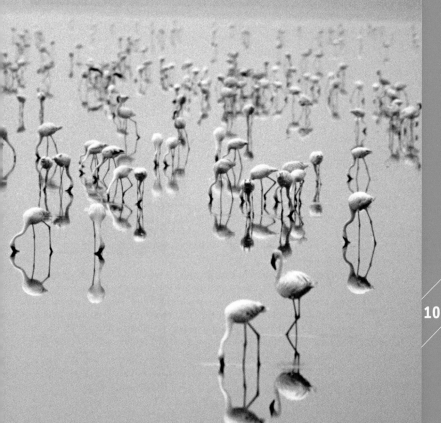

Updated by
Kate Turkington

In choosing to take a safari, you'll embark on one of the biggest travel adventures of your life. It's a big investment of both time and money—and planning well is crucial to ensure you have a good time. Even a basic question like "what should I wear?" is extremely important. In this safari section, we'll cover all the special considerations and lingo you'll need, with plenty of insider tips along the way.

Most people start planning a safari six to nine months in advance, but it's never too soon to start planning your trip. In fact, planning your trip 12 months in advance isn't unreasonable, especially if you want to travel during peak season—November through February in South Africa, July through October elsewhere—and have your heart set on a particular lodge.

Deciding where you want to go and choosing the safari operator in whose hands you'll place your trip are the most important things you need to do. Start planning for your safari the way you would any trip. Read travel books about the areas that most interest you. Talk to people who have been on a similar trip; word-of-mouth advice can be invaluable. Surf the Net. Get inspired. Line up your priorities. And find someone you trust to help plan your trip.

GETTING STARTED

AIR TRAVEL

Arriving by plane is the best and most viable means of transportation to most safari destinations. If you are visiting a game lodge deep in the bush, you will be arriving by light plane—and you really will be restricted in what you can bring. Excess luggage can usually be stored with the operator until your return. Don't just gloss over this: charter operators take weight very seriously, and some will charge you for an extra ticket if you insist on bringing excess baggage. ⇨ *For airline contact information and specific information for each country, see Air Travel, in the Getting Here and Around section of each chapter.*

AIR PASS

If you are planning to fly between a few of the countries mentioned in this book, consider the Star Alliance African Airpass, which can only be purchased by international passengers arriving to Africa on a Star Alliance carrier (Continental, United, US Airways, Air Canada, South African Airways, etc.); it's good for 3 to 10 flights. The flights are sold in segments, priced by the distance between cities. These are only economy-class seats and can be expensive when compared to the discount airline pricing within South Africa, but they are a bargain for the longer routes, such as from Nairobi to Johannesburg for under $300. If your itinerary includes more than 2 of the 26 cities served in Africa, this may be a good choice.

If you're flying on American Airlines or British Airways (there are 11 airlines in the alliance), another option is the Oneworld Alliance's Visit Africa Pass, which uses a zone system between cities in South Africa, Namibia, Zambia, and Zimbabwe. The minimum purchase is two segments and the maximum is 20. It's a great value when compared to regular fares.

Air Pass Info Oneworld Alliance (⊕ *www.oneworld.com*). **Star Alliance** (⊕ *www.staralliance.com*).

CHARTER FLIGHTS

Charter companies are a common mode of transportation when getting to safari lodges and remote destinations throughout Southern and East Africa. These aircraft are well-maintained and are almost always booked by your lodge or travel agent.

On-demand flights, those made at times other than those scheduled, are very expensive for independent travelers, as they require minimum passenger loads. If it is just two passengers, you will be charged for the vacant seats. Keep in mind that you probably won't get to choose the charter company you fly with. The aircraft you get depends on the number of passengers flying and can vary from very small (you will sit in the co-pilot's seat) to a much more comfortable commuter plane. Those with a severe fear of small planes might consider road travel instead.

Due to the limited space and size of the aircraft, charter carriers observe strict luggage regulations: luggage must be soft sided and weigh no more than 15 kg (33 lbs). Weight may vary by company, so be sure to ask what the limits are before packing.

⇨ *For information regarding charter companies in each country, see the Air Travel section, under Planning, in each country chapter.*

INTERNATIONAL DRIVER'S LICENSE

If you're taking a self-driving safari or renting a car in countries other than South Africa and Namibia, you'll need an international driver's license. These licenses are valid for one year and are issued at any American Automobile Association (AAA) office in the United States;

you must have a current U.S. driver's license. You need to bring two passport-type photographs with you for the license. A valid U.S. driver's license is accepted in South Africa and Namibia.

MONEY MATTERS

Most safaris are paid for in advance, so you need money only to cover personal purchases and gratuities. (The cash you take should include small denominations, like US$1, US$5, and US$10, for tips.) If you're self-driving, note that many places prefer to be paid in the local currency, so make sure you change money where you can. MasterCard and Visa are accepted almost everywhere; American Express is often refused in Botswana. Neither Diners Club nor Discover is recognized. *Throughout this guide, the following abbreviations are used: AE, American Express; DC, Diners Club; MC, MasterCard; and V, Visa.* ■ TIP→ It's a good idea to notify your credit-card company that you'll be traveling to Africa so that unusual-looking transactions aren't denied.

Reporting Lost Cards American Express (☎ 800/528-4800 in the U.S.; 336/393-1111 collect from abroad ⊕ www.americanexpress.com). **Diners Club** (☎ 800/234-6377 in the U.S.; 303/799-1504 collect from abroad ⊕ www.dinersclub.com). **MasterCard** (☎ 800/627-8372 in the U.S.; 636/722-7111 collect from abroad ⊕ www.mastercard.com). **Visa** (☎ 800/847-2911 in the U.S.; 410/581-9994 collect from abroad ⊕ www.visa.com).

PASSPORTS AND VISAS

A valid passport is a must for travel to any African country. ⚠ Certain countries, such as South Africa, won't let you enter with a soon-to-expire passport; also, you need two blank pages in your passport to enter South Africa. If you don't have a passport, apply immediately, because the process takes approximately five to six weeks. For a greatly increased fee, the application process can be shortened to as little as one week, but leaving this detail to the last minute can be stressful. If you have a passport, check the expiration date; if it's due to expire within six months of your return date, you need to renew it at once.

■ TIP→ If you're planning a honeymoon safari, make sure the bride's airline ticket, passport, and visas all use the same last name. Any discrepancies, especially between a passport and an airline ticket, will result in your trip being grounded before you ever take off. Brides may want to consider waiting to change their last name until after the honeymoon. Do be sure to let the lodge know in advance that you are on your honeymoon. You'll get lots of special goodies and extra-special pampering thrown in. ⇨ *For country-specific information regarding passports and visas, see the Passports and Visas section, under Planning, in each country chapter.*

U.S. Passport Information U.S. Department of State (☎ 877/487-2778 ⊕ www.travel.state.gov/passport).

U.S. Passport and Visa Expediters A. Briggs Passport & Visa Expediters (☎ 800/806-0581 or 202/338-0111 ⊕ www.abriggs.com). **American Passport**

DOCUMENT CHECKLIST

- Passport
- Visas, if necessary
- Airline tickets
- Proof of yellow-fever inoculation
- Accommodation and transfer vouchers
- Car-rental reservation forms
- International driver's license
- Copy of information page of your passport

- Copy of airline tickets
- Copy of medical prescriptions
- List of credit-card numbers and international contact information for each card issuer
- Copy of travel-insurance and medical-emergency evacuation policies
- Travel agent's contact numbers
- Notarized letter of consent from one parent if the other parent is traveling alone with their children

Express (☎ 800/455–5166 ⊕ www.americanpassport.com). **Passport Express** (☎ 800/362–8196 ⊕ www.passportexpress.com). **Travel Document Systems** (☎ 800/874–5100 or 202/638–3800 ⊕ www.traveldocs.com). **Travel the World Visas** (☎ 866/886–8472 or 202/223–8822 ⊕ www.world-visa.com).

SAFETY AND PRECAUTIONS

While most countries in Southern and East Africa are stable and safe, it's a good idea to do your homework and be fully aware of the areas you'll be traveling to before planning that once-in-a-lifetime trip.

The CIA's online *World Factbook* has maps and facts on the people, government, economy, and more for countries from Afghanistan to Zimbabwe. It's the fastest way to get a snapshot of a nation. It's also updated regularly and, obviously, well researched.

There's nothing like the local paper for putting your finger on the pulse. World-Newspapers.com has links to English-language newspapers, magazines, and Web sites in countries the world over.

The U.S. State Department's advice on the safety of a given country is probably the most conservative you'll encounter. That said, the information is updated regularly, and nearly every nation is covered. Just try to parse the language carefully. For example, a warning to "avoid all travel" carries more weight than one urging you to "avoid nonessential travel," and both are much stronger than a plea to "exercise caution." A travel warning is more permanent (though not necessarily more serious) than a so-called public announcement, which carries an expiration date.

At AllSafeTravels.com you can check the official travel warnings of several nations (for a more rounded picture), catch up on relevant news articles, and see what other travelers have to say. The site covers not only safety and security concerns but also weather hazards and health issues. For a small fee you can receive e-mail updates and emergency notifications for specific destinations.

10

ComeBackAlive.com, the Web site of author, filmmaker, and adventurer Robert Young Pelton is, as its name suggests, edgy, with information on the world's most dangerous places. Finding safety information on other seemingly safer places requires a little more fiddling around. There are forums where danger junkies share tips, and there are links to other relevant sites.

Travel Warnings AllSafeTravels.com (⊕ www.allsafetravels.com). **Central Intelligence Agency** (CIA ⊕ www.cia.gov). **ComeBackAlive.com** (⊕ www.comebackalive.com). **U.S. State Department** (⊕ www.travel.state.gov). **World-Newspapers.com** (⊕ www.world-newspapers.com).

TRAVEL INSURANCE

Get a comprehensive travel-insurance policy in addition to any primary insurance you already have. Travel insurance incorporates trip cancellation; trip interruption or travel delay; loss or theft of, or damage to, baggage; baggage delay; medical expenses; emergency medical transportation; and collision damage waiver if renting a car. These policies are offered by most travel-insurance companies in one comprehensive policy and vary in price based on both your total trip cost and your age.

It's important to note that travel insurance doesn't include coverage for threats of a terrorist incident or for any war-related activity. It's important that you speak with your operator before you book to find out how they would handle such occurrences. For example, would you be fully refunded if your trip was canceled because of war or a threat of a terrorist incident? Would your trip be postponed at no additional cost to you?

■ TIP➔ Purchase travel insurance within seven days of paying your initial trip deposit. For most policies this will not only ensure your trip deposit, but also cover you for any preexisting medical conditions and default by most airlines and safari companies. The latter two are not covered if your policy is purchased after seven days.

Many travel agents and tour operators stipulate that travel insurance is mandatory if you book your trip through them. This coverage is not only for your financial protection in the event of a cancellation but also for coverage of medical emergencies and medical evacuations due to injury or illness, which often involve use of jet aircraft with hospital equipment and doctors on board and can amount to many thousands of dollars.

If you need emergency medical evacuation, most travel-insurance companies stipulate that you must obtain authorization by the company prior to the evacuation. Unfortunately, many safari camps and lodges are so remote that they don't have access to a telephone, so getting prior authorization is extremely difficult, if not impossible. You should check with your insurance company before you leave to see whether it has this clause and if so, what can be done to get around it. Good travel agents and tour operators are aware of the issue and will address it.

Sign up with a medical-evacuation assistance company. A membership in one of these companies gets you doctor referrals, emergency

Pills & Vaccinations

	Yellow Fever	Malaria	Hepatitis A	Hepatitis B	Typhoid	Rabies	Polio	Other
Kenya	●	●	●	●	●	●	●	Meningitis
Tanzania	●	●	●	●	●	●	●	
South Africa	◐	●	●	●	●	●	●	
Botswana	◐	●	●	●	●	●	●	
Namibia	◐	●	●	●	●	●	●	
Zambia	◐	●	●	●	●	●	●	
Zimbabwe	◐	●	●	●	●	●	●	

KEY: ● = Necessary
● = Recommended
◐ = The government requires travelers arriving from countries where yellow fever is present to have proof that they got the vaccination

evacuation or repatriation, 24-hour hotlines for medical consultation, and other assistance. International SOS and AirMed International provide evacuation services and medical referrals. MedjetAssist offers medical evacuation.

Insurance Access America (⊕ www.accessamerica.com). **Travel Guard** (⊕ www.travelguard.com). **Expedia Package Protection Plus** (⊕ www.expedia. com). **HTH Worldwide** (⊕ www.hthworldwide.com). **International Medical Group** (⊕ www.imglobal.com). **Wallach & Company** (⊕ www.wallach.com).

Medical-Assistance Companies Air Med (⊕ www.airmed.com). **International SOS Assistance Emergency** (⊕ www.intsos.com). **MedJet Assistance** (⊕ www. medjetassist.com).

10

VACCINATIONS

Traveling overseas is daunting enough without having to worry about all the scary illnesses you could contract. But if you do your research and plan accordingly, there will be no reason to worry.

The Centers for Disease Control, or CDC, has an extremely helpful and informative Web site where you can find out country by country what you'll need. Remember that the CDC is going to be extremely conservative, so it's a good idea to meet with a trusted health-care professional to decide what you'll really need, which will be determined on your itinerary. We've also included the basic information on the countries we cover in the preceding chart.

Keep in mind that there is a time frame for vaccines. You should see your health provider four to six weeks before you leave for your trip. Also keep in mind that vaccines and prescriptions could run you anywhere from $1,000 to $2,000. It's important to factor this into your budget when planning, especially if you're plans include a large group.

You must be up to date with all of your routine shots such as measles/mumps/rubella (MMR) vaccine, diphtheria/pertussis/tetanus (DPT) vaccine, etc. If you're not up to date, usually a simple booster shot will bring you up to par. If you're traveling to northern Kenya December through June, don't be surprised if your doctor advises you to get inoculated against meningitis, as this part of the continent tends to see an outbreak during this time.

We can't stress enough the importance of taking malaria prophylactics. But be warned that all malaria medications are not equal. Chloroquine is NOT an effective antimalarial drug. And halofantrine (marketed as Halfan), which is widely used overseas to treat malaria, has serious heart-related side effects, including death. The CDC recommends that you do NOT use halofantrine. ⇨ *For more information on malaria, or other health issues while on safari, see Health below.*

Health Warnings Centers for Disease Control (*CDC* ☎ 877/394–8747 *international travelers' health line* ⊕ *www.cdc.gov/travel*).

HEPATITIS A AND B

Hepatitis A can be transmitted via contaminated seafood, water, or fruits and vegetables. According to the CDC, hepatitis A is the most common vaccine-preventable disease in travelers. Immunization consists of a series of two shots received six months apart. You need have received only the first one before you travel. This should be given at least four weeks before your trip.

The CDC recommends vaccination for hepatitis B only if you might be exposed to blood (if you are a health-care worker, for example), have sexual contact with the local population, stay longer than six months, or risk exposure during medical treatment. As needed, you should receive booster shots for tetanus-diphtheria (every 10 years), measles (you're usually immunized as a child), and polio (you're usually immunized as a child).

YELLOW FEVER

Yellow fever isn't inherent in any of the countries discussed in this book. Southern countries may, however, require you to present a valid yellow-fever inoculation certificate if prior to arrival you traveled to a region infected with yellow fever, so it's always best to carry one.

WHAT TO PACK

You'll be allowed one duffel-type bag, approximately 36 inches by 18 inches and a maximum of 26 kilos (57 pounds)—less on some airlines—so that it can be easily packed into the baggage pods of a small plane. One small camera and personal-effects bag can go on your lap. Keep all your documents and money in this personal bag.

■TIP➔ At O.R. Tambo International Airport in Johannesburg you can check bags at Lock-Up Luggage, one level below international departures. The cost is approximately US$7 per bag per day.

BINOCULARS

Binoculars are essential and come in many types and sizes. You get what you pay for, so avoid buying a cheap pair—the optics will be poor and the lenses usually don't stay aligned for long, especially if they get bumped, which they will on safari. Whatever strength you choose, pick the most lightweight pair, otherwise you'll be in for neck and shoulder strain. Take them with you on a night drive; you'll get great visuals of nocturnal animals and birds by the light of the tracker's spotlight. Many people find that when they start using binoculars and stop documenting each trip detail on film, they have a much better safari experience.

CLOTHING

You should need only three changes of clothing for an entire trip; almost all safaris include laundry as part of the package. If you're self-driving you can carry more, but washing is still easy and three changes of clothes should be ample if you use drip-dry fabrics that need no ironing. On mobile safaris you can wear tops and bottoms more than once, and either bring enough underwear to last a week between lodges, or wash as you go in the bathroom sink. Unless there's continual rain (unlikely), clothes dry overnight in the hot, dry African air.

■TIP➔ In certain countries—Botswana and Tanzania, for example—the staff won't wash underwear because it's against cultural custom.

For game walks, pack sturdy but light walking shoes or boots—in most cases durable sneakers suffice for this option. For a walking-based safari, you need sturdy, lightweight boots. Buy them well in advance of your trip so you can break them in. If possible, isolate the clothes used on your walk from the remainder of the clean garments in your bag. Bring a couple of large white plastic garbage bags for dirty laundry.

10

ELECTRICITY

Most of Southern Africa is on 220/240 volt alternating current (AC). The plug points are round. However, there are both large 15-amp three-prong sockets (with a ground connection) and smaller two-prong 5-amp sockets. Most lodges have adapter plugs, especially for recharging camera batteries; check before you go, or purchase a universal plug adapter before you leave home.

Safari hotels in the Serengeti, the private reserve areas outside Kruger National Park, and the less rustic private lodges in South Africa are likely to provide you with plug points and plugs, and some offer hair dryers and electric-razor sockets as well (check this before you go). Lodges on limited generator and solar power are usually able to charge camera batteries, as long as you have the right plug.

TOILETRIES AND SUNDRIES

Most hotels and game lodges provide toiletries such as soap, shampoo, and insect repellent, so you don't need to overpack these items. In the larger lodges in South Africa's national parks and private game reserves, stores and gift shops are fairly well stocked with clothing, film, and guidebooks; in self-drive and self-catering areas, shops also carry food and drink. In Botswana, lodges that belong to groups such as Wilderness Safaris or Gametrackers have small shops with a limited selection of books, clothing, film, and curios. Elsewhere in Africa you're not likely to find this type of amenity on safari.

On a canoe safari you're in the relentless sun every day and have to protect your legs, especially the tops of your thighs and shins, from sunburn. Bring a towel or, even better, a sarong, and place it over your legs. Sunscreen of SPF 30 or higher is de rigueur.

⚠ The African sun is harsh, and if you're even remotely susceptible to burning, especially coming from a northern winter, don't skimp on sunscreens and moisturizers. Also bring conditioner for your hair, which can dry out and start breaking off.

CAMERA SMARTS

All the safaris included in this book are photographic (game-viewing) safaris. That said, if you spend your entire safari with one eye closed and the other peering through a camera lens, you may miss all the other sensual elements that contribute to the great show that is the African bush. And more than likely, your pictures won't look like the photos you see in books about African safaris. A professional photographer can spend a full year in the field to produce a book, so you are often better off just taking snaps of your trip and buying a book to take home.

■ TIP➜ No matter what kind of camera you bring, be sure to keep it tightly sealed in plastic bags while you're traveling to protect it from dust. (Dust is especially troublesome in Namibia.) Tuck your equipment away when the wind kicks up. You should have one or more cloth covers while you're working, and clean your equipment every day if you can.

Learning some basics about the wildlife that you expect to see on your safari will help you capture some terrific shots of the animals. If you know something about their behavior patterns ahead of time, you'll be primed to capture action, like when the hippos start to roar. Learning from your guide and carefully observing the wildlife once you're there will also help you gauge just when to click your shutter.

PHOTOGRAPHY POINTERS

The trick to taking great pictures has three components: first is always good light. An hour after sunrise and before sunset are the magical times, because the light is softer and textures pop. For the few hours of harsh light each side of midday, you might as well put your camera away. The second component is framing. Framing a scene so that the composition is simple gives an image potency; with close-ups, fill the

Continued on page 584

SAFARI
STYLE

A frequently asked question on the Fodor's Forums is, "What do I wear on safari?" Your first thoughts might be of Meryl Streep in *Out of Africa* or Grace Kelly (seen here). But Hollywood didn't exactly get it right. Don't worry though, because we're here to help you figure out exactly what is and is not appropriate safari wear. Remember, khaki is the safari black.

WHAT TO WEAR

SUNGLASSES: The sun is bright here, and good UV protection is a must. Glasses also keep flying debris (like sand) out of your eyes. Plus you never know when you might see a spitting cobra—they aim for the eyes.

INSECT REPELLENT: Make sure yours has at least 20% DEET and is sweat resistant. We suggest OFF! Active. It has 25% DEET and comes in a 3-ounce pump spray bottle—perfect for those Transportation Security Administration (TSA) restrictions.

HAT: This is a must to keep off the sun and keep you in the shade. Make sure it has a brim all the way around and is packable and breathable. The Tilley hat (www.tilley.com) has been highly recommended in the Fodor's Forums.

CLOTHES: Make sure your clothes are cotton (read: breathable). Also we suggest you wear long pants in light earth colors—khaki and brown are best. Pants keep the bugs off, help prevent sunburn, and protect your legs from thorny bushes. Another thing to keep in mind: If you don't want to lug a bag, cargo pants are great for storage.

WALKING SHOES: The key words here are "sturdy," "support," and "traction." Though you probably won't be walking miles, you will be in and out of your vehicle and might be able to go on a walking safari. Hi-Tec (www.hi-tec.com) is an excellent brand with styles for all occasions.

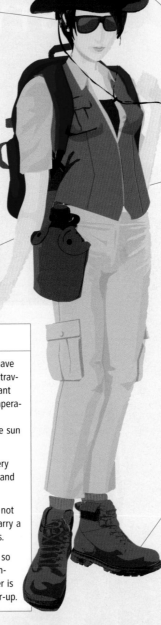

HOT...

- Usually your guide will have water for you, but if you're traveling alone it's very important that you bring water. It's imperative that you keep yourself hydrated when you're in the sun and heat.

- Bring layers. It can be very cold in the early mornings and late evenings.

- A photographer's vest is not a bad idea if you plan to carry a lot of film or memory cards.

- Most lodges have pools, so make sure you pack a swimsuit and a sarong. The latter is important to use as a cover-up.

WHAT NOT TO WEAR

LOTS OF MAKEUP:
Your daily regime should consist of slathering on sunscreen and spraying on insect repellent, not applying blush or foundation.

DESIGNER OUTFITS:
We think this goes without saying, but one never knows. Leave the fancy threads at home. They're bound to get ruined if you bring them.

CAMOUFLAGE: This is a big no-no. Warring factions in Africa wear camouflage, and you don't want to be confused with the military or appear to be making fun of the situation.

LEAVE THE BLING AT HOME: A safari is not a fashion show, and though you may get "dressed up" for dinner, there's no need for gold bracelets or diamonds. The shininess, not to mention the clinking of jewelry, will alert the animals to your presence. And when you're in the major cities, why invite trouble? You can live without your bling for a few days.

ANYTHING WITH HEELS: Prada or Gucci? Try L.L. Bean or EMS. You need sturdy, practical footwear. Again, a safari is not a fashion show. It's all about being comfortable and enjoying the experience.

...OR NOT

■ Don't wear clothes in any variation of blue or black, especially if you're traveling to tsetse-fly areas. These colors attract the pesky sleeping-sickness transmitters.

■ Don't wear perfume. Animals have an incredible sense of smell and will sense your arrival immediately and be gone before you can say "Greater Kudu."

■ Don't wear white. It reflects sunlight and startles animals.

■ Don't overpack. Most of the small airplanes you'll be taking to your camps have luggage-weight limits.

IN FOCUS SAFARI STYLE

10

PACKING CHECKLIST

Light, khaki, or neutral-color clothes are universally worn on safari and were first used in Africa as camouflage by the South African Boers, and then by the British Army that fought them during the South African War. Light colors also help to deflect the harsh sun and are less likely than dark colors to attract mosquitoes. Do not wear camouflage gear. Do wear layers of clothing that you can strip off as the sun gets hotter and put back on as the sun goes down.

■ Three cotton T-shirts

■ Two long-sleeve cotton shirts

■ Two pairs shorts or two skirts in summer

■ Two pairs long pants (three pairs in winter)

■ Optional: sweatshirt and sweatpants, which can double as sleepwear

■ Optional: a smart/casual dinner outfit

■ Underwear and socks

■ Walking shoes or sneakers

■ Sandals

■ Bathing suit

■ Warm thigh-length padded jacket and sweater in winter

■ Lightweight jacket in summer

■ Windbreaker or rain poncho

■ Camera equipment, plenty of film, and extra batteries

■ Contact lenses, including extras

■ Eyeglasses

■ Binoculars

■ Small flashlight

■ Personal toiletries

■ Malaria tablets

■ Sunscreen and lip balm with SPF 30 or higher, moisturizer, and hair conditioner

■ Antihistamine cream

■ Insect repellent

■ Basic first-aid kit (aspirin, bandages, antidiarrheal, antiseptic cream, etc.)

■ Tissues and/or premoistened wipes

■ Warm hat, scarf, and gloves in winter

■ Sun hat and sunglasses (Polaroid and UV-protected ones)

■ Documents and money (cash, credit cards), etc.

■ A notebook and pens

■ Travel and field guides

■ A couple of large white plastic garbage bags

■ Ziplock bags in various sizes

■ U.S. dollars in small denominations ($1, $5, $10) for tipping

frame for maximum impact. Using objects of known size in the foreground or middle ground will help establish scale. The third component is capturing sharp images: use a tripod or a beanbag to rest the camera on while in a vehicle. When using a long lens (upward of 200mm), you cannot hand-hold a steady shot; you must have some support if you want your photos to be clear.

DIGITAL CAMERAS

Good digital cameras and their memory cards or sticks may be more expensive than basic 35mm cameras, but the benefits of being able to preview shots, select what you want and delete what you don't, store them, and then adjust them on a computer can outweigh the initial cost. The resolution of nonprofessional digital images is approaching that of good film. Cameras with eight megapixels of resolution can print high-quality, smooth A4 or letter-size prints; images with five-megapixel resolution are fine as well.

Invest in a telephoto lens to shoot wildlife, as you tend to be too far away from the animals to capture any detail with the zoom lens generally built into most point-and-shoot digital cameras. This may mean upgrading to a more robust camera. A tripod or beanbag is another must-have; it will stabilize your camera, especially when a zoom lens is extended.

Buy or borrow as many memory cards as you can—you'll use them. You may want to use multiple smaller memory cards to minimize the risk of losing an entire card's worth of images. And, as always, bring extra batteries.

VIDEO CAMERAS

Video cameras these days are almost universally digital. The benefits of video are threefold: it's much easier to get basically pleasing results with moving images than with still photography; video cameras are much more light-sensitive than still cameras, so you can shoot in much lower light conditions; and you can edit your footage and show them on your DVD or computer at home. There's also the added benefit of the zoom-lens capability on most video cameras, which can give you almost as close a look at large animals as with binoculars (the zoom doesn't work as well with smaller, far-off subjects). Video cameras are hungry for batteries, however, and you may run into recharging problems in remote safari destinations.

Another problem with video cameras (but not for the person behind the lens) is that persistent videographers can become annoying to the other people in a group, so be sensitive about this. Don't go everywhere with your camera glued to your eye while simultaneously issuing nonstop commentary. Eventually someone is going to tell you to plug it, or worse. Resist poking your lens close to strangers' faces—it looks great through the lens but these are not paid actors, and they'll appreciate being given their own space.

10

ON SAFARI

The pieces are falling into place, but your idea of what life is like on safari may still be a golden-tinged haze. The whos, whats, and hows still need to come into focus. If you have questions like, Where's the best place to sit in a game-drive vehicle? or Can you get near a honey badger? then read on.

ACCOMMODATIONS

Price charts specific to each area are found in each chapter. We always list the facilities that are available—but we don't specify whether they cost extra: when pricing accommodations, always ask what's included. Price categories are based on a property's least expensive standard double room at high season (excluding holidays). Those indicated by a ⚠ are campgrounds with rustic camping accommodations (as opposed to the fairly luxurious safari tents at many private game lodges). Mailing addresses follow the street address or location, where appropriate. Be sure you understand the hotel's cancellation policy. Some places allow you to cancel without any kind of penalty—even if you prepaid to secure a discounted rate—if you cancel at least 24 hours in advance. Others require you to cancel a week in advance or penalize you the cost of one night. Small inns and B&Bs are most likely to require you to cancel far in advance. Always have written confirmation of your booking when you check in. ■TIP➔ Most hotels allow children under a certain age to stay in their parents' room at no extra charge, but others charge for them as extra adults, and some don't allow children under 12 at all. Ask about the policy on children before booking and make sure you find out the cutoff age for discounts.

Assume that hotels operate on the European Plan (EP, no meals) unless we specify that they use the Breakfast Plan (BP, with full breakfast), Continental Plan (CP, Continental breakfast), Full American Plan (FAP, all meals), Modified American Plan (MAP, breakfast and dinner), or are all-inclusive (AI, all meals and most activities).

BATHROOM BREAKS ON SAFARI

On safari, particularly when you stop for sundowners, you'll be pointed to a nearby bush (which the ranger checks out before you use it). Carry tissues and toilet paper with you, although these are usually available on the vehicle. Bury any paper you may use. If you have an emergency, ask your ranger to stop the vehicle and check out a suitable spot.

COMMUNICATIONS

INTERNET
Unless you have business in Africa, leave the laptop at home and take memory cards for your vacation photos. You can check e-mail for a few rand (or dollars) either in the comfort of your hotel or at a public Internet café. Most lodges will have a computer with Internet access, but remember that there's one computer for all the guests to use and

service is probably coming via satellite so availability may be limited.

PHONES

If you really want to save on international phone calls, the best advice is to provide a detailed itinerary back home and agree upon a schedule for calls. Internet calling like Skype also works well from the United States, but it's not always functional in Africa, unless you're on a reliable high-speed Internet connection, which isn't available everywhere. However, if you have a South African "free" cell phone (meaning you can receive calls for free; all phones using an SA SIM card do this), someone in the United States can call you from their Skype account, for reasonable per-minute charges—you won't be charged.

TELEPHONE COUNTRY CODES

- United States: 1
- Botswana: 267
- Kenya: 254
- Namibia: 264
- South Africa: 27
- Tanzania: 255
- Zambia: 260
- Zimbabwe: 263
- Note: When dialing from abroad, drop the initial 0 from local area codes.

MOBILE PHONES

Cell phones also can be rented by the day, week, or longer from the airport on your arrival, but this is an expensive option. If you plan on bringing a U.S. cell phone while you're traveling, know that plans change frequently, so try to gather as many details before leaving to figure out which plan is right for you. Some allow free calls to your number, but charge rates close to landline calls if you call the United States. If you don't text message at home, you'll learn to in Africa, where a simple text message costs a fraction of the cost of making an actual call. This is a handy option for meeting up with friends, but for making hotel reservations, it's best to make the call.

The least complicated way to make and receive phone calls is to obtain international roaming service from your cell-phone service provider before you leave home, but this can be expensive. ■TIP→ Verizon and Sprint customers cannot use their phones in Africa. Any phone that you take abroad must be unlocked by your company in order for you to be able to use it.

⇨ *For country-specific information regarding phones, see the Communication section, under Planning, in each country chapter.*

10

CUSTOMS AND DUTIES

Visitors traveling to South Africa or other Southern Africa Common Customs Union (SACU) countries (Botswana, Lesotho, Namibia, and Swaziland) may bring in new or used gifts and souvenirs up to a total value of R3,000 duty-free. For additional goods (new or used) up to a value of R12,000, a fee of 20% is levied. In addition, each person may bring up to 200 cigarettes, 20 cigars, 250 grams of tobacco, two liters of wine, one liter of other alcoholic beverages, 50 ml of perfume, and

250 ml of toilet water. The tobacco and alcohol allowance applies only to people 18 and over. If you enter a SACU country from or through another in the union, you are not liable for any duties. You will, however, need to complete a form listing items imported.

The United States is a signatory to CITES, a wildlife protection treaty, and therefore does not allow the importation of living or dead endangered animals, or their body parts, such as rhino horns or ivory. If you purchase an antique that is made partly or wholly of ivory, you must obtain a CITES preconvention certificate that clearly states the item is at least 100 years old. The import of zebra skin or other tourist products also requires a CITES permit.

U.S. Information U.S. Customs and Border Protection (⊕ *www.cbp.gov*). **U.S. Fish and Wildlife Service** (⊕ *www.fws.gov*).

GAME-VIEWING

GAME RANGERS AND TRACKERS

Game rangers (sometimes referred to as guides) tend to be of two types: those who have come to conservation by way of hunting and those who are professional conservationists. In both cases they have vast experience with and knowledge of the bush and the animals that inhabit it. Rangers work in conjunction with trackers, who sit in a special seat on the front of the 4x4, spot animals, and advise the rangers where to go.

For better or worse, the quality of your bush experience depends most heavily on your guide or game ranger and tracker. A ranger wears many hats while on safari: he's there to entertain you, protect you, and put you as close to the wilderness as possible while serving as bush mechanic, first-aid specialist, and host. He'll often eat meals with you, will explain animal habits and behavior while out in the bush, and, if you're on foot, will keep you alive in the presence of an excitable elephant, buffalo, hippo, or lion. This is no small feat, and each ranger has his particular strengths. Because of the intensity of the safari experience, with its exposure to potentially dangerous animals and tricky situations, your relationship with your guide or ranger is one of trust, friendliness, and respect. Misunderstandings may sometimes occur, but you're one step closer to ensuring that all goes well if you know the protocols and expectations.

Wondering how to treat your ranger? Acknowledge that your guide is a professional and an expert in the field, and defer to his knowledge. Instead of trying to show how much you know, follow the example of the hunter, which is to walk quietly and take notice of all the little signs around you. Save social chatter with the guide for when you're back at camp, not out on a game drive. Rangers appreciate questions, which give them an idea of your range of knowledge and of how much detail to include in their animal descriptions. However, if you like to ask a lot of questions, save some for later, especially as several other people are likely to be in the safari vehicle with you. Carry a pocket notebook on game drives and jot down questions as they occur; you can then bring

CLOSE UP

Tips for Tipping

Plan to give the local equivalents (U.S. dollars are also fine) of about US$10 per person per day to the ranger and not much less to the tracker; an additional tip of US$25 for the general staff would be sufficient for a couple staying two days. Mark Harris, managing director of Tanzania Odyssey, a London-based tour operator, suggests that tipping roughly $15 a day (per couple) into the general tip box and approximately $15 a day to your specific driver is generous.

Guides should be tipped at least US$5 per person per day.

It's also a good idea to bring some thank-you cards with you from home to include with the tip as a personal touch. Fodor's Forum member atravelynn adds, "Put bills in an envelope for your guide and in a separate envelope with your name on it for the camp staff. Sometimes the camps have envelopes, but bringing some from home is also a good idea."

---

them up at dinner or around the campfire, when your ranger has more time to talk and everyone can participate in the discussion.

Wondering how your ranger will treat you? Don't let your ranger get away with rote guiding, or "guiding by numbers"—providing only a list of an animal's attributes. Push him by politely asking questions and showing you'd like to know more. Even the best guides may experience "bush burnout" by the end of a busy safari season with demanding clients, but any guide worthy of the title always goes out of his way to give you the best possible experience. If you suspect yours has a case of burnout, or just laziness, you have a right to ask for certain things. There's never any harm in asking, and you can't expect your guide to read your mind about what you like. If, for example, you have a preference for birds, insects, or whatever, ask your guide to spend time on these subjects. You may be surprised by how happy he is to oblige.

GAME-VIEWING WITH A RANGER

At most Southern African camps and lodges, open vehicles with raised, stepped seating—meaning the seats in back are higher than the ones in front—are used for game drives. There are usually three rows of seats after the driver's row; the norm at a luxury lodge is to have two people per row. In the front row you'll have the clearest conversations with the ranger, but farther back you'll have a clearer, elevated view over the front of the car. Try not to get stuck in the very back, though; in that row you spend a lot of time ducking thorny branches, you're exposed to the most dust, you feel the most bumps, and communicating with your ranger is difficult because of the rows between you. In closed vehicles, which are used by private touring companies operating in Kruger National Park, sit as close to the driver-guide as possible so you can get in and out of the vehicle more easily and get the best views.

The tracker will be busy searching out animal tracks, spoor, and other clues to nearby wildlife while the guide drives and discusses the animals and their environment. As described in Luxury Lodge–Based Safaris (*see*

10

Chapter 1 for more information), rangers often communicate with each other via radio when someone has a good sighting.

Guided bush walks vary, but usually a maximum of eight guests walk in single file with the armed ranger up front and the tracker at the back. A bush walk is a more intimate experience than a drive. You are up close with the bush and with your fellow walkers and guides. Your guide will brief you thoroughly about where and how to walk, emergency procedures, and the like. If you are in a national park, you will most likely have to pay an additional fee to have an armed park ranger escort you on your walk.

GAME-VIEWING ON A SELF-DRIVE SAFARI

Although most animals in popular parks are accustomed to vehicles with humans in them and will carry on unperturbed in many cases, a vehicle should still approach any animal carefully and quietly, and the driver should "feel" the response. This is for your own and the animals' safety. A delicate approach also gives you a better chance of getting as close as possible without alarming the animal. Be conservative and err on the side of caution, stopping as soon as circumstances suggest.

Human presence among wild animals never goes unnoticed. Don't get out of the vehicle, even if the animals appear friendly, and don't feed the creatures. Animals don't associate people in a vehicle with the potential food source or possible threat that they do when people are out of the vehicle. But for this ruse to work you must be quiet and still. The smell of the exhaust fumes and noise of a vehicle mask the presence of the human cargo, so when the engine is off you need to exercise extra caution. This is especially true when closely viewing lions and elephants—the only two animals likely to attack a vehicle or people in a vehicle. When approaching lions or elephants, never leap out of your seat or talk loudly; you want to be able to get as close as possible without scaring them off, and you want to avoid provoking an attack.

It does take time to develop your ability to find motionless game in thick bush. On the first day you're less likely to spot an animal than to run it over. All those fancy stripes and tawny colors really do work. Slowly, though, you learn to recognize the small clues that give away an animal in the bush: the flick of a tail, the toss of a horn, even fresh dung. To see any of this, you have to drive *slowly,* 15 to 25 KPH (10 to 15 MPH). Fight the urge to pin back your ears and tear around a park at 50 KPH (30 MPH) hoping to find something big. The only way to spot game at that speed is if it's standing in the road or if you come upon a number of cars already at a sighting. But remember that being the 10th car at a game sighting is less exciting than finding the animal yourself. Not only do the other cars detract from the experience, but you feel like a scavenger—a sort of voyeuristic vulture.

The best time to find game is in the early morning and early evening, when the animals are most active, although old Africa hands will tell you that you can come across good game at any time of day. Stick to the philosophy "you never know what's around the next corner," and keep your eyes and ears wide open all the time. If your rest camp offers guided night drives on open vehicles with spotlights—go for it. You'll rarely be disappointed, seeing not only big game but also a lot of fascinating little critters that surface only at night. Book your night drive in advance or as soon as you get to camp.

HEALTH

Of all the horror stories and fantastic nightmares about meeting your end in the bush, the problem you're most likely to encounter will be of your own doing: dehydration. Also be wary of malaria, motion sickness, and intestinal problems. By taking commonsense precautions, your safari will be uneventful from a health perspective but memorable in every other way.

The Web site, Travel Health Online, is a good source to check out before you travel because it compiles primarily health and some safety information from a variety of official sources, and it's done by a medical publishing company. The CDC has information on health risks associated with almost every country on the planet, as well as what precautions to take. The World Health Organization (aka the WHO) is the health arm of the United Nations and has information by topic and by country. Its clear, well-written publication *International Travel and Health,* which you can download from the Web site, covers everything you need to know about staying healthy abroad.

Health Warnings Centers for Disease Control (*CDC* ☎ *877/394–8747 international travelers' health line* ⊕ *www.cdc.gov/travel*). **South African Airways Netcare Travel Clinics** (☎ *0860/638–2273 toll-free in South Africa* ⊕ *www.travelclinic.co.za*). **Travel Health Online** (⊕ *www.tripprep.com*). **World Health Organization** (*WHO* ⊕ *www.who.int*).

BUGS AND OTHER CREEPY CRAWLIES

In summer ticks may be a problem, even in open areas close to cities. If you intend to walk or hike anywhere, use a suitable insect repellent. After your walk, examine your body and clothes for ticks, looking carefully for pepper ticks, which are tiny but may cause tick-bite fever. If you are bitten, keep an eye on the bite. If the tick was infected, the bite will swell, itch, and develop a black necrotic center. This is a sure sign that you will develop tick-bite fever, which usually hits after about 8 to 12 days. Symptoms may be mild or severe, depending on the patient. This disease is not usually life-threatening in healthy adults, but it's horribly unpleasant. Most people who are bitten by ticks suffer no more than an itchy bump, so don't panic. ■TIP➔ **Check your boots for spiders and other crawlies and shake your clothes out before getting dressed.**

Always keep a lookout for mosquitoes. Even in nonmalarial areas they are extremely irritating. When walking anywhere in the bush, watch out for snakes. If you see one, give it a wide berth and you should be fine. Snakes really bite only when they are taken by surprise, so you don't want to step on a napping mamba.

DEHYDRATION AND OVERHEATING

The African sun is hot and the air is dry, and sweat evaporates quickly in these conditions. You might not realize how much bodily fluid you are losing as a result. Wear a hat, lightweight clothing, and sunscreen—all

10

of which will help your body cope with high temperatures. If you're prone to low-blood sugar or have a sensitive stomach, consider bringing along rehydration salts, available at camping stores, to balance your body's fluids and keep you going when you feel listless.

Drink at least two to three quarts of water a day, and in extreme heat conditions as much as three to four quarts of water or juice. Drink more if you're exerting yourself physically. Alcohol is dehydrating, so try to limit consumption on hot or long travel days. If you do overdo it at dinner with wine or spirits, or even caffeine, you need to drink even more water to recover the fluid lost as your body processes the alcohol. Antimalarial medications are also very dehydrating, so it's important to drink water while you're taking this medicine.

Don't rely on thirst to tell you when to drink; people often don't feel thirsty until they're a little dehydrated. At the first sign of dry mouth, exhaustion, or headache, drink water, because dehydration is the likely culprit. ■TIP➔ To test for dehydration, pinch the skin on the back of your hand and see if it stays in a peak; if it does, you're dehydrated. Drink a solution of ½ teaspoon salt and 4 tablespoons sugar dissolved in a quart of water to replace electrolytes.

Heat cramps stem from a low salt level due to excessive sweating. These muscle pains usually occur in the abdomen, arms, or legs. When a child says he can't take another step, ask if he has cramps. When cramps occur, stop all activity and sit quietly in a cool spot and drink water. Don't do anything strenuous for a few hours after the cramps subside. If heat cramps persist for more than an hour, seek medical assistance.

DON'T SWIM IN LAKES OR STREAMS
Many lakes and streams, particularly east of the watershed divide (i.e., in rivers flowing toward the Indian Ocean), are infected with *bilharzia* (schistosomiasis), a parasite carried by a small freshwater snail. The microscopic fluke enters through the skin of swimmers or waders, attaches itself to the intestines or bladder, and lays eggs. Avoid wading in still waters or in areas close to reeds. If you have been wading or swimming in dubious water, dry yourself off vigorously with a towel immediately upon exiting the water, as this may help to dislodge any flukes before they can burrow into your skin. Fast-moving water is considered safe. If you have been exposed, pop into a pharmacy and purchase a course of treatment and take it to be safe. If your trip is ending shortly after your exposure, take the medicine home and have a checkup once you get home. Bilharzia is easily diagnosed, and it's also easily treated in the early stages.

INTESTINAL UPSET
Microfauna and -flora differ in every region of Africa, so if you drink unfiltered water, add ice to your soda, or eat fruit from a roadside stand, you might get traveler's diarrhea. All reputable hotels and lodges have filtered, clean tap water or provide sterilized drinking water, and nearly all camps and lodges have supplies of bottled water. If you're traveling outside organized safari camps in rural Africa or are unsure of local water, carry plenty of bottled water and follow the CDC's advice for

fruits and vegetables: boil it, cook it, peel it, or forget it. If you're going on a mobile safari, ask about drinking water.

MALARIA

The most serious health problem facing travelers is malaria. The risk is medium at the height of the summer and very low in winter. All travelers heading into malaria-endemic regions should consult a health-care professional at least one month before departure for advice. Unfortunately, the malarial agent *Plasmodium sp.* seems to be able to develop a hardy resistance to new prophylactic drugs pretty quickly, so even if you are taking the newest miracle drug, the best prevention is to avoid being bitten by mosquitoes in the first place.

Treat your clothes with a mosquito-repellent spray or laundry wash before you leave home. Most of these last approximately 14 days and through several washings and contain the active ingredient permethrin, which is sold as Permanone and Duranon. This spray is specifically for clothes and shouldn't be used on skin. You can find it at camping and outdoor stores such as Eastern Mountain Sports.

After sunset wear light-colored (mosquitoes and tsetse flies are attracted to dark surfaces), loose, long-sleeve shirts, long pants, and shoes and socks, and apply mosquito repellent (that contains DEET) generously. Always sleep in a mosquito-proof room or tent, and if possible, keep a fan going in your room. If you are pregnant or trying to conceive, avoid malaria areas entirely.

Generally speaking, the risk is much lower in the dry season (May–October) and peaks immediately after the first rains, which should be in November, but El Niño has made that a lot less predictable.

If you have been bitten by an infected mosquito, you can expect to feel the effects anywhere from 7 to 90 days afterward. Typically you will feel like you have the flu, with worsening high fever, chills and sweats, headache, and muscle aches. In some cases this is accompanied by abdominal pain, diarrhea, and a cough. If it's not treated you could die. It's possible to treat malaria after you have contracted it, but this shouldn't be your long-term strategy for dealing with the disease. △ **If you feel ill even several months after you return home, tell your doctor that you have been in a malaria-infected area.**

MEDICAL CARE AND MEDICINE

As a foreigner, you'll be expected to pay in full for any medical services, so check your existing health plan to see whether you're covered while abroad, and supplement it if necessary. South African doctors are generally excellent. The equipment and training in private clinics rival the best in the world, but public hospitals tend to suffer from overcrowding and underfunding.

OVER-THE-COUNTER REMEDIES

You can buy over-the-counter medication in pharmacies and supermarkets, but your body may not react the same way to the African version of a product, even something as simple as a headache tablet. Bring your own supply for your trip and rely on pharmacies just for emergency medication.

A COMMON SAFARI AFFLICTION

In addition to the health hazards described in this section, there's a safari disease that's as well known as malaria: "khaki fever." Though this fever may not kill you, it can wreak havoc upon your sensibilities and your heart. In fact, it is part of the plotline in the 1953 film *Mogambo*, in which the married society girl (Grace Kelly) falls for the rugged, tanned game ranger (Clark Gable), who's already carrying on with a wild American (Ava Gardner).

When you're on safari, a magical world quite unlike the one to which you're accustomed reveals itself. When it does, a perpetual good mood might strike and with it, a feeling of euphoria and romance. We can't blame you. The campfire can be very seductive, and the bush is full of bewitching, sensual stimuli—a full moon hovers above the trees, a lion roars in the distance, a nightjar fills the velvety night with its trilling call. Then there's the tanned, knowledgeable ranger protecting you from the wilds of Africa, chauffeuring you around, and seemingly delivering your every wish.

Hey, heavenly things can happen . . . but if they do, just make sure you're prepared for the earthbound realities. AIDS in Africa is rife; if there's even the remotest chance of having a sexual encounter on safari, carry condoms. Better still, abstain.

MOTION SICKNESS

If you're prone to motion sickness, be sure to examine your safari itinerary closely. Though most landing strips for chartered planes are not paved but rather grass, earth, or gravel, landings are smooth most of the time. If you're going on safari to northern Botswana (the Okavango Delta, specifically), know that small planes and unpaved airstrips are the main means of transportation between camps; these trips can be very bumpy, hot, and a little dizzying even if you're not prone to motion sickness. If you're not sure how you'll react, take motion-sickness pills just in case. Most of the air transfers take an average of only 30 minutes and the rewards will be infinitely greater than the pains.

■TIP➜ When you fly in small planes, take a sun hat and a pair of sunglasses. If you sit in the front seat next to the pilot, or on the side of the sun, you will experience harsh glare that could give you a severe headache and exacerbate motion sickness.

VOCABULARY

Mastering the basics of just two foreign languages, Zulu and Swahili, should make you well equipped for travel through much of the region. Zulu is the most common of the Southern African Nguni family of languages (Zulu, Shangaan, Ndebele, Swazi, Xhosa) and is understood in South Africa and Zimbabwe. Swahili is a mixture of Arabic and Bantu and is used across East Africa. In Namibia, Botswana, and Zambia your best bet initially is to stick with English.

SAFARI SPEAK

Ablution blocks: public bathrooms

Banda: bungalow or hut

Big Five: buffalos, elephants, leopards, lions, and rhinoceros, collectively

Boma: a fenced-in, open-air eating area, usually circular

Braai: barbecue

Bushveld: general safari area in South Africa, usually with scattered shrubs and trees and lots of game; also referred to as the bush or the veld

Camp: used interchangeably with lodge

Campground: a place used for camping that encompasses several campsites and often includes some shared facilities

Campsite: may or may not be part of a campground

Concession: game-area lease that is granted to a safari company and gives it exclusive access to the land

Game guide: used interchangeably with ranger; usually a man

Hides: small, partially camouflaged shelters from which to view game and birds; blinds

Kopje/Koppies: hills or rocky outcrops

Kraal: traditional rural settlement of huts and houses

Lodge: accommodation in rustic yet stylish tents, rondavels, or lavish suites; prices at lodges usually include all meals and game-viewing

10

Marula: tree from which amarula (the liquor) gets its name

Mobile or overland safari: usually a self-sufficient, camping affair set up at a different location (at public or private campgrounds) each night

Mokoro: dugout canoe; plural *mekoro*

Ranger: safari guide with vast experience with and knowledge of the bush and the animals that inhabit it; used interchangeably with game guide

Rest camp: camp in a national park

Rondawel/rondavel: a traditional round dwelling with a conical roof

Sala: outdoor covered deck

Self-catering: with some kind of kitchen facilities, so you can store food and prepare meals yourself

Self-drive safari: budget-safari option in which you drive, and guide, yourself in a rented vehicle

Sundowner: cocktails at sunset

Tracker: works in conjunction with a ranger, spotting animals from a special seat on the front of the 4x4 game-viewing vehicle

Veld: a grassland; see bushveld

Vlei: wetland or marsh

SOUTH AFRICAN WORDS AND PHRASES

BASICS

Abseil: rappel

Berg: mountain

Boot: trunk (of a car)

Bottle store: liquor store

Bra/bru/my bra: brother (term of affection or familiarity)

Buck: antelope

Burg: city

Chommie: mate, chum

Dagga: marijuana, sometimes called *zol*

Djembes: drums

Dorp: village

Fanagalo: a mix of Zulu, English, Afrikaans, Sotho, and Xhosa

Highveld: the country's high interior plateau, including Johannesburg

Howzit?: literally, "how are you?" but used as a general greeting

Indaba: literally, a meeting but also a problem, as in "that's your indaba."

Ja: yes

Jol: a party or night on the town

Kloof: river gorge

Kokerbooms: quiver trees

Lekker: nice

Lowveld: land at lower elevation, including Kruger National Park

Mopane: nutrient-poor land

Muthi: (pronounced *mooti*) traditional (non-Western) medicine

Plaas: farm

Petrol: gasoline

Robot: traffic light

Sangoma: traditional healer or mystic

Shebeen: a place to drink, often used for taverns in townships

Sis: gross, disgusting

Sisi or usisi: sister (term of affection or respect)

Spaza shop: an informal shop, usually from a truck or container

Spar: name of grocery market chain in Africa

Stoep: veranda

Takkie: (pronounced *tacky*) sneaker

FOOD AND DRINK

Biltong: spiced air-dried (not smoked) meat, made of everything from beef to kudu

Bobotie: spiced, minced beef or lamb topped with savory custard, a Cape Malay dish

Boerewors: Afrikaner term for a spicy farmer's sausage, often used for a braai (pronounced boo-*rah-vorse*)

Bredie: a casserole or stew, usually lamb with tomatoes

Bunny chow: not a fancy name for salad—it's a half loaf of bread hollowed out and filled with meat or vegetable curry

Chakalaka: a spicy relish

Gatsby: a loaf of bread cut lengthwise and filled with fish or meat, salad, and fries

Kabeljou: one of the varieties of line fish

Kingklip: a native fish

Koeksister: a deep-fried braided, sugared dough

Malva: pudding

Melktert: a sweet custard tart

Moroho: mopane worms

Pap: also called *mielie pap*, a maize-based porridge

Peppadew: a patented vegetable, so you may see it under different names, usually with the word *dew* in them; it's a sort of a cross between a sweet pepper and a chili and is usually pickled.

Peri-peri: a spicy chili marinade, Portuguese in origin, based on the searing hot *piri-piri* chili; some recipes are tomato-based, others use garlic, olive oil, and brandy

Potjie: pronounced poy-*key* and also called *potjiekos*, a traditional stew cooked in a three-legged pot

Rocket: arugula

Rooibos: an indigenous, earthy-tasting red-leaf tea

Samp: corn porridge

Snoek: a barracudalike fish, often smoked, sometimes used for *smoorsnoek* (braised)

Sosaties: local version of a kebab, with spiced, grilled chunks of meat

Waterblommetjie: water lilies, sometimes used in stews

SWAHILI ESSENTIALS

ANIMALS

Buffalo: nyati

Cheetah: duma

Crocodile: mamba

Elephant: tembo

Giraffe: twiga

Hippo: kiboko

Impala: swala

Leopard: chui

Lion: simba

Rhino: kifalu

BASICS

Yes: ndio

No: hapana

Please: tafadhali

Excuse me: samahani

Thank you (very much): asante (sana)

Welcome: karibu

Hello: jambo

Beautiful: nzuri

Goodbye: kwaheri

Cheers: kwahafya njema

FOOD AND DRINK

Food: chakula

Water: maji

Bread: mkate

Fruit(s): (ma)tunda

Vegetable: mboga

Salt: chumvi

Sugar: sukari

Coffee: kahawa

Tea: chai

Beer: pombe

USEFUL PHRASES

What is your name?: Jina lako nani?

My name is . . . : Jina langu ni . . .

How are you?: Habari?

Where are you from?: Unatoka wapi?

I come from . . . : Mimi ninatoka . . .

Do you speak English?: Una sema kiingereza?

I don't speak Swahili.: Sisemi kiswahili.

I don't understand.: Sifahamu.

How do you say this in Kiswahili?: Unasemaje kwa Kiswahili?

How much is it?: Ngapi shillings?

May I take your picture?: Mikupige picha?

Where is the bathroom?: Choo kiko wapi?

I need . . . : Mimi natafuta . . .

I want to buy . . . : Mimi nataka kununua . . .

No problem.: Hakuna matata.

ZULU ESSENTIALS

BASICS

Yes: yebo

No: cha

Please/Excuse me: uxolo

Thank you: ngiyabonga

You're welcome: Nami ngiyabonga

Good morning/hello: sawubona

Goodbye: sala kahle

FOOD AND DRINK

Food: ukudla

Water: amanzi

Bread: isinkwa

Fruit: isthelo

Vegetable: uhlaza

Salt: usawoti

Sugar: ushekela

Coffee: ikhofi

Tea: itiye

Beer: utshwala

USEFUL PHRASES

What is your name?: Ubani igama lakho?

My name is . . . : Igama lami ngingu . . .

Do you speak English?: Uya khuluma isingisi?

I don't understand.: Angizwa ukuthi uthini.

How much is it?: Kuyimalini lokhu?

May I take your picture?: Mikupige picha?

Where is the bathroom?: Likuphi itholethe?

I would like . . . : Ngidinga . . .

10

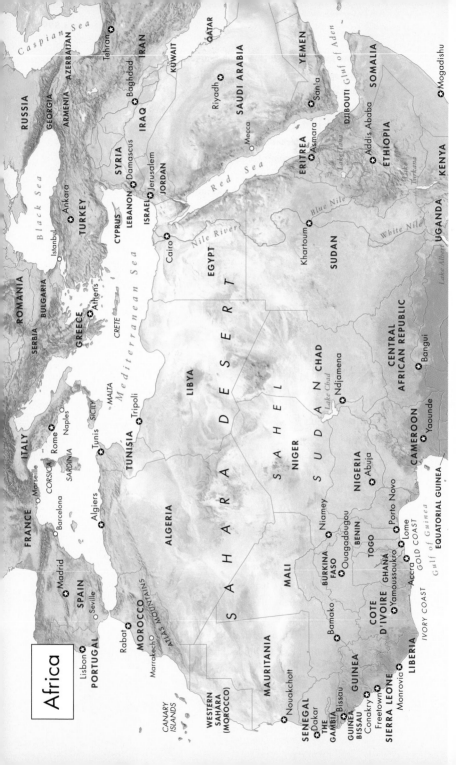

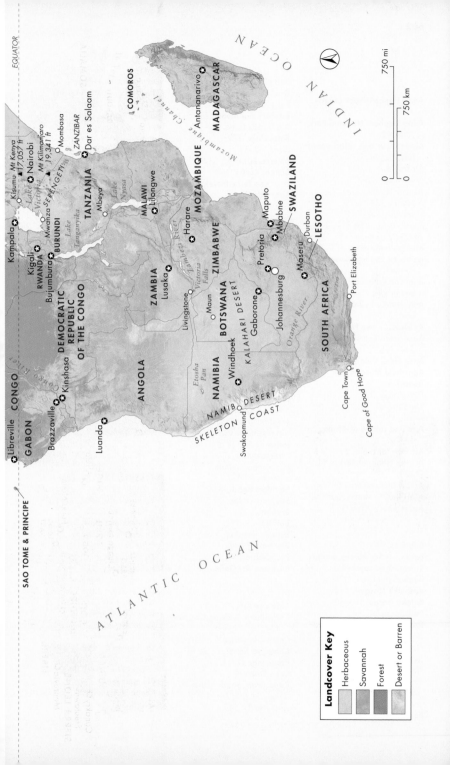

INDEX

PHOTO CREDITS

Alamy. 219, Debra Bouwer. 225, SuperStock. 230, Nicki Geigert, Fodors.com member. 234, BlueOrange Studio/iStockphoto. 239, brytta/iStockphoto. Chapter 5: South Africa 246-47, David Paynter/age fotostock. 248, PhotoSky 4t com/Shutterstock. 249, Nicolaas Weber/Shutterstock. 250, Djuma Game Reserve. 251 (bottom), Grootbos Private Nature Reserve. 251 (top), Hog Hollow Country Lodge. 252, Stacy Freeman, Fodors.com member. 257, jspiegel, Fodors.com member. 262, Images of Africa Photobank / Alamy. 270, Linda R. Hansen, Fodors.com member. 275, Walter Schmitz / Bilderberg/Aurora Photos. 276 (top), Singita Lebombo Lodge. 276 (bottom left and bottom right), Sweni Lodge. 277 (top), Protea Hotel. 277 (bottom), Rhino Post Plains Camp. 280, Adrian Bailey/AURORA Photos. 289, adkinsek, Fodors.com member. 293 (top), Leopard Hills/Sabi Sands Game Reserve. 293 (bottom left), Bush Lodge/Sabi Sands Game Reserve. 293 (bottom right), David Braun. 295, Eric Nathan / Alamy. 301, wlbox, Fodors.com member. 306 (top and bottom right), Hilltop Camp/Hluhluwe Game Reserve. 306 (bottom left), Impala Camp/Hluhluwe Game Reserve. 307 (all), CC Africa. 309, Nigel Dennis/age fotostock. 314, Karen Corby/Flickr. 320, Janice Kawka, Fodors.com member. 327 (top), Pascal Saez/ Sipa Press/Newscom. 327 (bottom) and 328 (left), Lebrecht Music and Arts Photo Library / Alamy. 328 (bottom right), JTB Photo Communications, Inc. / Alamy. 328 (top right), Reimar / Alamy. 329 (top left), Images of Africa Photobank / Alamy. 329 (bottom left), blickwinkel / Alamy. 329 (center right), Miguel Cuenca / Alamy. 329 (bottom right), Timothy Large/iStockphoto. 329 (top right), Perry Correll/ Shutterstock. 330 (top left), Bernard O'Kane / Alamy. 330 (bottom left), Eric Miller / Picturedesk International/Newscom. 330 (right), ALEXANDER JOE/AFP/Getty Images/Newscom. 331 (top), SIPHIWE SIBEKO / Reuters. 331, (bottom) Adrian de Kock/Pierre Tostee/ZUMA Press/Newscom. 332, Bruno Perousse/age fotostock. 341, larrya, Fodors.com member. 347, Stacy Freeman, Fodors.com member. 350, EcoPrint/Shutterstock. 356, Nicholas Pitt / Alamy. Chapter 6: Botswana 364-65, GlenRidgeDoug, Fodors.com member. 366, kolee5, Fodors.com member. 367, Beth Vorro, Fodors.com member. 368, Dana Allen/Wilderness Safaris. 369 (left), CC Africa. 369 (right), Sanctuary Lodges & Camps. 370, scott bredbenner, Fodors.com member. 376, panecott, Fodors.com member. 381, hslogan, Fodors.com member. 382 (all), Wilderness Safaris. 384, Des Curley / Alamy. 386, Beth Vorro, Fodors.com member. 389 (top and bottom right), Wilderness Safaris. 389 (bottom left), Julian Asher. 390, GlenRidgeDoug, Fodors.com member. 391, Kim Freedman, Fodors.com member. 392, GlenRidgeDoug, Fodors.com member. 397, wwhatmough, Fodors.com member. 398 (all), Wilderness Safaris. 399, CJ Thurman, Fodors.com member. 401 (all), Kwando Safaris. 407, DAleffi, Fodors.com member. 409 (top), Sylvain Grandadam/age fotostock. 409 (bottom), Meredith Lamb/Shutterstock. 410 (left), Bill Bachmann / Alamy. 410 (bottom right), Tom Grundy/Shutterstock. 410 (top right), Meredith Lamb/Shutterstock. 411 (top left), J Marshall - Tribaleye Images / Alamy. 411 (bottom left), Rick Matthews/age fotostock. 411 (top right), Sylvain Grandadam/age fotostock. 411 (bottom right), Ulrich Doering / Alamy. 412, Neil Moultrie/South African Tourism. Chapter 7: Namibia 416-17, Werner Bollmann/age fotostock. 418, Todd Cullen, Fodors.com member. 419, Heather Benfield, Fodors.com member. 420, NamidRand Safaris Ltd. 421 (left), Dana Allen/Wilderness Safaris. 421 (right), CC Africa. 422, Ashley Cullen, Fodors.com member. 427, jeep61, Fodors.com member. 430 and 437 (top and bottom left), Wilderness Safaris. 437 (bottom right), CC Africa. 439, Gianluca Basso/age fotostock. 440 (top), Namibia Tourism Board. 440 (2nd from top), Dave Humphreys/Namibia Tourism Board. 440 (3rd from top), Dave Humphreys/Namibia Tourism Board. 440 (bottom), Namibia Tourism Board. 440-441, Images of Africa Photobank / Alamy. 442, Roine Magnusson/age fotostock. 443 (top), Charles Sturge / Alamy. 443 (bottom), Richard Wareham Fotografie / Alamy. 444, Karsten Wrobel / Alamy. 448 (top and bottom right), Wilderness Safaris. 448 (bottom left), Vingerklip Lodge. 450, Ashley Cullen, Fodors.com member. 457, Morales/age fotostock. 459 (top), Wilderness Safaris. 459 (bottom left and right), Namibia Wildlife Resorts. 469, Britton Upham, Fodors.com member. 470, Rainer Kiedrowski/age fotostock. 479, World Travel / Alamy. 488, Gail Johnson/Shutterstock. Chapter 8: Victoria Falls 490-91, Berndt Fischer/age fotostock. 492 (left), Siankaba. 492 (right), globalvhc, Fodors.com member. 493, Lorrin, Fodors.com member. 494, CC Africa. 495 (left), Islands of Siankaba. 495 (right), Siankaba. 496, TXJL, Fodors.com member. 498, Pam Record, Fodors.com member. 500, James Mantock, Fodors.com member. 507, JTB Photo Communications, Inc. / Alamy. 515, Patrick Ward / Alamy. 516-17, Exactostock/SuperStock. 519, Chad Ehlers / Alamy. 521, Pam Record, Fodors.com member. 524, Lebrecht Music and Arts Photo Library / Alamy. Chapter 9: The Seychelles 528-29, Manfred Mehlig / age fotostock. 530 (top), victoria white2010/Flickr. 530 (bottom), Seycam, Wikimedia Commons. 531, The Leading Hotels of the World. 532, Fabio Calamosca/Flickr. 538, evhead/Flickr. 546 (top), The Leading Hotels of the World. 546 (bottom), Quentin Berryman/Four Seasons Resort Seychelles. 551, Sergey Khachatryan/Shutterstock. 555, fabio braibanti / age fotostock. 561, Tatiana Popova/Shutterstock. 564, Tobias/Wikimedia Commons. Chapter 10: On Safari 570-71, Bob Handelman / Alamy. 572, Kenya Tourist Board. 581, Everett Collection.

NOTES

NOTES

NOTES

NOTES

NOTES